Computational Intelligence in Industry 4.0 and 5.0 Applications

Industry 4.0 and 5.0 applications will revolutionize production, enabling smart manufacturing machines to interact with their environments. These machines will become self-aware, self-learning, and capable of real-time data interpretation for self-diagnosis and prevention of production issues. They will also self-calibrate and prioritize tasks to enhance production quality and efficiency.

Computational Intelligence in Industry 4.0 and 5.0 Applications examines applications that merge three key disciplines: computational intelligence (CI), Industry 4.0, and Industry 5.0. It presents solutions using Industrial Internet of Things (IIoT) technologies, augmented by CI-based techniques, modeling, controls, estimations, applications, systems, and future scopes. These applications use data from smart sensors, processed through enhanced CI methods, to make smart automation more effective.

Industry 4.0 integrates data and intelligent automation into manufacturing, using technologies like CI, the IoT, the IIoT, and cloud computing. It transforms data into actionable insights for decision-making and process optimization, essential for modern competitive businesses managing high-speed data integration in production processes. Currently, Industries 4.0 and 5.0 are undergoing significant transformations due to advances in applying artificial intelligence (AI), big data analytics, telecommunication technologies, and control theory. These applications are increasingly multidisciplinary, integrating mechanical, control, and information technologies. However, they face such technical challenges as parametric uncertainties, external disturbances, sensor noise, and mechanical failures. To address these, this book examines such CI technologies as fuzzy logic, neural networks, and reinforcement learning and their application to modeling, control, and estimation. It also covers recent advancements in IIoT sensors, microcontrollers, and big data analytics that further enhance CI-based solutions in Industry 4.0 and 5.0 systems.

Joseph Bamidele Awotunde is a Lecturer with the Computer Science Department, University of Ilorin, Ilorin, Nigeria. He has to his credit over 200 publications in reputable outlets such as Elsevier, Springer, Hindawi, and Taylor & Francis, among others, covering journals, edited conference proceedings, and chapters in books. He is also the editor of four books.

Kamalakanta Muduli is an Associate Professor and Head of the School of Mechanical Engineering at Papua New Guinea University of Technology.

Biswajit Brahma is a Senior Data and Visualization Engineer at McKesson, USA. His expertise is demonstrated by more than 50 publications in prestigious SCI/Scopus journals, showcasing his dedication to advancing knowledge in the fields of AI/ML and deep learning.

Advances in Computational Collective Intelligence

Edited by Subhendu Kumar Pani, Biju Patnaik University of Technology

Technologies for Sustainable Global Higher Education
Edited by Maria José Sousa, Andreia de Bem Machado, and Gertrudes Aparecida Dandolini

Social Media and Crowdsourcing: Application and Analytics
Edited by Sujoy Chatterjee, Thipendra P Singh, Sunghoon Lim, and Anirban Mukhopadhyay

Edge Computational Intelligence for AI-Enabled IoT Systems
Edited by Shrikaant Kulkarni, Jaiprakash Narain Dwivedi, Dinda Pramanta, and Yuichiro Tanaka

AI and IoT Technology and Applications for Smart Healthcare Systems
Edited by Alex Khang

Innovations and Applications of Technology in Language Education
Edited by Hung Phu Bui, Raghvendra Kumar, and Nilayam Kamila

Data-Driven Modelling and Predictive Analytics in Business and Finance: Concepts, Designs, Technologies, and Applications
Edited by Alex Khang, Rashmi Gujrati, Hayri Uygun, R. K. Tailor, and Sanjaya Gaur

Deep Learning Concepts in Operations Research
Edited by Biswadip Basu Mallik, Gunjan Mukherjee, Rahul Kar, and Aryan Chaudhary

Applications of Machine Learning and Deep Learning on Biological Data
Edited by Faheem Masoodi, Mohammad Quasim, Syed Bukhari, Sarvottam Dixit, and Shadab Alam

Deep Learning Applications in Operations Research
Edited by Aryan Chaudhary, Biswadip Basu Mallik, Gunjan Mukherjee, and Rahul Kar

Explainable Artificial Intelligence in Medical Imaging: Fundamentals and Applications
Edited by Amjad Rehman Khan and Tanzila Saba

Computational Intelligence in Industry 4.0 and 5.0 Applications: Trends, Challenges and Applications
Edited by Joseph Bamidele Awotunde, Kamalakanta Muduli, and Biswajit Brahma

For more information about this series, please visit: www.routledge.com/Advances-in-Computational-Collective-Intelligence/book-series/ACCICRC

Computational Intelligence in Industry 4.0 and 5.0 Applications

Trends, Challenges and Applications

Edited by

Joseph Bamidele Awotunde, Kamalakanta Muduli, and Biswajit Brahma

CRC Press
Taylor & Francis Group
AN AUERBACH BOOK

First edition published 2025
2385 NW Executive Center Drive, Suite 320, Boca Raton FL 33431

and by CRC Press
4 Park Square, Milton Park, Abingdon, Oxon, OX14 4RN

CRC Press is an imprint of Taylor & Francis Group, LLC

ISBN: 978-1-032-53922-5 (hbk)
ISBN: 978-1-032-94838-6 (pbk)
ISBN: 978-1-003-58196-3 (ebk)

DOI: 10.1201/9781003581963

Typeset in Times
by Newgen Publishing UK

Contents

Contributors

Mesfin Abebe
Adama Science and Technology University

Adama, Ethiopia
Abidemi Emmanuel Adeniyi
Bowen University
Iwo, Nigeria

Oluseyi Afolabi Adeyemi
University of South Wales
Treforest, United Kingdom

Sunday Adeola Ajagbe
Abiola Ajimobi Technical University
Ibadan, Nigeria

Solomon Olamilekan Akinola
University of Ibadan
Ibadan, Nigeria

Micheal Olaolu Arowolo
University of Missouri
Columbia, Missouri, USA
Hallelujah Oluwatobi Aworinde
Bowen University
Iwo, Nigeria

Joseph Bamidele Awotunde
University of Ilorin
Ilorin, Nigeria

Abdulrauf Olarenwaju Babatunde
University of Ilorin
Ilorin, Nigeria

Biswajit Brahma
McKesson Corporation
San Francisco, California, USA

Ming-Jer Chiang
Taoyuan, Chang Gung University
Taoyuan, Taiwan

Ronald Chiwariro
University of Zimbabwe
Harare, Zimbabwe

Ashish Kumar Dass
NISTUniversity, Berhampur
Odisha, India

Peace Busola Falola
University of Ibadan
Ibadan, Nigeria

Shashi Kant Gupta
Eudoxia Research University
Wilmington, Delaware, USA

Rendra Gustriansyah
Universitas Indo Global Mandiri
Palembang, Indonesia

Kingsley Theophilus Igulu
Kenule Beeson Saro-Wiwa Polytechnic
Bori, Nigeria

Abolaji Okikiade Ilori
Abiola Ajimobi Technical University
Ibadan, Nigeria

Rasheed Gbenga Jimoh
University of Ilorin
Ilorin, Nigeria

Siva Kumar Gowda Katta
Sreenidhi Institute of Science and Technology
Hyderabad, Telangana, India

R Kumar
National Institute of Technology Nagaland
Chumukedima, India

N. Vinaya Kumari
Malla Reddy Engineering College for Women
Hyderabad, Telangana, India

Brojo Kishore Mishra
NISTUniversity, Berhampur
Odisha, India

Nibedita Priyadarsini Mohapatra
NIST (Autonomous)
Berhampur, India

Hemant Narayan
National Institute of Technology Nagaland
Chumukedima, India

Manjushree Nayak
NIST University
Berhampur, Odisha, India

Deborah Olufemi Ninan
Obafemi Awolowo University
Ile-Ife, Nigeria

Odunayo Dauda Olanloye
Bowen University
Iwo, Nigeria

Oladeji Oluniyi Olanrele
Abiola Ajimobi Technical University
Ibadan, Nigeria

Adedoyin Oyebade
Bowen University
Iwo, Nigeria

Thipendra P.
Bennett University
Greater Noida, India

Sivakumar Annamalai Palanivel
Microsoft
Redmond, Washington, USA

Asish Panigrahi
NIST University, Berhampur
Odisha, India

R. S. M. Lakshmi Patibandla
Amrita Vishwa Vidyapeetham, Amaravati
Andhra Pradesh, India

Sudhir Ranajan Pattanaik
NIST (Autonomous)
Berhampur, India

M Prakash
National Institute of Technology Nagaland
Chumukedima, India

Bhanu Priya
University of Jammu
Jammu and Kashmir, India

Lokaiah Pullagura
Jain University, Bangalore
Karnataka, India

Shinta Puspasari
Universitas Indo Global Mandiri
Palembang, Indonesia

Dontha Madhusudhana Rao
Koneru Lakshmaiah Education Foundation
Andhra Pradesh, India

L. Ravikumar
Jain University, Bangalore
Karnataka, India

Demóstenes Zegarra Rodríguez
Federal University of Lavras
Lavras, Minas Gerais, Brazil

Ahmad Sanmorino
Universitas Indo Global Mandiri
Palembang, Indonesia

B Shakila
National Institute of Technology Nagaland
Chumukedima, India

Vivek Sharma
University of Jammu
Jammu and Kashmir, India

Thipendra P. Singh
Bennett University
Greater Noida, India

Daniel Dauda Wisdom
Chrisland University
Abeokuta, Nigeria

1 Industry 4.0

Challenges and Issues Encountered in Manufacturing and Testing of MEMS Devices

Hemant Narayan, M. Prakash, B. Shakila, R. Kumar, and Sivakumar Annamalai Palanivel

1.1 INTRODUCTION

Industry 4.0 has been discussed since the beginning of the century. The term "Industry 4.0" refers to the continual growth of the manufacturing and industrial sectors via the incorporation of digital technology, automation, and data exchange. It builds on the preceding three industrial revolutions, which resulted in substan tial advances in manufacturing processes. There are still some unclear areas concerning the implications and repercussions of this new manufacturing approach.

Industry 4.0 is characterized by the convergence of various technologies, including the IoT (Internet of Things), big data analytics, robotics, AI (artificial intelligence), and cloud computing. These technologies enable the creation of "smart factories" and facilitate the digitalization and interconnectedness of the entire value chain. It is built on the use of cutting-edge monitoring, information management, and transmission systems to enhance ongoing manufacturing processes [1]. Yet, despite increasing curiosity in the Industry 4.0 area, it still represents a quasi-idea. The adoption of Industry 4.0 technologies offers several potential benefits, including increased productivity, improved efficiency, enhanced flexibility, better quality control, reduced costs, and the ability to respond quickly to market demands. Industry 4.0 offers opportunities for innovation, improved efficiency, and enhanced functionality in the development, manufacturing, and utilization of MEMS devices. It enables the integration of MEMS into the digital ecosystem, fostering the growth of smart, interconnected systems and applications. Although it is the case that MEMS technology has evolved from integrated circuits fabrication techniques, these technologies' test approaches

DOI: 10.1201/9781003581963-1

are distinct. Because of the immersion of several domains, MEMS devices are complicated and diversified.

MEMS has exceptional adaptability and malleability in the miniaturization of devices, with the prospects of utilizing less energy and operating as envisioned. Designing smaller, lighter, and more powerful devices is now a popular micro/nano system trend [2].

1.2 KEY CONTRIBUTIONS OF THIS CHAPTER

The following are the most significant contributions of this chapter.

1. The chapter provides immense knowledge about Industry 4.0 and MEMS including its constituents, history, and applications.
2. The significant issues and challenges faced during MEMS manufacturing, testing, and packaging, in general, are discussed.
3. Biomedical applications of MEMS devices and their challenges are discussed in depth.

1.3 CHAPTER ORGANIZATION

Section 1.4 discusses a literature review for industry revolution and key components of Industry 4.0. Section 1.5 elaborates MEMS and its constituents, while Section 1.6 discusses the principles of the piezoelectric effect. The history of piezoelectric materials is discussed in Section 1.7 and Section 1.8 illustrates the key components of Industry 4.0 in MEMS. Section 1.9 depicts various methodologies of testing MEMS along with their breakdown and causes. Section 1.10 describes the difficulties encountered during the fabrication of MEMS devices and Section 1.11 describes MEMS testing concerns such as molding, dicing, designing, and wafer level issues. Section 1.12 depicts biomedical applications of MEMS devices and their issues and challenges. Lastly, Section 1.13 provides findings and gives research proposals for the future.

1.4 LITERATURE REVIEW

1.4.1 Industrial Revolution

Industry 3.0 represents the era of computerization and the use of electronics and IT in industrial processes. Key features include the introduction of computers, automation of production processes, and the use of early robotics. Industry 4.0, also known as the 4th Industrial Revolution, is characterized by the integration of smart technology, the Internet of Things (IoT), and cyber-physical systems into the manufacturing environment. It involves the extensive use of data, connectivity, and automation. Industry 5.0 is a concept that looks beyond pure automation and emphasizes the collaboration between humans and machines. It focuses on human-centric approaches, with AI and automation supporting human workers rather than replacing them entirely.

1.4.2 Key Components of Industry 4.0

Cyber-Physical Systems (CPS)

Machines and sensors are linked to the digital world, allowing for real-time monitoring, surveillance, and optimization of production processes.

Internet of Things (IoT)

Data are collected and exchanged by connected devices and sensors, allowing machines, goods, and systems to communicate with one another. The Internet of Things allows machines and things to interact, share information, and carry out activities without the need for direct human intervention. This collection of networked devices extends traditional computing's capabilities by allowing physical items to perceive, evaluate, and respond to their surroundings, making them "smart" and capable of interacting with the digital world.

Big Data Analytics

Large amounts of primary data acquired from many sources are analyzed in order to extract valuable information, optimize processes, and make educated choices.

Cloud Computing

Cloud-based services and platforms provide storage, computing power, and collaboration tools to support data processing and enable remote access to resources. Cloud computing is a model of computing that involves the delivery of computing resources and services over the internet ("the cloud"). Instead of hosting applications, data, and services on local servers or personal computers, cloud computing enables users to access and use these resources remotely via the internet. Cloud computing has revolutionized the way businesses and individuals utilize and manage IT resources, enabling more efficient, scalable, and cost-effective computing solutions.

ML (Machine Learning) and AI (Artificial Intelligence)

Machine learning is a branch of artificial intelligence (AI) that concentrates on the development of algorithms and statistical models that allow computers to gather information from data and make forecasts or assessments without being specifically programmed. Machine learning's major purpose is to enable computers to enhance their efficacy on a given activity through experience, despite human intervention. In machine learning, algorithms are trained on a dataset, which consists of input data (features) and corresponding output labels (targets). During the training process, the algorithm learns patterns and relationships in the data to make predictions or judgments on novel, unseen data.

AI is the imitation of human intellect in computers that are programmed to do tasks that would typically need human cognitive abilities. AI aims to create computer systems that can mimic human thinking, reasoning, learning, and problem-solving processes to perform tasks more efficiently and accurately. Machine learning, robotics, expert systems, computer vision, natural language processing, and other techniques and approaches are all part of the subject of artificial intelligence. These technologies allow AI systems to gather and analyze enormous volumes of data, detect patterns, forecast outcomes, and change their behavior depending on past experience.

Additive Manufacturing (3D Printing)
The ability to create complex objects layer by layer using 3D printing technology enables fast prototyping, customization, and decentralized production.

Virtual Reality (VR)
VR refers to a computer-generated simulation or a virtual environment that immerses users in a fully artificial, computer-generated 3D world. VR devices, such as head-mounted displays (HMDs) or VR goggles, block out the physical world and replace it with a digitally created environment, making users feel like they are present and interacting within that simulated world. Users can explore and interact with the virtual environment through head and hand movements, enabling a sense of presence and interaction with virtual objects and spaces. VR is commonly used in gaming, training, simulations, education, architecture, and various other fields where a realistic and immersive experience is desired.

Augmented Reality (AR)
Augmented reality overlays digital information onto the physical-world environment, enhancing or augmenting the user's perception of reality. AR technology allows users to see and interact with digital elements while still being aware of and able to interact with the real world. AR is typically experienced through smartphones, tablets, smart glasses, or other wearable devices that use cameras to capture the real-world scene and superimpose computer-generated graphics, images, or information on top of it. AR gives us a wide range of applications, including mobile gaming, navigation, industrial training, remote assistance, marketing, and interactive user manuals.

1.5 MICROELECTROMECHANICAL SYSTEMS

Microelectromechanical systems (MEMS) have undergone a rapid ascent to prominence as a vital technology over the last 10 years. MEMS is based on the greater volume efficiency and lower unit prices that the microelectronics industry has achieved in the past 60 years which may be transformed into devices that integrate mechanical and electrical components into a single silicon chip. Figure 1.1 illustrates the constituents of MEMS.

The majority of Si-based components, conductive metals, and some organic components have been used in MEMS devices since their functionality was mostly derived from intricate microstructures created by Si microfabrication processes. Functional materials, contrary to common belief, such as ferroelectric materials, are a form of piezoelectric material with impulsive electric polarization that may be inverted by an applied electric field. These materials are characterized by their ability to maintain a stable polarization state even after the external electric field is removed, making them useful for a broad area of applications, including sensors, actuators, memory devices, and energy-harvesting devices.

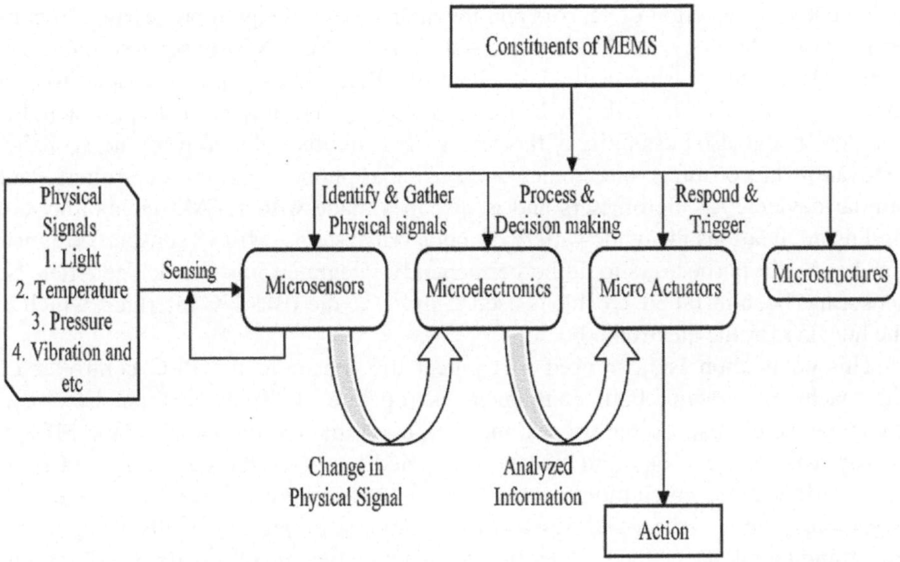

FIGURE 1.1 Constituents of MEMS [3].

These materials are typically crystalline in nature, and their unique properties arise from the asymmetry in their crystal structure, which leads to the presence of permanent electric dipoles within the material. The electric dipoles can align in multiple stable directions, resulting in the material having multiple polarization states or domains. These materials exhibit hysteresis behavior, which means that the polarization-versus-electric-field curve forms a loop when plotted. This hysteresis loop represents the ability of the material to switch between different polarization states with the application of an electric field and retain the polarization state after the field is removed. This property makes ferroelectric materials suitable for applications where stable and reversible polarization states are required.

Some common examples of ferroelectric materials include lithium niobate ($LiNbO_3$), lead zirconate titanate (PZT), barium titanate ($BaTiO_3$), and potassium niobate ($KNbO_3$), among others. These materials are widely used in various technologies, including sensors for pressure, acceleration, and temperature, ultrasonic transducers, actuators for precise motion control, nonvolatile ferroelectric memories, and energy-harvesting devices for converting mechanical vibrations or thermal gradients into electrical energy. Among these, piezoelectricity is very attractive in the application of microsensors and microactuators.

The implementation of digital technologies that can collect data in real time and analyze it is essential to the success of Industry 4.0. Providing the production system with information that is helpful to it in real time, temperature sensors, displacement sensors, pressure sensors, vibration sensors, torque sensors, power flow rate sensors, and variable sensors all make measurements that enable the creation of a digital representation of the manufacturing process. The objectives of the application should guide both the selection of sensors and the architecture of signal processing. In contemporary technology, MEMS sensors—such as the PulseNG sensor—significantly contribute to the measurement of acceleration. These sensors play a crucial role in monitoring signals. The ability to be manufactured in micro sizes, the requirement for less power, and also possibility of their integrated circuits and their usefulness, enable innovation in consumer electronics such as smartphones, gaming controllers, and similar devices. Accelerometers and gyroscopes made with MEMS technology are finding applications in a wide variety of industrial systems. MEMS sensors, designed for diagnostic purposes, should be permanently integrated into the device.After the sensor has been installed, a cable is used to link it to the IBU–NG interface, which is the housing for the electronic board.

This connection is later used to connect the sensor to the PLC controller of the machine, allowing both components to operate at the same time. Electrical components are responsible for reading the pulses that are produced by the MEMS sensor. The interface bus unit will be scheduled based on the data collected from the MEMS sensor, which monitors restrictions and vibrations. Once this information is gathered, the necessary settings will be configured programmatically.The policies governing maintenance have a significant impact on the rate of quality improvement. The manufacturers of vibration-monitoring and total productive maintenance/total quality management (TPM/TQM) systems will contribute to an increase in the life cycle of machine tools, which are employed in with high-quality performance. The MEMS sensor detects and quantifies vibrations by measuring acceleration on both the machine table and the spindle housing. These data are then used for information and predictive analysis [1]. Recently, countless research works have involving the applications of MEMS in the biomedical field, especially in microsurgery, microtherapy, artificial body parts, drug synthesis and delivery, and cell manipulation and characterization.

Piezoelectric energy harvesting is a sophisticated technology with great potential, and the performance of energy harvesting can be improved by adjusting a few important group parameters in terms of ceramic, polymer, single-crystal composite materials, and lead-free materials have their benefits and drawbacks. When it comes to piezoelectric polymers, PVDF-TrFE (polyvinylidene fluoride—trifluoroethylene) stands out as the most commonly utilized material among both PVDF and copolymers. Common PZT ceramics are made with hazardous lead. Consequently, it is important to look at potential alternatives to meet environmental regulations for new uses of existing materials. Consideration must also be given to the stability and state of the environment. Binding vibration mode is simple to tune at low frequency, and is used in these energy harvesters. High-voltage generators can benefit more from the impact design. Multiple potential ignition mechanisms have been investigated. Energy harvesters could one day power everything from personal electronics to entire smart cities, not to mention a wide variety of other uses in industries and the military. To fully utilize the potential of piezoelectric as sustainable energy sources, it will be necessary to optimize materials, make discoveries, create low-power devices, explore energy sources, increase energy output, and match applications [4].

Integrated circuits were employed in the development of devices and systems based on microelectromechanical systems (MEMS). These systems encompass design, fabrication techniques, and applications, including sensors and actuators. Procedures for processing in batches that are compatible, and sizes that span from micrometers to millimeters, are being created. MEMS technology derives from the tools and processes used to fabricate integrated circuits. Thermal sensors, pressure sensors, resonators, levers, and gear and gearbox systems, all of which are measured in microns, have the potential to be batch built together on the same chip as the processing unit. They make up a system on a chip in its own right, having numerous applications in the commercial sector. There is microfabrication of huge numbers of devices, each of which is capable of performing a single straightforward function. However, when combined, they are capable of performing complex functions. Not only do MEMS involve a reduction in the size of mechanical systems, they also constitute a novel approach to the design of mechanical devices and structures. Integrated microelectronic circuits are sometimes referred to as the "brains" of a device. There are several different types of MEMS devices, including sensors, actuators, bio-MEMS, microfluidic MEMS, RF MEMS, and optical MEMS. This forthcoming technological revolution of miniaturization known as MEMS has been acknowledged as providing valuable goods for a variety of commercial and government applications. The construction of micromachines that have small dimensions, low power consumption, and exquisite performance can only be accomplished with the assistance of devices that use MEMS technology [5].

1.6 PRINCIPLE OF THE PIEZOELECTRIC EFFECT

There are two distinct characteristics of piezoelectricity, direct and indirect piezoelectric effects (PE). The first effect is crucial for sensing and energy harvesting when a material is polarized under applied stress to procreate surface charges on the piezoelectric materials. In the second effect, electric potential induces mechanical strain or mechanical displacement in the material [6].

The piezoelectric constitutive equation shown below governs the direct and inverse piezoelectric effects.

$$\begin{bmatrix} S \\ D \end{bmatrix} = \begin{bmatrix} \alpha^E & \beta^t \\ \beta & \gamma^T \end{bmatrix} \begin{bmatrix} \mathrm{T} \\ \mathrm{E} \end{bmatrix} \tag{1.1}$$

This illustrates the relationship between strain (S), stress (T), electric displacement (D), and electric field (E) in the context of piezoelectric materials. It introduces parameters such as elastic compliance (α), piezoelectric coefficient (β), and dielectric constant (γ). Notably, superscripts E and T signify that certain constants are calculated at unaltered electric field and stress, respectively, while the superscript "t" indicates the transpose [7,8]. It highlights the impact of the direction of applied stress on the energy-harvesting performance of piezoelectric elements, emphasizing that for many piezoelectric materials, the polar axis is clearly defined. The direction of applied stress relative to this polar axis becomes crucial in determining the efficiency of energy scavenging. The text further notes that in ferroelectric ceramics or polymers like PVDF or PZT, the polar axis depends on the poling direction. On the other hand,

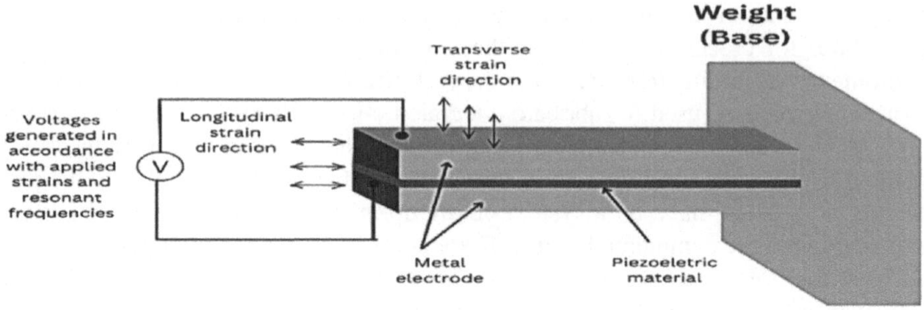

FIGURE 1.2 Mechanical work flows of piezoelectricity [8].

for non-ferroelectric crystalline materials such as ZnO or aluminum nitride (AlN), the polar axis is determined by the crystal orientation, specifically along the c-axis of the wurtzite crystal structure [9].

The mechanical function of piezoelectricity is shown in Figure 1.2, in which the transverse strain direction and longitudinal strain direction are mentioned and also the direction in which voltage is generated in accordance with applied strains and resonant frequencies.

1.7 PIEZOELECTRIC MATERIALS: HISTORY

The performance of micropiezoelectric materials over the last 10 years is shown in Figure 1.3. An assessment of various enhanced techniques is presented for cantilevers such as maximum resonant frequency cantilever, the 2-D cantilever beam with weight, the optimal device volume, and the four doubly clamped beams, including silicon-on-insulator (SOI) structures such as the addition of a SiO_2 layer and the bonding of bulk PZT oxide. It appears that significant searches are also being conducted for well-known piezoelectric materials such as potassium/sodium/niobium oxide (KNN), sodium niobium oxide ($NaNbO_3$) nanowires, AlN composites, PZT nanowires, $BaTiO_3$ nanogenerators, ZnO nanowire nanogenerators, and KNN/manganese oxide (Mn)/potassium (K) copper (C) tantalum (T) oxide (KCT) materials. Figure 1.3 compares various distinct methods of improvement, such as the hybrid model of electromagnetic-piezoelectric modifications like curved L-shaped and Si seismic weights on a uni-morph cantilever, and ad hoc options such as a blender caping with axial force and 12 bimorph actuators on a wind turbine [10].

As illustrated in Figure 1.3, the progressive advancement of micropiezoelectric energy harvesters over past 10 years demonstrates a favorable reaction to the system's potential. Power densities were obtained by using maximum resonant frequency cantilever, a two-dimensional cantilever beam with seismic mass, and optimum device volumes of 0.16, 0.24, and 0.31 mW/cm^3 were attained in the experiments. These findings were attained as a result of the cantilever constructions' low resonance frequencies, which were further minimized by the presence of mass at the cantilever's end. These piezoelectric devices frequently focus on low-frequency motions of the human body for their applications. In order to improve the resonance frequencies over a larger operational bandwidth and to

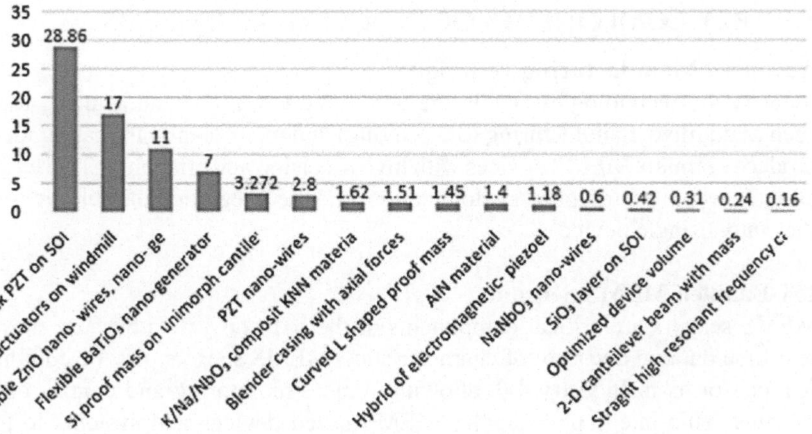

FIGURE 1.3 Power density (mWcm³) of piezoelectricity systems in the last decade [8].

offer higher output power, more precise piezoelectric structures are needed. This would make them appropriate for high-frequency applications. Lower Curie temperatures, lower relative densities, and decreased poling activity in perovskite-type ferroelectric $BaTiO_3$ materials all have the potential to diminish the piezoelectric performance. Its relatively high piezoelectric constant, however, may allow for its inclusion in piezoelectric modules. Using MEMS and soft lithography, Hwang [10] effectively created a flexible $BaTiO_3$ nanogenerator with up to 7 mW/cm³ of power conversion. Empirical studies on a flexible nanogenerator based on ZnO nanowires that was made using a scalable sweeping-printing technique were conducted. The power harvesting of the nanogenerator in this case scaled up to 11 mW/cm³, a value that is 12–22 times higher than that obtained by the standard PZT cantilever system [11,12].

In an experimental setup, it is evident that bulk PZT (lead zirconate titanate) is bonded to an SOI (silicon-on-insulator) structure, resulting in the formation of a unimorph cantilever. Implementing SOI results in a flatter overall contour for the structure. Following the bonding of the bulk piezo-ceramic to silicon wafers, it can be produced using micromachining procedures. It was found that this piezoelectric device's utilization of silicon wafer bonding machinery was particularly compatible with MEMS technology. The performance of micropiezoelectricity harvesters has improved significantly over the past 10 years because of the use of KNN/Mn/KCT material in a transformer application. With increased dielectric, piezoelectric, and ferroelectric characteristics and a high Curie temperature, KNN is a potential lead-free piezoelectric material. Through the co-doping of KNN with Mn and $K_{5.4}$ $Cu_{1.3}$ Ta_{10} (KCT) sintering aids, this technique improves the densification of KNN. The KNN/Mn/KCT material greatly increases the piezoelectric constant and electromechanical coupling factor. This discovery suggests that modest mechanical-to-electrical energy sensors can be used in applications on a large scale.

Because of these properties, piezoelectric materials are fundamentally sensors and actuators. As a result, incorporating piezoelectric materials into MEMS allows unique functionality, particularly in basic microstructures [13].

1.8 KEY COMPONENTS OF INDUSTRY 4.0 IN MEMS

Advanced Manufacturing Techniques

Industry 4.0 technologies enable the use of modernized manufacturing techniques, such as additive manufacturing (3D printing) and micro/nano fabrication methods, to produce complex MEMS devices with high precision and efficiency. These techniques allow for rapid prototyping, customization, and the integration of multiple functionalities into a single device.

IoT-Enabled MEMS Sensors

MEMS sensors are critical components of the IoT ecosystem because they provide real-time data on a variety of characteristics. MEMS sensors may be combined with IoT platforms in Industry 4.0, allowing remote monitoring and control of physical systems. This integration enables MEMS-based devices and systems to have predictive maintenance, optimal performance, and increased efficiency.

Data Analytics (DA) and Machine Learning (ML)

MEMS devices provide a large quantity of data, which Industry 4.0 uses to derive useful insights. Manufacturers may spot patterns, anomalies, and trends in sensor data generated by MEMS devices, enabling proactive decision-making, quality control, and process optimization.

Smart MEMS Devices

The 4th Industrial Revolution encourages the development of smart MEMS devices capable of communicating with other devices, systems, and humans. These smart MEMS devices may be combined with wireless communication modules to provide real-time data sharing and control.

Quality Control and Testing

Industry 4.0 techniques, such as computer vision and automated inspection systems, can be applied to MEMS manufacturing processes to ensure quality control and efficient testing. These techniques help detect defects, measure critical dimensions, and validate the performance of MEMS devices, reducing human error and enhancing product reliability.

1.9 TESTING

MEMS are examined at several stages during the manufacturing and fabrication processes. These tests are critical for analyzing and verifying device performance, as well as parametrically and functionally assessing system output data. During the fabrication process, the broad majority of MEMS devices can be created using three fabrication processes: surface micromachining, bulk micromachining, and the molding process. MEMS devices are tested with automatic test equipment (ATE) [14] during wafer-level manufacture by monitoring both AC and DC characteristics on the wafer level [15,16]. This test procedure separates the wafer for both positive and negative dying by utilizing designs for checking circuits in chips, self-assess mechanisms, and scan chains that are similar to integrated circuits.

Following dicing and wire bonding to test power efficiency, excellent devices are finally packed. Ultimately, these packaged devices undergo parametric retesting to verify their overall functionality. Prior to their actual utilization, functional testing and configuration are imperative for all MEMS devices. During the calibration process, the inherent parameters or values associated with device performance are established. This is accomplished by subjecting the devices to predetermined pneumatic and electrical stimulation to compare their resulting output responses. If there is a difference between the measured and estimated values, the device is regarded as unacceptable; otherwise, it is approved as an acceptable device. Figure 1.4 depicts the detailed fabrication and testing stages for the mass manufacture of a MEMS pressure sensor. In this diagram, steps 6 and 12 are for device assembly, while steps 3, 7, 9, and 16 are for device packaging, steps 2, 8, 11, 14, and 15 are for testing, and steps 4, 5, 10, and 13 are for microlevel fabrication [17].

Testing is important for ensuring the performance and dependability of the device during the MEMS production process, but it is quite expensive [18]. According to MEPTEC (Microelectronics Packaging and Test Engineering Council), the testing cost of MEMS is 20–45% of the total cost of element fabrication. According to Masi and Cortese [19], the total testing process consumes 25–35% of the material cost.

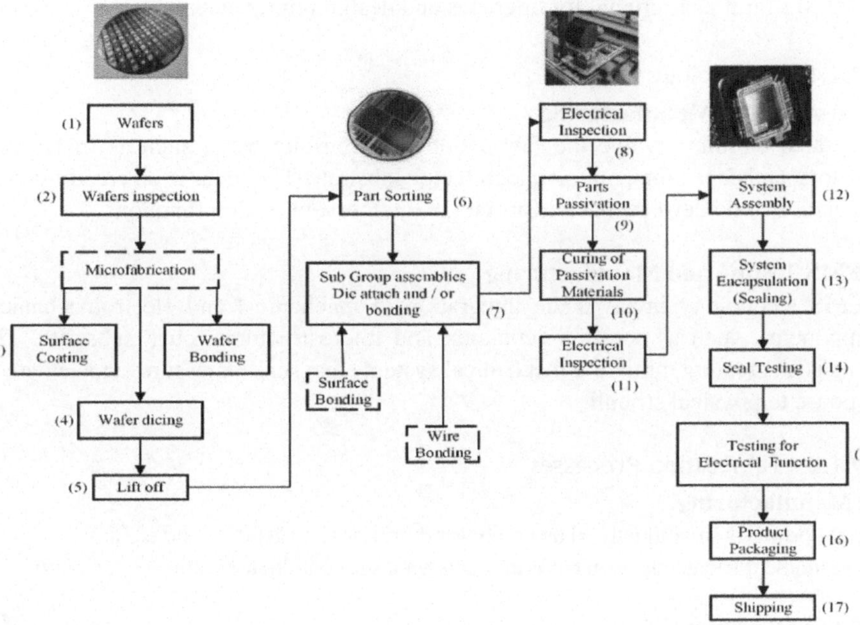

FIGURE 1.4 Detailed fabrication and testing stages for the mass manufacture of a MEMS pressure sensor [17].

According to Texas Instruments, for a digital micromirror device, the expense incurred for the final test, involving testing of the packaged device, amounts to 14% of the total cost. In contrast, the cost of inspecting the wafer at the wafer level accounts for 8% of the total cost [20]. However, according to the MIG (MEMS Industry Group) [21] for a MEMS test norm examination, testing costs at the stage of production can increase by up to 50% due to device design and sophistication.

1.9.1 The Differences among ICs versus MEMS Testing

Due to their multiphysics behavior, MEMS present numerous testing issues [22]. MEMS mechanical components are nonlinear, similar to analog electronic systems. MEMS requires analog and mixed signal tests [23], as well as verification and calibration. MEMS testing is complicated by their various qualities. A MEMS-based device's output, for example, is electrical in nature; yet, these signals are being generated by mechanical actuations in separate domains [24]. Consequently, utilizing electrical signals for testing purposes has proven advantageous in terms of controlling and observing mechanical components. In comparison to integrated circuits, MEMS technology is not as advanced. The monitoring and modeling of faults in MEMS devices are still in their early stages, lagging behind MEMS production and design. Despite being available since 1970, testing them remains a significant challenge. Conducting early-stage testing aids in production, fabrication, and even in packaging operations. The availability of analysis mechanism capable of identifying the causes of MEMS failures is crucial for upgrades and design improvements.

1.9.1.1 Technology Focus

IC Testing and Manufacturing

Integrated circuits involve the fabrication of electronic parts, such as transistors, resistors, and capacitors, on a semiconductor substrate. The focus is on creating functional electronic devices that perform logic, memory, or analog functions.

MEMS Testing and Manufacturing

MEMS technology involves the integration of mechanical and electromechanical components, such as sensors, actuators, and microstructures, on a substrate. The focus is on creating miniature mechanical systems that sense, measure, and actuate in response to physical stimuli.

1.9.1.2 Fabrication Processes

IC Manufacturing

ICs are primarily manufactured using photolithography, deposition, and etching processes to create the intricate electronic components on a semiconductor wafer (e.g., silicon).

MEMS Manufacturing

To manufacture mechanical and microelectronic components, MEMS devices are created utilizing various microfabrication techniques such as bulk micromachining, surface micromachining, and LIGA (lithography, electroplating, and molding).

1.9.1.3 Material Selection

ICs and MEMS

ICs are generally constructed of semiconductor materials like silicon that have been doped with certain impurities to provide the necessary electronic characteristics. To accomplish the requisite mechanical and electrical qualities, MEMS devices employ a variety of materials, including silicon, glass, metals, and polymers.

1.9.1.4 Testing Complexity

IC and MEMS Testing

IC testing focuses on electrical performance and functional testing to guarantee that digital logic or analog circuitry operates properly. Mechanical and electrical characterization are used in MEMS testing to confirm the mechanical behavior, sensing accuracy, and actuation capabilities of MEMS devices.

1.9.1.5 Device Architecture

ICs and MEMS

ICs are two-dimensional planar devices that are suited for electrical circuits and chip-scale integration. MEMS devices can have three-dimensional architectures because they frequently include movable or flexible components that enable mechanical functioning and sensing.

IC Packaging

ICs are typically encapsulated in hermetically sealed packages to protect them from environmental factors and ensure proper electrical connections.

MEMS Packaging

MEMS devices require specialized packaging to protect the delicate mechanical components and maintain their performance.

1.9.1.6 Application Areas

ICs

ICs are widely used in electronics, communication, computing, and other digital or analog applications.

MEMS

MEMS devices find applications in sensors, actuators, biomedical devices, automotive systems, consumer electronics, and IoT devices.

Failure modes [25] are as distinct as MEMS devices. Significant efforts have been expended in IC manufacturing to precisely assess and evaluate device performance in accordance with specified requirements. The fundamental distinction between testing MEMS and ICs is the environment. Integrated circuits undergo testing in diverse environments, subject to different temperature and moisture conditions in numerous scenarios. During the production process, somewhat similar testing and handling methods [26] are undertaken; nevertheless, the fundamental distinction arises from the unique environmental conditions in which the devices operate. In the

TABLE 1.1
Assessment Methodology of Microelectromechanical Systems [17]

Assessment Methodology	Digital Circuits	Analog Circuits	Microelectromechanical Systems
Fault method	Assertion, line, bus, redundancy, path, gate, behavioral, branch, cross-point, bridging, stuck-open, all are examples of delay	Catastrophic, hierarchical, macromodel, transistor, physical, behavioral, and parametric defects	Behavioral, electrothermal, and electromagnetic shorts and openings, structural fault level, parametric, operating functions, fatigue, and reliability models
Experiment method	BIST (built in self-test), HSPICE, VHDL, probabilistic, LFSR (linear feedback shift register), fault dictionary, are all examples of simulation techniques	ATPG, artificial neural network (ANN), HSPICE, SABRE, BIST (built-in self-test), Pole-Zero Analysis, VHDL-AMS	Device-level (FEM) and HDLs, as well as microelectronics system architecture, BIST, VHDL-AMS

test environment, any change can significantly impact the device's sensitivity and operation. The additional difficulty of mechanical motion necessitates extra caution during testing and handling (Table 1.1).

1.9.2 An Extensive Investigation into the Breakdown of MEMS Devicess

MEMS devices, unlike ICs, have dynamic characteristics; thus, unique methodologies and equipment are necessary for measuring mechanical responses at both the micro- and nanoscale. These technologies were used to analyze the device's behavior in depth, which aided in providing input to enhance the design. MEMS devices find extensive application across diverse global industries. Previously, there was an assumption that MEMS devices were part of the ICs family and might encounter similar failure concerns as ICs. On the other hand, MEMS devices have various breakdown mechanisms due to their complicated mechanical design and specific material, and they use explicit biasing approaches. Due to the complexity of these systems, the failure modes are classified into four groups.

Stationary MEMS devices that fall under Group A encompass stationary devices with no moving parts, including chemical sensors, microphones, and DNA sequencers. Particle contamination is the most common cause of failure in this group. Contaminated particles, being tiny and fundamentally nonelectrical, have a negative impact on device performance. Because particle contaminants are insulators, they cannot create an electrical connection across the device structure; due to this, contaminants are challenging to identify as short circuits.

Group B comprises of MEMS devices characterized by moving structures but lacking rubbing surfaces. This category includes comb drive accelerometers, where parts like hinges and microcantilever yoke regions are susceptible to fatigue failure. The focus of this group lies in examining structural failures caused by fatigue. Key components within this category include electrostatically actuated comb fingers featuring a perforated proof weight and a microcantilever featuring a notch. The critical aspect of examination involves the structural integrity of these components, specifically addressing the challenges posed by fatigue. In the case of electrostatically actuated comb fingers, the presence of a perforated proof weight adds complexity to the stress distribution. Similarly, the microcantilever, with its distinctive notch, becomes a focal point for analysis. The elevated stress levels at the notch are identified as the primary culprits triggering surface cracks on the microcantilever. These cracks, in turn, contribute to a restricted lifespan of the device and eventual failure attributable to fracture. Understanding and mitigating such fatigue-induced structural vulnerabilities are paramount for enhancing the reliability and longevity of MEMS devices in Group B.

MEMS devices having movable components and impact surfaces, including relays, valves, and thermal actuators, fall inside Group C. Such devices may be impacted by surface debris, fracture components, cracks [27], and so on. The device fails due to fracture caused by impact forces on the opposing structure.

Group D comprises of MEMS devices that involve translational components, rubbing motions, and impacting surfaces, such as micromirrors, optical shutters, and geared devices. The interaction of uneven surfaces in these devices leads to friction, causing material wear or the presence of debris. This friction-related wear and debris can result in various types of failures, including: (1) stiction of rubbing or contacting areas, (2) wear due to particles which impact motion tolerance, and (3) particle contamination (Table 1.2).

1.9.3 MEMS Device Reliability Testing

MEMS device functionality is determined by the structure's material, design, and actuating elements. As a result, the technology sector uses MEMS-based product reliability testing. MEMS device reliability testing is a significant challenge in bulk production and manufacturing. In this test, the failure analysis of the device under test (DUT) is conducted under particular circumstances that align with the device's application and within a particular duration. The product and application area greatly affect the causes of MEMS reliability failures. During the reliability test, it is necessary to employ an economical method for conducting prominent failure analysis to understand the characteristics of the DUT.

It is obvious that every type of MEMS device has failure processes caused by stiction, particle contamination, and other factors. As a result, understanding the causes of failure is far more significant than finding solutions to individual failures. Due to their distinct categories and nature, MEMS sensors and actuators exhibit separate

TABLE 1.2
Brief Details of Breakdowns, Causes, and Acquisition of Several MEMS Devices

Group	Application	Failure Cause	Reliability Testing	References
A	Nozzles, chemical sensors, microfluidics	Breakdown of dielectric	Flagellar microfluidic motors were tested for reliability under environmental settings. The rotational behavior was examined using a probabilistic mathematical model. The degradation time of the bacterial motor was anticipated to be 55 hours	[28]
A or B	Accelerometers	Structural changes and charging such as fracture, fatigue, change in friction	(a) The life duration was investigated practically for 1000 hours at temperatures ranging from 145°C to 200°C (b) Tytron 250 was utilized for fatigue testing. When the loads were increased from 2.05 to 2.83 GPa, the fatigue life ranged between 77.8k–14.8M cycles (c) Sandia National Laboratories created the SHiMMeR, which can test up to 256 MEMS parts at same time (d) X-ray diffraction was used to observe fatigue and creep. Stiction was measured using MIL-STD-883F. Wear was measured using DLC coating (Diamond Like Carbon), and contamination was measured using SAM (scanning acoustic microscope)	[29–31]
B	Pressure sensors	Structural changes like fracture, friction changes vibrations, shock, fatigue	It was discovered that fatigue can occur at equivalent stress and fracture levels in the constructed sensors functioning below the stress level (a) A three-axis gyroscope's reliability was evaluated under various shock loading circumstances (b) Temperature declines and changes in S/N ratio have also been recorded	[32–33]

TABLE 1.2 (Continued)
Brief Details of Breakdowns, Causes, and Acquisition of Several MEMS Devices

Group	Application	Failure Cause	Reliability Testing	References
	Gyroscopes	Vibrations and electric charge		
C	Thermal actuators	Vibration, shock, and structural deformation	(a) Testing for fracture on the beam using variable loads was analyzed using Weibull statistics (b) An experimental technique for observing malfunction due to electrical charge and creep was proposed for microswitches. (c) The effects of drawing voltages on beam bending and torsional modes were investigated. To determine the life duration, structural deformation and fatigue, experiments were done	[34–38]
	Microrelays	Structural deformation like fracture, electric charges, fatigue, shock, vibrations		
D	Electrostatic actuators	Structural deformation like fracture, electric charges, fatigue, shock, vibrations	The stochastic technique was used to analyze voltages in order to predict device life time	[39–42]
	Convex devices	Optical degradation, structural deformation like fracture, electric charges, fatigue, shock, vibrations	Texas Instruments (TI) created an optical analysis tool for DMD devices that inspects each pixel in the DMD array	
	Mechanical devices	Structural deformation like fracture, electric charges, fatigue, shock, vibrations	Simulations of sliding surfaces were used to avoid friction and wear	

TABLE 1.3
MEMS Mechanical Breakdown [17]

Mechanical Structural Breakdown					
Breakdown	Fatigue	Overload	Corrosion	Shock	
Reason	Structural damage due to periodic loading	Excessive stress	Oxidation, chemical reaction	Mechanical structure disorder, huge loading and drops	
Stiction					
Breakdown	Capillary forces	van der Waals forces	Residual stress	Chemical bond	Electrostatic charge
Reason	Capillary force is induced by a monolayer of moist or lubricant on the surfaces	Reactions of molecules at the surfaces of contact	Bending and deformation of structure during the release process	Surfaces contact bond	Electric potential at closed surfaces
Wear					
Breakdown	Surface fatigue	Corrosion	Lesion	Adherence	
Reason	Periodic loading rather than flat surfaces	Chemical synergy between two surfaces	Substance loss as a result of different surfaces sliding	interaction held within two surfaces	
Creep and Fatigue					
Breakdown	Thermal stress	Applied stress	Intrinsic stress		
Reason	Excess heating	Applied stress	Residual stress		

failure mechanisms. While in ICs, testing focuses solely on electrical parameters to identify defects, MEMS devices require comprehensive testing of both electrical and mechanical characteristics to address potential failures. Table 1.3 summarizes the MEMS failure causes throughout the reliability test.

1.9.4 MEMS Device Breakdown

These devices possess conductive or insulated flat layers, gears, hinges, cavities, and an electronic monitoring circuit. In contrast, multiple devices are integrated within a single chip. Moving on a single axis, MEMS architectures have been optimized to enable multiaxis movements. MEMS are becoming increasingly versatile in their design to accommodate a broader range of applications. Failure analysis plays a crucial role in comprehending the underlying causes of faulty device behavior throughout the testing operation, spanning from the wafer level to the last phase, i.e., packing of

TABLE 1.4
MEMS Electrical Breakdown [17]

Electric Circuit (Short and Open)				
Breakdown	Oxidation	Electromigration	ESD, high electric field	Degradation of dielectric material
Reason	Environment	Load variation	Overload	Capacitive discharges
Contamination				
Breakdown	Environment	Intrinsic (crystal growth)	Manufacturing-induced	
Reason	Variable temperature and humidity	Environment	Industry rough handling	

the device. The failure mechanism results in poor device performance due to defective interconnects and limited compatibility.

Table 1.3 lists the most common mechanical faults of MEMS devices. While MEMS failures extend beyond the mechanical aspects of the device, it is important not to overlook potential electrical failures. Contact failure, electro-migration, and dielectric degradation are the causes of these.

Table 1.4 lists the most common electrical breakdowns of MEMS devices. MEMS devices are the most difficult to test due to their multiphysics behavior. Recently, these gadgets have been tested using functional specifications. Variations can influence the specifications of the device in the manufacturing process, which is a detrimental condition in MEMS testing because process fluctuations might introduce a lot of faults. In addition, the device's specifications are diverse and the device's measurements at different testing stages can prolong the overall test duration. Consequently, a wide range of test methodologies is necessary to measure the attributes of performance of different devices, compelling manufacturers to acquire diverse test equipment for each product. To validate the DUT specifications, fast transient test approaches are necessary. Specifications in multistructured complicated devices are frequently altered due to fabrication process drifts and faults. Specification violations have occurred due to normal manufacturing changes for devices designed near the specification limits. Process monitoring systems have detected process drifts at an early point in the production phase. Defects serve as the root causes of catastrophic failures, which can be identified through parametric and functional failure analysis tests.

Some fields like shape memory alloys (SMAs) and shape memory polymers (SMPs) for micro- and nanotechnology applications have the capabilities to remember the predeformed shape. Current science has various techniques to form micro-sized as well as nano-sized SMA and SMP materials, usually in the form of thin films. The growing future of 3D printing technology and devices like micropumps and microactuators shows enormous potential in shape memory material nanotechnology [43]. Table 1.5 summarizes the issues in the SMAs-Based Thin Films and SMPs.

TABLE 1.5
Challenges in the SMAs-Based Thin Films and SMPs

S. no.	SMAs-Based Thin Films	Challenges in SMPs
1.	Problems with fatigue	Interaction between heat production and thermo-response, as well as structural and polymer network size issues in SMPs for nanotechnology applications
2.	Temperature-driven changes demonstrate significant hysteresis, which is affected by SMA preparation procedures and material composition	Difficulties with tensile testing (SMA/SMP). Internal stress created after the sampling process might lead free-standing samples to bend. These bent samples not only affect the test outcome, but they are also readily destroyed when clamped in the tensile test device
3.	Low actuation speed	Experiments on the shape memory effect and superelasticity in SMA/SMP at the nanoscale remain extremely difficult. For example, during the phase transformation, it is difficult to discern grain evolution/changes inside individual grains
4.	Challenges in separating the martensite and R-phase temperature domains	
5.	Handling the R-phase transformation temperatures and the minimal transformation strain poses challenges. Such challenges are limiting the R-phase's extensive adoption in current nanotechnology applications	
6.	The surface preparation required to avoid the release of poisonous Ni using the arc deposition process is a difficult undertaking because this technique could lead to the generation of microdroplets and also it requires precise control of the properties of plasma and the vacuum arc	
7.	Precise control of composition of ultrathin films during its preparation, especially at the nanoscale level, is a major issue because at nanoscale dimensions, the transformation behavior can significantly deviate	

TABLE 1.5 (Continued)
Challenges in the SMAs-Based Thin Films and SMPs

S. no.	SMAs-Based Thin Films	Challenges in SMPs
8.	Determination of nanoscale sample phase transformation temperatures. This may need the use of advanced devices such as nanocalorimeters. As a result, characterizing the shape memory and superelastic responses of micro-/nano-sized SMA and SMP samples is a difficult challenge. It necessitates precise measurements of forces and changes in displacement	
9.	Difficulties with tensile testing (SMA/SMP). Internal stress created after the sampling process might lead free-standing samples to bend. These bent samples not only affect the test outcome, but they are also readily destroyed when clamped in the tensile test device	
10.	Experiments on the shape memory effect and superelasticity in SMA/SMP at the nanoscale remain extremely difficult. For example, during the phase transformation, it is difficult to discern grain evolution/changes inside individual grains	

1.10 ISSUES DURING TESTING OF MEMS

MEMS are miniature devices that integrate mechanical and electrical components on a single chip. Testing MEMS devices can present several challenges due to their small size, complex structures, and the combination of mechanical and electrical functionality. Issues that can arise during the testing of MEMS are described below.

1.10.1 Fabrication Failures

Microfabrication techniques are essential in the manufacturing of MEMS. These techniques enable the precise and controlled fabrication of microstructures, sensors, actuators, and integrated circuits on a small scale. MEMS devices often involve complex and intricate structures that require specialized microfabrication processes as shown in Figure 1.5. Some common microfabrication techniques used in MEMS manufacturing described next.

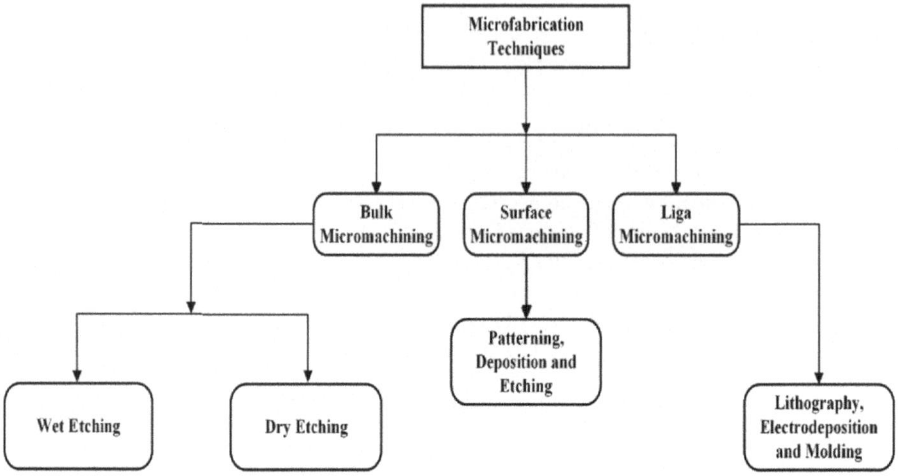

FIGURE 1.5 Microfabrication techniques for MEMS.

1.10.2 Photolithography

Photolithography is a crucial microfabrication process that uses light exposure and photoresist materials to form patterns on a substrate. It entails putting a photosensitive substance (photoresist) on the substrate, exposing it to light selectively through a photomask, and developing it to make the pattern of choice. The key features and layers of MEMS devices are created via photolithography.

1.10.3 Etching

Etching is the technique of removing material from a substrate selectively to form shapes and features. Wet etching involves soaking the substrate in a chemical solution that dissolves certain compounds, whereas dry etching removes material using plasma or ion beams. Etching is a technique used to determine the forms of MEMS components such sensors, actuators, and microfluidic channels.

1.10.4 Deposition

This requires depositing thin layers of materials onto a substrate in order to construct the desired MEMS structure. In MEMS production, typical deposition technologies include chemical vapor deposition (CVD), physical vapor deposition (PVD), and electroplating.

1.10.5 Oxidation

The process of oxidation is used to develop thin layers of oxide on a substrate, commonly silicon. This approach is utilized to build insulating layers as well as sacrificial layers for the release of MEMS systems.

1.10.6 Lithography

Lithography, like photolithography, involves producing patterns on a substrate via masks and light exposure. Lithography, on the other hand, is often utilized for patterning at higher sizes than photolithography, making it appropriate for some MEMS applications.

1.10.7 Bonding

Bonding methods are employed in MEMS devices to join substrates or layers of various materials. Bonding methods often utilized in MEMS production include wafer bonding, fusion bonding, and anodic bonding.

1.10.8 Surface Micromachining

Surface micromachining is the process of creating MEMS structures on a substrate's surface. Thin layers of material are deposited and patterned, and then further layers are created on top to make the required structures.

1.10.9 Bulk Micromachining

To construct 3D MEMS structures, bulk micromachining entails etching into the bulk of the substrate. This method is used to create gadgets that have moving components and mechanical functioning. These microfabrication techniques, along with other advanced processes, enable the precise and repeatable fabrication of MEMS devices with complex functionalities, making MEMS technology applicable in a wide range of industries, including electronics, healthcare, automotive, and consumer electronics.

Surface micromachining [44,45] is a direct evolution of the technology employed in manufacturing VLSI (very large-scale integration) devices using CMOS (complementary metal-oxide-semiconductor) technology. In such systems, thin layers of conductor, insulator, semiconductor, and passivation materials are deposited on doped silicon wafer substrates. In VLSI systems, these layers are coated, etched, and patterned to create highly cohesive electronic devices with smaller component sizes.

On the other hand, in surface micromachined MEMS, these layers are etched and shaped to construct electromechanical components that act as sacrificial layers, enabling the passage of mechanical layers. By utilizing CMOS-compliant processes and materials, the coupling of mechanical with electronic devices required for data processing and power transmission can be achieved, adding value to the overall system. Examples of commercially available extensively integrated micromachined surface devices include microaccelerometers chips used to control the activation of vehicle airbags and mirror arrays utilized in movable projectors. Figure 1.6 shows a surface micromachines process, which depicts amorphous, silicon carbide, and photoresist layers. These micromachining processes are often confined to thickness layers below 5 mm, limiting the ability to build devices that can distribute significant mechanical force.

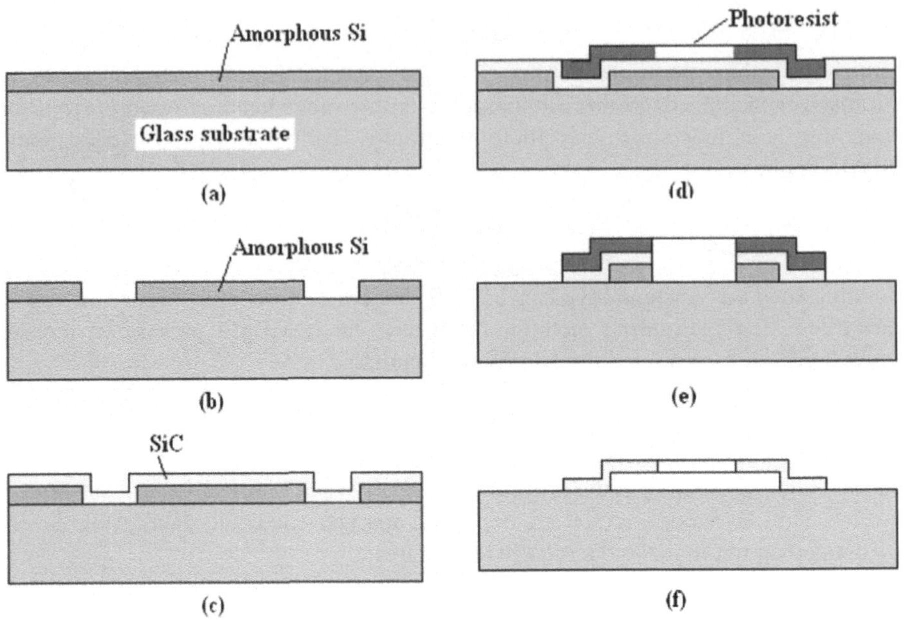

FIGURE 1.6 Typical surface micromachines process [47].

Bulk micromachining [46] involves the direct etching of a silicon wafer or another substrate. When integrated electrical functionalities are desired, the microelectronic components on the topmost layer of the silicon wafer are typically fabricated using CMOS methods. The remaining sides of the wafer are then used for bulk micromachining to construct mechanical elements like slim diaphragms, beams, or fluid flow tunnels. For many years, this technology has been employed to produce compact optical pressure sensors. Capacitive or piezoresistive techniques are utilized to gauge the bending of a slender membrane on an entire micromachined cavity. The cavity is sealed and vented to form a relative or absolute pressure sensor. Figure 1.7 provides a schematic representation of bulk micromachining that allows for the use of wider and thicker features compared to surface micromachining, primarily due to the silicon substrate serving as the foundation for physical system components. This is particularly advantageous in MEMS applications that require higher mechanical forces or strength levels, or in fluid applications like inkjet printer nozzles, where flow through small channels is achieved by surface micromachining and can lead to significant losses.

1.11 MOLDING PROCESS ISSUES

The production of the mechanical components of MEMS devices using a micromold is the third most prevalent industrial method. The term "LIGA" is derived from the German abbreviations for the primary process phases: lithography, galvanoforming (electroforming), and molding. The fundamental procedure entails lithography to

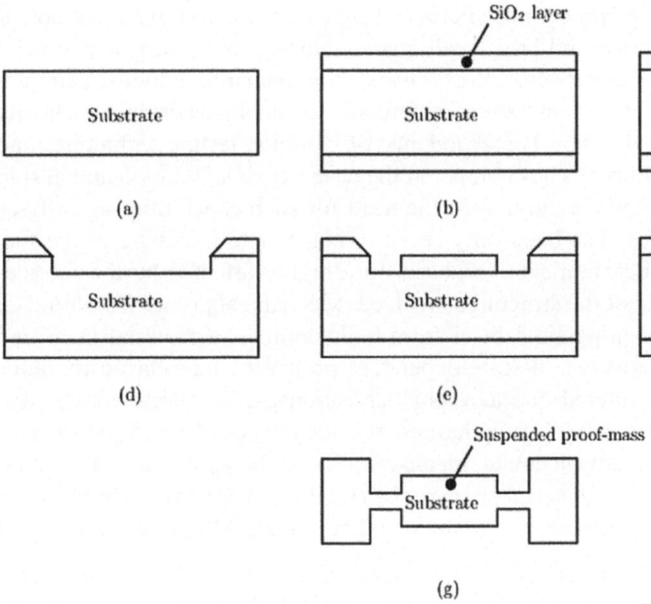

FIGURE 1.7 Schematic diagram of bulk micromachining [48].

create polymer molds [47] and subsequently electroplating metals into the cavities of these molds. The concept of using a molding mechanism is not limited to the deposition method. Certain substances, includes polycrystalline silicons and silicon carbides, can be processed using CVD and refractory ceramic structures generated by the sludge process approach.

1.11.1 Dicing Issues

The swift advancement and increased accessibility of cost-effective wafers, novel electrode materials, and thin-film targets with superior electrical output and compatibility with semiconductor processing pose challenges for MEMS devices. Achieving elevated temperature stability and resistance to perpetual deformation in MEMS devices is crucial. However, these requirements exceed the capabilities of delicate mechanisms. The MEMS industry is currently dealing with the most serious issue: device breakage during dicing.

1.11.2 Designing Issues

The ease and certainty with which complicated devices can be developed without the need for extensive prototypes is an essential goal for the continuous advancement of technology as well as the economic development of the microelectronic sectors [48]. The reliability of the existing modeling tools, along with the extensively characterized electrical properties of the materials used and the manufacturing techniques employed, greatly facilitate the design process of microelectronic devices. To unlock the potential of low component price and large-scale manufacturing in MEMS, it is crucial to adopt a similar design approach. In response to this demand, numerous simulation tools have been developed and are commercially available, catering specifically to the design of MEMS devices. The abundance of common testing techniques and material characteristics libraries has hampered the usability of simulation and design methodologies. Despite the recognition of the need for such capabilities as early as 1986, convincing progress has been only recently made. The issues lie in the fact that the properties of microfabricated materials are highly affected by the fabrication process and the scale of the structures involved. Mechanical properties estimated at the micro scale can significantly differ from bulk samples of material measured at the macro size. Moreover, non-scale-dependent properties like elastic modulus and density [49] can be altered due to vapor deposition gas, substrate effects, and nonequilibrium microstructure. To fully harness the advantages of rapid and systematic simulators for MEMS advancement, methodologies are being developed to establish connections between the material characteristics achieved and the assemblies and materials used. Figure 1.8 provide a schematic diagram of MEMS design. The initial

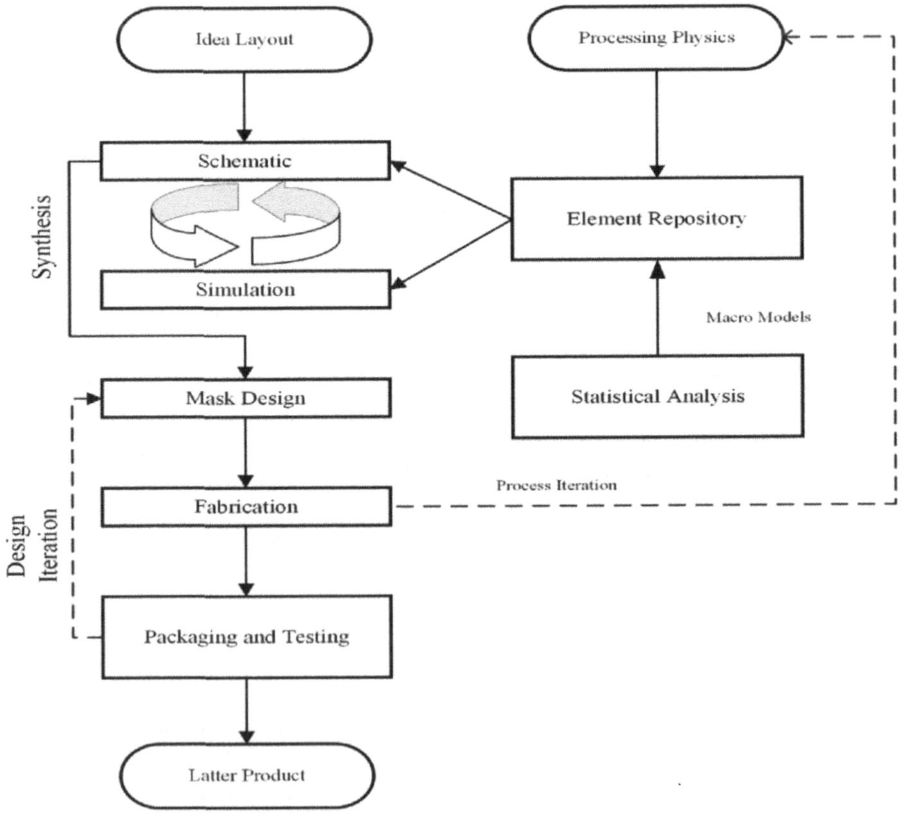

FIGURE 1.8 Schematic diagram of MEMS design [3].

step involves establishing graded testing protocols to characterize the structural properties of micromechanical manufactured materials using procedures and criteria specific to the intended applications. This will enable the creation of verified product and process databases, as well as the linkage of manufacturing paths and assets, to enable simulation-based design. Various studies have focused on key design issues such as elastic properties, strength characterization, bond strength, residual stress, fatigue, adhesion, surface forces, and tribology.

1.11.3 Testing at Wafer Level Issues

Comparing packaging of MEMS devices at the wafer level to bare die MEMS devices is not appropriate. Testing every sample die on the whole wafer substrate is challenging and time-consuming, which may result in inadequately testing wafer-level packaged products. Furthermore, there are additional obstacles to overcome, for example, consider the limited area between wire bonding and the handling challenges. The fundamental challenge in testing packed wafer-level devices is developing a system capable of evaluating numerous dye in a single test cycle.

1.11.4 Packaging and Handling

MEMS devices have a tendency to be sensitive and must be handled with care during testing and packing. They are susceptible to environmental conditions including humidity, tremors, and temperature. During testing, certain care must be taken to safeguard the equipment from damage or contamination.

1.11.5 Test Structure Design

Creating an appropriate test framework for MEMS devices may be difficult. Access to both electrical and mechanical interfaces must be provided by the test structure, permitting functional testing of the device's components. It might be difficult to design adequate test structures that do not interfere with the device's performance or modify its behavior.

1.11.6 Sensor Calibration

Calibration is required for many MEMS devices, such as gyroscopes, pressure sensors, and accelerometers, to guarantee precise measurement. Calibration is the process of analyzing the device's reaction and changing its output to meet established reference values. It can be difficult to develop calibration techniques and equipment that can manage the small size and complicated behavior of MEMS sensors.

1.11.7 Electrical and Mechanical Coupling

Mechanical and electrical components of MEMS devices frequently interact in complex ways. Testing these devices necessitates assessing both electrical and mechanical performance at the same time. During testing, it might be difficult to identify and isolate the impacts of each component.

1.11.8 Test Equipment Limitations

Because of their small size and particular properties, conventional test equipment may not be adequate for evaluating MEMS devices. To precisely access and test MEMS devices, specialized equipment such as microprobes, microscopes, and environmental chambers may be necessary. Such technology can be costly and may need specialized knowledge to operate efficiently.

1.11.9 Yield and Reliability

MEMS devices are mass-produced, therefore maintaining high yield and dependability is critical. Testing assists in identifying any manufacturing flaws or variances that may have an impact on the performance or dependability of the devices. Developing effective testing procedures to reduce false positives and false negatives and increase yield can be difficult.

1.12 CHALLENGES ENCOUNTERED DURING THE MANUFACTURING OF MEMS DEVICES

MEMS device manufacture presents various obstacles due to its complicated architecture, tiny size, and integration of multiple components. Figure 1.9 depicts the MEMS manufacturing procedures. Some frequent issues faced during MEMS device production include:

Process complexity: MEMS production entails complex techniques such as deposition, etching, lithography, and bonding. It might be difficult to coordinate these activities and ensure their compliance with the required device structure. To obtain the necessary mechanical and electrical properties of the device, the manufacturing procedures must be properly regulated.

Miniaturization and precision: MEMS devices are often made at the microscale, necessitating tremendous accuracy. It can be difficult to achieve the appropriate feature sizes, such as submicron diameters, and to maintain consistency across large batches of devices. The sensitivity to process changes is likewise increased by miniaturization, making process control crucial.

Material selection and compatibility: MEMS devices frequently necessitate the use of several materials with varied mechanical, electrical, and chemical capabilities. It might be difficult to select appropriate materials that can endure manufacturing procedures and perform consistently in the device's intended environment. Material compatibility, stress mismatch, and variances in thermal expansion must all be carefully examined.

Packaging and hermetic process: It is an enormous challenge to package MEMS devices so that they are protected from external conditions while remaining functional. Moisture, particulates, and impurities may all influence the performance

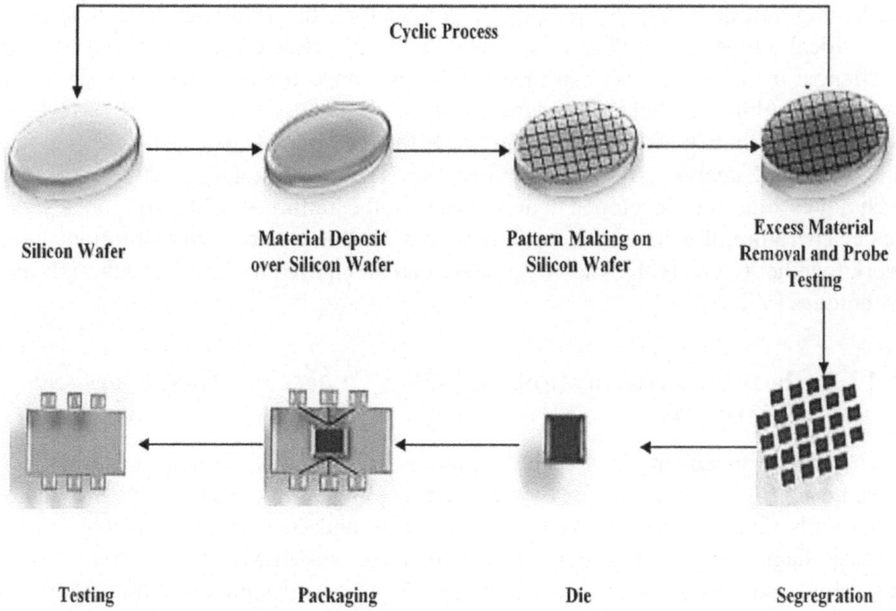

FIGURE 1.9 MEMS manufacturing process [3].

and dependability of MEMS devices. It is critical yet difficult to achieve a hermetic seal to prevent impurities from entering the device without affecting its mechanical or electrical behavior.

Yield improvement: MEMS production frequently includes batch processing, in which a large number of devices are produced on a wafer at the same time. Due to process differences, material difficulties, and complicated device designs, achieving high yield and eliminating defects over the whole wafer can be difficult. To improve production efficiency, yield enhancement methods such as defect identification, process optimization, and statistical process control are required.

Testing and characterization: Validating the functionality and performance of MEMS devices is essential during manufacturing. However, testing complex MEMS structures can be challenging due to their small size, the integration of mechanical and electrical components, and the need for specialized equipment. Developing reliable and efficient testing methodologies to ensure the quality and reliability of each device can be demanding.

Future challenges faced by the MEMS failure analysis in six distinct categories based on their applications are sensors, actuators, RF MEMS, optical MEMS, microfluidic MEMS, and bio-MEMS. A major challenge for failure analysis common to all these categories is to develop a technique that performs multiple measurements on single and several devices in parallel at the same time. For sensors, a major hurdle is simulating the chemical behavior of the devices designed to sense. Other major areas are packaging and depackaging/decapping. In actuators, the challenge is to determine the critical temperature, whereas in the case of RF MEMS and optical MEMS the challenges include analysis of surface roughness, nondestructive analysis of adhesion or stiction failures, and charge accumulation.

Similarly, challenges for microfluidic MEMS and bio-MEMS include functional and structural analysis, biocompatibility, etc. Therefore, nondestructive tools and techniques must be developed that can assess the failure mechanisms on a large scale. Therefore, the industries, academia, and various government institutions must work together to create the knowledge base that is required to develop such tools and techniques [50].

1.12.1 Biomedical Applications of MEMS Devices and Their Issues and Challenges

Technical advancements in the field of biomedical MEMS, known as bio-MEMS, have been growing over the last two decades as efficient microscale as well as nanoscale tools for the precise, fast, highly sensitive, and cost-efficient alternatives for disease diagnoses and processing. In Figure 1.10, bio-MEMS includes the biology discipline and MEMS, and it has been developed and designed for the upliftment of diagnostic devices and biosensors, surgical tools, microfluidic devices, inertial sensors for biomechanics, ultrasound transducers, drug-delivery systems, and lab-on-a-chip (LOC) devices [51].

Lab-on-a-chip (LOC) devices: MEMS-based lab-on-a-chip devices enable the miniaturization and integration of complex laboratory processes, such as sample preparation, mixing, separation, and detection, onto a single microfluidic chip. LOC devices have applications in medical diagnostics, DNA analysis, drug discovery, and point-of-care testing, offering faster, cost-effective, and portable solutions.

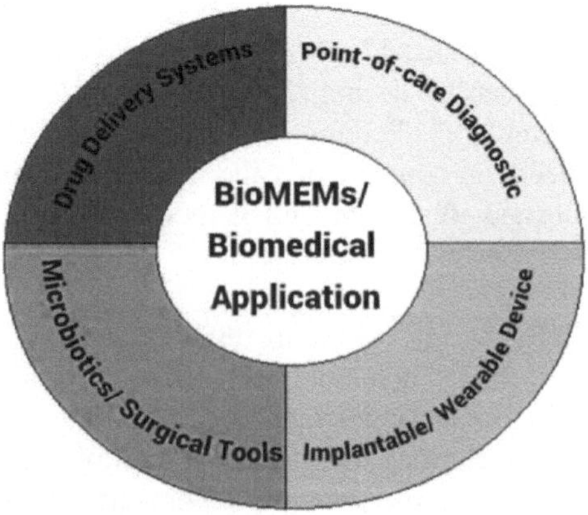

FIGURE 1.10 MEMS applications in the biomedical field.

Biosensors: MEMS biosensors are capable of detecting and quantifying biological molecules, cells, and pathogens with high sensitivity and specificity. Submicron-range MEMS are being developed so that they can be useful in miniaturized diagnostic devices. These biosensors find applications in detecting biomarkers for various diseases, monitoring glucose levels, analyzing DNA sequences, and identifying infectious agents. Specific MEMS components, such as micropumps, micromixers, and microvalves, are used in these applications to regulate and analyze liquids, fluids, and chemical processes. For disease diagnosis, body fluids such as blood, serum, urine, saliva, or liquid biopsies are frequently introduced into the microchip. Biosensors have been used to detect and monitor glucose, hemoglobin, urea, amino acids, bodily gases, viruses, bacteria, and cancer biomarkers. BioMEMS, on the other hand, can be employed as wearable or implanted devices for fixed and continuous measurement of blood oxygen, intraocular or aortic pressure, electrical impulses, or metabolic processes. Wearable MEMS have become an important component of chronic patients' everyday life since they may remotely track vital statistics such as blood and intracranial pressure, glucose levels, heart and respiration rate, body temperature, and O_2 saturation [52–60].

Implantable devices: MEMS-based implantable devices are used in various medical applications, including neural prosthetics, pacemakers, drug-delivery systems, and intraocular pressure sensors for glaucoma patients. Their miniaturization allows for minimally invasive procedures and reduced risk of complications.

Microfluidic devices: MEMS-based microfluidic devices enable precise manipulation and control of fluids at the microscale. They are used for applications such as cell sorting, drug delivery, organ-on-chip models, and analysis of single cells, contributing to advancements in personalized medicine and drug development.

Inertial sensors for biomechanics: Wearable gadgets use MEMS accelerometers and gyroscopes to track human movements and measure physical activity. These sensors are used to monitor sports and fitness, as well as for rehabilitation and gait analysis.

Ultrasound transducers: MEMS-based ultrasound transducers enable the creation of smaller, portable ultrasound devices while improving imaging capabilities. They have medical imaging uses, such as point-of-care ultrasonography and less invasive treatments.

Drug-delivery systems: MEMS-based drug-delivery systems have the ability to precisely regulate drug release rates and dosages, hence improving therapeutic efficacy and decreasing adverse effects. They have uses in cancer therapy, insulin administration for diabetic management, and other controlled-release medicines.

Bio-MEMS: Bio-MEMS have demonstrated tremendous potential in numerous aspects of infectious illness detection, diagnosis, monitoring, and treatment, including during the coronavirus (COVID-19) pandemic caused by the SARS-CoV-2 virus.

Diagnostic testing: Bio-MEMS-based lab-on-a-chip devices have been developed for rapid and sensitive detection of the SARS-CoV-2 virus. These devices use microfluidic technology to miniaturize and integrate the different steps of the diagnostic process, enabling faster and point-of-care testing. Polymerase chain reaction (PCR) amplification, isothermal amplification, and CRISPR-based detection methods have been integrated into bio-MEMS devices for COVID-19 testing.

Wearable health monitoring: Wearable bio-MEMS devices, such as biosensors and microfluidic patches, have been explored for continuous monitoring of biomarkers related to COVID-19, such as body temperature, respiratory rate, and cytokine levels. These devices can provide early indications of infection or disease progression and help in monitoring patient health remotely.

1.13 CONCLUSION AND FUTURE SCOPE

The most significant improvements in MEMS could come from technological advancements that allow for the production of larger instruments at unit prices comparable to those of current microelectronics. Mesoscale devices, which possess greater capacity and strength than modern MEMS, present an opportunity in Industry 4.0 to expand the range of materials and refine fabrication procedures. Material sciences must focus on improving methodologies for material selection and characterization in the context of microfabricated structures. While some testing tools and methods for IC technology can be applied for testing in MEMS, there is a need for new diagnostic tools to address specific challenges. The cost of testing must be reduced and value-added techniques implemented in Industry 4.0 and 5.0 to facilitate the adoption of MEMS as an emerging technology. Standard electrical testing is insufficient to capture MEMS devices' mechanical behavior, necessitating specialized techniques for flow, motion, and pressure testing. As device complexity increases with multifunction integration, testing becomes more challenging. Different testing approaches are employed throughout MEMS development's design, prototype, and production cycles. In Industry 4.0, Design for Test (DFT) is crucial to address cost and time-to-market pressures, and a comprehensive understanding of testing requirements is essential during the design phase to ensure cost-effectiveness and reliable prediction of device performance. Resolving these challenges in Industry 4.0 requires a holistic view of MEMS as a system, ensuring that material solutions align with the entire production process and application needs.

ACKNOWLEDGMENT

The authors acknowledge endorsement provided by National Institute of Technology Nagaland to complete this work.

REFERENCES

[1] Wszołek, Grzegorz, Piotr Czop, Jakub Słoniewski, and Halit Dogrusoz. "Vibration monitoring of CNC machinery using MEMS sensors." *Journal of Vibroengineering* 22, no. 3 (2020): 735–750.

[2] Pattanaik, Priyabrata, and Manoj Ojha. "Review on challenges in MEMS technology." *Materials Today: Proceedings* 81, (2021): 224–226.

[3] Podder, Itilekha, Tamas Fischl, and Udo Bub. "Artificial intelligence applications for MEMS-based sensors and manufacturing process optimization." In *Telecom*, 4, no. 1, pp. 165–197. MDPI, 2023.

[4] Chircov, Cristina, and Alexandru Mihai Grumezescu. "Microelectromechanical systems (MEMS) for biomedical applications." *Micromachines* 13, no. 2 (2022): 164.

[5] Li, Tao, and Pooi See Lee. "Piezoelectric energy harvesting technology: From materials, structures, to applications." *Small Structures* 3, no. 3 (2022): 2100128.

[6] Mishra, Manish Kumar, Vikas Dubey, P. M. Mishra, and Isharat Khan. "MEMS technology: A review." *Journal of Engineering Research and Reports* 4, no. 1 (2019): 1–24.

[7] Mahapatra, Susmriti Das, Preetam Chandan Mohapatra, Adrianus Indrat Aria, Graham Christie, Yogendra Kumar Mishra, Stephan Hofmann, and Vijay Kumar Thakur. "Piezoelectric materials for energy harvesting and sensing applications: Roadmap for future smart materials." *Advanced Science* 8, no. 17 (2021): 2100864.

[8] Raju, S. Srinivasulu, M. Umapathy, and G. Uma. "Cantilever piezoelectric energy harvester with multiple cavities." *Smart Materials and Structures* 24, no. 11 (2015): 115023.

[9] Liu, Shuang, Bingkun Hu, Dawei Liu, Fu Li, Jing-Feng Li, Bo Li, Liangliang Li, Yuan-Hua Lin, and Ce-Wen Nan. "Micro-thermoelectric generators based on through glass pillars with high output voltage enabled by large temperature difference." *Applied Energy* 225 (2018): 600–610.

[10] Erturk, Alper, and Daniel J. Inman. *Piezoelectric energy harvesting*. John Wiley & Sons, 2011.

[11] Hwang, Geon-Tae, Joonseok Yang, Seong Ho Yang, Ho-Yong Lee, Minbok Lee, Dae Yong Park and Jae Hyun Han. "A reconfigurable rectified flexible energy harvester via solid-state single crystal grown PMN–PZT." *Advanced Energy Materials* 5, no. 10 (2015): 1500051.

[12] Zhu, Guang, Rusen Yang, Sihong Wang, and Zhong Lin Wang. "Flexible high-output nanogenerator based on lateral ZnO nanowire array." *Nano Letters* 10, no. 8 (2010): 3151–3155.

[13] Song, HuaiBing, Ilbey Karakurt, Minsong Wei, Nathaniel Liu, Yao Chu, Junwen Zhong, and Liwei Lin. "Lead iodide nanosheets for piezoelectric energy conversion and strain sensing." *Nano Energy* 49 (2018): 7–13.

[14] Choudhary, Vikas, and Krzysztof Iniewski, eds. *Mems: Fundamental technology and applications*. CRC Press, 2017.

[15] Tseng, Ampere A., Kuan Chen, Chii D. Chen, and Kung J. Ma. "Electron beam lithography in nanoscale fabrication: Recent development." *IEEE Transactions on Electronics Packaging Manufacturing* 26, no. 2 (2003): 141–149.

[16] Saburo Muroga. "CMOS." In *The VLSI handbook second edition*, Wai-Kai Chen, Routledge Taylor & Francis Group, 2006.

[17] Vai, M. Michael. *VLSI design*. CRC press, 2017.

[18] Shoaib, Muhammad, Nor Hisham Hamid, Aamir Farooq Malik, Noohul Basheer Zain Ali, and Mohammad Tariq Jan. "A review on key issues and challenges in devices level MEMS testing." *Journal of Sensors* 1 (2016): 1639805.

[19] Moyer, B. "The MEMS testing quagmire." *Electronic Engineering Journal* (Online) (2011).

[20] Wynnyckyj, S. "MEMS testing challenges & cost of test." In *Proceedings of the 13th Annual MEPTEC MEMS Technology Symposium*. 2015.

[21] Ciganda Brasca, Lyl M., Paolo Bernardi, Matteo Sonza Reorda, Dimitri Barbieri, Luciano Bonaria, Roberto Losco, Luciano Marcigot, and Maurizio Straiotto. "A

parallel tester architecture for accelerometer and gyroscope MEMS calibration and test." *Journal of Electronic Testing* 27 (2011): 389–402.

[22] Bennett, H., M. Gaitan, and Y. Obeng. "MEMS testing standards: A path to continued innovation." *MEMS Industry Group: Pittsburgh, PA, USA* (2011).

[23] Zhang, Jian-hong, Dong-guang Li, and Xue-jun Cui. "Failure analysis of micro-structure under shock load." In *2012 Proceedings of International Conference on Modelling, Identification and Control*, pp. 86–90. IEEE, 2012.

[24] Pierce, David M., Benedikt Zeyen, Brent M. Huigens, and Alissa M. Fitzgerald. "Predicting the failure probability of device features in MEMS." *IEEE Transactions on Device and Materials Reliability* 11, no. 3 (2011): 433–441.

[25] Lellouchi, Djemel, Xavier Lafontan, Jeremie Dhennin, F. Beaudoin, and Francis Pressecq. "MEMS failure analysis case studies using the IR-OBIRCH method-Short circuit localization in a MEMS pressure sensor." In *2009 16th IEEE International Symposium on the Physical and Failure Analysis of Integrated Circuits*, Suzhou, China, pp. 827–831. IEEE, 2009, doi: 10.1109/IPFA.2009.5232714

[26] Broué, Adrien, Jérémie Dhennin, Cédric Seguineau, Xavier Lafontan, Christel Dieppedale, Jean-Michel Desmarres, Patrick Pons, and Robert Plana. "Methodology to analyze failure mechanisms of ohmic contacts on MEMS switches." In *2009 IEEE International Reliability Physics Symposium*, pp. 869–873. IEEE, 2009.

[27] De Wolf, Ingrid, Anne Jourdain, Piet De Moor, H. A. C. Tilmans, and Laurent Marchand. "Hermeticity testing and failure analysis of MEMS packages." In *2007 14th International Symposium on the Physical and Failure Analysis of Integrated Circuits*, pp. 147–154. IEEE, 2007.

[28] Jan, M. Tariq, Nor Hisham B. Hamid, Mohd Haris B. Md Khir, Muhammad Shoaib, and Asif Mirza. "Influence of crack growths on the performances of cantilever based MEMS devices: Design and simulations." In *2014 5th International Conference on Intelligent and Advanced Systems (ICIAS)*, pp. 1–4. IEEE, 2014.

[29] Al-Fandi, Mohamed, Jin-Woo Kim, Ajay P. Malshe, Steve Tung, Jerry Jenkins, and Ryan Pooran. "Chemo-sensitivity and reliability of flagellar rotary motor in a MEMS microfluidic actuation system." *Sensors and Actuators B: Chemical* 114, no. 1 (2006): 229–238.

[30] Xiong, Xingguo, Yu-Liang Wu, and Wen-Ben Jone. "Material fatigue and reliability of MEMS accelerometers." In *2008 IEEE International Symposium on Defect and Fault Tolerance of VLSI Systems*, pp. 314–322. IEEE, 2008.

[31] Hartley, F. T., S. Arney, and F. Sexton. "Microsystems reliability, test and metrology." *International Technology Roadmap for Semiconductors* (2001).

[32] Wolffenbuttel, R. F., & van Mullem, C. J. The relationship between microsystem technology and metrology. *IEEE Transactions on Instrumentation and Measurement, 50,* no. 6, 1469–1474.

[33] Bemis, Andy, Alex Ned, Sorin Stefanescu, Nathaniel Wilson, and Adam Kane. "The effect of silicon fatigue on Kulite silicon pressure sensor's reliability application note: AN 101," 3/20/12, https://kulite.com/.

[34] Li, Jue, Mikael Broas, Joonas Makkonen, Toni T. Mattila, Jussi Hokka, and Mervi Paulasto-Kröckel. "Shock impact reliability and failure analysis of a three-axis MEMS gyroscope." *Journal of Microelectromechanical Systems* 23, no. 2 (2013): 347–355.

[35] Patel, Chandradip, Patrick McCluskey, and David Lemus. "Performance and reliability of MEMS gyroscopes at high temperatures." In *2010 12th IEEE Intersociety Conference on Thermal and Thermomechanical Phenomena in Electronic Systems*, pp. 1–5. IEEE, 2010.

[36] Kapels, Hergen, Robert Aigner, and Josef Binder. "Fracture strength and fatigue of polysilicon determined by a novel thermal actuator [MEMS]." *IEEE Transactions on Electron Devices* 47, no. 7 (2000): 1522–1528.

[37] van Gils, Marcel, Jeroen Bielen, and Gavin McDonald. "Evaluation of creep in RF MEMS devices." In *2007 International Conference on Thermal, Mechanical and Multi-Physics Simulation Experiments in Microelectronics and Micro-Systems. EuroSime 2007*, pp. 1–6. IEEE, 2007.

[38] Min, Qi, Junyong Tao, and Xun Chen. "A parallel-plate actuated test structure for fatigue analysis of MEMS." In *2011 International Conference on Quality, Reliability, Risk, Maintenance, and Safety Engineering*, pp. 297–301. IEEE, 2011.

[39] Kam, Hei, Vincent Pott, Rhesa Nathanael, Jaeseok Jeon, Elad Alon, and Tsu-Jae King Liu. "Design and reliability of a micro-relay technology for zero-standby-power digital logic applications." In *2009 IEEE International Electron Devices Meeting (IEDM)*, pp. 1–4. IEEE, 2009.

[40] Tariq Jan, Mohammad, Nor Hisham Bin Hamid, Mohd Haris Md Khir, Khalid Ashraf, and Mohammad Shoaib. "Reliability and fatigue analysis in cantilever-based MEMS devices operating in harsh environments." *Journal of Quality and Reliability Engineering*, 987847, 16 pages, 2014.

[41] Mardivirin, David, Arnaud Pothier, M. El Khatib, A. Crunteanu, O. Vendier, and P. Blondy. "Reliability of dielectric less electrostatic actuators in RF-MEMS ohmic switches." In *2008 European Microwave Integrated Circuit Conference*, pp. 490–493. IEEE, 2008.

[42] Boloni, Francisc Attila, Abdelkader Benabou, and Abdelmounaïm Tounzi. "Stochastic modeling of the pull-in voltage in a MEMS beam structure." *IEEE Transactions on Magnetics* 47, no. 5 (2011): 974–977.

[43] Huang, Yunhan, Arvind Sai Sarathi Vasan, Ravi Doraiswami, Michael Osterman, and Michael Pecht. "MEMS reliability review." *IEEE Transactions on Device and Materials Reliability* 12, no. 2 (2012): 482–493.

[44] Yang, Ping, and NingBo Liao. "Surface sliding simulation in micro-gear train for adhesion problem and tribology design by using molecular dynamics model." *Computational Materials Science* 38, no. 4 (2007): 678–684.

[45] Stachiv, Ivo, Eduardo Alarcon, and Miroslav Lamac. "Shape memory alloys and polymers for MEMS/NEMS applications: Review on recent findings and challenges in design, preparation, and characterization." *Metals* 11, no. 3 (2021): 415.

[46] Chen, Weiqiang, Raymond HW Lam, and Jianping Fu. "Photolithographic surface micromachining of polydimethylsiloxane (PDMS)." *Lab on a Chip* 12, no. 2 (2012): 391–395.

[47] Chen, Bangtao, Francis EH Tay, and Ciprian Iliescu. "Development of thick film PECVD amorphous silicon with low stress for MEMS applications." In *Micro- and Nanotechnology: Materials, Processes, Packaging, and Systems IV*, vol. 7269, pp. 130–140. SPIE, 2008.

[48] Antonello, Riccardo, and Roberto Oboe. "MEMS gyroscopes for consumers and industrial applications." In *Microsensors*. IntechOpen, 2011.

[49] Tseng, Ampere A., Kuan Chen, Chii D. Chen, and Kung J. Ma. "Electron beam lithography in nanoscale fabrication: Recent development." *IEEE Transactions on Electronics Packaging Manufacturing* 26, no. 2 (2003): 141–149.

[50] Kaeslin, Hubert. *Top-down digital VLSI design: From architectures to gate-level circuits and FPGAs*. Morgan Kaufmann, 2014.

[51] Hopcroft, Matthew A., William D. Nix, and Thomas W. Kenny. "What is the Young's Modulus of Silicon?" *Journal of Microelectromechanical Systems* 19, no. 2 (2010): 229–238.

[52] Walraven, Jeremy A. "Future challenges for MEMS failure analysis." In *International Test Conference, 2003. Proceedings. ITC 2003*, pp. 850–850. IEEE Computer Society, 2003.

[53] Paul, Suprio R., Suraj K. Nayak, Arfat Anis, and Kunal Pal. "MEMS-based controlled drug delivery systems: A short review." *Polymer-Plastics Technology and Engineering* 55, no. 9 (2016): 965–975.

[54] Leichle, Thierry, Liviu Nicu, and Thomas Alava. "MEMS biosensors and COVID-19: Missed opportunity." *ACS Sensors* 5, no. 11 (2020): 3297–3305.

[55] Shende, P., and P. Kasture. "Dendrimeric biosensor for detection of E. coli O157: H7 in diet." Biointerface Research in Applied Chemistry 10 (2020): 5128–5131.

[56] Chircov, Cristina, Alexandra Cătălina Bîrcă, Alexandru Mihai Grumezescu, Bogdan Stefan Vasile, Ovidiu Oprea, Adrian Ionuţ Nicoară, Chih-Hui Yang, Keng-Shiang Huang, and Ecaterina Andronescu. "Synthesis of magnetite nanoparticles through a lab-on-chip device." *Materials* 14, no. 19 (2021): 5906.

[57] Sonetha, Vaibhavi, Poorvi Agarwal, Smeet Doshi, Ridhima Kumar, and Bhavya Mehta. "Microelectromechanical systems in medicine." *Journal of Medical and Biological Engineering* 37 (2017): 580–601.

[58] Pachkawade, Vinayak. "Ultra-precise MEMS based bio-sensors." *Biosensor-Current and Novel Strategies for Biosensing* (2020). IntechOpen, 5 May 2021. Crossref, doi:10.5772/intechopen.93931.

[59] Chircov, Cristina, Alexandra Cătălina Bîrcă, Alexandru Mihai Grumezescu, and Ecaterina Andronescu. "Biosensors-on-chip: An up-to-date review." *Molecules* 25, no. 24 (2020): 6013.

[60] Podlevsky, Jennie Hewitt Appel. "Diagnostic and Therapeutic MEMS (Micro-Electro-Mechanical Systems) Devices for the Identification and Treatment of Human Disease." PhD diss., Arizona State University, 2018.

2 The Industrial Internet of Things (IIoT)

Overview, Architecture, Challenges, and Possible Solutions

Oladeji Oluniyi Olanrele, Sunday Adeola Ajagbe, Abolaji Okikiade Ilori, and Oluseyi Afolabi Adeyemi

2.1 INTRODUCTION

The Industrial Internet of Things (IIoT) is a paradigm shift that is revolutionizing smart electricity, manufacturing, healthcare, and transportation [1,2]. Smart gadgets use the Internet to connect with one another, which increases their computing and storage capability while reducing the size of their individual components. The IIoT has huge potential to improve productivity, efficiency, and operational performance across a variety of industries by enabling seamless communication, real-time data collection, and intelligent decision-making [3,4]. The fundamental concept underlying the IIoT is to connect industrial equipment, machinery, and systems to enable communication and information sharing over a densely connected network. Due to this connectedness, massive amounts of data may be gathered from multiple sources, including sensors built into machinery, equipment, and production lines. Insightful information about the operational status, performance indicators, and environmental circumstances in industrial contexts is provided by the collected data [5,6]. The IIoT, on the other hand, goes beyond merely collecting data to rely on cutting-edge analytics methods to glean useful insights and promote reasoned decision-making. IIoT systems may recognize patterns, locate anomalies, forecast maintenance requirements, enhance operations, and even enable autonomous control by applying advanced algorithms and machine learning models to the gathered data. In Sundmaeker et al. [7], the method increases overall productivity by improving quality control, reducing downtime, and maximizing resource usage.

Numerous sectors, including industry, energy, transportation, agriculture, and healthcare, can use IIoT applications. In manufacturing industries, the IIoT enables "smart factories" with networked machinery, leading to more efficient operations

DOI: 10.1201/9781003581963-2

with higher productivity [8]. The IIoT in the energy sector enables remote monitoring of power generating and distribution systems, smart grid management, and energy optimization [9,10]. For increased effectiveness and safety in transportation, the IIoT enables fleet management, logistics optimization, and vehicle tracking [11]. Despite the enormous potential benefits of the IIoT, there are still issues that need to be resolved. The interconnectedness of gadgets and the importance of industrial activities give rise to security and privacy problems. Important factors to take into account include ensuring data protection, securing communication routes, and protecting against cyber threats [12]. Interoperability between various industrial systems and legacy infrastructure also continues to be difficult, necessitating efforts in standardization and integration [13,14].

In this chapter, we will delve into the architecture and applications of the IIoT, exploring its various components, technologies, and real-world use cases. We will examine the layered architecture of IIoT systems, discuss key enabling technologies, and highlight the low points and requirements for implementation. At the end, readers will gain a comprehensive understanding of the IIoT and its potential to revolutionize industries, drive innovation, and shape the future of industrial systems. Through this exploration, this study provides resources for researchers, industry professionals, and enthusiasts toward grasping the fundamental concepts, practical implementations, and future directions of the IIoT.

One of the significant advantages of the IIoT is its ability to improve efficiency and productivity. By monitoring and optimizing manufacturing processes, identifying bottlenecks, and reducing downtime, IIoT devices empower manufacturers to enhance their operational efficiency. In this book contribution, we will delve into the architecture and applications of the IIoT, exploring its various components, technologies, and real-world use cases. We will examine the layered architecture of IIoT systems, discuss key enabling technologies, and highlight the challenges and considerations associated with its implementation. By the end, readers will gain a comprehensive understanding of the IIoT and its potential to revolutionize industries, drive innovation, and shape the future of industrial systems. Through this exploration, we aim to provide a valuable resource for researchers, industry professionals, and enthusiasts seeking to grasp the fundamental concepts, practical implementations, and future directions of the IIoT.

2.1.1 Research Questions and Methodology

The following are the research questions that will enable us to achieve the proposed chapter:

i. How does the implementation of IIoT architectures impact the efficiency and cost-effectiveness of manufacturing processes?
ii. In what ways does the IIoT contribute to improving the quality of products in manufacturing industries?
iii. What are effective computational techniques in analyzing the vast amount of data generated by IIoT devices?

These research questions align well with the themes of the chapter, providing a basis for further investigation within the context of the Industrial Internet of Things and its applications in manufacturing industry. And this informs the methodology adopted, which is a systematic and comprehensive identification, selection, and analysis of relevant sources to develop a clear understanding of the existing body of knowledge. A specific focus is placed on identifying challenges associated with IIoT implementation, as the understanding of these is crucial for establishing ways to address them.

2.1.2 Chapter Organization

The remainder of the chapter is organized as follows: Section 2.2 provides an overview of IIoT technology. Section 2.3 describes features of IIoT architecture and Section 2.4 explains the challenges of IIoT-based implementation. The chapter conclusion, implications, and future scope are presented in Section 2.5.

2.2 OVERVIEW OF IIOT TECHNOLOGY

The definitions that follow, written by several writers, offer a variety of viewpoints on the nature and reach of the IIoT. The IIoT is a network of items integrated with software and sensors, and other technologies that allow them to gather and exchange data. It is possible to increase productivity, efficiency, and decision-making in industrial settings by integrating physical and digital systems [15,16].

According to Javaid et al. [3], the IIoT refers to the convergence of industrial systems with Internet technologies, enabling the seamless integration of devices, sensors, and machines to gather, analyze, and utilize data for process monitoring, optimization, and automation with significant impact on different areas of industry, as shown in Figure 2.1.

The IIoT, on the other hand, is defined by Lee et al. [17] as the Internet-enabled networking and communication of physical objects, industrial machinery, and infrastructure that enables the integration of data-driven analytics, automation, and control systems in a variety of industrial domains. The IIoT is also defined as the implementation of Internet-connected devices [18], data analytics, and automation technologies to improve industrial processes by enabling real-time monitoring, predictive maintenance, and adaptive control. The term "Industrial Internet of Things" (IIoT) refers to the integration of smart devices, sensors, and communication technologies in extensive contexts to facilitate data-driven decision-making, process optimization, and increased operational efficiency [19,20].

The origins of the IIoT can be traced back to the convergence of industrial systems and Internet technology [21]. The IIoT has evolved since its inception, with breakthroughs in connectivity, data analytics, cybersecurity, and interoperability. It has revolutionized how industrial operations are monitored, managed, and optimized in a variety of industries, including manufacturing, energy, transportation, healthcare, and agriculture [22,23]. The emergence of the IIoT may be traced back to when SCADA systems were first introduced. Using centralized computers, these systems

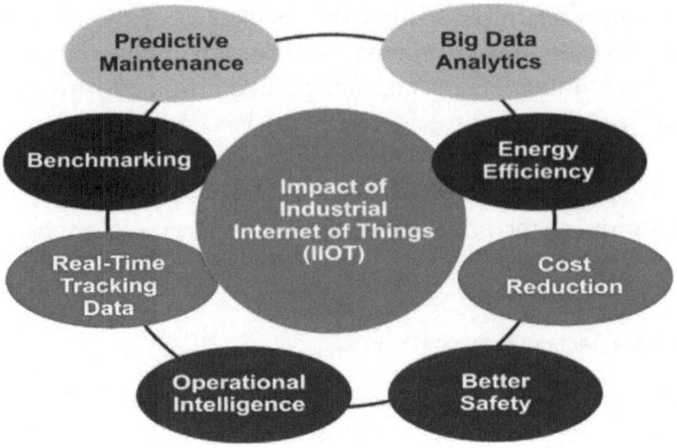

FIGURE 2.1 Significant impact of the Industrial Internet of Things (IIoT).

provided remote monitoring and control of industrial processes [24]. Advances in telecommunications and networking technology resulted in the emergence of Machine-to-Machine (M2M) communication protocol. M2M enables machines and gadgets to connect with one another, facilitating data and control signal interchange [25].

The term "Industrial Internet" was first used by General Electric (GE) in 2011 to highlight the use of IoT technologies especially in industrial sectors. By fusing data analytics, networking, and automation, the Industrial Internet was created to enhance industrial operations and efficiency. According to Rehman et al. [26], the IIoT refers to the fusion of industrial systems and IoT technologies. To enable data-driven decision-making and process optimization, the IIoT improved traditional industrial automation capabilities by incorporating advanced analytics, cloud computing, edge computing, and artificial intelligence (AI) [27]. The Industrial Internet promises to change our world once more in the 21st century. The Industrial Revolution's invention of the global industrial system and the Internet Revolution's development of open computing and communication systems have combined to create new opportunities to increase productivity, decrease waste and inefficiency, and improve the quality of human labor [28,29]

2.2.1 Benefits of IIoT Technology

The Industrial Internet of Things holds significant importance in today's industrial landscape, and this lies in its potential to transform industries, drive operational efficiencies, enable data-driven decision-making, and unlock new opportunities for innovation and sustainability. The key reasons highlighting its significance are presented next.

2.2.1.1 Enhanced Efficiency and Productivity

By increasing productivity and efficiency through a variety of methods, IIoT effects are obvious in a number of sectors. The IIoT provides better decision-making, process optimization, and higher operational efficiency by utilizing real-time data, connectivity, and advanced analytics. Predictive maintenance is a crucial component, as the IIoT allows for real-time asset and equipment monitoring, anomaly detection, and failure prediction. This proactive approach aids in avoiding unscheduled downtime, cutting maintenance costs, and improving resource usage [30]. By fusing machines, systems, and processes, the IIoT also makes workflow automation and optimization possible. Data may be gathered, analyzed, and acted upon through the implementation of networked devices, enabling streamlined operations, quicker response times, and better resource allocation [31]. A further benefit of the IIoT is remote monitoring and management, which enables businesses to access and manage their industrial assets from any location. In Chui et al. [32], remote accessibility increases operational flexibility, lowers travel expenses, and enables effective resource allocation.

2.2.1.2 Improved Decision-Making

Decision-making processes in companies have significantly improved because of the IIoT. The IIoT provides more informed and data-driven decision-making by leveraging the power of real-time data, connectivity, and advanced analytics. The IIoT makes it possible to gather enormous amounts of data from numerous sources, such as sensors, gadgets, and manufacturing systems. Machine learning algorithms and predictive analytics can be introduced to analyze these data and produce insightful results. With the aid of these insights, firms are better able to comprehend their processes, spot trends and abnormalities, and take preventative action [33]. Additionally, the IIoT makes it possible to integrate data from other components of the industrial ecosystem, including supply chains, production lines, and consumer reviews. Decision-makers can make more accurate and fast decisions because of the comprehensive information that this holistic viewpoint gives them in real time [34]. Decision-makers may now access vital information and oversee operations from any location at any time thanks to the IIoT's remote monitoring and control capabilities. This accessibility improves decision-making agility and reactivity, as well as the capacity to handle problems and speed up procedures [35]. Organizations may improve operational efficiency, optimize resource allocation, strengthen quality control, and boost innovation by utilizing the possibilities of the IIoT.

2.2.1.3 Operational Visibility and Control

Organizations are given improved operational visibility and control via the IIoT, as it enables them in managing and monitoring of processes in a timely manner. The IIoT facilitates the collecting of real-time data from multiple points within the industrial ecosystem through the deployment of sensors, devices, and interconnected systems. These data include details about the operation of the equipment, production metrics, environmental factors, and other things. Organizations may spot bottlenecks, inefficiencies, and future problems with the use of these real-time data, which gives them a full perspective of their operations [36]. The IIoT enables remotely monitoring and management of industrial systems and processes. This has provided operators and managers the freedom to monitor operations and make adjustments as necessary by having access to real-time data and control systems from any place. According to Nagy et al. [37], this competence enables businesses to adjust quickly to shifting circumstances, optimize procedures, and maintain operational continuity.

The IIoT also makes it easier for industrial systems to be automated and controlled on their own. The IIoT offers smooth communication and coordination across many components by merging devices and systems. Organizations can streamline processes, minimize manual involvement, and enhance system performance thanks to this automation and control capacity [38]. Organizations are able to make data-driven decisions, maximize resource usage, boost productivity, and guarantee operational efficiency thanks to the operational visibility and control given by the IIoT.

2.2.1.4 Safety and Risk Mitigation

The IIoT, which enables proactive monitoring, real-time alerts, and preventive interventions, is essential for improving safety and risk reduction in industrial environments. Sensors and linked devices can be deployed as part of the IIoT to continually monitor factors such as temperature, pressure, humidity, and gas levels. The early identification of irregularities and potential safety risks is made possible by this real-time monitoring. Instant alarms can be provided, allowing for prompt risk mitigation and accident prevention [39]. Patterns and trends in data can be found by combining the IIoT with advanced analytics and machine learning techniques. By using data analysis, prospective equipment breakdowns or safety issues can be predicted, enabling predictive maintenance. Organizations can reduce downtime and avoid safety issues by proactively addressing maintenance needs [40].

Remote monitoring and control system implementation is also made easier by the IIoT. Real-time data are accessible to operators and safety personnel, who may also remotely manage and control equipment and vital operations. With this capability, less manual intervention is required in dangerous areas, allowing for safer and more effective operations [41]. The deployment of thorough safety standards and compliance monitoring are also made possible by the IIoT. To make sure that safety requirements and standards are being followed, data generated from IIoT devices can be evaluated. Organizations can spot areas for improvement and implement preventative steps to reduce hazards by keeping a steady stream of data and tracking safety performance [42,43]. Utilizing IIoT capabilities allows businesses to improve safety, reduce hazards, make workplaces safer for workers, safeguard assets, and safeguard infrastructure.

2.2.1.5 Innovation and New Business Models

Businesses now have more opportunities to implement innovative business models thanks to the IIoT, which has sparked a wave of innovation. Large volumes of data from linked devices, sensors, and equipment may be gathered and analyzed by businesses thanks to the IIoT. This extensive data ecosystem offers insights into market trends, consumer behavior, and operational effectiveness. Organizations can use these data to uncover new business possibilities, create cutting-edge products and services, and improve current workflows [44]. With the IIoT, businesses can switch from established product-centric models to ones that are outcome- or service-based.

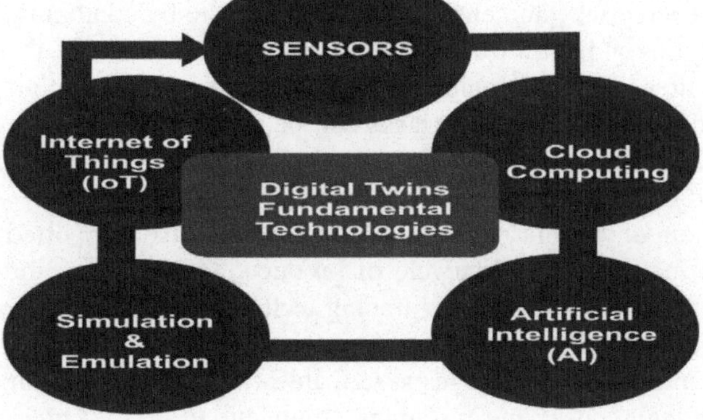

FIGURE 2.2 Digital twin fundamental technologies.

Organizations can provide predictive maintenance services, performance optimization solutions, or even pay-per-use models by monitoring the performance and consumption of equipment through the IIoT. Organizations are able to stand out in the market and develop new revenue streams thanks to this transition from selling items to providing value-added services [45]. The IIoT encourages collaboration among many industrial ecosystem stakeholders. To co-create creative solutions, businesses can exchange data and insights with suppliers, clients, and other industry stakeholders. The development of new business models based on ecosystem cooperation is made possible by this collaborative approach, which also promotes open innovation [46].

Additionally, the IIoT enables enterprises to create digital twins of their physical assets by integrating physical and digital systems. Virtual reproductions known as "digital twins" allow for the examination, modeling, and real-time monitoring of actual assets. This technology lowers the costs and dangers associated with physical experimentation by enabling enterprises to test novel concepts, enhance workflows, and investigate creative scenarios in a virtual setting [47], the digital twin fundamentals are shown in Figure 2.2. Organizations may open up new revenue streams, improve consumer experiences, and create market disruption by embracing the IIoT and investigating creative business models.

2.2.1.6 Sustainability and Resource Optimization

When it comes to encouraging sustainability and improving resource use in industrial operations, the IIoT is important. The IIoT offers real-time monitoring and data collecting of energy use, emissions, and resource usage by integrating diverse equipment, sensors, and devices. According to Abdel-Basset et al. [48], enterprises can use this data-driven strategy to evaluate performance, discover inefficiencies, and make data-driven decisions that will maximize resource use and minimize the environmental impact. The IIoT makes it easier to develop intelligent, automated systems that can adapt operations on the fly depending on real-time data. The IIoT, for instance, can optimize production schedules, modify energy usage, and reduce waste output in manufacturing operations. Organizations can increase operational efficiency, lower energy use, and eliminate resource waste by combining the IIoT with advanced analytics and optimization algorithms [49]. Additionally, the IIoT provides predictive maintenance, which aids businesses in anticipating equipment faults and performance decline. Maintenance tasks can be scheduled on time using data with predictive analytics, reducing downtime and making the best use of resources like spare parts and maintenance staff [50].

The adoption of circular economy principles is also supported by the IIoT. Organizations may trace the lifecycle of products and materials through the integration of the IIoT and tracking and tracing technology, enabling effective resource recovery, recycling, and remanufacturing processes. According to Kamble et al. [51], this closed-loop method encourages sustainable consumption and production while reducing waste and conserving resources. Simonetto et al. [52] presented a closed-loop supply chain 4.0, which is shown in Figure 2.3. Organizations may meet sustainability objectives, optimize resource usage, and support a more resource- and environment-conscious industrial ecosystem by leveraging the power of the IIoT.

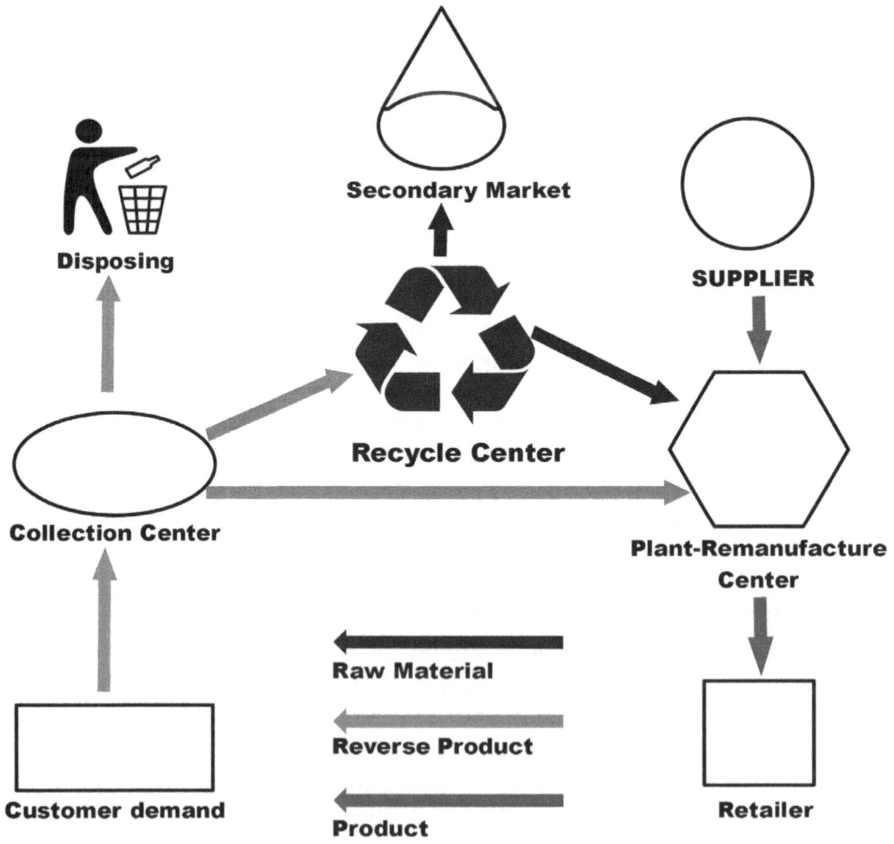

FIGURE 2.3 A closed loop supply chain for Industry 4.0.

2.2.2 Key Concepts in the IIoT

The IIoT encompasses key concepts that include connectivity, data collection, data analytics, automation and control, and interoperability, security and privacy, scalability, and flexibility [15]. These concepts form the foundation of the IIoT, enabling seamless communication, data-driven decision-making, adaptive control, and integration of diverse industrial components. By leveraging these concepts, the IIoT offers transformative potential for optimizing industrial processes and improving efficiency [53].

2.2.2.1 Connectivity

Connectivity is a fundamental concept in the IIoT which means the ability of systems to establish and maintain communication with each other. It involves the networking infrastructure and protocols that enable data exchange and interaction among interconnected components within an industrial environment [54]. In the IIoT, connectivity allows for real-time monitoring, control, and collaboration between various industrial assets, such as machines, equipment, and sensors. Connectivity can be made possible in the IIoT through various technologies, including wired (Ethernet, fieldbus) and wireless (Wi-Fi, cellular, Bluetooth, Zigbee) networks. These networks provide the means to establish reliable and secure connections, facilitating the transfer of data and enabling remote access and control of industrial systems. The concept of connectivity in the IIoT emphasizes the importance of establishing robust and reliable communication channels that enable the integration and interoperability of diverse devices and systems. It forms the foundation for data-driven decision-making, automation, and optimization within industrial processes.

2.2.2.2 Data Collection

The IIoT revolves around the concept of data collection, which entails compiling information from numerous sources within an industrial setting. It includes the gathering of information from sensors, tools, processes, and other pertinent sources. Real-time operational data, performance indicators, environmental conditions, and other information can all be found in the collected data [55]. Organizations can obtain insights into their operations, track performance, spot patterns, spot abnormalities, and make well-informed decisions for industrial process optimization thanks to data collection in the IIoT.

2.2.2.3 Data Analytics

The IIoT depends largely on data analytics, which enables businesses to gain useful insights from the data gathered [56]. The IIoT enables the identification of patterns, trends, and correlations within the data thorough data analytics solutions algorithms, which facilitates predictive maintenance, anomaly detection, and optimization of industrial processes [57]. Organizations can use data analytics in the IIoT to make data-driven choices, increase operational effectiveness, and improve overall performance.

2.2.2.4 Automation and Control

The IIoT is built on reliable algorithms, sensors, actuators to monitor and optimize industrial processes, and automation and control are key ideas in this context [58]. Automation is the practice of using technology and systems to complete jobs and processes without the involvement of a human. Control involves keeping an eye on, policing, and changing business operations to guarantee maximum effectiveness. In the framework of the IIoT, devices, sensors, and data analytics capabilities are connected with automation and control systems. This makes it possible to monitor industrial assets in real time, make data-driven decisions, and implement adaptive control based on pre-established rules or algorithms. Operators can now monitor and modify operations from any location thanks to the IIoT's remote access and control capabilities. According to Usman et al. [59], automation and control in the IIoT have many advantages, including higher production, better product quality, lower operating costs, improved safety, and optimal resource usage.

2.2.2.5 Interoperability

Interoperability is a key concept in the IIoT that emphasizes the capability of devices to seamlessly interact, exchange data, and work together [60,61]. It involves the establishment of standardized protocols, interfaces, and data formats to enable interoperability between heterogeneous components within an industrial environment [62,63]. In the IIoT, interoperability ensures that diverse devices, sensors, machines, and software systems can connect and collaborate effectively, regardless of their manufacturer or technology. It enables data sharing, integration of functionalities, and coordinated operations across different parts of the industrial ecosystem [64]. Interoperability in the IIoT is crucial for achieving efficient and flexible industrial processes, facilitating data-driven decision-making, enabling system scalability, and promoting the adoption of innovative technologies and solutions [63].

2.2.2.6 Security and Privacy

IIoT security and privacy concerns the protection of data, systems, and infrastructure in industrial environments [65]. Implementing safeguards against unwanted access, data breaches, and cyber threats is part of maintaining security in the IIoT. This comprises strong authentication and access control techniques, data encryption, secure communication protocols, and intrusion detection systems. The objective is to guarantee the availability, confidentiality, and integrity of data and systems in IIoT installations [66]. The protection of personal and sensitive data gathered by IIoT devices and systems is a key component of IIoT privacy. To defend individual privacy rights, it entails putting in place privacy-enhancing technology, data anonymization methods, and consent management frameworks [67]. Building trust, upholding regulatory compliance, and reducing the dangers of data breaches, industrial espionage, and unauthorized access are all reliant on security and privacy in the IIoT. The IIoT can help enterprises fully utilize the advantages of linked industrial systems while maintaining the protection of sensitive data by solving these issues.

2.2.2.7 Scalability and Flexibility

To facilitate the extension and adaptability of networked industrial systems, the IIoT relies on scalability and flexibility [68]. Scalability is the ability of an IIoT ecosystem to accept an increasing number of devices, data, and connections without sacrificing functionality or performance [69]. Flexibility, on the other hand, relates to how readily IIoT implementations may be changed, expanded, or reconfigured to meet changing business needs and technological advancements. The scalability and adaptability of the IIoT enable organizations to extend operations, incorporate new gadgets and technologies, and quickly adjust to changing market conditions [70]. These fundamental ideas serve as the IIoT's cornerstone and demonstrate how it has the power to alter industries by facilitating data-driven decision-making, process optimization, and increased operational effectiveness.

2.3 IIOT ARCHITECTURES

IIoT architectures offer the foundation for integrating and connecting industrial settings' various systems, equipment, and services. They make it possible for data, communication, and control to flow smoothly throughout the IIoT ecosystem. The choice is based on criteria such as data volume, latency needs, security issues, scalability, and unique use case requirements. Each design has advantages and considerations.

2.3.1 Centralized Architecture

One of the popular strategies for IIoT deployments is centralized architecture. In this design, information is gathered from field sensors and devices and sent to a central server or data center for processing, archiving, and analysis. Centralized monitoring and control of industrial processes are made possible by the server, which serves as a communication hub for all linked equipment [71]. A centralized repository for data storage and retrieval, simpler management and control, and quicker data processing and analysis are just a few advantages of this design. It enables standard data formats and protocols, promoting compatibility between hardware and software. Additionally, by utilizing the processing power and storage capability of the centralized server, it offers a scalable option for large-scale deployments.

The centralized architecture does, however, have significant drawbacks. As the entire system depends on the performance of the centralized server, it may be vulnerable to single points of failure. In situations where real-time decision-making or control is necessary, latency may be an issue. Furthermore, the centralized strategy could necessitate more communication and bandwidth, particularly if a lot of data needs to be sent to the central server [57]. The centralized architecture offers a simple and centralized method for IIoT installations, enabling effective data administration and control. However, its appropriateness is determined by the particular requirements, size, and type of industrial operations involved.

2.3.2 Distributed Architecture

An alternative strategy frequently utilized in IIoT systems is distributed architecture. This architecture distributes processing power and intelligence among a number of IIoT network nodes or devices. Each device or node in the network can process, filter, and analyze data locally in a distributed design [72]. To share information and work together on projects, these nodes can communicate with one another. The advantages of this decentralized strategy include increased scalability, fault tolerance, and lessened network traffic. The design can manage massive volumes of data and support more connected devices by dispersing intelligence over the network [73]. In situations where low-latency processing, real-time control, and autonomous decision-making are essential, distributed architectures are especially advantageous. For instance, distributed architectures can offer quicker and more effective processing in industrial settings with time-sensitive activities or where responsiveness is crucial. This architecture also encourages resilience by preventing single points of failure because the system can keep running even if one or more nodes or devices fail [74].

In contrast to a centralized strategy, managing a distributed architecture can be more difficult. In order to provide consistency and dependability in data processing and decision-making, it necessitates coordination and synchronization among the distributed nodes. To further safeguard the distributed network from potential threats and weaknesses, security measures must be put in place. For applications that need responsiveness and fault tolerance, distributed architectures in the IIoT offer a decentralized and scalable solution that offers on-time processing and an effective decision process [75].

2.3.3 Edge Computing Architecture

IIoT systems frequently employ a computing architecture, which places data processing and analysis at the network's edge, closer to the data source [76]. This architecture enables real-time processing and analysis without the need to transmit all data to a centralized server or cloud by placing computing resources and intelligence at the network edge, generally on edge devices or gateways [77]. The edge computing architecture has a number of advantages. By processing data locally, it first lowers latency, enabling quicker response times and real-time insights. In time-sensitive applications where quick action is required, this is extremely important. It also saves bandwidth and lessens network congestion by lowering the amount of data transported to the centralized server [78]. This can be especially helpful in situations with poor network connectivity or plenty of data. By storing sensitive data locally and reducing data exposure to external networks, edge computing also enhances privacy and security. In an edge computing architecture, edge devices or gateways have enhanced analytics capabilities in addition to processing power and storage capacity. These gadgets are capable of data filtering, aggregation, and analysis, producing useful information at the edge. Additionally, by serving as a local control point, they can provide autonomous control without ongoing connection with the server [79].

With regard to edge computing architecture, there are other factors to take into account. To guarantee data consistency and dependability, managing a dispersed network of edge devices calls for rigorous orchestration and coordination. To shield edge devices from potential assaults or illegal access, security measures must be put in place. Additionally, more resources and knowledge might be needed for the development and upkeep of edge computing infrastructure [80]. In IIoT systems, edge computing design generally moves computation, analytics, and decision-making closer to the data source, enabling real-time insights, decreased latency, enhanced privacy, and bandwidth optimization.

2.3.4 Cloud-based Architecture

IIoT systems frequently use cloud-based architecture, where data processing, storing, and analysis are carried out in the cloud infrastructure. This architecture enables scalable and centralized data management by sending sensor data and other pertinent information from connected devices to the cloud for processing and storage. The advantages of cloud-based architectures are numerous [81]. The ability to store and interpret massive amounts of unprocessed information produced by devices in the IIoT is made possible through practically unlimited storage capacity. Cloud-based designs facilitate simple scalability since more computer resources may be added as needed to meet expanding data and processing demands. Third, enterprises can often acquire useful insights from the collected data thanks to cloud-based solutions' frequent inclusion of machine learning and advanced analytics features [82]. As authorized stakeholders can access and analyze data from any location with an Internet connection, cloud-based architectures also make it easier for teams to share and collaborate on data.

IIoT devices often gather data and send it to the cloud infrastructure via communication protocols in a cloud-based architecture. The servers, databases, and other services that deal with data management make up the cloud infrastructure. To install their IIoT applications on the cloud, businesses can use the platforms and services offered by large providers like Amazon Web Services (AWS), Microsoft Azure, or Google Cloud Platform (GCP) [83]. There are issues with cloud-based designs, though. Dependence on Internet connectivity is an important consideration because using cloud services and sending data both require a steady and dependable Internet connection. As opposed to local processing at the edge, latency may also be an issue because data processing and analysis in the cloud may cause some delay. When sending sensitive data to the cloud, enterprises must also address security and privacy concerns and put in place the necessary safeguards to protect the data [84]. All things considered, cloud-based architectures in IIoT systems offer scalability, storage capacities, advanced analytics, and data-sharing opportunities, making them suited for enterprises seeking flexible and centralized data management.

2.3.5 Hybrid IIoT Architecture

A combination of many architectural strategies, including centralized, distributed, edge, and cloud-based architectures, is referred to as hybrid architecture in the context

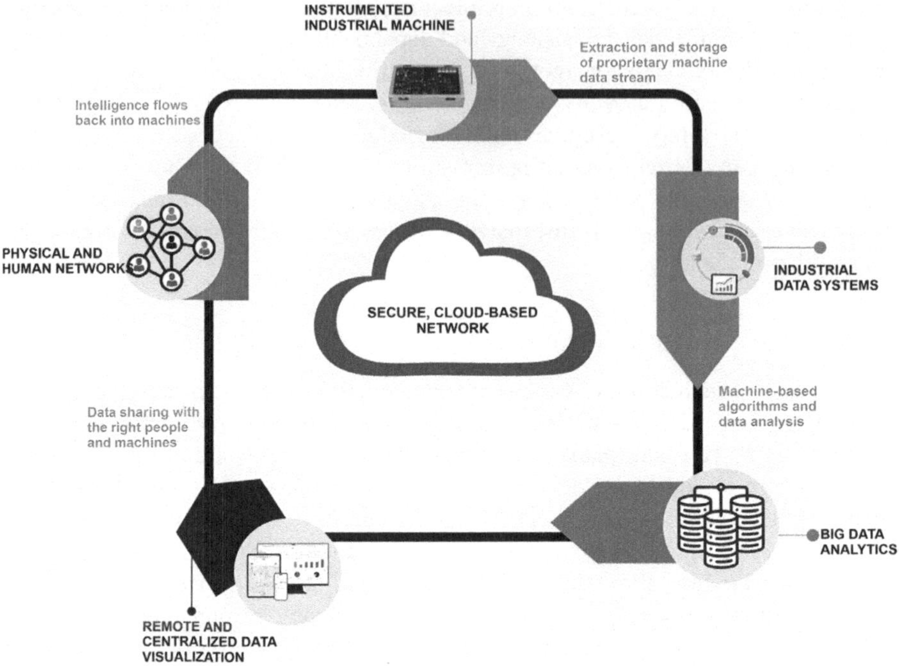

FIGURE 2.4 Secure, cloud-based network.

of the Industrial Internet of Things. It makes use of the advantages of each architecture to build a flexible and scalable system that satisfies requirements and maximizes resource use. In a hybrid architecture, some elements or processes might be deployed centrally while others are dispersed throughout the network or moved to the edge [85]. Data sensitivity, latency concerns, scalability requirements, and cost considerations are just a few examples of the variables that influence which architecture is best for each component or process.

The utilization of edge computing for real-time data processing and control while utilizing cloud-based services for storage, analytics, and long-term data analysis is an illustration of a hybrid architecture. This method eliminates the requirement for constant communication with the cloud by having edge devices perform instant local processing. After processing, the data can be sent selectively to the server for analysis, predictive modeling, and archiving. Multiple benefits are provided by hybrid designs [86–88]. They enable enterprises to improve resource allocation depending on particular application requirements by balancing local processing and centralized data management. This strategy can improve data privacy and security, decrease latency and bandwidth usage, and make better use of available resources possible. Hybrid designs also provide flexibility, enabling businesses to modify and extend their IIoT systems as necessary. Activity around a secured, cloud-based network is shown in Figure 2.4.

To enable seamless communication and coordination across various components and designs however, the implementation of a hybrid architecture necessitates careful planning and integration. It might include more complicated system deployment, management, and design. To choose the best hybrid architecture for their IIoT applications, organizations must carefully assess their unique demands, objectives, and technological capabilities.

2.4 CHALLENGES OF IIOT-BASED IMPLEMENTATION

The potential provided by the IIoT holds enormous promise, but there are a number of obstacles that must be overcome, which should be the focus of future study. The primary difficulties are caused by the need for effective energy management, great performance in a dynamic context, the requirement for interaction, and providing apps security and protecting users' privacy, as mentioned below.

2.4.1 Efficient Energy Management

With the increase in the high level of competition due to new regulations, and focus on net zero energy [89], numerous IIoT implementations need to operate on batteries. Low power consumption sensors are therefore needed. In recent years, a number of energy-efficient sensor strategies have been described [90–92], however, the IIoT does not instantly benefit from these ideas. In the IIoT, energy-efficient systems are important for managing energy usage. This will reduce pollution and in turn makes our environment greener. LPWAN IoT solutions employ a number of energy-efficient design strategies to operate at low power levels. First, they often create a star topology, which eliminates the energy used by multiloop networks for packet routing. Second, they delegate the complexity to the gateway, keeping the node architecture straightforward. Third, they employ narrowband channels to reduce noise and increase transmission range [93]. Energy management is a viable strategy in the IIoT. The availability of the matching energy source is necessary for harvesting from such environmental sources. However, RF energy harvesting might have advantages due to its wirelessness, accessibility, affordability, and include portable devices.

2.4.2 Interoperability and Coexistence

There will be a lot of devices placed relatively close to each other and deployed, due to rapid IIoT connectivity construction. The impending difficulty of coexisting in the congested Industrial, Scientific, and Medical (ISM) bands is brought about by this. In order to keep devices functional, interference between them must be managed. The IIoT will not benefit from the extensive work on wireless coexistence that has been done with WiFi, Bluetooth, and IEEE802.15.4 networks [94]. These devices may be exposed to an unparalleled amount of interference sources because of their widespread and dense installations. Each IIoT technology has unique qualities that could present additional difficulties. Future IIoT devices must be able to detect, identify, and eliminate external interference in order to ensure peaceful coexistence. Recently, some research on classifying interference on IIoT devices using spectrum sensing [95] has been presented, but the majority of this work falls short because the sensing methods require a larger memory than is presently available, which has very long sampling windows [96]. Additionally, IEEE802.15.4-based devices do not currently support forward error correction (FEC), which would increase the systems' reliability. A lot of research has gone into error control codes for industrial sensor networks, and the outcomes unmistakably demonstrate that FEC will increase reliability and coexistence [97–99].

The demand for interoperability is partly a result of the IIoT technologies' quick development. In particular, future frictionless data usage and sharing with a system will be necessary for a fully effective digital ecosystem. The difficulty and expense of IIoT deployment and integration will dramatically grow due to the lack of compatibility across IIoT devices. Various industrial facilities will require either refurbishing or total equipment replacement to be able to work with the newest technologies, and this will make the transformation or keying into these technologies much more challenging. Multimode radios, flexible software, and cross-technology communication can all be used to overcome the issues posed by device variety in the IIoT [100]. Multimode radios enable communication between various IIoT devices. For effective communication, cross-technology communication has recently been researched without the need for additional hardware [101]. Future research is required to enable cross-technology communication in IIoT devices because such approaches are technology-specific.

2.4.3 Timely Data Acquisition and Management

Environmental data acquisition and transmission must be done on time, this is established through a good reliability criterion that an IIoT must adhere to [102]. Unexpected disruptions can be divided into internal disturbances within the network architecture and environmental disturbances external to the system being observed. Numerous centralized scheduling systems have been described to cater to the internally manifested disturbances [103]. A few publications have also been released about crucial control systems that must respond to outside disruptions.

2.4.4 Security

Security is a key issue in the IIoT in addition to the demands for real-time performance and energy economy [63]. Due to this, security measures, such as secure protocols, are insufficient to protect the intricate IIoT systems [68], including privacy assurance and light encryption [104]. This problem is especially pressing in applications that include large-scale data sharing and real-time demands. One might argue for a comprehensive approach, as mentioned in [63,105].

i. The IIoT device's storage should be secured from attackers by encrypting the data to maintain privacy.
ii. IIoT devices must be impervious to physical attacks such as passive secret theft and unauthorized reprogramming, while allowing authorized users to upgrade the device's secure firmware.

iii. Only authorized parties should be able to access IIoT resources thanks to effective identification and authorization processes in the IIoT infrastructure.
iv. Even if malicious users physically harm the equipment, the system ought to be usable in normal operation. This ensures the IIoT' s resilience.
v. To maintain confidentiality and integrity, the IIoT device communication network needs to be protected.

2.5 CONCLUSIONS AND FUTURE DIRECTION

As we have seen, the Industrial Internet of Thing is a disruptive technology transforming operations by fusing conventional manufacturing methods with cutting-edge information and communication technologies. It has numerous advantages, such as increased effectiveness and productivity, enhanced safety, better decision-making, predictive maintenance, real-time monitoring and control, and higher-quality products. The many IIoT architectures, such as centralized, distributed, edge computing, cloud-based, and hybrid architectures, have also been covered. Each design has special benefits and applications that meet various industrial needs and specifications. To enable the effective deployment and operation of IIoT systems, we have identified the security and privacy problems, interoperability issues, data management challenges, and scalability considerations that must be addressed. The chapter concludes by highlighting the enormous potential of the IIoT to change industries and boost operational effectiveness. Businesses can open up new opportunities, improve operations, cut costs, and sharpen their competitive edge by embracing the IIoT and its accompanying infrastructures. Stakeholders must be abreast of recent advancements and improvements as the IIoT continues to develop and advance. Organizations can use the IIoT to promote innovation, develop new business models, and achieve sustainable growth in the dynamic and linked world of industrial automation by tackling its obstacles and maximizing its advantages. This chapter provides valuable insight to both academics and industry. Academics can use the findings to enrich their research in manufacturing processes and technology integration, development of curriculum in engineering-related disciplines, and engage students in applied learning bridging the gap between theoretical knowledge and practical applications. Meanwhile industry professionals can apply the insights to process optimization, quality improvement, and making informed data-driven decisions.

The IIoT is a promising field with promising future directions that can expand its capabilities and impact in industrial settings. Future studies could look at how well deep learning can handle different sorts of data, including image data, data from sensors, and data on consumer behavior. Better planning and even real-time choices that could affect the entire system could be made as a result. Thanks to the IIoT, significant new advancements in edge intelligence, AI integration, blockchain security, digital twins, standardization, sustainability, human–machine collaboration, and other areas are now conceivable. By following these avenues, researchers and practitioners can achieve the full potential of the IIoT in altering industrial processes and fostering sustainable and successful operations.

REFERENCES

[1] S. Schneider, "The Industrial Internet of Things (IIoT)," in *Internet of Things and Data Analytics Handbook*, Wiley, 2017, pp. 41–81.

[2] Tarek Gaber, Joseph B. Awotunde, Sakinat O. Folorunso, Sunday A. Ajagbe and Esraa Eldesouky, "Industrial Internet of Things Intrusion Detection Method Using Machine Learning and Optimization Techniques," *Wireless Communications and Mobile Computing*, vol. 2023, no. 1, pp. 1–15, 2023. https://onlinelibrary.wiley.com/doi/10.1155/2023/3939895

[3] M. Javaid, R. P. Abid Haleem, S. R. Singh and S. Rajiv, "Upgrading the Manufacturing Sector via Applications of Industrial Internet of Things (IIoT)," *Sensors International*, vol. 2, p. 100129, 2021.

[4] R. Maqbool, R. S. Mohammed and A. Saleha, "Emerging Industry 4.0 and Internet of Things (IOT) Technologies in the Ghanaian Construction Industry: Sustainability, Implementation Challenges, and Benefits," *Environmental Science and Pollution Research*, vol. 30, no. 13, pp. 37076–37091, 2022.

[5] W. Qin, S. Chen and M. Peng, "Recent Advances in Industrial Internet: Insights and Challenges," *Digital Communications and Networks*, vol. 6, no. 1, pp. 1–13, 2020.

[6] M. Vijarania, S. Gupta, A. Agrawal, M. O. Adigun, S. A. Ajagbe and J. B. Awotunde, "Energy Efficient Load-Balancing Mechanism in Integrated IoT–Fog–Cloud Environment," *Electronics*, vol. 12, no. 11, p. 2543, 2023.

[7] H. Sundmaeker, P. Guillemin, P. Friess and S. Woelfflé, "Vision and Challenges for Realizing the Internet of Things. European Commission, Directorate-General for Communications Networks," *Content and Technology*, pp. 11–23, 2010. http://dx.doi.org/10.2759/26127

[8] W. Cheng, "Intelligent Manufacturing Production Line Data Monitoring System for Industrial Internet of Things," *Computer Communications*, vol. 151, pp. 31–41, 2020.

[9] M. A. M. Sadeeq and S. Zeebaree, "Energy Management for Internet of Things via Distributed Systems," *Journal of Applied Science and Technology Trends (JASTT)*, vol. 2, no. 2, pp. 59–71, 2021.

[10] J. B. Awotunde, J. C. Chakraborty and A. Adeniyi, "Intrusion Detection in Industrial Internet of Things Network-Based on Deep Learning Model with Rule-Based Feature Selection," *Wireless Communications & Mobile Computing*, vol. 2021, no. 1, pp. 1–17, 2021.

[11] D. Oladimeji, G. Khushi, A. Nuri, K. Kose, L. G. Gundogan and L. Fan, "Smart Transportation: An Overview of Technologies and Applications," *Sensors*, vol. 23, no. 8, p. 3880, 2023.

[12] T. Gebremichael, P. L. Lehlogonolo, H. E. Mohamed, P. H. Gerhard, P. Nuno, G. Mikael and A. Johan, "Security and Privacy in the Industrial Internet of Things: Current Standards and Future Challenges," *IEEE Access*, vol. 8, pp. 152351–152366, 2020.

[13] A. Zeid, S. Sarvesh, M. Mohsen, K. Sagar and M. Tucker, "Interoperability in Smart Manufacturing: Research Challenges," *Machines*, vol. 7, no. 2, p. 21, 2021.

[14] G. Embia, A. Mohamed, B. R. Moharana and K. Muduli, "Edge Computing-Based Conditional Monitoring," in *Intelligent Manufacturing Management Systems: Operational Applications of Evolutionary Technologies in Mechanical and Industrial Engineering*, K. Muduli, V. P. Kommula, K. Devendra, M. Yadav, C. P. Selvan and J. Kandasamy, Eds., pp. 249–270, 2023. https://doi.org/10.1002/9781119836780.ch10

[15] S. Li, X. Da and Z. Shanshan, "The Internet of Things: A Survey," *Information Systems Frontiers*, vol. 17, no. 2, pp. 243–259, 2015.
[16] P. Chhotaray, B. C. Behera, B. R. Moharana, K. Muduli and F. T. R. Sephyrin, "Enhancement of Manufacturing Sector Performance with the Application of Industrial Internet of Things (IIoT)," in *Smart Technologies for Improved Performance of Manufacturing Systems and Services*, CRC Press, 2024, pp. 1–19.
[17] J. Lee, B. Behrad and K. Hung-An, "A Cyber-Physical Systems Architecture for Industry 4.0-Based Manufacturing Systems," *Manufacturing Letters*, vol. 3, pp. 18–23, 2015.
[18] F. Tao, C. Jiang, Q. Qinglin, Z. Meng, Z. He and S. Fangyuan, "Digital Twin-Driven Product Design, Manufacturing and Service with Big Data," *The International Journal of Advanced Manufacturing Technology*, vol. 9, no. 12, pp. 3563–3576, 2017.
[19] M. Naphade, B. Guruduth, H. Colin, P. Jurij and M. Robert, "Smarter Cities and Their Innovation Challenges," *Computer*, vol. 44, no. 6, pp. 32–39, 2011.
[20] K. N. Galgal, M. Ray, B. R. Moharana, B. C. Behera and K. Muduli, "Quality Control in the Era of IoT and Automation in the Context of Developing Nations," in *Smart Technologies for Improved Performance of Manufacturing Systems and Services*, CRC Pres, 2023, pp. 21–37.
[21] H. Boyes, H. Bil, C. Joe and W. Tim, "The Industrial Internet of Things (IIoT): An Analysis Framework," *Computers in Industry*, vol. 101, pp. 1–12, 2018.
[22] S. Werbińska-Wojciechowska and K. Winiarska, "Maintenance Performance in the Age of Industry 4.0: A Bibliometric Performance Analysis and a Systematic Literature Review," *Sensors*, vol. 23, no. 3, p. 1409, 2023.
[23] S. Jeschke, C. Brecher, T. Meisen, D. Özdemir, T. Eschert, "Industrial Internet of Things and Cyber Manufacturing Systems," In: S. Jeschke, C. Brecher, H. Song, D. Rawat, D. (eds) *Industrial Internet of Things*, Springer Series in Wireless Technology. Springer, Cham. pp. 3–19, 2016. https://doi.org/10.1007/978-3-319-42559-7_1
[24] S. D. Anton, F. Daniel, L. Christoph, P. Frederic, Z. Marc and D. S. Hans, "Two Decades of SCADA Exploitation: A Brief History," in *2017 IEEE Conference on Application, Information and Network Security (AINS)*, 2017.
[25] S. Chen, R. Ma, H. -H. Chen, H. Zhang, W. Meng and J. Liu, "Machine-to-Machine Communications in Ultra-Dense Networks—a Survey," *IEEE Communications Surveys & Tutorials*, vol. 19, no. 3, pp. 1478–1503, 2017. http://dx.doi.org/10.1109/COMST.2017.2678518
[26] M. Rehman, I. Y., S. Khaled, I. Muhammad, J. Prem and P. Charith, "The Role of Big Data Analytics in Industrial Internet of Things," *Future Generation Computer Systems*, vol. 99, pp. 247–259, 2019.
[27] O. Peter, P. Anup and M. Charles, "Industrial Internet of Things (IIoT): Opportunities, Challenges, and Requirements in Manufacturing Businesses in Emerging Economies," *Procedia Computer Science*, vol. 217, pp. 856–865, 2023.
[28] J. Vrana and S. Ripudaman, "NDE 4.0—a Design Thinking Perspective," *Journal of Nondestructive Evaluation*, vol. 40, no. 1, pp. 1–24, 2021.
[29] M. Akkaraboina, S. R. Kodari, A. Barve and K. Muduli, "Securing Data of Online Learners Using Blockchain Technology," in *Advancements in Artificial Intelligence, Blockchain Technology, and IoT in Higher Education: Mitigating the Impact of COVID-19*, Taylor & Francis, 2023.
[30] H. Tran-Dang, K. Nicolas, C. Patrick and K. Dong-Seong, "The Internet of Things for Logistics: Perspectives, Application Review, and Challenges," *IETE Technical Review*, vol. 39, no. 1, pp. 93–121, 2020.

[31] N. Savic, P. Goran and T. Ana, "Smart, Connected Products as a New Competitive Advantage: Challenges for Serbia," *Ekonomika preduzeca*, vol. 64, no. 1–2, pp. 143–155, 2016.
[32] M. Chui, M. Löffler and R. Roberts, "The Internet of Things," *The McKinsey Quarterly*, vol. 2, no. 47, pp. 1–9, 2010.
[33] D. Miorandi, S. Sabrina, D. P. Francesco and C. Imrich, "Internet of Things: Vision, Applications and Research Challenges," *Ad Hoc Networks*, vol. 10, no. 7, pp. 1497–1516, 2012.
[34] S. Chauhan, S. Rajesh, G. Anita, V. Shaik, B. T. Akram and P. Neeraj, "Digitalization of Supply Chain Management with Industry 4.0 Enabling Technologies: A Sustainable Perspective," *Processes*, vol. 11, no. 1, p. 96, 2022.
[35] S. Ahmetoglu, C.-C. Zaihisma and N. Ali, "A Systematic Review of Internet of Things Adoption in Organizations: Taxonomy, Benefits, Challenges and Critical Factors," *Applied Sciences*, vol. 12, no. 9, p. 4117, 2022.
[36] E. Borgia, "The Internet of Things Vision: Key Features, Applications and Open Issues," *Computer Communications*, vol. 54, pp. 1–31, 2014.
[37] J. Nagy, O. Judit, E. Edina, M. Domicián and P. József, "The Role and Impact of Industry 4.0 and the Internet of Things on the Business Strategy of the Value Chain—the Case of Hungary," *Sustainability*, vol. 10, no. 10, p. 3491, 2018.
[38] L. D. Xu, H. Wu and L. Shancang, "Internet of Things in Industries: A Survey," *IEEE Transactions on Industrial Informatics*, vol. 10, no. 4, pp. 2233–2243, 2014.
[39] F. Wortmann and F. Kristina, "Internet of Things," *Business & Information Systems Engineering*, vol. 57, no. 3, pp. 221–224, 2015.
[40] B. Debasis and J. Sen, "Internet of Things: Applications and Challenges in Technology and Standardization," *Wireless Personal Communications*, vol. 58, no. 1, pp. 49–69, 2011.
[41] H. Ramzey, B. Mahmoud, E. Mostafa and A. E. Adel, "I2OT-EC: A Framework for Smart Real-Time Monitoring and Controlling Crude Oil Production Exploiting IIoT and Edge Computing," *Energies*, vol. 16, no. 4, pp. 1–29, 2023.
[42] A. J. Jara, A. Z. Miguel and F. S. Antonio, "An Internet of Things–Based Personal Device for Diabetes Therapy Management in Ambient Assisted Living (AAL)," *Personal and Ubiquitous Computing*, vol. 15, pp. 431–440, 2011.
[43] O. O. Olanrele, O. A. Adeaga, O. A. Adeyemi, O. K. Ajayi and A. O. Mowemi, "An IoT Based Weather Station Using an Embedded System," *Quantum Journal of Engineering, Science and Technology*, vol. 3, no. 3, pp. 31–40, 2022.
[44] H. Lasi, F. Peter, K. Hans-Georg, F. Thomas and H. Michael, "Industry 4.0," *Business & Information System Engineering*, vol. 6, pp. 239–242, 2014.
[45] P. Qvist-Sørensen, "Applying Iiot and AI - Opportunities, Requirements and Challenges for Industrial Machine and Equipment Manufacturers to Expand Their Services," *Central European Business Review*, vol. 9, no. 2, pp. 46–77, 2020.
[46] O. Ogiemwonyi, N. Mohammad, I. E. Alam, N. A. Hago, F. H. Azizan and H. Sazzad, "Green Innovation Behaviour: Impact of Industry 4.0 and Open Innovation," *Heliyon*, vol. 9, no. 6, pp. 1–17, 2023.
[47] D. Piromalis and K. Antreas, "Digital Twins in the Automotive Industry: The Road toward Physical-Digital Convergence," *Applied System Innovation*, vol. 5, no. 4, p. 65, 2022.
[48] A.-B. Mohamed, G. Manogaran and M. Mohamed, "Retracted: Internet of Things (IOT) and Its Impact on Supply Chain: A Framework for Building Smart, Secure and Efficient Systems," *Future Generation Computer Systems*, vol. 86, pp. 614–628, 2018.

[49] F. Shrouf, J. Ordieres and G. Miragliotta, "Smart Factories in Industry 4.0: A Review of the Concept and of Energy Management Approached in Production Based on the Internet of Things Paradigm," in *2014 IEEE International Conference on Industrial Engineering and Engineering Management*, IEEM 2014, Selangor Darul Ehsan, Malaysia, December 9–12, pp. 697–701, 2014.

[50] M. Paolanti, L. Romeo, A. Felicetti, A. Mancini, E. Frontoni and J. Loncarski, "Machine Learning Approach for Predictive Maintenance in Industry 4.0," in *2018 14th IEEE/ASME International Conference on Mechatronic and Embedded Systems and Applications (MESA)*, Oulu, Finland, pp. 1–6, 2018.

[51] S. S. Kamble, G. Angappa and A. G. Shradha, "Achieving Sustainable Performance in a Data-Driven Agriculture Supply Chain: A Review for Research and Applications," *International Journal of Production Economics*, vol. 219, pp. 179–194, 2020.

[52] M. Simonetto, S. Fabio, B. Daria and G. Kannan, "Closed Loop Supply Chains 4.0: From Risks to Benefits through Advanced Technologies. A Literature Review and Research Agenda," *International Journal of Production Economics*, vol. 253, p. 108582, 2022.

[53] A. Al-Fuqaha, G. Mohsen, M. Mehidi, A. Mohammed and A. Moussa, "Internet of Things: A Survey on Enabling Technologies, Protocols, and Applications," *IEEE Communications Surveys & Tutorials*, vol. 17, pp. 2347–2376, 2015.

[54] S. Yi, L. Cheng and L. Qun, "A Survey of Fog Computing," in *Proceedings of the 2015 Workshop on Mobile Big Data*, 2015.

[55] M. Talabis and M. Jason, "Information Security Risk Assessment: Data Collection," in *Information Security Risk Assessments Toolkit*, M. Talabis and J. Martin, Eds., Elsevier, pp. 63–104, 2013.

[56] A. Al-Fuqaha, G. Mohsen, M. Mehdi, M. A. and A. Moussa, "Internet of Things: A Survey on Enabling Technologies, Protocols, and Applications," *IEEE Communications Surveys & Tutorials*, vol. 17, no. 4, pp. 2347–2376, 2015.

[57] S. Wang, W. Jiafu, Z. Daqiang, L. Di and Z. Chunhua, "Towards Smart Factory for Industry 4.0: A Self-Organized Multi-Agent System with Big Data Based Feedback and Coordination," *Computer Networks*, vol. 101, pp. 158–168, 2016.

[58] O. Vermesan and P. Friess, "Internet of Things: Converging Technologies for Smart Environments and Integrated Ecosystems," in *Series in Communication and Networking*, River Publishers, 2013.

[59] M. Usman, S. S. Muhammad, H. Usman, U. A. Muhammad and J. Saleha, "Automatic Hybrid Access Control in SCADA-Enabled IIOT Networks Using Machine Learning," *Sensors*, vol. 23, no. 8, p. 3931, 2023.

[60] A. Karmakar, N. Dey, T. Baral, M. Chowdhury and M. Rehan, "Industrial Internet of Things: A Review," in *International Conference on Opto-Electronics and Applied Optics (Optronix)*, Kolkata, India, 2019.

[61] A. H. Eyeleko and T. Feng, "A Critical Overview of Industrial Internet of Things Security and Privacy Issues Using a Layer-Based Hacking Scenario," *IEEE Internet of Things Journal*, vol. 10, no. 24, pp. 21917–21941, 2023.

[62] E. Sisinni, S. Abusayeed, H. Ssong, J. Ulf and G. Mikael, "Industrial Internet of Things: Challenges, Opportunities, and Directions," *IEEE Transactions on Industrial Informatics*, vol. 14, no. 11, pp. 4724–4734, 2018.

[63] S. A. Ajagbe, S. Misra, O. F. Afe and K. I. Okesola, "Internet of Things (IoT) for Secure and Sustainable Healthcare Intelligence: Analysis and Challenges," in *5th International Conference on Applied Informatics (ICAI 2022)*, Peru, 2022.

[64] B. Farahani and K. M. Amin, “Smart and Collaborative Industrial IoT: A Federated Learning and Data Space Approach,” *Digital Communications and Networks*, vol. 9, no. 2, pp. 436–447, 2023.

[65] S. Kumar, T. V. Alampalayam and S. Harshit, “Security in Internet of Things: Challenges, Solutions and Future Directions,” in *2016 49th Hawaii International Conference on System Sciences (HICSS)*, 5–8 January, Koloa, HI, USA, pp. 5772–5781, 2016.

[66] R. Roman, J. Zhou and J. Lopez, “On the Features and Challenges of Security and Privacy in Distributed Internet of Things,” *Computer Networks*, vol. 57, pp. 2266–2279, 2013.

[67] K. Gafu and C. Tai-Myoung, “Comprehensive Survey on Internet of Things, Architecture, Security Aspects, Applications, Related Technologies, Economic Perspective, and Future Directions,” *Journal of Information Processing Systems*, vol. 15, no. 4, pp. 797–819, 2019.

[68] J. Gubbi, R. Buyya, S. Marusic and M. Palaniswami, “Internet of Things (IoT): A Vision, Architectural Elements, and Future Directions,” *Future Generation Computer Systems*, vol. 29, no. 7, pp. 1645–1660, 2013.

[69] A. Mirani, G. Ali, A. A. Velasco-Hernandez and W. Joseph, “Key Challenges and Emerging Technologies in Industrial IoT Architectures: A Review,” *Sensors*, vol. 22, no. 15, p. 5836, 2022.

[70] C. Perera, H. L. Chi, J. Srimal and C. Min, “A Survey on Internet of Things from Industrial Market Perspective,” *IEEE Access*, vol. 2, pp. 1660–1679, 2014.

[71] M. Islam, N. Sheikh, K. Fakhri and M. Ghulam, “Internet of Things: Device Capabilities, Architectures, Protocols, and Smart Applications in Healthcare Domain,” *IEEE Internet of Things Journal*, vol. 10, no. 4, pp. 3611–3641, 2023.

[72] A. M. Buttar and N. Arshad, “Industrial 4.0 Adaptation and Challenges in Pattern Recognition, Computer Vision, and IoT,” in *Investigations in Pattern Recognition and Computer Vision for Industry 4.0*, IGI Global, 2023, pp. 90–126.

[73] G. Radoglou, I. Panagiotis, G. S. Panagiotis and D. M. Ioannis, “Securing the Internet of Things: Challenges, Threats and Solutions,” *Internet of Things*, vol. 5, pp. 41–70, 2019.

[74] J. O. Kephart and D. M. Chess, “The Vision of Autonomic Computing,” *Computer*, vol. 36, no. 1, pp. 41–50, 2003.

[75] E. Welbourne, B. Leilani, C. Garret, G. Kayla, R. Kyle, R. Samuel, B. Magdalena and B. Gaetano, “Building the Internet of Things Using RFID: The RFID Ecosystem Experience,” *IEEE Internet Computing*, vol. 13, no. 3, pp. 48–53, 2009.

[76] A. Pradeep, “Exploring the Future of Edge Computing: Advantages, Limitations, and Opportunities,” In: Shaw, R.N., Paprzycki, M., Ghosh, A. (eds) Advanced Communication and Intelligent Systems, Second International Conference (ICACIS) 2023, Warsaw, Poland, June 16–17, vol. 1921, pp. 196–209, 2023.

[77] P. Sethi and R. S. Smruti, “Internet of Things: Architectures, Protocols, and Applications,” *Journal of Electrical and Computer Engineering*, vol. 2017, pp. 1–25, 2017.

[78] P. Baronti, P. Prashant, W. C. Vince, C. S. Chook, A. Gotta and Y. F. Hu, “Wireless Sensor Networks: A Survey on the State of the Art and the 802.15.4 and Zigbee Standards,” *Computer Communications*, vol. 30, no. 7, pp. 1655–1695, 2007.

[79] D.-M. Han and L. Jae-Hyun, “Design and Implementation of Smart Home Energy Management Systems Based on Zigbee,” *IEEE Transactions on Consumer Electronics*, vol. 56, no. 3, pp. 1417–1425, 2010.

[80] L. Atzori, L. Antonio and M. Giacomo, "Siot: Giving a Social Structure to the Internet of Things," *IEEE Communications Letters*, vol. 15, no. 11, pp. 1193–1195, 2011.

[81] A. Mohammad and E.-N. Huh, "Fog Computing and Smart Gateway Based Communication for Cloud of Things," in *2014 International Conference on Future Internet of Things and Cloud* (FiCloud), Barcelona, Spain, pp. 464–470, 2014.

[82] J. Soldatos, N. Kefalakis, M. Hauswirth, M. Serrano, J. P. Calbimonte, M. Riahi, K. Aberer, P. P. Jayaraman, A. Zaslavsky, I. P. Žarko, L. Skorin-Kapov & R. Herzog, "OpenIoT: Open Source Internet-of-Things in the Cloud," In: I. Podnar Žarko, K. Pripužić, M. Serrano (eds) *Interoperability and Open-Source Solutions for the Internet of Things*, vol. 9001, pp. 13–25, 2015.

[83] L. N. Sai and N. Pounambal, "Integrated Publish/Subscribe and Push-Pull Method for Cloud Based IOT Framework for Real Time Data Processing," *Measurement: Sensors*, vol. 27, p. 100699, 2023.

[84] L. Bréhon–Grataloup, K. Rahim and B. André-Luc, "Mobile Edge Computing for V2X Architectures and Applications: A Survey," *Computer Networks*, vol. 206, p. 108797, 2022.

[85] K. Szum, "IoT-Based Smart Cities: A Bibliometric Analysis and Literature Review," *Engineering Management in Production and Services*, vol. 13, no. 2, pp. 115–136, 2021.

[86] D. Wu, W. R. David, W. Lihui and S. Dirk, "Cloud-Based Design and Manufacturing: A New Paradigm in Digital Manufacturing and Design Innovation," *Computer-Aided Design*, vol. 59, pp. 1–14, 2015.

[87] K. Muduli, S. Luthra, J. A. Garza-Reyes and D. Huisingh, "Application of Blockchain Technology for Addressing Reverse Logistics Challenges: Current Status and Future Opportunities," *Supply Chain Forum: An International Journal*, vol. 24, no. 1, pp. 1–6, 2023.

[88] P. Evans and M. Annunziata, "Pushing the Boundaries of Minds and Machines," *General Electric Reports*, pp. 1–37, 2012. www.researchgate.net/profile/Marco-Annunziata/publication/271528854_Industrial_Internet_Pushing_the_Boundaries_of_Minds_and_Machines/links/566342e608ae418a786bb015/Industrial-Internet-Pushing-the-Boundaries-of-Minds-and-Machines.pdf. Accesed November 1, 2023.

[89] O. Adeyemi, I. A. Ayoade, E. O. Adeyemi, O. O. Olanrele, I. Eweoya and J. Mathew, "Adoption of Artificial Intelligence in Operations Management: A Design-Oriented Review," in *Advances in Manufacturing Technology*, XXXVI, 20ed ed., 2023, pp. 17–23.

[90] T. Rault, A. Bouabdallah and Challal, "Energy Efficiency in Wireless Sensor Networks: A Top-Down Survey," *Computer Networks*, vol. 67, pp. 104–122, 2014.

[91] O. O. Alabi, O. A. Adeaga, S. A. Ajagbe, S. T. Adekunle and M. O. Adigun, "Performance of the Solar PV Module of the Dual Solar Axis Tracker of a Smart Home Monitoring System," *Journal of Hunan University (Natural Science)*, vol. 50, no. 9, pp. 21–29, 2023.

[92] R. Rawat, O. Oki, R. K. Chakrawarti, T. S. Adekunle, J. M. Lukose and S. A. Ajagbe, "Autonomous Artificial Intelligence Systems for Fraud Detection and Forensics in Dark Web Environments," *Informatica*, vol. 47, no. 9, pp. 51–62, 2023.

[93] A. Saifullah, M. Rahman, D. Ismail, C. Lu, R. Chandra and J. Liu, "SNOW: Sensor Network Over White Spaces," SenSys '16: The 14th ACM Conference on Embedded Network Sensor Systems, Stanford CA USA, November 14–16, pp. 272–285, 2016.

[94] D. Yang, Y. Xu and M. Gidlund, "Coexistence of IEEE 802.15.4 Based Networks: A Survey," in *IECON 2010-36th Annual Conference on IEEE Industrial Electronics Society*, Glendale, AZ, USA, pp. 2107–2113, 2010.

[95] T. M. Chiwewe, C. F. Mbuya and G. P. Hancke, "Using Cognitive Radio for Interference-Resistant Industrial Wireless Sensor Networks: An Overview," *IEEE Transaction Industrial Information*, vol. 11, no. 6, pp. 1466–1481, 2015.

[96] S. Grimaldi, A. Mahmood and M. Gidlund, "An SVM-Based Method for Classification of External Interference in Industrial Wireless Sensor And Actuator Networks," *Journal Sensor Actuator Networks*, vol. 6, no. 2, p. 9, 2017.

[97] F. Barac, M. Gidlund and T. Zhang, "Ubiquitous, Yet Deceptive: Hardware-Based Channel Metrics on Interfered WSN Links," *IEEE Transactions on Vehicular Technology*, vol. 64, no. 5, pp. 1766–1778, 2015.

[98] F. Barac, S. Caiola, M. Gidlund, E. Sisinni and T. Zhang, "Channel Diagnostics for Wireless Sensor Networks in Harsh Industrial Environments," *IEEE Sensors Journal*, vol. 14, no. 11, pp. 3983–3995, 2014.

[99] T. Olofsson, A. Ahlen and M. Gidlund, "Modeling of the Fading Statistics of Wireless Sensor Network Channels in Industrial Environments," *IEEE Transactions on Signal Processing*, vol. 64, no. 12, pp. 3021–3034, 2016.

[100] L. Ascorti, S. Savazzi, G. Soatti, M. Nicoli, E. Sisinni and S. Galimberti, "A Wireless Cloud Network Platform for Industrial Process Automation: Critical Data Publishing and Distributed Sensing," *IEEE Transactions on Instrumentation and Measurement*, vol. 66, no. 4, pp. 592–603, 2017.

[101] S. M. Kim and T. He, "Freebee: Cross-Technology Communication Via Free Side-Channel," MobiCom '15: Proceedings of the 21st Annual International Conference on Mobile Computing and Networking, Paris, France, pp. 317–330, 2015.

[102] P. Ferrari, A. Flammini, E. Sisinni, S. Rinaldi, D. Brandao and M. S. Rocha, "Delay Estimation of Industrial IoT Applications Based on Messaging Protocols," *IEEE Transactions on Instrumentation and Measurement*, vol. 67, no. 9, pp. 2188–2199, 2018.

[103] F. Dobslaw, T. Zhang and M. Gidlund, "End-to-End Reliability-Aware Scheduling for Wireless Sensor Networks," *IEEE Transactions on Industrial Informatics*, vol. 12, no. 2, pp. 758–767, 2016.

[104] S. A. Ajagbe, H. Florez and J. Awotunde, "A New Cryptography Key for Electronics Health Record Security," AESRSA: A New Cryptography Key for Electronic Health Record Security," 5th International Conference, ICAI 2022, Arequipa, Peru, October 27–29, 2022 vol 1643. Springer, Cham, 2022.

[105] A. W. Atamli and A. Martin, "Threat-Based Security Analysis for the Internet of Things," in *2014 International Workshop on Secure Internet of Things, (SIoT 2014)*, 10 September 2014, Wroclaw, Poland, pp. 35–43, 2014.

3 Artificial Intelligence in Industry 5.0

Transforming Manufacturing through Machine Learning and Robotics in Collaborative Age

Bhanu Priya, Vivek Sharma, Joseph Bamidele Awotunde, and Abidemi Emmanuel Adeniyi

3.1 INTRODUCTION

Industrial revolutions are the mother of the technological world which exists today. These revolutions started in the 18th century with the introduction of machines to the present-day technologies such as artificial intelligence, robotics, financial technologies, IoT, digital printing, etc. [1]. They have changed not only the entire world physically but also have had a greater impact on societies. The introduction of teamwork and mechanization in the 18th century marked the beginning of the First Industrial Revolution, which had a profound impact on manufacturing industries [2].

The 18th century saw the First Industrial Revolution, marked by team power and mechanization, which transformed the manufacturing sector, leading to the emergence of factories [3]. The late 19th century saw rapid idea transfer and machine replacement, characterized by mass production using electricity, assembly lines, and transportation infrastructure [4,5]. With the widespread adoption of computers in society, the Third Industrial Revolution, sometimes known as the "digital revolution," began in the 1970s with the introduction of digital logic such as integrated circuit chips and digital cellular phones and the Internet, and the automation of various manufacturing processes [6]. The Fourth Industry Revolution significantly transformed the world by integrating advanced technologies, physical products, artificial intelligence, IoT, robotics, and digital transformation [7]. Through the application of cutting-edge digital technologies like robotics, the Internet of Things (IoT), and artificial intelligence (AI), the Fourth Industrial Revolution, often known as Industry 4.0, brought

DOI: 10.1201/9781003581963-3

about enormous changes to manufacturing [8]. Industry 5.0 is nearing completion, aiming to elevate the transformation process by integrating human intelligence with advanced technologies [9]. The upcoming manufacturing era will see the integration of AI to enhance human capabilities, enabling more flexible and personalized production processes [10,11]. This chapter focuses on the transformative impact of AI in Industry 5.0, and the opportunities and challenges associated with its adoption in the manufacturing sector. The major research questions are:

Q1: What are the various AI technologies and how they can be used to create Industry 5.0?
Q2: What are the potential applications of AI in optimizing operations and increasing efficiency within the framework of Industry 5.0?
Q3: How can AI help in achieving the star pillars of human centricity, sustainability, and resilience of Industry 5.0?

The chapter therefore adds to the literature by exploring various AI technologies and their roles in creating Industry 5.0. It also investigates the potential applications of AI in optimizing operations and increasing efficiency within the framework of Industry 5.0, and examines how AI can contribute to achieving the star pillars of human-centricity, sustainability, and resilience within Industry 5.0. Therefore, the chapter contributes to the understanding of how AI can be integrated into Industry 5.0 to enhance manufacturing processes, improve efficiency, and achieve broader societal goals such as sustainability and resilience.

3.1.1 Structure of the Chapter

This chapter is split into five sections. Section 3.2 portrays the background of Industry 5.0. Section 3.3 presents the data analysis and results. In Section 3.4, the conceptual framework is built, drawing from the use of dynamic capability theory and the research findings in Section 3.5. To end, conclusions, along with contributions made to academic theory and industrial practice, are summarized in Section 5.6.

3.2 REVIEW OF THE LITERATURE

3.2.1 Background of Industry 5.0

The concept of the Fifth Industrial Revolution, also known as Industry 5.0, is a relatively new one and refers to the incorporation of cutting-edge technology like automation, the IoT, and AI into industry [12]. This new wave of innovation aims to create a more collaborative and sustainable production process, with a focus on human–machine interaction and ethical considerations [13,14]. The Fifth Industrial Revolution is anticipated to significantly alter the labor market, favoring highly skilled and creative jobs necessitating specialized knowledge and technical expertise [15]. The fifth Industrial Revolution builds on the advancements of the first, with the potential to significantly transform our lives and work in the 21st century.

The Fifth Industrial Revolution builds on previous revolutions, incorporating AI, machine learning, robotics, and the Internet of Things for a more integrated manufacturing process [16,17]. The proposed system will foster a more efficient, responsive, and adaptive production system, integrating machines with human workers to foster a harmonious and collaborative environment. Intelligent automation will enhance quality control, resource management, and waste reduction, leading to a more sustainable and environmentally friendly production process [18].

One of the key aspects of the fifth Industrial Revolution (5IR) is the emphasis on ethical considerations and social responsibility, while keeping in view the sustainability aspects [19]. Technology's transformative effects on society and the workplace must be balanced with the aim of minimizing negative effects on individuals, communities, and the planet. The process involves assessing the potential social, economic, and environmental impacts of new technologies and devising strategies to mitigate any adverse effects.

The Fifth Industrial Revolution is a ground-breaking advancement that has the potential to revolutionize the manufacturing sector, paving the way for a new era of innovation and progress. Technological change presents challenges and risks, but its benefits are expected to outweigh any negative effects, creating a bright future for those willing to embrace and adapt (Figure 3.1) [12,20,21].

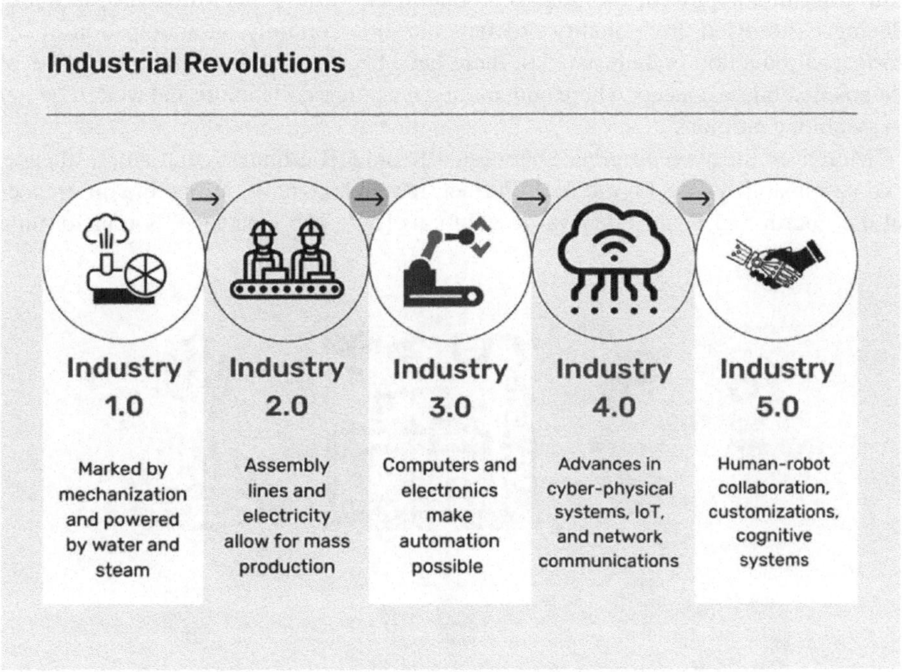

FIGURE 3.1 An overview of Industrial Revolutions from 1.0 to 5.0.

3.2.2 Industry 5.0

Industry 5.0 philosophy was developed in 2020 through virtual workshops, and officially published in January 2021, following debates and idea sharing in the European Commission (EC) [22]. Industry 5.0, launched by Michael Rada in 2015, was legitimized by the EC in 2021 to meet the European Union's 2030 targets, with various definitions developed by industry practitioners [23]. 5IR promotes harmonious human–machine cooperation, prioritizing the well-being of various stakeholders including society, companies, employees, and customers. It therefore prepares the way for a revolution in how humans and machines collaborate for improved societal well-being [24]. Industry 5.0, a shift from Industry 4.0, focuses on digitalization and AI-driven technologies to enhance production flexibility and efficiency, shifting away from social justice and sustainability principles.

Industry 5.0 has recently started getting more attention aiming to overcome the limitations of Industry 4.0. It is defined as a concept of future industry that should involve human-centric, resilient, and sustainable production systems and services [25,26]. Therefore, it has been concluded that Industry 5.0 should be, unlike Industry 4.0, around three core values, namely human-centricity, sustainability, and resilience, calling on industries to rethink their positions and roles in society. In terms of sustainability, Industry 5.0 has the potential to become the first human-driven industrial revolution, characterized by the principle of industrial recycling, known as the 6Rs policy: Recognize, Reconsider, Realize, Reduce, Reuse, and Recycle. By following this approach, the goal is to minimize waste while simultaneously producing customized, high-quality products [27,28]. Certainly, in anticipation of the formal introduction of Industry 5.0, there have been discussions about the "Age of Augmentation," a concept where humans and machines collaborate and work together in symbiotic harmony.

Moreover, the main difference between 4IR and 5IR is human centrism, resilience, and sustainability (see Figure 3.2). Further, researchers have outline the differences in the Fourth and Fifth Industrial Revolutions [29]. The metaverse is transforming

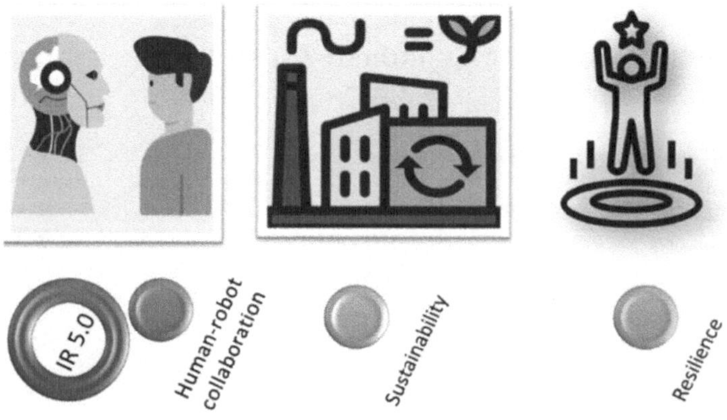

FIGURE 3.2 Pillars of the Fifth Industrial Revolution.

the future of technology in industrial services, focusing on sustainability and sustainability [30,31]. Industry 5.0 will enhance workplace inclusivity, resilience, and sustainability by promoting resilience, sustainability, and human-centricity within industry [32–33].

3.2.3 Artificial Intelligence and Industry 5.0

AI is a crucial technology in Industry 5.0, combining human intelligence and advanced technologies to drive industrial development. There are two primary types of AI: general artificial intelligence (AGI) and narrow artificial intelligence (ANI) [34]. AGI aims to create computers that can think and reason like humans in various tasks and domains. ANI focuses on creating machines capable of performing specific tasks and emulating human-like thinking and reasoning within those specific domains [35–37]. AI is continuously being used for predicting maintenance, and to improve quality control and reduce wastage in manufacturing processes. Additionally, it can be used in process optimization wherein with the help of AI algorithms data can be analyzed from sensors and other devices to identify inefficiencies in the production process and suggest changes to improve performance [38]. Apart from this, AI can be used to enhance the collaboration between humans and machines in manufacturing processes. Machines are capable of handling routine and repetitive tasks, which in turn liberates human workers from these mundane activities [39]. As a result, humans can direct their attention toward more intricate tasks that demand creativity and problem-solving skills [40].

Humans and robots possess distinct strengths that can be enhanced through a synergistic connection, necessitating a systematic approach for its full realization. The architecture should incorporate forecasting, explainable artificial intelligence, active learning, simulated reality, decision-making, and human feedback modules [41]. The integration of artificial intelligence in manufacturing is revolutionizing jobs and fostering human–machine cooperation, highlighting the complementary nature of machine and human capabilities [42–43]. The active learning paradigm enables human–machine cooperation by optimizing artificial intelligence models by selecting a small number of data instances to meet learning objectives [44]. Active learning is utilized in manufacturing for quality control, predictive modeling, and demand forecasting, such as predicting local chip displacement between layers [45,46] or to assist a model in predicting the shape control of a composite fuselage [47]

3.2.4 Research Model of How AI Works in Industry 5.0

Industry 5.0 prioritizes human-centricity, focusing on AI as a transformative force that will revolutionize manufacturing processes and redefine the relationship between humans and technology. AI-driven automation is expected to enhance efficiency, reduce waste, and streamline workflows in Industry 5.0 by optimizing production lines. AI algorithms predict maintenance needs, prevent downtime, and ensure uninterrupted production cycles. AI-enabled robotics enhances safety, collaboration, and a dynamic manufacturing environment. ML-based algorithms will analyze large datasets to provide valuable insights, enabling manufacturers to make data-driven decisions and swiftly adapt to evolving market demands [48]. Moreover, AI-powered quality control systems will accurately detect defects, ensuring products meet rigorous standards and reducing recall risks and customer dissatisfaction. AI algorithms are set to revolutionize personalized production processes by optimizing manufacturing parameters based on individual customer preferences and requirements [49,50]. AI-driven supply chain management systems will improve transparency, traceability, and sustainability, fostering collaboration and resilience in Industry 5.0 [51]. The integration of AI into design and prototyping phases will expedite innovation cycles, enabling manufacturers to quickly and efficiently introduce new products to the market [52,53]. Manufacturers will be guided in making strategic decisions by AI-driven insights into market trends and customer behavior, which will help them foresee changes in demand and maintain their competitiveness. AI will drive Industry 5.0 by enabling manufacturers to utilize advanced technologies while prioritizing human-centric values like safety, sustainability, and flexibility (Figure 3.3).

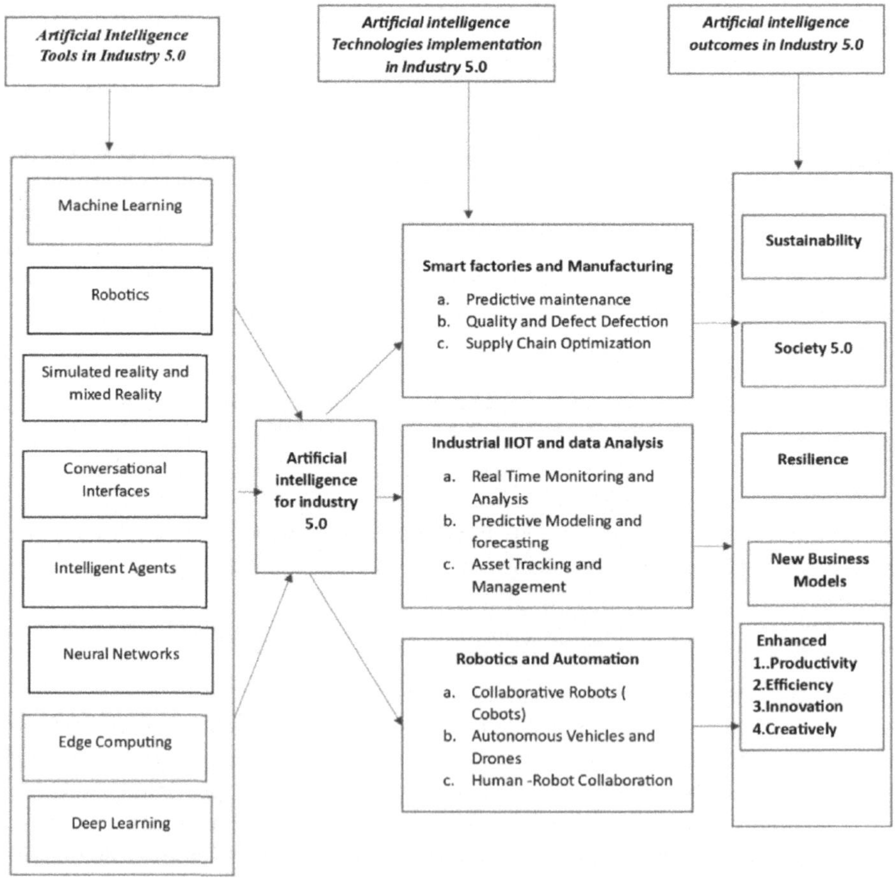

FIGURE 3.3 Model showing tools, technologies, and outcomes of AI in Industry 5.0.

3.2.5 Artificial Intelligence and Industry 5.0

Artificial intelligence (AI) technologies have been rapidly evolving and transforming various industries over the past few decades [54]. Industry 4.0, a digitalization of manufacturing processes, has significantly benefited from AI's role in enhancing automation, increasing efficiency, and reducing costs. Industry 5.0, a shift toward human-centered manufacturing, is expected to significantly enhance productivity, work quality, and worker well-being through the use of AI technologies. AI techniques like machine learning, automation, robotics, machine vision, data mining, big data, and expert systems have proven effective in manufacturing industries [55]. AI techniques, aided by data acquisition technologies, robotic systems, and computer science, are being increasingly utilized in digital manufacturing to enhance system controllability and product quality. AI systems use various methodologies, including machine learning, simulated and mixed realities, robotics, intelligent agents, conversational interfaces, edge computing, and deep learning, to analyze and predict sensor outputs [56,57]. Manufacturing data are extracted from documents using natural language processing, and knowledge graphs of manufacturing resource data are built and embedded in cloud manufacturing environments.

3.2.6 Machine Learning

Machine learning has emerged as a crucial technology in Industry 5.0, the latest phase of the industrial revolution, where human–machine collaboration is central to the production process. Markets and research predict the global machine learning market to reach USD 190.61 billion by 2025, with a 36.6% CAGR from 2020 to 2025 [58,59]. ML-based models significantly enhance productivity, reduce costs, and improve product and service quality in industries like healthcare, manufacturing, and finance. ML-based methods have received immense attention as potential models for modeling different manufacturing systems in Industry 5.0 [60]. ML-based algorithms are a popular technique that is utilized in medical diagnosis, image processing, prediction, classification, learning association, regression, and other applications [61]. For instance, in the healthcare industry, machine learning algorithms are used to analyze patient data and support clinical decision-making processes, while in manufacturing, they are used to optimize production processes and minimize defects [62,63]. These examples illustrate the vast potential of machine learning in Industry 5.0, making it a vital technology for businesses to stay competitive and improve their bottom line.

Furthermore, machine learning has enabled businesses to implement predictive maintenance, a proactive maintenance strategy that can significantly reduce downtime and improve asset reliability [64]. By leveraging ML algorithms, businesses can analyze sensor data from machines and predict when maintenance is needed, reducing unplanned downtime and increasing operational efficiency. Researchers and academicians have also shown how machine learning can help in predictive maintenance, highlighting its benefits and limitations [65]. Moreover, machine learning is driving automation in various industries, including logistics and transportation, where it is used to optimize route planning and reduce fuel consumption. Research and markets predict the global autonomous vehicle market will reach USD 65.3 billion by 2027, growing at a CAGR of 63.1% from 2020 to 2027 [66].

3.2.7 Robotics

Robotics and AI are essential components of Industry 5.0, which is the next evolution in manufacturing that emphasizes human–machine collaboration and the use of advanced technologies. The integration of robotics and AI is driving innovation, increasing productivity, and changing the way we work in various industries. The rapid development of robotics, AI, and Industry 5.0 has been a game changer for many industries. The global market for collaborative robots is predicted to reach $11.2 billion by 2025, fueled by their enhanced safety and productivity capabilities [67]. A study has indicated that AI and automation could boost global productivity by 1.4% annually, potentially adding $16 trillion to the global economy by 2030 [68,69]. According to a study described in Ref. [70], the integration of robotics and AI in the automotive industry has led to increased productivity, cost savings, and improved safety. Similarly, a recent study by Kim et al. found that the application of AI and Industry 5.0 in manufacturing industries has led to increased automation, quality control, and supply chain optimization. Furthermore, the healthcare industry has also seen significant benefits from the use of robotics and AI, as reported in a study described in Ref. [71], which found that the use of AI in medical image analysis has improved diagnostic accuracy and patient outcomes. Studies have revealed the potential of robotics, AI, and Industry 5.0 in transforming industries and driving economic growth, emphasizing the need for businesses to stay competitive and innovative.

In addition to the studies mentioned above, there are several other chapters that highlight the importance of robotics, AI, and Industry 5.0 in today's world. For instance, a study described in Ref [72], found that the use of robotics and AI in the logistics industry has led to significant improvements in transportation efficiency and cost reduction. Similarly, a study by authors of Ref. [73] highlighted the potential of Industry 5.0 in enabling smart manufacturing and sustainable production processes. Moreover, the field of robotics has also seen significant advancements, as reported in Ref. [74], which highlights the potential of soft robotics for creating flexible and adaptable robots for various applications. These studies demonstrate the broad applicability of robotics, AI, and Industry 5.0 in various industries and the significant impact they can have on enhancing productivity, improving quality, and promoting sustainability. As such, it is clear that these technologies will continue to play a critical role in shaping the future of work and society as a whole.

Undeniably, these technologies will continue to play a pivotal role in shaping the trajectory of both work and society in their entirety. Particularly, soft robotics in industrial applications, adept at manipulating delicate objects, emerges as a significant domain. This facilitates a meticulous and nuanced approach to manipulation. Furthermore, the deployment of Industry 4.0 technologies, embracing a worker-centric ethos, strives to strike a balance between capital and labor welfare. Concurrently, the utilization of AI in mobile robotics engenders resilient solutions, bolstering overall operational efficiency and adaptability. By embracing these cutting-edge advancements, we can pave the path toward a more productive, streamlined, and employee-oriented future. These studies demonstrate the broad applicability of robotics, AI, and Industry 5.0 in various industries and the significant impact they can have on enhancing productivity, improving quality, and promoting sustainability. As such, it is clear that these technologies will continue to play a critical role in shaping the future of work and society as a whole.

However, the integration of robotics and AI in Industry 5.0 also poses some challenges and risks, such as ethical considerations, data privacy and security, and potential job displacement, which need to be addressed. Therefore, there is an urgent need for further research and development, collaboration between academia, industry, and government, and regulatory frameworks to ensure safe and ethical adoption of robotics and AI in Industry 5.0.

3.2.8 Simulated Reality

Simulated reality, also known as virtual reality, refers to a computer-generated environment that simulates a physical environment, allowing users to interact with it in a realistic way. In Industry 5.0, simulated reality can be used to create immersive training and simulation environments, enabling workers to learn and practice new skills in a safe and controlled environment [74]. Simulated reality can also be used to enhance human–machine collaboration by creating virtual interfaces that allow humans to interact with machines in a more natural and intuitive way [75]. For example, virtual reality headsets can be used to control and monitor industrial equipment, allowing workers to visualize and interact with complex machinery in a more intuitive way. In addition, simulated reality can be used to improve safety and efficiency in industrial environments [76–78]. For example, virtual reality simulations can be used to train workers on safety procedures and emergency response protocols, allowing them to practice these procedures in a realistic and controlled environment. Overall, simulated reality is an important technology for Industry 5.0 because it can enhance human–machine collaboration, improve safety and efficiency, and provide workers with new training and learning opportunities [9]. By leveraging the power of simulated reality, Industry 5.0 can create a more immersive and interactive environment that fosters collaboration and innovation, while also prioritizing safety and sustainability [79]. In the realm of simulated reality, we grasp the concept of any program or process endowed with the capacity to engender data that bear a semblance to a distinct facet of actuality. This intricate process adeptly assimilates inputs and in turn yields outputs, exemplified by synthetic data or outcomes, artfully mimicking diverse scenarios or transformations in various processes [80]. Machine learning models can solve complex tasks with high-quality data, but acquiring it can be costly and challenging due to defects, wear, and human error. Synthetic data offer a solution to these challenges.

3.2.9 Conversational Interfaces

Spoken dialog systems and conversational multimodal interfaces leverage artificial intelligence and can reduce friction and enhance human–machine interactions [81] by approximating a human conversation. However, in practice, conversational interfaces mostly act as the first level of support and cannot offer much help as a knowledgeable human. They can be classified into three broad categories: (i) basic-bots, (ii) text-based assistants, and (iii) voice-based assistants. Conversational interfaces refer to computer programs that enable communication between humans and machines in natural language. These interfaces can take various forms, including chatbots, voice assistants, and virtual agents. Industry 5.0 is a concept that describes the next phase of industrialization, where human and machine collaboration is at the forefront.

This phase is focused on creating sustainable and ethical solutions that benefit both society and the environment. Conversational interfaces can play a crucial role in Industry 5.0 by facilitating communication between humans and machines in a more intuitive and natural way. This can lead to more efficient and effective collaboration between humans and machines, enabling them to work together seamlessly. For example, conversational interfaces can be used to control and monitor industrial equipment and processes, provide real-time feedback and insights, and facilitate collaboration between human workers and machines. By leveraging the power of conversational interfaces, Industry 5.0 can create a more human-centric approach to industrialization that prioritizes sustainability, safety, and social responsibility.

3.2.10 Intelligent Agents

Intelligent agents are becoming increasingly popular in Industry 5.0 due to their ability to perform tasks autonomously and efficiently. In manufacturing industries, intelligent agents are being used to optimize production processes, reduce downtime, and improve quality control [82]. Moreover, intelligent agents are being used in logistics and supply chain management to optimize routes, track inventory, and monitor delivery times [83]. These applications of intelligent agents in Industry 5.0 have shown significant improvements in efficiency and productivity while reducing operational costs. However, the ethical and social implications of using intelligent agents in the workplace need to be addressed to ensure safe and responsible adoption. Intelligent agents are also being used in customer services to provide personalized assistance and improve customer satisfaction.

In the healthcare industry, intelligent agents are being used to assist physicians in diagnosis and treatment recommendations [84]. Moreover, intelligent agents are being used in the financial sector to detect fraud, analyze risks, and make investment recommendations [85,86]. These applications of intelligent agents are transforming various industries, improving efficiency, and enabling new business models. However, the widespread adoption of intelligent agents requires overcoming technical, ethical, and regulatory challenges. Therefore, there is a need for further research and development to ensure the safe and responsible adoption of intelligent agents in Industry 5.0. Intelligent agents are also being used in the field of education to personalize learning experiences and provide targeted support to students. For instance, intelligent tutoring systems use AI to adapt the learning content to the needs of each individual student, providing immediate feedback and guidance [87]. Moreover, intelligent agents are being used in the field of HR to automate recruitment and talent management processes, reducing bias and increasing efficiency [88]. In addition, intelligent agents are being used in the field of agriculture to monitor crop health, optimize irrigation, and reduce water usage [89].

These applications of intelligent agents in various fields demonstrate their potential to transform industries and improve outcomes. However, challenges such as data privacy, transparency, and bias need to be addressed to ensure the ethical and responsible adoption of intelligent agents in Industry 5.0. One of the key benefits of intelligent agents in Industry 5.0 is their ability to continuously learn and adapt to changing circumstances. This is enabled by machine learning algorithms that allow intelligent agents to improve their performance over time based on feedback and data analysis. This means that as intelligent agents are used more extensively in various industries, their performance will improve, resulting in increased efficiency and productivity. However, this also raises concerns about the impact of intelligent agents on the job market and the need for reskilling and upskilling of the workforce to adapt to this new technological landscape. Henceforth, the judicious assimilation of intelligent agents within Industry 5.0 necessitates a holistic approach, wherein not only the technical dimensions but also the social, ethical, and economic implications of their utilization are duly taken into profound consideration.

3.2.11 Neural Networks

Neural networks stand as a pivotal cornerstone of AI's assimilation in the context of Industry 5.0. They embody intricately designed computer systems that strive to emulate the sophisticated operations of the human brain, thus endowing them with the ability to glean insights from data and render astute predictions or decisions based on the acquired knowledge. In Industry 5.0, neural networks are being used to solve complex problems and automate processes in various industries. For instance, in manufacturing industries, neural networks are harnessed for the purpose of optimizing intricate production processes and elevating the standards of quality control [90]. In the healthcare industry, neural networks are being used to analyze medical images and assist in diagnosis and treatment [91]. Moreover, neural networks are being used in the financial industry to detect fraud, predict market trends, and make investment decisions [92].

The potential applications of neural networks in Industry 5.0 are vast and varied, offering the opportunity to improve efficiency, accuracy, and decision-making. However, challenges such as data quality, interpretability, and privacy need to be addressed to ensure the responsible and ethical use of neural networks in Industry 5.0. Neural networks have become a crucial component of Industry 5.0, with applications in diverse fields such as transportation, energy, agriculture, and logistics. In the transportation sector, neural networks are being utilized to optimize traffic flow and enhance safety while minimizing congestion [93]. In the energy industry, neural networks are being used to predict energy consumption and optimize energy production, leading to cost savings and reduced environmental impact [94]. In agriculture, neural networks are being used to analyze soil data and optimize crop yields [91]. In logistics, neural networks are being used to optimize supply chain operations, reduce costs, and improve delivery times [95]. These examples demonstrate the vast potential of neural networks to solve complex problems and automate processes in various industries [96]. However, it is important to address challenges such as data privacy, transparency, and bias to ensure the ethical and responsible use of neural networks in Industry 5.0. The post-COVID-19 world is expected to see a surge in digital transformation, accelerating the integration of neural networks into Industry 5.0 [97]. The pandemic has also highlighted the need for remote work and virtual operations, which can be enabled by AI and neural networks. For instance, in the healthcare industry, neural networks can be used for remote monitoring of patients, telemedicine, and drug discovery [98]. In manufacturing, the use of neural networks can help companies reduce their reliance on human labor and increase automation [99].

3.2.12 Edge Computing

Edge computing has emerged as a critical technology for the development of Industry 5.0, also known as the "human-centric era" of manufacturing. Edge computing involves processing data closer to where it is generated, thereby reducing the latency and enabling real-time decision-making in the production process. Seeing the successful application of AI in various fields, EC researchers start to set their sights on AI, especially from a perspective of machine learning, a branch of AI that has gained increased popularity in recent decades [94]. As the production process becomes more complex and human–machine interaction becomes more critical, the role of edge computing is becoming increasingly important. The conceptualization and implementation of an intelligent manufacturing system are considered paramount in securing competitive advantages for the manufacturing industries of major countries in the context of Industry 5.0. Employing a multi-access edge computing (MEC)-enabled framework paves the way for the development of a knowledge-sharing DT machine tool (DTMT) swarm, which proves instrumental in fostering intelligent manufacturing capabilities [100,101] provides a comprehensive review of various edge computing architectures and technologies that can be used in Industry 5.0 and suggested that edge computing can be used to develop a range of smart applications for the manufacturing industry, such as real-time monitoring of production processes, predictive maintenance, and quality control. Furthermore, the potential of edge computing is also highlighted to enable real-time decision-making and improve operational efficiency in the production process.

Also, for implementing edge computing in Industry 5.0, Ref. [102] provides a case study of a smart factory that uses edge computing to monitor and control the production process in real time and suggested that edge computing can be used to collect and analyze vast amounts of data from machines and other devices on the production floor, thereby enabling real-time decision-making and improving worker safety. Along the same line, researchers also suggested that edge computing can enable the development of a range of smart applications for the manufacturing industry, such as real-time monitoring of production processes, predictive maintenance, and quality control [102]. As the production process becomes more complex and human–machine interactions become more critical, the role of edge computing is becoming increasingly important. Therefore, further research is needed to explore the potential of edge computing in Industry 5.0 and to develop new technologies and applications to support the growth of this emerging field.

3.3 INTEGRATION OF AI WITH OTHER ADVANCED TECHNOLOGIES

3.3.1 Digital Twins

Digital twins have been identified as a critical technology for the success of Industry 5.0, which seeks to integrate advanced manufacturing with a human-centric approach. Digital twins are virtual representations of physical systems, allowing for real-time monitoring and optimization of industrial processes. They can be used for a range of applications, such as predictive maintenance, process optimization, and quality control. According to a report by research and markets, the digital twin market is expected to grow from $3.1 billion in 2020 to $48.2 billion by 2026 [103], with industries such as aerospace and defense, automotive, and healthcare being the major contributors to this growth. According to a recent study [104], the use of digital twins can lead to a significant reduction in production downtime and an increase in efficiency by up to 30%. In addition, digital twins can enhance collaboration between humans and machines, enabling a more flexible and adaptive manufacturing process [105]. A review [93] highlighted the importance of digital twins in enabling sustainable manufacturing practices, such as reducing waste and energy consumption.

3.3.2 6G Technology

6G is the next generation of wireless technology that is expected to succeed 5G in the coming years and can offer significant value-added services to Industry 5. 0. While 5G promises faster data speeds and lower latency, 6G is expected to take things to the next level with even higher data rates, greater capacity, and lower latency. The integration of 6G and Industry 5.0 has the potential to transform manufacturing and other industries. The 6G network is expected to meet with the intelligent information standard that provides high energy efficiency, high reliability, plus high capacity of traffic [105].

By offering intelligent spectrum management, mobile EC powered by AI, and intelligent mobility, 6G networks efficiently and effectively assist Industry5.0 apps in improving application performance [27]. According to Ref. [102], 6G can enable ultra-reliable and low-latency communication, which is crucial for Industry 5.0 applications such as real-time monitoring and control of manufacturing processes. Additionally, 6G can support machine-type communication (MTC) applications in Industry 5.0, which require high reliability, low latency, and high data rates [106]. Moreover, studies have also found that 6G can enable more efficient and sustainable manufacturing practices, by enabling energy-efficient communication [107]. Therefore, 6G can play an important role in allowing the vision of Industry 5.0, by enabling new applications, improving communication reliability and speed, and enabling more sustainable manufacturing practices.

3.3.3 Explainable Artificial Intelligence

Explainable artificial intelligence (XAI), a specialized domain within the realm of artificial intelligence, delves into extensive research on techniques and methodologies aimed at elucidating insights into the underlying reasoning of artificial intelligence models or providing an approximation thereof [108]. XAI is a field of AI that focuses on developing AI systems that can explain their decision-making processes in a way that humans can understand. This is important because AI systems are becoming increasingly complex and are making important decisions in areas such as healthcare, finance, and security. XAI can help ensure that these decisions are transparent and trustworthy. Industry 5.0 is a concept that emphasizes human–machine collaboration and the integration of new technologies, such as AI, to create sustainable and ethical solutions. XAI can play a crucial role in Industry 5.0 by ensuring that AI systems are transparent and explainable, which is important for building trust between humans and machines.

For example, in manufacturing, AI systems can be used to optimize production processes, monitor equipment performance, and detect quality issues. XAI can help ensure that these systems are transparent and that the decisions they make are explainable to human operators. This can help build trust between humans and machines, leading to more effective collaboration and better outcomes. XAI can also play a role in ensuring that AI systems are developed and deployed in an ethical and socially responsible way. By making AI systems more transparent and explainable, XAI can help ensure that these systems are not biased or discriminatory, and that they are designed to benefit society as a whole. Overall, XAI is an important technology for Industry 5.0 because it can help ensure that AI systems are transparent, trustworthy, and ethical, which is critical for building effective human–machine collaboration and creating sustainable solutions for the future.

3.3.4 Blockchain

Blockchain is a distributed ledger technology which gained prominence as an evaluation of bitcoin, which is an automated distributed transaction platform that manages a large number of requests without the intervention of a centralized or third party. Blockchain was used by SME as a secure infrastructure or a ledger that records occurrences of node transactions and logs changes in SMEs' expert status [109].

Blockchain technology has several potential use cases in Industry 5.0, including supply chain management, quality control, intellectual property protection, smart contracts, and decentralized manufacturing. Blockchain can be used to track and verify the authenticity of goods as they move through the supply chain, which helps in reducing fraud [75]. Blockchain can be used to store and track data related to product quality and testing that can help to ensure that products meet regulatory standards and customer expectations while protecting intellectual property by creating a permanent, tamper-proof record of ownership and usage rights as well as customers benefiting from blockchain technology by tracking orders, payments, production, and so on.

In order to circumvent redundant efforts and maintain a unified database system, network participants uphold distributed ledger records of transactions [105]. Researchers and academicians handling blockchain studies also maintain that blockchain (BC) is a frontrunner for Industry 5.0 ecosystems as a security enabler because of its innate capacity to provide immutability, chronology, and auditability in industrial systems [27]. Moreover, blockchain can be utilized for effective subscriber management in Industry 5.0 by creating digital identities for various people and businesses. It is required for access management and stakeholder authentication in any industrial activities conducted via a public network [27]. Additionally, blockchain can also solve the problems of privacy. To address the problems of privacy in blockchain, FusionFedBlock (the Fusion of Blockchain and Federated Learning to Protect Privacy in Industry 5.0) was created [98]. This model works in a way that the industry's divisions (production, quality control, and distribution) connect with the global model at the federated layer and enable local learning updates with network automation.

Apparently, miners in the blockchain networks then verify this information. In this way, federated learning offers the protection of privacy amongst the many departments and sectors indicated and at the cloud layer, the Distributed Hash Table (DHT) offers decentralized secure storage. Blockchain can be used to create smart contracts that automate complex processes, such as payment and delivery, and ensure that all parties involved in a transaction are held accountable. The utilization of a blockchained smart contract pyramid-driven multi-agent autonomous process control (BSCP-MAAPC) approach is implemented to enhance the timeliness and adaptability of control mechanisms, fostering resilience and individualized manufacturing in the process [76]. Furthermore, blockchain can be used to create decentralized manufacturing networks that enable smaller, independent manufacturers to collaborate and share resources, such as equipment and expertise [77].

3.3.5 Security Cover by Artificial Intelligence

In Industry 5.0, security is a critical concern, given the increasing use of digital technologies and the growing risk of cyber-attacks. AI can play a crucial role in enhancing security in Industry 5.0, by providing real-time threat detection, fraud prevention, access control, and cybersecurity [110]. AI can be used to detect and prevent security threats in real time, by analyzing large volumes of data from various sources, including sensors, cameras, and social media. AI algorithms can identify patterns and anomalies that may indicate security threats and alert security personnel. Further, AI can be used to improve access control by analyzing user behavior and identifying anomalies that may indicate unauthorized access attempts. AI algorithms can also be used to monitor access patterns and flag suspicious activity. In addition, AI can be used to enhance cybersecurity in Industry 5.0 by identifying and preventing cyber threats, such as malware, ransomware, and phishing attacks. AI algorithms can analyze network traffic and identify patterns that may indicate a cyber-attack. Additionally, AI can be used to enhance security in Industry 5.0 by providing predictive maintenance. By analyzing data from sensors and other sources, AI can identify potential security vulnerabilities in equipment and machinery before they become a threat, as well as improve video surveillance in Industry 5.0 by analyzing video data in real time and identifying potential security threats, such as suspicious behavior or unattended packages.

3.4 ARTIFICIAL INTELLIGENCE APPLICATIONS IN INDUSTRY 5.0

3.4.1 Smart Factories and Manufacturing Processes

Smart factories and manufacturing processes are integral components of Industry 5.0, and the transformative power of AI holds immense promise for revolutionizing these operations. The concepts of "smart factories" and "Industry 5.0" have motivated global enterprises to embrace automation and intelligent robots, leading to enhanced manufacturing capabilities, improved product quality, and increased overall productivity. Undeniably, AI emerges as a vital tool in augmenting manufacturing endeavors, enabling seamless research and development, elevated quality standards, error reduction, and efficient supply chain management through demand forecasting and outcome simulations. These advancements are pivotal in securing a competitive advantage in a fiercely competitive market landscape [111]. Smart factories can help manufacturers stay ahead of the competition by leveraging real-time data and analytics to improve efficiency and productivity.

AI can play a critical role in this by enabling predictive maintenance, quality control, and process optimization [112,113]. In addition, the Industrial Internet of Things (IIoT) and machine learning can be used to create intelligent manufacturing systems that adapt to changing conditions and improve over time [114]. However, the adoption of AI in manufacturing also presents challenges, including data privacy concerns and the need for skilled personnel [101]. Nonetheless, research has shown that the benefits of AI in smart manufacturing can far outweigh the costs, including reduced downtime, increased throughput, and improved quality [112]. The role of AI in the manufacturing sector in Industry 5.0 are described below.

3.4.1.1 Predictive Maintenance

Predictive maintenance is a critical aspect of ensuring maximum uptime and operational efficiency in the manufacturing sector. AI has emerged as a powerful tool for predictive maintenance, as it can analyze vast amounts of sensor data in real time to identify patterns and anomalies that could signal impending equipment failure [115,116]. By using machine learning algorithms, AI systems can learn from historical data to predict future equipment failures and schedule maintenance proactively, reducing the need for costly emergency repairs and downtime [117]. Moreover, AI can also optimize maintenance schedules by taking into account factors such as the impact of maintenance on production and the availability of spare parts [118]. The use of AI for predictive maintenance has been shown to significantly reduce maintenance costs, increase equipment lifespan, and improve overall equipment effectiveness [119]. As such, it is a critical component of Industry 5.0, where smart factories rely on data-driven insights to maximize efficiency and productivity.

3.4.1.2 Quality Control and Defect Detection

AI has been proven to play a significant role in quality control in manufacturing, helping to improve the accuracy, efficiency, and speed of the inspection process [120]. Early defect detection, effective production, and quality assurance are necessities for meeting rising industrial process demands. When more sensors, smart devices, and cyber-physical networks are connected during the manufacturing process, more data are generated. These data could be utilized to optimize manufacturing methods and product quality. Algorithms for machine learning could enhance quality control (QA). The automated visual inspection technique is also used to guarantee optical quality with a machine learning-based framework for automated quality control [121].

Through defect detection, predictive maintenance, process optimization, and supply chain management, industries can harness the power of AI to enhance efficiency, minimize downtime, and streamline operations, ultimately leading to improved productivity and cost-effectiveness.

AI can improve product quality, reduce costs, and gain a competitive edge in the marketplace [13]. AI algorithms can be trained to identify defects automatically, enabling manufacturers to detect and correct quality issues early in the production process [113]. Additionally, AI predictive capabilities enable manufacturers to anticipate and forecast potential equipment failures. This foresight empowers them to proactively schedule maintenance tasks before any breakdowns occur, ensuring optimal equipment performance and reducing costly downtime. improving product quality by ensuring that equipment is operating at peak performance [115]. Overall, AI can help manufacturers to achieve a more efficient and effective quality control system, enhancing the production process and ultimately benefiting the business as a whole.

One study [122] examined the use of AI-based methods for defect detection and classification in manufacturing processes. The study found that these methods can significantly improve defect detection rates, reduce inspection times, and improve the overall quality of products. Another study [123] examined the use of machine vision and artificial intelligence-based methods for defect detection in steel products. The study found that these methods can detect defects with high accuracy, and are effective in reducing the time and cost associated with manual inspection. Furthermore, another study [104] explored the use of AI-based methods for process optimization in manufacturing industries. The study found that these methods can improve production efficiency and reduce waste, ultimately leading to better product quality and increased profitability. AI can have a significant impact on quality control in manufacturing, improving defect detection rates, reducing inspection times, and improving the overall efficiency of the production process. AI-based methods can significantly improve machine uptime, reduce maintenance costs, and improve product quality, and can effectively detect defects in the production process and improve products [124].

3.4.1.3 Supply Chain Optimization

The application of AI in supply chain management (SCM) has enabled significant improvements in supply chain optimization. Supply chain optimization refers to the process of finding the most efficient and effective way of delivering products and services to customers while minimizing costs [85,125]. AI-powered systems can also help in demand forecasting by analyzing data from various sources such as sales trends, weather patterns, and customer behavior, and this can result in significant cost savings and reduced lead times [126]. This enables companies to reduce inventory levels and the risk of stock-outs or excess inventory, leading to lower costs and increased customer satisfaction [127]. Additionally, it can also help to optimize supplier selection and performance by analyzing supplier performance data such as on-time delivery, quality, and pricing that lead to reduced costs and improved supplier relationships [128].

3.4.2 Industrial Internet of Things (IIoT) and Data Analytics

Industry 5.0 represents the next evolutionary phase of industry, amalgamating human intelligence with cutting-edge technologies like the IIoT and data analytics. By harmoniously integrating human expertise and technological prowess, Industry 5.0 seeks to unleash unprecedented levels of productivity, innovation, and efficiency in the industrial landscape. Precisely, the fusion of human intelligence and technological advancements in Industry 5.0 is anticipated to yield substantial improvements in the efficiency and productivity of manufacturing processes. Moreover, this synergy is poised to elevate the overall quality of products manufactured, leading to enhanced customer satisfaction and competitiveness in the global market. The collaborative capabilities of humans and advanced technologies promise to revolutionize the industrial domain, fostering a new era of innovation and progress.

IIoT technologies can be used to develop smart factories, which enable real-time data analysis and decision-making. Smart factories are designed to integrate all aspects of the manufacturing process, from raw materials to finished products, and provide real-time monitoring of production lines to optimize performance. Data analytics plays a critical role in Industry 5.0 by providing insights into the massive amounts of data generated by IIoT devices and can be used to improve production processes, reduce downtime, and enhance product quality. The IIoT and data analytics can be used to implement predictive maintenance in Industry 5.0 which can be used to analyze the performance of equipment and predict when maintenance is required. The IIoT and data analytics can also be used to improve supply chain management in Industry 5.0 as well as being used to monitor and optimize the performance of supply chains, reducing costs, and improving efficiency. Finally, the IIoT and data analytics can be used to improve product quality in Industry 5.0 to monitor production lines in real time, identify defects, and optimize production processes to enhance product quality.

3.4.2.1 Real-Time Monitoring and Analysis

Real-time monitoring and analysis play a critical role in Industry 5.0 by enabling efficient and effective decision-making, improving productivity, and reducing downtime [129]. Industry 5.0 is the latest paradigm shift in the manufacturing industry, focusing on the integration of human intelligence and creativity with advanced technologies such as the IoT, AI, and robotics [130]. Real-time monitoring and analysis are essential components of this new paradigm, allowing manufacturers to collect and analyze data in real time to optimize their operations and improve product quality.

3.4.2.2 Predictive Modeling and Forecasting

Predictive modeling and forecasting play a significant role in Industry 5.0 by helping manufacturers anticipate future events, optimize their operations, and make data-driven decisions. In Industry 5.0, manufacturers rely on advanced technologies such as the IoT, AI, and big data analytics to collect and analyze vast amounts of data. Predictive modeling and forecasting techniques are then used to extract insights from these data and predict future outcomes. Researchers [131–133] have examined the role of predictive modeling and forecasting in identifying potential equipment failures and optimizing maintenance schedules, which helps in improving the overall efficiency of manufacturing operations.

3.4.2.3 Asset Tracking and Management

Asset tracking and management solutions help manufacturers to track their assets in real time, monitor their performance, and make data-driven decisions. Asset-tracking solutions provide real-time location data, enabling manufacturers to track their assets as they move through the supply chain. These data can be used to optimize transportation routes, improve delivery times, and reduce costs.

Moreover, asset-tracking solutions (ATSs) can also be used to monitor asset performance, identifying potential issues before they cause downtime that enables manufacturers to schedule maintenance proactively, reducing unplanned downtime and improving overall productivity. They can help manufacturers to optimize their inventory management processes by tracking inventory in real time, so that manufacturers can reduce the risk of stockouts, minimize excess inventory, and improve supply chain efficiency. Further, ATSs provide manufacturers with real-time visibility into their assets, enabling them to make data-driven decisions. This enhanced visibility and transparency can help manufacturers to identify areas for improvement, optimize their operations, and reduce costs.

3.4.3 Robotics and Automation

3.4.3.1 Collaborative Robots (Cobots)

Current technological trends are enabling increasingly more physical contact between humans and machines. Humans and machines act together and communicate with each other not only through gestures and speech but mainly through the haptic channel [74,134]. This has resulted in the development of a new type of robot, the collaborative robot (cobot), which is geared toward human collaboration. This term describes a robot capable of working and collaborating with humans. These collaborative robots will be aware of human presence and will therefore take care of safety and risk criteria. In Industry 5.0, which emphasizes the collaboration between humans and machines, cobots play a critical role in facilitating human–robot collaboration. Cobots are designed to work alongside humans, helping them in repetitive, dangerous, and physically demanding tasks while allowing humans to focus on higher-level tasks that require creativity and problem-solving skills. Research on cobots and Industry 5.0 has revealed potential benefits of human–robot collaboration, including improved manufacturing efficiency, reduced lead time, and increased throughput [135]. This leads to enhanced productivity and enhanced product quality.

3.4.3.2 Autonomous Vehicles and Drones

AI is a critical technology not only for autonomous vehicles and drones, but also for the emerging Industry 5.0, which focuses on the integration of AI and automation technologies into traditional manufacturing processes. According to a report by McKinsey & Company, AI-enabled autonomous vehicles have the potential to reduce traffic fatalities by up to 90%, while also improving traffic flow and reducing energy consumption [136]. AI algorithms can process data from various sensors, such as cameras, lidar, and radar, to create a real-time map of the environment and make decisions on how to navigate through it. In addition, AI can be used to predict the behavior of other vehicles and pedestrians on the road, allowing the autonomous vehicle to anticipate and respond to potential hazards. In one study [137], the investigation delved into a routing protocol designed for autonomous systems, implementing advanced computational intelligence methodologies, and the results unveiled its noteworthy efficacy, surpassing existing techniques in critical domains, encompassing data delivery, data loss, energy consumption, and latency parameters. On the other hand, autonomous vehicles (AVs) are prone to malicious attacks, posing a great threat to the future of mobility and data protection. In resolving this challenge, AI and blockchain operate in tandem to address numerous security and privacy concerns of AVs.

AI plays a pivotal role in optimizing the construction of the blockchain, rendering it more efficient, secure, and energy-efficient. On the other hand, blockchain offers data immutability and a trust mechanism for AI-driven solutions, enhancing their transparency, trustworthiness, and explainability [138]. Together, these technologies form a robust synergy that fortifies AV systems, ensuring heightened security and reliability in their operations. Similarly, in the case of drones, AI can help them navigate through complex environments and avoid obstacles, such as buildings and trees, as well as enhance their tracking capabilities [139]. Drones are one of the emerging technologies used in smart cities. Thus, AI is an essential technology for the safe and efficient operation of autonomous vehicles and drones.

3.4.3.3 Human–Robot Collaboration

In the era of Industry 5.0, a revolutionary paradigm emerges, wherein humans and machines collaborate, synergizing their efforts to enhance the efficiency of industrial production. Industry 5.0 builds upon the advantages of Industry 4.0, utilizing technology to facilitate the transition, while simultaneously expanding its scope through a human-centric approach.

Industry 5.0 represents a shift away from using robots solely for automation purposes and instead emphasizes the integration of robots that collaborate and work alongside humans [140]. In its advancement from Industry 4.0 automation, Industry 5.0 enriches the capabilities of automation by complementing speed, accuracy, scalability, predictive capabilities, and repetitive tasks with the augmentation of human attributes.

These include agility, dexterity, creativity, improvisation, leadership, social talent, and soft skills. By combining the strengths of both humans and technology, Industry 5.0 aims to achieve unprecedented levels of productivity and efficiency in the industrial landscape. AI plays a critical role in facilitating human–machine collaboration by enabling machines to understand and interpret human inputs and communicate insights back to humans in a meaningful way. Natural language processing (NLP) is one of the key AI technologies used in human–machine collaboration, allowing machines to understand and interpret human language in various forms, including text, speech, and even nonverbal cues. NLP can be used to analyze unstructured data sources, such as customer feedback or social media posts, and provide insights that can inform human decision-making. In addition, AI-powered chatbots and virtual assistants can provide real-time support to human workers, helping them to complete tasks more efficiently and effectively [141]. For example, chatbots can answer common questions from customers, freeing up human workers to focus on more complex issues that require human intelligence and creativity. Thus, AI is an essential technology for enabling effective human–machine collaboration.

3.5 OUTCOMES OF AI IN INDUSTRY 5.0

3.5.1 Sustainability

The attainment of sustainability is predicated upon the symbiotic interplay of three interdependent factors: the environment, the economy, and society. The concept of Industry 5.0 has recently arisen as a vision of a future industry that values environmental and societal protection. Industry 5.0 supporters believe that Industry 4.0 is insufficient for attaining sustainable growth. Furthermore, recent studies, such as Ref. [142], clearly explain such Industry 4.0 constraints or negative sustainability implications. Also, while scholars widely believe that Industry 5.0 builds on the technological constituents of Industry 4.0, it is associated with radical technological advancements in cognitive artificial intelligence (CAI), energy transition technologies, and smart materials, to name a few [27].

A content-centric literature highlighted 16 functions that Industry 5.0 can use to further sustainable development principles, particularly those related to human centricity, environmental sustainability, and resilience, and developed a model that describes how Industry 5.0 can extend beyond delivering efficiency and productivity to promote socioenvironmental development meaningfully. Industry 5.0, encompassing 16 interdependent functions, from micro-technical to macro-operational, can contribute to sustainable development through their complementary roles in real-time communication and supply chain adaptability.

AI can play a crucial role in increasing sustainability in Industry 5.0 through various applications. it can optimize the use of resources in Industry 5.0, such as energy, water, and raw materials, by analyzing data and providing insights into how to minimize waste and maximize efficiency. For example, AI algorithms can optimize production schedules, logistics routes, and supply chain management to reduce environmental impact and enhance sustainability. AI can enable predictive maintenance of industrial equipment, reducing the risk of unplanned downtime and minimizing resource waste. By analyzing sensor data and other relevant data, AI algorithms can detect patterns and anomalies, providing early warnings of potential equipment failures and allowing for timely maintenance, thus extending the lifespan of machinery and reducing waste. AI can facilitate the implementation of circular economy principles in Industry 5.0.

For example, AI can support the tracking and traceability of materials and products throughout their lifecycle, enabling effective recycling, remanufacturing, and waste reduction strategies. AI can assist in designing more sustainable products by analyzing data on materials, manufacturing processes, and product lifecycle impacts. AI algorithms can provide recommendations for eco-friendly materials, energy-efficient designs, and end-of-life disposal strategies, leading to more sustainable product development. AI can optimize energy consumption in Industry 5.0 by analyzing data from sensors, smart grids, and energy management systems. AI algorithms can predict energy demand, optimize energy generation and consumption, and enable demand–response strategies, contributing to more efficient and sustainable energy usage. AI has the potential to play a significant role in achieving environmental sustainability. Below are some examples of how AI is being used to address environmental challenges.

3.5.2 Environmental Sustainability

3.5.2.1 Climate Modeling and Prediction

AI is being used to create more accurate climate models and predictions, which can help policymakers make informed decisions about how to mitigate and adapt to climate change. Machine learning algorithms are used to improve the accuracy of climate models and predict future temperature and precipitation patterns [143]. Various scholars and researchers using AI techniques like ML, EC, FL, ES, SVM, and neurofuzzy have explored various AI applications in areas like carbon emissions, natural disasters, ocean and cryosphere, atmosphere forecasting, and other climate change scenarios [128,144].

3.5.2.2 Energy Efficiency

AI can help reduce energy consumption by optimizing building and transportation systems. Machine learning algorithms have been used to develop an energy-saving control system for HVAC (heating, ventilation, and air conditioning) in buildings [92]. Various researchers have explained how AI components like machine learning can be used in domains like energy production and distribution, energy planning and design, operation and maintenance, building energy use, and renewable energy [145,146].

3.5.2.3 Renewable Energy Integration

AI can help integrate renewable energy sources into power grids more efficiently. Deep learning algorithms to predict the solar power output for photovoltaic systems could help grid operators manage energy flows and reduce waste [127]. AI can be used in smart farms, which is a novel idea for providing energy in rural areas using artificial intelligence and renewable energy management using an artificial neural network (ANN) for process optimization based on the agroeconomic profile of farms [147,148].

3.5.2.4 Environmental Monitoring

AI can help monitor environmental conditions and detect pollution in real time. For example, researchers in Canada used machine learning algorithms to analyze satellite imagery and detect oil spills in the ocean [149]. Several environmental problems (monitoring, analysis, diagnosis, forecasting, planning, and control) can be solved efficiently using AI techniques. The authors of Ref. [150] assessed air quality and control systems by using AI techniques that can be applied to forecasting problems solving such as artificial neural networks (ANNs), fuzzy logic, case-based reasoning, fuzzy inference systems (ANFISs), expert systems, and adaptive neurofuzzy systems [128,150].

In sustainable agriculture AI can help farmers improve crop yields and reduce waste by providing real-time insights into soil conditions, weather patterns, and pest infestations. The agriculture industry is utilizing AI technology to grow healthier crops, control pests, monitor soil and growth conditions, analyze data for farmers, and improve various management tasks associated with the food supply chain. AI aids farmers in selecting the best seed for given weather conditions as well as providing data on weather forecasts to assist farmers in increasing crop quality, producing more with less resources, and reducing the time it takes for products to reach the market. AI also helps in understanding soil properties which aids farmers by recommending the required nutrients [147].

3.5.2.5 Society 5.0

Society 5.0 is a future society that is being envisioned by Japan as a human-centered society that balances economic advancement with the resolution of social issues. Society 5.0 integrates new technologies in businesses and social activities, aiming for economic development based on the United Nations' Sustainable Development Goals and addressing significant social issues [151]. Society 5.0 aims to place human beings at the midpoint of innovation, exploiting the impact of technology and Industry 4.0 results with the technological integration to improve quality of life, social responsibility, and sustainability [29]. Society 5.0 and Industry 5.0 are significant shifts in communities and economies, aiming to balance economic development with social and environmental issues, and eliminate human–machine interaction and talent matching obstacles [152]. One of the most contentious issues is whether or not AI will replace people in value-added activities and the influence of future AI on businesses and society.

Society 5.0 places a strong emphasis on putting the person at the center of innovation, technological revolution, and industrial automation, which is fueled by artificial intelligence and Industry 5.0. This new Society 5.0 paradigm will be crucial in building a happier, more satisfied, fulfilled, and thus more productive society by utilizing sophisticated technology from artificial intelligence and Industry 5.0 for the benefit of humanity, in order to foster a link between people and systems in cyberspace. Apart from that, manufacturing and business processes are also increasingly using cloud and mobile technologies, the IoT, AI, and data analytics, which herald Industry 5.0. Society 5.0 entails a human-centric community capable of finding a balance between economic proliferation and resolving societal liabilities through the fundamental mix of cyber and physical space. Industry 5.0 provides digital transformation to the perspective of Industry 4.0, which leaps into a digital revamp that extends to the various segement of the industrial evolution [153]. AI is playing a crucial role in building Society 5.0 by offering innovative solutions to complex problems in various sectors. Below are a few examples.

Healthcare: AI is helping to improve healthcare by enabling faster and more accurate diagnoses, personalized treatment plans, and improved patient outcomes. For example, AI algorithms can analyze medical images to detect and diagnose diseases such as cancer, and AI chatbots can provide patients with medical advice and triage services.

Transportation: AI is helping to build a smarter transportation system that is safe, efficient, and sustainable. For example, AI algorithms can analyze traffic patterns and optimize traffic flows to reduce congestion, and self-driving cars powered by AI can improve road safety and reduce accidents.

Education: AI is helping to revolutionize education by offering personalized learning experiences to students. For example, AI-powered chatbots can provide students with real-time feedback on their work, and AI algorithms can analyze student data to create personalized learning paths that cater to individual learning styles and needs.

Energy: AI is helping to build a sustainable energy system by optimizing energy usage and reducing waste. For example, AI algorithms can analyze energy consumption patterns and identify areas where energy can be saved, and AI-powered smart grids can optimize energy distribution and reduce energy waste.

Agriculture: AI is helping to improve agriculture by enabling precision farming, which involves using data and technology to optimize crop yields and reduce resource waste. For example, AI algorithms can analyze soil and weather data to predict crop yields, and AI-powered drones can monitor crops and identify areas that require attention.

Manufacturing: AI is helping to create a more efficient and productive manufacturing industry by optimizing supply chain management, improving quality control, and enabling predictive maintenance. For example, AI algorithms can analyze data from sensors on manufacturing equipment to predict when maintenance is needed, and AI-powered robots can automate manufacturing processes to increase efficiency and reduce costs.

Finance: AI is helping to create a more transparent and efficient financial system by enabling predictive analytics, fraud detection, and personalized financial advice. For example, AI algorithms can analyze financial data to predict market trends and make investment recommendations, and AI-powered chatbots can provide customers with personalized financial advice and help with banking transactions.

Smart cities: AI is helping to create smarter and more sustainable cities by enabling predictive maintenance, traffic optimization, and energy efficiency. For example, AI algorithms can analyze data from sensors on infrastructure to predict maintenance needs, and AI-powered traffic management systems can optimize traffic flow to reduce congestion and improve air quality.

Environmental monitoring: AI is helping to monitor and protect the environment by enabling real-time data analysis and predictive modeling. For example, AI algorithms can analyze data from sensors on air and water quality to predict pollution levels and identify areas that require attention, and AI-powered drones can monitor wildlife populations and help with conservation efforts.

Disaster response: AI is helping to improve disaster responses by enabling faster and more accurate predictions of natural disasters and providing real-time assistance during emergencies. For example, AI algorithms can analyze weather patterns and seismic activity to predict earthquakes and hurricanes, and AI-powered chatbots can provide real-time emergency assistance and support during disasters.

Overall, AI is helping to build Society 5.0 by enabling more efficient and sustainable systems across a wide range of sectors, from healthcare and education to finance and the environment. By leveraging the power of AI, we can create a more equitable and human-centered society that benefits everyone.

3.5.4 Resilience and IR5

Resilience is a key factor in the success and longevity of any organization, and this is particularly true in the context of Industry 5.0 [154]. The concept of resilience is increasingly important in the context of Industry 5.0, as this new era of manufacturing brings with it new challenges and opportunities. Resilience can be defined as the ability to adapt and recover from disruptions and changes in the environment, and it is a critical factor in the success of any organization. In the context of Industry 5.0, resilience is closely linked to the ability to adopt and implement new technologies, such as AI, the IoT, and robotics. By leveraging these technologies, companies can gain greater visibility into their operations and respond more quickly to changes in market conditions and customer demands.

As new technologies and innovations continue to emerge, it is essential that companies are able to adapt and evolve in response to changing market conditions and customer demands. This requires a willingness to embrace new ideas and approaches, and to be open to learning and experimentation. One of the key benefits of Industry 5.0 is its ability to promote resilience by creating a more flexible and adaptive production process. By leveraging technologies like AI and the IoT, companies can gain greater visibility into their operations and make real-time adjustments to optimize efficiency and productivity. This enables them to respond more quickly to changes in demand, supply chain disruptions, and other external factors that can impact their business.

Another way that Industry 5.0 can promote resilience is by fostering collaboration and partnerships between different stakeholders. By working together to share knowledge and resources, companies can create a more robust and interconnected ecosystem that is better able to weather challenges and overcome obstacles. This requires a shift away from traditional silos and hierarchies toward a more collaborative and inclusive approach to business. Figure 3.4 displays the revolution of Industry 5.0.

3.5.5 New Business Models

Industry 5.0 is a future industrial revolution that emphasizes the importance of human intelligence and collaboration with machines to create a more sustainable and equitable manufacturing industry. AI-based model is playing a key role in building new business models in Industry 5.0 by enabling new levels of efficiency, personalization,

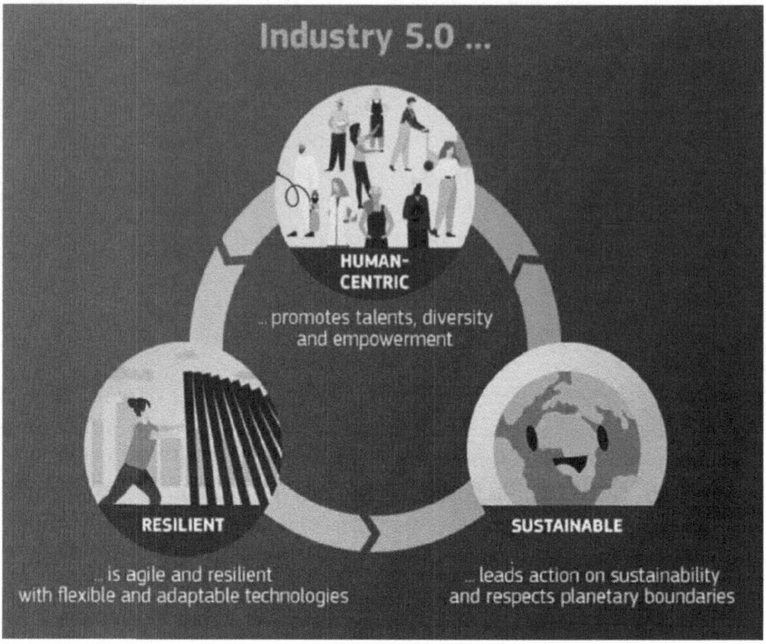

FIGURE 3.4 Industry 5.0.

and sustainability. AI-powered predictive maintenance helps businesses to reduce downtime, increase machine lifespan, and improve product quality. By analyzing data from sensors on machines and predicting when maintenance is needed, businesses can perform maintenance proactively, reducing the risk of breakdowns and reducing costs. AI-powered customization helps businesses to create more personalized products and services for customers. By analyzing customer data and using machine learning algorithms to identify patterns and preferences, businesses can offer tailored products and services that meet individual needs and preferences.

AI-powered logistics helps businesses to optimize the supply chain by improving visibility, reducing waste, and increasing efficiency. By analyzing data from sensors on products, trucks, and warehouses, businesses can optimize delivery routes, reduce inventory costs, and improve the speed and accuracy of deliveries. AI-powered quality control helps businesses to improve product quality by identifying defects and inconsistencies. By analyzing data from sensors on products and using machine learning algorithms to identify patterns, businesses can identify defects early on, reducing the risk of product recalls and improving customer satisfaction. AI-powered sustainable production helps businesses to reduce waste, conserve resources, and improve sustainability. By analyzing data from sensors on energy usage, emissions, and waste, businesses can identify areas where improvements can be made, reducing their environmental impact and improving their bottom line.

Overall, AI is helping businesses to build new business models in Industry 5.0 by enabling new levels of efficiency, personalization, and sustainability. By leveraging the power of AI, businesses can create more value for their customers, reduce their environmental impact, and stay competitive in a rapidly changing market.

3.5.6 Key Takeaways

The literature review suggests that Industry 4.0 and 5.0 technologies can be categorized into three groups: core technologies, supporting technologies, and beneficial technologies. Core technologies like the IoT, IoE, AIoT, AI, cognitive computing, automation, and robotics form the foundation of the next industrial revolution. Supporting technologies such as cloud computing, edge computing, big data, blockchain, 6G, and cyber security provide critical infrastructure for core technologies. Beneficial technologies like cyber-physical systems, additive manufacturing, cobots, digital twins, smart sensors, and extended reality rely on core and supporting technologies for functionality.

Industry 5.0 enablers seem like minor improvements or upgrades of Industry 4.0 technologies. However, they emphasize the inclusion of humans, environmental consciousness, and social responsibility. Environmental, social, and governance (ESG) and sustainability are key themes, with ESG evolving from sustainability. Both concepts entail "doing good" for the environment and society, with human inclusion being a central focus.

3.5.7 Challenges of Industry 5.0

Industry 5.0 presents some distinct issues that have never been seen before, like social diversity in terms of accepted ideals, measurement of the creation of social and environmental value, integration of entire value chains into small and medium-sized enterprises (SMEs); fostering interdisciplinary collaboration across research disciplines and grappling with system complexity; and adopting an ecosystem-oriented innovation strategy with agile, outcome-oriented processes [155]. The incorporation of standardization and legalization measures will serve to mitigate potential conflicts between technology, society, and businesses. The implementation of AI in Industry 5.0, which highlights the significance of human intelligence and cooperation with machines, presents its unique array of challenges. Below some of the main challenges are outlined.

Data quality and availability: AI relies heavily on data, and the quality and availability of data can impact the accuracy and effectiveness of AI systems. Obtaining high-quality data can be difficult, particularly for smaller companies with limited resources.

Bias and fairness: AI systems can be biased, reflecting the biases present in the data used to train them. This can lead to unfair outcomes, particularly in areas such as hiring and lending. Ensuring that AI systems are fair and unbiased requires careful attention to the data used to train them.

Explainability and transparency: AI systems can be complex and difficult to understand, particularly when they use deep learning algorithms. Ensuring that AI systems are transparent and explainable is important for building trust in these systems and ensuring that they are used ethically.

Regulation and compliance: As with any new technology, AI raises ethical and regulatory concerns, such as data privacy, cybersecurity, and the impact of automation on jobs. Companies must navigate these issues carefully to ensure that their use of AI is ethical and compliant with regulations.

Workforce reskilling: Implementing AI systems can require a highly skilled workforce with expertise in areas such as data science and machine learning. Reskilling and retraining a large workforce can be time-consuming and expensive.

Overall, implementing AI in Industry 5.0 presents challenges related to data quality and availability, bias and fairness, explainability and transparency, regulation and compliance, and workforce reskilling. Addressing these challenges will require collaboration between industry, government, and academia to ensure that AI can be implemented in a way that is ethical, sustainable, and beneficial for everyone.

3.5.8 Future Directions

Future research directions in academia related to AI are likely to focus on several key areas that reflect the evolving challenges, opportunities, and advancements in the field. Below are some potential future research directions.

3.5.8.1 Ethical AI and Responsible Innovation

As AI technologies become increasingly integrated into society, there is a growing need for research on ethical AI frameworks, principles, and guidelines. Future research may explore topics such as fairness, accountability, transparency, privacy, and bias mitigation in AI systems. Additionally, there will be a focus on developing ethical AI design methodologies and tools to ensure responsible innovation and deployment of AI technologies.

3.5.8.2 Explainable AI (XAI)

Explainable AI is a critical research area aimed at improving the transparency and interpretability of AI models and decisions. Future research may focus on developing new XAI techniques and methodologies that enable users to understand and trust AI systems. This includes research on model interpretability, feature importance analysis, and interactive visualization techniques for explaining AI predictions and behaviors.

3.5.8.3 AI for Social Good and Sustainability

There is a growing interest in leveraging AI technologies to address pressing societal challenges and promote sustainability. Future research directions may include the application of AI for healthcare, education, environmental conservation, disaster response, poverty alleviation, and humanitarian aid. This research will involve interdisciplinary collaborations between AI researchers, domain experts, policymakers, and communities to develop impactful AI solutions that benefit society as a whole.

3.5.8.4 AI and Human-Centered Computing

Human-centered computing is an interdisciplinary field that explores the design, development, and evaluation of AI systems with a focus on human needs, capabilities, and experiences. Future research may investigate topics such as human–AI interaction, user-centered design methodologies, personalized AI systems, adaptive interfaces, and AI-mediated communication. This research will contribute to the development of AI technologies that enhance human productivity, creativity, well-being, and inclusivity.

3.5.8.5 AI and Augmented Intelligence

Augmented intelligence is an emerging paradigm that emphasizes the synergistic collaboration between humans and AI systems to enhance cognitive capabilities and decision-making processes. Future research directions may include the development of hybrid intelligence systems that combine the strengths of humans and AI algorithms. This research will explore novel approaches for human–AI collaboration, cognitive augmentation, decision support, and adaptive learning in diverse application domains.

3.5.8.6 AI Safety and Robustness

Ensuring the safety, reliability, and robustness of AI systems is a critical research challenge that requires interdisciplinary collaboration between AI researchers, computer scientists, engineers, and ethicists. Future research may focus on developing techniques for verifying and validating AI systems, detecting and mitigating adversarial attacks, ensuring system resilience to uncertainties and errors, and designing fail-safe mechanisms for autonomous AI systems.

3.5.8.7 AI and Cognitive Science

Cognitive science provides valuable insights into human cognition, perception, learning, and decision-making processes, which can inform the design and development of AI systems. Future research directions may include interdisciplinary collaborations between AI researchers and cognitive scientists to study the fundamental principles of intelligence, consciousness, emotion, and creativity. This research will advance our understanding of both natural and artificial intelligence and inspire new approaches for designing more human-like AI systems.

The use of AI technologies in Industry 5.0 can support sustainability goals by reducing waste, improving efficiency, and enabling more informed decision-making. Manufacturers that prioritize sustainability in their operations can not only meet consumer demand but also position themselves as leaders in the industry. AI technologies have transformed the manufacturing industry in Industry 5.0, enabling manufacturers to achieve new levels of efficiency, productivity, and innovation. The use of AI technologies will continue to shape the future of manufacturing, driving further advancements and opportunities for growth and development. AI technologies play a critical role in Industry 5.0 by enabling manufacturers to collect and analyze vast amounts of data, optimize their operations, and make data-driven decisions.

3.6 CONCLUSION

The use of AI technologies such as machine learning, natural language processing, and computer vision has transformed the manufacturing industry, enabling manufacturers to achieve new levels of efficiency, productivity, and innovation. AI technologies are used in a wide range of applications in Industry 5.0, including predictive maintenance, quality control, supply chain optimization, asset tracking, and predictive modeling and forecasting. By leveraging these technologies, manufacturers can improve their operations, reduce downtime, and increase productivity, thereby achieving a competitive advantage in the market. However, the implementation of AI technologies in Industry 5.0 also presents challenges, such as data privacy and security concerns, the need for specialized skills and training, and the potential for job displacement. To overcome these challenges, it is important for manufacturers to develop comprehensive strategies for the ethical and responsible use of AI technologies, while also investing in the training and development of their workforce. Another important point to consider in the use of AI technologies in Industry 5.0 is sustainability. As the world increasingly prioritizes sustainability, manufacturers are under pressure to reduce their environmental footprint and operate more efficiently. AI technologies can play a significant role in achieving these goals. AI-powered predictive maintenance solutions can help manufacturers reduce the amount of waste generated by repairing equipment before it fails, thereby minimizing the need for replacement parts and reducing environmental impact. Similarly, AI-powered optimization solutions can help manufacturers reduce energy consumption by optimizing production processes and identifying areas for improvement. AI-based technologies have been used to support sustainable sourcing and supply chain management. By analyzing data on suppliers and materials, manufacturers can make more informed decisions about their supply chain and identify opportunities to reduce waste and environmental impact.

REFERENCES

[1] Falola, P. B., Adeniyi, A. E., Madamidola, O. A., Awotunde, J. B., Olukiran, O. A., & Akinola, S. O. (2024). Artificial Intelligence in Agriculture: The Potential for Efficiency and Sustainability, with Ethical Considerations. In *Exploring Ethical Dimensions of Environmental Sustainability and Use of AI* (pp. 307–329). IGI Global.

[2] Ghobakhloo, M. (2020). Industry 4.0, digitization, and opportunities for sustainability. *Journal of Cleaner Production, 252*, 119869.

[3] Awotunde, J. B., Ayo, E. F., Ajamu, G. J., Jimoh, T. B., & Ajagbe, S. A. (2023). The Influence of Industry 4.0 and 5.0 for Distance Learning Education in Times of Pandemic for a Modern Society. In *Advances in Distance Learning in Times of Pandemic* (pp. 177–214). Chapman and Hall/CRC.

[4] Sony, M., & Naik, S. (2020). Key ingredients for evaluating Industry 4.0 readiness for organizations: A literature review. *Benchmarking: An International Journal, 27*(7), 2213–2232.

[5] Coelho, P., Bessa, C., Landeck, J., & Silva, C. (2023). Industry 5.0: The arising of a concept. *Procedia Computer Science, 217*, 1137–1144.

[6] Capello, R., & Lenzi, C. (2021). Industry 4.0 and servitisation: Regional patterns of 4.0 technological transformations in Europe. *Technological Forecasting and Social Change*, *173*, 121164.

[7] Abikoye, O. C., Bajeh, A. O., Awotunde, J. B., Ameen, A. O., Mojeed, H. A., Abdulraheem, M., ... & Salihu, S. A. (2021). Application of Internet of Thing and Cyber Physical System in Industry 4.0 Smart Manufacturing. In *Emergence of Cyber Physical System and IoT in Smart Automation and Robotics: Computer Engineering in Automation* (pp. 203–217). Springer International Publishing.

[8] Bajeh, A. O., Mojeed, H. A., Ameen, A. O., Abikoye, O. C., Salihu, S. A., Abdulraheem, M., ... & Awotunde, J. B. (2021). Internet of robotic things: its domain, methodologies, and applications. In *Emergence of Cyber Physical System and IoT in Smart Automation and Robotics: Computer Engineering in Automation* (pp. 135–146). Springer International Publishing.

[9] Wang, B., Zhou, H., Li, X., Yang, G., Zheng, P., Song, C., ... & Wang, L. (2024). Human digital twin in the context of Industry 5.0. *Robotics and Computer-Integrated Manufacturing*, *85*, 102626.

[10] Kumari, P., Anand, A., Praveen, P., Verma, A. R., & Godiyal, A. (2024). Infrastructure Potential and Human-Centric Strategies in the Context of Industry 5.0. In *Infrastructure Possibilities and Human-Centered Approaches With Industry 5.0* (pp. 199–214). IGI Global.

[11] Awotunde, J. B., Folorunso, S. O., Imoize, A. L., Odunuga, J. O., Lee, C. C., Li, C. T., & Do, D. T. (2023). An ensemble tree-based model for intrusion detection in industrial internet of things networks. *Applied Sciences*, *13*(4), 2479.

[12] Raja Santhi, A., & Muthuswamy, P. (2023). Industry 5.0 or industry 4.0 S? Introduction to industry 4.0 and a peek into the prospective industry 5.0 technologies. *International Journal on Interactive Design and Manufacturing (IJIDeM)*, *17*(2), 947–979.

[13] Wang, H., Lv, L., Li, X., Li, H., Leng, J., Zhang, Y., ... & Luo, G. (2023). A safety management approach for Industry 5.0′ s human-centered manufacturing based on digital twin. *Journal of Manufacturing Systems*, *66*, 1–12.

[14] Abdulraheem, M., Adeniyi, E. A., Awotunde, J. B., Imoize, A. L., Jimoh, R. G., Oladipo, I. D., & Falola, P. B. (2024). Artificial Intelligence of Medical Things for Medical Information Systems Privacy and Security. In *Handbook of Security and Privacy of AI-Enabled Healthcare Systems and Internet of Medical Things* (pp. 63–96). CRC Press.

[15] Hein-Pensel, F., Winkler, H., Brückner, A., Wölke, M., Jabs, I., Mayan, I. J., ... & Zinke-Wehlmann, C. (2023). Maturity assessment for Industry 5.0: A review of existing maturity models. *Journal of Manufacturing Systems*, *66*, 200–210.

[16] Rath, K. C., Khang, A., & Roy, D. (2024). The Role of Internet of Things (IoT) Technology in Industry 4.0 Economy. In *Advanced IoT Technologies and Applications in the Industry 4.0 Digital Economy* (pp. 1–28). CRC Press.

[17] Ahmad, M. H., Moshood, T. D., & Nawanir, G. (2024). The influence of Industrial Revolution 4.0 in the implementation of the learning factory at the University of Malaysia Pahang. *Journal of Applied Research in Higher Education*, *16*(1), 89–103.

[18] Golovianko, M., Terziyan, V., Branytskyi, V., & Malyk, D. (2023). Industry 4.0 vs. Industry 5.0: Co-existence, transition, or a hybrid. *Procedia Computer Science*, *217*, 102–113.

[19] Nel-Sanders, D. (2023). Revolutionising public private partnerships: A transition to the fifth industrial revolution. *International Journal of Innovation in Management, Economics and Social Sciences*, *3*(1), 12–29.

[20] Beaudry, A., & Pinsonneault, A. (2005). Understanding user responses to information technology: A coping model of user adaptation. *MIS Quarterly, 29*(3), (Sep., 2005), 493–524.
[21] Awotunde, J. B., Imoize, A. L., Jimoh, R. G., Adeniyi, E. A., Abdulraheem, M., Oladipo, I. D., & Falola, P. B. (2024). AIoMT Enabling Real-Time Monitoring of Healthcare Systems: Security and Privacy Considerations. In *Handbook of Security and Privacy of AI-Enabled Healthcare Systems and Internet of Medical Things* (pp. 97–133). CRC Press, Taylors and Francis.
[22] Pluta-Zaremba, A., & Szelagowska, A. (2021). Transformation of the Economy: Towards Era 5.0. In *The Economics of Sustainable Transformation*. Taylor & Francis.
[23] Tallat, R., Hawbani, A., Wang, X., Al-Dubai, A., Zhao, L., Liu, Z., ... & Alsamhi, S. H. (2023). Navigating industry 5.0: A survey of key enabling technologies, trends, challenges, and opportunities. *IEEE Communications Surveys & Tutorials, 26*(2), pp. 1080–1126, Secondquarter 2024, doi: 10.1109/COMST.2023.3329472
[24] Noble, S. M., Mende, M., Grewal, D., & Parasuraman, A. (2022). The Fifth Industrial Revolution: How harmonious human–machine collaboration is triggering a retail and service [r] evolution. *Journal of Retailing, 98*(2), 199–208.
[25] Alves, J., Lima, T. M., & Gaspar, P. D. (2023). Is Industry 5.0 a human-centred approach? A systematic review. *Processes, 11*(1), 193.
[26] Agote-Garrido, A., Martín-Gómez, A. M., & Lama-Ruiz, J. R. (2023). Manufacturing system design in Industry 5.0: Incorporating sociotechnical systems and social metabolism for human-centered, sustainable, and resilient production. *Systems, 11*(11), 537.
[27] Maddikunta, P. K. R., Pham, Q. V., Prabadevi, B., Deepa, N., Dev, K., Gadekallu, T. R., ... & Liyanage, M. (2022). Industry 5.0: A survey on enabling technologies and potential applications. *Journal of Industrial Information Integration, 26*, 100257.
[28] Ajagbe, S. A., Awotunde, J. B., Opadotun, A. T., & Adigun, M. O. (2023, March). Cybersecurity in the Supply Chain and Logistics Industry: A Concept-Centric Review. In *International Conference on Advances in IoT and Security with AI* (pp. 39–50). Springer Nature Singapore.
[29] Carayannis, E. G., & Morawska-Jancelewicz, J. (2022). The futures of Europe: Society 5.0 and Industry 5.0 as driving forces of future universities. *Journal of the Knowledge Economy, 13*(4), 3445–3471.
[30] Gaber, T., Awotunde, J. B., Torky, M., Ajagbe, S. A., Hammoudeh, M., & Li, W. (2023). Metaverse-IDS: Deep learning-based intrusion detection system for Metaverse-IoT networks. *Internet of Things, 24*, 100977.
[31] Pachouri, V., Singh, R., Gehlot, A., Pandey, S., Akram, S. V., & Abbas, M. (2024). Empowering sustainability in the built environment: A technological Lens on industry 4.0 Enablers. *Technology in Society, 76*, 102427.
[32] Ivanov, D. (2023). The Industry 5.0 framework: Viability-based integration of the resilience, sustainability, and human-centricity perspectives. *International Journal of Production Research, 61*(5), 1683–1695.
[33] Narkhede, G. B., Pasi, B. N., Rajhans, N., & Kulkarni, A. (2024). Industry 5.0 and sustainable manufacturing: A systematic literature review. *Benchmarking: An International Journal, 2023*(2), 100–118.
[34] Ajagbe, S. A., Awotunde, J. B., Oladipupo, M. A., & Oye, O. E. (2022). Prediction and Forecasting of Coronavirus Cases Using Artificial Intelligence Algorithm. In *Machine Learning for Critical Internet of Medical Things: Applications and Use Cases* (pp. 31–54). Springer International Publishing.

[35] Awotunde, J. B., Ajagbe, S. A., & Florez, H. (2022, October). Internet of Things with Wearable Devices and Artificial Intelligence for Elderly Uninterrupted Healthcare Monitoring Systems. In *International Conference on Applied Informatics* (pp. 278–291). Springer International Publishing.

[36] Rožanec, J. M., Fortuna, B., & Mladenić, D. (2022). Knowledge graph-based rich and confidentiality preserving Explainable Artificial Intelligence (XAI). *Information Fusion, 81*, 91–102.

[37] Rožanec, J. M., Novalija, I., Zajec, P., Kenda, K., Tavakoli Ghinani, H., Suh, S., ... & Soldatos, J. (2023). Human-centric artificial intelligence architecture for industry 5.0 applications. *International Journal of Production Research, 61*(20), 6847–6872.

[38] Awotunde, J. B., Folorunso, S. O., Ajagbe, S. A., Garg, J., & Ajamu, G. J. (2022). AiIoMT: IoMT-based system-enabled artificial intelligence for enhanced smart healthcare systems. In: Al-Turjman, F., Nayyar, A. (eds) *Machine Learning for Critical Internet of Medical Things*. Springer, Cham, 229–254. https://doi.org/10.1007/978-3-030-80928-7_10

[39] Awotunde, J. B., Adeniyi, E. A., Ajamu, G. J., Balogun, G. B., & Taofeek-Ibrahim, F. A. (2022). Explainable Artificial Intelligence in Genomic Sequence for Healthcare Systems Prediction. In *Connected e-Health: Integrated IoT and Cloud Computing* (pp. 417–437). Springer International Publishing.

[40] Reiter-Palmon, R., & Illies, J. J. (2004). Leadership and creativity: Understanding leadership from a creative problem-solving perspective. *The Leadership Quarterly, 15*(1), 55–77.

[41] Górriz, J. M., Álvarez-Illán, I., Álvarez-Marquina, A., Arco, J. E., Atzmueller, M., Ballarini, F., ... & Ferrández-Vicente, J. M. (2023). Computational approaches to explainable artificial intelligence: Advances in theory, applications and trends. *Information Fusion, 100*, 101945.

[42] Vrontis, D., Christofi, M., Pereira, V., Tarba, S., Makrides, A., & Trichina, E. (2022). Artificial intelligence, robotics, advanced technologies and human resource management: A systematic review. *The International Journal of Human Resource Management, 33*(6), 1237–1266.

[43] Awotunde, J. B., Oluwabukonla, S., Chakraborty, C., Bhoi, A. K., & Ajamu, G. J. (2022). Application of Artificial Intelligence and Big Data for Fighting COVID-19 Pandemic. In: Hassan, S.A., Mohamed, A.W., Alnowibet, K.A. (eds) *Decision Sciences for COVID-19*. International Series in Operations Research & Management Science, vol 320. Springer, Cham. (pp. 3–26). https://doi.org/10.1007/978-3-030-87019-5_1

[44] Krishnakumar, A. (2007). Active learning literature survey. *Technical reports, University of California, Santa Cruz., 42*.

[45] Lughofer, E., Zavoianu, A. C., Pollak, R., Pratama, M., Meyer-Heye, P., Zörrer, H., ... & Radauer, T. (2019). Autonomous supervision and optimization of product quality in a multi-stage manufacturing process based on self-adaptive prediction models. *Journal of Process Control, 76*, 27–45.

[46] Lee, J., Singh, J., Azamfar, M., & Pandhare, V. (2020). Industrial AI and Predictive Analytics for Smart Manufacturing Systems. In *Smart Manufacturing* (pp. 213–244). Elsevier.

[47] Yue, X., Wen, Y., Hunt, J. H., & Shi, J. (2020). Active learning for Gaussian process considering uncertainties with application to shape control of composite fuselage. *IEEE Transactions on Automation Science and Engineering, 18*(1), 36–46.

[48] Awotunde, J. B., Misra, S., Ayeni, F., Maskeliunas, R., & Damasevicius, R. (2021, December). Artificial Intelligence Based System for Bank Loan Fraud Prediction.

In *International Conference on Hybrid Intelligent Systems* (pp. 463–472). Springer International Publishing.

[49] Sarkar, K., Shiuly, A., & Dhal, K. G. (2024). Revolutionizing concrete analysis: An in-depth survey of AI-powered insights with image-centric approaches on comprehensive quality control, advanced crack detection and concrete property exploration. *Construction and Building Materials*, *411*, 134212.

[50] Awotunde, J. B., & Misra, S. (2022). Feature Extraction and Artificial Intelligence-Based Intrusion Detection Model for a Secure Internet of Things Networks. In *Illumination of Artificial Intelligence in Cybersecurity and Forensics* (pp. 21–44). Springer International Publishing.

[51] Adel, A. (2023). Unlocking the future: Fostering human–machine collaboration and driving intelligent automation through industry 5.0 in smart cities. *Smart Cities*, *6*(5), 2742–2782.

[52] J. Joosten, V. Bilgram, A. Hahn and D. Totzek (2024). Comparing the ideation quality of humans with generative artificial intelligence. *IEEE Engineering Management Review*, *52*(2), 153-164, April 2024, doi: 10.1109/EMR.2024.3353338

[53] Awotunde, J. B., Jimoh, R. G., Matiluko, O. E., Gbadamosi, B., & Ajamu, G. J. (2021). Artificial Intelligence and An Edge-IoMT-Based System for Combating COVID-19 Pandemic. In *Intelligent Interactive Multimedia Systems for e-Healthcare Applications* (pp. 191–214). Springer Singapore.

[54] Awotunde, J. B., Folorunso, S. O., Jimoh, R. G., Adeniyi, E. A., Abiodun, K. M., & Ajamu, G. J. (2021). Application of artificial intelligence for COVID-19 epidemic: an exploratory study, opportunities, challenges, and future prospects. In: Oliva, D., Hassan, S.A., Mohamed, A. (eds) Artificial Intelligence for COVID-19. Studies in Systems, Decision and Control, vol 358. Springer, Cham, 47–61. https://doi.org/10.1007/978-3-030-69744-0_4

[55] Javaid, M., Haleem, A., Singh, R. P., & Suman, R. (2022). Artificial intelligence applications for industry 4.0: A literature-based study. *Journal of Industrial Integration and Management*, *7*(01), 83–111.

[56] Šumak, B., Brdnik, S., & Pušnik, M. (2021). Sensors and artificial intelligence methods and algorithms for human–computer intelligent interaction: A systematic mapping study. *Sensors*, *22*(1), 20.

[57] Ribeiro de Oliveira, T., Biancardi Rodrigues, B., Moura da Silva, M., Antonio N. Spinassé, R., Giesen Ludke, G., Ruy Soares Gaudio, M., ... & Mestria, M. (2023). Virtual reality solutions employing artificial intelligence methods: A systematic literature review. *ACM Computing Surveys*, *55*(10), 1–29.

[58] Miro, J. P. (2020). *FPGA-Based Accelerators for Convolutional Neural Networks on Embedded Devices* (Doctoral dissertation, University of Colorado Colorado Springs).

[59] AbdulRaheem, M., Oladipo, I. D., Imoize, A. L., Awotunde, J. B., Lee, C. C., Balogun, G. B., & Adeoti, J. O. (2023). Machine learning assisted snort and zeek in detecting DDoS attacks in software-defined networking. *International Journal of Information Technology*, *16*, 1627–1643. https://doi.org/10.1007/s41870-023-01469-3.

[60] Elsheikh, A. H. (2023). Applications of machine learning in friction stir welding: Prediction of joint properties, real-time control and tool failure diagnosis. *Engineering Applications of Artificial Intelligence*, *121*, 105961.

[61] Jiang, J. (2023). A survey of machine learning in additive manufacturing technologies. *International Journal of Computer Integrated Manufacturing*, *36*(9), 1258–1280. https://doi.org/10.1080/0951192X.2023.2177740.

[62] Javeed, A., Dallora, A. L., Berglund, J. S., Ali, A., Ali, L., & Anderberg, P. (2023). Machine learning for dementia prediction: A systematic review and future research directions. *Journal of Medical Systems*, *47*(1), 17.

[63] Ashton, J. J., Young, A., Johnson, M. J., & Beattie, R. M. (2023). Using machine learning to impact on long-term clinical care: Principles, challenges, and practicalities. *Pediatric Research*, *93*(2), 324–333.

[64] Herm, L. V., Heinrich, K., Wanner, J., & Janiesch, C. (2023). Stop ordering machine learning algorithms by their explainability! A user-centered investigation of performance and explainability. *International Journal of Information Management*, *69*, 102538.

[65] Kaur, R., Karmakar, G., Xia, F., & Imran, M. (2023). Deep learning: Survey of environmental and camera impacts on internet of things images. *Artificial Intelligence Review*, *56*, 9605–9638 (2023). https://doi.org/10.1007/s10462-023-10405-7

[66] Narayanan, S., Chaniotakis, E., & Antoniou, C. (2020). Shared autonomous vehicle services: A comprehensive review. *Transportation Research Part C: Emerging Technologies*, *111*, 255–293.

[67] Tate, S., Daugherty, D., Tuttle, M., & Lyon-Hill, S. (2023). *Feasibility Analysis and Action Plan for a Regional Robotics Innovation Hub*, 1–72.

[68] Chitturu, S., Lin, D. Y., Sneader, K., Tonby, O., & Woetzel, J. (2017). Artificial intelligence and Southeast Asia's future. *Singapore Summit*, 1–40.

[69] Redek, T., Marčič, E., Maldonado, A. C. B., da Silva, A. R. P., & Shenstone, P. M. J. (2023). Artificial intelligence in brief: The development and impact of AI technologies. *Beyond Bits and Algorithm*, 33–53.

[70] Chakraborty, A., Bhattacharyya, S., De, D., Sarigiannidis, P., & Banerjee, J. S. (2023). Confluence of Artificial Intelligence and Robotic Process Automation: Concluding Remarks. In *Confluence of Artificial Intelligence and Robotic Process Automation* (pp. 389–399). Springer Nature Singapore.

[71] Saini, S., & Saxena, N. (2023). A survey of threats to research literature dependent medical AI solutions. *ACM Computing Surveys*, *55*(14s), 1–26.

[72] Bernardo, R., Sousa, J. M., & Gonçalves, P. J. (2022). Survey on robotic systems for internal logistics. *Journal of Manufacturing Systems*, *65*, 339–350.

[73] Lu, Y., Zheng, H., Chand, S., Xia, W., Liu, Z., Xu, X., ... & Bao, J. (2022). Outlook on human-centric manufacturing towards Industry 5.0. *Journal of Manufacturing Systems*, *62*, 612–627.

[74] Panagou, S., Neumann, W. P., & Fruggiero, F. (2024). A scoping review of human robot interaction research towards Industry 5.0 human-centric workplaces. *International Journal of Production Research*, *62*(3), 974–990.

[75] Leng, J., Zhu, X., Huang, Z., Xu, K., Liu, Z., Liu, Q., & Chen, X. (2023). ManuChain II: Blockchained smart contract system as the digital twin of decentralized autonomous manufacturing toward resilience in Industry 5.0. *IEEE Transactions on Systems, Man, and Cybernetics: Systems*, *53*(8), 4715–4728.

[76] Adeniyi, J. K., Adeniyi, T. T., Awotunde, J. B., Abiodun, M. K., & Atanda, O. G. (2023, April). Agrolend: A Blockchain Implementation Approach of Smart Contract Farming Platform. In *2023 International Conference on Science, Engineering and Business for Sustainable Development Goals (SEB-SDG)* (Vol. 1, pp. 1–7). IEEE.

[77] Awotunde, J. B., Misra, S., & Pham, Q. T. (2022, November). A Secure Framework for Internet of Medical Things Security Based System Using Lightweight Cryptography Enabled Blockchain. In *International Conference on Future Data and Security Engineering* (pp. 258–272). Springer Nature Singapore.

[78] Pérez, L., Diez, E., Usamentiaga, R., & García, D. F. (2019). Industrial robot control and operator training using virtual reality interfaces. *Computers in Industry*, *109*, 114–120.

[79] Tiwari, S., Bahuguna, P. C., & Walker, J. (2022). Industry 5.0: a macroperspective approach. In *Handbook of Research on Innovative Management Using AI in Industry 5.0*.

[80] Zhao, J., Han, X., Ouyang, M., & Burke, A. F. (2023). Specialized deep neural networks for battery health prognostics: Opportunities and challenges. *Journal of Energy Chemistry*.

[81] Klopfenstein, L. C., Delpriori, S., Malatini, S., & Bogliolo, A. (2017, June). The Rise of Bots: A Survey of Conversational Interfaces, Patterns, and Paradigms. In *Proceedings of the 2017 Conference on Designing Interactive Systems* (pp. 555–565).

[82] Mukherjee, S., & Chittipaka, V. (2022). Analysing the adoption of intelligent agent technology in food supply chain management: An empirical evidence. *FIIB Business Review*, *11*(4), 438–454.

[83] Sharma, R., Shishodia, A., Gunasekaran, A., Min, H., & Munim, Z. H. (2022). The role of artificial intelligence in supply chain management: Mapping the territory. *International Journal of Production Research*, *60*(24), 7527–7550.

[84] Awotunde, J. B., Bhoi, A. K., Jimoh, R. G., Ajagbe, S. A., Ayo, F. E., & Adebisi, O. A. (2023). Internet of Things Based Enabled Convolutional Neural Networks in Healthcare. In *IoT-enabled Convolutional Neural Networks: Techniques and Applications* (pp. 329–357). River Publishers.

[85] Sawwalakhe, R., Arora, S., & Singh, T. P. (2023). Opportunities and Challenges for Artificial Intelligence and Machine Learning Applications in the Finance Sector. In *Advanced Machine Learning Algorithms for Complex Financial Applications* (pp. 1–17).

[86] AbdulRaheem, M., Awotunde, J. B., Chakraborty, C., Adeniyi, E. A., Oladipo, I. D., & Bhoi, A. K. (2023). Security and Privacy Concerns in Smart Healthcare System. In *Implementation of Smart Healthcare Systems using AI, IoT, and Blockchain* (pp. 243–273). Academic Press.

[87] VanLehn, K. (2011). The relative effectiveness of human tutoring, intelligent tutoring systems, and other tutoring systems. *Educational Psychologist*, *46*(4), 197–221.

[88] Chowdhury, S., Dey, P., Joel-Edgar, S., Bhattacharya, S., Rodriguez-Espindola, O., Abadie, A., & Truong, L. (2023). Unlocking the value of artificial intelligence in human resource management through AI capability framework. *Human Resource Management Review*, *33*(1), 100899.

[89] Javaid, M., Haleem, A., Khan, I. H., & Suman, R. (2023). Understanding the potential applications of Artificial Intelligence in agriculture sector. *Advanced Agrochem*, *2*(1), 15–30.

[90] Jiang, J., Chen, M., & Fan, J. A. (2021). Deep neural networks for the evaluation and design of photonic devices. *Nature Reviews Materials*, *6*(8), 679–700.

[91] Zeng, C., Zhang, F., & Luo, M. (2022). A deep neural network-based decision support system for intelligent geospatial data analysis in intelligent agriculture system. *Soft Computing*, *26*(20), 10813–10826.

[92] Chen, C., Hu, Y., Karuppiah, M., & Kumar, P. M. (2021). Artificial intelligence on economic evaluation of energy efficiency and renewable energy technologies. *Sustainable Energy Technology Assessments,* 47, 101358.

[93] Liu, S., Bao, J., & Zheng, P. (2023). A review of digital twin-driven machining: From digitization to intellectualization. *Journal of Manufacturing Systems*, *67*, 361–378.

[94] Hua, H., Li, Y., Wang, T., Dong, N., Li, W., & Cao, J. (2023). Edge computing with artificial intelligence: A machine learning perspective. *ACM Computing Surveys*, *55*(9), 1–35.

[95] Zhou, X., Wei, X., Lin, J., Tian, X., Lev, B., & Wang, S. (2021). Supply chain management under carbon taxes: A review and bibliometric analysis. *Omega*, *98*, 102295.

[96] Ajagbe, S. A., Awotunde, J. B., & Florez, H. (2023). Ensuring intrusion detection for IoT services through an improved CNN. *SN Computer Science*, *5*(1), 49.

[97] Awokola, A. J., Falola, B. P., Adeniyi, A. E., Abiodun, M. K., Madamidola, A. O., Awotunde, J. B., ... & Omolehin, P. (2023, April). Development of an android-based reminder system for the covid-19 Management. In *2023 International Conference on Science, Engineering and Business for Sustainable Development Goals (SEB-SDG)* (Vol. 1, pp. 1–11). IEEE.

[98] Singh, S. A., & Desai, K. A. (2023). Automated surface defect detection framework using machine vision and convolutional neural networks. *Journal of Intelligent Manufacturing*, *34*(4), 1995–2011.

[99] Maqsood, M., Mehmood, I., Kharel, R., Muhammad, K., Lee, J., & Alnumay, W. S. J. H. C. C. I. S. (2021). Exploring the role of deep learning in industrial applications: A case study on coastal crane casting recognition. *Human-centric Computing and Information Sciences*, *11*, 1–14.

[100] Zhang, C., Zhou, G., Li, J., Chang, F., Ding, K., & Ma, D. (2023). A multi-access edge computing enabled framework for the construction of a knowledge-sharing intelligent machine tool swarm in Industry 4.0. *Journal of Manufacturing Systems*, *66*, 56–70.

[101] Chander, B., Pal, S., De, D., & Buyya, R. (2022). Artificial intelligence-based internet of things for industry 5.0. *Artificial intelligence-based internet of things systems*, 3–45.

[102] Hao, Y., Cao, J., Wang, Q., & Du, J. (2021). Energy-aware scheduling in edge computing with a clustering method. *Future Generation Computer Systems*, *117*, 259–272.

[103] Mihai, S., Yaqoob, M., Hung, D. V., Davis, W., Towakel, P., Raza, M., ... & Nguyen, H. X. (2022). Digital twins: A survey on enabling technologies, challenges, trends and future prospects. *IEEE Communications Surveys & Tutorials*.

[104] Wang, P., Yang, Y., & Moghaddam, N. S. (2022). Process modeling in laser powder bed fusion towards defect detection and quality control via machine learning: The state-of-the-art and research challenges. *Journal of Manufacturing Processes*, *73*, 961–984.

[105] Adel, A. (2022). Future of industry 5.0 in society: Human-centric solutions, challenges and prospective research areas. *Journal of Cloud Computing*, *11*(1), 1–15.

[106] Shahzadi, S., Iqbal, M., & Chaudhry, N. R. (2021). 6g vision: Toward future collaborative cognitive communication (3c) systems. *IEEE Communications Standards Magazine*, *5*(2), 60–67.

[107] Aslam, A. M., Chaudhary, R., Bhardwaj, A., Budhiraja, I., Kumar, N., & Zeadally, S. (2023). Metaverse for 6G and beyond: The next revolution and deployMent ChallenGes. *IEEE Internet of Things Magazine*, *6*(1), 32–39.

[108] Henin, C., & Le Métayer, D. (2021). Beyond explainability: Justifiability and contestability of algorithmic decision systems. *AI & SOCIETY*, 1–14.

[109] Khan, M., Haleem, A., & Javaid, M. (2023). Changes and improvements in Industry 5.0: A strategic approach to overcome the challenges of Industry 4.0. *Green Technologies and Sustainability*, *1*(2), 100020.

[110] Yadav, M., Vardhan, A., Chauhan, A. S., & Saini, S. (2023, February). A Study on Creation of Industry 5.0: New Innovations Using Big Data through Artificial Intelligence, Internet of Things and Next-Origination Technology Policy. In *2023 IEEE International Students' Conference on Electrical, Electronics and Computer Science (SCEECS)* (pp. 1–12). IEEE.

[111] Jauhar, S. K., Jani, S. M., Kamble, S. S., Pratap, S., Belhadi, A., & Gupta, S. (2023). How to use no-code artificial intelligence to predict and minimize the inventory distortions for resilient supply chains. *International Journal of Production Research*, 1–25.

[112] Zhang, B., Zhu, J., & Su, H. (2023). Toward the third generation artificial intelligence. *Science China Information Sciences*, *66*(2), 121101.

[113] Singh, A., Dwivedi, A., Agrawal, D., & Singh, D. (2023). Identifying issues in adoption of AI practices in construction supply chains: Towards managing sustainability. *Operations Management Research*, 1–17.

[114] Peter, O., Pradhan, A., & Mbohwa, C. (2023). Industrial internet of things (IIoT): Opportunities, challenges, and requirements in manufacturing businesses in emerging economies. *Procedia Computer Science*, *217*, 856–865.

[115] Kim, S. W., Kong, J. H., Lee, S. W., & Lee, S. (2022). Recent advances of artificial intelligence in manufacturing industrial sectors: A review. *International Journal of Precision Engineering and Manufacturing*, 1–19.

[116] Polenghi, A., Cattaneo, L., & Macchi, M. (2023). A framework for fault detection and diagnostics of articulated collaborative robots based on hybrid series modelling of Artificial Intelligence algorithms. *Journal of Intelligent Manufacturing*, 1–19.

[117] Zonta, T., Da Costa, C. A., da Rosa Righi, R., de Lima, M. J., da Trindade, E. S., & Li, G. P. (2020). Predictive maintenance in the Industry 4.0: A systematic literature review. *Computers & Industrial Engineering*, *150*, 106889.

[118] Su, J., Huang, J., Adams, S., Chang, Q., & Beling, P. A. (2022). Deep multi-agent reinforcement learning for multi-level preventive maintenance in manufacturing systems. *Expert Systems with Applications*, *192*, 116323.

[119] van Dinter, R., Tekinerdogan, B., & Catal, C. (2022). Predictive maintenance using digital twins: A systematic literature review. *Information and Software Technology*, 107008.

[120] Azamfirei, V., Psarommatis, F., & Lagrosen, Y. (2023). Application of automation for in-line quality inspection, a zero-defect manufacturing approach. *Journal of Manufacturing Systems*, *67*, 1–22.

[121] Arora, A., & Gupta, R. (2022, September). A Comparative Study on Application of Artificial Intelligence for Quality Assurance in Manufacturing. In *2022 4th International Conference on Inventive Research in Computing Applications (ICIRCA)* (pp. 1200–1206). IEEE.

[122] Sundaram, S., & Zeid, A. (2023). Artificial intelligence-based smart quality inspection for manufacturing. *Micromachines*, *14*(3), 570.

[123] Leberruyer, N., Bruch, J., Ahlskog, M., & Afshar, S. (2023). Toward Zero Defect Manufacturing with the support of Artificial Intelligence—Insights from an industrial application. *Computers in Industry*, *147*, 103877.

[124] Powell, D., Eleftheriadis, R., & Myklebust, O. (2021). Digitally enhanced quality management for zero defect manufacturing. *Procedia CIRP*, *104*, 1351–1354.

[125] Razzaq, A., Quach, S., & Thaichon, P. (2022). Artificial Intelligence (AI)-Integrated Operation; Insights Into Supply Chain Management. In *Artificial Intelligence for Marketing Management* (pp. 96–119). Routledge.

[126] Singh, S. P., Rawat, J., Mittal, M., Kumar, I., & Bhatt, C. (2022). Application of AI in SCM or Supply Chain 4.0. In *Artificial Intelligence in Industrial Applications: Approaches to Solve the Intrinsic Industrial Optimization Problems* (pp. 51–66).

[127] Jain, M., Sharma, D. K., & Sharma, N. (2022). Artificial Intelligence Computing and Nature-Inspired Optimization Techniques for Effective Supply Chain Management. In *Data Analytics and Artificial Intelligence for Inventory and Supply Chain Management* (pp. 63–80). Springer Nature Singapore.

[128] Kumari, N., & Pandey, S. (2023). Application of artificial intelligence in environmental sustainability and climate change. In *Visualization Techniques for Climate Change with Machine Learning and Artificial Intelligence* (pp. 293–316). Elsevier.

[129] Arputharaj, J. V., & Pal, S. K. Transforming Industry 5.0: Real Time Monitoring and Decision Making with IIOT. In *Sustainability in Industry 5.0* (pp. 76–106). CRC Press.

[130] Zizic, M. C., Mladineo, M., Gjeldum, N., & Celent, L. (2022). From industry 4.0 towards industry 5.0: A review and analysis of paradigm shift for the people, organization and technology. *Energies*, *15*(14), 5221.

[131] Ayvaz, S., & Alpay, K. (2021). Predictive maintenance system for production lines in manufacturing: A machine learning approach using IoT data in real-time. *Expert Systems with Applications*, *173*, 114598.

[132] Çınar, Z. M., Abdussalam Nuhu, A., Zeeshan, Q., Korhan, O., Asmael, M., & Safaei, B. (2020). Machine learning in predictive maintenance towards sustainable smart manufacturing in industry 4.0. *Sustainability*, *12*(19), 8211.

[133] Kumar, A., Shankar, R., & Thakur, L. S. (2018). A big data driven sustainable manufacturing framework for condition-based maintenance prediction. *Journal of Computational Science*, *27*, 428–439.

[134] Prassida, G. F., & Asfari, U. (2022). A conceptual model for the acceptance of collaborative robots in industry 5.0. *Procedia Computer Science*, *197*, 61–67.

[135] Pizoń, J., & Gola, A. (2023). Human–machine relationship—Perspective and Future Roadmap for Industry 5.0 Solutions. *Machines*, *11*(2), 203.

[136] Bathla, G., Bhadane, K., Singh, R. K., Kumar, R., Aluvalu, R., Krishnamurthi, R., ... & Basheer, S. (2022). Autonomous vehicles and intelligent automation: Applications, challenges, and opportunities. *Mobile Information Systems*, 2022.

[137] Haseeb, K., Rehman, A., Saba, T., Bahaj, S. A., Wang, H., & Song, H. (2023). Efficient and trusted autonomous vehicle routing protocol for 6G networks with computational intelligence. *ISA Transactions*, *132*, 61–68.

[138] Bendiab, G., Hameurlaine, A., Germanos, G., Kolokotronis, N., & Shiaeles, S. (2023). Autonomous vehicles security: Challenges and solutions using blockchain and artificial intelligence. *IEEE Transactions on Intelligent Transportation Systems*.

[139] Soori, M., Arezoo, B., & Dastres, R. (2023). Artificial intelligence, machine learning and deep learning in advanced robotics, A review. *Cognitive Robotics*.

[140] Aheleroff, S., Huang, H., Xu, X., & Zhong, R. Y. (2022). Toward sustainability and resilience with Industry 4.0 and Industry 5.0. *Frontiers in Manufacturing Technology*, *2*, 951643.

[141] Sinha, N., Singh, P., Gupta, M., & Singh, P. (2020). Robotics at workplace: An integrated Twitter analytics–SEM based approach for behavioral intention to accept. *International Journal of Information Management*, *55*, 102210.

[142] Grybauskas, A., Stefanini, A., & Ghobakhloo, M. (2022). Social sustainability in the age of digitalization: A systematic literature review on the social implications of industry 4.0. *Technology in Society*, *70*, 101997.

[143] Tebaldi, C., Debeire, K., Eyring, V., Fischer, E., Fyfe, J., Friedlingstein, P., ... & Ziehn, T. (2020). Climate model projections from the scenario model intercomparison project (ScenarioMIP) of CMIP6. *Earth System Dynamics Discussions*, *2020*, 1–50.

[144] Calabrese, A., Costa, R., Tiburzi, L., & Brem, A. (2023). Merging two revolutions: A human-artificial intelligence method to study how sustainability and Industry 4.0 are intertwined. *Technological Forecasting and Social Change*, *188*, 122265.

[145] Caspart, R., Ziegler, S., Weyrauch, A., Obermaier, H., Raffeiner, S., Schuhmacher, L. P., ... & Debus, C. (2022, May). Precise Energy Consumption Measurements of Heterogeneous Artificial Intelligence Workloads. In *International Conference on High Performance Computing* (pp. 108–121). Springer International Publishing.

[146] Charef, N., Mnaouer, A. B., Aloqaily, M., Bouachir, O., & Guizani, M. (2023). Artificial intelligence implication on energy sustainability in Internet of Things: A survey. *Information Processing & Management*, *60*(2), 103212.

[147] Javaid, M., Haleem, A., Singh, R. P., & Suman, R. (2022). Enhancing smart farming through the applications of Agriculture 4.0 technologies. *International Journal of Intelligent Networks*, *3*, 150–164.

[148] Mohamed, E. S., Belal, A. A., Abd-Elmabod, S. K., El-Shirbeny, M. A., Gad, A., & Zahran, M. B. (2021). Smart farming for improving agricultural management. *The Egyptian Journal of Remote Sensing and Space Science*, *24*(3), 971–981.

[149] Shamsudeen, T. Y. (2020). Advances in remote sensing technology, machine learning and deep learning for marine oil spill detection, prediction and vulnerability assessment. *Remote Sensing*, *12*(20), 3416.

[150] Patel, D., Kulwant, M., Shirin, S., Kumar, A., Ansari, M. A., & Yadav, A. K. (2022). Artificial intelligence for air quality and control systems: Status and future trends. *Modeling and Simulation of Environmental Systems*, 133–152.

[151] Kasinathan, P., Pugazhendhi, R., Elavarasan, R. M., Ramachandaramurthy, V. K., Ramanathan, V., Subramanian, S., ... & Alsharif, M. H. (2022). Realization of sustainable development goals with disruptive technologies by integrating Industry 5.0, Society 5.0, smart cities and villages. *Sustainability*, *14*(22), 15258.

[152] Saikia, B. (2023). Industry 5.0–Its Role Toward Human Society: Obstacles, Opportunities, and Providing Human-Centered Solutions. In *Fostering Sustainable Businesses in Emerging Economies: The Impact of Technology* (pp. 109–126). Emerald Publishing Limited.

[153] Nair, M. M., Tyagi, A. K., & Sreenath, N. (2021, January). The Future with Industry 4.0 at the Core of Society 5.0: Open Issues, Future Opportunities and Challenges. In *2021 International Conference on Computer Communication and Informatics (ICCCI)* (pp. 1–7). IEEE.

[154] Sindhwani, R., Afridi, S., Kumar, A., Banaitis, A., Luthra, S., & Singh, P. L. (2022). Can industry 5.0 revolutionize the wave of resilience and social value creation? A multi-criteria framework to analyze enablers. *Technology in Society*, *68*, 101887.

[155] Banholzer, V. M. (2022). From „Industry 4.0 "to „Society 5.0 "and „Industry 5.0 ": Value-and mission-oriented poli-cies. *Technological and Social Innovations–Aspects of Systemic Transformation. IKOM WP*, *3*(2), 2022.

4 Computational Intelligence in the Industrial Internet of Things

Nibedita Priyadarsini Mohapatra, Sudhir Ranajan Pattanaik, Mesfin Abebe, and Ming-Jer Chiang

4.1 INTRODUCTION

The entire world is now afflicted with the novel pandemic illness SARSCoV-2, also known as COVID-19 [1]. In late December 2019, Wuhan, China, was the birth place of the virus. Since then, it has become the infectious disease with the fastest rate of spread worldwide, presenting a fresh risk to public health worldwide [2]. The COVID-19 pandemic has brought attention to and exposed the weaknesses of current organizations. Having destroyed the economy and impacted millions of lives globally, the COVID-19 pandemic is unmatched. The World Health Organization (WHO) has made comprehensive technical guidelines available to all countries for the diagnosis and treatment of patients based on experiences with severe acute respiratory syndrome (SARS) and Middle East respiratory syndrome (MERS). WHO has worked with its international partners to expedite the development of essential health protocols and equipment [3]. Their committee came to the conclusion that in order to keep systems functioning properly, additional COVID-19 tests, therapies, and immunizations are required. In order to prepare for the present and upcoming crises, our society must make use of the numerous research opportunities and challenges that this epidemic has produced. In this global health disaster, researchers and medical professionals are currently looking for novel instruments to detect and contain unpredictable pandemic outbreaks. Healthcare professionals and public health officials must keep an eye out for viral infections in order to guarantee proper patient isolation and timely containment measures. Devastating effects have been caused by the COVID-19 pandemic; a therapeutic drug having a track record of usage in treating patients would be a quick cure for the illness. Usually, Internet of Things (IoT) designers are not entirely familiar with the power of the CI

DOI: 10.1201/9781003581963-4

algorithms in solving composite IoT frameworks, and researchers are unaware of real-time dilemmas and their demands. This divergence causes difficulties in team work and advancements. There are countless real-time implementations which have been already executed in IoT frameworks using CI approaches. We require pivoting on matters and provocations faced while applying CI methods in IoT frameworks and CI ranking. The IoT life cycle and its general construction, organizing tools, programming languages, and existing CI approaches to the IoT environment along with their constraints need to be understood. The IoT is a grid of networks which includes numerous devices such as actuators, sensors, RFID tags, smart cells, back-end servers, etc. All these gadgets are interconnected together for the design, collection, and sharing of information. The extreme advancement of the IoT has modified into a grid of connected devices to gather information from the real world. These gadgets interrelate with other devices using cyber protocols and standards. The intensification of the IoT leads to smart future Industry 4.0,which singly carries out composite tasks. Industry 4.0 unites smart mechanisms like artificial intelligence, the IIoT, and big data, to maximize the performance, quality, controlling capability, and lucidity of manufacturing processes.

4.1.1 Key Contributions of the Chapter

This chapter highlights different key points. In every aspect the authors have attempted to prevent ambiguity in concepts. We are thankful to Dr. Awotunde Joseph Bamidele, Dr. Kamalakanta Muduli, and Biswajit Brahma for giving us this opportunity to write a chapter for such a book which covers almost all the facts about computational intelligence in Industry 4.0 and 5.0 applications.

4.1.2 Chapter Organization

Section 4.2 presents the basics of computational intelligence (CI) and the Industrial Internet of Things (IIoT), and Section 4.3 outlines the motivation and role of CI for Industry 4.0 (IIoT). Section 4.4 presents the transformation of classical industry to smart industry, while Section 4.5 contains the concluding remarks.

4.2 BASICS OF COMPUTATIONAL INTELLIGENCE (CI) AND THE INDUSTRIAL INTERNET OF THINGS (IIOT)

Computational intelligence (CI) is a subgroup of artificial intelligence (this concept was first described by Bezdek in 1994). Computational intelligence is broadly classified into two types: one is machine intelligence, which is mostly based on hard computing methods, and the other is computational and primarily depends upon soft computing techniques, which enable a system to adapt to several situations.

Computational intelligence is the term used to describe a computer's ability to learn a given task using experimental data. The primary goal of computational intelligence is to understand the theory that makes intelligent behavior in real or virtual systems

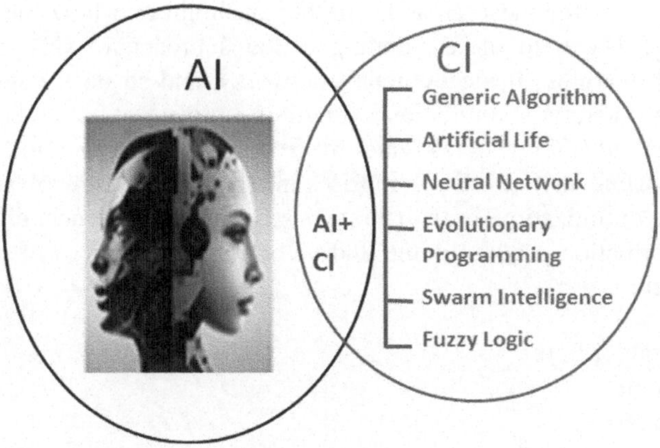

FIGURE 4.1 Classification of CI subset of AI.

feasible. The main presumption is that computation is interpretation. Computational intelligence methods are concerned with the exercise of a computing device to enable an appliance to replicate human adaptation. The most notable blueprint utilization comprises AI systems, fuzzy logic artificial neural networks, computer vision, evolutionary computing techniques, chaos engineering artificial life, and adaptive intelligence. The above-mentioned knowledge-based calculus smart techniques have produced immense ownership among application engineers and experts due to several processes such as conception, transformation, organized self-repair, fault toleration, and evolutionary features. Flourishing convention of different knowledge-based applications, designs, and strategies will assist engineers and experts in finding global and cost-effective answers to complicated challenges. This chapter furnishes a fresh preface to computational intelligence principles. Conventionally, the three foremost support systems of CI have been neural networks, evolutionary computation, and fuzzy systems. However, over time several inspired computational models have been developed. Hence, CI is a progressive field which offers add-ons to the three dominant factors, it enhances measuring models such as context smartness, imitative life, synthetic learning, unnatural endocrine networks, civic reasoning, and artificial hormonal networks. CI incorporates games and empirical advancement models to recreate a crucial function in developing effective smarter models. There has been a recent surge in research on hierarchical learning, particularly in deep learning neural networks. Currently, machine learning is the gold standard approach to artificial intelligence. In actuality, CI is the foundation of some highly promising mass AI models (Figure 4.1) [17].

4.2.1 Neural Networks

The synthetic neural networks (NNs) are generally parallel dispersed networks whose models have the capability to learn and hypothesize from samples. Here the motivational factor for these areas is the human brain and how the human brain is functioning. The field of fact-finding contains proactive NNs, self-organized NNs, machine learning, intricacy neural networks, and so on. Evolutionary computation utilizes natural evolution as a origin of motivation, while the evolutionary computing method (EC) resolves issues by creating, estimating, and transforming a number of possible answers. EC comprises inherent methods, evolvable hardware, multiobjective optimization, growth strategies, swarm intelligence, differential evolution, transformation programming, and so on. Five prototypes of computational intelligence are:

- Genetic algorithm.
- Fuzzy logic.
- Input pattern.
- Fuzzy logic controller.
- Predicate logic.

The knowledge required for creating machines to do tasks needs intelligence like creative intelligence in humans. It includes thinking processes, findings, and customization in all tasks. Three diverse methodologies, artificial evolution, artificial intelligence, and artificial life, have been used to shape machines in order to enable them to act like humans, or other species. Artificial intelligence explores most of the smart delegates. A delegate is an entity that realizes an action. The significant sides of the delegates are highlighted here. Delegates are partly autonomous: Each delegate has some duties in task solving with less or no awareness of what other delegates do or how the task is done. Delegates are situated at different geographical positions, every delegate has a keen interest for knowing its neighbor climate and generally has less awareness about the overall environment specifications of all delegates. Delegates collaborate on a specific task. The beauty of intellect in this environment is criticality: The overall group result of the delegate associations can be visualized as being more than the sum value of its individual contributors. A delegate has reasoning abilities such as: being able to deduce conclusions and make decisions depending on its surrounding environment, acquiring knowledge for improving its performance, and transmitting information with other delegates for making decisions and resolve problems.

Due of its exploratory nature, computing intelligence (CI) has been regarded as a factual study. We must establish acceptable assumptions and conduct research based on them since computational intelligence involves difficult tasks. The usage of symbols or subsymbolism, sequential or parallel computing, being based on logic or something else, are only a few of the significant assumptions that have been made in artificial intelligence, as will be detailed in the remainder of this chapter. It is also possible to use other facets of human intellect, despite the fact that using human intelligence as a metaphor is common. In its numerous paradigms, which are organized as follows in this chapter, computational intelligence as a rich body of knowledge is illustrated. The next section provides a brief outline of the essential ideas in classical AI, the connection between AI and CI, and our key findings for categorizing CI paradigms. In the following sections, we quickly go over a number of representatives

(Figure 4.1). The IEEE Computational Intelligence Society (IEEE-CIS, 2021) defines computational intelligence (CI) as the theory, design, application, and development of computational methods that are biologically and linguistically motivated. Three key pillars are identified in CI: artificial neural networks, fuzzy systems, and evolutionary algorithms.

4.2.2 Industrial Internet of Things (IIoT)

Understanding the fundamentals of the Industrial Internet of Things (IIoT) is crucial given the impending Fourth Industrial Revolution. Its primary objective is to offer manufacturing industries intelligent solutions. The IIoT provides a number of advantages for manufacturing, including innovation, reduced unproductive time, increased efficiency, and cheaper maintenance costs. IoT equipment can considerably assist businesses in enhancing their operations. This technology has a wide range of uses and is constantly developing. When a company uses sophisticated tracking tools, monitoring the movement of commodities can enhance operations. By keeping an eye on their position, state, and condition, these gadgets can even track consumer satisfaction. Additionally, if a business rents out equipment, they can automate the process. IoT-connected gadgets are already being used by numerous multinational corporations. For instance, to develop a proof-of-concept device, Ericsson worked with a manufacturer of outdoor power tools and an equipment rental company. Over time, the Industrial IoT aids enterprises in improving the effectiveness of maintenance and manufacturing procedures.

The IIoT includes industrial applications such as software-defined production processes, robots, and medical technologies. Beyond the conventional consumer electronics and physical device interconnectivity often associated with the Internet of Things, there is more to the IIoT. Intelligent assets, a data communications infrastructure, analytics and applications to interpret and act on the data, and people are the four core components of any IIoT system. Machines or other assets having sensors, processors, memory, and communications capabilities are considered intelligent assets. The three main industrial Internet components are radios, controllers, and software. The IIoT is a matrix of networks connecting equipment and devices, collecting data via sensor technologies, analyzing them, and integrating them back into platforms as service (Figure 4.2).

It is driven by the convergence of information technologies (IT) and operational technology (OT).

4.2.3 The IoT (Internet of Things)

Physical devices that are embedded with sensors, software, and other technologies to transfer data and communicate among devices through the Internet are referred to as IoT devices. Cellphones, laptops, home appliances, and a plethora of other electronic devices are among the examples. The usage of the Internet of Things in industrial applications and sectors is referred to as the Industrial Internet of Things (IIoT). Networked sensors, other devices, industrial computers, and gadgets mostly

FIGURE 4.2 Industrial IoT 4.0.

utilized in manufacturing are referred to as IIoT equipment. A few examples are the warehouses of Amazon and Airbus, smart robotics, etc.

Comparison

The IoT often emphasizes consumer convenience. While the IIoT concentrates on ROI to ensure that organizations get the most out of using the IIoT, the following observations can be made when the IoT and IIoT are compared in terms of complexity, expense, and requirements.

Cost

In essence, hardware components like sensors, internet connections, and embedded systems are what the IoT and IIoT rely on. However, the IoT is less expensive than the IIoT since IoT devices require less precision than IIoT devices. Because the IIoT operates in crucial business sectors such as manufacturing, machinery monitoring, etc., it requires more advanced devices for greater precision.

Complexity

Applications for the IIoT are more sophisticated than those for the IoT. This complexity increases along with technological development. Applications for the IIoT are therefore more complicated than those for the IoT.

- Consumer convenience is an IoT end requirement; while the RoI, or return on investment, is an IIoT end requirement.
- The IoT focuses on controlling home equipment that makes consumers lives more convenient by conserving resources like power.

- The IIoT focuses on crucial systems such as those in healthcare, aerospace, and factory automation, as well as on connecting people and machines and using data analytics.
- The IIoT aims for less downtime and more uptime for business operations.

4.3 MOTIVATION AND ROLE OF CI FOR INDUSTRY 4.0 (IIOT)

Implementation

The application of these two technologies differs between the IoT and IIoT. The IoT provides user convenience through the utilization of low-cost linked sensors and devices. The IIoT extends current production and supply chain management systems with more advanced devices, offering greater visibility, automated controls, and increasingly skilled analytics. Both technologies enable real-time data capture for users and boost productivity. Because IIoT systems and applications are made to withstand harsh conditions found in industrial settings, they are extremely dependable and beneficial for preventative maintenance. Most of the time, these devices enable remote access and automated infrastructure monitoring, transmitting all big data analytics to the cloud platform. They need stricter communication protocols than IoT devices as a result.

Integration

By combining both technologies, IIoT solutions are intended to improve user experience while streamlining industrial operations. IIoT systems incorporate field sensors, whereas IoT systems connect and monitor devices using cloud computing. The quality of the products and services in smart factories is then improved by these devices, with the use of data analytics to find patterns. Industrial operations already employ this strategy. The IIoT is also anticipated to hasten the adoption of smart goods and services, particularly in the manufacturing sector. Platforms for the Industrial IoT allow for the development and use of new goods that are customized for certain uses. The degree of integration is another distinction between the IIoT and IoT. The IIoT is typically more sophisticated, but the IoT is typically more flexible. IIoT devices are essential for the future of any industry since they have a wide range of additional uses and possibilities.

Applying Pool

The IIoT, in contrast to the IoT, is a network of smart, connected devices used in industrial applications. The IIoT is a network of interconnected industrial processes, whereas the IoT is a network of consumer-based gadgets. Technology of this kind is employed to gather data and enhance industrial procedures. The IIoT is more expensive and sophisticated. It makes predictions to improve production and forecasts trends in the area of digital transformation using sensors and analytics. The scope of technology will expand also, but more sophisticated devices will cost more to produce. Since IIoT devices have so many extra uses and applications, they are crucial for the future of any industry. The IIoT, or the applying pool, is a network of intelligent, connected devices used in industrial applications as opposed to the

IoT. The IoT is a network of consumer-based devices, whereas the IIoT is a network of connected industrial processes. Such technology is used to collect data and improve business processes. The IIoT is more costly and advanced. Using sensors and analytics, it analyses trends in the area of digital transformation and offers predictions to increase productivity. The reach of technology will also grow, but more advanced products will cost more to make. Numerous industries, including agriculture, cutting-edge technology, the auto industry, leading industrial IoT companies, smart cities, power generation, and robotics companies, can be transformed by the IIoT. IIoT initiatives frequently seek to automate, conserve, or improve processes. These initiatives support business objectives and strategies, such as innovation, customer-focused service delivery, and data-driven revenue. Businesses may participate in the digital transformation of whole industries thanks to the Industrial IoT, which also aids in the creation of value-adding ecosystems for them.

Construction Industry

Process engineers profit from the IIoT. Data collecting, energy management, and more can all be facilitated by a digital manufacturing project in the engineering sector. In conventional methods, engineers must manually gather data, combine them with other data, analyze them, and then carry out manual data visualization. However, these tasks can be automated using wearable technology and IoT-enabled operations, allowing staff to concentrate on process improvement rather than data analysis.

Mining Sector

The IIoT offers significant benefits to the mining sector also. There is growing demand on the mining sector to generate additional raw materials. The IoT will assist in managing these resources throughout the ensuing decade. Balancing the many diverse parts of a situation will be achievable with the use of cameras, sensors, and long-term evolution (LTE) networks. Finally, mining operations will be able to switch from manual processes to algorithms thanks to technology. Regardless of the company's specialization, IoT adoption in mining is beneficial. IoT devices help businesses to increase production, lower expenses, and increase efficiency whether they are underground, close to the surface, or in the field. The mining industry is able to gather more data than ever before by linking machinery and vehicles to the cloud. This illustrates that devices can be operated remotely, possibly even using a smart phone app. Mining firms will benefit from the identification and process optimization provided by AI analytics. Machine learning will have a place in the IIoT data ecosystem, allowing mining businesses to make better decisions.

Manufacturing Industry

The IIoT can also benefit manufacturing businesses. RFID tags can be used in their facilities by IoT-enabled sensors to monitor temperature and pressure and make sure they stay within set parameters. Similarly, factories can save money and energy by using IIoT-enabled sensors. The system can optimize the utilization of various facilities and reduce operational risk by keeping track of equipment performance. The IIoT has the potential to fundamentally alter how goods are produced if properly applied. For manufacturing, the IIoT provides sensors that may identify hazardous working situations and notify employees and managers. To increase productivity, some industrial businesses have begun incorporating the IIoT into their manufacturing operations. For instance, a car with an IoT-enabled system may determine how long a trip will take and assess the traffic situation. Air conditioning systems may automatically adjust to the outside temperature, and refrigerators can correlate temperature with desired temperatures. Production processes are heavily utilizing this new technology, so when the products are put on the market, they already have sensors built in.

Logistics

Devices with Internet access are essential for managing logistics. These IIoT devices can be used for RF truck identification, tracking the movement of physical products, and even ensuring the safety of traveling employees. The IIoT is revolutionizing our society and is quickly becoming a crucial part of the digital economy. Even though the Internet of Things has transformed several businesses, logistics remains one of the top sectors. Businesses can monitor their supply chains and increase employee productivity with the aid of IoT devices. As can be seen, the industrial gateway IoT, smart equipment, and artificial intelligence apps can help logistics organizations track and manage their inventory while also enhancing the safety of their customers and employees.

When discussing logistics, it is important to keep in mind that it encompasses more than just vehicles and land transportation. IoT-based industrial security systems are now being used by aircraft manufacturing companies to identify problems and enhance performance. Consequently, without adding more staff, this machine-to-machine innovative technology can boost production.

Healthcare

Manufacturing and logistics are the two most prevalent sectors in this area, however the IoT is not just used in these sectors. IoT technology, for instance, is widely used in the healthcare sector. IoT industrial applications can track medical kit components, components used in the manufacture of specific medications, and other crucial healthcare procedures. IoT industrial technology can be the simplest and most effective solution for medical equipment, but it requires close supervision and monitoring. A variety of medical institutes already employ the IoT. As an illustration, the global medical equipment maker Mediators effectively incorporated IoT technology into its services. Without increasing its number of employees, the company observed a 78% increase in service issues and occurrences. Without adding additional staff, such an increase is not only beneficial but also economical.

Other Industries

A variety of other industries that the IoT can be used in must also be mentioned. The Industrial IoT can shorten lead times and improve production flexibility. It can aid factories in managing inventory and assets more effectively. Additionally, it can reduce operating costs and increase energy efficiency. The IoT is a terrific tool for monitoring the health and safety of production areas in addition to manufacturing. IoT sensors can be used by manufacturing organizations to collect data from various sources and analyze them. Some sectors can employ IoT devices to monitor assets in production lines and distant locations. Even operational technology, such as smart packaging, can be integrated with it.

Additionally, IoT technology can be used in the financial sector. When sensors are used, a bank can identify which of its ATMs is the most effective. Also, IoT devices will dramatically improve cyber security in the financial sector. These are just a few of the many industries that can benefit from the IoT. Manufacturing is increasingly relying on the IoT. It has both technological and financial benefits, and it is already beginning to influence a number of industries, including aviation. Long term, it will continue to be a crucial tool for producers. Manufacturers will be able to lower costs and boost product quality with the help of the IoT. One of the most common reasons for decreased product quality is improper setup or calibration.

Intelligent devices can be useful in analyzing measured machine signals, which are a reliable indicator of machine performance. In order to improve workplace safety, the IoT will assist in monitoring these signals and reporting any deviations from optimal working conditions. Therefore, careful machinery supervision will guarantee that the product quality and dependability are maintained. New revenue sources may also result from IoT use. For instance, connected items can aid manufacturers in the transition from selling tangible goods to offering experiences, a crucial business strategy for the market of today. The IoT makes it feasible to predict problems before they happen and even stop them from happening. What sets it apart is the intersection of information technology (IT) and operational technology (OT). The networking of industrial control systems (ICSs), such as distributed control systems (DCSs), supervisory control and data acquisition (SCADA) systems, programmable logic controllers (PLCs), and human–machine interfaces (HMIs), is known as operations procedures (OT).The confluence of IT and OT benefits industries through automation and optimization, as well as enhanced supply chain and logistics visibility. Monitoring and managing physical infrastructures in industrial activities, such as those in manufacturing, transportation, utilities, healthcare, and agriculture, is made easier by smart sensors and actuators, remote access, and control.

In the context of Industry 4.0,, the IIoT is critical to how big data and analytics will transform cyber-physical systems and industrial processes. Real-time data from sensors and other information sources are useful for decision-making, which is the process of gaining knowledge and carrying out predetermined actions, in industrial equipment and infrastructure. Moreover, machines can now automate tasks that humans were unable to perform throughout previous industrial revolutions. More broadly, use cases involving interconnected environments or ecosystems such as the conversion of cities into smart cities and factories into smart factories require the IIoT.

There are several opportunities for growth for organizations and industries due to the frequent gathering and sharing of data across smart machines and devices. By using the data, industries and companies may quickly fix errors or inefficiencies in the supply chain, for example, and promote continuous operational and financial efficiency. When properly integrated, the IIoT can anticipate problem areas, maximize

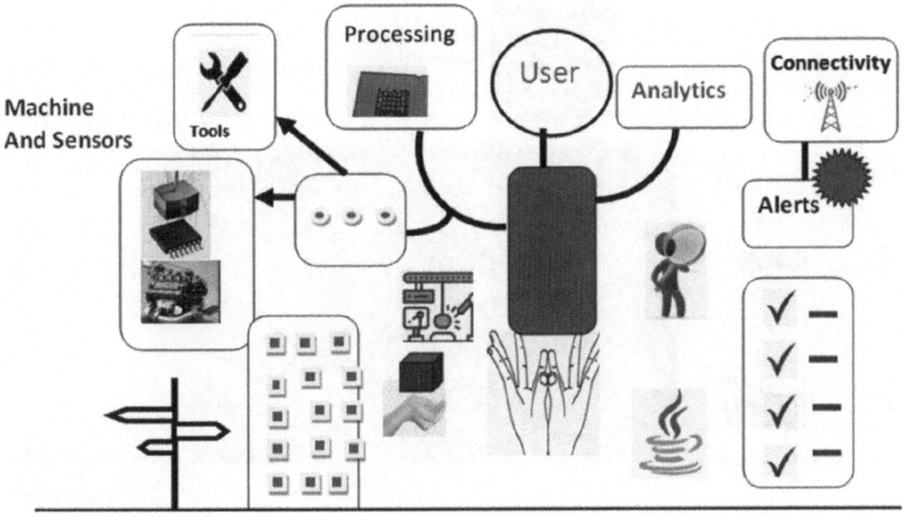

FIGURE 4.3 Industrial IoT.

asset use, and even initiate maintenance operations automatically. By using connected and intelligent devices, businesses can collect and evaluate more data faster. This will close the gap between general offices and production floors and enhance performance and scalability. Through the integration of the IIoT, industrial entities can obtain a more precise understanding of the state of their operations and utilize those data by integrating the IIoT, and industrial entities can get a more accurate picture of how their operations are progressing and use that information to make smarter business decisions.

Industrial operations may already be accustomed to availability and scalability because they are well-established or have been in the business for some time. However, businesses can run into security issues when integrating the IIoT into their operations. One example of this is the widespread usage of antiquated technologies and practices by many businesses. Many technologies exist for a longer period of time and haven't been updated with new requirements, making them obsolete (Figure 4.3).

Additionally, the growth of smart gadgets has increased security flaws and raised questions about security accountability. Adopters of the IIoT are de facto responsible for protecting the installation and use of their connected devices, but device manufacturers are also responsible for safeguarding their customers when they release new goods.

Security Issues and Difficulties That Arise When Implementing the IIoT

The IIoT has the power to completely change the way industries operate, but as connectivity increases, it becomes more challenging to advance digital transformation programs while maintaining security. It is reasonable to presume that companies and sectors dealing with operational technologies have some understanding of matters such as product quality and worker safety. The integration of OT with the Internet has

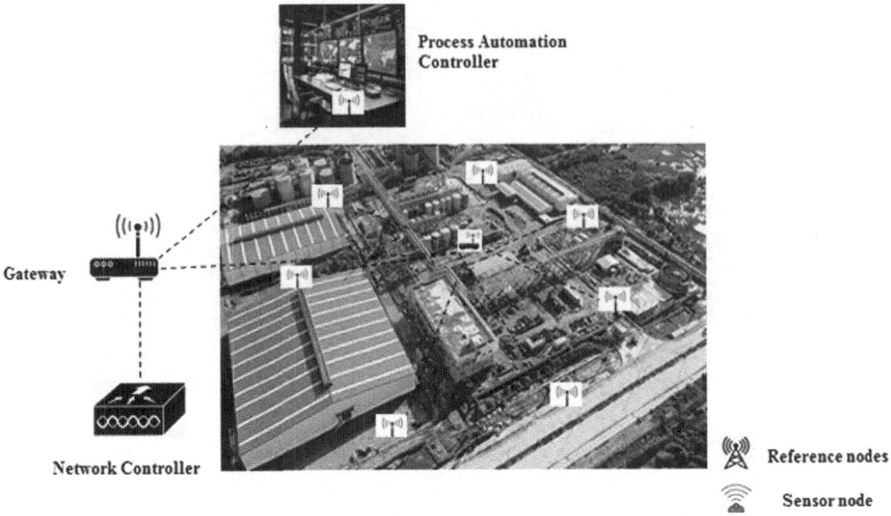

FIGURE 4.4 Network architecture for Industrial IoT.

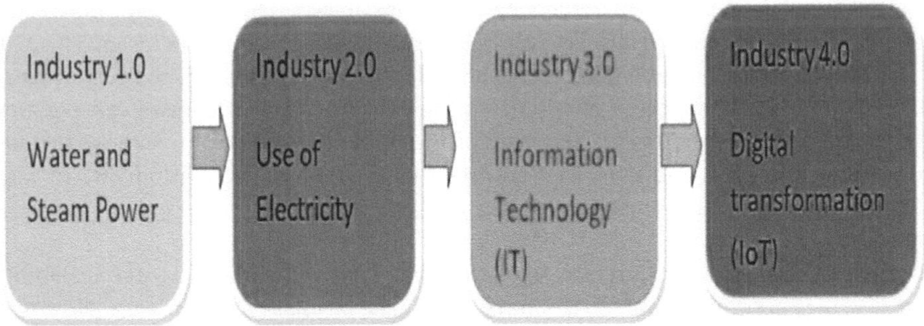

FIGURE 4.5 Industrial evolution.

led to the introduction of more intelligent and automated equipment at work. This has created a number of new difficulties for companies that require an understanding of the inner workings of the IIoT (Figures 4.4 and 4.5).

Three things need to be prioritized with IIoT implementations: availability, scalability, and security (Figure 4.6).

Manufacturers should be able to guarantee user security and offer precautions or fixes should security problems occur. As more important security events come to light over time, the need for cyber security is further highlighted. When hackers get access to networked systems, the firm is not only at risk of a significant data breach but also of having operations suspended. Enterprises and sectors adopting the IIoT need to think like tech businesses in order to securely manage both digital and physical components [46,47]. For IIoT systems, improving operational productivity is crucial, but security must also be taken into account. Connecting OT to the Internet could

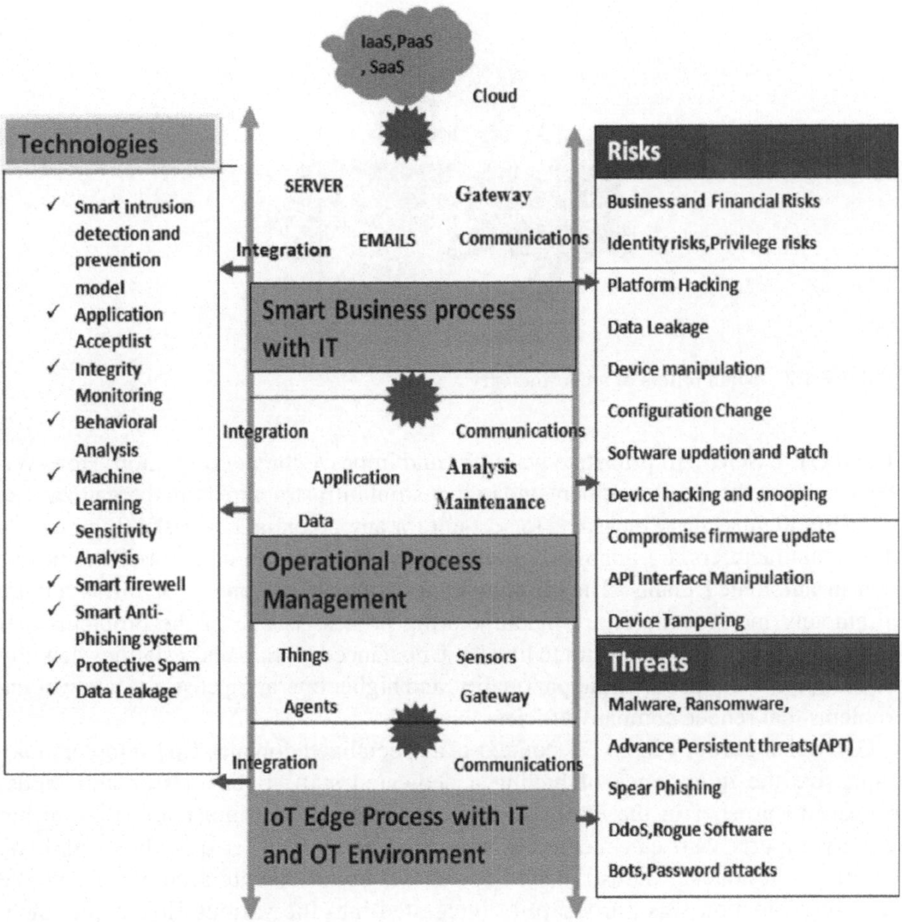

FIGURE 4.6 IoT infrastructure with operational features and risks.

improve an organization's survivability because of the many sensors and connected devices in use and the real-time data they produce. However, reducing cyber security costs could outweigh the benefits. Security by design and embedded security strategies should be used in this situation.

In order to proactively monitor and protect against the wide spectrum of threats that affect networked environments, it is essential to have a security operations center (SOC) (Figures 4.4–4.6) With the help of this centralized unit, businesses and industries can manage the large number of notifications they could receive and enable prompt action.

SOCs are especially beneficial to facilities that need to monitor their security position continuously and with more visibility. SOC teams seek to detect anomalies in activity or security issues so they may quickly address them and prevent a potential compromise. This method addresses the issues that poor reaction times, low system visibility, and legacy systems may bring. In order to help businesses manage both

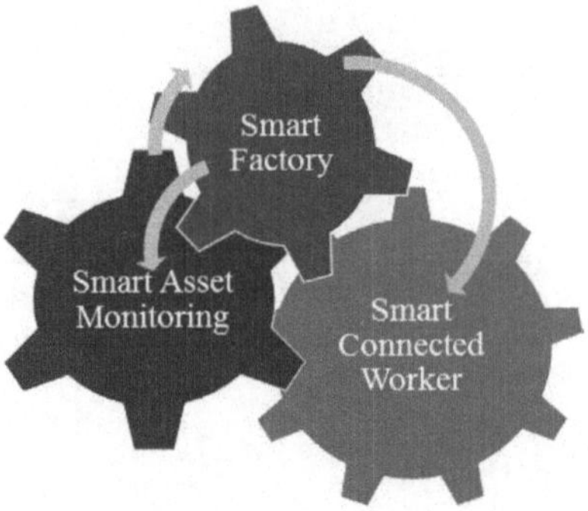

FIGURE 4.7 Main pillars of smart industry.

IT and OT, a SOC will prioritize warnings and improve threat correlation. However, changes in the threat environment and in industrial infrastructures force organizations to modify their security measures to account for any potential new risks (Figure 4.7). Most manufacturers are unable to maximize production and meet customer needs, even in automated plants. The absence of appropriate equipment or infrastructure to remotely monitor the entire manufacturing process is one of the problems that stakeholders are finding difficult to handle. Unbalanced workloads at stations, lengthy production cycle times with subpar quality, and higher operating costs are a few of the problems that reduce company efficiency.

Given that security in an OT context is a specialized domain, IIoT adopters may emphasize the importance of having a dedicated staff. If businesses and industries are to prosper in the era of IT/OT convergence, they must prioritize hiring security experts who can recognize various dangers and act quickly to mitigate the effects of attacks. Industries and businesses could operate securely if a whole stack of protection was purposefully integrated into the various IIoT deployment tiers [43–45]. The cloud, the network, and the device all fall under these security layers. The device layer is where the IIoT apps and devices that are introduced from different manufacturers and service providers typically reside. IIoT adopters ought to be aware of the data transmission and storage practices used by their providers of goods and services. In order for enterprises to take the appropriate action, manufacturers and service providers also need to be able to actively notify them of any security risks.

Device data are collected by the gateway, which is situated on the network area. Next-generation intrusion prevention systems are necessary for enterprises to monitor and identify possible attacks (IPSs). The gateway usually has a control panel as well, which is used to deliver commands to other devices.

Organizations should install security hardening in the control center, which is the most important location, to protect against malware infection and hacker control (Figure 4.8).

Finally, but just as importantly, cloud providers ought to implement server-based protection to lower the likelihood of hackers gaining access to servers and the data that are kept there. This draws attention to the concern that companies may be subject

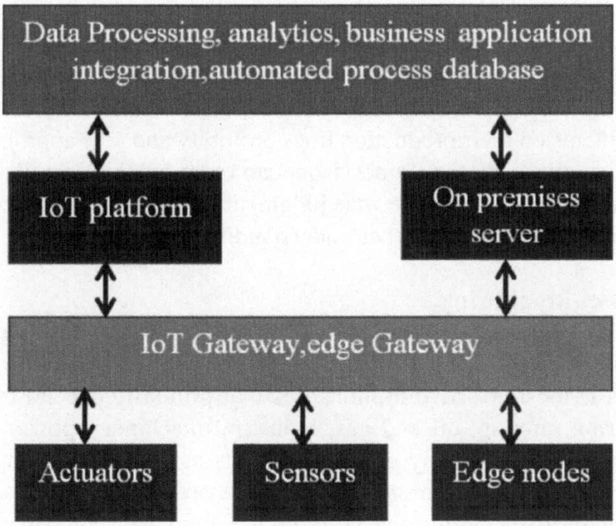

FIGURE 4.8 IoT infrastructure.

to data privacy-related legal consequences. Thus, for the security of IIoT systems, end-to-end protection from the gateway to the endpoint must be able to offer:

- Enhanced threat visibility and early anomaly detection.
- Continual monitoring and detection in the event of malware infection.
- Safe data transfer and proactive protection against attacks and threats between IT and OT.
- Putting in place, processes that enable quicker time to market.
- Maintaining a balance between upkeep and throughput.
- Ensuring customer satisfaction.

Today's industries confront several major issues, including:

- A lack of real-time data and heterogeneous data systems.
- Keeping up with rules and maintaining compliance.

Organizations are having a difficult time keeping up with client demands and market expansion as a result of the aforementioned difficulties.

Solution

Company executives are looking for a workable system in their factories that can specifically handle and carry out all these tasks, be it data to track activities on the production line, recent job statistics, or regular report updates. The statistical analysis and quality control functions of a smart factory solution are compatible with almost all production line stations. As a result, next-generation intrusion prevention systems

(IPSs) are utilized to prevent attacks by exploiting security flaws in servers and applications throughout data centers and cloud infrastructure. A smart factory system may give real-time, continuous, and standardized work-level data, which allows supervisors to thoroughly analyze factory performance. Supervisors are better able to recognize problems on their production lines promptly and take appropriate action to adapt to the changing scenario. Supervisors can more quickly identify trouble spots on their production lines and make wise judgments to meet the changing demands of production lines if they have a deeper understanding of those lines.

Intelligent Asset Monitoring

At this time, smart asset monitoring is all the rage. The attributes and features of the solution are viewed as the X factor that will provide a competitive advantage. This approach is most effective in industries that primarily depend on assets, such as manufacturing, mining, oil and gas, industrial machinery, power, and utilities. An industry's success is largely dependent on its assets, and a company may not be able to meet its profit margin goals if its assets are lost, damaged, or ineffective. Before intelligent asset monitoring systems were created, companies had trouble keeping tabs on asset performance, exercising little control over assets, preventing asset loss, and planning efficient maintenance schedules. If employees have a good understanding of the above issues, then the demands of production lines can be met more easily..

Solution

An IoT-enabled smart asset monitoring system enhances customer experiences, reduces operating expenses, boosts productivity, and helps businesses to better manage their machinery and equipment. Using a smart asset monitoring technology, businesses may obtain greater insights into the location, productivity, availability, and state of their assets. What makes the solution so popular is its ability to track all of the previously mentioned features from a single perspective. The capacity to keep track of every active asset, eliminate any ghost assets, and provide precise information on how assets are being used in every process is the cherry on top of an intelligent asset monitoring system.

Intelligent Connected Worker

The protection of field worker safety is one of the most difficult issues that organizations are facing today. Organizations must contend with the challenge of tracking and overseeing worker activity in the field in addition to ensuring their safety. Industries are scrambling to find a solution that can match the criteria in an efficient and effective manner. By reducing the amount of time employees spend on unproductive tasks and providing them with a safer working environment, organizations also hope to increase their overall effectiveness. Among the main challenges that industries must solve are unanticipated field accidents; enhancing worker performance; improving employee experience; tracking worker whereabouts and minimizing the risk of errors; improving data quality; and generating visibility in the process job state. In addition to having a completely connected system, being able to link industrial workers is now a viable solution to ensure worker productivity and safety and

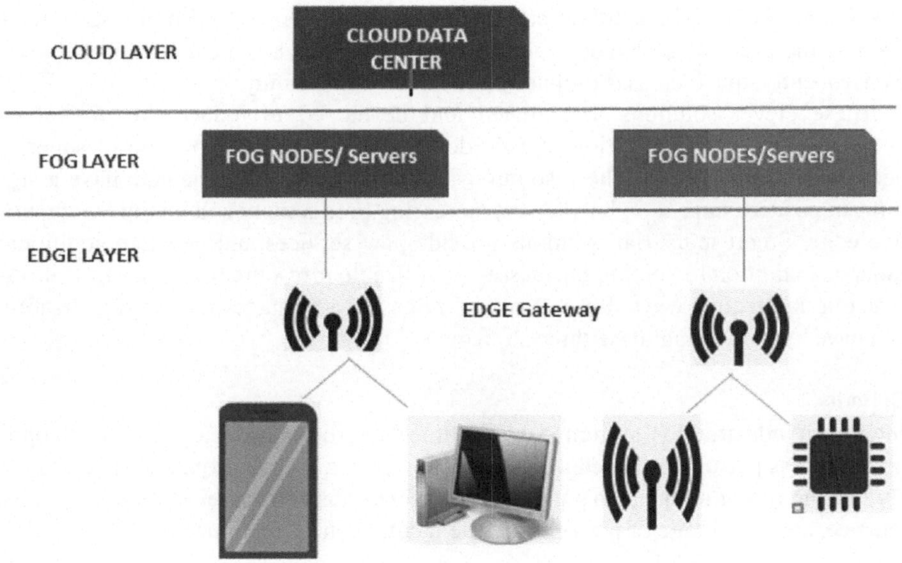

FIGURE 4.9 Computing infrastructure.

improve operational effectiveness. Linked workers not only provide real-time health and activity monitoring, but they also enhance company regulatory compliance.

The three solutions that can turn a sector into a smart sector are now known to us and are built on an enterprise IoT platform. To better grasp the main benefits of all these solutions combined, for example, consider a factory where a large number of workers collaborate with several tools and machinery. Overall factory productivity depends on each employee and every piece of equipment operating flawlessly. There can be a significant loss of time, resources, and money when any asset malfunctions or is otherwise disrupted in its operation. Stakeholders may encounter difficulties such as: production line breakdown, asset availability, loss of final product, and injured labor. How, therefore, can stakeholders overcome these obstacles? Here, clever solutions are really helpful. When implemented jointly, before harm is done, smart factory, smart asset monitoring, and smart connected worker may predict incidents, thoroughly investigate them, and take the necessary action (Figure 4.9).

A smart factory solution, on the other hand, can assist stakeholders in anticipating any occurrence long before it really happens. The solution capacity is to perform predictive analysis which can help with this. The solution assesses the equipment's working pattern and forecasts any anomalies in the operation of assets using data collected from various machines and stations on the shop floor. By tracking their position, utilization, and availability, a smart asset monitoring solution can keep an eye on assets that are set up on-site or off-shore. This guarantees the best possible use of all organizational resources. The tracking and monitoring of the assets guarantee their security in addition to their safety and deters theft. However, a knowledgeable, connected employee maintains business operations while making sure that everyone is safe and secure. The solution can be to find the employee and notify the supervisor in the event of an incident, injury, or if the employee enters a restricted area. Consequently, this increases output and ensures worker safety.

These clever solutions are created and developed to reduce the difficulties associated with data collection, insight development, and the provision of superior decision-making criteria. These solutions, when properly implemented, have a significant positive impact on businesses, increasing productivity and giving a competitive edge. Smart industrial solutions provide new services and generate additional money in addition to helping businesses to utilize their resources and business infrastructure in creative ways. Let us now examine the advantages that an organization can have by combining these three strategies.

Benefits

Intelligent industrial IoT systems use real-time data from sensors to monitor and optimize process performance, reduce the need for human intervention, and save energy. By making use of all the data gathered, downtime caused by asset availability, maintenance, and a shortage of personnel in the factory can be minimized.

Increased Safety and Security

With the use of sensors and video cameras to monitor equipment, these solutions help firms improve worker safety, guard against physical threats, and expedite crisis resolution through several teams.

More Rapid Decision-Making

Real-time operational analytics can help businesses make quicker, more informed decisions, while also cutting expenses. All business decisions can be prioritized and distributed with the aid of these IoT-enabled technologies.

Increased Business Intelligence

Smart solutions can be utilized as a forecasting tool for improved decision-making by continually collecting, aggregating, and evaluating data from several sensors dispersed across the facility or available to the entire workforce. These sensors help managers collect data in real time, giving firms insights into different operations and the ability to begin taking preventative action.

One of the biggest changes is the widespread adoption of the IoT, which enables organizations to frame analyses in accordance with their needs. The fundamental idea driving every industrial development is Industry 4.0. By improving production efficiency, industrialists are boosting innovation and expanding their firms. They are planning how to apply IoT ideas in order to achieve targeted commercial goals. They are now able to implement a sustainable solution that increases production overall and satisfies customer demand. Additionally, it improves the performance of the current SCADA and PLC systems.

The potential economic value of employing IoT technology in the businesses is predicted to increase and expand by $12.6 trillion by the year 2030, according to McKinsey. Industries will gain from better operational efficiency, physical asset management, employee wellness, and general well-being. The IoT is the driving force behind digital transformations.

System Infrastructure Improvement

Sectors are completely free to engage in different jobs and increase efficiency by using cloud-based solutions. Through IoT technology, which enables quick answers to industrial requirements and aids in maintaining overall efficiency, management looks to strengthen the system infrastructure.

Sustainable Remedy

By encouraging innovation, increasing industry productivity, and enhancing infrastructure, the IoT is achieving goals for sustainable development. Installing cutting-edge sensor technology to improve industrial assets is revolutionizing industries by offering consumers improved sustainability.

Remote Control

Many companies aim to run their operations remotely in order to produce better outcomes with more affordable prices. Even though industrialists may have millions of devices, the IoT enables remote real-time monitoring of every unit. Additionally, it protects the data and streamlines procedures with less manual labor.

Predictive Analytics for the IoT

Almost all companies need efficient tools or systems to manage massive amounts of data and use those data to infer outcomes depending on various circumstances. IoT technology includes sensors and sophisticated gateway communication, which give managers well-informed insights. Better judgment and quick answers are made possible.

Easily Maintained

The IoT encourages efficient asset management tactics and improves their performance by providing managers with useful data. This lessens their effort by automating all of the industrial processing instead of having them perform each task manually. Therefore, it results in relatively lower asset upkeep and streamlines the decision-making process.

Gathering and Analyzing Data

The sensor devices gather data from the assets and transmit them to the connected dashboard via the gateway. This enhances cloud-based platform data storage and further processes it in a user-friendly language, enabling efficient productivity. The managers find it simple to analyze these data and talk about the commercial defects to urge adjustments to business tactics.

Real-Time Tracking and Observation

The restructuring of industries has also made it possible for businesspeople to follow their top priorities in real time and check on each piece of equipment with a single click. The IoT is a unique technology that links data and management choices for increased efficiency via sensors and gateways.

Connectivity

The IoT is centered on recreating everything around us in order to create the most modern hardware and software, keeping businesses ahead of the competition. Technology must be more adaptable and scalable in Industry 4.0 so that it can adapt to changes in both the supply chain and the entire manufacturing line. Connectivity is the primary distinction that distinguishes IoT and Industry 4.0 technologies as the foundational elements of the advanced industrial transformation. Industry 4.0 refers to the concept of integrating sensors, actuators, control units, logistic services, other planning systems, etc. The IoT aims to connect everything to the Internet. Due to industries' massive data production, they need a secure and dependable system that can process and store data on the cloud for easier accessibility.

4.4 TRANSFORMATION OF CLASSICAL INDUSTRY TO SMART INDUSTRY

When it comes to the Industrial IoT, businesses of all sizes can profit greatly. For instance, in the global process industry, early malfunction detection can save millions of dollars. Additionally, with the capacity to send out alerts when something goes wrong, operators can respond quickly to solve the issue before it becomes worse. Equipment rental businesses can perform preventive maintenance with the use of IoT sensors and systems. Monitoring solutions could assist in preventing expensive breakdowns by lowering the expense of sending mechanics into the field activity. As can be seen, IIoT solutions can dramatically lower costs while improving the production process. Predictive maintenance is one of the key uses for the IIoT. Millions of dollars in lost productivity can be attributed to malfunctioning machinery. Predictive maintenance can be automated using IIoT devices, requiring less manual intervention.

Enhancing Operational Effectiveness

Another advantage of the Industrial IoT is its ability to improve manufacturing processes, in addition to financial savings. It does, however, create a number of practical difficulties, which would make it difficult for most businesses to benefit from it. The majority of businesses currently use operational technology, which is not meant to connect to anything outside of the local network. The data stream produced by these devices must also be redirected into already in-place data management software systems. It is important to choose Industrial IoT automation systems carefully if you want to work effectively with linked equipment. There are many advantages to the Industrial IoT. It aids in city resource management. For instance, it makes it possible for garbage trucks to plan their routes more efficiently and emit fewer emissions. Cities that use Industrial IoT technologies can better manage resources and increase productivity.

Optimization of Processes

Businesses can enhance processes with the use of the Industrial IoT. By gathering information from sensors, businesses may automate procedures and improve manufacturing lines. Industrial IoT sensors are typically linked to a cloud computing platform. Companies are able to access the information in this way from any location. They can employ predictive maintenance and monitor their production line. They can then automate and monitor their supply chain. Additionally, they can cut costs by minimizing human interaction thanks to the numerous opportunities offered by IIoT technologies. Manufacturing is only one of the numerous ways a business can use the IoT. For instance, a manufacturer might keep track of employee productivity. Factories may monitor their performance by utilizing the IoT. Additionally, it might raise the standards of goods and services. Safety may be increased in industrial environments by using the IoT. Employers can keep an eye on the security of their staff by installing an IoT-based mobile device. Advantages of the IIoT could be visualized by the following points. The IIoT has several advantages, ranging from better efficiency to increased safety. These advantages include:

- Generating accurate data. The IIoT enables businesses to collect enormous (and accurate) amounts of data that are beneficial for operations, energy use, and efficiency.
- Analysis of businesses can use crucial data to make judgments, otherwise they may not be able to make crucial business decisions.
- The capacity to identify patterns. The IIoT enables businesses to anticipate consumer behavior, maximizing earnings, marketing initiatives, and even customer satisfaction.
- Preventative upkeep. Preventive maintenance is made possible by the massive amount of data being collected every second, which is precise and affordable.
- Cost reductions, people can be assigned to more essential jobs (and kept safer at work) when basic, repetitive, or extremely risky tasks are handled by automated machinery rather than by people.

4.4.1 Drawbacks of the IIoT

The drawbacks of the Industrial Internet of Things include:

- Risk: The risk of virtual attacks increases as more gadgets are connected to the Internet. These assaults have the potential to jeopardize sensitive and important data and possibly stop equipment from operating completely.
- Profound overhauls: Old technologies or equipment with no technology must be updated for IIoT compatibility in order to function efficiently.
- Problems with the workforce: Connected machinery could be problematic if your team lacks the technological aptitude.

4.4.2 Convergence of AI and IIoT 4.0

Industrial enterprises must improve the connectivity of their workforce to decision-making resources and digitize labor and business processes. The main goal of industrial technology projects is to help different members of the organization make decisions that will improve company success by utilizing the industrial data that have previously been gathered. All areas of production, including design engineering, operations and maintenance, supply chain management, and human resources, are affected by this dynamic. To properly leverage AI, one must possess data science abilities, which adds another layer of complexity to an already complex environment. If an AI system established for industrial operations is not sufficiently knowledgeable about a facility or process, or about the right controls and safety measures, it could lead to a potentially dangerous situation.

Data science organizational expertise has not generally been developed in industrial manufacturing. Large data analysis is a skill that engineers are good at, but creating production-ready machine learning systems is challenging. The phrase AIoT describes the combination of artificial intelligence (AI) with the Internet of Things (IoT), which in industrial settings moves intelligence from the edge to the cloud and transforms data into insightful knowledge that facilitates improved decision-making. Where processing is most required, it is done there. The ability to routinely gather enormous amounts of data and to make these integrated datasets portable and available for use in strategic decision-making throughout the whole business is the cornerstone of the Industrial IoT. With the convergence of data science and IT, large-scale software provisioning, and OT domain expertise, AIoT aims to democratize AI and machine learning in the industrial domain.

Artificial intelligence serves as the system brain, and the IIoT as its digital nervous system. The only systems utilized in the past were the networks, control systems, and process historian infrastructure that make up this digital nervous system. But today, the industry is pilfering from IT again, along with cloud-based methods and architectures designed for business systems. By utilizing a scalable data infrastructure to fuel industrial AI models from training to product values, these systems help the industry integrate AI into operational technology. This enables users to resolve industrial issues without necessitating major advancements in industrial organizations or data science competencies. Aspen Technology introduced the Aspen AIoT Hub, an industry-ready, cloud-ready, and purpose-built Industrial AI infrastructure solution, with the integration of data science. Aspen AIoT Hub is made up of many popular and cutting-edge technologies. Aspen InfoPlus.21, which combines cloud-native connectivity, AI-driven tools for creating and implementing IoT applications, and advanced corporate workflows, analytics, and governance specifically designed for industrial firms, is at the center of it all. Among the main features of the Aspen AIoT Hub are the following.

Integration of Data and Mobility: Organizations will have access to and use of fully integrated data from sensors to the edge and cloud across the whole business thanks to the Aspen AIoT Hub.The AIoT Hub offers enterprise-speed and scale industrial AI application development, production-grade AI environment, and edge and cloud infrastructure (Figure 4.10).

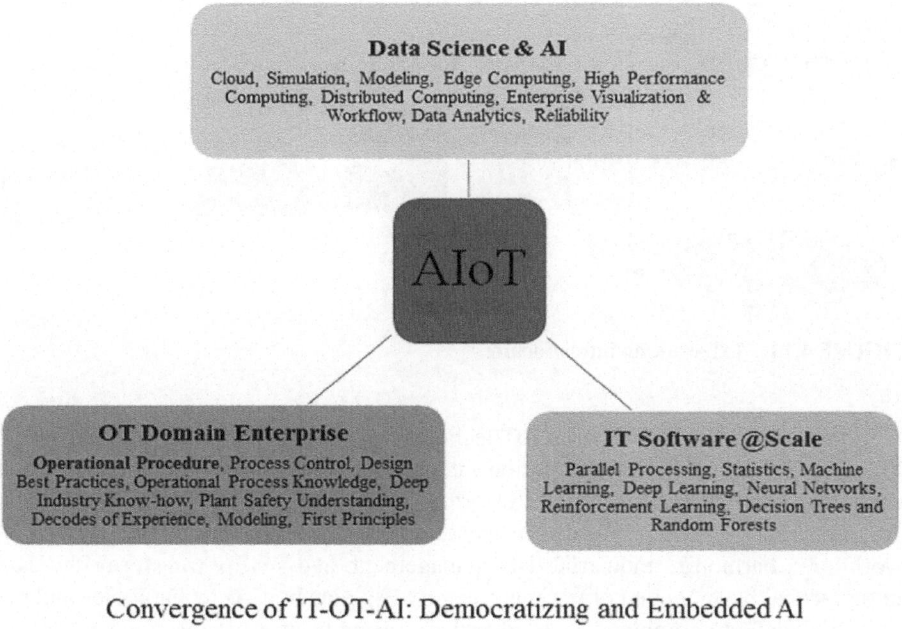

FIGURE 4.10 Computing infrastructure.

Cloud-ready Framework: In order to scale AI, more infrastructure, tools, and workflows for data science, development, and infrastructure skills like CloudOps, DevOps, MLOps, and others must be made available.

Visualization Across the Entire Organization
Enterprise users may get real-time data and analytics through the Aspen AIoT Hub, which can be used to improve operations, project efficiency, and collaboration. This is made possible by the promise of quicker insights and richer visualizations.

4.4.3 Industrial AI Ecosystem Applications

Theseallows users to train and quickly build machine learning (ML) models, and provides them with access to an embedded workbench that makes collaboration and versioning easier. This makes it possible for subject matter experts to collaborate with data scientists at customers and partners on data-rich AI applications. Organizational accountability, change leadership, and expertise face problems according to a recent survey on digital transformation conducted among 157 process manufacturers. The ARC Advisory Group research indicates that manufacturing has a great deal of interest in artificial intelligence (AI); nonetheless, the study also discovered that these three fields face major obstacles. Because of this gap between ambition and capacity, industrial organizations are searching for ways to use Industrial AI to democratize AI applications, just like Industrial IoT has done with data access.

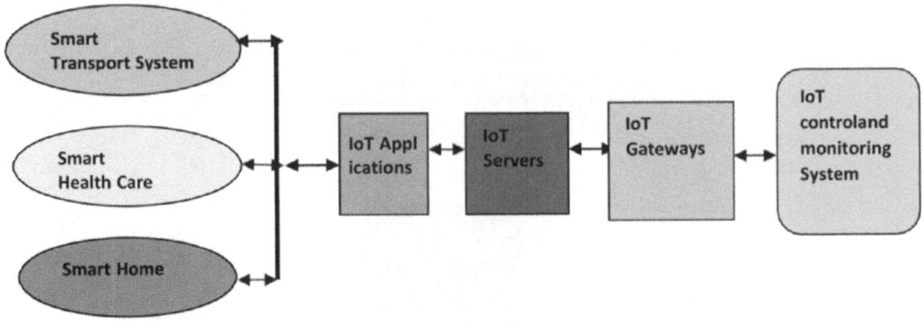

FIGURE 4.11 IoT working infrastructure.

Converging AI with Industrial IoT technical aspects, the Artificial Intelligence of Things (AIoT) is a new digital solution category focused on unlocking the unrealized economic value in industrial data. In order to build the next-generation Industrial AI infrastructure, which enables businesses to facilitate seamless human–machine workflows, harmonize industrial data management, and swiftly transform raw data into practical business outcomes, this category explains how AI technologies and the Industrial IoT are combined.The industry is currently at a tipping point where its traditional methods are becoming obsolete. To stay ahead of the curve and maintain a competitive edge, companies need to take use of the disruptive power of emerging technology.

Information technology (IT) and operations technology (OT) are combining to generate AIoT, along with AI and Industrial IoT. This presents both new potential and fresh challenges. Utilizing previously gathered data is a major factor driving the convergence of Industrial IoT and AI. When defending an AIoT strategy, industrial users should take into account the following business factors, according to the ARC Advisory Group (Figure 4.11).

Although the IoT has a lot of potential, it also poses several risks to the security and privacy of data. Evolutionary computation and other kinds of artificial intelligence will play a crucial role in helping the subfields of business intelligence and cyber security to reach their full potential [18]. The biggest problems that CI-enabled cyber security solutions are currently facing are also covered in this study,along with prospective future research topics[19,42]. Information security is beginning to pay more attention to cyber threat intelligence and cyber behavior profiling defense intelligence,both of which are made possible by computer intelligence.

Computer-gathered data are used to derive both of these types of intelligence. Cyber criminals, in particular, use techniques for detecting cyber intrusions in order tobetter predict future behavior from people. By using CI techniques, a crucial part ofcyber-behavioral modeling,it will be feasible to more precisely estimate temporal correlations in data and spend less time training. The task of making cyberspace safer will likewise heavily rely on CI techniques[20]. Techniques for privacy-preserving data aggregation are ways to protect private information while gathering data from IoT devices with constrained resources.

Intelligent sensors, smart meters, and other similar gadgets are some of these devices. As aconsequence of our investigation, we learned that computational intelligence is already being used to protect IoT devices from hacker attacks. The findings of ourstudy also point to the need for further investigation in this field because it has the ability to grow and diversify while also offering even better security solutions for IoT-connected devices. In view of the ongoing increase in the frequency of cyber-attacks, computational intelligence[22] may be able to help make industrial IoT devices safer.

Because edge devices frequently move around in environments that support 5G-IoT, it is challenging to localize threat monitoring, detection, and prevention for IoT nodes in these settings.However,proximity-based authentication and identity management are highly effective in this situation. Due to the current atmosphere, this is challenging to do. This entails the capacity to carry out secure operations in a setting that combines people and things, aswell as the flexibility to modify security precautions immediately. The use of CI techniques is detailed for creating cyber defenses that are meant to protect IoT-connected devices.

With the help of CI cyber defense, vulnerabilities can be found and defenses against threats and attacks online can be developed. Potential cyber security vulnerabilities can be more easily addressed thanks to cutting-edge CI algorithms that can evolve over time. Since these technologies employ learning algorithms, they can recognize the most recent malware variants, online threats, and cyber-attacks. They can also make sure the tools are up to date with the most recent traits of dangerous malware[23]. Over the past 10 years, computer-aided information security has been a significant area of academic research due to a rise in the demand for safe and intelligent systems.Fuzzy logic can be used to reduce a sizable numerical input space into a more manageable search area by using language-based definitions and understandings of numerical information. Researchers have the added advantage of being able to explain details about normal or abnormal behavior in a clear way by using linguistic qualities. Information security is made more resilient because of the fuzziness and imprecision of fuzzy logic ability to distinguish between legitimate and erroneous data. Both the emergence of evolutionary computing and artificial neural networks have received influence from natural systems. Without having any prior knowledge of regularities, they can deduce behavior patterns from data by using biological metaphors.

As a result, the IoT is recognized as having contributed tothe conception of cognitive intelligence (CI). Here, we examine the state of cyber security concerns as well as new IoT research advancements made feasible by artificial intelligence.Combining CI algorithms with those of other technologies like advanced analytics, the IoT, robots, and edge computing is a practice that is becoming increasingly widespread. It is crucial to keep CI and cyber security-based efforts in mind when designing the IoT for resilience and security.

The process of importing and exporting experiences with others in order to strengthen the industrial ecosystem as a whole is known as knowledge transfer. Organizations need assistance in learning more about the potential benefits and workable solutions for creating integrated platforms for automatic data interchange between IT systems, particularly with cooperating organizations (i.e., suppliers and clients). Moreover, research has shown that businesses require assistance in disseminating information regarding Industry 4.0 technologies, existing IT infrastructure, and potential operational applications of artificial intelligence (AI). This implies that industrial enterprises don't have a clear way or open platform to communicate their positive experiences with a given technology. Developers can share technological knowledge surprisingly easily thanks to the abundance of public repositories and open data platforms [38,39]. If you are trying to meet these requirements, this can be a fantastic place to start.The training also fills in the knowledge gaps that companies now have, which makes it possible for them to use new EC, AI, and IoT technologies. This last point is crucial. Industry 4.0 really mandates that employers integrate new job profiles into industrial work environments, including data scientists, data architects, data analysts, and data engineers[40,41].

Businesses often find it difficult to decide which tasks to assign to these new profiles and how to integrate them into the team because most of them did not exist in the past. Companies also find it difficult to retrain current employees given the abundance of available knowledge on AI, IoT, and EC for Industry 4.0. It has been determined that organizations require assistance in creating training materials for both present and potential employees to acquire the hard (technical) and soft skills necessary for the efficient use of Industry 4.0 solutions. It would be prudent to integrate industry professionals and Industry 4.0 experts into a single training program in order to meet this requirement. Through superior skill complementation, both profiles would become fluent in each other's language and contribute to Industry 4.0 actualization in the real world.

4.5 CONCLUDING REMARKS

Because of Industry 4.0, the way industrial processes are implemented is changing. With the help of automation, artificial intelligence, and the Internet of Things (IoT), businesses can now provide their customers with better products and services. Forinstance, smart factories have the ability to continuously monitor their equipment, rapidlyspot any issues, and modify output levels as necessary. This contributes to cost-effective efficiency growth. Additionally, firms may more accurately adapt their services thanks to Industry 4.0 technology, which helps them understand their clients purchasing trends. The whole experience for both producers and consumers is greatly enhanced as a result of this level of digital transformation.

It follows that it is not surprising that Industry 4.0 has evolved into a crucial element of contemporary industry. Because of its capacity to simplify operations, increase accuracy and efficiency, and lower costs, Industry4.0 is swiftly taking the lead in establishing itself as the foundation of smart industry. As new technologies are developed and those already in use are refined, it is always changing, enabling businessesto stay at the forefront of innovation and to compete in their specific markets. Businesses must maintain their agility and adopt a change-oriented culture to realize these benefits.Companies that commit to this will be well-positioned for many years to come to take advantage of Industry 4.0 opportunities.

Industry 4.0 is redefining what it means to be a smart industry in the modern dayand opening up opportunities that were previously unthinkable. Utilizing its potential canhelp businesses enhance operations and maintain an edge over rivals. Businesses who adopt this change will experience enormous long-term benefits.

Industry 5.0 is centered on the Fourth Industrial Revolution and how it has affected international trade and industry. The goal of this revolution is to increase production efficiency across a variety of industries by utilizing linked technology, automation, artificial intelligence, robots, analytics, machine learning, and other technologies. By utilizing these new technologies and deploying them strategically, businesses can increase output quality and productivity while gaining more meaningful insights into their operations. Industry 5.0 also emphasizes proactive measures that firmsmay take to better position themselves for future technological developments that willfurther optimize processes and open up new growth prospects. Companies that embrace this shift toward digital transformation will benefit from cost savings and enhanced consumer experiences, giving them a competitive edge.Asa result,companies should start putting up plans to take advantage of Industry 5.0 prospects and stay competitive in a constantly shifting environment. Companies who foresee changes and put solid strategies into place will be well-positioned to succeed in this new era of industry. To maximize productivity and enhance consumer engagement, businesses should focus on creating clever solutions that incorporate diverse technologies.

To safeguard their intellectual property from cyber-attacks and stay one stepahead of bad actors, firms must prioritize data security. For businesses to succeed, value must be consistently created while offering clients novel experiences. A successful approach must therefore incorporate projects thatmake use of cutting-edge technology and give staff members cutting-edge skill sets. Businesses who adopt the proper strategy may make sure they stay at the forefront of Industry 5.0 and profit from long-term planning.

IIoT Potential in the Near and Long Term

It seems incredible that the demand for IoT-based asset tracking devices will increase by three times over the course of the upcoming year. The Industrial IoT is setting the standard in several areas by real-time monitoring of products and industrial operations. Numerous sectors are changing their organizational structures from SCADA/PLCs to modern, automated ones for a variety of reasons, including cost-cutting, improved ROIs, analytical decision-making, data-driven approach, and storming of technology-based ideas. The adoption of the IIoT in today's world suggests improved operational adjustments,cost management, and reducing production lags at any time and from any location, thereby outlining a clear course of action to satisfy the population's increasing needs. By putting these cutting-edge ideas into practice,waste and pointless chores that could impede current industrial processes are reduced. Enterprises stand to gain significantly from Industry 5.0, but in order to prosper, enterprises must take immediate action. By embracing this transition toward digital transformation, businesses can make sure they are well-positioned to take advantage of developing technology and prosper in this new era of the industry.Industry5.0 can help businesses succeed.

REFERENCES

[1] Pedrycz, W., *Computational Intelligence: An Introduction*, CRC Press, Boca Raton, 1998.
[2] Shastri, L. (Guest ed.), A fuzzy logic symposium, IEEE Expert, vol. 9, no. 4, pp. 2–49, 1994.
[3] Schwefel, H.-P., Back, T. D., Periaux, J., Poloni, C., and Winter, G. (Eds.), Artificial evolution: How and why?, *Chapter 1 in Uagliarela, Genetic Algorithms and Evolution Strategies in Engineering and Computer Science*, pp. 1–20, 1998.
[4] Chen, Z., Fanelli, A. M., Castellano, G., and Jain, L. C, Introduction to computational intelligence paradigms, in Baba, N., Jain, L. C. (eds) *Computational Intelligence in Games. Studies in Fuzziness and Soft Computing*, vol 62 . Physica, Heidelberg. https://doi.org/10.1007/978-3-7908-1833-8_1, 2001.
[5] Khalil, R. A., and Saeed, N., Network optimization for industrial internet of things (IIoT), *IEEE Sensors Letters*, doi:10.1109/lsens.2020.3002232
[6] Lucas-Estañ, M. C. and Gozalvez, J., Load balancing for reliable self-organizing industrial IoT networks, *IEEE Trans. Ind. Informat.*, vol. 15, no. 9, pp. 5052–5063, 2019.
[7] Saeed, N., Alouini, M., and Al-Naffouri, T. Y., Accurate 3-D localization of selected smart objects in optical internet of underwater things, *IEEE Internet of Things J.*, vol. 7, no. 2, pp. 937–947, 2020.
[8] Saeed, N., Nam, H., Haq, M. I. U., and Muhammad Saqib, D. B., A survey on multi-dimensional scaling, *ACM Comput. Surv.*, vol. 51, no. 3, pp. 1–25, 2018.
[9] Lucas-Estañ, M. C., and Gozalvez, J., Load balancing for reliable self-organizing industrial IoT networks, *IEEE Trans. Ind. Informat.*, vol. 15, no. 9, pp. 5052–5063, 2019.
[10] Sisinni, E., Saifullah, A., Han, S., Jennehag, U., and Gidlund, M., Industrial internet of things: Challenges, opportunities, and directions, *IEEE Trans. Ind. Informat.*, vol. 14, no. 11, pp. 4724–4734, 2018.
[11] Boyes, H., Hallaq, B., Cunningham, J., and Watson, T., The industrial internet of things (IIoT): An analysis framework, *Comput. Industry*, vol. 101, pp. 1–12, 2018.
[12] Gilchrist, A., *Industry 4.0: The Industrial Internet of Things*, Apress, Berkeley, CA, 2016.
[13] Baba N and Jain L. A., *Computational Intelligence in Games*© Physica-Verlag Heidelberg, 2001.
[14] Wojcicki, K., Bieganska, M., Paliwoda, B. and Gorna, J., Internet of things in industry:Research profiling, application, challenges and opportunities–a review, February 2022, *Energies*, vol. 15, no. 5, pp. 1–24, https://doi.org/10.3390/en15051806
[15] Stentoft, J., Adsbøll Wickstrøm, K., Philipsen, K., and Haug, A. Drivers and barriers for Industry 4.0 readiness and practice: Empirical evidence from small and medium-sized manufacturers, *Prod. Plan. Control*, vol. 32, pp. 811–828, 2021.
[16] Namrata G. D. et al. *An Improved Approch for Fraud Detection in Health Insurance Using Data Mining Techniques*. no. 5, 27–32, 2017.
[17] Potgantwar, A. D, A standalone RFID and NFC based healthcare. *Int. J. Interactive Mobile Technol.*, vol. 7, no. 2, pp. 73–79, 2013. https://doi.org/10.3991/ijim.v7i2.2314
[18] Bhaladhare, P. R. and Jinwala, D. C., Novel approaches for privacy preserving data mining in k-anonymity model. *J. Inf. Sci. Eng.* vol. 32, pp. 63–78, 2016.

[19] Adeniyi, A. E., Jimoh, R. G., Awotunde, J. B., Olagunju, M., Ninan, D. O., Olanloye, O. D., ... & Babatunde, A. O. Computational Models Enabling Smart Teaching and Learning in Wireless Communication Systems. In *Computational Modeling and Simulation of Advanced Wireless Communication Systems* (pp. 322–351). CRC Press, 2024.

[20] Bhaladhare, P. R. and Jinwala, D. C., A clustering approach using fractional calculus-bacterial foraging optimization algorithm for k-anonymization in privacy preserving data mining. *Censorship, Surveillance, and Privacy: Concepts,Methodologies, Tools, and Applications, edited by Information Resources Management Association*, IGI Global, pp. 587–608, 2019, https://doi.org/10.4018/978-1-5225-7113- 1.ch031

[21] Gite S. N., Dharmadhikari D. D., and Kumar, R., Educational decision making based on GIS, *Int. J. Recent Technol. Eng*, ISSN: 2277–3878, vol. 1, no. 1, Apr. 2012.

[22] Kumar, R., Kumar, S., and Kolte V. S., A model for intrusion detection based on undefined distance, *Int. J. Soft Comput. Eng.*, vol. 1 no. 5, pp. 2231–2307, Nov. 2011.

[23] Mahajan, V., Dwivedi, A., Kulkarni, S., Ali, M. A., Solanki, R. K. Face mask detection using machine learning, *Int. Res. J. Modern. Eng. Technol. Sci.*, vol: 04, no. 05, pp. 435–445, May, 2022.

[24] Zhao, S., Li, S., Qi, L., and Xu, L. D., Computational intelligence enabled cybersecurity for the internet of things, in *IEEE Trans. Emerg. Topics Comput. Intell.*, vol. 4, no. 5, pp. 666–674, Oct. 2020, https://doi.org/10.1109/TETCI.2019.2941757.

[25] H. He, H., Maple, C., Watson, T., Tiwari, A., Mehnen, J., Jin, Y., & Gabrys, B., The security challenges in the IoT enabled cyber-physical systems and opportunities for evolutionary computing & other computational intelligence, *IEEE Congress on Evolutionary Computation (CEC),* 2016, pp. 1015–1021, https://doi.org/10.1109/CEC.2016.7743900.

[26] Chanal, P. M., Kakkasageri, M. S., & Manvi, S. K. S., Security and privacy in the internet of things: Computational intelligent techniques-based approaches, in *ScienceDirect* (pp. 111–127), Academic Press, 2021, www.sciencedirect .com / science /article /pii /B9780128228449000098#, Accessed 16 Nov. 2021.

[27] Wang, R. and Ji, W., Computational intelligence for information security: A survey, in *IEEE Trans. Emerg. Topics Comput. Intell.*, vol. 4, no. 5, pp. 616–629, Oct. 2020, https://doi.org/10.1109/TETCI.2019.2923426.

[28] Ranjan, P., and Om, H., Computational intelligence based security in wireless sensor networks: Technologies and design challenges. *Stud. Comput. Intell.*, vol. 676, 2017, pp. 131–151, https://doi.org/10.1007/978-3-319-47715-2_6. Accessed 20 Nov. 2021.

[29] Iram, R., Sheikh, M. I., Jabbar, S., and Minhas, A. A., Computational intelligence based optimization in wireless sensor network, *2011 International Conference on Information and Communication Technologies*, pp. 1–6, 2011, https://doi.org/10.1109/ICICT.2011.5983561. Electronic copy available at: https://ssrn.com/abstract=4187998

[30] Rajawat, A. S., Bedi, P., Goyal, S. B., Shukla, P. K., Jamal, S. S., Alharbi, A. R., and Aljaedi, A. Securing 5G-IoT device connectivity and coverage using Boltzmann machine keys generation, *Math. Prob. Eng.*, vol. 2021, Article ID 2330049, 10 pages, 2021, https://doi.org/10.1155/2021/2330049

[31] Rajawat, A. S., Jain, S., and Barhanpurkar, K. Fusion protocol for improving coverage and connectivity WSNs, *IET Wireless Sensor Syst.*, vol. 11, no. 4, 16 Mar. 2021, pp. 161–168, https://doi.org/10.1049/wss2.12018.

[32] Rajawat, A. S., Bedi, P., Goyal, S. B., Alharbi, A. R., Aljaedi, A., Jamal, S. S., and Shukla, P. K. Fog big data analysis for IoT sensor application using fusion deep

learning, *Math. Prob. Eng.*, vol. 2021, Article ID 6876688, 16 pages, 2021, https://doi.org/10.1155/2021/6876688

[33] Singh Rajawat, A., Bedi, P., Goyal, S. B., Shukla, P. K., Zaguia, A., Jain, A., and Monirujjaman Khan, M. Reformist framework for improving human security for mobile robots in Industry 4.0, *Mobile Inf. Syst.*, vol. 2021, Article ID 4744220, 10 pages, 2021, https://doi.org/10.1155/2021/4744220

[34] Kumar, S., Tiwari, P., and Zymbler, M. Internet of Things is a revolutionary approach for future technology enhancement: A review, *J Big Data*, vol. 6, pp. 111, 2019, https://doi.org/10.1186/s40537-019-0268-2

[35] Rajawat, S., Barhanpurkar, K., Mukhopadhyay, D., and Ghosh, A., Scheme Invisible Internet Protocol (I2P) using blockchain techniques for tracking darkweb user activities, *2021 IEEE 4th International Conference on Computing, Power and Communication Technologies (GUCON)*, pp. 1–5, 2021, https://doi.org/10.1109/GUCON50781.2021.9573880.

[36] Rajawat, A. S., Mohammed, O., and Bedi, P. FDLM: Fusion deep learning model for classifying obstructive sleep apnea and type 2 diabetes, *2020 Fourth International Conference on I-SMAC (IoT in Social, Mobile, Analytics and Cloud) (ISMAC)*, pp. 835–839, 2020, https://doi.org/10.1109/I-SMAC49090.2020.9243553.

[37] Rajawat, A. S., Mohammed, O., and Bedi, P. Web personalization model using modified S3VM algorithm for developing recommendation process, 2nd International Conference on Data, Engineering and Applications (IDEA), pp. 1–6, 2020, https://doi.org/10.1109/IDEA49133.2020.9170701.

[38] Nair, A. R. and Potgantwar, A. D. Masked face detection using the Viola Jones Algorithm: A progressive approach for less time consumption. *Int. J. Recent Contribut. Eng. Sci.*, vol. 6, no. 4, pp. 4–14, 2018, https://doi.org/10.3991/ijes.v6i4.9317.

[39] Dabbish, L., Stuart, C., Tsay, J., and Herbsleb, J. Social coding in GitHub: Transparency and collaboration in an open software repository, in *Proceedings of the ACM 2012 Conference on Computer Supported Cooperative Work*, Seattle, WA, USA, 11–15, February 2012.

[40] Sicilia, M.-A., García-Barriocanal, E., and Sánchez-Alonso, S. Community curation in open dataset repositories: Insights from Zenodo, *Procedia. Comput., Sci.*, vol. 106, pp. 54–60, 2017, [CrossRef]

[41] Corea, F. *An Introduction to Data: Everything You Need to Know About AI: Big Data and Data Science*, Springer Nature Switzerland AG: Geneva, Switzerland, 2019.

[42] Chhotaray, P., Behera, B. C., Moharana, B. R., Muduli, K., and Sephyrin, F. T. R. Enhancement of manufacturing sector performance with the application of industrial internet of things (IIoT), in *Smart Technologies for Improved Performance of Manufacturing Systems and Services*. CRC Press, pp. 1–19, 2024.

[43] Embia, G., Mohamed, A., Moharana, B. R., and Muduli, K. Edge computing-based conditional monitoring. *Intelligent Manufacturing Management Systems: Operational Applications of Evolutionary Digital Technologies in Mechanical and Industrial Engineering*,John Wiley: Newark, pp. 249–270, 2023.

[44] Embia, G. J., Moharana, B. R., Behera, B. C., Mohmaed, N. H., Biswal, D. K., and Muduli, K. Reliability prediction using machine learning approach, in *Smart Technologies for Improved Performance of Manufacturing Systems and Services*. CRC Press: London, pp. 21–37, 2023.

[45] Galgal, K. N., Ray, M., Moharana, B. R., Behera, B. C., and Muduli, K. Quality control in the era of IoT and automation in the context of developing nations, in *Smart*

Technologies for Improved Performance of Manufacturing Systems and Services. CRC Press, pp. 39–50, 2023.

[46] Akkaraboina, M., Kodari, S. R., Barve, A., and Muduli, K. Securing data of online learners using blockchain technology, in *Advancements in Artificial Intelligence, Blockchain Technology, and IoT in Higher Education: Mitigating the Impact of COVID-19*. Apple Academic Press, pp. 181–202, 2023.

[47] Muduli, K., Luthra, S., Garza-Reyes, J. A., and Huisingh, D. Application of blockchain technology for addressing reverse logistics challenges: current status and future opportunities, *Supply Chain Forum Int. J.*, vol. 24, no. 1, pp. 1–6, 2023.

5 Security, Privacy, Trust, and Other Issues in Industries 4.0 and 5.0

Abidemi Emmanuel Adeniyi, Rasheed Gbenga Jimoh, Joseph Bamidele Awotunde, Deborah Olufemi Ninan, Hallelujah Oluwatobi Aworinde, Adedoyin Oyebade, Peace Busola Falola, and Abdulrauf Olarenwaju Babatunde

5.1 INTRODUCTION

The industrial environment is experiencing major changes. We are witnessing the growth of Industry 4.0, which is being driven by the convergence of sophisticated technologies such as cyber-physical systems, artificial intelligence, and big data [1,2]. Industry 5.0 is on the horizon. This progress offers new levels of efficiency, productivity, and human–machine collaboration, but it also provides a complex interplay of opportunities and difficulties, necessitating a closer examination of their underlying principles and their repercussions. The emergence of industrial revolutions has demonstrated human inventiveness and technical advancement [3]. From the First Industrial Revolution, which brought mechanized production, to the current Industry 4.0, which is distinguished by the incorporation of digital technology into industrial processes, each phase has substantially transformed the production environment. Now, as we approach Industry 5.0, it is critical to comprehend both the current status and the future direction of industrial growth.

5.1.1 Industry 4.0: Automation, Interconnectedness, and Smart Production

The following basic pillars produce major benefits, including better efficiency, lower costs, higher product quality, and more adaptability. However, Industry 4.0 raises concerns about employment displacement, cybersecurity risks, and the moral consequences of technology and decision-making based on data [4].

i. **Automation:** Robots, sophisticated production technologies, and self-optimizing processes take center stage, minimizing human participation in

DOI: 10.1201/9781003581963-5

repetitive activities while increasing precision and consistency [5]. This is demonstrated by automated manufacturing lines equipped with adaptive robots and real-time feedback loops [6].

ii. **Interconnectivity:** Industrial facilities evolve into sophisticated cyber-physical systems in which machines, sensors, and software systems exchange real-time data via the Industrial Internet of Things [7,8]. This allows for data-driven decision-making, predictive maintenance, and efficient resource allocation.

iii. **Smart production:** Big data analytics, artificial intelligence, and machine learning algorithms turn acquired data into insights that drive intelligent manufacturing processes [9]. Predictive maintenance, self-adjusting production settings, and real-time anomaly detection have become widespread [10,11].

5.1.2 Industry 5.0: Human-Centered Interaction, Sustainability, Resilience, and Adaptability

While Industry 4.0 emphasized technology improvements, Industry 5.0 takes a broader perspective. It acknowledges the limitations of full automation while emphasizing the critical role of humans in the industrial environment.

Human-centric collaboration: Rather than replacing humans, Industry 5.0 envisions a future in which humans and robots collaborate in a symbiotic partnership. AI and automation improve human capacities, allowing people to focus on jobs that require creativity, critical thinking, and social intelligence [12–15].

Sustainability emphasizes environmental and social responsibility. Industry 5.0 encourages the development of environmentally friendly technology and manufacturing methods that reduce environmental impact and resource usage. Circular economy ideas, green manufacturing methods, and closed-loop systems are being adopted [16,17].

Resilience and adaptability: In an increasingly uncertain environment, Industry 5.0 prioritizes flexibility and resilience. Advanced technologies are employed to create adaptive systems that can handle disruptions, shifting market needs, and unexpected obstacles [18,19].

The shift to Industry 5.0 necessitates tackling various issues, including upskilling and reskilling employees to adapt to new tasks, building ethical structures for human–machine teamwork, and eliminating institutional resistance to embracing environmentally friendly procedures [20]. The move from Industry 4.0 to Industry 5.0 brings both enormous obstacles and tremendous opportunities.

5.1.3 Challenges of the Shift from Industry 4.0 to Industry 5.0

Jobs and skills: Automation may result in job losses, necessitating considerable reskilling and upskilling efforts to enable a seamless transition for the workforce [21].

Data privacy and security: Increased data collecting and analysis raises concerns about privacy and security risks. Strong data governance structures and cybersecurity safeguards are essential [22].

Ethical considerations: The use of AI and automation poses ethical concerns around bias, transparency, and accountability. Ethical frameworks and appropriate AI development procedures are critical.

Sustainability: Integrating environmental and social responsibility into industrial processes would necessitate significant investments in new technology and manufacturing methods.

5.1.4 Opportunities of Shifting from Industry 4.0 to Industry 5.0

Enhanced productivity and efficiency: Improved procedures, data-driven decision-making, and intelligent automation can result in considerable productivity and efficiency improvements [23]. New technology and collaborative settings promote creativity and provide opportunities for disruptive company models [24].

Improved product quality and customer satisfaction: Personalized production, real-time quality control, and data-driven insights can result in greater product quality and increased customer satisfaction. Figure 5.1 depicts a layered approach to addressing security, privacy, trust, and other critical issues in Industries 4.0 and 5.0.

The architecture emphasizes a holistic approach to security, privacy, trust, and other critical issues in Industries 4.0 and 5.0 by building upon each layer.

5.1.5 Evolution and Key Characteristics

The growth of industry from its early stages to the present day is a monument to human ingenuity and technical progress [25]. Industry 4.0 and Industry 5.0 refer to different stages of this progression, each with its own set of characteristics and paradigms. Understanding the progression and important characteristics of these

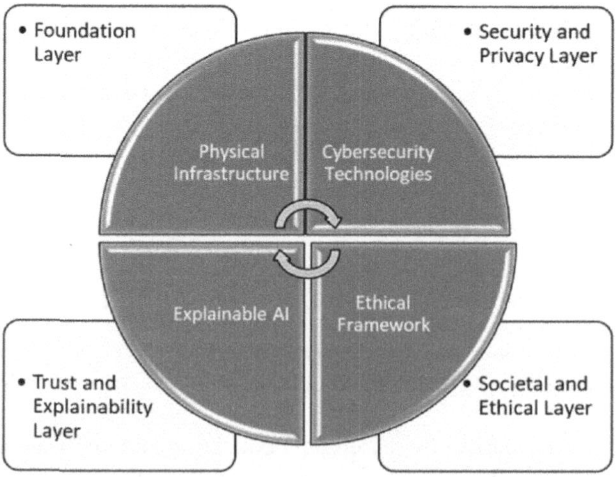

FIGURE 5.1 Architecture diagram of security and privacy in Industries 4.0 and 5.0.

stages is critical for understanding the current and future trends in industrial growth. The industrial landscape is not static. Each revolution expands on the preceding one, pushing the limits of what is possible and transforming our reality. We are on the verge of another disruptive transition, highlighted by the rise of Industry 4.0 and, on the horizon, Industry 5.0.

5.1.6 Evolution of Industrial Revolutions

The First Industrial Revolution (late 18th to early 19th centuries) represented the move from manual to machine-based manufacturing, which was predominantly powered by steam and water. It transformed sectors such as textiles and fueled the rise of factories.

The Second Industrial Revolution (late nineteenth to early twentieth centuries), also known as the Technological Revolution, was propelled by the introduction of electricity and mass industrial techniques. This era witnessed great breakthroughs in steel manufacturing, railroads, and telegraphy.

The Third Industrial Revolution, sometimes known as the Digital Revolution, occurred in the late twentieth century. With the emergence of computers, the internet, and information technology, it was defined by a shift from analog and mechanical technology to digital technology.

Industry 4.0 (twentieth century): The integration of digital technology into production defines the Fourth Industrial Revolution. It depicts the transition from centralized to decentralized manufacturing.

Industry 5.0 (emerging): While still in its early phases, Industry 5.0 expands on Industry 4.0 by shifting the emphasis from pure technology and efficiency to human collaboration and sustainability.

5.1.7 From Forges to Bits: The Rise of Industry 4.0

Industry 4.0, often known as the Fourth Industrial Revolution, did not emerge suddenly [26]. Its roots were sowed far earlier, with the advent of the steam engine ushering in the First Industrial Revolution, followed by mass production lines and assembly lines of the Second and Third Industrial Revolutions, respectively. Each step resulted in improved automation, mechanization, and efficiency. However, with Industry 4.0, the emphasis changes from physical brilliance to digital integration and cyber-physical systems. This revolution is based on four essential pillars:

1. Interconnectivity: The Industrial Internet of Things (IIoT) develops as the factory's nervous system, with smart sensors implanted in equipment, goods, and surroundings. These sensors are continually collecting and transmitting data, resulting in a real-time, linked environment.
2. Big data and analytics: This massive amount of data becomes the lifeblood of intelligent decision-making [27]. Advanced analytics techniques, such as machine learning and artificial intelligence, derive insights from data, enhance processes, and anticipate possible problems before they occur.

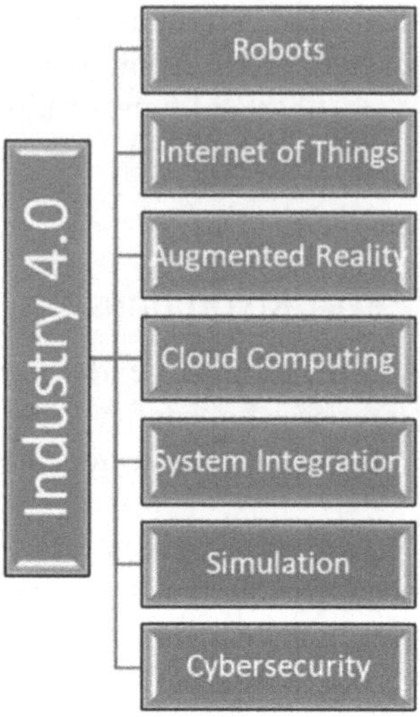

FIGURE 5.2 Elements of industry 4.0.

3. Automation and robotics: Physical machines are being replaced by or complemented with robots, capable of completing complicated tasks with increased precision and speed. This automation extends beyond the production floor to include shipping, warehousing, and supply chain management.
4. Human–machine collaboration: While automation takes the spotlight, people remain essential. Industry 4.0 proposes a dynamic cooperation between humans and machines, with human creativity, critical thinking, and problem-solving abilities complementing automation's efficiency and accuracy. Figure 5.2 displays various elements of Industry 4.0.

5.1.8 The Advantages of Industry 4.0

Increased productivity and efficiency: Real-time data analysis and streamlined procedures result in considerable production improvements and waste reductions.

Improved product quality: Machine-controlled manufacturing and improved quality control techniques ensure that products are consistent and exceptional.

Enhanced agility and flexibility: Connected systems and data-driven insights enable rapid responses to changing market needs and unexpected disruptions.

Innovation and new business models: The convergence of technology creates an environment conducive to innovation, resulting in the birth of novel goods, services, and business models. However, this shift is not without its hurdles.

Concerns about automation displacing human occupations require upskilling and reskilling measures to enable a seamless workforce transition.

Data privacy and security: The large volume of data gathered raises worries about privacy violations and cyberattacks. Strong data governance structures and cybersecurity safeguards are critical.

Ethical considerations: The employment of AI and automation raises concerns about bias, transparency, and responsibility. Building ethical foundations for responsible AI development is critical.

Concerns about automation displacing human occupations require upskilling and reskilling measures to enable a seamless workforce transition.

Data privacy and security: The large volume of data gathered raises concerns about privacy violations and cyberattacks. Strong data governance structures and cybersecurity safeguards are critical.

Ethical considerations: The employment of AI and automation raises concerns about bias, transparency, and responsibility. Building ethical foundations for responsible AI development is critical.

5.1.9 Human at the Helm: The Dawn of Industry 5.0

Industry 5.0 builds on the basis of Industry 4.0 while introducing a significant shift: a renewed emphasis on the human aspect [26,27]. It acknowledges that, while technology is a powerful instrument, it must be developed and applied in accordance with human values and ethics. Here are the major characteristics of Industry 5.0 [28].

1. Human-centric collaboration: Rather than just boosting human skills, Industry 5.0 focuses on synergy and co-creation. Humans and robots collaborate as partners, exploiting one another's abilities to generate greater results.
2. Sustainability and the circular economy: Environmental responsibility takes center stage. Industry 5.0 encourages the development of green technology and closed-loop systems, therefore reducing environmental effects and resource usage. This involves reducing waste, using renewable energy, and applying sustainable industrial processes.
3. Resilience and adaptability: In an increasingly uncertain environment, resilience is critical. Industry 5.0 focuses on developing flexible and adaptive systems capable of successfully responding to shocks, market swings, and unexpected obstacles. This includes adopting modularity, decentralized production, and agile manufacturing processes.
4. Ethical and responsible innovation: Transparency, accountability, and fairness are core values. Ethical issues drive technological developments, ensuring that AI, robots, and other new technologies are developed and used responsibly.

5.1.10 The Convergence of Physical and Digital Systems of Industries 4.0 and 5.0

The confluence of physical and digital systems, commonly referred to as Industry 4.0 and the Internet of Things (IoT), is one of the most disruptive movements in today's technology world [29]. This phenomenon, the outcome of decades of change in both the physical and digital worlds, has far-reaching consequences for companies, economies, and society. This section dives into the history, evolution, and important characteristics of this confluence, emphasizing its importance and influence. The distinction between the physical and digital worlds is eroding. What was formerly separate, with physical items operating in the physical world and digital information living in the ethereal cyberspace, is fast clashing and combining. The confluence of physical and digital systems represents a dramatic transition, altering businesses, economies, and even our view of the world around us [30]. Table 5.1 displays a comparative summary of security, privacy and trust of Industries 4.0 and 5.0.

TABLE 5.1
Summary of the Security, Privacy, and Trust Issues in Industries 4.0 and 5.0

Issue	Industry 4.0	Industry 5.0
Data Security	Limited data security standards and protocols– Vulnerable to data breaches and cyberattacks	Focus on human-centric security and privacy by design Stronger data encryption and access controls– Blockchain technology for secure data sharing
Data Privacy	Privacy concerns with data collection and usage– Lack of transparency in data ownership and control	Greater emphasis on data ownership and control– Individualized privacy settings and opt-out mechanisms– Development of privacy-preserving technologies
Trust in Automation	Lack of transparency in AI decision-making– Concerns about algorithmic bias and fairness	Development of explainable and transparent AI systems– Human oversight and control over AI decision-making– Focus on building trust through responsible AI development
Algorithmic Bias	Potential for bias in algorithms used for automation– Discrimination based on race, gender, or other factors	Mitigation of algorithmic bias through diverse data and training– Fair and unbiased AI algorithms– Regular audits and monitoring for bias
Cybersecurity Threats	Increased vulnerability to cyberattacks on interconnected systems– Lack of robust cybersecurity measures	Enhanced cybersecurity measures for human–machine collaboration– Secure communication protocols and intrusion detection systems– Continuous vulnerability assessment and patching

TABLE 5.1 (Continued)
Summary of the Security, Privacy, and Trust Issues in Industries 4.0 and 5.0

Issue	Industry 4.0	Industry 5.0
Job Displacement	Job losses due to automation and AI adoption– Need for workforce reskilling and upskilling	Reskilling and upskilling initiatives for workforce adaptation– Creation of new jobs in AI-powered industries– Focus on human-centered workplaces that complement automation
Ethical Considerations	Ethical dilemmas surrounding AI and automation– Concerns about job displacement, social inequality, and misuse of technology	Alignment of AI with human values and ethical principles– Responsible development and deployment of AI– Public engagement and dialog about AI ethics
Digital Divide	Unequal access to technology and its benefits Widening gap between the tech-savvy and the tech-excluded	Bridging the digital divide through inclusive technology access– Digital literacy programs and initiatives– Affordable and accessible broadband internet

5.1.11 From Separate Realms to Intertwined Worlds: A Historical Perspective

The roots of this confluence were planted more than a century ago, with the introduction of the telegraph, which sparked the first murmurs of connection beyond physical distances. Early incarnations, such as the Babbage difference engine and Hollerith tabulator, hinted at the integration of physical equipment with numerical calculation. The advent of the transistor accelerated the shift, allowing for shrinking and the widespread use of digital technology [31].

The major acceleration, however, occurred with the introduction of the personal computer and the internet. These transformational technologies put immense computing power and connection at our fingertips, blurring the physical and digital divide. The emergence of smartphones and omnipresent sensors further entrenched this convergence, integrating digital intelligence into tangible items. Today, this confluence takes center stage in numerous ways, as outlined below.

The Internet of Things (IoT): Devices and objects outfitted with sensors and actuators link to the internet, delivering and receiving data, resulting in a massive network of intelligent physical systems. From smart houses to linked autos, the Internet of Things combines real things with digital capabilities, automating chores and providing useful information.

Cyber-physical systems (CPS): Physical and digital systems are intimately interconnected, sharing data and responding in real time. Robots work alongside people in industries, and intelligent traffic systems optimize vehicle flow in cities, blurring the distinction between physical infrastructure and digital control.

Digital twins: Virtual representations of actual things and systems that are fed real-time data allow for simulations and forecasts, improving performance, forecasting maintenance needs, and even training workers in controlled digital settings. The integration of physical assets with digital equivalents enables improved monitoring, analysis, and control.

5.1.12 Applications Redefining Industries and Our Lives

The repercussions of this confluence extend far beyond technological curiosity. It transforms industries and reshapes our everyday lives in a variety of ways.

Smart factories use robots, intelligent machinery, and real-time data analysis to optimize production, increase efficiency, and customize goods. This "smart manufacturing" transforms whole sectors, resulting in flexible and responsive production processes [32].

Digital healthcare: Medical equipment gather and transmit patient data, allowing for remote monitoring, real-time diagnostics, and individualized treatment programs. Connected gadgets and wearables encourage preventative care and enable people to take control of their own health [33].

Smart cities: By combining traffic management systems, digital infrastructure, and networked sensors, urban settings become more responsive and efficient [34]. The digitization of physical places has enormous potential for minimizing energy usage and improving public safety.

Augmented reality (AR) and virtual reality (VR): Digital information overlays the real environment, blurring the distinction between the two. AR applications improve our perception of actual settings, but VR produces immersive digital experiences that alter industries such as education, entertainment, and even medical training [35].

5.1.13 Challenges and Opportunities: Navigating the New Landscape

While the confluence of physical and digital systems gives enormous benefits, it also poses issues that require careful consideration.

Cybersecurity: Increased connection presents vulnerabilities to cyberattacks, endangering key infrastructure, personal data, and even physical safety. Robust security mechanisms and ethical frameworks are essential for navigating this digital war [32].

Privacy concerns: The massive volume of data acquired by networked devices raises concerns about privacy infringement and the exploitation of personal information. Transparent data governance procedures and individual control over data utilization are critical for fostering trust and ethical growth.

The digital divide must be bridged in order for everyone to reap the benefits of convergence. Bridging the digital gap through infrastructure development, education, and skill training is critical for preventing additional socioeconomic inequities.

5.1.14 A Look into the Future: Evolving Together

The convergence of physical and digital systems is a continuous evolutionary process, rather than a single event. As technology improves, the distinction between the two worlds will become increasingly blurred, resulting in more complex and transformational applications.

Imagine smart cities that adapt in real time to changing requirements, self-driving automobiles that navigate dynamic metropolitan landscapes, and medical implants that continually monitor and optimize body systems. These are not distant apocalyptic visions, but probable realities on the horizon as the physical and digital worlds become increasingly intertwined.

5.1.15 Key Contributions of this Chapter

This chapter delves deeply into Industries 4.0 and 5.0, highlighting the critical role of new technologies and their consequences for reshaping the industrial environment. The conversation focuses on many aspects of these industrial revolutions, such as the integration of digital technology and the transition to a human-centric, sustainable manufacturing paradigm. Here are the main contributions of this chapter:

i. The chapter began by describing the transition from Industry 4.0's digitized and networked world to Industry 5.0's collaborative, human-centered approach.
ii. It stresses that Industry 5.0 is not a replacement, but rather an enhancement and extension of Industry 4.0's digital breakthroughs, with a renewed emphasis on customization and sustainability.
iii. This chapter makes a significant addition to the literature by explaining the roles of new technologies such as AI, ML, big data, blockchain, and the IoT in Industries 4.0 and 5.0.
iv. It emphasizes how new technologies drive efficiency, innovation, and change in industrial processes, while simultaneously addressing the problems and ethical concerns they raise.
v. The chapter explores blockchain's potential for increasing trust and security in industrial transactions and data management.
vi. It investigates applications such as supply chain transparency, quality assurance, and the facilitation of smart contracts.
vii. Finally, this chapter helps to provide a full grasp of Industries 4.0 and 5.0. It focuses on the transformational influence of new technology while also taking into account the problems and ethical concerns that arise. The insights presented here are critical for anybody trying to understand current trends and future directions in industrial growth, laying the groundwork for further inquiry and invention in these dynamic and developing domains.

5.1.16 Chapter Structure

The remainder of the chapter is divided into a further nine sections; Section 5.2 discuss cybersecurity threats and vulnerabilities in Industries 4.0 and 5.0. Data privacy in industrial applications: balancing progress with protection is discussed in Section 5.3. Emerging technologies and their implications: AI and machine learning in Industries 4.0 and 5.0 are discussed in Section 5.4. Section 5.5 discusses the emerging technologies and their implications: blockchain for enhanced security and trust in Industries 4.0 and 5.0. Section 5.6 discusses emerging technologies and their implications, while lessons learnt from the chapter are discussed in Section 5.7. Key findings from the chapter are discussed in Section 5.8. Future trends are discussed in Section 5.9, while Section 5.10 concludes the chapter.

5.2 CYBERSECURITY THREATS AND VULNERABILITIES IN INDUSTRIES 4.0 AND 5.0

Industry 4.0 and Industry 5.0 have transformed the industrial landscape by integrating cutting-edge technologies like the Internet of Things (IoT), artificial intelligence (AI), big data analytics, and cloud computing into manufacturing and production processes [36]. While these innovations provide unparalleled efficiency, customization, and automation, they also greatly increase cybersecurity concerns. This section presents an overview of the cybersecurity risks and vulnerabilities that exist in Industries 4.0 and 5.0, emphasizing the challenges of safeguarding industrial systems in an increasingly linked world. The industrial environment is experiencing a fundamental transformation. Industry 4.0, powered by cyber-physical systems, big data, and artificial intelligence, promises to revolutionize efficiency and automation. However, this linked environment creates a terrifying new frontier for hackers, with vulnerabilities and risks lurking in the shadows of every connected device and system. Understanding these cybersecurity problems is becoming increasingly important as we get closer to Industry 5.0, which emphasizes human-centric collaboration and sustainability. This thorough introduction looks into the intricate web of vulnerabilities, examines the changing threat picture, and proposes alternative risk-mitigation and resilience-building solutions in these revolutionary industrial times.

5.2.1 The Fabric of Industry 4.0: A Landscape of Interconnected Vulnerabilities

Industry 4.0 is distinguished by its hyperconnectivity. Industrial Internet of Things (IIoT) devices, sensors, and machines exchange real-time information, eroding the distinction between the physical and digital worlds. This interconnection, while facilitating automation and data-driven decision-making, also offers a large attack surface with several possible entry points for malevolent actors [37]. Industries 4.0 and 5.0 reflect a move from traditional production to a more linked, digitalized, and automated world. Cyber-physical systems (CPS), which combine physical processes with digital control systems, are at the heart of this shift. These systems improve operational efficiency while also exposing industrial surroundings to cyber risks formerly exclusive to the digital world.

5.2.1.1 Key Technological Components and Their Vulnerabilities

Internet of Things (IoT): IoT devices, which are critical in Industry 4.0 for data gathering and sharing, sometimes lack strong security, making them ideal targets for cyber-attacks.

Cloud computing: Businesses are increasingly relying on cloud services for data storage and processing. While cloud systems provide scalability and flexibility, they also bring weaknesses in data privacy and security.

Artificial intelligence and machine learning: AI and ML systems, which are critical for predictive maintenance and process optimization, can be compromised by manipulated data inputs, resulting in incorrect decision-making.

Big data: The vast amount of data collected and processed in these businesses makes them a desirable target for hackers. Data breaches can result in severe intellectual property theft and privacy concerns.

Network and connectivity: The widespread usage of wireless and wired networks broadens the attack surface, exposing weaknesses in communication protocols and network infrastructure.

Device vulnerabilities: Legacy equipment with obsolete software and unpatched vulnerabilities is still a serious threat. Outdated firmware in industrial control systems (ICS) can be used to obtain unauthorized access and control vital operations.

Software vulnerabilities: Bugs and security weaknesses in SCADA systems, HMIs, and other industrial software can serve as backdoors for attackers.

Network vulnerabilities: Insecure network protocols, misconfigured firewalls, and ineffective authentication techniques make vital data and systems vulnerable to man-in-the-middle assaults, denial-of-service attacks, and data breaches.

Insider threats: Disgruntled workers or hostile actors with valid access can inflict major harm through deliberate data modification, sabotage, or illegal access.

5.2.1.2 The Changing Threat Landscape: Traditional Attacks to Advanced Threats

Cybercriminals are continually evolving their strategies, taking advantage of the specific vulnerabilities of Industry 4.0 environments. Some of the most common risks are:

Targeted attacks: Nation-states and sophisticated criminal groups are increasingly focused on high-value targets for industrial espionage, sabotage, and critical infrastructure disruption.

Ransomware: Attacks on vital systems such as electricity grids and manufacturing facilities can cripple operations and demand excessive ransoms, resulting in considerable economic and societal damage.

AI-driven assaults: As AI becomes increasingly common in industrial processes, attackers might use it to launch sophisticated assaults, alter algorithms, and exploit AI system flaws.

Supply chain attacks: Targeting weaknesses in software or hardware supply chains can jeopardize whole ecosystems, affecting several enterprises and sectors.

5.2.1.3 Human Factor: The Weakest Link in the Chain

Beyond technology weaknesses, human factors play an important role in cybersecurity concerns. Personnel lack of knowledge, insufficient training in secure procedures, and social engineering approaches can all be used to acquire access and compromise systems [38].

5.2.1.4 Navigating the Storm: Building Resilience in Industry 4.0 and Beyond

Mitigating these dangers and establishing resilience in Industry 4.0 and 5.0 calls for a multilayered approach:

Implementing comprehensive cybersecurity frameworks, such as the NIST Cybersecurity Framework or ISO 27001, provides an organized way to identifying, assessing, and managing cybersecurity risks.

Patch management: Proactive patching of software and firmware vulnerabilities is critical to preventing attackers from exploiting known flaws.

Segmentation and access control: Implementing network segmentation and rigorous access control measures reduces the attack surface and prevents unauthorized access to key systems.

Security awareness and training: Educating personnel on cybersecurity best practices, phishing schemes, and social engineering techniques enhances awareness and lowers the risk of human error.

Threat intelligence and monitoring: Continuously monitoring systems for suspicious behavior and utilizing threat intelligence feeds gives early warning of prospective assaults and allows for proactive security methods.

5.2.2 Case Studies of Security Breaches in Industries 4.0 and 5.0: A Landscape of Growing Risk

The interconnected nature of Industries 4.0 and 5.0, characterized by automation, data exchange, and cyber-physical systems, presents a fertile ground for cyberattacks [39]. While these advancements offer unparalleled efficiency and productivity, they also create an expanded attack surface and new vulnerabilities. This report examines specific case studies of security breaches in these industries, highlighting the evolving threats, potential impacts, and lessons learned.

Case Study 1: NotPetya Ransomware Attack on Maersk (2017)

i. **Target:** Maersk, a global shipping giant, heavily reliant on Industry 4.0 technologies like connected containers and automated port systems.
ii. **Attack:** The NotPetya ransomware exploited vulnerabilities in outdated software and infected Maersk's IT systems, disrupting port operations, freezing cargo deliveries, and causing financial losses exceeding $300 million.
iii. **Impact:** This attack demonstrated the ripple effect of cyberattacks in interconnected ecosystems, highlighting the dependence of global supply chains on secure digital infrastructure.
iv. **Lessons Learned:** The importance of patching outdated software, implementing robust cyber hygiene practices, and diversifying IT systems to minimize the impact of future attacks.

Case Study 2: Supply Chain Attack on SolarWinds (2020)

i. **Target:** SolarWinds, a software provider for critical infrastructure, including energy grids and government agencies.
ii. **Attack:** Hackers compromised SolarWinds' Orion software supply chain, injecting backdoor code that allowed them to infiltrate systems of numerous customers worldwide, including Fortune 500 companies and government agencies.
iii. **Impact:** This attack highlighted the vulnerability of supply chains in Industry 4.0 environments and the potential for widespread damage through targeted compromise of critical infrastructure.
iv. **Lessons Learned:** The need for robust supply chain security measures, including code signing, vulnerability assessments, and increased transparency within the software development and distribution ecosystem.

Case Study 3: AI-Powered Phishing Attack on Tesla (2022)

i. **Target:** Tesla, a pioneer in electric vehicles and autonomous driving technology, heavily reliant on AI and data-driven systems.
ii. **Attack:** Deepfakes and impersonation techniques were used to create synthetic voicemails and emails, targeting Tesla employees to gain access to sensitive data and potentially disrupt operations.
iii. **Impact:** This case highlights the emerging threat of AI-powered social engineering attacks, targeting knowledge workers and exploiting the vulnerabilities of human trust in AI-generated content.
iv. **Lessons Learned:** The need for employee awareness training, robust authentication measures, and continuous monitoring of AI systems to detect and mitigate fraudulent activities.

5.2.2.1 Emerging Threats in Industries 4.0 and 5.0

i. **Ransomware attacks targeting industrial control systems (ICS)** can disrupt critical infrastructure and cause widespread economic and societal harm.
ii. **Zero-day attacks** exploiting unknown vulnerabilities in connected devices and software pose a significant challenge for traditional security measures.
iii. **Social engineering tactics** targeted at employees with access to critical systems pose a growing threat, especially when combined with AI-powered manipulation techniques.
iv. **Vulnerable supply chains** within complex manufacturing and software ecosystems can be exploited to compromise entire networks and cause widespread damage.

Recommendations for Mitigating Security Risks

i. **Implement a comprehensive cybersecurity framework:** Employing established frameworks like NIST Cybersecurity Framework or ISO 27001 provides a structured approach to identify, assess, and manage risks.
ii. **Prioritize patch management:** Proactively patch vulnerabilities in software and firmware to prevent attackers from exploiting known weaknesses.
iii. **Segment networks and enforce access control:** Minimize the attack surface by segmenting networks and implementing strict access control mechanisms to limit unauthorized access to critical systems.
iv. **Educate and train employees:** Raise awareness among personnel about cybersecurity best practices, phishing scams, and social engineering tactics to reduce the risk of human error.
v. **Monitor systems for suspicious activity:** Continuously monitor systems for anomalies and suspicious behavior to detect potential attacks early and take proactive measures.
vi. **Collaborate and share information:** Share threat intelligence and best practices across industries and government agencies to foster collaboration and strengthen collective defenses.

5.3 DATA PRIVACY IN INDUSTRIAL APPLICATIONS: BALANCING PROGRESS WITH PROTECTION

The rise of Industries 4.0 and 5.0, characterized by hyper-connectivity, data-driven decision-making, and intelligent automation, is revolutionizing industrial landscapes. Sensors embedded in every stage of production, interconnected machines exchanging data, and real-time monitoring powered by AI generate vast amounts of valuable data [40]. While these data promise efficiency gains, improved product quality, and predictive maintenance capabilities, they also raise crucial concerns about data privacy in industrial applications. Navigating this intricate landscape requires a balanced approach, maximizing the benefits of data-driven technologies while upholding individual privacy rights and building trust in these transformative applications.

5.3.1 Unlocking Value: The Power of Industrial Data

The data generated in industrial applications provide a wealth of insights for optimizing processes, identifying inefficiencies, and predicting potential issues. Real-time access to data enables quick adjustments to production parameters, optimizes resource utilization, and facilitates predictive maintenance, minimizing downtime and maximizing productivity [41]. Advanced analytics can identify patterns and trends within the data, revealing hidden inefficiencies and suggesting targeted improvements across the entire production chain. Moreover, these data can be used to personalize products and services to individual customer needs, creating innovative business models and enhancing customer satisfaction.

5.3.2 The Shadow Side: Privacy Concerns in the Industrial Realm

While the potential of data-driven technologies is undeniable, concerns regarding data privacy are equally significant. Industrial data often contain sensitive information, including employee IDs, location data, production parameters, and even intellectual property secrets. Improper collection, storage, or use of these data can lead to various privacy violations:

i. **Employee Surveillance:** Tracking employee movements, monitoring productivity, and analyzing communication patterns can intrude upon individual privacy and create an oppressive work environment.
ii. **Data Breaches and Misuse:** Industrial systems are increasingly targeted by cybercriminals, and data breaches can expose sensitive information, potentially leading to identity theft, financial losses, and reputational damage for individuals and organizations.
iii. **Algorithmic Bias and Discrimination:** Unconscious biases embedded in algorithms used for decision-making within industrial processes can lead to discriminatory outcomes, impacting individual opportunities and perpetuating social inequalities.

5.3.3 Striving for Harmony: Building a Framework for Data Privacy in Industrial Applications

Finding a balance between utilizing the value of industrial data and protecting individual privacy requires a multipronged approach:

i. **Transparency and Control:** Organizations must be transparent about their data collection practices, inform individuals about how their data are used, and provide mechanisms for individuals to access, rectify, and erase their data.
ii. **Data Minimization and Anonymization:** Collecting only the minimum data necessary for specific purposes and anonymizing data whenever possible can reduce the risk of privacy violations and minimize the potential harm in case of a data breach.

iii. **Secure Data Storage and Management:** Implementing robust cybersecurity measures, including encryption, access control, and regular vulnerability assessments, is crucial for protecting sensitive data from unauthorized access and malicious attacks.
iv. **Privacy-Enhancing Technologies (PETs):** Utilizing technologies like homomorphic encryption, secure multiparty computation, and differential privacy enables data analysis without revealing individual information, ensuring both insights and privacy protection.
v. **Collaboration and Education:** Fostering collaboration and information sharing between industry stakeholders, policymakers, and privacy experts is vital for developing robust data privacy frameworks and promoting best practices across the industrial landscape.

5.3.4 The Road Ahead: Building Trust in a Data-Driven Industrial Future

Data privacy in industrial applications is not just a technical challenge; it is also a social and ethical responsibility [40]. Successfully navigating this landscape requires a shift in mindset, moving from solely focusing on data-driven optimization to prioritizing data privacy as an integral part of responsible technological development. By building trust through transparency, implementing robust privacy protections, and promoting ethical data practices, we can unlock the full potential of data-driven technologies in industries while ensuring individual privacy remains a cornerstone of our increasingly interconnected world.

5.3.5 Building Trust and Reliability in Industries 4.0 and 5.0

The advent of Industry 4.0 and the growing concept of Industry 5.0 have heralded a new era of networked, intelligent production. This transformation is distinguished by the integration of cutting-edge technologies such as the Internet of Things (IoT), artificial intelligence (AI), big data, and cyber-physical systems. While these advancements offer more efficiency, customization, and automation, they also pose substantial hurdles in establishing confidence and assuring reliability. This chapter delves into the techniques and practices required to cultivate trust and reliability in the Industry 4.0 and 5.0 landscapes. The integration of automated technologies in Industries 4.0 and 5.0 constitutes a watershed moment in production and service delivery. While new technologies offer enhanced efficiency, production, and creativity, they also present difficulties in establishing trust among stakeholders. This section digs into the methods and best practices for building confidence in the automated systems that underpin Industries 4.0 and 5.0.

5.3.6 Challenges of Trust and Reliability in Industries 4.0 and 5.0

Integration of digital technology in industrial processes presents specific challenges, as described below.

Cybersecurity risks: The networked structure of Industry 4.0 and 5.0 systems renders them vulnerable to cyber-attacks, increasing concerns about data security and system integrity.

System complexity: Advanced technologies such as AI and machine learning can be difficult to understand and forecast due to their complexity and opacity.

Data integrity and privacy: The massive volumes of data collected and used pose questions about data veracity, privacy, and ethical use.

Dependence on technology: Overreliance on automated systems might create risks in the case of a technical breakdown or malfunction.

5.3.7 Building Trust in Industries 4.0 and 5.0

To solve these difficulties, numerous trust-building strategies might be implemented:

Robust cybersecurity frameworks: Implementing sophisticated cybersecurity measures, conducting regular security audits, and using encryption technologies can help protect against cyber-attacks.

Transparency and explainability: Making AI and machine learning processes more accessible and intelligible builds confidence among users and stakeholders.

Data governance: Implementing strong data governance principles assures data integrity and privacy, instilling trust in the systems that rely on it.

Standards and regulations: Creating and adhering to industry standards and regulatory regulations can offer a foundation for dependable and ethical technology use.

Collaboration and partnerships: Working with technology suppliers, regulatory authorities, and cybersecurity specialists may help to build a culture of trust and shared accountability.

5.3.8 Ensuring Reliability in Industries 4.0 and 5.0

Reliability in these sectors may be improved by:

Resilient system design: Designing systems with built-in redundancies and fail-safes assures that they will continue to operate even in unfavorable situations.

Continuous monitoring and maintenance: Regular monitoring and predictive maintenance of systems can help to prevent breakdowns and guarantee constant operation.

Quality assurance: New technologies and systems must undergo rigorous testing and quality assurance to ensure dependability.

Training and skill development: Providing the workforce with the skills and knowledge required to operate and manage sophisticated technology efficiently.

Human-centered design: Creating technologies that prioritize human demands and usability can improve system dependability in real-world applications.

Building trust and dependability in Industries 4.0 and 5.0 is crucial for the effective implementation and optimization of these sophisticated technologies. This necessitates a multidimensional strategy that includes effective cybersecurity, transparency, resilient system design, and strong governance structures. As we go forward into a more digital and linked industrial future, adherence to these principles will be critical to realize the full promise of Industries 4.0 and 5.0 while mitigating the inherent hazards these technologies provide.

5.4 EMERGING TECHNOLOGIES AND THEIR IMPLICATIONS: AI AND MACHINE LEARNING IN INDUSTRIES 4.0 AND 5.0

The Fourth and Fifth Industrial Revolutions, known as Industry 4.0 and 5.0, are distinguished by the incorporation of digital technology into manufacturing and production processes. Artificial intelligence (AI) and machine learning (ML) are at the vanguard of these transitions, serving as not only emergent technologies but also fundamental change drivers [42]. This chapter investigates the roles and consequences of AI and machine learning in Industries 4.0 and 5.0, focusing on how they transform industrial landscapes, challenge conventional paradigms, and provide new possibilities and challenges.

5.4.1 The Roles of AI and Machine Learning in Industries 4.0 and 5.0

In Industry 4.0, AI and machine learning have played critical roles in automating and improving production processes. They evaluate massive volumes of data provided by IoT devices to improve manufacturing efficiency, predictability, and adaptability. In Industry 5.0, the emphasis turns to a more collaborative, human-centric approach, with AI and ML used not only for efficiency, but also to improve human capacities and stimulate creativity.

5.4.1.1 Key Applications for Industries 4.0 and 5.0

Predictive maintenance: AI algorithms anticipate equipment breakdowns, lowering downtime and maintenance costs.

Quality control: ML models trained on large datasets may detect and correct flaws more effectively than manual inspection.

Supply chain optimization: Artificial intelligence improves supply chain efficiency by forecasting demand, optimizing inventory, and automating procurement procedures.

Personalized production: In Industry 5.0, AI allows for large-scale customization of products to specific client preferences.

Collaborative robots (cobots): These robots collaborate with people, learning and adapting to their requirements using AI and ML.

5.4.2 Implications of AI and Machine Learning in Industrial Settings

Increased efficiency and productivity: AI and ML simplify operations, decreasing manual labor and error rates while increasing productivity.

Job transformation: While AI and ML automate mundane jobs, they also generate a demand for new skill sets in AI management and decision-making.

Data security and privacy: The reliance on data for AI and ML poses privacy issues as well as the vulnerability to cyber assaults.

Ethical and social considerations: AI systems' decision-making raises ethical concerns, notably those related to prejudice, transparency, and accountability.

Sustainability: AI and machine learning can improve resource usage, resulting in more sustainable industrial practices.

5.4.2.1 Challenges and Considerations

Integration with existing systems: Integrating AI and machine learning with legacy systems presents substantial technological obstacles.

Skill gap: There is a demand for experts who can create, run, and maintain AI and ML systems.

Establishing the dependability of AI choices and fostering confidence among users and stakeholders is critical.

Regulatory compliance: Industries must traverse a complicated regulatory framework governing AI and data use.

5.4.2.2 Future Outlook

Looking ahead, AI and ML will remain important to the advancement of Industries 4.0 and 5.0. Their responsibilities are anticipated to increase and become more complex as deep learning, neural networks, and AI-driven design improve. The future holds more collaboration between humans and machines, with AI not just augmenting human talents but also driving innovation in product design, supply chain management, and consumer contact. Table 5.2 provides a high-level comparison between the roles and characteristics of ML and AI in Industry 4.0 and Industry 5.0.

5.5 EMERGING TECHNOLOGIES AND THEIR IMPLICATIONS: BLOCKCHAIN FOR ENHANCED SECURITY AND TRUST IN INDUSTRIES 4.0 AND 5.0

As we move toward Industries 4.0 and 5.0, the convergence of modern technology and industrial processes is resulting in unparalleled efficiency and productivity. Among these technologies, blockchain stands out for its ability to profoundly change how businesses work, notably in terms of security and trust. Blockchain technology is fundamentally a decentralized, distributed ledger that records transactions across several

TABLE 5.2
Industries 4.0 and 5.0 ML and AI Characteristics

Aspect	Industry 4.0	Industry 5.0
Primary Focus	Automation and efficiency	Collaboration, personalization, and sustainability
ML/AI Applications	Predictive maintenance Quality control Supply chain optimization Process automation	Human–AI collaboration Customized production AI in ergonomics Sustainable resource management
Data Utilization	High-volume data analysis for operational efficiency	Data analysis for enhancing human–machine interaction and sustainable practices
Key Technologies	IoT, cyber-physical systems, cloud computing	IoT, advanced robotics, augmented reality, cloud computing
Challenges	Integration with legacy systems, data security, scalability	Ethical AI use, advanced AI training, human-centric design challenges
AI/ML Goals	Improve production efficiency, reduce downtime, optimize resource use	Enhance human capabilities, personalize production, promote eco-friendly practices
Workforce Impact	Job displacement in routine tasks, increased demand for AI/ML expertise	Creation of new roles focusing on AI–human collaboration, emphasis on creativity and innovation
Cybersecurity Focus	Protecting industrial automation systems and data integrity	Securing collaborative systems and sensitive personalization data
Innovation Drivers	Technological advancements in automation and data processing	Technological advancements combined with human ingenuity and ethical considerations

computers in such a way that the registered transactions cannot be changed retrospectively. This technology, which supports cryptocurrencies like Bitcoin, provides transparency, security, and immutability, which are extremely beneficial in industrial applications.

5.5.1 Application of Blockchain in Industry 4.0

Industry 4.0 is distinguished by the incorporation of digital technology into production processes, resulting in what is known as "smart factories." In this scenario, blockchain can play an important role.

Supply chain management: Blockchain technology can create a transparent and immutable record of products movement from manufacture to delivery, improving traceability and accountability.

Quality assurance: By monitoring components and materials, blockchain can assist to ensure quality and compliance throughout the production process.

Data security: Blockchain's decentralized design makes it highly resistant to cyber-attacks, ensuring the protection of important industrial data.

Smart contracts: These are self-executing contracts in which the terms of the agreement are directly expressed in code. In Industry 4.0, smart contracts can automate many operations, decreasing the need for middlemen.

5.5.2 Blockchain for Industry 5.0

While Industry 4.0 focuses on automation and efficiency, Industry 5.0 promotes customization, human-centeredness, and environmentally friendly practices. Blockchain's function in Industry 5.0 involves:

Customization and personalization: Blockchain can safeguard and manage client data required to customize products while maintaining privacy and trust.

Cooperation: Blockchain enables safe and transparent cooperation among many stakeholders, such as customers, manufacturers, and suppliers.

Sustainability tracking: Blockchain may be used to verify sustainable practices and ethical material procurement, which increases customer confidence.

5.5.3 Challenges and Considerations

Despite its potential, the integration of blockchain in industrial processes is not without hurdles.

Scalability: Blockchain networks may experience scalability challenges, particularly when managing huge quantities of transactions effectively.

Integration with existing systems: Integrating blockchain into existing industrial systems and standards may be difficult and expensive.

Regulatory compliance: Understanding the regulatory landscape, particularly in industries with strict data protection rules, is critical for blockchain applications.

Energy consumption: Some blockchain implementations, particularly those based on proof-of-work consensus algorithms, are energy-intensive.

The future of blockchain in Industries 4.0 and 5.0 is bright, with continuous developments resolving present restrictions. More energy-efficient consensus processes, improved scaling solutions, and more comprehensive integration tools are on the way. As these developments become reality, blockchain's role in establishing safe, transparent, and efficient industrial ecosystems is set to expand enormously.

Blockchain technology has the ability to transform companies in the era of Industries 4.0 and 5.0 by providing increased security, transparency, and trust [43]. Its applications in supply chain management, quality assurance, data security, and other areas can help modern enterprises overcome some of their most pressing difficulties

[44]. While there remain obstacles to mainstream acceptance, ongoing developments in this technology pave the way for its vital position in the future of industrial operations. As companies progress toward more interconnected, sustainable, and human-centric models, blockchain is a vital technology in accomplishing these aims.

5.6 EMERGING TECHNOLOGIES AND THEIR IMPLICATIONS: THE ROLE OF BIG DATA AND ANALYTICS IN INDUSTRIES 4.0 AND 5.0

The progress of Industry 4.0 and the early stages of Industry 5.0 are inextricably tied to the rise of new technologies, particularly big data and analytics. These technologies are critical in ushering traditional production into a new era marked by efficiency, customization, and sustainability. This section investigates the roles of big data and analytics in Industries 4.0 and 5.0, including their consequences, problems, and future possibilities.

5.6.1 The Rise of Big Data and Analytics

Big data refers to the massive amounts of data created by a variety of sources, including IoT devices, sensors, and online transactions. When combined with analytics, the capacity to analyze and evaluate data, big data becomes a powerful tool for insights and decision-making. This combination is transforming industries by allowing for more informed, data-driven decisions.

5.6.2 Role in Industry 4.0

Big data and analytics play a critical role in Industry 4.0, which combines digital technology with conventional industrial methods. Predictive maintenance uses analytics to forecast equipment breakdowns before they occur, decreasing downtime and saving money. Big data allows for more effective and responsive supply chain management by forecasting demand, managing stock levels, and spotting possible interruptions.

5.6.3 Expansion to Industry 5.0

Industry 5.0 signifies a transition toward a more human-centric strategy that emphasizes customization, sustainability, and automation. Here, big data and analytics play a separate yet crucial role:

Customization and personalization: Analytics enables product customization to fit specific consumer preferences by evaluating customer data and feedback.

Human–machine collaboration: Data-driven insights can help designers create more effective human–machine interfaces and collaboration models.

Sustainable operations: Analytics promotes sustainability by improving resource consumption and decreasing waste via efficient process design.

Big data and analytics are crucial to the changes of Industries 4.0 and 5.0. Their capacity to convert massive volumes of data into useful insights is helping companies become more efficient, adaptable, and customer-centric [45,46]. As we progress through these industrial revolutions, big data and analytics will play an increasingly important role in driving innovation, efficiency, and sustainability in the industry. The success of this trip, however, is dependent on overcoming the obstacles of data management, security, and talent development.

5.7 LESSONS LEARNT FROM THIS CHAPTER

The lessons learnt in this chapter emphasize the significance of a comprehensive strategy to managing security, privacy, and trust in Industries 4.0 and 5.0. The use of modern technology provides tremendous benefits while also introducing difficult obstacles that must be properly addressed. Understanding these lessons allows industry to better prepare for these difficulties, creating a safe, private, and trustworthy environment for all stakeholders. The key lessons learned are outlined below:

1. The huge volumes of data created and used in Industries 4.0 and 5.0 raise privacy issues, particularly about how it is kept, processed, and shared.
2. Trust is fundamental to the connection between industries and its stakeholders, which include consumers, workers, and partners.
3. While connection in Industries 4.0 and 5.0 provides several benefits, it also introduces dangers, since a breach in one section of the network might affect the entire system.
4. AI, IoT, and blockchain technologies provide both security and privacy benefits.
5. Cyber dangers in Industries 4.0 and 5.0 are continually changing, necessitating adaptable and proactive security solutions.
6. The human element is still an important role in security and privacy, both as a possible risk (e.g., human error) and a solution (e.g., awareness and training).

5.8 KEY FINDINGS FROM THE CHAPTER

These significant findings highlight the difficulties and interdependence of security, privacy, and trust in the context of Industries 4.0 and 5.0. They emphasize the importance of taking an integrated, proactive, and collaborative approach to navigating the obstacles posed by today's sophisticated technology world. Understanding and utilizing these results is critical for firms to prosper in this ever-changing industrial environment while being secure and responsible. The following are the key findings of this chapter:

1. Human factors have a tremendous impact on security and privacy. Regular training and awareness initiatives are required to reduce risks associated with human error and to improve the overall security culture inside enterprises.

2. Trust is an important factor in the interaction between industries and their stakeholders. Transparency, ethical use of technology, and constant stakeholder involvement are critical to establishing and keeping confidence.
3. Addressing the difficulties of security, privacy, and trust in Industries 4.0 and 5.0 necessitates a joint effort. Sharing knowledge, best practices, and working toward shared standards will help us solve these difficulties more effectively.
4. Cyber dangers in these businesses are more sophisticated and widespread. To combat these increasing threats, cybersecurity tactics must be constantly updated and the most up-to-date technologies implemented.

5.9 FUTURE TRENDS

The future trends in security, privacy, and trust in Industries 4.0 and 5.0 hint toward an era of more intelligent, proactive, and integrated methods. These patterns highlight the need for ongoing innovation, collaboration, and adaptability in the face of changing technology environments and increasing dangers. As industries evolve, staying ahead in these areas will be critical for preserving resilience, trustworthiness, and a competitive edge.

The possible rise of quantum computing may cause substantial changes in the cybersecurity environment. While it provides improved processing capacity, it may also provide new obstacles to data encryption and security methods.

Future trends point to an increased usage of artificial intelligence (AI) and machine learning (ML) in cybersecurity. These technologies will be critical for anticipating and mitigating cyber-attacks, improving real-time security monitoring, and automating response tactics.

As data privacy concerns rise, the research and use of privacy-enhancing technologies (PETs) are expected to become increasingly common. These technologies will seek to enable data processing and analytics while maintaining individual privacy.

The use of blockchain technology is likely to grow, with decentralized security models that guarantee transparency, immutability, and resistance to manipulation and fraud.

5.10 CONCLUSION

Industries 4.0 and 5.0 usher in a new era of tremendous technological innovation, with promises of automation, hyperconnectivity, and the merger of human and artificial intelligence. However, along with this enthusiasm, there is a complex web of obstacles, including concerns about security, privacy, trust, and the real human cost of advancement. To traverse this terrain, we must take a comprehensive approach that encourages responsible innovation while ensuring that benefits are distributed equitably. Building safe and resilient systems is critical. Robust cyber defenses, strict data governance, and privacy-enhancing technologies are essential for protecting sensitive information and preventing bad actors from exploiting weaknesses. We must go beyond only data protection to ensure individual autonomy and control over their personal information.

Building confidence in technology necessitates openness and accountability. Explainable AI systems that simplify decision-making processes are critical for reducing worries of bias and prejudice. Human monitoring and control systems must be in place to ensure that AI serves our ideals rather than the opposite. This chapter shed light on the issues of security, privacy, and trust in the context of Industries 4.0 and 5.0. It provided a deep grasp of the problems faced by developing technology and detailed solutions for avoiding risks while maximizing rewards. As industries expand, the ideas and experiences learned from this chapter will be useful in directing future improvements, ensuring that industrial sectors thrive and innovate in a secure, responsible, and sustainable manner.

The success of Industries 4.0 and 5.0 is dependent on our capacity to face these issues straight on. By putting security, privacy, trust, ethics, and social responsibility first, we can harness the power of technology for good, creating a more inclusive, wealthy, and truly human-centered future. This is more than a technological undertaking; it is also a social and ethical necessity that necessitates collaboration across disciplines, industries, and countries. In this collaborative attitude, we can traverse the crossroads of innovation and responsibility, ensuring that Industries 4.0 and 5.0 lead to a brighter future for everybody.

REFERENCES

[1] K. Zhang, Y. Shi, S. Karnouskos, T. Sauter, H. Fang, & A. W. Colombo. Advancements in industrial cyber-physical systems: An overview and perspectives. *IEEE Transactions on Industrial Informatics*, 2022. *19*(1), 716–729.

[2] J. E. Agolla. Human capital in the smart manufacturing and industry 4.0 revolution. *Digital Transformation in Smart Manufacturing*, 2018. (2), 41–58.

[3] P. A. Schulte, J. M. Streit, F. Sheriff, G. Delclos, S. A. Felknor, S. L. Tamers, ... & R. Sala. Potential scenarios and hazards in the work of the future: A systematic review of the peer-reviewed and gray literatures. *Annals of Work Exposures and Health*, 2020. 64(8), 786–816.

[4] H. ElMaraghy, L. Monostori, G. Schuh, & W. ElMaraghy. Evolution and future of manufacturing systems. *CIRP Annals*, 2021. 70(2), 635–658.

[5] C. Schlick, V. Stich, R. Schmitt, G. Schuh, M. Ziefle, C. Brecher, ... & C. Schlick. Cognition-enhanced, self-optimizing production networks. In *Integrative Production Technology: Theory and Applications* (pp. 645–743). Cham: Springer International Publishing. 2017.

[6] H. Xu, W. Yu, D. Griffith, & N. Golmie. A survey on industrial Internet of Things: A cyber-physical systems perspective. *IEEE Access*, 2018. 6, 78238–78259.

[7] Y. J. Lin, C. B, Lan, & C. Y. Huang. A realization of cyber-physical manufacturing control system through Industrial Internet of Things. *Procedia Manufacturing*, 2019. 39, 287–293.

[8] J. Wang, C. Xu, J. Zhang, & R. Zhong. Big data analytics for intelligent manufacturing systems: A review. *Journal of Manufacturing Systems*, 2022. 62, 738–752.

[9] A. Carlsen. A self-assessment model for intelligent predictive maintenance analytics: An update of the Analyses Module in the Maintenance Baseline Study *(Master's thesis, University of Stavanger, Norway)*. 2020

[10] J. B. Awotunde, A. E. Adeniyi, R. O. Ogundokun, G. J. Ajamu, & P. O. Adebayo. MIoT-based big data analytics architecture, opportunities and challenges for

enhanced telemedicine systems. *Enhanced Telemedicine and e-Health: Advanced IoT Enabled Soft Computing Framework*, 2021. vol 410. Springer, Cham. 199–220. https://doi.org/10.1007/978-3-030-70111-6_10

[11] M. H. Jarrahi. Artificial intelligence and the future of work: Human-AI symbiosis in organizational decision making. *Business Horizons*, 2018. 61(4), 577–586.

[12] Z. Su, G. Togay, & A. M. Côté. Artificial intelligence: A destructive and yet creative force in the skilled labour market. *Human Resource Development International*, 2021. 24(3), 341–352.

[13] A. Singh, & T. Chouhan. Artificial Intelligence in HRM: Role of emotional–social intelligence and future work skill. In *The Adoption and Effect of Artificial Intelligence on Human Resources Management, Part A* (pp. 175–196). Emerald Publishing Limited. 2023. https://doi.org/10.1108/978-1-80382-027-920231009

[14] M. Abdulraheem, E. A. Adeniyi, J. B. Awotunde, A. L. Imoize, R. G. Jimoh, I. D. Oladipo, & P. B. Falola. Artificial intelligence of medical things for medical information systems privacy and security. In *Handbook of Security and Privacy of AI-Enabled Healthcare Systems and Internet of Medical Things* (pp. 63–96). CRC Press, Boca Raton. 2024.

[15] S. Atif. Analysing the alignment between circular economy and industry 4.0 nexus with industry 5.0 era: An integrative systematic literature review. *Sustainable Development*, 2023. *31*(4), 2155–2175.

[16] M. K. Abiodun, J. B. Awotunde, R. O. Ogundokun, E. A. Adeniyi, & M. O. Arowolo. Security and information assurance for IoT-based big data. In *Artificial Intelligence for Cyber Security: Methods, Issues and Possible Horizons or Opportunities* (pp. 189–211). Cham: Springer International Publishing. 2021.

[17] J. Fiksel, & J. R. Fiksel. *Resilient by design: Creating businesses that adapt and flourish in a changing world.* Island Press. 2015.

[18] J. B. Awotunde, S. O. Folorunso, R. G. Jimoh, E. A. Adeniyi, K. M. Abiodun, & G. J. Ajamu. Application of artificial intelligence for COVID-19 epidemic: an exploratory study, opportunities, challenges, and future prospects. *Artificial Intelligence for COVID-19*, 2021, vol 358. Springer, Cham. 47–61. https://doi.org/10.1007/978-3-030-69744-0_4

[19] I. P. Pradhan, & P. Saxena. Reskilling workforce for the Artificial Intelligence age: Challenges and the way forward. In *The Adoption and Effect of Artificial Intelligence on Human Resources Management, Part B* (pp. 181–197). Emerald Publishing Limited. 2023.

[20] M. AbdulRaheem, J. B.. Awotunde, C. Chakraborty, E. A. Adeniyi, I. D. Oladipo, & A. K. Bhoi. Security and privacy concerns in smart healthcare system. In *Implementation of Smart Healthcare Systems using AI, IoT, and Blockchain* (pp. 243–273). Academic Press. 2023.

[21] A. Bousdekis, K. Lepenioti, D. Apostolou, & G. Mentzas. A review of data-driven decision-making methods for industry 4.0 maintenance applications. *Electronics*, 2021. 10(7), 828.

[22] C. Li, Y. Chen, & Y. Shang. A review of industrial big data for decision making in intelligent manufacturing. *Engineering Science and Technology, An International Journal*, 2022. 29, 101021.

[23] M. R. Blagojević, & A. Tufegdžić. The new technology era requirements and sustainable approach to industrial heritage renewal. *Energy and Buildings*, 2016. 115, 148–153.

[24] I. Moll. The myth of the fourth industrial revolution. *Theoria*, 2021. 68(167), 1–38.

[25] G. Edison. Transforming medical decision-making: A comprehensive review of AI's impact on diagnostics and treatment. *BULLET: Jurnal Multidisiplin Ilmu*, 2023. 2(4), 1121–1133.

[26] S. Nahavandi. Industry 5.0—A human-centric solution. *Sustainability*, 2019. 11(16), 4371.

[27] F. Longo, A. Padovano, & S. Umbrello. Value-oriented and ethical technology engineering in industry 5.0: A human-centric perspective for the design of the factory of the future. *Applied Sciences*, 2020. 10(12), 4182.

[28] P. K. R. Maddikunta, Q. V. Pham, B. Prabadevi, N. Deepa, K. Dev, T. R. Gadekallu, ... & M. Liyanage. Industry 5.0: A survey on enabling technologies and potential applications. *Journal of Industrial Information Integration*, 2022. 26, 100257.

[29] O. Vermesan, & P. Friess. *Digitising the Industry Internet of Things connecting the physical, digital and virtual worlds*. CRC Press. 2022.

[30] J. B. Awotunde, A. E. Adeniyi, S. A. Ajagbe, & A. González-Briones. Natural computing and unsupervised learning methods in smart healthcare data-centric operations. In *Cognitive and Soft Computing Techniques for the Analysis of Healthcare Data* (pp. 165–190). Academic Press, Sciencedirect. 2022

[31] W. Cao, H. Bu, M. Vinet, M. Cao, S. Takagi, S. Hwang,... & K. Banerjee. The future transistors. *Nature*, 2023. 620(7974), 501–515.

[32] B. Gbadamosi, R. O. Ogundokun, E. A. Adeniyi, S. Misra, & N. F. Stephens. Medical data analysis for IoT-based datasets in the cloud using Naïve Bayes classifier for prediction of heart disease. In *New Frontiers in Cloud Computing and Internet of Things* (pp. 365–386). Cham: Springer International Publishing. 2022.

[33] R. O. Ogundokun, J. B. Awotunde, E. A. Adeniyi, & S. Misra. Application of the Internet of Things (IoT) to fight the COVID-19 pandemic. In *Intelligent Internet of Things for Healthcare and Industry* (pp. 83–103). Cham: Springer International Publishing. 2022.

[34] M. AbdulRaheem, J. B. Awotunde, C. Chakraborty, E. A. Adeniyi, I. D. Oladipo, & A. K. Bhoi. Security and privacy concerns in smart healthcare system. In *Implementation of Smart Healthcare Systems using AI, IoT, and Blockchain* (pp. 243–273). Academic Press, Sciencedirect. 2023.

[35] A. E. Adeniyi, M. Olagunju, J. B. Awotunde, M. K. Abiodun, J. Awokola, & M. O. Lawrence. Augmented intelligence multilingual conversational service for smart enterprise management software. In *International Conference on Computational Science and Its Applications* (pp. 476–488). Cham: Springer International Publishing. 2022.

[36] K. M. Abiodun, E. A. Adeniyi, J. B. Awotunde, C. Chakraborty, D. R. Aremu, A. A. Adebiyi, & M. O. Adebiyi. Blockchain and Internet of Things in healthcare systems: Prospects, issues, and challenges. *In Digital Health Transformation with Blockchain and Artificial Intelligence* (pp. 1–22). CRC Press, Taylors and Francis. 2022.

[37] M. Nankya, R. Chataut, & R. Akl. Securing industrial control systems: Components, cyber threats, and machine learning-driven defense strategies. *Sensors*, 2023, 23(21), 8840.

[38] I. Momoh, G. Adelaja, & G. Ejiwumi. Analysis of the Human Factor in Cybersecurity: Identifying and Preventing Social Engineering Attacks in Financial Institution. 2023.

[39] V. Liagkou, C. Stylios, L. Pappa, & A. Petunin. Challenges and opportunities in industry 4.0 for mechatronics, artificial intelligence and cybernetics. *Electronics,* 2021. 10(16), 2001.

[40] A. E. Adeniyi, R. G. Jimoh, & J. Awotunde. A Review on Elliptic Curve Cryptography Algorithm for Internet of Things: Categorization, Application Areas, and Security. Application Areas, and Security. 2024.

[41] J. Lee, J. Ni, J. Singh, B. Jiang, M. Azamfar, & J. Feng. Intelligent maintenance systems and predictive manufacturing. *Journal of Manufacturing Science and Engineering*, 2022. 142(11), 110805.

[42] V. Biagini, M. Subasic, A. Oudalov, & J. Kreusel. The autonomous grid: Automation, intelligence and the future of power systems. *Energy Research & Social Science*, 2020. 65, 101460.

[43] J. B. Awotunde, R. O. Ogundokun, S. Misra, E. A. Adeniyi, & M. M. Sharma. Blockchain-based framework for secure transaction in mobile banking platform. In Hybrid Intelligent Systems: *20th International Conference on Hybrid Intelligent Systems*, Springer International Publishing (pp. 525–534). (HIS 2020), December 14-16, 2020.

[44] E. A. Adeniyi, P. B. Falola, M. S. Maashi, M. Aljebreen, & S. Bharany. Secure sensitive data sharing using RSA and ElGamal cryptographic algorithms with hash functions. *Information*, 2022. 13(10), 442.

[45] S. Aheleroff, H. Huang, X. Xu, & R. Y. Zhong. Toward sustainability and resilience with Industry 4.0 and Industry 5.0. *Frontiers in Manufacturing Technology*, 2022. 2, 951643.

[46] M. Hattinger, & K. Stylidis. Transforming Quality 4.0 towards resilient operator 5.0 needs. *Procedia CIRP*, 2023. 120, 1600–1605.

6 Fine-Tuning for a Deep Learning Model in Optimizing Ransomware Attack Detection in the Industry 4.0 and 5.0 Era

Ahmad Sanmorino, Rendra Gustriansyah, Shinta Puspasari, Joseph Bamidele Awotunde, and Demóstenes Zegarra Rodríguez

6.1 INTRODUCTION

The emergence of Industry 4.0 and its subsequent progression into Industry 5.0 has marked the onset of a fresh era of innovation and productivity within the industrial sector. These models encompass the seamless fusion of smart systems, the internet, and cutting-edge technologies, facilitating real-time data exchange and decision-making across diverse industrial operations. This transformation has led to increased productivity, reduced costs, and improved overall performance across industries. However, the widespread adoption of smart technologies has also presented unprecedented challenges, most notably in the domain of cybersecurity. Ransomware attacks have become a significant concern for various industries in the Industry 4.0 and 5.0 era [1–3]. Ransomware is a dangerous app designed to encrypt vital data and systems, rendering them inaccessible to users until a ransom is paid to the individuals responsible. These attacks have the potential to cause substantial financial damage, disrupt essential operations, and even compromise human safety, especially in industrial settings where critical infrastructure and sensitive data are at stake.

In order to reduce the severe impacts of ransomware attacks, it is crucial to create resilient and flexible detection systems. Conventional methods reliant on specific signatures frequently face challenges in keeping up with the ever-changing

DOI: 10.1201/9781003581963-6

ransomware variations and evasion strategies. Consequently, there is a growing demand for more sophisticated and efficient approaches, leading to the exploration of deep learning (DL) models for ransomware detection. DL, a subfield of AI, has witnessed significant advancements recently [4,5]. Deep NNs, particularly CNNs and RNNs, have shown remarkable effectiveness across a range of fields, such as NLP, image recognition, and anomaly detection, as evidenced in Refs. [6,7]. These models are highly proficient at autonomously acquiring intricate patterns and representations from extensive datasets, rendering them ideal for addressing intricate cybersecurity issues.

In ransomware detection, DL models have shown promising results by learning to identify unique patterns and behaviors indicative of ransomware attacks. Unlike traditional rule-based approaches, DL models can adapt and evolve their representations based on new data, making them more adept at handling novel and previously unseen ransomware strains. While DL models hold great potential, training them from scratch for ransomware detection often requires a significant amount of labeled ransomware samples, which may be scarce or challenging to obtain due to the sensitive nature of such data. Fine-tuning, a transfer learning technique, addresses this limitation by leveraging pretrained neural networks and adapting them to a target domain with limited labeled data. Transfer learning involves using the knowledge gained from a primary task to enhance performance in a related secondary task. Fine-tuning extends this concept by taking a preexisting model, usually trained on a comprehensive and varied dataset (e.g., ImageNet for image recognition), and fine-tuning its parameters using a smaller dataset of ransomware-related samples [8–10]. This process allows the model to retain the general knowledge acquired during pretraining while tailoring its representations to the specific characteristics of ransomware attacks. To achieve optimal performance in ransomware detection, several critical factors need to be considered when applying fine-tuning. In cases where there is an insufficient supply of labeled ransomware samples, techniques for data augmentation can be applied to artificially increase the size of the dataset. These techniques involve applying transformations, such as rotation, flipping, and scaling, to the existing samples, creating additional variations of the data. Such augmentation helps enhance the model's capacity to generalize to ransomware instances it hasn't encountered before. The choice of a pretrained model plays a crucial role in the success of fine-tuning. Models pretrained on tasks closely related to ransomware detection, such as malware classification or cybersecurity, are more likely to yield better results when fine-tuned for ransomware attack detection. Fine-tuning encompasses the configuration of hyperparameters, such as learning rates, batch sizes, and optimization algorithms, which influence both the model's convergence and its ability to generalize [11]. Proper hyperparameter tuning is essential to achieve the best performance. Next, we would like to submit research questions related to the discussion in the following sections.

Research Question 1:
How effective is the performance of deep learning models, specifically fine-tuned neural networks using transfer learning, in the context of ransomware detection within the industrial settings of Industries 4.0 and 5.0?

Research Question 2:
What are the key factors influencing the effectiveness of fine-tuning for ransomware detection in the context of Industries 4.0 and 5.0, and how can these factors be optimized, including the selection of pretrained models, and tuning of hyperparameters, to enhance the overall cybersecurity measures in the industrial ecosystem?

6.1.1 Key Contributions of the Chapter

Below are the notable contributions made by this chapter:

1. The chapter provides a comprehensive exploration of fine-tuning for DL models in optimizing ransomware attack detection in the context of Industries 4.0 and 5.0.
2. The chapter discuss various pretrained models suitable for ransomware detection, and proposes an optimized fine-tuning approach with data augmentation and hyperparameter tuning.
3. The chapter also evaluates the performance of fine-tuned models against traditional approaches and assesses their efficacy in detecting ransomware attacks.
4. The knowledge acquired from this chapter will play a role in improving the cybersecurity measures for Industry 4.0 and 5.0 businesses, fortifying their defenses against the growing risk of ransomware attacks.

6.1.2 Implications of This Research

Below are the implications of this research:

1. Enhanced Ransomware Detection Methodology: Academicians can incorporate the optimized fine-tuning methodology into their academic curricula, ensuring that students are exposed to cutting-edge techniques in ransomware detection. Industry professionals can apply this methodology to improve the cybersecurity measures in Industry 4.0 and 5.0 environments, leading to more robust defenses against ransomware attacks.
2. Model Selection Guidance: The comparison of various deep learning models (CNN, RNN, Faster R-CNN, LSTM) provides valuable insights into their respective strengths and weaknesses in the context of ransomware detection. This information can guide both academia and industry in selecting appropriate models based on specific requirements and constraints.
3. Performance Evaluation Metrics: The evaluation metrics presented in the study offer a comprehensive assessment of the fine-tuned models' performance. Academicians can use these metrics as benchmarks for future research, and industry professionals can leverage them to objectively evaluate and compare different ransomware detection solutions.
4. Dataset Quality Importance: The emphasis on the quality and diversity of the dataset for effective fine-tuning is a crucial takeaway. Academicians can integrate this knowledge into their discussions on dataset preparation for

machine learning projects. Industry practitioners can use this insight to ensure their datasets accurately represent the complexities of Industry 4.0 and 5.0 environments.

5. Identification of Future Research Avenues: The study identifies several future research directions, such as real-world deployment, model robustness, interpretability, adversarial testing, ensemble methods, and data balancing. Academicians can use these suggestions to guide their research agenda, while industry professionals can stay informed about potential advancements and trends in ransomware detection.
6. Collaboration Opportunities: The call for collaboration with industry partners and practitioners provides a bridge between academia and real-world application. Joint efforts can validate and refine the proposed fine-tuned models in diverse industrial settings, fostering a collaborative environment that benefits both researchers and industry professionals.
7. Practical Implementation Strategies: The recommendations for deploying and monitoring fine-tuned models in real Industry 4.0 and 5.0 environments offer practical insights for industry professionals. This information can guide the implementation process, ensuring a smooth transition from research findings to real-world application.

6.1.3 Chapter Organization

The upcoming parts of this chapter are organized in the following manner: Section 6.2 provides a brief introduction to Industries 4.0 and 5.0, addresses security issues related to ransomware attacks, and examines research related to ransomware detection utilizing deep learning and transfer learning techniques. Section 6.3 delves into the fundamentals of DL models and the concept of fine-tuning. Section 6.4 outlines the proposed methodology for fine-tuning DL models for ransomware attack detection in Industry 4.0 and 5.0 environments. Section 6.5 presents the experimental setup and evaluation metrics. In Section 6.6, the findings and discussions are showcased, and this is followed by Section 6.7, which wraps up the chapter while outlining possible avenues for future research.

6.2 RELATED WORK

6.2.1 Industries 4.0 and 5.0: A Brief Overview

Industry 4.0 and the forthcoming Industry 5.0 represent transformative paradigms in the industrial sector. This chapter provides a concise overview of these concepts, highlighting their key characteristics, technological foundations, and potential implications for the future of manufacturing and beyond. The document delves into the essential concepts at the core of Industry 4.0, including aspects like connectivity, interoperability, data analysis, and cyber-physical systems (CPS). It also introduces the nascent notion of Industry 5.0, highlighting its emphasis on production systems centered around human needs and the amalgamation of advanced technologies. This summary lays the foundation for a more profound grasp of the obstacles and possibilities linked to the ongoing industrial transformation.

The advent of Industry 4.0 and the subsequent development of Industry 5.0 have revolutionized the manufacturing sector by leveraging advanced technologies and innovative approaches. These concepts aim to transform traditional industries into highly interconnected, intelligent, and adaptive systems. Systems in Industry 4.0 involve the fusion of CPS, wherein physical components are seamlessly integrated with digital technologies. This integration facilitates real-time data exchange and empowers autonomous decision-making capabilities. This connectivity facilitates improved efficiency, flexibility, and productivity within industrial processes [12].

Industry 4.0 fosters compatibility among diverse components and systems, facilitating smooth communication and cooperation throughout various phases of the value chain. Standardization of protocols, interfaces, and data formats is vital to achieve effective integration and interoperability [13]. The abundance of data generated by interconnected systems and devices in Industry 4.0 necessitates advanced data analytics techniques for deriving meaningful insights. AI and ML algorithms are employed to process and analyze large volumes of data, enabling predictive maintenance, optimization, and intelligent decision-making [14].

Industry 5.0 builds upon the foundations of Industry 4.0 by giving significant importance to integrating both humans and machines into manufacturing systems. It focuses on harmonious collaboration between human workers and state-of-the-art technologies such as robotics, AI, and AR to leverage human creativity, problem-solving skills, and adaptability [15]. Industry 5.0 emphasizes the shift toward individualized and customer-centric manufacturing. By leveraging advanced technologies, such as additive manufacturing and flexible production systems, companies can respond to individual customer needs and produce personalized products in a cost-effective manner [16].

The adoption of Industry 4.0 and 5.0 principles enables streamlined processes, reduced waste, improved resource allocation, and enhanced productivity. Automation, data-driven decision-making, and optimized supply chains contribute to increased efficiency and competitiveness [17]. Incorporating cutting-edge advancements in Industries 4.0 and 5.0 have the potential to bring about changes in job roles and a requirement for upskilling the workforce. As routine tasks become automated, workers are required to acquire new skills, such as data analysis, system monitoring, and collaboration with intelligent machines [18].

Industries 4.0 and 5.0 represent transformative visions for the industrial sector, driven by advancements in connectivity, data analytics, AI, and human–machine collaboration. It is crucial for organizations to grasp the fundamental concepts and consequences of these models in order to navigate the ongoing industrial revolution effectively and fully exploit the emerging technologies.

6.2.2 Challenges in Ensuring Security for Industries 4.0 and 5.0

The swift embrace of Industry 4.0 and the imminent emergence of Industry 5.0 have revolutionized industrial processes, leveraging CPS and the IoT. However, these advancements have also introduced significant cybersecurity challenges. This chapter explores the key challenges faced in Industry 4.0 and anticipates potential trials in Industry 5.0. It discusses vulnerabilities, threats, and their implications, and presents potential solutions to mitigate the risks. Through effective cybersecurity measures, the transition towards Industry 4.0 and Industry 5.0 can be facilitated while ensuring the safety and security of critical industrial systems.

The integration of CPS and IoT technologies in Industry 4.0 and the forthcoming Industry 5.0 has led to interconnected industrial systems that offer increased productivity, efficiency, and automation [19]. However, this integration has also expanded the attack surface and introduced new cybersecurity challenges that must be addressed to safeguard critical infrastructure. The interconnectivity of devices, networks, and systems in Industry 4.0 presents challenges in maintaining secure communications and data exchange. The heterogeneous nature of industrial systems, comprising diverse technologies from different vendors, makes achieving seamless interoperability and standardization difficult, leading to potential security gaps [20].

The vast amounts of data generated and processed in Industry 4.0 raise concerns regarding data security and privacy. Safeguarding sensitive information from unauthorized access, data breaches, or tampering is crucial to maintaining the trust of stakeholders. Additionally, ensuring data privacy while promoting data sharing for collaborative purposes poses a complex challenge [21]. Many industrial systems and infrastructures were not originally designed with cybersecurity in mind. Retrofitting security measures onto legacy systems can be challenging due to incompatible protocols, limited resources for updates, and the risk of disrupting critical operations. Incorporating security by design principles from the early stages of system development is vital to prevent vulnerabilities [22].

Advanced persistent threats (APTs) pose a significant threat to Industry 4.0 and are expected to evolve in Industry 5.0. APTs are sophisticated, persistent, and targeted attacks aimed at infiltrating systems, stealing sensitive data, or disrupting operations. Adversaries continuously adapt their tactics to bypass traditional security measures, making it crucial to employ advanced threat intelligence and detection techniques [23]. The increasing reliance on technology and automation in Industries 4.0 and 5.0 amplifies the risk of insider threats. Individuals with ill intent from within an organization, like dissatisfied employees or contracted personnel, can misuse their authorized access to systems, undermining data integrity or causing disruptions in operations. To mitigate insider threats [24], it is crucial to enforce stringent access controls, monitor user activities, and regularly conduct employee awareness programs.

Industry 5.0 embraces advanced technologies, quantum computing emerges as both a solution and a challenge. While quantum computing offers unprecedented computational power, it also poses a threat to current encryption algorithms and cryptographic protocols. Organizations must anticipate quantum computing-related vulnerabilities and invest in quantum-safe encryption and post-quantum cryptography [25]. In the context of Industry 5.0, the AI security sector envisions a widespread application of AI algorithms for autonomous decision-making and enhancing system efficiency. However, AI models remain susceptible to adversarial attacks, in which malicious actors manipulate inputs to mislead the AI system or exploit weaknesses in AI algorithms. Developing robust AI security mechanisms, including adversarial training and explainable AI, is crucial to safeguard critical industrial processes [26].

Employing a defense-in-depth tactic, which involves the integration of various security measures like network division, intrusion detection systems, encryption, and access controls, can effectively reduce cybersecurity vulnerabilities. This strategy guarantees that in case one layer is breached, additional layers offer supplementary safeguards [27]. The utilization of security automation and AI technologies within security operations enables organizations to promptly detect and counteract cyber threats. Automated surveillance, incident management, and threat investigation can substantially boost the efficiency and effectiveness of cybersecurity defenses [28].

The transition toward Industry 4.0 and the upcoming Industry 5.0 present remarkable opportunities for industrial growth. However, these advancements bring new cybersecurity challenges that must be addressed proactively. By understanding the vulnerabilities, threats, and emerging challenges and implementing comprehensive cybersecurity strategies, organizations can secure critical industrial systems and drive the future of digitalized industries.

6.2.3 Ransomware Attacks: Threats to Industry 4.0 and 5.0 Systems

Ransomware attacks have emerged as a significant cybersecurity threat to Industry 4.0 and pose even greater risks to the forthcoming Industry 5.0. This chapter explores the growing menace of ransomware attacks, their potential impact on industrial systems, and the challenges they present in the context of Industries 4.0 and 5.0. The chapter discusses the techniques employed by ransomware attackers, their motivations, and the vulnerabilities exploited in industrial environments. It also highlights the implications of successful ransomware attacks on critical infrastructure and proposes strategies to enhance cybersecurity measures to mitigate these threats effectively.

Ransomware attacks have evolved into one of the most prevalent and damaging cyber threats, targeting organizations across various sectors, including industry (see Table 6.1). The incorporation of cyber-physical systems, the IoT, and enhanced connectivity in Industries 4.0 and 5.0 makes industrial systems more susceptible to ransomware attacks, thus requiring the implementation of strong security measures. Ransomware attacks often begin with phishing emails and social engineering tactics, tricking users into downloading malicious attachments or clicking on malicious links. This initial entry point enables the attackers to gain a foothold within the targeted industrial network [29].

Ransomware attackers frequently exploit software vulnerabilities to gain unauthorized access to industrial systems. Unpatched or outdated software, including operating systems and industrial control systems (ICS), is particularly vulnerable to these attacks [30]. Attackers leverage weak or misconfigured remote desktop protocol (RDP) connections to gain unauthorized access to industrial networks. Once inside, they can deploy ransomware payloads and encrypt critical files and systems [31].

TABLE 6.1
Ransomware Attacks in Recent Years

Attack Name	Year	Target	Impact
WannaCry	2017	Global	Affected over 200,000 systems across 150 countries
NotPetya	2017	Global	Caused widespread disruptions in various industries
Bad Rabbit	2017	Russia, Ukraine	Targeted corporate networks and critical infrastructure
SamSam	2018	United States	Targeted healthcare organizations and government agencies
Ryuk	2018	Global	Demanded high ransoms from targeted organizations
GandCrab	2018–2019	Global	Infected numerous victims through exploit kits
LockerGoga	2019	Global	Targeted industrial and manufacturing companies
Maze	2019	Global	Employed double extortion tactics against victims
Sodinokibi/REvil	2019–2021	Global	Conducted large-scale attacks on various sectors
DarkSide	2021	Colonial Pipeline (US)	Led to the shutdown of a major fuel pipeline in the US
Conti	2021	Global	Affected numerous organizations, including in the healthcare sector

Successful ransomware attacks can cause severe operational disruptions and downtime in industrial environments. Production processes may come to a halt, leading to financial losses, reputational damage, and delays in meeting customer demands [32]. In industrial systems, ransomware attacks can compromise the safety and integrity of critical processes, leading to potential physical harm, accidents, or environmental damage. For instance, a ransomware attack targeting a manufacturing plant's control systems can disrupt safety protocols and compromise worker safety [33]. Ransomware attacks targeting industrial systems can spread across interconnected supply chains, affecting multiple organizations. Such disruptions can lead to delays in product delivery, financial losses, and reputational damage for the entire supply chain ecosystem [34].

Establishing a culture of cybersecurity awareness among both employees and stakeholders is of paramount importance. Consistent training initiatives can provide personnel with knowledge regarding the dangers associated with ransomware attacks, phishing methods, and secure computing habits, thereby decreasing the chances of successful attacks [35]. Implementing regular and automated backup procedures for critical data and systems can mitigate the impact of ransomware attacks. Secure offsite backups and regularly tested recovery processes enable organizations to restore operations quickly in the event of an attack [36].

By employing robust network segmentation and access controls, the lateral movement of ransomware within industrial networks can be restricted. Restricting user privileges, segregating critical systems, and employing firewalls can reduce the attack surface and contain the spread of ransomware [37]. Frequently implementing security patches and updates for software and systems is crucial for dealing with acknowledged vulnerabilities. Carrying out regular vulnerability assessments and penetration tests can help detect and resolve potential weaknesses proactively, preventing attackers from taking advantage of them [38].

Ransomware attacks pose a significant threat to Industry 4.0 and 5.0 systems, with the potential to disrupt operations, compromise safety, and cause financial losses. It is imperative for organizations to understand the techniques employed by ransomware attackers, enhance security measures, and adopt proactive strategies to mitigate the risks effectively. By implementing robust cybersecurity practices and staying vigilant, industrial systems can withstand the growing menace of ransomware attacks.

6.2.4 DL for Ransomware Attack Detection

DL has emerged as a potent and adaptable approach for tackling intricate problems across various domains. This chapter provides an extensive overview of the core concepts and methodologies in DL. It delves into the structure and constituents of deep neural networks, the training process, and the associated challenges in DL. The chapter also examines the applications and influence of DL in diverse domains and underscores the latest advancements and future trajectories in this swiftly evolving field. DL is a subset of ML dedicated to teaching deep NNs to comprehend and depict intricate data patterns and associations. This segment introduces the concept of DL and its significance in dealing with intricate problems. DL is founded on ANNs, mathematical models influenced by the structure and operation of biological NNs. ANNs consist of interconnected layers of artificial neurons, with each neuron processing a weighted combination of inputs and using an activation function to generate an output [39].

Deep NNs are characterized by their depth, featuring multiple concealed layers situated between the input and output layers. This section delves into various kinds of deep neural network architectures, encompassing feedforward NNs, CNNs, RNNs, and GANs. BPNNs are foundational algorithms employed for the training of deep NNs, involving the iterative adjustment of network parameters guided by the gradient of the loss function with respect to the weights. This section clarifies the BPNN algorithms and their role in enhancing the network's parameters. Activation functions introduce non-linearity into deep NNs, empowering them to comprehend intricate data relationships. This section discusses prominent activation functions, such as sigmoid, ReLU, and softmax, and their impact on network performance [40]. To counteract overfitting in deep NNs, regularization techniques are employed. In this section, we delve into techniques such as L1 and L2 regularization, dropout, and batch normalization, all of which improve the overall capacity of deep models to generalize effectively.

Deep NNs can confront challenges like vanishing or exploding gradients during training, hampering the learning process. This section analyzes the origins of gradient instability and suggests techniques, including gradient clipping and normalization, to mitigate these issues. Overfitting occurs when a deep neural network excels in training data but encounters difficulties in applying its knowledge to unfamiliar data. On the other hand, underfitting signifies the network's failure to grasp fundamental data patterns. This section elucidates approaches such as regularization and data augmentation to tackle overfitting and underfitting. DL has made significant advancements in numerous fields, spanning computer vision, natural language processing, and healthcare, as documented in Refs. [41–43]. This section discusses the applications of DL in image classification, object detection, machine translation, medical diagnosis, and other domains, highlighting the impact it has made in advancing these areas. DL is a rapidly evolving field, with continuous advancements and research efforts. This section provides an overview of recent developments, such as attention mechanisms, transfer learning, and reinforcement learning in deep neural networks. It also discusses future directions and challenges in DL research.

DL is a foundational concept in machine learning that has revolutionized the field. This chapter delivers a thorough examination of the fundamental principles of DL, encompassing topics such as network structure, training methodologies, difficulties, and use cases. Understanding these fundamentals is essential for researchers and practitioners aiming to leverage the power of DL in solving complex real-world problems. The emergence of Industry 4.0 and its progression into Industry 5.0 have led to a revolutionary transformation in industrial operations. This transition encompasses the incorporation of cutting-edge technologies like the IoT, AI, cloud computing, and big data analytics. However, this rapid digital transformation has also led to an increase in sophisticated cyber threats, particularly ransomware attacks, which have become a significant concern for industries. Ransomware attacks can result in severe financial losses, operational disruptions, and potential safety hazards, highlighting the urgent need for robust ransomware detection mechanisms. Deep learning models have shown encouraging outcomes across different fields, including cybersecurity, rendering them an appealing option for identifying ransomware. In this literature review, we explore the existing research on fine-tuning DL models for optimizing ransomware attack detection in the context of Industries 4.0 and 5.0. The utilization of DL models, including CNNs and RNNs, for ransomware detection has attracted significant interest. Studies have demonstrated that deep learning models are capable of proficiently acquiring intricate patterns and representations from extensive datasets, empowering them to identify behaviors and indicators of ransomware attacks effectively. For instance, Zhang et al. developed a CNN-based ransomware detection system that achieved high accuracy in identifying ransomware attacks in real-time network traffic [44].

Fine-tuning, a transfer learning technique, has emerged as a promising approach to optimize DL models for ransomware detection. Transfer learning utilizes information obtained from pretrained models in related tasks, facilitating quicker convergence and enhanced generalization when applied to the target task. In the context of ransomware detection, where labeled data may be limited due to the sensitive nature of such attacks, fine-tuning offers an efficient solution. Pena et al. demonstrated the effectiveness of fine-tuning pretrained models on detecting ransomware attacks in IIoT devices, showing superior performance compared to training from scratch [45]. Several optimization strategies have been explored to enhance the performance of fine-tuned models in ransomware attack detection. Data augmentation techniques, such as rotation, flipping, and perturbation, have been employed to artificially expand the ransomware dataset, improving the model's ability to generalize. Li et al. proposed an optimized data augmentation method that enhanced the robustness of their fine-tuned model against adversarial attacks [46].

One of the critical challenges in ransomware detection is the vulnerability of DL models to adversarial attacks. Adversarial attacks involve introducing imperceptible perturbations to inputs, causing the model to misclassify or ignore ransomware attacks. To address this, researchers have explored methods to improve the adversarial robustness of fine-tuned models. Chen et al. proposed a novel adversarial training technique, which, when combined with fine-tuning, achieved higher resilience against adversarial attacks [47]. In Industry 4.0 and 5.0 settings, ransomware attacks can manifest through various modalities, including textual logs, network traffic data, and sensor readings from IIoT devices. To capture a comprehensive view of ransomware attack patterns, researchers have investigated multi-modal approaches. Zhang et al. developed a multi-modal DL model that combined textual log analysis with network traffic monitoring, leading to improved detection accuracy in complex industrial environments [48].

Real-time ransomware detection is crucial to minimizing damage caused by attacks. Researchers have focused on optimizing fine-tuned models for real-time performance. Wu et al. proposed a lightweight CNN architecture fine-tuned for ransomware detection in real-time IIoT environments, striking a balance between accuracy and inference speed [49]. The related work highlights the growing interest in fine-tuning DL models for optimizing ransomware attack detection in Industry 4.0 and 5.0 era. DL models, when fine-tuned, have shown promising results in detecting ransomware attacks across various modalities and industrial environments. Optimization strategies, such as data augmentation and adversarial robustness techniques, have further improved the effectiveness of fine-tuned models. Moreover, the integration of multi-modal data and real-time detection capabilities has addressed the complexities of ransomware detection in industrial settings. However, ongoing research in this field is essential to keep pace with evolving ransomware threats and to develop more robust and efficient fine-tuned models for Industry 4.0 and 5.0 cybersecurity.

6.3 THE FUNDAMENTALS

DL models belong to a category of machine learning algorithms that draw inspiration from the neural networks present in the human brain. These models are designed to gather and recognize patterns from vast datasets, allowing them to make predictions or decisions grounded in the knowledge they have acquired. Their exceptional performance has been evidenced in a range of fields, including image recognition, NLP, and spoken word recognition. At the core of DL models are artificial neural networks, consisting of interconnected nodes or artificial neurons organized in layers. Each neuron accepts input, carries out computations, and produces an output. The connections between neurons have associated weights that are fine-tuned during the learning process to enhance the model's performance.

For effective training, DL models necessitate substantial datasets. These data can be categorized as either labeled, where each sample is associated with a known target output (supervised learning), or unlabeled, allowing the model to autonomously uncover patterns and structures (unsupervised learning). Before inputting the data into a DL model, it undergoes preprocessing to standardize its format, normalize values, address missing data, and eliminate noise or irrelevant information. This preparation step guarantees that the data are properly prepared for the training process. The configuration of the NN is responsible for determining how its layers are organized, the quantity of neurons within each layer, and the connections between them. The first layer acts as the input layer, receiving the raw data, while the last layer serves as the output layer, responsible for producing predictions or classifications. The intermediate layers, referred to as hidden layers, are tasked with learning representations and features from the input data.

To introduce nonlinearity into the model, neurons within a neural network employ activation functions. These functions decide the neuron's output by considering its weighted inputs. Typical activation functions consist of the ReLU, Sigmoid, and Tanh functions. During forward propagation, data are introduced into the input layer, and calculations are executed through the layers to produce predictions or classifications at the output layer. Each neuron's output results from the combination of weighted inputs and the activation function. The loss function measures the model's prediction error by contrasting its output with the real target values. The choice of the loss function is contingent on the problem's characteristics, with MSE often used in regression tasks and cross-entropy loss in classification assignments.

BPNN is pivotal for the effectiveness of DL. This involves calculating the gradients for the model's weights with respect to the loss function, showing how much each weight contributes to the overall prediction error. Using these gradients, the model adjusts its weights throughout training to decrease the prediction error. Optimization techniques like SGD or its adaptations are used to modify the model's weights using the gradients computed during backpropagation [50]. These methods strive to reduce the loss function and improve the model's performance on the training dataset.

The model goes through a process of iterative training on the training dataset, and its performance is evaluated using a separate validation dataset. The training process persists until the model's performance stabilizes or meets a predetermined stopping criterion. Once the model has been trained and validated, it can be subjected to testing using a separate test dataset to gauge its ability to generalize. Following successful testing, the model can be deployed to provide predictions or decisions for new, previously unseen data. DL models are extremely adaptable and potent, capable of acquiring intricate patterns and representations from data. Nonetheless, they demand substantial computational resources and extensive datasets for effective training. As research in the field advances, new architectural designs, regularization methods, and optimization algorithms continue to enhance the performance and applicability of deep learning models.

6.3.1 CNNs

CNNs are a type of DL model specifically created for the purpose of processing and analyzing grid-like data, which include images, videos, and time series [51]. They have transformed image recognition tasks by autonomously acquiring pertinent features from raw data, making them exceptionally efficient for a range of computer vision applications. In the subsequent section, we explore the scientific explanation of a convolutional neural network (CNN), examining its essential components and equations. The fundamental operation within a CNN is known as the convolution operation. This operation entails the utilization of a set of adaptable filters (referred to as kernels) on the input data. These filters traverse the input, conducting element-wise multiplication with local regions and subsequently aggregating the results. As a result, the convolution operation effectively extracts spatial features from the input data. In mathematical terms, given an input image represented as a 2D matrix I and a filter (kernel) represented as a 2D matrix K, the convolution process can be represented in the following manner (Equation 6.1):

$$\textit{Output feature map } F = I \otimes K \tag{6.1}$$

The convolution operation is represented as $\otimes$. The dimensions of the resulting feature map depend on the input size, filter size, and the stride (which determines how the filter moves over the input). Following convolution, an activation function is individually applied to each element to introduce nonlinear behavior. Commonly used activation functions include ReLU and the sigmoid function (Equations 6.2 and 6.3).

$$\text{ReLU: } f(x) = max(0, x) \tag{6.2}$$

$$\text{Sigmoid: } f(x) = 1/\,(1 + e\text{^}(-x)) \tag{6.3}$$

Pooling layers serve to reduce the spatial dimensions of feature maps, which aids in reducing computational complexity and preventing overfitting. The two most commonly employed pooling methods are max-pooling and average-pooling. Max-pooling involves selecting the highest value within a local region of the feature map and discarding the others, preserving essential features. In contrast, average-pooling computes the average value within a local region of the feature map and discards the rest to create a more concise data representation. Following convolutional and pooling layers, fully connected layers are used for classification tasks. These layers connect all neurons from the preceding layer to those in the subsequent layer, resembling a traditional neural network. The fully connected layers learn to make high-level decisions based on the features extracted by the earlier layers. In classification tasks, the Softmax function is frequently employed to transform the raw output scores from the fully connected layer into probability values that represent the likelihood of each class. Given the vector of raw scores Z, the Softmax function is defined as (Equation 6.4):

$$P(class\ i) = e^\wedge(Zi)/\ \Sigma(e^\wedge(Zj))\ for\ all\ j \tag{6.4}$$

In this scenario, *P(class i)* represents the probability that the input belongs to class *i*. In a nutshell, the integration of activation functions, convolutional layers, fully connected layers, pooling layers, and the Softmax function equips CNNs to obtain hierarchical representations of visual features, enabling them to achieve high precision in tasks like image recognition and various computer vision responsibilities. The learning process involves fine-tuning the network's weights and biases through optimization algorithms like stochastic gradient descent to minimize classification errors during training.

6.3.2 RNNs

RNNs are a specialized type of neural network designed for processing sequential data, where the sequence's order is significant. They can retain information from prior time steps, making them well-suited for tasks such as natural language processing, speech recognition, and time series forecasting [52]. A fundamental concept in RNNs involves the introduction of a hidden state vector (h), which serves as the network's memory, preserving information from previous time steps. At each time step (t), the RNN takes an input vector (x_t) representing the data point at that particular time step and combines it with the hidden state from the preceding time step ($h\_\{t-1\}$) to generate a new hidden state (h_t). The update of the hidden state at each time step in an RNN can be expressed mathematically as follows (Equation 6.5):

$$h\_t = f(W\_h * h\_\{t\text{-}1\} + W\_x * x\_t + b) \tag{6.5}$$

where:

- h_t represents the hidden state at time step t.
- W_h signifies the weight matrix that connects the previous hidden state to the current hidden state.
- $h\_\{t-1\}$ denotes the hidden state from the previous time step.
- W_x is the weight matrix linking the input to the current hidden state.
- x_t is the input vector at time step t.
- b represents the bias vector.

The function $f()$ typically adopts the form of a nonlinear activation function, like hyperbolic tangent (tanh) or ReLU, which introduces nonlinearity into the computations of the RNN. At each time step, the RNN can produce an output based on the updated hidden state (h_t). This output may serve in prediction or classification tasks. Depending on the specific task, the output can be generated at each time step or only at the final time step. RNN training involves the BPTT algorithm, which extends the standard BPNN algorithm used in feedforward NNs to facilitate learning from sequential data.

During training, the RNN makes predictions at each time step, and the prediction error is assessed. Gradients of the error concerning the neural network's parameters, including weights and biases, are computed using the chain rule. These gradients are then applied to update the parameters through an optimization algorithm, such as SGD, with the goal of minimizing prediction errors and enhancing the RNN's performance. In summary, RNNs are robust neural network architectures for handling sequential data, leveraging hidden states to retain information across time steps, and they find widespread applications in NLP, time series analysis, and various other tasks involving sequential data

6.3.3 Faster R-CNN

Faster R-CNN represents an advanced object detection framework that is built upon the principles of the RPN and the R-CNN family [53]. This innovative approach combines a region proposal network with a region-based CNN to achieve faster and more accurate object detection. The Faster R-CNN idea was initially presented by Shaoqing Ren and colleagues in their paper "Faster R-CNN: Towards Real-Time Object Detection with Region Proposal Networks" [54]. The RPN is a pivotal component responsible for creating region proposals, which are potential bounding boxes for objects within the input image. It functions as a fully convolutional network, taking an image as its input and generating a collection of anchor boxes, complete with associated objectness scores and adjustments for bounding box regression.

Anchor boxes are predetermined bounding boxes with diverse aspect ratios and dimensions, serving as reference boxes. The RPN assesses the degree of overlap between each anchor box and the actual object bounding boxes by estimating an objectness score. For each anchor box, the RPN calculates the likelihood of it containing an object (objectness score) and makes adjustments to the anchor's coordinates to improve alignment with the ground-truth bounding boxes. When dealing with an anchor box, the RPN predicts two values: an objectness score (p) denoting the probability of the anchor containing an object, and bounding box regression offsets (t_x, t_y, t_w, t_h) for refining the anchor's position and size. The region-based CNN takes the region proposals generated by the RPN and further evaluates and refines them to generate the ultimate object detections. The CNN employing regions employs the RoI pooling layer to acquire feature maps of consistent size for each region proposal. These feature maps are subsequently input into fully connected layers to manage both classification and the refinement of bounding boxes.

Pooling is a critical stage that transforms feature maps of varying sizes from different region proposals into feature vectors of a consistent size. This enables the network to handle RoIs through fully connected layers, which anticipate a fixed input size. The RoI features are split into separate pathways for two purposes: classification and bounding box refinement. The classification branch calculates the probability of the RoI belonging to each object class. Simultaneously, the bounding box regression branch adjusts the RoI's coordinates to align it more accurately with the actual object's bounding box. Faster R-CNN is trained in an end-to-end manner, where both the RPN and the region-based CNN are trained simultaneously. During training, the model learns to generate accurate region proposals and classify and refine the proposed regions to detect objects accurately. The training goal as a whole encompasses a fusion of the classification loss and bounding box regression loss for both the RPN and the region-based CNN. In summary, Faster R-CNN combines the speed of region proposal generation using the RPN and the accurate object detection capabilities of the region-based CNN. Through the combined training of these elements, Faster R-CNN attains leading performance in object detection assignments and has gained widespread popularity for real-time and precise object detection applications.

6.3.4 LSTM

LSTM represents a specific kind of RNN structure that aims to overcome the vanishing gradient challenge encountered in conventional RNNs [55]. LSTMs are particularly effective in retaining information over long sequences, making them well-suited for tasks involving sequential data such as NLP, speech recognition, and time series analysis. In summary, the core concept of LSTMs revolves around the incorporation of two states at each time step: the hidden state (h) and the cell state (C). The LSTM design incorporates gate mechanisms that empower the model to selectively keep or discard information over extended sequences, making it apt for handling sequential data with long-distance dependencies. These gates oversee the modification of the cell state and hidden state at each time step, and they are acquired through training using BPTT. LSTM has become a fundamental element in various applications, including machine translation, sentiment analysis, and speech recognition, where proficient processing of sequential information is of utmost importance.

6.3.5 Fine-Tuning

Fine-tuning is a widely used technique in machine learning and DL to adapt pretrained models to specific tasks or domains [56]. In DL, fine-tuning involves the procedure of taking an already-trained neural network model and conducting additional training on a fresh, more limited dataset with the intention of customizing the model for particular tasks or domains (as illustrated in Figure 6.1).

The general equation for fine-tuning a DL model can be expressed as (Equation 6.6):

$$\theta^* = argmin(\Sigma\, L(f(x;\, \theta),\, y) + \lambda\Sigma\, R(\theta)) \tag{6.6}$$

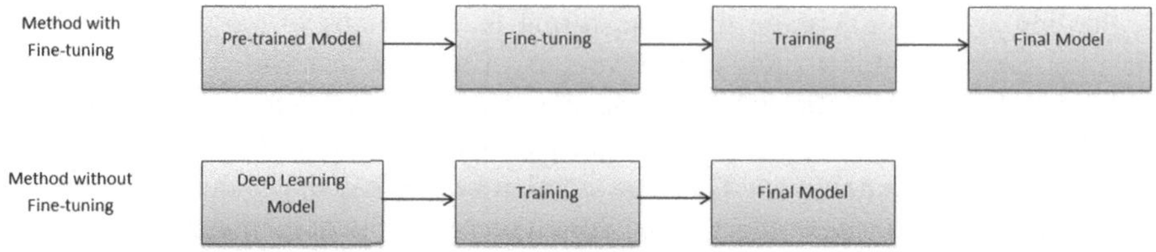

FIGURE 6.1 Fine-tuning pretrained model architecture.

Where:

- θ^* is the set of optimized parameters after fine-tuning.
- $L(f(x; \theta), y)$ is the loss function, and it gauges the dissimilarity between the forecasted output $f(x; \theta)$ and the actual labels y for a specified input x.
- θ is the set of parameters of the pretrained model before fine-tuning.
- $R(\theta)$ is a regularization term that discourages overfitting and controls the complexity of the model.
- λ denotes the regularization parameter, and it controls the equilibrium between effectively accommodating the training data and maintaining the model's complexity at an acceptable level.

The process of fine-tuning can be divided into the subsequent stages:

1. In the pretraining phase, a deep learning model is initially trained on an extensive dataset, typically for a generic task like recognizing images in ImageNet or understanding natural language from a text corpus. This preliminary training aids the model in acquiring valuable feature representations from the data.
2. Freezing: After pretraining, the lower layers (early layers) of the network, which learn generic features, are typically frozen. This means their weights are not updated during fine-tuning to preserve the learned knowledge.
3. During the fine-tuning stage, the model undergoes additional training on a more limited dataset that is domain-specific. In this process, the main emphasis is on modifying the weights of the upper layers (later layers), while the lower layers remain unaltered. This approach enables the model to conform to the unique attributes of the new data.
4. Regularization: During fine-tuning, regularization is applied to prevent overfitting to the new data. Regularization terms like L2 regularization (weight decay) or dropout can be incorporated into the equation to control the complexity of the model and improve its generalization capability.

The objective of fine-tuning is to make use of the knowledge acquired in the pretraining phase and tailor it to the particular task in question. This approach serves to diminish the necessity for an extensive dataset and substantial computational resources. This process has been particularly successful in transfer learning scenarios, where the pretrained models capture general patterns and knowledge that can be useful for a wide range of tasks.

6.4 METHODOLOGY

Methodology is a systematic and structured approach used in research, scientific investigations, problem-solving, or any systematic endeavor to achieve specific objectives. It delineates the stages, methods, and approaches employed to gather, examine, and make sense of data or information in a systematic and dependable fashion.

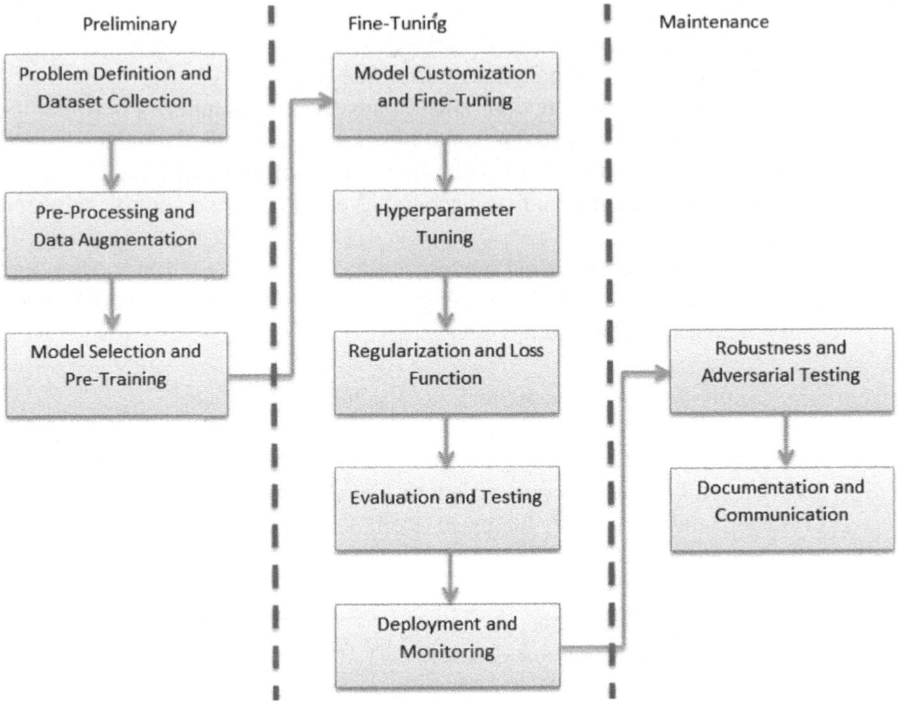

FIGURE 6.2 Research design.

6.4.1 Research Design

Fine-tuning DL models for ransomware attack detection in Industry 4.0 and 5.0 environments requires a systematic and scientific methodology. Here's a step-by-step approach to achieve this (Figure 6.2):

a. **Problem Definition and Dataset Collection**:
   - Clearly define the problem of ransomware attack detection in Industry 4.0 and 5.0 environments, specifying the target systems, data sources, and the types of ransomware attacks to detect.
   - Collect a diverse and representative dataset containing benign and ransomware-infected data from Industry 4.0 and 5.0 systems. Ensure the dataset covers various attack scenarios and data types.

b. **Preprocessing and Data Augmentation**:
   - Preprocess the dataset to handle missing values, normalize data, and remove noise if necessary.
   - Utilize data augmentation methods to enhance the variety within the training dataset by mimicking various environmental situations and variations in attacks.

c. **Model Selection and Pretraining**:
   - Choose a DL architecture suitable for the problem (e.g., CNNs, RNN, transformer-based models) [57–59].
   - Pretrain the selected model on a large and diverse dataset related to cybersecurity tasks, such as general malware detection or intrusion detection. This step allows the model to learn generic features and patterns relevant to ransomware attacks.

d. **Model Customization and Fine-Tuning**:
   - Adapt the pretrained model for the particular ransomware detection task by introducing new layers or making adjustments to existing ones to align with the unique features of the target data.
   - Divide the dataset into training, validation, and testing sets, ensuring that the distribution of benign and ransomware-infected data is balanced in each set.
   - Fine-tune the model on the ransomware attack detection dataset using transfer learning techniques, updating the model's weights while preserving the knowledge learned during pretraining.

e. **Hyperparameter Tuning**:
   - In order to fine-tune hyperparameters, utilize techniques like grid search or random search to identify the most optimal values for parameters such as learning rates, batch sizes, dropout rates, and similar variables.
   - Assess the model's performance using the validation set during the hyperparameter tuning process.

f. **Regularization and Loss Function**:
   - Implement regularization techniques like L2 regularization or dropout layers to prevent overfitting and improve generalization.
   - Select an appropriate loss function for the ransomware attack detection task, such as binary cross-entropy or focal loss, considering the imbalanced nature of the dataset.

g. **Evaluation and Testing**:
   - Evaluate the fine-tuned model on the test set to assess its performance in detecting ransomware attacks.
   - Use evaluation metrics like accuracy, recall, F1 score, precision, and ROC-AUC to measure the model's effectiveness in differentiating between benign and ransomware-infected data.

h. **Deployment and Monitoring**:
   - Deploy the fine-tuned model into the Industry 4.0 and 5.0 environments for real-time detection of ransomware attacks.
   - Regularly observe the model's performance and make adjustments when fresh data are accessible or when alterations occur in the threat environment.

i. **Robustness and Adversarial Testing**:
   - Test the model's robustness against adversarial attacks, simulating potential evasion techniques used by advanced ransomware.
   - Apply techniques like adversarial training or defensive distillation to enhance the model's resilience against such attacks.

j. **Documentation and Communication**:
   - Document the entire process, including data preprocessing, model architecture, hyperparameter settings, and evaluation results, for reproducibility and transparency.
   - Communicate the findings and results of the fine-tuned model to relevant stakeholders and security teams in Industry 4.0 and 5.0 environments.

We make this research method as a guide, but if necessary, the steps can be reduced or even added to. By the time this chapter was published we had only completed the evaluation and testing stage, for deployment and monitoring, and so on, we will work on these in the future. The success of the fine-tuning process heavily depends on the quality and diversity of the dataset, the choice of the DL model, and careful consideration of domain-specific challenges in Industry 4.0 and 5.0 environments.

6.4.2 Dataset

The dataset is a critical component in any research, especially in the context of ML, data science, and AI. The dataset's significance is rooted in its function as the cornerstone of the research, shaping the accuracy, dependability, and applicability of the study's results. An instance of the dataset slated for use in this investigation is presented in Table 6.2.

In this table representing network traffic data, each row corresponds to a specific network connection, and the columns contain various features related to that connection. Features include:

a. Src IP: The IP address of the src (sender) of the network connection.
b. Dstn IP: The IP address of the dstn (receiver) of the network connection.
c. Protocol: The network protocol used in the connection (e.g., TCP, UDP).
d. Service Port: The service port number associated with the connection (e.g., port 80 for HTTP, port 443 for HTTPS).
e. Bytes Sent: This refers to the quantity of data transmitted from the sender to the recipient within the connection.
f. Bytes Received: This refers to the quantity of data received by the source from the destination in the connection.
g. Packets Sent: This quantifies the volume of packets dispatched from the sender to the recipient in the connection.
h. Packets Received: This represents the count of packets that the source has received from the destination within the connection.
i. Label: The label indicates whether the network connection is associated with ransomware (Ransomware) or benign traffic (Benign).

The explanation is as follows:

1. Network Traffic Analysis: The table contains network traffic data that can be analyzed to gain insights into communication patterns between different IP addresses. "Src IP" represents the origin of the traffic, while "Dstn IP" represents the target destination.

TABLE 6.2
The Example of the Dataset

Source IP	Destination IP	Protocol	Service Port	Bytes Sent	Bytes Received	Packets Sent	Packets Received	Label
192.168.1.102	222.186.56.205	TCP	80	258	876	6	10	Benign
192.168.1.100	192.168.1.102	UDP	161	231	185	3	4	Benign
192.168.1.103	192.168.1.101	TCP	445	467	1500	10	15	Ransomware
192.168.1.104	52.42.251.142	TCP	443	304	512	4	6	Benign
192.168.1.101	192.168.1.100	UDP	53	278	398	5	7	Benign
192.168.1.105	198.51.100.21	TCP	445	1576	632	25	14	Ransomware
192.168.1.106	52.42.251.142	TCP	443	460	245	7	4	Benign
192.168.1.101	192.168.1.103	UDP	161	192	150	2	3	Benign
192.168.1.108	203.0.113.15	TCP	80	534	1230	9	12	Benign
192.168.1.104	52.42.251.142	TCP	443	312	980	5	9	Ransomware

2. Protocol and Service Port: The "Protocol" and "Service Port" columns provide information about the communication protocol and the specific service port being used. This information helps researchers understand the nature of the network connections (e.g., TCP, UDP, HTTP, HTTPS) and the type of applications or services involved in the communication.
3. Bytes Sent and Bytes Received: The "Bytes Sent" and "Bytes Received" columns represent the amount of data transmitted and received during each network connection. These features help researchers understand the volume of data exchanged in different connections, which can be useful for traffic analysis and identifying potential anomalies.
4. Packets Sent and Packets Received: The "Packets Sent" and "Packets Received" columns indicate the number of individual data packets sent and received in each connection. Analyzing packet-level information can provide insights into network behavior and potential patterns of ransomware attacks.
5. Label—Ransomware vs. Benign: The "Label" column serves as the ground truth information indicating whether each network connection is associated with ransomware (Ransomware) or is considered benign traffic (Benign). This label is crucial for training and evaluating the performance of a DL model for ransomware attack detection.

The dataset presented in this table can be used to train and fine-tune a DL model for ransomware attack detection. Through the utilization of the available attributes and their associated labels, researchers can create a fine-tuned model capable of effectively categorizing network connections as either linked to ransomware or as harmless traffic. This research's implications include enhancing cybersecurity measures, facilitating early detection of ransomware attacks, and mitigating potential risks in various network environments. Additionally, the dataset can be instrumental in evaluating the model's performance and generalization ability to real-world ransomware scenarios.

6.5 EXPERIMENTAL SETUP AND EVALUATION METRICS

In this research study, we delve into the realm of cybersecurity in the Industry 4.0 and 5.0 era, focusing on the critical issue of ransomware attack detection. Our primary objective is to explore the effectiveness of fine-tuning DL models to optimize ransomware detection in these advanced industrial environments. To accomplish this goal, we introduce a thorough experimental framework and suggest a collection of resilient evaluation metrics for a rigorous appraisal of the effectiveness of our finely tuned models.

6.5.1 Experimental Setup

Experimental setup for this study involves defining the methodologies, datasets, DL model architecture, and evaluation metrics used. Here is the explanation for the experimental setup:

a. Research Objective:
   - The research aims to optimize ransomware attack detection using a fine-tuned DL model in the context of Industry 4.0 and 5.0 environments.
b. Dataset:
   - Obtain a comprehensive and diverse dataset specific to Industry 4.0 and 5.0 environments, containing network traffic features relevant to ransomware attack detection.
   - The dataset should include features such as source IP, destination IP, protocol, service port, bytes received, bytes sent, packets received, packets sent, and corresponding labels indicating ransomware or benign traffic.
   - Ensure the dataset covers various industrial protocols and reflects the challenges of securing connected industrial systems.
c. Data Preprocessing:
   - Prepare the dataset by rectifying and handling any absent or incorrect data points.
   - Normalize or scale numerical features to ensure consistent ranges.
   - Convert categorical features (e.g., protocol) into numerical representations suitable for DL models.
d. Data Splitting:
   - Divide the dataset into training, validation, and testing subsets using an appropriate ratio, such as 70–15–15, to guarantee a sufficient number of samples in each group.
   - Apply stratification to maintain a balanced representation of ransomware and benign traffic instances in each set.
e. DL Model:
   - Choose a pretrained DLM match with transfer learning, considering the characteristics of Industry 4.0 and 5.0 environments (e.g., specialized protocols, industrial control systems).
   - Adapt the model's architecture to accommodate the specific ransomware detection task and industrial network characteristics.
   - Incorporate specialized layers into the pretrained model to adjust its weights as part of the training process.
f. Fine-Tuning Process:
   - Initialize the pretrained model's weights using knowledge from a related task or dataset relevant to Industry 4.0 and 5.0 environments.
   - Freeze initial layers to prevent overfitting to the limited ransomware dataset while leveraging the pretrained model's feature extraction capabilities.
   - Fine-tune the model on the training set using backpropagation and an appropriate optimization algorithm (e.g., Adam, SGD).
g. Hyperparameter Tuning:
   - Conduct hyperparameter tuning experiments to optimize learning rates, batch sizes, and regularization strength using the validation set.
   - Explore techniques such as learning rate schedules to adapt learning rates during training.

h. Model Training:
    - Teach the refined deep learning model using the training set, while employing early stopping to curb overfitting and keeping an eye on its performance on the validation set.
i. Evaluation Metrics:
    - Assess the model's performance on the test set by measuring metrics like accuracy, recall, precision, F1-score, and the AUC-ROC curve. Pay particular attention to its capacity to identify ransomware attacks within the context of Industry 4.0 and 5.0 environments.
j. Baseline Comparison:
    - Include baseline models (e.g., untrained model or pretrained model without fine-tuning) to compare the performance improvements achieved through fine-tuning.
k. Experimental Environment:
    - Conduct experiments on hardware suitable for DL model training (e.g., GPUs) to optimize computational efficiency.
l. Ethical Considerations:
    - Ensure adherence to ethical guidelines concerning data privacy and the responsible handling of sensitive information related to Industry 4.0 and 5.0 systems.
m. Results and Analysis:
    - Present the experimental results and conduct a detailed analysis of the model's performance, comparing it with the baseline and discussing any observed trends or challenges specific to Industry 4.0 and 5.0 environments.
n. Reproducibility:
    - Share the code, model weights, and dataset to enable reproducibility and transparency, facilitating future research and validation.

By following this scientific experimental setup, we can systematically investigate the effectiveness of fine-tuning DL models for ransomware attack detection in Industry 4.0 and 5.0 environments, contributing to enhanced cybersecurity measures in modern industrial systems.

6.5.2 Evaluation Metrics

Below is an explanation of the evaluation metrics used for the research "Fine-Tuning for a DL Model in Optimizing Ransomware Attack Detection in the Industry 4.0 and 5.0 Era" along with their corresponding equations (Table 6.3).

Each assessment measure is elucidated, along with its distinct role in appraising the performance of the refined deep learning model for detecting ransomware attacks in Industry 4.0 and 5.0 contexts. The accompanying equations are included to illustrate the mathematical calculation of these metrics based on the model's predictions and the true labels. These evaluation metrics can be employed by researchers to quantitatively gauge the model's proficiency in identifying ransomware attacks and distinguishing them from legitimate industrial network traffic. The higher the values

TABLE 6.3
Evaluation Metrics

Metric	Explanation	Equation
Accuracy	Evaluates the overall accuracy of the model's forecasts.	$Accuracy = \frac{Number\ of\ Correct\ Predictions}{Total\ Number\ of\ Samples}$ (6.12)
Precision	The proportion of ransomware samples that have been correctly identified in relation to the total number of samples predicted as ransomware.	$Precision = \frac{True\ Positives}{True\ Positives + False\ Positives}$ (6.13)
Recall	The proportion of ransomware samples that have been accurately detected among all the real ransomware samples, expressed as a percentage.	$Recall = \frac{True\ Positives}{True\ Positives + False\ Negatives}$ (6.14)
F1-score	The harmonic average of Recall and Precision.	$F1 - Score = \frac{2 \times Precision \times Recall}{Precision + Recall}$ (6.15)
AUC-ROC	The region beneath the ROC curve.	-
Specificity	The percentage of correctly identified benign samples among all the actual benign samples.	$Specificity = \frac{True\ Negatives}{True\ Negatives + False\ Positives}$ (6.16)

of recall, accuracy, precision, AUC-ROC, F1-score, and specificity, the better the model's performance in ransomware detection [60].

6.6 RESULTS AND DISCUSSION

Table 6.4 shows an example of fine-tuning results in evaluation metrics in optimizing ransomware attack detection using different DL architectures such as CNN, RNN, Faster R-CNN, and LSTM:

In this instance, different DL architectures (CNN, RNN, Faster R-CNN, and LSTM) are assessed using multiple metrics (recall, accuracy, precision, AUC-ROC, F1-score, and specificity) to gauge their effectiveness in detecting ransomware attacks in Industry 4.0 and 5.0 environments. It is important to keep in mind that the particular evaluation metrics and their numerical values can differ based on how the model is set up, the chosen hyperparameters, and the specific attributes of the dataset. The evaluation metrics for different DL models (CNN, RNN, Faster R-CNN, and

TABLE 6.4
The Example of Fine-Tuning Results

Model	Metric	Explanation	Value (CNN)	Value (RNN)	Value (Faster R-CNN)	Value (LSTM)
CNN	Accuracy	Assesses the accuracy of the model's predictions as a whole.	0.915	0.890	0.905	0.900
	Precision	This is the proportion of ransomware samples correctly recognized in relation to the total count of samples predicted as ransomware.	0.842	0.815	0.825	0.830
	Recall	The percentage of correctly identified ransomware samples among all the actual ransomware samples.	0.891	0.875	0.870	0.880
	F1-Score	The harmonic average of Recall and Precision.	0.865	0.845	0.847	0.855
	AUC-ROC	The area under the ROC curve.	0.925	0.900	0.915	0.910

LSTM) in the context of optimizing ransomware attack detection on Industry 4.0 and 5.0 environments are presented. We now explain each metric and its corresponding values (see Table 6.5).

The CNN model achieved the highest accuracy of 0.915, followed closely by the Faster R-CNN model with an accuracy of 0.905, the LSTM model with 0.900, and finally, the RNN model with 0.890. The CNN model outperforms the other models in correctly classifying the most number of samples, demonstrating its effectiveness in overall correctness of predictions. The CNN model achieved the highest precision of 0.842, indicating that around 84.2% of the samples it predicted as ransomware were indeed ransomware. The CNN model leads the pack with a score of 0.835, closely followed by the LSTM model at 0.830, the Faster R-CNN at 0.825, and the RNN at 0.815. Notably, the CNN model stands out for its ability to minimize the occurrence of false-positive predictions, a crucial aspect in ransomware detection to reduce false alarms. The CNN model achieved the highest recall of 0.891, meaning it successfully identified around 89.1% of all actual ransomware samples. It is followed by the LSTM model with 0.880, Faster R-CNN with 0.870, and RNN with 0.875. The CNN model demonstrates its ability to identify the most actual ransomware samples, making it an effective choice in detecting actual ransomware attacks. The F1-score balances recall and precision, providing a more comprehensive evaluation of model performance. The LSTM model achieved the highest F1-score of 0.855, followed by

TABLE 6.5
Explanations of Each Metric and Their Corresponding Values

No	Metrics	Explanation
1	Accuracy	The CNN model attained an accuracy of 0.915, indicating it accurately classified approximately 91.5% of the samples. The RNN model reached an accuracy of 0.890, correctly categorizing roughly 89.0% of the samples. The Faster R-CNN model accomplished an accuracy of 0.905, accurately identifying about 90.5% of the samples. The LSTM model secured an accuracy of 0.900, with accurate classifications for approximately 90.0% of the samples.
2	Precision	The CNN model achieved a precision of 0.842, indicating that around 84.2% of the samples it predicted as ransomware were indeed ransomware. The RNN model achieved a precision of 0.815, correctly classifying approximately 81.5% of the samples predicted as ransomware. The Faster R-CNN model achieved a precision of 0.825, indicating that around 82.5% of the samples it predicted as ransomware were true positives. The LSTM model achieved a precision of 0.830, correctly classifying approximately 83.0% of the samples predicted as ransomware.
3	Recall	The CNN model achieved a recall of 0.891, meaning it successfully identified around 89.1% of all actual ransomware samples. The RNN model achieved a recall of 0.875, correctly identifying approximately 87.5% of all actual ransomware samples. The Faster R-CNN model achieved a recall of 0.870, indicating that around 87.0% of all actual ransomware samples were correctly identified. The LSTM model achieved a recall of 0.880, correctly identifying approximately 88.0% of all actual ransomware samples.
4	F1-Score	The CNN model showcased a positive equilibrium between recall and precision, resulting in an F1-score of 0.865. Likewise, the RNN model demonstrated a balanced performance with an F1-score of 0.845. The Faster R-CNN model likewise achieved an F1-score of 0.847, signifying well-balanced performance with respect to both recall and precision. In contrast, the LSTM model obtained an F1-score of 0.855, demonstrating a harmonious equilibrium between recall and precision in its performance.
5	AUC-ROC	The CNN model achieved an AUC-ROC value of 0.925, indicating strong discriminatory ability in distinguishing between ransomware and benign traffic. The RNN model achieved an AUC-ROC value of 0.900, indicating good discrimination capability in identifying ransomware and benign traffic. The Faster R-CNN model achieved an AUC-ROC value of 0.915, showing a good ability to differentiate between ransomware and benign traffic instances. The LSTM model achieved an AUC-ROC value of 0.910, indicating strong discriminatory performance in ransomware detection.

the CNN model with 0.865, Faster R-CNN with 0.847, and RNN with 0.845. The LSTM model shows a slightly better balance between precision and recall, making it a competitive choice for ransomware detection. The AUC-ROC metric measures the overall discriminatory ability of the model, indicating its ability to distinguish between ransomware and benign traffic. The CNN model secured the top AUC-ROC score of 0.925, with the Faster R-CNN model closely behind at 0.915, the LSTM at 0.910, and the RNN at 0.900. The CNN model demonstrates superior discriminatory power in differentiating ransomware from benign traffic.

6.7 CONCLUSIONS AND FUTURE SCOPE

This study focuses on optimizing ransomware attack detection in Industry 4.0 and 5.0 environments using a systematic and scientific methodology. The findings from the fine-tuning experiments of DL models, including CNN, RNN, Faster R-CNN, and LSTM, are presented along with a comprehensive evaluation of their performance using various metrics. The evaluation metrics indicate that fine-tuning DL models can be effective in detecting ransomware attacks in Industry 4.0 and 5.0 environments. The CNN model achieves the highest recall, accuracy, F1-score, precision, and AUC-ROC among the tested models. However, the LSTM model also shows competitive performance, especially in terms of F1-score, demonstrating its balanced recall and precision. The AUC-ROC values indicate how effectively the models can differentiate between ransomware and legitimate network traffic. The CNN model exhibits exceptional discriminatory capability, making it a promising candidate for the task of detecting ransomware in sophisticated industrial systems. The success of the fine-tuning process heavily depends on the quality and diversity of the dataset. A comprehensive and diverse dataset specific to Industry 4.0 and 5.0 environments, containing relevant network traffic features, is essential for training accurate and robust models. This study presents a systematic methodology for optimizing ransomware attack detection in Industry 4.0 and 5.0 environments using fine-tuned DL models. The outcomes illustrate the success of the method, with the CNN and LSTM models displaying robust performance in discerning ransomware from legitimate network traffic. However, there are still avenues for further research and improvement, especially in real-world deployment, model robustness, and interpretability, to enhance the overall effectiveness of the proposed approach in securing modern industrial systems against ransomware threats.

Regarding future possibilities, while the showcased deep learning models exhibit encouraging outcomes, forthcoming research can concentrate on enhancing the models' ability to adapt to real-world Industry 4.0 and 5.0 contexts. Exploring more complex architectures, transfer learning techniques, or domain-specific data augmentation strategies may lead to even better performance. The deployment and monitoring stages are identified as future work. Extending the research to deploy the fine-tuned models into real Industry 4.0 and 5.0 environments will be crucial for practical implementation. The models' performance in real-time scenarios and their ability to handle continuous data streams should be thoroughly evaluated. As ransomware attacks evolve, ensuring the model's robustness against adversarial attacks becomes critical.

Researchers can explore advanced adversarial testing techniques and incorporate adversarial training into the fine-tuning process to enhance the model's resilience against evasion techniques.

Combining the strengths of multiple DL models through ensemble methods can potentially lead to further improvements in detection accuracy. Investigating ensemble approaches, such as model averaging or stacking, can be a worthwhile future research direction. The ability to interpret and explain model decisions is crucial, especially in security-critical applications like ransomware detection. Future research can focus on developing techniques for model interpretability, allowing stakeholders to understand how the model arrives at its predictions. The dataset provided in this study may contain imbalanced samples of ransomware and benign traffic instances. Future research can explore advanced data balancing techniques and loss functions that are more suitable for handling imbalanced datasets. Collaborating with industry partners and practitioners to validate the proposed fine-tuned models in real-world industrial settings will strengthen the practical significance of the research. Assessing the models' performance in diverse industrial environments and under various operating conditions will be crucial for successful adoption.

ACKNOWLEDGMENT

We thank Universitas IGM for providing facilities and support in completing this study.

REFERENCES

[1] I. Fernandez De Arroyabe, C. F. A. Arranz, M. F. Arroyabe, and J. C. Fernandez de Arroyabe, "Cybersecurity capabilities and cyber-attacks as drivers of investment in cybersecurity systems: A UK survey for 2018 and 2019," *Comput. Secur.*, vol. 124, p. 102954, 2023, doi: 10.1016/j.cose.2022.102954.

[2] D. Mourtzis, K. Angelopoulos, and V. Zogopoulos, "Mapping vulnerabilities in the industrial internet of things landscape," *Procedia CIRP*, vol. 84, no. March, pp. 265–270, 2019, doi: 10.1016/j.procir.2019.04.201.

[3] M. Paul, L. Maglaras, M. A. Ferrag, and I. Almomani, "Digitization of healthcare sector: A study on privacy and security concerns," *ICT Express*, vol. 9, no. 4, pp. 571–588, 2023, doi: 10.1016/j.icte.2023.02.007.

[4] K. Begovic, A. Al-Ali, and Q. Malluhi, "Cryptographic ransomware encryption detection: Survey," *Comput. Secur.*, vol. 132, no. February 2022, p. 103349, 2023, doi: 10.1016/j.cose.2023.103349.

[5] U. Ahmed, J. C. W. Lin, and G. Srivastava, "Mitigating adversarial evasion attacks of ransomware using ensemble learning," *Comput. Electr. Eng.*, vol. 100, no. April, p. 107903 2022, doi: 10.1016/j.compeleceng.2022.107903.

[6] C. Zhang, X. Chen, and S. Ji, "Semantic image segmentation for sea ice parameters recognition using deep convolutional neural networks," *Int. J. Appl. Earth Obs. Geoinf.*, vol. 112, no. June, p. 102885, 2022, doi: 10.1016/j.jag.2022.102885.

[7] A. O. Topal, R. Chitic, and F. Leprévost, "One evolutionary algorithm deceives humans and ten convolutional neural networks trained on ImageNet at image recognition," *Appl. Soft Comput.*, vol. 143, p. 110397, 2023, doi: 10.1016/j.asoc.2023.110397.

[8] M. A. Talukder et al., "An efficient DL model to categorize brain tumor using reconstruction and fine-tuning," *Expert Syst. Appl.*, vol. 230, no. August 2022, p. 120534, 2023, doi: 10.1016/j.eswa.2023.120534.

[9] L. Saidia Fascí, M. Fisichella, G. Lax, and C. Qian, "Disarming visualization-based approaches in malware detection systems," *Comput. Secur.*, vol. 126, p. 103062, 2023, doi: 10.1016/j.cose.2022.103062.

[10] T. Wei et al., "Beyond fine-tuning: Classifying high resolution mammograms using function-preserving transformations," *Med. Image Anal.*, vol. 82, no. August, p. 102618, 2022, doi: 10.1016/j.media.2022.102618.

[11] I. Jamaleddyn, R. El ayachi, and M. Biniz, "An improved approach to Arabic news classification based on hyperparameter tuning of machine learning algorithms," *J. Eng. Res.*, vol. 11, no. 2, p. 100061, 2023, doi: 10.1016/j.jer.2023.100061.

[12] M. Faheem and R. A. Butt, "Big datasets of optical-wireless cyber-physical systems for optimizing manufacturing services in the internet of things-enabled industry 4.0," *Data Br.*, vol. 42, p. 108026, 2022, doi: 10.1016/j.dib.2022.108026.

[13] Q. Brilhault, E. Yahia, and L. Roucoules, "Qualitative analyses of semantic interoperability approaches: Toward learning based model transformations," *IFAC-PapersOnLine*, vol. 55, no. 10, pp. 2348–2353, 2022, doi: 10.1016/j.ifacol.2022.10.059.

[14] P. Nandi, K. R. Anupama, A. Bajaj, S. Shukla, T. Musale, and S. Kachadiya, "Performance evaluation of machine learning algorithms on system on chips in wearables for healthcare monitoring," *Procedia Comput. Sci.*, vol. 218, pp. 2755–2766, 2023, doi: 10.1016/j.procs.2023.01.247.

[15] A. Tóth, L. Nagy, R. Kennedy, B. Bohuš, J. Abonyi, and T. Ruppert, "The human-centric Industry 5.0 collaboration architecture," MethodsX, vol. 11, no. March, p. 102260, 2023, doi: 10.1016/j.mex.2023.102260.

[16] M. Golovianko, V. Terziyan, V. Branytskyi, and D. Malyk, "Industry 4.0 vs. Industry 5.0: Co-existence, transition, or a hybrid," *Procedia Comput. Sci.*, vol. 217, no. 2022, pp. 102–113, 2023, doi: 10.1016/j.procs.2022.12.206.

[17] V. Pandey, A. Sircar, N. Bist, K. Solanki, and K. Yadav, "Accelerating the renewable energy sector through Industry 4.0: Optimization opportunities in the digital revolution," *Int. J. Innov. Stud.*, vol. 7, no. 2, pp. 171–188, 2023, doi: 10.1016/j.ijis.2023.03.003.

[18] J. Ordieres-Meré, M. Gutierrez, and J. Villalba-Díez, "Toward the industry 5.0 paradigm: Increasing value creation through the robust integration of humans and machines," *Comput. Ind.*, vol. 150, no. May, p. 103947, 2023, doi: 10.1016/j.compind.2023.103947.

[19] M. Javaid, A. Haleem, R. P. Singh, and R. Suman, "An integrated outlook of cyber–physical systems for Industry 4.0: Topical practices, architecture, and applications," *Green Technol. Sustain.*, vol. 1, no. 1, p. 100001, 2023, doi: 10.1016/j.grets.2022.100001.

[20] S. Ainslie, D. Thompson, S. Maynard, and A. Ahmad, "Cyber-threat intelligence for security decision-making: A review and research agenda for practice," *Comput. Secur.*, vol. 132, p. 103352, 2023, doi: 10.1016/j.cose.2023.103352.

[21] Q. Miao, H. Lin, J. Hu, and X. Wang, "An intelligent and privacy-enhanced data sharing strategy for blockchain-empowered Internet of Things," *Digit. Commun. Networks*, vol. 8, no. 5, pp. 636–643, 2022, doi: 10.1016/j.dcan.2021.12.007.

[22] C. M. Patterson, J. R. C. Nurse, and V. N. L. Franqueira, "Learning from cyber security incidents: A systematic review and future research agenda," *Comput. Secur.*, vol. 132, 2023, doi: 10.1016/j.cose.2023.103309.

[23] D. T. Salim, M. M. Singh, and P. Keikhosrokiani, "A systematic literature review for APT detection and Effective Cyber Situational Awareness (ECSA) conceptual model," *Heliyon*, vol. 9, no. 7, p. e17156, 2023, doi: 10.1016/j.heliyon.2023.e17156.

[24] N. J. Rowan et al., "Digital transformation of peatland eco-innovations ('Paludiculture'): Enabling a paradigm shift towards the real-time sustainable production of 'green-friendly' products and services," *Sci. Total Environ.*, vol. 838, no. April, 2022, doi: 10.1016/j.scitotenv.2022.156328.

[25] C. Mangla, S. Rani, N. M. Faseeh Qureshi, and A. Singh, "Mitigating 5G security challenges for next-gen industry using quantum computing," J. *King Saud Univ. Comput. Inf. Sci.*, vol. 35, no. 6, p. 101334, 2023, doi: 10.1016/j.jksuci.2022.07.009.

[26] M. S. Müller, T. Jung, N. Jazdi, and M. Weyrich, "Safeguarding autonomous systems: Emerging approaches, assumptions and metrics - A systematic literature review," *IFAC-PapersOnLine*, vol. 55, no. 6, pp. 743–754, 2022, doi: 10.1016/j.ifacol.2022.07.216.

[27] X. Ning and J. Jiang, "Defense-in-depth against insider attacks in cyber-physical systems," *Internet Things Cyber-Physical Syst.*, vol. 2, no. October, pp. 203–211, 2022, doi: 10.1016/j.iotcps.2022.12.001.

[28] R. Kaur, D. Gabrijelčič, and T. Klobučar, "Artificial intelligence for cybersecurity: Literature review and future research directions," *Information Fusion*, vol. 97, no. January, p. 101804, 2023, doi: 10.1016/j.inffus.2023.101804.

[29] B. Naqvi, K. Perova, A. Farooq, I. Makhdoom, S. Oyedeji, and J. Porras, "Mitigation strategies against the phishing attacks: A systematic literature review." *Computers & Security*," vol. 132, p. 103387, 2023, doi: 10.1016/j.cose.2023.103387.

[30] A. Zimba, Z. Wang, and H. Chen, "Multi-stage crypto ransomware attacks: A new emerging cyber threat to critical infrastructure and industrial control systems," *ICT Express*, vol. 4, no. 1, pp. 14–18, 2018, doi: 10.1016/j.icte.2017.12.007.

[31] G. Mott et al., "Between a rock and a hard(ening) place: Cyber insurance in the ransomware era," *Comput. Secur.*, vol. 128, no. November 2022, p. 103162, 2023, doi: 10.1016/j.cose.2023.103162.

[32] M. Safaei Pour, C. Nader, K. Friday, and E. Bou-Harb, "A comprehensive survey of recent internet measurement techniques for cyber security," *Comput. Secur.*, vol. 128, p. 103123, 2023, doi: 10.1016/j.cose.2023.103123.

[33] R. Prasad and Y. Moon, "Architecture for preventing and detecting cyber attacks in cyber-manufacturing system," *IFAC-PapersOnLine*, vol. 55, no. 10, pp. 2246–2251, 2022, doi: 10.1016/j.ifacol.2022.10.042.

[34] T. R. Reshmi, "Information security breaches due to ransomware attacks - A systematic literature review," *Int. J. Inf. Manag. Data Insights*, vol. 1, no. 2, p. 100013, 2021, doi: 10.1016/j.jjimei.2021.100013.

[35] M. H. (Miles) Chung et al., "Enhancing cybersecurity situation awareness through visualization: A USB data exfiltration case study," *Heliyon*, vol. 9, no. 1, p. e13025, 2023, doi: 10.1016/j.heliyon.2023.e13025.

[36] C. Lee, J. G. Song, C. K. Lee, and P. H. Seong, "Development of a method for securing the operator's situation awareness from manipulation attacks on NPP process data," *Nucl. Eng. Technol.*, vol. 54, no. 6, pp. 2011–2022, 2022, doi: 10.1016/j.net.2021.12.011.

[37] R. Kirner and P. Puschner, "A qualitative cybersecurity analysis of time-triggered communication networks in automotive systems," *J. Syst. Archit.*, vol. 136, no. October 2022, p. 102835, 2023, doi: 10.1016/j.sysarc.2023.102835.

[38] S. Khalid Khan, N. Shiwakoti, P. Stasinopoulos, and M. Warren, "Modelling cybersecurity regulations for automated vehicles," *Accid. Anal. Prev.*, vol. 186, no. August 2022, p. 107054, 2023, doi: 10.1016/j.aap.2023.107054.

[39] S. Sohail, Z. Fan, X. Gu, and F. Sabrina, "Multi-tiered artificial neural networks model for intrusion detection in smart homes," *Intell. Syst. with Appl.*, vol. 16, no. October, p. 200152, 2022, doi: 10.1016/j.iswa.2022.200152.

[40] S. Elfwing, E. Uchibe, and K. Doya, "Sigmoid-weighted linear units for neural network function approximation in reinforcement learning," *Neural Netw.*, vol. 107, pp. 3–11, 2018, doi: 10.1016/j.neunet.2017.12.012.

[41] A. Sharma et al., "Computer vision based healthcare system for identification of diabetes & its types using AI," *Meas. Sensors*, vol. 27, no. February, p. 100751, 2023, doi: 10.1016/j.measen.2023.100751.

[42] S. Siddique, S. Islam, E. E. Neon, T. Sabbir, I. T. Naheen, and R. Khan, "DL-based bangla sign language detection with an edge device," *Intell. Syst. with Appl.*, vol. 18, no. February, p. 200224, 2023, doi: 10.1016/j.iswa.2023.200224.

[43] N. Sharma, R. Sharma, and N. Jindal, "Machine learning and DL applications - A vision," *Glob. Transitions Proc.*, vol. 2, no. 1, pp. 24–28, 2021, doi: 10.1016/j.gltp.2021.01.004.

[44] L. Zhang, J. Wang, and Y. Liu, "DL-based ransomware detection system for industrial networks," In Proceedings of the International Conference on Industrial Engineering and Operations Management, pp. 1984–1990, 2019.

[45] C. Pena, D. Morales, and S. Siller, "Fine-tuning DL Models for ransomware detection in industrial IoT devices," *J. Cybersecurity Inf Manage.*, vol. 15, no. 3, pp. 267–278, 2020.

[46] X. Li, Q. Wang, and G. Xu, "Optimization of fine-tuning for ransomware attack detection using data augmentation," In Proceedings of the IEEE International Conference on Cybersecurity and Privacy, pp. 120–128, 2021.

[47] W. Chen, M. Zhang, S. Liu, "Enhancing adversarial robustness of fine-tuned ransomware detection models," *ACM Trans. Priv. Secur.*, vol. 25, no. 1, pp. 1–18, 2022.

[48] H. Zhang, S. Chen, and L. Wang, "Multi-modal DL for ransomware detection in Industry 4.0 environments," *IEEE Trans. Ind. Inform.*, vol. 16, no. 4, pp. 2456–2465, 2020.

[49] Q. Wu, J. Zhao, and Y. Li, "Real-time ransomware detection in industrial iot environments using fine-tuned CNNs," *J. Comput. Netw. Commun.*, pp. 1–10, 2021.

[50] I. Chakroun, T. Haber, and T. J. Ashby, "SW-SGD: The sliding window stochastic gradient descent algorithm," *Procedia Comput. Sci.*, vol. 108, pp. 2318–2322, 2017, doi: 10.1016/j.procs.2017.05.082.

[51] F. Marini, *Non-linear Modeling: Neural Networks*, Second Edition., vol. 3, no. January. Elsevier, 2020, doi: 10.1016/b978-0-12-409547-2.14893-0.

[52] A. Sherstinsky, "Fundamentals of Recurrent Neural Network (RNN) and Long Short-Term Memory (LSTM) network," *Phys. D Nonlinear Phenom.*, vol. 404, p. 132306, 2020, doi: 10.1016/j.physd.2019.132306.

[53] N. S. Ouf, "Leguminous seeds detection based on convolutional neural networks: Comparison of Faster R-CNN and YOLOv4 on a small custom dataset," *Artif. Intell. Agric.*, vol. 8, pp. 30–45, 2023, doi: 10.1016/j.aiia.2023.03.002.

[54] S. Ren, K. He, R. Girshick, and J. Sun, "Faster R-CNN: Towards real-time object detection with region proposal networks," *IEEE Trans. Pattern Anal. Mach. Intell.*, vol. 39, no. 6, pp. 1137–1149, 2017, doi: 10.1109/TPAMI.2016.2577031.

[55] S. Wijaya, Y. Heryadi, Y. Arifin, W. Suparta, and Lukas, "Long short-term memory (LSTM) model-based reinforcement learning for nonlinear mass spring damper system control," *Procedia Comput. Sci.*, vol. 216, no. 2022, pp. 213–220, 2023, doi: 10.1016/j.procs.2022.12.129.

[56] A. K. Shahade, K. H. Walse, V. M. Thakare, and M. Atique, "Multi-lingual opinion mining for social media discourses: An approach using DL based hybrid fine-tuned smith algorithm with adam optimizer," *Int. J. Inf. Manag. Data Insights*, vol. 3, no. 2, p. 100182, 2023, doi: 10.1016/j.jjimei.2023.100182.

[57] J. B. Awotunde, T. Gaber, L. N. Prasad, S. O. Folorunso, and V. L. Lalitha, "Privacy and security enhancement of smart cities using hybrid deep learning-enabled blockchain," *Scalable Comput. Prac. Exp.*, vol. 24, no. 3, pp. 561–584, 2023.

[58] J. B. Awotunde, R. Panigrahi, S. Shukla, B. Panda, and A. K. Bhoi, "Big data analytics enabled deep convolutional neural network for the diagnosis of cancer," *Knowl. Inf. Syst.*, vol. 66, no. 2, pp. 905–931, 2023.

[59] J. K. Adeniyi, T. T. Adeniyi, J. B. Awotunde, M. K. Abiodun, and O. G. Atanda, "Agrolend: A blockchain implementation approach of smart contract farming platform," In 2023 International Conference on Science, Engineering and Business for Sustainable Development Goals (SEB-SDG), IEEE, vol. 1, pp. 1–7, 2023.

[60] G. Abdiyeva-Aliyeva, J. Aliyev, and U. Sadigov, "Application of classification algorithms of Machine learning in cybersecurity," *Procedia Comput. Sci.*, vol. 215, pp. 909–919, 2022, doi: 10.1016/j.procs.2022.12.093.

7 Blockchain in Industry 4.0 and Industry 5.0

A Paradigm Shift towards Decentralized Efficiency and Autonomous Ecosystems

Manjushree Nayak, Asish Panigrahi, Ashish Kumar Dass, Brojo Kishore Mishra, and Shashi Kant Gupta

7.1 INTRODUCTION TO INDUSTRIES 4.0 AND 5.0

Industry 4.0 and Industry 5.0 are two distinct phases in the evolution of industrial systems and manufacturing processes. Industry 4.0, known as the Fourth Industrial Revolution, represents the fast digital technologies in manufacturing, including the Internet of Things (IoT), artificial intelligence (AI), robotics, and big data analytics. It aims to create smart factories and interconnected systems that optimize efficiency, productivity, and customization. On the other hand, Industry 5.0 envisions a future where humans and machines collaborate harmoniously. It emphasizes the value of human skills, productivity, and emotional intelligence, complemented by technologies like advanced robotics, augmented reality, and additive manufacturing. Industry 5.0 seeks to combine the strengths of both humans and machines, fostering innovation, flexibility, and a more fulfilling work environment. While Industry 4.0 is already being implemented, Industry 5.0 serves as an aspirational framework for the next phase of industrial development.

7.1.1 What Is Industry 4.0?

The manufacturing and industrial sectors are undergoing a transformative period known as "Industry 4.0," or the "Fourth Industrial Revolution," which is being driven by the sum of modern technology and digital systems. It builds upon the foundation laid by the previous industrial revolutions but takes it to new heights by leveraging the power of connectivity and automation. At its core, Industry 4.0 aims to create smart factories and intelligent manufacturing systems that are highly flexible, efficient, and responsive to dynamic market demands. The Internet of Things (IoT),

 DOI: 10.1201/9781003581963-7

artificial intelligence (AI), big data analytics, cloud computing, and cyber-physical systems are some of the key technologies that underpin Industry 4.0. The Internet of Things enables the interconnection of various devices, sensors, and machines within the manufacturing environment, facilitating real-time data collection and communication. This connectivity allows for seamless coordination and control of the entire production process, from raw material sourcing to final product delivery. Artificial intelligence and machine learning play a vital role in Industry 4.0 by enabling machines and systems to analyze enormous volumes of data and come to wise decisions. AI algorithms can optimize production workflows, predict maintenance needs, and identify patterns and anomalies in manufacturing processes, leading to enhanced efficiency and reduced downtime.

Big data analytics gives meaningful insights from the enormous volumes [3] of data generated by industrial operations. By analyzing and interpreting these data, manufacturers can uncover correlations that can drive process improvements, quality enhancements, and cost savings. Cloud computing serves as a critical infrastructure in Industry 4.0, enabling the storage, processing, and sharing of data across different devices and locations. It provides scalable and secure platforms for data management, software deployment, and collaboration, ensuring that relevant information is accessible to all stakeholders in real time. Cyber-physical systems, which encompass the integration of physical machinery with digital systems, form the backbone of Industry 4.0. These systems combine hardware, software, and network connectivity to create intelligent and autonomous production environments. Cyber-physical systems enable machines and processes to communicate, cooperate, and make decentralized decisions, resulting in increased productivity, flexibility, and customization capabilities. The benefits of Industry 4.0 are wide-ranging. It offers manufacturers the potential to optimize resource utilization, reduce waste, and achieve higher levels of productivity.

The ability to analyze data allows for predictive maintenance, minimizing equipment failures and unplanned downtime. Industry 4.0 also enables mass customization, where products can be tailored to individual customer requirements without sacrificing efficiency or cost-effectiveness. While Industry 4.0 presents numerous opportunities, it also brings forth challenges that need to be addressed, and ensuring equitable access to technological advancements across different regions and industries.

7.2 THE EMERGENCE OF INDUSTRY 5.0

Industry 5.0, the envisioned next phase of industry development, represents a paradigm shift in the relationship between humans and machines. Building upon the foundation laid by Industry 4.0, Industry 5.0 seeks collaboration between human and advanced technologies, combining [2] the unique strengths of both to drive innovation and productivity to new heights. At its core, Industry 5.0 recognizes the price of human skills and emotional intelligence in the manufacturing process. It envisions a future where humans and machines work side by side in a collaborative and symbiotic manner, leveraging the capabilities of each to achieve optimal results. Advanced robotics plays a key role in Industry 5.0, where robots are designed to assist and augment human capabilities rather than replace them. These robots are equipped with advanced sensors, perception capabilities, and dexterity to perform intricate tasks in coordination with human operators. By handling repetitive or physically demanding tasks, robots free up human workers to focus on more complex, creative, and cognitive aspects of production.

Technologies such as augmented reality (AR) and virtual reality (VR) are instrumental in Industry 5.0, providing immersive interfaces that enhance human–machine interaction. AR and VR enable real-time information overlays, digital work instructions, and remote collaboration, improving operational efficiency and reducing errors. Additive manufacturing, or 3D printing, is another key technology in Industry 5.0. It empowers manufacturers to produce highly customized and on-demand products, allowing for greater personalization and responsiveness to customer needs. Additive manufacturing also facilitates decentralized production and reduces the reliance on centralized factories, enabling local manufacturing and reducing supply chain complexities. Industry 5.0 envisions a work environment that prioritizes fulfilling and meaningful jobs. By leveraging technology to automate repetitive tasks, Industry 5.0 aims to create opportunities for upskilling and reskilling the workforce. This approach not only enhances job satisfaction but also empowers workers to embrace new roles that require creativity, critical thinking, problem-solving, and adaptability.

Furthermore, Industry 5.0 recognizes the importance of ethical considerations and sustainability. It seeks to develop environmentally friendly and socially responsible manufacturing practices, incorporating circular economy principles and reducing waste throughout the product lifecycle. While Industry 5.0 is still a conceptual framework, its vision provides a guidepost for the future of manufacturing. It holds the promise of revolutionizing the workplace, creating innovative products, and fostering a more inclusive and empowering industrial landscape. As the world continues to advance technologically, Industry 5.0 serves as a catalyst for reshaping industries and maximizing the potential of human–machine collaboration (Figures 7.1 and 7.2).

7.3 KEY TECHNOLOGIES AND TRENDS

In the context of Industry 4.0 and the emerging Industry 5.0, several key technologies and trends are shaping the future of industrial development and manufacturing. These technologies and trends include:

1. The Internet of Things (IoT): The IoT forms the backbone of interconnected systems in Industry 4.0 and Industry 5.0. It enables the integration of sensors, devices, and machines, allowing for real-time data collection, communication, and control. The IoT facilitates smart monitoring, predictive maintenance, and enhanced operational efficiency (Figure 7.3).
2. Artificial Intelligence (AI) and Machine Learning: These play a critical role in Industry 4.0 and beyond. They enable machines to analyze large datasets, identify patterns, make autonomous decisions, and continuously improve

FIGURE 7.1 3D printing.

FIGURE 7.2 Blockchain technology.

performance. AI-powered systems optimize production processes, enable predictive analytics, and support intelligent automation.

3. Big Data Analytics: The availability of vast amounts of data generated by industrial processes presents immense opportunities for insights and optimization. Big data analytics tools and techniques enable the extraction, processing, and analysis of data to uncover patterns, trends, and correlations. This information drives informed decision-making, predictive maintenance, and operational improvements.

FIGURE 7.3 The Internet of Things.

4. Robotics and Automation: Robotics and automation technologies have significantly transformed manufacturing processes. Advanced robots equipped with sensors, vision systems, and AI capabilities collaborate with humans, enhancing productivity, precision, and safety. Automation streamlines workflows, reduces errors, and enables greater production flexibility.
5. Additive Manufacturing (3D Printing): Additive manufacturing allows for the production of complex, customized, and on-demand parts and products. It eliminates traditional manufacturing constraints, reduces waste, and enables decentralized production. 3D printing empowers designers and manufacturers to rapidly prototype, iterate, and innovate.
6. Virtual Reality (VR) and Augmented Reality (AR): These improve training, visualization, and human–machine interaction. They provide immersive experiences, overlay digital information in real time, and enable remote collaboration. AR and VR improve operational efficiency, training effectiveness, and maintenance procedures.
7. Cybersecurity: With increased connectivity, securing industrial systems and data becomes crucial. Cybersecurity includes safeguards against cyber threats and protects sensitive information, ensuring the reliability, integrity, and confidentiality of industrial operations.
8. Sustainable Manufacturing: Environmental consciousness and sustainability are key considerations in modern manufacturing. Industries are adopting sustainable practices, such as energy-efficient processes, waste reduction, recycling, and the use of renewable resources. Circular economy principles, including product life extension and recycling, are gaining prominence.

These technologies and trends are shaping the future of industrial development, driving productivity, efficiency, customization, and innovation. They provide a foundation for the transition from Industry 4.0 to Industry 5.0, where human–machine collaboration, creativity, and ethical considerations take center stage.

7.3.1 Understanding Blockchain Technology

Blockchain [1,4] technology is a concept that has gained widespread attention and recognition in recent years. Blockchain is fundamentally a transparent technology, which makes it immutable and safe. Blockchain functions on a peer-to-peer network, assuring trust and doing away with the need for middlemen, in contrast to traditional centralized systems, which depend on a single authority or intermediary. Blockchain technology is based on blocks, which are collections of transactions or other data. Cryptographic techniques are used to connect each block to the one before it, resulting in a chain of blocks that goes by the name "blockchain." By replicating and storing the ledger across numerous computers or nodes, this linkage produces a distributed ledger that is extremely resistant to manipulation or illegal adjustments. One of the key features of blockchain technology is its transparency. Additionally, the decentralized [17] nature of blockchain enhances security by eliminating a single point of failure.

As each transaction is validated by multiple nodes in the network through consensus mechanisms, the chances of malicious activities or data manipulation are significantly reduced. Blockchain technology also offers immutability, meaning that once a transaction or data is recorded on the blockchain, it becomes virtually. This feature ensures the integrity of the information stored on the blockchain and builds trust among participants who can rely on the accuracy and reliability of the data. Blockchain [18] potential applications extend far beyond cryptocurrencies like Bitcoin. Smart contracts, which are self-executing agreements with predefined conditions written into the blockchain, further expand the possibilities of automation and trust in various domains. While blockchain [19] technology holds immense promise. It also has to deal with issues including energy usage, scalability, and regulatory concerns.

7.3.2 Basics of Blockchain

Blockchain operates on a network of computers, often referred to as nodes, which collaborate to maintain and validate the integrity of the blockchain. The core concept of blockchain [20] revolves around blocks, which are containers of information. Block contains a batch of data, and these blocks are cryptographically [21] linked together in a chronological order, forming a chain. This linking process ensures that the blocks are tamper-resistant since any change in a previous block [22] would require altering subsequent blocks, which becomes increasingly difficult as the chain grows. Consensus procedures are used to preserve the blockchain integrity. These protocols guarantee that all network users concur on the legitimacy of transactions and the sequence in which they should be added to the blockchain. Proof of work (PoW) and proof of stake (PoS) are two popular consensus mechanisms that use computational or stake-based techniques, respectively, to obtain an agreement. A block cannot be removed or changed after it is put to the blockchain without the approval of the majority of the network. This property makes the block unchangeable. Because of its immutability, which offers a high degree of security and trust, blockchain technology is well suited for uses where data integrity and transparency are essential. Decentralization is yet another crucial aspect of blockchain technology.

Blockchain distributes the data among several network nodes. Because it is decentralized, there is no longer a need for middlemen, there is less chance of a single point of failure, and it creates a more unfriendly atmosphere where users may communicate with each other directly. Because blockchain technology is linked to cryptocurrencies like Bitcoin, it has attracted a lot of attention. Its promise goes far beyond virtual currency, though. Blockchain is being investigated by a number of industries, including finance, real estate, supply chain management, and healthcare, in order to improve security, expedite workflows, and build more transparent and efficient systems. Blockchain has a lot going for it, but it also has drawbacks, like energy consumption, scalability, and regulatory issues. Scalability is the capacity of a blockchain network to effectively manage a high volume of transactions. Additionally, the regulatory landscape surrounding blockchain is still evolving, and policymakers are working to establish frameworks that balance innovation and consumer protection.

7.3.3 Decentralization and Consensus Mechanisms

Decentralization and consensus mechanisms are two fundamental components of blockchain technology that contribute to its unique characteristics and capabilities. Decentralization [23] is the dispersion of power and management among a group of nodes in a network as opposed to their concentration in a single central figure or middleman. Decentralization promotes transparency, trust, and resilience, making blockchain suitable for applications where security and autonomy are crucial. Consensus methods are essential to preserving consensus in a decentralized blockchain network and guaranteeing the legitimacy of transactions. Consensus is essential to prevent double-spending, where a user spends the same digital asset or cryptocurrency more than once. Different consensus mechanisms employ various algorithms and protocols to achieve agreement among network participants.

One widely known consensus mechanism is proof-of-work (PoW), which is used by Bitcoin and many other cryptocurrencies. PoW requires network participants. This computational work helps secure the blockchain by making it computationally expensive to attack or manipulate the network. Another popular consensus mechanism is proof-of-stake (PoS), where the probability of creating a new block and validating transactions is determined by the stake or ownership of a cryptocurrency held by participants. In PoS, validators are chosen based on their economic stake, and they are incentivized to maintain the security as they have a stake at risk. With regard to decentralization, security, scalability, and energy efficiency, each mechanism has pros and cons of its own. Consensus mechanisms facilitate agreement among participants without relying on a central authority or intermediary, ensuring that the blockchain network functions effectively and securely. They enable trust and integrity in a decentralized environment, where participants can transact and interact with confidence, knowing that the consensus of the network validates their actions (Figure 7.4).

FIGURE 7.4 Decentralized mechanism of blockchain.

7.3.4 Smart Contracts and Distributed Ledger Technology

Smart contracts and distributed ledger technology (DLT) are integral components of blockchain systems that enhance automation, transparency, and efficiency in various industries. These contracts are agreed upon by the involved parties without the need for intermediaries. Smart contracts enable the automation of business processes, eliminating manual intervention and reducing the potential for errors or disputes. They can facilitate a wide range of activities, such as financial transactions, intellectual property rights, and more. By leveraging smart contracts, businesses can streamline operations, increase trust, and reduce costs. Distributed ledger technology refers to the underlying infrastructure that supports the transparent nature of blockchain systems. In a distributed ledger, copies of the entire blockchain are maintained across multiple nodes or computers within a network. Each node has access to an identical copy of the ledger and independently verifies and validates transactions. By guaranteeing that everyone has access to the same data, this distributed consensus promotes openness and does away with the need for a central authority to keep track of or reconcile records.

DLT provides several benefits, including enhanced security and resilience. Since the ledger is distributed across multiple nodes, it becomes highly resistant to tampering, hacking, or data loss. Even if one or more nodes fail or are compromised, the remaining nodes ensure the availability and integrity of the ledger. This robustness makes DLT suitable for applications where data integrity and security are paramount. Furthermore, DLT enables improved traceability and auditability. Each transaction is recorded on the distributed ledger. This feature allows participants to trace the origin and movement of assets, products, or information, ensuring transparency and accountability. Auditing processes can also be simplified as auditors can directly access and verify transactions on the distributed ledger, reducing the reliance on manual record-keeping and reconciliation. By leveraging the automation and transparency provided by smart contracts, businesses can streamline operations, reduce costs, and create more efficient and trustworthy systems. Distributed ledger technology ensures the integrity, security, and availability of data, fostering trust among participants and enabling new business models. However, it is important to consider the challenges associated with smart contracts and distributed ledger technology, such as legal and regulatory implications, scalability, and interoperability. As these technologies continue to evolve, efforts aim to address these challenges and unlock the full potential of smart contracts and distributed ledger technology in driving innovation and transforming industries.

7.4 BLOCKCHAIN IN INDUSTRY 4.0: TRANSFORMING MANUFACTURING PROCESSES

Blockchain technology is transforming manufacturing processes in Industry 4.0 by revolutionizing supply chain management, enhancing quality control, enabling digital twins and remote monitoring, and optimizing predictive maintenance and asset tracking. One of the key applications of blockchain in Industry 4.0 is supply chain management and traceability. With blockchain, each step in the supply chain can be securely recorded with a verified record of product movement. This transparency enables stakeholders to track and authenticate products, verify their origin, and ensure compliance with regulations. Blockchain-based smart contracts can automate processes such as payment settlements, reducing administrative costs and streamlining transactions within the supply chain. Quality control and product authentication are also significantly improved through blockchain implementation. By recording product information, quality certifications, and test results on the blockchain, manufacturers can create an immutable record of a product's journey, ensuring its authenticity and quality. This enhances consumer trust and helps combat issues such as counterfeit products or unauthorized substitutions. Smart contracts can automate quality checks and trigger alerts for non-compliant products, facilitating quick actions to rectify any quality-related issues.

Digital twins, virtual representations of physical assets or processes, integrated with blockchain, provide manufacturers with real-time insights and remote monitoring capabilities. By securely linking digital twins to their physical counterparts through blockchain, manufacturers can remotely monitor equipment performance, analyze real-time data, and optimize maintenance schedules. This proactive approach minimizes downtime, improves operational efficiency, and extends the lifespan of assets, ultimately reducing costs and enhancing productivity. Predictive maintenance and asset tracking are further enhanced by blockchain technology in Industry 4.0. Real-time data from sensors embedded in machinery or products can be recorded on the blockchain, allowing for predictive analytics to identify patterns and potential maintenance requirements. Smart contracts can automatically trigger maintenance requests or order replacement parts when predefined conditions are met. Additionally, blockchain-based asset tracking provides a transparent and auditable record of an asset's lifecycle, enabling more efficient inventory management and reducing losses.

By leveraging blockchain technology in Industry 4.0, manufacturers can achieve greater transparency, efficiency, and trust in their operations. Blockchain's inherent features of decentralization, transparency, and immutability enable secure and reliable data sharing, streamline processes, and enhance collaboration among stakeholders. However, challenges such as scalability, regulatory considerations, and cultural barriers need to be addressed to fully unlock the potential of blockchain in transforming manufacturing processes in Industry 4.0. Blockchain technology has the ability to completely transform the industrial sector through further study, development, and use. This would result in more output, lower prices, and more general efficiency.

7.4.1 Supply Chain Management and Traceability

Supply chain management and traceability are critical aspects of modern business operations, and blockchain technology is revolutionizing these areas by providing enhanced transparency, accountability, and efficiency. Traditional supply chains often involve numerous stakeholders, including manufacturers, suppliers, distributors, retailers, and consumers. The complexity and lack of visibility in these supply chains can lead to challenges such as counterfeiting, product recalls, supply chain disruptions, and ethical concerns. Blockchain technology addresses these challenges by creating a decentralized and transparent ledger where all transactions and activities within the supply chain can be recorded securely. Through blockchain, each transaction and movement of goods can be immutably recorded on the distributed ledger. This creates a transparent and auditable trail of the product's journey from its origin to the end consumer. Blockchain enables the verification and authentication of products. By recording product details, such as batch numbers, serial numbers, manufacturing dates, and certifications, it can easily trace and assure the quality of products. This capability is particularly crucial in industries where counterfeit products pose significant risks, such as pharmaceuticals, luxury goods, and electronics.

Smart contracts play a vital role in supply chain management on the blockchain. Smart contracts can automate various aspects of supply chain processes, such as payment settlements, quality control checks, and delivery confirmations. This automation reduces administrative overheads, eliminates the need for intermediaries, and speeds up transaction times, resulting in more efficient supply chain operations. Blockchain-based supply chain management systems also facilitate proactive measures to address issues such as product recalls or supply chain disruptions. In the event of a product recall, the immutable nature of the blockchain ensures that accurate and timely information can be shared across the supply chain, enabling rapid identification and removal of affected products. Similarly, during supply chain disruptions and logistical information, it can enable stakeholders to make informed decisions and minimize disruptions. The adoption of traceability offers several benefits. It enhances transparency, reduces fraud, improves efficiency, and fosters trust among stakeholders. Additionally, blockchain-based systems can enable more sustainable and ethical supply chains by verifying and validating compliance with social and environmental standards. By leveraging blockchain technology, businesses can streamline their supply chain processes, ensure product authenticity, and meet the growing demands of consumers for transparency and accountability.

7.4.2 Quality Control and Product Authentication

Quality control and product authentication are critical aspects of ensuring consumer confidence and maintaining brand reputation. Blockchain technology is playing a significant role in enhancing this product information. With blockchain, manufacturers can create a quality certification, and test results. This information can be securely stored on the blockchain, making it accessible to all authorized stakeholders in the supply chain. By recording quality control data on the blockchain, manufacturers can ensure the integrity and authenticity of their products. Product authentication is another area where blockchain technology shines. Counterfeit products pose a significant threat to businesses and consumers alike, leading to financial losses and potential harm to consumers. Blockchain-based systems provide a transparent and immutable record of a product's journey from its origin to the end consumer. This record includes information such as the manufacturer, production dates, shipping details, and quality certifications. Consumers can easily verify the authenticity of a product by scanning a unique identifier or QR code and accessing the corresponding blockchain data.

By leveraging smart contracts, manufacturers can automate quality control processes and enforce compliance with established standards. Smart contracts can be programmed to trigger alerts or notifications when specific quality parameters are not met, enabling quick actions to rectify any issues. This automation streamlines quality control procedures, reduces human error, and ensures consistent adherence to quality standards throughout the production and distribution processes. Blockchain technology also facilitates supply chain traceability, which is closely linked to quality control and product authentication. With blockchain, stakeholders can track and verify the movement of products at each stage of the supply chain. This transparency enables early detection of potential issues, such as unauthorized substitutions or deviations from quality standards, allowing for timely corrective actions.

The implementation of blockchain technology in quality control and product authentication offers numerous benefits. It enhances consumer trust by providing verifiable and transparent information about product origins, quality, and authenticity. Manufacturers can demonstrate their commitment to delivering high-quality products and differentiate themselves in the market. Moreover, the decentralized nature of blockchain eliminates the need for intermediaries and reduces the risk of data manipulation or fraud. As blockchain continues to evolve, it holds immense potential for revolutionizing quality control and product authentication processes. By leveraging this technology, businesses can establish a robust framework for maintaining quality standards, combating counterfeiting, and safeguarding consumer interests.

7.4.3 Digital Twins and Remote Monitoring

Digital twins and remote monitoring are key components of Industry 4.0, and blockchain technology is playing a transformative role in enhancing these capabilities. By combining digital twins with blockchain, manufacturers can achieve real-time monitoring, analysis, and optimization of their assets, leading to improved operational efficiency and reduced downtime. It captures data embedded in the physical asset and mirrors its behavior in the virtual world. Blockchain technology can securely link the digital twin to its physical counterpart, ensuring data integrity and immutability. This integration enables manufacturers to monitor and analyze the performance, condition, and usage patterns of their assets remotely. Through blockchain-based digital twins, manufacturers can gain valuable insights into assets. Real-time data from sensors, such as temperature, pressure, or vibration, can be recorded on the blockchain, creating an auditable and transparent history of the asset's behavior. These data can be analyzed using advanced analytics and machine learning algorithms to detect anomalies, predict maintenance requirements, and optimize asset utilization.

Remote monitoring is a crucial aspect of digital twin implementation, and blockchain technology enhances the security and trustworthiness of remote monitoring systems. Manufacturers and authorized stakeholders can access the blockchain-based data and monitor asset performance remotely, enabling timely decision-making and proactive maintenance actions. Furthermore, blockchain-based digital twins facilitate collaboration and information sharing among stakeholders. Multiple parties, such as equipment manufacturers, maintenance providers, and operators, can access and contribute to the digital twin's data on the blockchain. This transparency and collaboration foster a holistic approach to asset management, enabling stakeholders to work together to optimize asset performance, reduce maintenance costs, and extend asset lifecycles.

Blockchain technology also offers opportunities for monetizing data generated by digital twins. Manufacturers can securely share selected data points from their digital twins with trusted partners or service providers through blockchain-based data marketplaces. This data sharing can lead to new revenue streams, collaborative innovation, and the development of value-added services. Overall, the integration of digital twins with blockchain technology revolutionizes remote monitoring and asset management in Industry 4.0. It empowers manufacturers with real-time insights, predictive analytics, and collaborative capabilities. By leveraging blockchain-based digital twins, manufacturers can optimize asset performance, reduce maintenance costs, and enhance operational efficiency, ultimately contributing to the success and competitiveness of their businesses in the era of digital transformation.

7.4.4 Predictive Maintenance and Asset Tracking

Predictive maintenance and asset tracking are critical aspects of efficient operations in Industry 4.0, and blockchain technology is proving to be a game-changer in these areas. By leveraging blockchain for predictive maintenance and asset tracking, manufacturers can optimize maintenance schedules, reduce downtime, and improve overall asset performance. Predictive maintenance involves leveraging data analytics and machine learning algorithms to identify patterns and anomalies in equipment behavior, allowing for timely maintenance interventions. Blockchain technology plays a vital role in predictive maintenance by securely recording and storing real-time sensor data on the distributed ledger. These data include information such as temperature, vibration, performance metrics, and usage patterns. By storing these data on the blockchain, they become immutable and transparent, ensuring the integrity and accuracy of the maintenance records.

With blockchain-based predictive maintenance, manufacturers can proactively identify maintenance requirements and address them before they lead to critical failures or unplanned downtime. Smart contracts can be programmed to automatically trigger maintenance alerts or work orders based on predefined conditions, such as abnormal sensor readings or deviation from performance thresholds. This automation streamlines maintenance processes, reduces response times, and optimizes resource allocation. Asset tracking is another crucial application of blockchain technology in Industry 4.0. Traditional asset tracking methods often involve complex and centralized systems, leading to challenges such as data silos, inefficiencies, and limited transparency. By securely recording asset information, such as serial numbers, location, ownership history, and maintenance records, on the blockchain, manufacturers can have a comprehensive and auditable view of their assets.

Each time an asset changes hands or moves to a different location, the transaction is recorded on the blockchain, creating a transparent and tamper-proof history. This enhanced visibility improves inventory management, reduces the risk of asset loss or theft, and enables efficient asset utilization. These data can be accessed by authorized stakeholders to track asset status, monitor performance metrics, and make informed decisions regarding maintenance, replacement, or optimization. By leveraging blockchain for predictive maintenance and asset tracking, manufacturers can optimize their operations, reduce maintenance costs, and extend asset lifecycles. The decentralized and transparent nature of blockchain enhances data integrity, eliminates information asymmetry, and fosters collaboration among stakeholders. With real-time insights and proactive maintenance strategies, manufacturers can minimize downtime, improve asset performance, and ensure the continuous and efficient operation of their assets in the era of Industry 4.0.

7.5 ENHANCING COLLABORATION AND SECURITY IN INDUSTRY 4.0 WITH BLOCKCHAIN

In an increasingly interconnected and digitized environment, where multiple stakeholders and systems need to collaborate seamlessly, blockchain offers a trusted framework that fosters collaboration while ensuring data integrity and security. The aim is to enhance through is its ability to eliminate the need for intermediaries and facilitate peer-to-peer interactions. Blockchain enables direct transactions and data sharing between participants without relying on centralized authorities or intermediaries. This decentralized nature of blockchain streamlines collaboration, reduces costs, and accelerates decision-making processes. Smart contracts, embedded within the blockchain, automate and enforce predefined rules and conditions, further enhancing collaboration by removing the need for manual interventions and reducing the risk of disputes. Blockchain also enhances data security and privacy in Industry 4.0. The cryptographic algorithms used in blockchain ensure the integrity and confidentiality of data.

Each transaction recorded on the blockchain is cryptographically secured. However, the adoption of blockchain in Industry 4.0 still faces challenges, including scalability, interoperability, and regulatory considerations. Overcoming these challenges will require further research, development, and collaboration among industry players, policymakers, and standardization bodies. Nonetheless, as blockchain technology continues to evolve, it holds significant promise for enhancing collaboration and security in Industry 4.0, enabling organizations to leverage the benefits of a trusted and decentralized infrastructure for seamless collaboration, secure data sharing, and robust cybersecurity.

7.5.1 Interoperability and Data Sharing

Interoperability and data sharing are critical aspects of Industry 4.0, where diverse systems, technologies, and stakeholders need to collaborate seamlessly. Blockchain technology is emerging as a promising solution to address the challenges associated with interoperability and data sharing in this complex ecosystem. Interoperability refers to the ability of different systems, devices, and applications to communicate, exchange data, and work together effectively. In Industry 4.0, where various technologies such as IoT devices, AI systems, and cloud [6] platforms coexist, achieving interoperability is essential for seamless operations and efficient data flow. Blockchain provides a decentralized and standardized platform that can facilitate interoperability among disparate systems. Blockchain distributed ledger technology serves as a shared infrastructure that enables different stakeholders to interact and exchange data in a secure and transparent manner. Through blockchain, participants can establish common data formats, protocols, and smart contracts that define how data are shared and processed across the network.

This standardized approach to data sharing and interoperability promotes seamless integration and collaboration among various systems and stakeholders. Moreover, blockchain's decentralized nature eliminates the need for a centralized authority or intermediary to manage data sharing and interoperability. Instead, blockchain allows for peer-to-peer interactions, where participants can directly exchange data and assets without relying on a single point of control. This decentralized approach enhances data sovereignty, privacy, and security, as participants maintain ownership and control over their data while securely sharing it with authorized parties. Blockchain-based data-sharing protocols and frameworks further enhance interoperability by providing secure and standardized mechanisms for data exchange. These protocols enable seamless integration of diverse data sources and formats, ensuring compatibility and consistency in data transactions.

Smart contracts embedded in the blockchain automate and enforce predefined rules and conditions for data sharing, facilitating trust and reliability in the interoperability process. By leveraging blockchain for interoperability and data sharing, Industry 4.0 stakeholders can unlock new possibilities for collaboration, innovation, and value creation. The ability to share data seamlessly across systems and organizations opens up opportunities for cross-domain applications, improved supply chain visibility, and enhanced decision-making based on real-time and reliable data. Furthermore, blockchain immutability and transparency provide an audit trail for data transactions, enabling traceability, accountability, and compliance with regulations and standards. While challenges remain, such as scalability, performance, and governance, the ongoing development of blockchain protocols, interoperability standards, and industry collaborations is paving the way for overcoming these obstacles. As blockchain technology continues to mature, it holds significant promise for achieving seamless interoperability and secure data sharing in Industry 4.0, driving innovation and unlocking the full potential of this transformative era.

7.5.2 Intellectual Property and Rights Management

Intellectual property (IP) and rights management are crucial considerations in the digital age, particularly in Industry 4.0, where the exchange and utilization of digital assets are prevalent. Blockchain technology offers innovative solutions for managing and protecting intellectual property rights, fostering trust, transparency, and efficiency in IP-related processes. By registering IP-related information on the blockchain, creators and innovators can establish an immutable and time-stamped record of their creations, proving ownership and establishing a digital trail of evidence. This decentralized approach mitigates the risk of fraudulent claims and disputes, as the blockchain acts as a trusted and auditable source of truth. Smart contracts are self-executing agreements that automatically enforce predefined conditions and rules. They enable automated royalty distribution, licensing agreements, and usage permissions, streamlining the licensing and monetization of IP assets. With smart contracts, creators can define the terms and conditions for the usage of their intellectual property, ensuring fair compensation and control over its utilization. Blockchain also facilitates secure licensing and transfer of IP rights. Through blockchain-based marketplaces, creators can directly connect with potential licensees or buyers, eliminating intermediaries and reducing transaction costs. Blockchain's decentralized nature enhances trust between parties and reduces the risk of unauthorized use or infringement.

Additionally, blockchain transparency and immutability provide a reliable mechanism for IP enforcement and protection. Any changes or transactions related to IP assets are recorded on the blockchain, creating an auditable history of ownership and usage. This feature can serve as valuable evidence in the event of IP disputes or infringements, simplifying legal proceedings and reducing the burden of proof. Blockchain's tamper-proof nature ensures the integrity and authenticity of IP-related records, safeguarding against unauthorized modifications or tampering.

Furthermore, blockchain technology enables the creation of decentralized IP registries and repositories. These distributed databases store IP-related information, such as patents, trademarks, and copyrights, in a secure and transparent manner. By decentralizing IP registries, blockchain reduces the risk of data loss or manipulation, enhances accessibility and discoverability of IP assets, and streamlines the process of searching and verifying existing IP rights. While blockchain technology offers significant advantages in IP and rights management, challenges such as legal frameworks, standardization, and interoperability need to be addressed for broader adoption. Collaboration between technology providers, legal experts, and regulatory bodies is crucial to establishing appropriate regulations and frameworks that govern IP transactions on the blockchain (Figure 7.5).

FIGURE 7.5 Intellectual property and rights management.

7.5.3 Cybersecurity and Data Integrity

Cybersecurity and data integrity are paramount concerns in the digital landscape, particularly in Industry 4.0, where vast amounts of sensitive data are generated, exchanged, and stored. Blockchain technology offers robust solutions to enhance cybersecurity and ensure data integrity, addressing the challenges posed by cyber threats and data manipulation. One of the key strengths of blockchain in cybersecurity lies in its decentralized architecture. Conventional centralized systems have single points of failure, which leaves them open to data leaks and cyberattacks. This decentralized structure makes it extremely difficult for attackers to compromise the integrity of the data or manipulate transactions, since they would need to simultaneously target multiple nodes, each with its unique cryptographic key.

Additionally, blockchain employs maintained data integrity. Transactions recorded on the blockchain are encrypted and linked together in a chain of blocks, forming a tamper-proof record. Once a block is added to the chain, it becomes computationally impractical to alter the data without consensus from the majority of network participants. This cryptographic immutability ensures that data stored on the blockchain remains secure and tamper-proof. Furthermore, blockchain introduces transparency and auditability, which are crucial for cybersecurity and data integrity. All transactions recorded on the blockchain are transparent and visible to the network participants, enhancing accountability and facilitating the detection of any unauthorized changes or suspicious activities. The distributed nature of the blockchain also enables participants to independently verify the integrity of the data by comparing their local copies with others in the network, reducing the reliance on centralized authorities for data validation.

Blockchain technology also offers secure identity management solutions that can mitigate cybersecurity risks. This eliminates the need for centralized identity management systems, reducing the risk of identity theft and unauthorized access. Additionally, blockchain-based authentication mechanisms can enhance the security

FIGURE 7.6 Cybersecurity.

of digital transactions and protect against fraudulent activities. While blockchain technology provides robust cybersecurity measures, it is not without challenges. Scalability and performance limitations, as well as vulnerabilities in the implementation of blockchain protocols and smart contracts, need to be addressed. Moreover, as with any technology, the human factor remains a critical aspect of cybersecurity. Adequate user education, awareness, and adherence to best practices are essential to ensure the secure utilization of blockchain technology.

Blockchain technology has emerged as a powerful tool for enhancing cybersecurity and ensuring data integrity in Industry 4.0. Its decentralized architecture, cryptographic algorithms, transparency, and secure identity management capabilities contribute to a more resilient and trustworthy digital ecosystem. By leveraging blockchain, organizations can protect their sensitive data, mitigate cyber threats, and build trust with their stakeholders in an increasingly digitized and interconnected world (Figure 7.6).

7.5.4 Tokenization and Value Exchange

Tokenization and value exchange are key aspects of Industry 4.0, where digital assets and transactions play a central role. Blockchain technology enables the tokenization of assets, representing them as digital tokens on the blockchain, and facilitates efficient and secure value exchange between participants. These tokens can represent a wide range of assets, including physical assets such as real estate or commodities, financial instruments, intellectual property rights, or even digital assets like digital art or collectibles. By tokenizing assets, their ownership, value, and transferability can be recorded and managed on the blockchain, enabling fractional ownership, liquidity, and efficient trading. Blockchain-based tokenization provides several benefits in Industry 4.0. This fractionalization enhances liquidity and accessibility, as it enables individuals to invest in or trade assets that would otherwise be prohibitively expensive or illiquid. Tokenization also opens up new avenues for investment and financing, as it enables the creation of asset-backed tokens that can be traded on blockchain-based markets, providing investors with greater flexibility and diversification opportunities. Moreover, tokenization enables programmable assets through the use of smart contracts. Smart contracts embedded within the tokens can define and automate the conditions and rules for value exchange. This programmability enhances the efficiency and transparency of transactions, as the execution of predefined conditions is automatically enforced by the blockchain network.

For example, smart contracts can automate revenue sharing, royalty payments, or compliance requirements, streamlining complex value exchange processes. The decentralized nature of the blockchain eliminates the need for intermediaries, reducing transaction costs and the risk of fraud. This transparency fosters trust among participants and enhances the integrity of value exchange processes. Additionally, blockchain-based tokenization facilitates cross-border transactions and interoperability. Tokens can be easily transferred and traded across different blockchain networks and platforms, enabling seamless value exchange between diverse ecosystems. This interoperability unlocks new possibilities for global collaboration, investment, and trade, as it eliminates the barriers and inefficiencies associated with traditional cross-border transactions. While blockchain-based tokenization offers significant opportunities, challenges such as regulatory frameworks, standardization, and scalability need to be addressed for broader adoption.

Clear regulations and guidelines are necessary to ensure compliance and protect investors. Standardization efforts are crucial to enable interoperability among different token standards and platforms. Scalability solutions are required to handle the high transaction volumes associated with tokenized assets in a cost-effective and efficient manner. Blockchain-based tokenization revolutionizes value exchange in Industry 4.0 by enabling fractional ownership, programmability, and transparent transactions. It unlocks liquidity, enhances accessibility, and opens up new avenues for investment and financing. As blockchain technology matures and regulatory frameworks evolve, tokenization is expected to transform various industries, creating new economic models, and democratizing access to assets and value exchange opportunities.

7.6 BLOCKCHAIN APPLICATIONS IN INDUSTRY 5.0: HUMAN–MACHINE INTEGRATION

Blockchain technology holds immense potential in driving where collaborative and symbiotic relationships between humans and intelligent systems are at the forefront. By leveraging blockchain, Industry 5.0 can facilitate secure, transparent, and decentralized interactions, enabling a range of applications that enhance human–machine integration. One of the key areas where blockchain can contribute to human–machine integration is in the development of peer-to-peer networks and decentralized autonomous organizations (DAOs). Blockchain decentralized networks are where individuals and machines can interact directly without the need for intermediaries. This decentralized approach promotes autonomy, trust, and transparency in the interactions between humans and machines. DAOs, powered by blockchain, enable collective decision-making and governance, where stakeholders can participate in the decision-making process and influence the actions of autonomous systems.

Personalized manufacturing and customization are also areas where blockchain can make a significant impact. Blockchain technology enables the secure and efficient exchange of personal data between individuals and machines, ensuring privacy and consent. Through blockchain-based identity management systems, individuals can maintain control over their personal data and share it with machines or systems for customized manufacturing or personalized services. This facilitates the seamless integration of personal preferences, needs, and requirements into the manufacturing processes, resulting in tailored products and services that align with individual preferences. Immutable digital identities and reputation systems are another application of blockchain in Industry 5.0. These digital identities and reputation systems enhance trust and accountability in human–machine interactions, allowing for seamless collaboration and coordination between different entities in Industry 5.0. Furthermore, blockchain technology can enable secure and efficient value exchange in the context of Industry 5.0. With the integration of blockchain, machines can autonomously transact and exchange value with each other or with humans. Smart contracts on the blockchain can facilitate automated and trusted transactions, ensuring fairness, transparency, and traceability.

This enables machines to participate in economic activities, negotiate contracts, and exchange value without the need for human intervention. As Industry 5.0 continues to evolve, blockchain technology will play a pivotal role in fostering human–machine integration. By providing a decentralized, transparent, and secure infrastructure, blockchain enables trust, autonomy, and collaboration between humans and machines. The applications mentioned above are just a glimpse of the potential of blockchain in Industry 5.0, and as the technology advances, we can expect further innovation and transformation in how humans and machines interact and work together to drive industrial progress (Figure 7.7).

7.6.1 The Shift toward Human-Centric Work Environments

The shift toward human-centric work environments is a significant aspect of Industry 5.0, emphasizing the importance of placing humans at the center of industrial processes and systems. Blockchain technology can contribute to the realization of human-centric work environments by enabling transparency, trust, and empowerment. Blockchain's transparent and decentralized nature fosters transparency in work processes, allowing individuals to have greater visibility into the operations and decision-making processes within organizations. This transparency helps build trust between employees and employers, as well as among different stakeholders, by providing a shared and immutable record of activities and transactions. Employees can have a better understanding of how their work contributes to the overall goals of the organization, fostering a sense of purpose and empowerment.

Moreover, blockchain can facilitate the establishment of decentralized and autonomous decision-making structures within organizations. Through the use of blockchain-based smart contracts and decentralized autonomous organizations (DAOs), decision-making processes can become more inclusive, participatory, and democratic. Employees can actively contribute to decision-making processes,

FIGURE 7.7 Human–machine integration.

propose changes or improvements, and have a say in the direction of their work environment. This distributed decision-making approach empowers employees and promotes a sense of ownership and engagement. Blockchain secure identity management capabilities also play a vital role in human-centric work environments. This enables personalized experiences, tailored services, and customized work environments that align with individual preferences and needs. Employees can have greater control over their professional identities and career trajectories, allowing for more flexible and fulfilling work experiences.

Furthermore, blockchain can address issues of fairness and equity in human-centric work environments. By utilizing blockchain-based systems for tracking and recording work-related activities, such as task completion, contributions, or achievements, organizations can establish transparent and verifiable systems for performance evaluation and rewards distribution. This helps ensure fairness in recognizing and rewarding employees' efforts and contributions, promoting a culture of meritocracy and motivation. As Industry 5.0 continues to shape the future of work, the integration of blockchain technology holds immense promise in creating human-centric work environments. By leveraging blockchain transparency, decentralization, and identity management capabilities, organizations can foster trust, empowerment, and inclusivity among employees. The shift towards human-centric work environments not only enhances the well-being and satisfaction of individuals but also contributes to increased productivity, innovation, and overall organizational success.

7.6.2 Peer-to-Peer Networks and Decentralized Autonomous Organizations

Peer-to-peer networks and decentralized autonomous organizations (DAOs) are key components of Industry 5.0, facilitating collaborative and autonomous interactions between humans and machines. Blockchain technology plays a pivotal role in enabling the establishment and operation of such networks and organizations, promoting decentralization, transparency, and trust. Peer-to-peer networks, powered by blockchain, allow direct interactions and transactions between individuals or entities without the need for intermediaries. Blockchain's decentralized architecture eliminates the need for centralized authorities, enabling direct peer-to-peer exchanges of information, goods, or services. This peer-to-peer model enhances efficiency, reduces costs, and eliminates unnecessary intermediation, fostering a more direct and collaborative environment for conducting business and sharing resources.

Decentralized autonomous organizations (DAOs) take peer-to-peer networks a step further by leveraging blockchain-based smart contracts to processes. DAOs are self-governing entities that operate on the blockchain, with rules and regulations encoded in smart contracts. These smart contracts define the organization's operations, decision-making mechanisms, and distribution of resources. The DAOs allow for collective decision-making, where stakeholders can participate, vote, and influence the organization's actions and direction. Blockchain technology provides several advantages for peer-to-peer networks and DAOs. Firstly, blockchain ensures transparency by recording all transactions and activities on a shared and immutable ledger. This transparency builds trust among network participants and DAO members, as everyone can verify the accuracy and integrity of the recorded data. It also promotes accountability, as the actions and decisions made within the network or organization are transparent and auditable.

Additionally, blockchain enables secure and efficient value exchange within peer-to-peer networks and DAOs. Through the use of digital tokens and smart contracts, blockchain facilitates peer-to-peer transactions, automating processes and ensuring trust and reliability in value exchange. Smart contracts enforce predefined rules and conditions, eliminating the need for intermediaries and reducing the risk of fraud or manipulation. Moreover, blockchain decentralized architecture enhances the resilience and robustness of peer-to-peer networks and DAOs. This decentralized structure ensures the continuity of operations and data availability even in the face of failures or malicious attempts. Overall, the integration of blockchain technology enables the development of peer-to-peer networks and decentralized autonomous organizations, transforming how humans and machines collaborate in Industry 5.0. These networks and organizations foster direct interactions, transparent governance, and efficient value exchange, empowering individuals and promoting collective decision-making. As blockchain technology continues to evolve, we can expect further advancements in peer-to-peer networks and DAOs, unlocking new possibilities for collaboration, innovation, and value creation in Industry 5.0.

7.6.3 Personalized Manufacturing and Customization

Personalized manufacturing and customization are key drivers of Industry 5.0, where the focus shifts toward meeting individualized customer needs and preferences. Blockchain technology plays a significant role in enabling personalized manufacturing and customization by providing secure data exchange, traceability, and transparency throughout the production process. Blockchain facilitates the secure exchange of personal data and preferences between customers and manufacturers. Through blockchain, customers can have a transparent view of the manufacturing process. Each step of the production journey, from design to sourcing materials to manufacturing and distribution, can be recorded on the blockchain. This provides customers with visibility into the entire supply chain, ensuring transparency and building trust. Customers can verify the authenticity and origin of products, ensuring they meet their desired specifications and ethical standards.

Blockchain also enables the creation of digital twins, virtual representations of physical products or assets. Digital twins can be linked to the blockchain, providing a secure and tamper-proof record of their specifications and history. This allows customers to have a comprehensive understanding of the product they are purchasing and enables manufacturers to track and manage personalized features or modifications requested by customers. Smart contracts on the blockchain automate the customization process by executing predefined rules and conditions. Manufacturers can define customization options and parameters within smart contracts, ensuring that the final product aligns with customers' preferences. These smart contracts can automatically trigger specific manufacturing processes, adjust product configurations, or calculate pricing based on personalized features.

Furthermore, blockchain-based decentralized marketplaces can facilitate personalized manufacturing and customization. Customers can connect directly with manufacturers or suppliers through peer-to-peer interactions on the blockchain, eliminating intermediaries and streamlining the customization process. Blockchain ensures transparency, trust, and accountability in these interactions, as all transactions and agreements are recorded on the distributed ledger. Personalized manufacturing and customization enabled by blockchain technology provide several benefits. Customers can enjoy products tailored to their unique preferences, enhancing their overall satisfaction and experience. Manufacturers can differentiate themselves by offering personalized products and services, leading to increased customer loyalty and brand value. The transparent and traceable nature of blockchain also contributes to sustainability efforts, as customers can make informed choices based on the environmental and ethical impact of the production process.

As Industry 5.0 continues to evolve, personalized manufacturing and customization will become increasingly prevalent. Blockchain technology offers a robust foundation for secure data exchange, traceability, and automation, enabling the seamless integration of personalization into the manufacturing process. The combination of blockchain and personalized manufacturing holds immense potential for transforming industries and meeting the evolving demands of individual customers in Industry 5.0.

7.6.4 Immutable Digital Identities and Reputation Systems

Immutable digital identities and reputation systems are integral components of Industry 5.0, where trust and accountability are crucial in human–machine interactions. Blockchain technology provides a reliable and secure platform for establishing and managing immutable digital identities and reputation systems, enhancing the overall integrity and transparency of transactions and interactions. Blockchain enables the creation of digital identities that are tamper-proof and resistant to fraud or manipulation. Each individual or entity can have a unique digital identity stored on the blockchain, which includes verified information such as personal details, qualifications, or certifications. These digital identities are cryptographically secured and cannot be altered without consensus from the network participants, ensuring the authenticity and integrity of the information.

With immutable digital identities on the blockchain, reputation systems can be developed to assess and track the trustworthiness and reliability of individuals or machines. Reputation scores or ratings can be assigned based on past interactions, transactions, or performance. These reputation systems provide a transparent and objective measure of credibility, enabling others to make informed decisions when engaging in collaborations, transactions, or partnerships. Blockchain-based reputation systems foster trust and accountability in Industry 5.0. Individuals and machines are incentivized to maintain a good reputation as it directly influences their opportunities and interactions within the ecosystem. This promotes responsible behavior, ethical practices, and high-quality performance, leading to a more trustworthy and efficient environment for human–machine integration.

Moreover, blockchain allows for the interoperability of reputation systems across different platforms or ecosystems. Reputation scores or ratings recorded on one blockchain network can be recognized and accepted by other networks, enabling seamless reputation transfer and recognition. This promotes cross-platform collaboration and trust, as reputation information can be securely and reliably shared between different entities. The combination of immutable digital identities and reputation systems has far-reaching implications in Industry 5.0. It enables personalized experiences, where individuals can tailor their interactions and collaborations based on the reputation and credibility of others. Machines can also benefit from reputation systems, allowing them to select reliable partners or service providers for enhanced performance and efficiency. Furthermore, immutable digital identities and reputation systems can address challenges related to data privacy and security.

With blockchain, individuals have control over their personal information, deciding what data to share and with whom. By providing a transparent record of data access and usage, blockchain enhances data privacy and mitigates the risk of unauthorized access or misuse. Blockchain technology plays a vital role in establishing immutable digital identities and reputation systems in Industry 5.0. These systems foster trust, transparency, and accountability in human–machine interactions, enabling more reliable and efficient collaborations. As blockchain continues to evolve, we can expect further advancements in the integration of digital identities and reputation systems, revolutionizing the way individuals and machines establish trust and engage in Industry 5.0 ecosystems.

7.7 CHALLENGES AND OPPORTUNITIES OF BLOCKCHAIN ADOPTION IN INDUSTRIES 4.0 AND 5.0

The adoption of blockchain technology in Industries 4.0 and 5.0 brings with it both challenges and opportunities. On one hand, scalability and performance issues pose significant challenges. Blockchain networks must be capable of handling large-scale transactions and processing high volumes of data in real time. Solutions like sharding, off-chain transactions, and consensus algorithm improvements are being explored to address these challenges. Additionally, regulatory and legal implications surrounding data privacy, security, and cross-border transactions require careful consideration. Collaboration between governments, industry stakeholders, and regulatory bodies is essential to establish clear frameworks that foster innovation while ensuring compliance. On the other hand, blockchain adoption presents immense opportunities.

Blockchain's decentralized nature promotes trust, transparency, and data integrity, enhancing supply chain management, traceability, and quality control. It enables secure data sharing, collaboration, and interoperability among different stakeholders, leading to streamlined processes and improved efficiency. Moreover, blockchain's potential to revolutionize intellectual property and rights management opens up new possibilities for creators and innovators to protect their work and monetize their assets in a transparent and decentralized manner. By addressing these challenges and leveraging the opportunities, industries can harness the full potential of blockchain technology in Industries 4.0 and 5.0, leading to transformative advancements and competitive advantages.

7.7.1 Scalability and Performance Issues

The transaction processing capacity of these networks is limited, often resulting in network congestion during periods of high demand. This limitation hinders the scalability of blockchain technology for industries that require fast and high-volume transactions, such as supply chain management or financial services. However, there are ongoing efforts to address these scalability challenges. One approach is the development of layer-two solutions, such as payment channels and sidechains, which enable off-chain transactions that can later be settled on the main blockchain. These solutions help alleviate congestion on the main blockchain and improve transaction throughput. Another approach is the exploration of new consensus algorithms, such as proof of stake (PoS) or directed acyclic graphs (DAGs), that offer improved scalability and performance compared to traditional proof of work (PoW) systems. PoS algorithms allow network participants to validate transactions based on their stake in the network, reducing the need for extensive computational resources.

DAG-based blockchain, on the other hand, enables parallel transaction processing, increasing the network's capacity to handle a higher volume of transactions. Furthermore, the development of specialized blockchain platforms and protocols tailored for specific industries or use cases is gaining traction. These industry-specific blockchains are designed to address scalability and performance requirements unique to their respective domains. By focusing on specific industry needs, these solutions can provide faster transaction processing and higher throughput, enabling widespread blockchain adoption in industries such as supply chain, healthcare, or energy. While scalability and performance issues have been significant challenges for blockchain adoption in Industries 4.0 and 5.0, ongoing research and development efforts are addressing these limitations. The introduction of layer-two solutions, new consensus algorithms, and industry-specific blockchain holds promise for overcoming scalability challenges and improving the performance of blockchain networks, making them more suitable for enterprise-scale applications. As these solutions mature, the scalability and performance concerns associated with blockchain technology are expected to diminish, unlocking its full potential in transforming industries.

7.7.2 Regulatory and Legal Implications

The adoption of blockchain technology in Industries 4.0 and 5.0 brings forth a range of regulatory and legal implications that need to be addressed for its successful integration. As blockchain-based systems involve the storage, transfer, and processing of data and assets, regulatory frameworks must be developed to ensure compliance, protect consumer rights, and mitigate potential risks. One of the primary challenges is determining the jurisdiction and applicable laws for blockchain-based transactions, especially in cases where multiple parties from different jurisdictions are involved. Harmonizing legal frameworks and establishing international standards can help create a consistent and predictable environment for blockchain adoption. Data privacy and protection are crucial considerations when implementing blockchain solutions.

Striking a balance between the transparency of blockchain and the need to protect sensitive information is an ongoing challenge that requires careful design and implementation. Smart contracts, a core component of blockchain technology, also raise legal considerations. These self-executing contracts are governed by code and operate automatically based on predefined conditions. Ensuring the legal enforceability of smart contracts and clarifying the liabilities and responsibilities of the involved parties are important aspects that regulators and legal systems need to address. Intellectual property rights and licensing present another area of concern. With blockchain's ability to facilitate secure and transparent transactions, issues related to copyright, patent, and trademark protections arise. Establishing mechanisms for intellectual property rights management and licensing within blockchain networks is essential to protect the rights of innovators and creators.

Fraud, security breaches, and illegal activities are additional concerns that regulators and legal authorities must address in the context of blockchain adoption. While blockchain technology provides inherent security features, it is not immune to vulnerabilities and malicious activities. Establishing frameworks to detect and mitigate fraudulent or illegal activities while maintaining the immutability and integrity of the blockchain is a complex challenge that requires collaboration between technology developers, regulators, and law enforcement agencies. Furthermore, blockchain adoption may require modifications to existing regulations or the introduction of new laws to accommodate the unique features and potential benefits of this technology. Collaborative efforts between governments, industry stakeholders, and legal experts are crucial to develop regulatory frameworks that encourage innovation, protect consumer interests, and mitigate risks associated with blockchain implementation.

The regulatory and legal implications of blockchain adoption in Industries 4.0 and 5.0 are multifaceted. Establishing clear and adaptable regulatory frameworks that balance innovation and compliance is essential. Addressing data privacy, intellectual property rights, enforceability of smart contracts, security concerns, and jurisdictional challenges are key aspects in creating an environment that fosters blockchain adoption while ensuring legal and regulatory compliance. Collaborative efforts among stakeholders are crucial to navigating these challenges and unlocking the full potential of blockchain technology in transforming industries.

7.7.3 Cultural and Organizational Barriers

Cultural and organizational barriers are significant challenges that must be addressed for successful blockchain adoption in Industries 4.0 and 5.0. The integration of blockchain technology often requires a shift in mindset, changes in organizational structures, and the cultivation of a culture that embraces decentralized, transparent, and collaborative systems. One of the primary cultural barriers is resistance to change. Industries that have long relied on centralized models and traditional business processes may be hesitant to adopt blockchain technology due to concerns about disrupting established practices. Overcoming this resistance requires education and awareness about the potential benefits of blockchain, showcasing real-world use cases, and highlighting the long-term advantages it offers, such as increased efficiency, transparency, and trust.

Another cultural barrier is the lack of trust in decentralized systems. Blockchain's core value proposition lies in its ability to provide a trustless environment, where transactions and data are verified by a network of participants rather than relying on a centralized authority. However, building trust in this new paradigm requires industry stakeholders to understand the underlying technology, its security features, and the benefits it brings in terms of eliminating intermediaries and reducing the potential for fraud or manipulation. Organizational barriers also pose challenges to blockchain adoption. Traditional hierarchical structures and siloed departments may hinder the implementation of blockchain-based solutions, as they require cross-functional collaboration and the sharing of data and resources. Embracing blockchain often necessitates rethinking organizational structures, fostering a culture of collaboration and transparency, and breaking down internal barriers to facilitate information sharing and decision-making.

Moreover, blockchain implementation may require interoperability with existing legacy systems and technologies. Integration challenges can arise when attempting to connect blockchain networks with existing IT infrastructure, databases, or software solutions [7]. Overcoming these technical [8] barriers involves careful planning, collaboration with IT teams, and ensuring compatibility between blockchain systems and legacy technologies. Addressing cultural and organizational barriers requires a top-down approach, with strong leadership support and a clear vision for blockchain integration. Education and training programs can help employees understand the benefits and potential of blockchain technology, easing their concerns and building confidence in the adoption process. Collaborative efforts between different departments, along with the involvement of industry associations and experts, can foster knowledge sharing and best practices.

Furthermore, industry-wide collaborations and partnerships can facilitate blockchain adoption by establishing standards, protocols, and governance frameworks that enable interoperability and seamless integration across organizations and sectors. These collaborations can also address regulatory concerns, share resources and expertise, and collectively overcome the challenges associated with blockchain implementation. Cultural and organizational barriers pose significant challenges to blockchain adoption in Industries 4.0 and 5.0. Overcoming resistance to change, building trust in decentralized [9] systems, rethinking organizational structures, and addressing interoperability concerns require concerted efforts from industry leaders, stakeholders, and employees. By fostering a culture of innovation, collaboration, and knowledge sharing, organizations can navigate these barriers and unlock the transformative potential of blockchain technology in revolutionizing industries [10].

7.7.4 Potential Solutions and Future Developments

In addressing the challenges of blockchain [10] adoption in Industries 4.0 and 5.0, there are potential solutions and ongoing developments that hold promise for the future of this technology. One potential solution is the advancement [11] of blockchain scalability through the development of layer-two solutions and alternative consensus algorithms. Layer-two solutions, such as payment channels and sidechains, allow for off-chain transaction processing, reducing congestion on the main blockchain and increasing scalability. Additionally, new consensus algorithms like proof of stake (PoS) and directed acyclic graphs (DAGs) offer improved scalability and performance compared to traditional proof of work (PoW) systems, enabling higher transaction throughput. Interoperability frameworks are also being explored to address the issue of compatibility between different blockchain networks [12]. These frameworks aim to establish standard protocols and communication channels, allowing for seamless integration and data exchange across diverse blockchain platforms. This interoperability will facilitate collaboration and information sharing among organizations, enabling the development of robust blockchain ecosystems.

Another area of focus is the development of regulatory frameworks and legal standards specifically tailored to blockchain technology. Governments and regulatory bodies are actively working to create supportive environments for blockchain adoption by establishing clear guidelines for compliance, data privacy, and consumer protection. These efforts will help build trust in the technology and provide a solid foundation for its widespread implementation. These cryptographic techniques allow for secure data sharing, confidential transactions, and the protection of sensitive information, making blockchain more viable for industries with stringent security requirements. Furthermore, advancements in user-friendly interfaces and developer tools are simplifying the process of building and deploying blockchain applications. User experience (UX) improvements and intuitive development frameworks are lowering the barriers to entry for businesses and developers, making it easier to integrate blockchain solutions into existing workflows and systems. The integration of blockchain with AI enables secure and transparent data sharing, enhancing the trustworthiness and reliability of AI-driven applications. Similarly, combining blockchain with IoT devices allows for secure and decentralized management of connected devices, enabling new levels of automation, efficiency, and data integrity.

Potential solutions and future developments in blockchain technology offer promising avenues to overcome the challenges of adoption in Industries 4.0 and 5.0. Scalability improvements, interoperability frameworks, regulatory frameworks, enhanced security measures, improved user interfaces, and the convergence with AI and the IoT are all driving the advancement and maturation of blockchain technology. As these solutions continue to evolve, the potential for blockchain to revolutionize industries and create new business models becomes increasingly tangible.

7.8 CASE STUDIES: REAL-WORLD EXAMPLES OF BLOCKCHAIN IMPLEMENTATION

One notable case study of blockchain implementation is the partnership between Walmart and IBM. They joined forces to create a system for tracing food products. By leveraging blockchain technology, they aimed to enhance transparency, improve food safety, and reduce the time it takes to trace the origin of contaminated products. The blockchain solution enables real-time tracking of food products from farm to store, allowing Walmart to quickly identify and remove potentially unsafe items from their shelves. This implementation has significantly improved traceability and accountability in the food supply chain, providing consumers with greater confidence in the safety and authenticity of the products they purchase.

7.8.1 Manufacturing and Supply Chain: Success Stories

One of the most notable success stories of blockchain implementation in the manufacturing and supply chain industry is the collaboration between IBM and Maersk. Together, they developed a blockchain-based platform called TradeLens, which aims to digitize and streamline global trade processes. By utilizing blockchain technology, TradeLens provides a decentralized, transparent, and secure network that connects various stakeholders, including shippers, freight forwarders, customs authorities, port operators, and more. The platform allows for real-time tracking and visibility of shipments, documentation, and trade-related transactions, eliminating the need for manual paperwork and reducing administrative burdens. With TradeLens, participants in the supply chain can securely share and access information, enabling greater efficiency, reduced costs, and improved compliance. The immutable nature of blockchain ensures the integrity and authenticity of data, mitigating the risk of fraud and tampering. TradeLens has gained significant traction, with over 150 organizations joining the platform, facilitating the exchange of information for millions of shipments worldwide. This successful implementation demonstrates the transformative potential of blockchain in revolutionizing supply chain management, enhancing transparency, trust, and collaboration among stakeholders across the globe.

7.8.2 Industry 5.0 Innovations and Blockchain Integration

In the context of Industry 5.0, the integration of blockchain technology has the potential to bring about innovative solutions and transformations across various sectors. One such example is the application of blockchain in the field of renewable energy and microgrids. By combining blockchain with smart grid technologies, energy producers and consumers can engage in peer-to-peer energy trading, allowing for more efficient and decentralized energy distribution. Blockchain enables transparent tracking of energy generation and consumption, ensuring the integrity of transactions and providing a secure platform for participants to trade excess energy. This integration promotes sustainability, empowers local communities, and encourages the adoption of renewable energy sources. Additionally, blockchain can play a crucial role in the healthcare industry, particularly in securing medical records and enhancing data interoperability. Blockchain-based platforms provide a tamper-proof and decentralized repository for health records, ensuring privacy, security, and efficient data sharing between healthcare providers.

Patients have greater control over their health data, enabling them to securely share records with different providers and improving the quality of care through comprehensive and accurate information. Moreover, blockchain integration in the field of intellectual property management is gaining momentum. With blockchain, artists, musicians, and creators can establish proof of ownership and track the usage and distribution of their digital assets. This enables them to protect their intellectual property rights, receive fair compensation, and maintain a transparent record of transactions. The integration of blockchain technology with Industry 5.0 innovations offers immense potential for enhancing efficiency, transparency, and trust in various sectors, fostering a more sustainable, interconnected, and equitable future.

7.8.3 Lessons Learned and Best Practices

Lessons learned and best practices from real-world blockchain implementations can provide valuable insights for organizations looking to adopt this technology in Industries 4.0 and 5.0. One important lesson is the need for clear use cases and a deep understanding of the problem blockchain aims to solve. It is essential to identify specific pain points, such as inefficiencies, lack of transparency, or trust issues, and determine how blockchain can address them effectively. Starting with smaller, focused projects that showcase tangible benefits can help build confidence and support for broader implementation.

Another key lesson is the importance of collaboration and ecosystem building. Successful blockchain implementations often involve multiple stakeholders working together to create a network or consortium that fosters trust, data sharing, and standardization. Collaboration can help overcome challenges such as interoperability and establish governance frameworks that ensure fairness and accountability. Additionally, privacy-enhancing techniques such as zero-knowledge proofs or differential privacy can be utilized to protect sensitive data while still allowing for verification and transparency. Education and awareness play a crucial role in driving blockchain adoption. Investing in training programs and workshops can help stakeholders understand the technology's potential and limitations, debunk myths, and address concerns. Promoting a culture of learning and innovation enables employees to embrace blockchain and actively contribute to its successful implementation.

Moreover, regulatory compliance should be a priority. Organizations must navigate the legal and regulatory landscape to ensure their blockchain initiatives align with existing laws and standards. Engaging with regulators and industry associations can provide guidance and foster an environment that supports blockchain innovation while addressing concerns around consumer protection, data privacy, and financial regulations. Continuous evaluation and adaptation are vital. Blockchain technology is evolving rapidly, and organizations must stay updated on the latest developments, research, and emerging best practices. Regular assessments of the implemented solutions, along with feedback from stakeholders, can help identify areas for improvement and drive further innovation.

Lessons learned from real-world blockchain implementations highlight the importance of clear use cases, collaboration, security, education, regulatory compliance, and ongoing evaluation. By adopting these best practices, organizations can navigate the challenges and maximize the benefits of blockchain technology in Industries 4.0 and 5.0, driving transformation and unlocking new opportunities in various sectors.

7.9 THE FUTURE OF INDUSTRY: SYNERGIES BETWEEN BLOCKCHAIN, AI, AND THE IOT

The future of industry holds great potential in harnessing the synergies between blockchain, artificial intelligence (AI), and the Internet of Things (IoT). These transformative technologies, when combined, can revolutionize various sectors, enabling enhanced efficiency, automation, and data-driven decision-making. Blockchain can provide a secure and transparent framework for managing and verifying the vast amounts of data generated by IoT devices. By leveraging blockchain immutability and decentralization, the integrity and trustworthiness of IoT data can be ensured, facilitating secure transactions [14], supply chain traceability, and data sharing across multiple stakeholders. AI, on the other hand, can leverage the rich data stored on blockchain to drive predictive analytics, optimize processes, and enable autonomous decision-making. The integration of AI algorithms with blockchain can enhance data analysis, anomaly detection, and pattern recognition, leading to improved operational efficiency and intelligent automation. Together, blockchain, AI, and the IoT create a powerful ecosystem that enables seamless connectivity, automation, and intelligent decision-making in Industry 4.0 and beyond. This convergence paves the way for smart factories [14], predictive maintenance, optimized logistics, and personalized manufacturing, ultimately driving innovation, productivity, and sustainable growth in the future of industry.

7.9.1 Convergence of Emerging Technologies

The convergence of emerging technologies is reshaping the future of industries and creating unprecedented opportunities for innovation and growth. One notable convergence is between blockchain, AI, and the IoT. These three technologies, when combined, have the potential to revolutionize various sectors and drive the next wave of industrial transformation. Blockchain provides a decentralized [15] and secure framework for data storage, verification, and transactions. By leveraging its immutability and transparency, blockchain can enhance trust, traceability, and data integrity in a wide range of applications. When integrated with AI, blockchain can enable advanced analytics, predictive modeling, and machine learning. AI algorithms can process vast amounts of data stored on the blockchain, extracting valuable insights and driving intelligent decision-making. The IoT, with its network of connected devices and sensors, generates massive volumes of data. By integrating the IoT with blockchain and AI, organizations can create a secure and efficient ecosystem for managing and analyzing IoT data.

The convergence of these technologies opens up new possibilities across industries. In healthcare, for example, blockchain can enable secure sharing of patient data, while AI can analyze these data to drive personalized medicine and improved diagnostics. In supply chain management, blockchain can provide end-to-end traceability and transparency, while AI can optimize logistics and predict demand patterns. In energy management, blockchain can facilitate peer-to-peer energy trading, while AI can optimize energy consumption and predict energy demand. However, the convergence of these technologies also presents challenges. Interoperability, scalability, and privacy concerns need to be addressed to fully harness the potential of this convergence. Moreover, ethical considerations, regulatory frameworks, and standardization efforts are crucial for ensuring responsible and inclusive adoption. The convergence of blockchain, AI, and IoT represents a powerful force that is transforming industries and driving innovation. This convergence enables secure data sharing, advanced analytics, and intelligent decision-making, leading to enhanced efficiency, personalized experiences, and sustainable growth. As organizations continue to explore and embrace this convergence, they have the opportunity to unlock new levels of productivity, agility, and competitive advantage in the digital age.

7.9.2 Intelligent Automation and Autonomous Systems

Intelligent automation refers to the integration of AI and robotics to automate complex tasks and workflows. By leveraging machine learning algorithms, robots and machines can analyze vast amounts of data, make intelligent decisions, and perform tasks with precision and accuracy. This automation enhances productivity, reduces errors, and frees up human workers to focus on higher-value activities. Autonomous systems take intelligent automation to the next level by enabling machines and devices to operate independently, without human intervention. These systems leverage AI, sensors, and connectivity to perceive their environment, make decisions, and execute actions. Examples include autonomous vehicles, drones, and smart appliances that can adapt to changing conditions, optimize their performance, and interact with other systems seamlessly.

The integration of blockchain technology with intelligent automation and autonomous systems further enhances their capabilities. Blockchain's decentralized and immutable nature provides a secure and transparent framework for recording and verifying transactions and data. This enables autonomous systems to interact and transact with each other in a trustless and tamper-proof manner. For example, autonomous vehicles can securely share data about their location, speed, and behavior on a blockchain, enabling a decentralized [16] and reliable network for communication and coordination. The benefits of intelligent automation and autonomous systems are far-reaching. In manufacturing, these technologies enable highly efficient and flexible production lines, predictive maintenance, and real-time quality control. In logistics and supply chain management, autonomous systems optimize inventory management, route planning, and last-mile delivery.

In healthcare, they facilitate telemedicine, remote patient monitoring, and robotic surgery. The potential applications span across industries, transforming the way we work, live, and interact with technology. However, the adoption of intelligent automation and autonomous systems also poses challenges. Ethical considerations, safety concerns, and regulatory frameworks need to be addressed to ensure responsible and secure deployment. Additionally, upskilling and retraining the workforce to adapt to these new technologies is crucial for successful implementation. Intelligent automation and autonomous systems are revolutionizing industries by enhancing efficiency, productivity, and reliability. The integration of AI, machine learning, robotics, and blockchain is enabling machines and devices to operate independently, make intelligent decisions, and collaborate with each other securely. As these technologies continue to advance, they have the potential to reshape industries, create new business models, and unlock unprecedented levels of productivity and innovation.

7.9.3 Blockchain-Enabled AI and Machine Learning

Blockchain-enabled technologies have emerged as a powerful combination that holds significant potential for various industries. By integrating blockchain technology with AI and machine learning algorithms, organizations can enhance the efficiency of their data-driven processes. Blockchain's decentralized and immutable nature addresses key challenges in AI and machine learning, such as data privacy, trust, and the verifiability of algorithms and models. It provides a secure and tamper-proof ledger where data can be stored and shared among multiple parties without compromising its integrity. This is particularly valuable in scenarios where sensitive data need to be accessed and processed by AI algorithms while maintaining privacy and confidentiality. Blockchain enables transparent and auditable data provenance, allowing organizations to trace the origin and history of data inputs used in AI and machine learning models. This transparency enhances trust and accountability, as stakeholders can verify the accuracy and fairness of the algorithms and ensure compliance with regulations and ethical standards.

Furthermore, blockchain facilitates data sharing and collaboration in AI and machine learning initiatives. Traditional data silos and access restrictions can impede the development of robust AI models. With blockchain, organizations can securely share data, incentivize data contributors through tokenization, and establish unreliable data marketplaces. This collaborative approach promotes the availability of diverse and high-quality datasets, leading to more accurate and robust AI models. Blockchain also introduces opportunities for federated learning, a decentralized approach to machine learning. Instead of centralizing data in a single location, federated learning allows data to remain on the devices or servers where they are generated. Blockchain can enable secure aggregation of models trained on decentralized data sources, preserving privacy and enabling collective intelligence without compromising sensitive information. The integration of blockchain with AI and machine learning introduces new dimensions of security, transparency, and collaboration. By leveraging blockchain's decentralized and immutable characteristics, organizations can enhance the privacy, reliability, and trustworthiness of their AI and machine learning initiatives.

7.9.4 The Internet of Things and Blockchain Integration

With blockchain, individuals can have ownership and control over their IoT-generated data, deciding who can access it and under what conditions. This empowers individuals to share data selectively and securely, promoting privacy and data sovereignty. Moreover, blockchain facilitates trust and interoperability in IoT ecosystems. With a shared blockchain ledger, IoT devices can establish trust and verify the identity and authenticity of other devices, ensuring secure and seamless interactions. Blockchain also enables the establishment of smart contracts, which can automate and enforce agreements between IoT devices, ensuring compliance and enabling autonomous decision-making. Additionally, blockchain can enhance the scalability and efficiency of IoT networks. By leveraging blockchain distributed architecture, IoT networks can handle large-scale deployments and accommodate a growing number of devices without relying on a centralized authority.

This scalability helps in reducing bottlenecks and increasing the overall efficiency of IoT systems. Furthermore, the integration of IoT and blockchain can enable new business models and value creation. With blockchain, IoT devices can participate in decentralized marketplaces, exchanging data or services in a secure and transparent manner. This opens up possibilities for monetizing IoT data, enabling micro transactions, and fostering peer-to-peer interactions. However, challenges exist in integrating the IoT and blockchain, including scalability, interoperability, and resource constraints. The sheer number of IoT devices and the volume of data they generate pose scalability challenges for blockchain networks. Interoperability between different IoT devices and blockchain platforms also needs to be addressed for seamless integration.

Moreover, resource-constrained IoT devices may have limitations in terms of computational power and energy efficiency, requiring innovative solutions for blockchain integration. Integration of the IoT and blockchain offers significant advantages in terms of data security, privacy, trust, and interoperability. It enables secure and transparent interactions between IoT devices, enhances data ownership and control, and unlocks new possibilities for value creation. As this integration continues to evolve, it has the potential to reshape industries, drive innovation, and create a more connected and efficient future.

7.10 CONCLUSION

In conclusion, the convergence of blockchain technology with Industry 4.0 and Industry 5.0 concepts holds immense promise for transforming industries into more transparent, efficient, and inclusive ecosystems. Blockchain decentralized and immutable nature addresses critical challenges such as data security, trust, and transparency, enabling secure and tamper-proof transactions, data sharing, and collaboration. In Industry 4.0, blockchain is revolutionizing supply chain management, quality control, digital twins, and predictive maintenance, leading to streamlined processes, improved traceability, and optimized resource utilization. In Industry 5.0, blockchain is facilitating human–machine integration, personalized manufacturing, peer-to-peer networks, and immutable digital identities, enabling a shift toward human-centric work environments and empowering individuals. However, regulatory implications, cultural barriers, and technical limitations need to be addressed for widespread blockchain adoption. Through collaborative efforts, innovative solutions, and continuous advancements, the future of industry is poised to leverage the synergies between blockchain, AI, and the IoT, creating a more transparent, efficient, and inclusive world of interconnected systems and intelligent automation. The following key subpoints highlight the significance of blockchain in empowering Industry 4.0 and beyond:

1. Transforming Manufacturing Processes: Blockchain is revolutionizing supply chain management, quality control, digital twins, and predictive maintenance in Industry 4.0. It enables end-to-end traceability, enhances product authentication, enables remote monitoring through digital twins, and facilitates predictive maintenance and asset tracking.
2. Enhancing Collaboration and Security: Blockchain enhances collaboration and security in Industry 4.0 by enabling interoperability and data sharing, ensuring intellectual property and rights management, strengthening cybersecurity and data integrity, and enabling tokenization and value exchange.
3. Pioneering Industry 5.0: Blockchain applications in Industry 5.0 enable human–machine integration, personalized manufacturing, peer-to-peer networks, and immutable digital identities. This shift toward human-centric work environments fosters collaboration, customization, and the development of reputation systems.
4. Overcoming Challenges and Embracing Opportunities: The adoption of blockchain in Industry 4.0 and beyond faces challenges such as scalability and performance issues, regulatory and legal implications, cultural and organizational barriers. However, by identifying potential solutions and embracing future developments, these challenges can be overcome, paving the way for widespread adoption and innovation.
5. Realizing Real-World Impact: Real-world case studies demonstrate the successful implementation of blockchain in manufacturing, supply chain management, and Industry 5.0 innovations. These success stories provide valuable insights and lessons learned for future implementations.

6. Synergies with Emerging Technologies: The future of industry lies in the synergies between blockchain, AI, and the IoT. The convergence of these emerging technologies enables intelligent automation, autonomous systems, blockchain-enabled AI and machine learning, and seamless integration with the Internet of Things. Together, they create a powerful ecosystem that drives efficiency, productivity, and innovation.

In summary, blockchain technology is a game-changer for Industry 4.0 and beyond. It empowers manufacturing processes, enhances collaboration and security, pioneers Industry 5.0 innovations, overcomes challenges, realizes real-world impact, and synergizes with other emerging technologies. As organizations and industries embrace blockchain's potential, they can unlock new levels of transparency, efficiency, and inclusivity, driving the next wave of industrial transformation. The future is bright, as blockchain revolutionizes the way we work, interact, and build the industries of tomorrow.

REFERENCES

[1] S. Nakamoto, A. Bitcoin, A peer-to-peer electronic cash system, Bitcoin (2008). https://bitcoin.org/bitcoin.pdf, 4.

[2] G. Wood, et al., Ethereum: a secure decentralised generalised transaction ledger, Ethereum project yellow paper 151 (2014) (2014) 1–32.

[3] M.-C. Valiente Blazquez, S. Hassan, J. Pavon Mestras, *Evaluating the Software Frameworks for Developing Decentralized Autonomous Organizations*, Complutense University of Madrid, 2020.

[4] D. Kronovet, *Aragon, DAOstack, Colony, Moloch*. Kronosapiens. http://kronosapiens.github.io/blog/2019/06/16/aragon-daostack-colony-moloch.html, 2019.

[5] S. Farshidi, S. Jansen, R. De Jong, S. Brinkkemper, A decision support system for cloud service provider selection problem in software producing organizations, in: 2018 IEEE 20th Conference on Business Informatics (CBI), vol. 1, IEEE, 2018, pp. 139–148.

[6] S. Farshidi, S. Jansen, A decision support system for pattern-driven software architecture, in: Proceedings of the 14th European Conference on Software Architecture, ECSA 2020, ACM, 2020, pp. 1–12.

[7] J. B. Awotunde, T. Gaber, L. N. Prasad, S. O. Folorunso, V. L. Lalitha, Privacy and security enhancement of smart cities using hybrid deep learning-enabled blockchain, Scalable Comput. Prac. Exp. 24 (3) (2023) 561–584.

[8] S. Farshidi, S. Jansen, R. de Jong, S. Brinkkemper, Multiple criteria decision support in requirements negotiation, in: 23rd International Conference On Requirements Engineering, Foundation for Software Quality (REFSQ), 2018. E. Baninemeh et al. Blockchain: Research and Applications 4 (2023) 100127 18.

[9] V. Buterin, et al., A next-generation smart contract and decentralized application platform, White Paper 3 (37) (2014)., 1–37.

[10] J. K. Adeniyi, T. T. Adeniyi, J. B. Awotunde, M. K. Abiodun, O. G. Atanda, Agrolend: A blockchain implementation approach of smart contract farming platform, in: 2023 International Conference on Science, Engineering and Business for Sustainable Development Goals (SEB-SDG), Vol. 1, IEEE, April 2023, pp. 1–7.

[11] V. Dhillon, D. Metcalf, M. Hooper, The hyperledger project, in: Blockchain Enabled Applications, Springer, 2017, pp. 139–149.

[12] W. Mougayar, An operational framework for decentralized autonomous organizations, Startup Manag (2015). http://startupmanagement.org/2015/02/ 04/an-operational-framework-for-decentralizedautonomous-organizations.

[13] K. Chen, R. Stegerean, R.-L. Nistor, A modern management approach in internet era, in: Proceedings of the 11th International Management Conference, 2017, pp. 2–4. Bucharest, Romania: Bucharest University of Economic Studies.

[14] R. v. Pelt, S. Jansen, D. Baars, S. Overbeek, Defining blockchain governance: A framework for analysis and comparison, *Inf. Syst. Manag.* 38 (1) (2021) 21–41.

[15] Y. Faqir-Rhazoui, J. Arroyo, S. Hassan, A comparative analysis of the platforms for decentralized autonomous organizations in the ethereum blockchain, *J. Internet. Serv. Appl.* 12 (1) (2021) 1–20.

[16] J. B. Awotunde, S. Misra, Q. T. Pham, A secure framework for Internet of medical things security based system using lightweight cryptography enabled blockchain, in: International Conference on Future Data and Security Engineering, Springer Nature Singapore, November 2022, pp. 258–272.

[17] P. Kutsyk, K. Redchenko, R. Voronko, Management control and modern decentralized technologies, *Baltic J. Econ. Stud.* 6 (4) (2020) 98–102.

[18] O. Rikken, M. Janssen, Z. Kwee, Governance challenges of blockchain and decentralized autonomous organizations, *Inf. Polity* 24 (4) (2019) 397–417.

[19] W. A. Kaal, C. Calcaterra, Crypto transaction dispute resolution, *Bus. Lawyer* 73 (1) (2017) 109–152.

[20] S. Wang, W. Ding, J. Li, Y. Yuan, L. Ouyang, F.-Y. Wang, Decentralized autonomous organizations: Concept, model, and applications, *IEEE Trans. Comput. Soc. Sys.* 6 (5) (2019) 870–878.

[21] P. De Filippi, G. McMullen, Governance of Blockchain Systems: Governance Of and by Distributed Infrastructure. PhD Thesis, Blockchain Research Institute and COALA, Toronto, Canada, 2018.

[22] F. Machart, The State of Blockchain Governance, 2020. https://medium.com/greenfield-one/the-state-of-blockchain-governance-governance-by-and-of-blockchains-f6418c46077/.

[23] Y. El Faqir, J. Arroyo, S. Hassan, An overview of decentralized autonomous organizations on the blockchain, in: Proceedings of the 16th International Symposium on Open Collaboration, 2020, pp. 1–8. Association for Computing Machinery (ACM).

8 Integration of Digital of Twins in Industries 4.0 and 5.0

Joseph Bamidele Awotunde, Abidemi Emmanuel Adeniyi, and Peace Busola Falola

8.1 INTRODUCTION

The growth of technological innovation has resulted in numerous new technologies. Digital twins utilize data like physical designs, sensor modifications, and operational history to combine interdisciplinary, multiphysical, multiscale, and multiprobability simulation procedures [1]. The mapping is performed in a virtual environment to precisely depict the whole life cycle of the matching actual devices. Digital twins utilize simulation technology to collect real-world data from physical models, mapping a digital body to the actual object on the screen. Digital twins enable real-time monitoring of digital entities, parameter monitoring, and simulation of virtual worlds using artificial intelligence (AI), subsequently transferring results to real-world scenarios [2]. Numerous scholars have conducted research in this area. Digital twins are increasingly being used in the construction of smart cities, as 85% of Internet of Things (IoT) gadgets globally utilize them for the surveillance of security [3]. Infrastructure, the foundation of urban development, is the most difficult region to assess and reach with the IoT. The existing development management system does not sufficiently satisfy the needs of the times and society. Thus, digital twins may considerably improve the growth of the facilities business by providing an excellent basis for constructing analysis models [4,5].

The manufacturing industry has undergone significant transformation, necessitating global manufacturers to enhance productivity. In 2011, Germany launched Industry 4.0 to increase its manufacturing competitiveness [6,7]. Industry 4.0 is a transition in technological advancement that began with Industry 1.0's introduction of the steam locomotive period. Industry 2.0 transformed power, Industry 3.0 brought about the digital era, and Industry 4.0 utilized intelligence to enhance industrial upgrades. The European Union proposed, in 2021, that the Fifth Industrial Revolution (Industry 5.0 or 5IR) will combine the Internet with artificial intelligence in industrial engineering and production [8]. The focus is on people orientation, sustainability, and flexibility [9–11], with studies revealing that Industry 4.0 is predominantly driven by

DOI: 10.1201/9781003581963-8

technological devices, whereas Industry 5.0 is value driven. Mourtzis [12] suggests that 5IR should focus on creating a framework for process optimization using big data and semantic integration. The Industry 5.0 industrial vision is still largely unfulfilled in developed countries due to their limited efficiency and productivity. The specific focus is on enhancing the industry's position and influence in society. Most enterprises are still focusing on Industry 5.0 as a future orientation, aiming to fully utilize the potential of Industry 4.0 [13]. Hence, digitalization facilitates the transition from technology to leadership, coordinating resources, handling operational intelligence data, and providing more predictable work units and factories.

Digital twins have their roots in the realm of industrial manufacturing [14,15] and it is believed that digital twins can provide real-time visualization of manufacturing systems through 3D simulations. Digital twins are used to model, create, and products through simulation experiments. Digital twins possess the ability to increase manufacturing by enabling simulation of equipment operation and parameter adjustment. Digital twins possess an opportunity to improve products' reliability and availability, and reduce development and manufacturing risks [16,17]. Digital twins have played a crucial role in the servicing stage, continually gathering and assessing operational information to forecast optimal maintenance times. The maintenance cycle reference basis could then be provided [18,19]. Meanwhile, digital twins were utilized as a reference for calculating fault sites and probabilities. Digital twins provide considerable benefits and lower costs in manufacturing industries, assisting manufacturers. Investigation into the usage of digital twins in manufacturing is mostly focused on troubleshooting and exploring the virtual world [20,21].

The goal is to optimize the machine's operation and its related content for optimal performance. The design procedure and summarized examinations of digital twins' applicability in manufacturing industries are scarce. Therefore, this chapter investigates the key principles, challenges, and opportunities linked with the integration of digital twins in Industries 4.0 and 5.0, shedding light on their transformative potential in modeling the prospect of industrial operations. The discussion spans from the foundational concepts of Industry 4.0 to the developing landscape of Industry 5.0, offering intuitions into how digital twins serve as a connection between these two eras. Through a comprehensive examination of case studies and technological advancements, this chapter seeks to provide a thorough understanding of the strategic deployment of digital twins in achieving enhanced efficiency, productivity, and innovation in the evolving industrial landscape.

8.1.1 Key Contributions of the Chapter

The following are notable contributions of the chapter:

i. This chapter explores the incorporation of digital twins in Industries 4.0 and 5.0.
ii. The chapter discusses challenges and prospects related to the incorporation of digital twins in Industries 4.0 and 5.0,

iii. The chapter explores the role of digital twins in bridging the gap between Industry 4.0 and Industry 5.0, focusing on its foundational concepts.
iv. The chapter also describes lessons learned and future research difficulties for integrating digital twins in Industries 4.0 and 5.0.

8.2 THE MOTIVATION FOR THE EVOLUTION OF INDUSTRY 4.0 TO INDUSTRY 5.0

Industry 1.0 emerged in the 18th century, encompassing various industries such as textiles, metals, cement, chemicals, fossil fuels, glass, paper, mining, farming, and transport using steam. The industrial era which started in the 19th century, transformed farming, transportation, and economic expansion, and Industry 2.0 developed [22]. The emphasis was on diverse industries such as steel, railways, electricity, machinery, documents, petrochemicals, marine technology, rubber, cars, fertilizers, engines, generators, telecommunications, and contemporary corporate governance [23,24]. Industry 3.0, characterized by the widespread adoption of electronic and information technologies, revolutionized mass production by dividing component processing and assembly [25,26]. The extensive use of computers and data technologies substantially improved the automated control of production processes [27,28].

Industry 4.0, introduced in 2011, focuses on intelligent manufacturing. The primary objective is to enhance performance through labor-intensive massive manufacturing using developing technology [29]. Sharma and Villányi [30] proposed a secure, end-to-end, two-way authorized data transfer mechanism for Industry 4.0. The technology was found to maintain the system's integrity and stability following the scaling-out phenomena. This approach has the lowest overheads for communication, calculation cost, and time for the return trip. According to research by Javaid et al. [31], Industry 4.0 improves versatility in production and allows enterprises to quickly adjust to consumer developments. The industrial control system automatically changes output based on varying participation rates, hence lowering manufacturing expenses. According to Javaid and Haleem [32], 5IR reflects the industrial field's future orientation, intending to harness human inventiveness to work with effective and intelligent gadgets. Figure 8.1 shows the evolution from Industry 1.0 to Industry 5.0.

The 21st century has seen rapid advancements in advanced information technologies such as the Internet of Things, cloud computing, big data, wireless internet, and artificial intelligence. Mourtzis and Doukas [33] examined the growth of manufacturing frameworks, concepts, and their connections, considering technological advancements and sociopolitical factors throughout each era. In 2011, Germany introduced Industry 4.0, highlighting the transformative impact of digital, data-driven, and interconnected industries on the advancement of information technology [34,35]. Industry 4.0 uses a cyber-physical system (CPS) to digitalize industrial supply, manufacture, and sales, enabling rapid, effective, and personalized product supply [36,37]. The manufacturing industry has been fully transformed through the use of CPS for digital and intelligent advancements [38,39]. Industry 4.0 integrates digital and

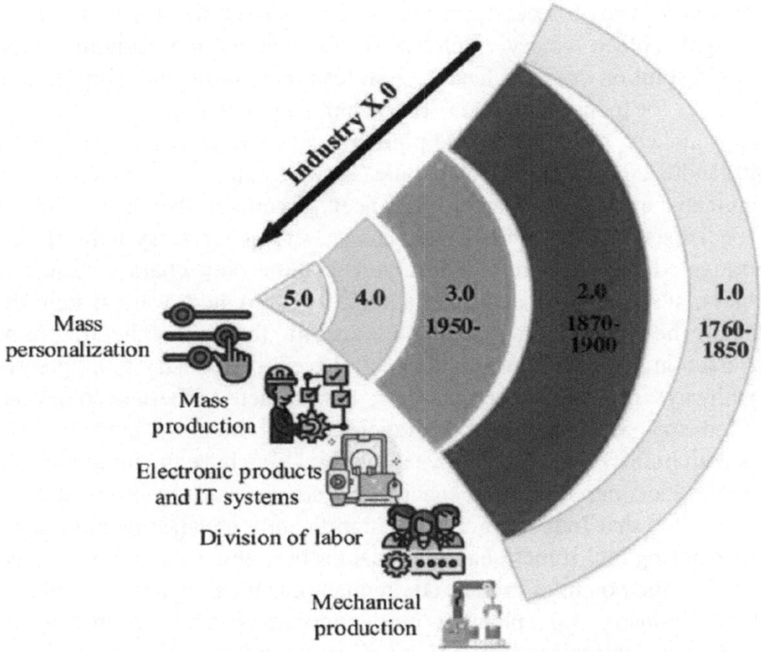

FIGURE 8.1 The Industrial Revolution, from Industry 1.0 to Industry 5.0.

physical worlds, guiding European innovation in industry, technical advancement, and digital evolution, as acknowledged by large economies worldwide [40–43]. This posited that Industry 4.0 could enhance manufacturing industry intelligence by enabling machine interconnection and mutual control over machinery across its entire cycle. Industry 4.0 emphasizes the automation of processes, which reduces human participation in the production process.

Industry 4.0 encourages autonomy of systems and questions the significance of human intelligence. This raises the issue of the essential role human intellect ought to have in different facets of life. What is the best way to address the job issue once humans are replaced by machines? The employment problem can be effectively addressed by implementing strategies that address the shift from manual labor to automation. Mourtzis et al. [44] propose Industry 5.0 as a framework for integrating industry and emerging social trends, facilitating transitioning from Industry 4.0 to Community 5.0. Liao et al. [45] proposed the digital twins paradigm to improve cloud-edge device cooperation dependability and effectiveness of communication in low-carbon energy-managing devices. The trials demonstrated its superior efficacy concerning loss function, communication effectiveness, and greenhouse gas reductions. Zhou et al. [46] proposed a federated learning-based digital twins architecture and a safe and efficient digital twins-assisted resource allocation method. The model demonstrated superiority in 5G edge computing permission, where efficiency is measured by cumulative repetition delay, digital twin loss function, usage of energy, and a lack of access precedence. Zemtsov et al. [47] proposed that the industry might replace factory employees while encouraging economic expansion. The proposed solution does not lead to significant environmental damage, pollution, or health issues for industrial workers or the human population.

Decision-makers, researchers, and politicians have explored Industry 5.0 to successfully handle the challenges of people and the natural surroundings in industrial manufacturing. The Industry 5.0 concept leverages the distinctive skills of human specialists to work with smart, clever, and accurate systems. Leng et al. [48] investigated the evolution of 5IR and its three key characteristics: people-centeredness, sustainability, and adaptability. They created a 3D system that correctly depicts the technical, realistic, and pragmatic features of the 5IR framework. The conversation went into the fundamental drivers of Industry 5.0, potential integration pathways, prospective applications, and obstacles experienced in real-world settings. Industry 5.0 technology is anticipated to merge advanced, high-speed machines with human critical cognitive thinking. Users have the option to select and customize products based on their specific preferences and requirements. Kaasinen et al. [49] posited that Industry 5.0 could significantly enhance manufacturing efficiency by fostering multifunctional relationships between machines and individuals. The device has the potential to facilitate human–machine engagement and constant surveillance. Industry 5.0 enhances production quality by automating complex mechanical tasks and incorporating transforming human thoughts into thought-provoking challenges.

The evolution from Industry 4.0 to Industry 5.0 is driven by the relentless pursuit of enhanced human–machine collaboration and the desire to consider the constraints of purely automated systems. Industry 4.0 marked a significant shift toward smart, interconnected manufacturing processes, leveraging innovations such as the Internet of Things, intelligent machines, and advanced robotics. While Industry 4.0 brought about increased efficiency and automation, it also generated concerns around job relocation and the diminishing role of human workers in certain industries.

The motivation for Industry 5.0 lies in finding a more balanced and synergistic interaction between robotics and human beings. Recognizing the irreplaceable qualities of human intuition, creativity, and adaptability, Industry 5.0 seeks to integrate these capabilities into the manufacturing landscape. This evolution aims to create a collaborative environment where machines and humans complement each other, fostering innovation, problem-solving, and a more sustainable approach to industrial processes. By focusing on human-centric solutions, Industry 5.0 envisions a future in which technologies enhances human potential rather than replaces it.

Moreover, Industry 5.0 is motivated by the growing importance of ethical considerations and social responsibility in technological advancements. As the impact of automation on the workforce becomes more pronounced, there is a need for a shift toward a more inclusive and ethical approach to technology adoption. Industry 5.0 emphasizes the creation of meaningful, socially responsible jobs, and the development of technologies that prioritize environmental sustainability. This evolution reflects a broader societal awareness of the need to harmonize technological progress with human values, ethics, and a sustainable future.

8.3 KEY TECHNOLOGIES AND COMPONENTS OF DIGITAL TWINS FOR INDUSTRY 4.0 AND INDUSTRY 5.0

Digital twins technology is a critical component of both the current Industry 4.0 and the proposed Industry 5.0. It includes developing virtual reproductions of actual resources, procedures, or structures to mimic, observe, and improve performance. Digital twins technology serves as a cornerstone in both Industry 4.0 and the evolving paradigm of Industry 5.0, albeit with differing emphases. In Industry 4.0, key components of digital twin include IoT sensors for data acquisition, cloud computing for storage and processing, advanced analytics for real-time insights, and augmented reality for visualization and interaction. This setup enables virtual duplicates of actual resources or procedures, encouraging proactive upkeep, optimization, and simulation. However, Industry 5.0 integrates human-centered approaches, emphasizing collaboration between humans and machines. Here, digital twins are enriched with AI-driven interfaces for seamless human–machine interaction, incorporating natural language processing and gesture recognition [50,51]. Additionally, emotional analytics and empathy models enhance the understanding and response to human needs, amplifying the synergy between human ingenuity and technological prowess.

Digital twin technology revolutionizes Industry 4.0 by creating virtual replicas of physical entities, providing insights, and enabling data visualization, analysis, and manipulation for informed decision-making. The digital twin is a vital tool for modern businesses and industries, serving as a bridge between the real-world and electronic spheres [52]. The digital twin, at the core of Industry 4.0, comprises physical entities, virtual replicas, and data integration and analysis [53]. The integration of physical and digital worlds enables efficient monitoring and optimization of complex systems through virtual replicas, promoting informed decision-making and reduced risks. Digital twins offer more than just cost reduction; they facilitate stakeholder collaboration, provide real-time insights, and lead to innovative solutions and new business models. Digital twin is a transformative technology, gaining momentum due to IoT and AI adoption, and the growing demand for predictive maintenance and process optimization [54,55].

Digital twin technology is a crucial component of Industry 4.0, enabling businesses to generate digital reproductions of actual systems, goods, or processes in real-time insights and analysis (Figure 8.2) [56,57]. Technology has revolutionized businesses by utilizing digital twins to enhance product understanding, identify potential issues, and implement proactive measures for growth and innovation. Digital twin technology enhances reliability, reduces downtime, and boosts productivity, making it critical for firms to keep viable in the continually shifting industry [58]. Here are key technologies and components associated with digital twins in both Industry 4.0 and Industry 5.0:

Internet of Things Sensors: IoT sensors are used to get real-time information from physical assets or systems [59]. These sensors monitor various characteristics such as temperature and pressure, vibration, and more. The data collected by these sensors form the basis for creating digital twins. IoT sensors play an

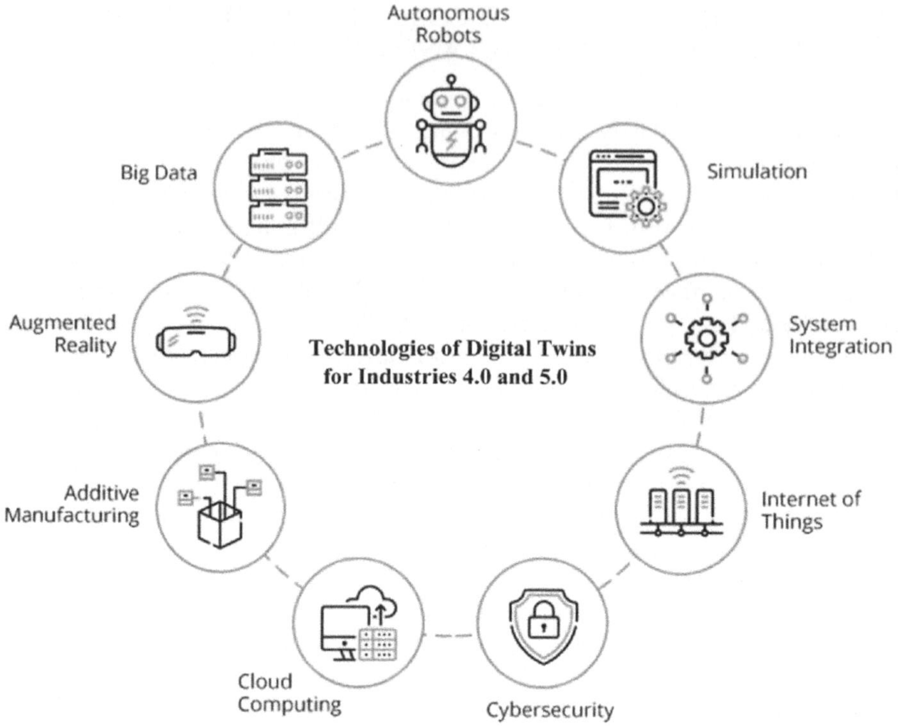

FIGURE 8.2 The technologies and components of digital twins for Industries 4.0 and 5.0.

important role for handling physical possessions by capturing data as they occur on temperature, pressure, humidity, and vibration. The data generated create a digital twin that accurately represents the asset's performance, offering a comprehensive view for businesses and researchers. In the context of Industry 4.0 and its evolution into Industry 5.0, the integration of IoT sensors with digital twins represents a transformative synergy [60]. IoT sensors are deployed across industrial environments to collect massive volumes of timely information from machines, processes, and assets [61,62]. These data are then utilized to create digital twins, virtual replicas that mirror their physical counterparts in the digital realm. Through advanced analytics, using machine learning and intelligence-based techniques, these digital twins can mimic, anticipate, and optimize various aspects of industrial operations, facilitating predictive maintenance, performance monitoring, and process optimization. In Industry 5.0, this integration extends beyond mere optimization to enable more holistic human–machine collaboration, where digital twins serve as virtual companions aiding human decision-making processes and fostering a symbiotic relationship between humans and machines, thereby enhancing productivity, efficiency, and innovation in industrial settings [44].

Cloud Computing: Cloud computing infrastructure is essential for gathering, organizing, and analyzing the massive volumes of data created by the Internet of Things sensors [63]. It provides the scalability and flexibility required to handle the dynamic nature of digital twin applications. Digital twin relies heavily on cloud platforms for data storage and processing, ensuring scalability, accessibility, real-time analysis, and remote access for efficient data management [64,65]. In the progression from Industry 4.0 to Industry 5.0, the integration of cloud computing with sensors and digital twins marks a pivotal advancement in industrial operations. Cloud computing provides the infrastructure and resources necessary for storing, processing, and interpreting enormous amounts of data supplied by sensors deployed throughout industrial environments [66]. These data are leveraged to create and refine digital twins' virtual replicas of actual resources and operations. Through cloud-based platforms, digital twins gain enhanced capabilities, including real-time monitoring, predictive analytics, and simulation of various scenarios. In Industry 5.0, this integration extends further, facilitating seamless collaboration between humans and digital twins in decision-making processes, enabling dynamic adjustments to operations based on real-time insights, and fostering a more responsive and adaptable industrial ecosystem that prioritizes human–machine symbiosis for enhanced productivity, innovation, and sustainability.

Big Data Analytics: Digital twins rely on advanced analytics techniques to extract meaningful insights from the collected data. Big data analytics tools and algorithms are used to identify patterns, trends, anomalies, and correlations within the data, enabling predictive and prescriptive maintenance strategies [67]. Data analytics utilizes advanced technologies like machine learning and AI to analyze sensor data, detect patterns, predict maintenance, optimize performance, and enhance efficiency and productivity in businesses [68]. In the progression from Industry 4.0 to Industry 5.0, the convergence of big data analytics with digital twins heralds a significant evolution in industrial practices [69]. Big data analytics harnesses advanced methods and strategies for processing and extracting useful insights from vast and diverse datasets generated by industrial processes, equipment, and systems [70]. By integrating big data analytics with digital twins, industries gain the capability to create highly accurate and dynamic virtual depictions of tangible assets and operations. These digital twins are empowered to not only simulate real-world scenarios but also leverage historical and real-time data to predict future outcomes, optimize performance, and facilitate proactive decision-making [71]. In Industry 5.0, this synergy between big data analytics and digital twins transcends traditional optimization, fostering a paradigm where human expertise is augmented by machine intelligence, leading to more adaptive, efficient, and collaborative industrial ecosystems that prioritize human-centric values, creativity, and innovation [72].

Machine Learning and AI: Machine learning and artificial intelligence techniques play an important role in digital twins by enabling autonomous decision-making, predictive modeling, and adaptive control [73,74]. These technologies help optimize real-time performance data for tangible possessions and procedures. During the transition from Industry 4.0 to Industry 5.0, connectivity of ML and AI with digital twins represents a transformative shift in industrial practices [75].

ML and AI techniques enable digital twins to evolve from static representations to dynamic entities capable of autonomously learning from and adapting to new data. By leveraging ML algorithms, digital twins can analyze vast datasets collected from sensors and historical records to identify patterns and anomalies, and optimize performance. In Industry 5.0, this integration advances further, facilitating more sophisticated decision-making processes where digital twins act as intelligent assistants, collaborating seamlessly with human operators to address complex challenges, predict outcomes, and drive continuous improvement [76,77]. This symbiotic relationship between ML/AI and digital twins fosters a more agile, adaptive, and human-centered industrial environment, where innovation flourishes, and productivity is maximized through enhanced collaboration and decision-making [78,79].

Simulation and Modeling Simulation and modelling tools generate virtual representations of physical systems, continuously updated with real-world data, enabling experts to predict complex system behaviors, driving innovation and scientific discovery in various fields. The integration of simulation and modeling with digital twins signifies a pivotal advancement in both Industry 4.0 and its evolution into Industry 5.0 [80]. Simulation and modeling techniques enable the creation of highly accurate virtual representations of physical assets and processes within digital twins, allowing for predictive analysis, optimization, and scenario planning [81]. In Industry 4.0, this integration facilitates proactive maintenance strategies, process optimization, and resource allocation based on simulated outcomes. In Industry 5.0, the sophistication of simulation and modeling within digital twins extends further, enabling dynamic adaptation to real-time data inputs, fostering human–machine collaboration in decision-making processes, and facilitating agile responses to changing operational environments [82]. This synergy empowers industries to achieve unprecedented levels of efficiency, resilience, and innovation by leveraging the predictive and adaptive capabilities of digital twins enhanced through simulation and modeling techniques [83,84].

Augmented Reality (AR) and Virtual Reality (VR): AR and VR technologies enhance the visualization and interaction capabilities of digital twins [85]. They enable users to overlay digital data on their actual surroundings or immerse themselves in simulated copies, facilitating training, maintenance, and troubleshooting activities. AR/VR technology can enhance business performance by integrating with digital twins for immersive training, maintenance, and remote monitoring, promoting real-time interaction with virtual objects [87]. The integration of AR and VR technologies with digital twins represents a significant advancement in both Industry 4.0 and its evolution into Industry 5.0. AR and VR offer immersive visualization and interaction capabilities that enable users to interact with digital twins in simulated or augmented environments. In Industry 4.0, AR and VR enhance training, maintenance, and troubleshooting processes by providing technicians with intuitive interfaces to interact with digital twins overlaid onto physical equipment. They also facilitate remote monitoring and collaboration, enabling experts to assist field personnel in real time. In Industry 5.0, AR and VR play an even more crucial role, bridging the gap between humans and digital twins by providing intuitive interfaces for data visualization, analysis, and decision-making [88]. This integration fosters a collaborative ecosystem where human expertise is augmented by digital twins, enabling more efficient problem-solving, innovation, and adaptability in industrial operations [89].

Blockchain: Blockchain innovation may be used for security and to authenticate the data exchanged between different components of the digital twin ecosystem [90]. It ensures data integrity, transparency, and traceability, which are critical for maintaining trust in digital twin applications. Blockchain innovation improves the accuracy of information and transparency in the digital twin, particularly in supply chain and manufacturing scenarios, offering strong and transparent infrastructure transaction recording and tracking [91]. Blockchain technology in digital twin can revolutionize supply chain and manufacturing processes, enhancing efficiency, transparency, and trust for businesses. The integration of blockchain technology with digital twins signifies a transformative advancement in both Industry 4.0 and its progression into Industry 5.0. Blockchain, with its decentralized and irreversible registry platform, guarantees safe and transparent transactions and data exchange among stakeholders [92]. In Industry 4.0, blockchain-enabled digital twins enhance supply chain management, ensuring the integrity and traceability of data across the entire value chain, from raw material sourcing to product delivery [93,94]. This fosters trust, reduces fraud, and enhances efficiency. In Industry 5.0, blockchain further enables decentralized decision-making and collaboration, facilitating the autonomous exchange of data and services between interconnected digital twins and human operators [95,96]. This integration empowers industries to create more resilient, transparent, and collaborative ecosystems where digital twins serve as trusted intermediaries, driving innovation and value creation through secure data exchange and interoperability [97,98].

Edge Computing: Edge computing puts computing power nearer to the data source, decreasing latency and allowing for actual time processing and analysis of data generated by IoT sensors [99]. It is particularly important for applications where immediate action is required based on the insights derived from digital twins. Edge computing, or data processing near the data source, decreases latency and enhances instantaneous decision-making, particularly in urgent situations [100]. The integration of edge computing with digital twins marks a significant advancement in both Industry 4.0 and its evolution into Industry 5.0. The use of edge computing moves computational capacity closer to the data source, allowing for real-time processing and analysis of data generated by sensors and devices at the edge of the network [101]. In Industry 4.0, edge computing-enabled digital twins enhance responsiveness and efficiency by processing data locally, reducing latency and bandwidth requirements while enabling rapid decision-making in time-sensitive applications such as predictive maintenance and quality control [102]. Industry 5.0 integrates digital twins with autonomous decision-making capabilities, fostering decentralized, adaptive systems. This collaboration with human operators drives agility, resilience, and innovation in industrial operations [103]. This synergy between edge computing and digital twins creates more dynamic and responsive industrial ecosystems, optimizing resource utilization and enhancing overall productivity and performance.

Cybersecurity Solutions: Securing digital twin environments against cyber threats is essential to secure critical data and prevent illegal access or tampering. Cybersecurity solutions encompass a range of technology including encryption, access control, and detection of intruders, and threat intelligence. Digital twins' data collection and processing necessitate robust cybersecurity regulations such as authentication, authorization, and systems for detecting intrusions to protect against cyber threats. The integration of cybersecurity measures with digital twins represents a critical advancement in both Industry 4.0 and its evolution into Industry 5.0. In Industry 4.0, robust cybersecurity protocols ensure the security, privacy, and accessibility of information transmitted and stored within digital twins, safeguarding against unwanted access and data losses, and sabotage. As industries transition to Industry 5.0, where digital twins play an even more central role in decision-making and collaboration, cybersecurity becomes paramount in ensuring the trustworthiness and resilience of interconnected digital twin ecosystems. This integration enhances data protection, identity management, and threat detection capabilities, fostering a secure and trustworthy environment where human–machine interactions are safeguarded, and innovation can thrive without compromising on security and privacy.

Interoperability Standards: Standardization efforts play a key role in ensuring interoperability and compatibility between different digital twin implementations. Standards define standard protocols, data structures, and gateways to enable smooth connectivity with existing systems and interoperability across various domains. The integration of interoperability standards with digital twins represents a pivotal advancement in both Industry 4.0 and its progression into Industry 5.0. Interoperability standards establish common frameworks techniques that allow for smooth connection and data sharing between heterogeneous systems and devices, ensuring compatibility and integration across various platforms and technologies. In Industry 4.0, adherence to interoperability standards facilitates the integration of diverse digital twin implementations within complex industrial ecosystems, enabling interoperable data sharing and collaboration across organizational boundaries. As industries transition to Industry 5.0, where the interconnectedness of digital twins and human operators becomes more pronounced, interoperability standards play a crucial role in fostering a cohesive and adaptable ecosystem where digital twins can collaborate seamlessly with humans and other digital twins, driving innovation, agility, and efficiency. This integration enhances scalability, flexibility, and resilience, enabling industries to harness the full potential of digital twins to address complex challenges and unlock new opportunities for growth and competitiveness.

3D Visualization: 3D visualization improves predictions by providing a realistic representation of physical systems, facilitating complex system analysis, and enhancing decision-making and outcomes. The integration of 3D visualization with digital twins represents a significant advancement in both Industry 4.0 and its evolution into Industry 5.0. 3D visualization technology allows for the creation of highly immersive and interactive representations of physical assets and processes within digital twins, providing stakeholders with intuitive and detailed insights into complex industrial environments. In Industry 4.0, 3D visualization enhances situational awareness, enabling operators to monitor and analyze processes more effectively, identify potential bottlenecks, and optimize resource allocation. As industries transition to Industry 5.0, collaboration between humans and machines is central, 3D visualization further facilitates intuitive interaction with digital twins, enabling stakeholders to visualize and manipulate virtual representations in real time, fostering more knowledgeable decision-making and collaboration. This integration enhances communication, problem-solving, and innovation, empowering industries to attain advanced ranks of effectiveness, productivity, and adaptability in dynamic and interconnected industrial ecosystems.

Digital Thread: The digital twin is a key constituent of the digital thread, connecting all phases of a product's lifespan to enhance efficiency and collaboration. This allows for seamless information flow between design, manufacturing, operation, and maintenance. Digital twin technology offers a simulated illustration of the physical product, allowing businesses to test and optimize various scenarios without incurring significant costs. By leveraging this approach, companies may streamline processes, lower expenses, and enhance their bottom line. The incorporation of the digital thread concept with digital twins represents a foundational advancement in both Industry 4.0 and its progression into Industry 5.0. The digital thread refers to the seamless flow of data through the invention growth, from design and engineering to industrial, operation, and preservation. By intertwining digital twins with the digital thread, industries achieve a holistic view of the product lifecycle, enabling real-time surveillance, evaluation, and improvement across every stage. In Industry 4.0, this integration enhances traceability, quality control, and process optimization, enabling agile responses to changing demands and market conditions. As industries transition to Industry 5.0, where human-centric values and collaboration are emphasized, the digital thread-enabled digital twins foster greater transparency, accountability, and collaboration among stakeholders, driving continuous improvement, innovation, and value creation throughout the product lifecycle. This integration enhances efficiency, agility, and sustainability, empowering industries to adapt and thrive in an ever-evolving and interconnected global marketplace.

Communication Protocols: MQTT and OPC UA are standardized communication protocols that facilitate data exchange between devices, sensors, and the digital twin, enhancing IoT efficiency, cost reduction, and productivity. The integration of communication protocols with digital twins signifies a critical advancement in both Industry 4.0 and its progression into Industry 5.0. Communication protocols establish standardized methods for devices and systems to exchange data, ensuring seamless connectivity and interoperability across diverse industrial environments. In Industry 4.0, adherence to communication protocols facilitates the integration of disparate digital twin implementations within complex industrial ecosystems, enabling efficient data exchange and collaboration across organizational boundaries. As industries transition to Industry 5.0, interaction among humans and machines is central, and communication protocols perform an important part in allowing seamless interaction between humans and digital twins. This integration fosters real-time collaboration, decision-making, and problem-solving, driving innovation, agility, and productivity in dynamic and interconnected industrial ecosystems. By leveraging communication protocols, industries can realize the entire potential of virtual twins to handle difficult issues and leverage upcoming development opportunities and competitiveness.

Human–Machine Interaction: Natural language processing and conversational AI technologies have significantly improved the use of digital twins, enabling efficient access to information and insights, enhancing business operations and becoming increasingly important in various industries. The integration of human–machine interaction (HMI) with digital twins represents a transformative advancement in both Industry 4.0 and its evolution into Industry 5.0. HMI encompasses the interfaces and interactions through which humans and machines communicate and collaborate. In Industry 4.0, HMI-enabled digital twins facilitate intuitive control, monitoring, and decision-making, empowering operators to interact with the real-time simulated versions of actual assets and operations. As industries transition to Industry 5.0, where human-centric values and collaboration are paramount, HMI becomes even more critical in fostering seamless collaboration between humans and digital twins. This integration enhances the accessibility, usability, and adaptability of digital twins, enabling more intuitive and personalized interactions that leverage human expertise while augmenting decision-making processes with machine intelligence. By enabling effective human–machine collaboration, HMI-enabled digital twins drive innovation, efficiency, and productivity in industrial operations, ultimately creating more adaptive, resilient, and sustainable ecosystems that prioritize human well-being and empowerment.

Semantic Data Integration: Semantic technologies organize and unify data from diverse sources, enhancing comprehension and decision-making. Integrating them in business and academia streamlines data management, improves analysis accuracy, and supports informed decision-making. The integration of semantic data integration with digital twins marks a significant advancement in both Industry 4.0 and its progression into Industry 5.0. Semantic data integration involves linking and harmonizing data from disparate sources using standardized vocabularies and ontologies, enabling a deeper understanding of data relationships and context. In Industry 4.0, semantic data integration enhances interoperability and data consistency within digital twins, facilitating more comprehensive insights and analysis across complex industrial environments. As industries transition to Industry 5.0, where collaboration and agility are emphasized, semantic data integration becomes even more critical in facilitating seamless data altercation and collaboration between interconnected digital twins and human operators. This integration fosters a more holistic and contextual understanding of industrial data, driving more informed decision-making, innovation, and collaboration. By leveraging semantic data integration, industries can realize the full capacity of digital replicas to handle difficult issues and benefit from emergent opportunities for development and competitiveness in dynamic and interconnected industrial ecosystems.

8.4 THE VITAL ROLES AND OPPORTUNITIES OF THE INTEGRATION OF DIGITAL TWINS IN INDUSTRIES 4.0 AND 5.0

The integration of digital twins within Industries 4.0 and 5.0 presents a transformative paradigm for manufacturing and industrial processes. In Industry 4.0, digital twins are synthetic reproductions of actual assets, structures, or operations that enable continuous evaluation, analysis, and improvement. Digital twins use data from sensors, IoT gadgets, and various other resources to enable predictive maintenance, fault detection, and performance optimization, thereby reducing downtime and enhancing operational efficiency. Moreover, they facilitate simulation and scenario testing, empowering businesses to explore different strategies and outcomes before implementing changes in the physical environment. As Industry 4.0 transitions to Industrial 5.0, digital twins become even more integral, fostering effortless interaction between people and robots through advanced technology like AI and robots, and augmented reality. This integration enables dynamic and adaptive manufacturing ecosystems where virtual twins serve a major role in orchestrating processes, coordinating resources, and responding to changing demands in real time.

The integration of digital twins in Industries 4.0 and 5.0 also opens up new possibilities for development and generating value across various sectors. For instance, in manufacturing, digital twins enable the design of more efficient and sustainable products by simulating their lifecycle, from conception to disposal. This not only reduces time-to-market but also enhances product quality and customization while minimizing environmental impact. Additionally, digital twins facilitate the development of smart cities and infrastructure by modeling urban environments, optimizing resource allocation, and improving citizen services. In healthcare, they promote individualized medication by developing virtual representations of patients, enabling tailored treatment plans and predictive healthcare analytics. Furthermore, in the power industry, digital twins optimize the efficiency of renewable energy sources, grid systems, and infrastructure, promoting sustainability and resilience in the face of climate change. Overall, the integration of digital twins in Industries 4.0 and 5.0 catalyzes innovation, efficiency, and sustainability across diverse domains, shaping the future of digital transformation and industrial advancement. The digital twin is a crucial tool in Industries 4.0 and 5.0, integrating digital technologies, data-driven decision-making, and automation, enhancing performance, efficiency, and reducing errors, thereby enhancing business competitiveness. The digital twin is a crucial tool in facilitating transformation and contributing significantly to Industries 4.0 and 5.0.

Real-Time Monitoring and Control: In essence, a digital twin is a digital twin of a real-world thing, like a machine or a factory. It uses real-time sensor data to constantly track what's going on. This allows businesses to spot problems early, fix them before they break, and run things more smoothly. This gives them a big advantage and helps them come up with new ideas. Digital twins are especially important in modern factories (Industries 4.0 and 5.0) because they allow companies to keep a close eye on everything and make adjustments as needed. By using real-time data, digital twins can predict problems, optimize operations, and minimize downtime. They also allow remote monitoring and control, giving businesses more flexibility. With advanced analytics and machine learning, digital twins can even suggest improvements and make decisions on their own, leading to even greater efficiency and innovation.

Predictive Maintenance: Digital twins are game-changers for predictive maintenance in Industries 4.0 and 5.0. These virtual mirrors of physical assets allow continuous monitoring and analysis of performance data. By combining real-time sensor readings with historical trends, digital twins predict equipment issues before they happen, enabling proactive maintenance. This approach minimizes downtime, reduces costs, and extends asset life. Additionally, digital twins enable condition-based monitoring and diagnostics, pinpointing root causes for optimized maintenance strategies, boosting reliability and efficiency. Advanced analytics and machine learning further empower digital twins, offering prescriptive actions and even autonomous decision-making. This translates to operational excellence and a competitive edge in the Industries 4.0 and 5.0 era.

Product Development and Testing: Digital twins aid product development by enabling virtual simulation and testing before physical realization, expediting design, reducing prototyping costs, and enabling iterative improvements based on simulations. Digital twins play crucial roles in product development and testing in Industries 4.0 and 5.0 by providing virtual representations of physical products and processes, facilitating simulation, prototyping, and testing in a digital environment. By creating digital replicas of products, companies can conduct virtual tests to assess performance, functionality, and durability before physical prototypes are built, significantly reducing time and costs associated with traditional testing methods. Digital twins enable iterative design improvements based on real-time feedback, allowing for rapid innovation and customization to meet evolving customer needs. Moreover, by simulating various scenarios and environments, digital twins help optimize product design, manufacturing processes, and supply chain logistics, ensuring products are market-ready and competitive in an increasingly dynamic and interconnected global marketplace. This integrated approach to product development and testing empowers companies to accelerate time-to-market, enhance product quality, and drive sustainable growth in the Industries 4.0 and 5.0 era.

Process Optimization: The digital twin is a powerful tool for optimization, allowing manufacturers to simulate and improve processes, fine-tune parameters, and optimize supply chain and resource allocation, thereby improving efficiency and decision-making. Digital twins play pivotal roles in process optimization within Industries 4.0 and 5.0 by providing real-time insights into the performance and behavior of manufacturing processes. By creating digital replicas of production systems, companies can simulate different operational scenarios, identify inefficiencies, and optimize workflows to maximize productivity and minimize costs. Digital twins enable continuous monitoring of process parameters and equipment condition, facilitating predictive maintenance to prevent downtime and improve asset reliability. Moreover, by integrating with data insights and artificial intelligence techniques, digital twins empower companies to identify concealed patterns, improve the utilization of resources, and make data-driven decisions for continuous improvement. This holistic approach to process optimization enhances operational agility, flexibility, and competitiveness in an increasingly dynamic and interconnected industrial landscape, driving sustainable growth and innovation in Industry 4.0 and beyond.

Quality Control: Digital twins aid in real-time product quality monitoring and management by comparing actual data with virtual twin specifications, detecting deviations, addressing them promptly, minimizing defects, and improving overall product quality, leading to cost savings and customer satisfaction. Digital twins play indispensable roles in quality control within Industries 4.0 and 5.0 by offering real-time monitoring and analysis capabilities throughout the manufacturing process. By creating digital replicas of products and production environments, companies can conduct virtual inspections and simulations to detect defects, deviations, and potential issues early on. This proactive approach allows for immediate corrective actions, ensuring adherence to quality standards and regulatory requirements while minimizing scrap and rework. Digital twins enable continuous monitoring of product parameters, production metrics, and environmental conditions, facilitating root cause analysis and process optimization to improve overall product quality and customer satisfaction. Moreover, by integrating with advanced analytics and artificial intelligence, digital twins empower companies to predict quality trends, optimize quality control strategies, and drive continuous improvement initiatives, ultimately enhancing competitiveness and fostering innovation in the Industries 4.0 and 5.0 landscape.

Resource Efficiency: Industry 4.0 prioritizes sustainability. Digital twins are key tools, providing real-time data and optimization for resource use. By mirroring factories, processes, and supply chains digitally, companies can analyze consumption, identify waste, and minimize environmental impact. Predictive analytics and simulations help optimize energy, materials, and production, aiding sustainable practices. Additionally, digital twins connect with IoT sensors and data platforms, enabling companies to monitor resource performance, track progress, and continuously improve efficiency in this digital age.

Customization and Personalization: Digital twins unlock mass customization, especially in cars and fashion. They boost efficiency, accuracy, and innovation, all within virtual model limits. By creating digital twins of products and processes, manufacturers can personalize for each customer in Industries 4.0 and 5.0. Analyzing customer data (behavior, preferences, usage) lets companies tailor products, services, and experiences. Digital replicas allow configuring products to exact needs, offering high customization without sacrificing efficiency. Furthermore, digital twins enable real-time adjustments, so companies can adapt to evolving customer demands. This personalization translates to happy customers, brand loyalty, and standing out from the competition, fueling growth in the digital age.

Data Analysis and AI Integration: Digital twins leverage advanced analytics and AI to generate vast data, providing businesses with deeper insights, accurate predictions, and process optimization, enhancing efficiency and competitiveness. Digital twins are data analysis and AI powerhouses in Industries 4.0 and 5.0. These virtual twins pump out real-time data, feeding advanced analytics for smart decisions. By mirroring real-world assets, digital twins continuously collect sensor data. Machine learning then analyzes these data to find hidden patterns, predict trends, and optimize choices. Digital twins are the launchpad for AI, providing the structure for intelligent automation, autonomous decisions, and adaptable control. This data–AI combination fuels innovation, boosts efficiency, and unlocks new growth opportunities in the digital age.

Remote Operation and Troubleshooting: Digital twins are crucial tools for remote operation and troubleshooting equipment, especially in hazardous environments like offshore oil rigs or space exploration. They allow real-time monitoring of performance metrics, enhancing operational efficiency, safety, and cost savings. Digital twins play vital roles in remote operation and troubleshooting within Industries 4.0 and 5.0 by providing real-time visibility and control over physical assets and processes from anywhere in the world. By creating digital replicas of equipment and systems, companies can remotely monitor performance metrics, diagnose issues, and troubleshoot problems without the need for physical presence on-site. This capability enhances operational efficiency, reduces downtime, and reduces the requirement for expensive and time-consuming travel. Moreover, digital twins enable remote collaboration among teams, experts may give instruction and help in actual time, regardless of the geographical location. By leveraging remote operation and troubleshooting capabilities, companies can improve responsiveness, agility, and resilience in the face of unforeseen challenges, ultimately driving operational excellence and competitiveness in the digital era.

Continuous Improvement: Industry 4.0 utilizes advanced technologies, including digital twins, for highly automated manufacturing environments. It enhances productivity, quality, and profitability by providing a feedback loop for continuous optimization and market competitiveness. Digital twins play crucial roles in facilitating continuous improvement within Industries 4.0 and 5.0 by providing a dynamic platform for ongoing optimization and innovation. By creating digital replicas of physical assets and processes, companies can continuously monitor performance, gather real-time data, and analyze insights to identify areas for enhancement. Digital twins enable predictive analytics and simulation modeling to predict future scenarios, optimize decision-making, and drive proactive interventions. Moreover, by integrating with sophisticated machine learning and analytics techniques digital twins empower companies to uncover hidden patterns, optimize processes, and drive autonomous decision-making. This iterative approach to continuous improvement creates a culture of inventiveness, agility, and flexibility, allowing firms to compete and prosper in quickly changing industrial landscapes.

Sustainability and Environmental Impact: Digital twins help companies maximize resource utilization and reduce the ecological impact by simulating the effects of different operational strategies and technologies. By modeling energy consumption, emissions, and waste generation, companies can identify opportunities to minimize their ecological impact and meet environmental objectives. Digital twins play pivotal roles in promoting sustainability and mitigating the environmental impact within Industries 4.0 and 5.0 by providing a comprehensive understanding of resource consumption, emissions, and waste generation throughout the entire lifecycle of products and processes. By developing digital duplicates of actual assets and supply chain networks, businesses may simulate numerous situations and improve processes to decrease energy usage, reduce emissions, and optimize resource utilization. Digital twins enable predictive analytics and simulation modeling to assess the environmental footprint of various strategies and technologies, facilitating informed decision-making to achieve sustainability goals. Moreover, by integrating with IoT sensors and data analytics platforms, digital twins empower companies to monitor environmental performance in real time, discover places for enhancement, and implement proactive measures to enhance environmental stewardship and corporate responsibility. This integrated approach to sustainability not only drives cost savings and operational efficiency but also fosters innovation and enhances brand reputation in the context of a rapidly evolving global landscape focused on environmental conservation and sustainable development.

Data-driven Insights and Analytics: Digital twins create massive volumes of data, which may be studied to get useful insights into the efficiency of assets, usage patterns, and customer behavior. By using modern analytical methods like machine learning and artificial intelligence, companies can detect concealed patterns and opportunities for improvement. Digital twins serve as crucial enablers for data-driven insights and analytics within Industries 4.0 and 5.0 by providing a digital representation of physical assets and procedures. By constantly gathering and analyzing information gathered by gadgets, sensors, and networks embedded in physical assets, digital twins offer real-time visibility into operational performance and behavior. This data goldmine fuels performance tracking, maintenance predictions, process tweaks, and smarter supply chains. Digital twins also team up with machine learning and AI, uncovering hidden trends and turning data into actionable insights. With these data-powered decisions, companies can streamline operations, make smarter choices, and unlock innovation for a digital age advantage.

Supply Chain Management: Digital twins streamline how goods move. By modeling the supply chain, companies cut inventory, speed up deliveries, and boost overall efficiency. They're a game-changer for Industries 4.0 and 5.0, creating a digital twin of the entire chain, from suppliers to customers. Companies see everything in real time, allowing for proactive decisions and tweaks. Digital twins predict demand, optimize stock, and allocate resources better, leading to faster deliveries, fewer stockouts, and overall smoother operations. Plus, with sensors and blockchain, they track goods throughout the journey, building trust and meeting regulations. This joined-up approach makes the supply chain agile, resilient, and responsive, letting companies adapt to a changing market and deliver value in the digital age.

Product Lifecycle Management: Digital twins support product lifecycle management by providing a digital representation of physical products throughout their lifecycle. This enables companies to track product performance, monitor usage patterns, and gather feedback for product improvement and innovation. Digital twins serve as indispensable tools for product lifecycle management within Industries 4.0 and 5.0 by providing a digital representation of products across every phase of their lives, from design and production to usage and disposal. By creating digital replicas of physical products, companies can track and monitor product performance, usage patterns, and maintenance history in real time, enabling proactive decision-making and optimization. Digital twins facilitate collaboration across multidisciplinary teams by providing a centralized platform for sharing data, insights, and feedback throughout the product development process. Moreover, by integrating with IoT sensors and data analytics platforms, digital twins enable predictive maintenance, personalized services, and continuous product improvement, ensuring that products are aligned with customer needs and market trends. This integrated approach to product lifecycle management fosters innovation, enhances customer satisfaction, and drives sustainable growth in the digital age.

8.5 THE CHALLENGES ASSOCIATED WITH THE INTEGRATION OF DIGITAL TWINS IN INDUSTRIES 4.0 AND 5.0

The integration of digital twins presents numerous challenges in both Industry 4.0 and the evolving landscape of Industry 5.0. One significant challenge lies in data integration and interoperability. In Industry 4.0, this involves integrating data from disparate sources such as sensors, machinery, and enterprise systems, often with varying formats and protocols. Ensuring seamless interoperability among these systems is crucial for effective decision-making and optimization. In Industry 5.0, the challenge is further compounded by the exponential growth of data generated by an even wider array of interconnected devices, including IoT sensors, AI algorithms, and edge computing platforms. Managing and integrating this massive volume of diverse data streams pose significant hurdles for organizations aiming to leverage digital twins for advanced analytics and insights.

As Industries 4.0 and 5.0 connect more machines and processes, security risks rise. This vast, digital landscape creates more openings for cyberattacks. To protect sensitive data and critical systems, strong security measures are essential. In Industry 5.0, the proliferation of interconnected devices further heightens security risks, as each node becomes a potential entry point for cyberattacks. Strengthening security protocols and implementing stringent access controls are essential to mitigate these risks and protect digital twin ecosystems from unauthorized access, data breaches, and other cyber threats.

Another challenge is scalability, particularly in Industry 5.0, where the scale and complexity of interconnected systems reach unprecedented levels. As the number of devices, sensors, and data sources proliferates, establishments must guarantee that their digital twin infrastructure can scale efficiently to accommodate the growing volume of data and support real-time processing and analytics. Achieving scalability requires robust infrastructure, advanced data management capabilities, and scalable computing resources to handle the increasing demands of digital twin applications in

Industry 5.0. Additionally, organizations need to consider the long-term scalability of their digital twin solutions to support future growth and technological advancements in the rapidly evolving industrial landscape. Table 8.1 show the challenges with the integration of digital twins in Industries 4.0 and 5.0.

TABLE 8.1
Challenges of Digital Twins' Integration in Industries 4.0 and 5.0

Challenges	Industry 4.0	Industry 5.0
Data Integration and Interoperability	Making digital twins work in Industry 4.0 isn't easy. The challenge? Combining data from sensors, machines, and different computer systems, all speaking different languages. We need smooth data flow to unlock the full potential of digital twins: better processes, smarter decisions, and a more efficient Industry 4.0.	Handling exponentially increasing data from diverse sources like the IoT, AI, and edge computing. This presents a significant challenge in the integration of digital twins in Industry 5.0 due to the diverse and extensive sources of data generated by interconnected devices, AI algorithms, and edge computing platforms, requiring seamless integration across multiple systems and formats. Ensuring interoperability among these disparate data sources is crucial for enabling effective decision-making, optimization, and collaboration within the composite and dynamic environments of Industry 5.0.
Security and Privacy	Ensuring data security against cyber threats. Security and privacy present significant challenges in integrating digital twins into Industry 4.0's super-connected factories bring big benefits, but also security risks. As machines and processes talk more online, data breaches and attacks become a growing threat. Implementing robust security measures and stringent access controls is crucial to safeguarding digital twin ecosystems, safeguarding key infrastructure, and maintaining the confidentiality of sensitive data in Industry 4.0 environments.	Enhancing security measures due to the proliferation of interconnected devices and systems. Security and privacy become even more critical challenges in incorporating digital twins into Industry 5.0 due to the proliferation of interconnected devices and systems, creating a vast attack surface for cyber threats and potential breaches of sensitive data. Strengthening security protocols, implementing advanced encryption techniques, and ensuring compliance with privacy regulations are essential to mitigate risks and safeguard digital twin ecosystems in the complex and dynamic environments of Industry 5.0.

(*Continued*)

TABLE 8.1 (Continued)
Challenges of Digital Twins' Integration in Industries 4.0 and 5.0

Challenges	Industry 4.0	Industry 5.0
Scalability	Adapting to large-scale data processing requirements. Scalability poses a notable challenge in integrating digital twins into Industry 4.0 due to the need to adapt to large-scale data processing requirements stemming from diverse sources such as sensors, machinery, and enterprise systems. Ensuring that digital twin infrastructure can efficiently scale to handle the growing volume and variety of data is crucial for enabling real-time analytics, decision-making, and optimization in Industry 4.0 environments.	Managing scalability challenges with the massive growth in interconnected devices and data. Scalability emerges as a significant challenge in integrating digital twins into Industry 5.0 due to the exponential growth of interconnected devices and data sources, necessitating robust infrastructure and scalable computing resources to handle the increasing volume and complexity of data. Ensuring that digital twin solutions can seamlessly scale to accommodate the evolving demands of Industry 5.0 is essential for supporting real-time processing, analytics, and decision-making across interconnected systems and environments.
Real-time Data Processing	Processing data in real time to enable timely decision-making. Real-time data processing presents a significant challenge in integrating digital twins into Industry 4.0 due to the necessity for timely real-time data crunching which is key to unlocking the full power of digital twins. By swiftly processing and analyzing data, companies can optimize industrial processes and make smarter decisions with improved efficiency, productivity, and responsiveness in Industry 4.0 environments.	Ensuring real-time processing capabilities for immediate feedback and responsiveness. Real-time data processing remains a critical challenge in integrating digital twins into Industry 5.0 due to the vast influx of data from diverse interconnected devices and systems, necessitating advanced computing capabilities to ensure immediate feedback and responsiveness for decision-making and automation in dynamic environments. Ensuring seamless real-time processing is essential to leverage the full potential of digital twins in Industry 5.0 for optimizing operations and driving innovation.

TABLE 8.1 (Continued)
Challenges of Digital Twins' Integration in Industries 4.0 and 5.0

Challenges	Industry 4.0	Industry 5.0
AI and Analytics Integration	Integrating AI and analytics for predictive maintenance and optimization. AI and analytics integration poses a challenge in integrating digital twins into Industry 4.0 due to the complexity of leveraging AI algorithms to extract actionable insights from the diverse and voluminous data generated by digital twin systems. Ensuring seamless integration of AI and analytics is crucial for enhancing predictive maintenance, process optimization, and decision-making capabilities in Industry 4.0, requiring advanced data processing techniques and scalable infrastructure to derive meaningful insights from digital twin data.	Advancing AI integration for more sophisticated decision-making and automation. AI and analytics integration presents a challenge in integrating digital twins into Industry 5.0 due to the need for sophisticated algorithms and models to extract actionable insights from vast and complex data streams generated by interconnected devices. Ensuring seamless integration of AI and analytics is crucial for enhancing making choices, proactive upkeep, and optimization procedures in Industry 5.0, requiring robust infrastructure and advanced algorithms to derive meaningful insights from digital twin data.
Model Accuracy and Validation	Ensuring accuracy and reliability of digital twin models through validation against real-world data. Model accuracy and validation integration present a challenge in integrating digital twins into Industry 4.0 due to the need for ensuring the reliability of digital twin models against real-world data, which can be complex and dynamic. Achieving accurate and validated models is crucial for leveraging digital twins effectively in Industry 4.0 to support decision-making, predictive maintenance, and optimization processes, requiring continuous validation and refinement to ensure alignment with actual industrial operations.	Continuously validating and improving digital twin models for dynamic and evolving environments. Model accuracy and validation integration remains a challenge in integrating digital twins into Industry 5.0 due to the dynamic and interconnected nature of systems, which require continuous validation and refinement of digital twin models to ensure their reliability in complex environments. Ensuring accurate and validated models is crucial for leveraging digital twins effectively in Industry 5.0 for predictive analytics, decision-making, and optimization, necessitating ongoing validation against real-time data streams from diverse interconnected devices and systems.

(*Continued*)

TABLE 8.1 (Continued)
Challenges of Digital Twins' Integration in Industries 4.0 and 5.0

Challenges	Industry 4.0	Industry 5.0
Lifecycle Management	Managing the lifecycle of digital twins from creation to decommissioning. Lifecycle management poses a challenge in integrating digital twins into Industry 4.0 due to the need for managing the entire lifecycle of digital twin systems, including creation, deployment, monitoring, and eventual decommissioning, amidst rapidly evolving technologies and processes. Ensuring efficient lifecycle management is crucial for maximizing the longevity and effectiveness of digital twins in Industry 4.0, requiring robust strategies and frameworks to adapt to changing requirements and technological advancements.	Handling the complexity of lifecycle management across interconnected systems and environments. Lifecycle management presents a challenge in integrating digital twins into Industry 5.0 due to the complexity of managing interconnected systems and environments throughout their lifecycle, from creation to decommissioning. Ensuring efficient lifecycle management is crucial for maintaining the relevance and effectiveness of digital twins in Industry 5.0, requiring robust strategies and processes to handle the evolution and integration of digital twin systems within dynamic industrial ecosystems.
Human–Machine Interaction	Facilitating human interaction with digital twins for effective control and monitoring. Human–machine interaction presents a challenge in integrating digital twins into Industry 4.0 due to the need for effective collaboration and communication between humans and digital twin systems to optimize industrial processes and decision-making. Ensuring seamless and intuitive interfaces for human interaction with digital twins is crucial for leveraging their potential to enhance efficiency, productivity, and innovation in Industry 4.0 environments.	Enhancing human–machine interaction for seamless collaboration and decision-making. Human–machine interaction remains a challenge in integrating digital twins into Industry 5.0 due to the increasing complexity and autonomy of interconnected systems, requiring sophisticated interfaces and intuitive communication channels for effective collaboration and decision-making between humans and digital twin systems. Ensuring seamless interaction between humans and digital twins is crucial for leveraging their capabilities to drive innovation, optimize processes, and enhance productivity in the dynamic and interconnected environments of Industry 5.0.

TABLE 8.1 (Continued)
Challenges of Digital Twins' Integration in Industries 4.0 and 5.0

Challenges	Industry 4.0	Industry 5.0
Cost and ROI	Justifying investment costs with tangible returns through efficiency gains and reduced downtime. Cost and ROI present a significant challenge in the integration of digital twins in Industry 4.0 due to the substantial investment required for developing and deploying digital twin infrastructure, as well as for maintaining and updating the systems over time. Justifying these costs with tangible returns, such as increased operational efficiency, reduced downtime, and improved decision-making, becomes essential for organizations to realize the full potential of digital twin technology.	Balancing investment costs with long-term benefits in a rapidly evolving technological landscape. This poses a considerable challenge in the integration of digital twins in Industry 5.0 due to the complex and expansive nature of interconnected systems, which often require substantial investment in infrastructure, data management, and cybersecurity measures. Organizations must carefully assess the long-term benefits and strategic value of implementing digital twin solutions to ensure that the investment aligns with their overall business objectives and delivers tangible returns amidst the rapidly evolving technological landscape of Industry 5.0.

8.6 THE LESSONS LEARNED FROM THE INTEGRATION OF DIGITAL TWINS IN INDUSTRIES 4.0 AND 5.0

The integration of digital twins within Industry 4.0 and its evolution into Industry 5.0 has yielded crucial lessons for organizations across various sectors. Firstly, it has emphasized the fundamental importance of data quality and integrity. Accurate data are the lifeblood of digital twins. Companies understand that reliable data collection, cleaning, and management are key to trustworthy simulations and predictions. Furthermore, the integration has highlighted the significance of interconnectivity and integration between different systems and technologies. Successful implementation requires seamless connectivity between digital twins, IoT devices, production machinery, supply chain management systems, and other relevant data sources to create comprehensive digital representations of the physical world. Organizations have realized that fostering interoperability and collaboration between disparate technologies and stakeholders is critical for leveraging the full potential of digital twin ecosystems.

Secondly, the integration of digital twins has underscored the importance of agility and adaptability in response to dynamic operational environments. Digital twins allow for continuous tracking, evaluation, and improvement of resources and processes, empowering organizations to proactively identify issues, optimize performance, and make data-driven decisions in near real time. Organizations have learned the value of implementing agile methodologies and flexible architectures to quickly respond to changing market conditions, technological advancements, and business requirements. Additionally, digital twins facilitate virtual simulations and scenario planning, allowing organizations to test different strategies, assess potential risks, and optimize operations without disrupting physical assets or processes. This capability has emphasized the importance of leveraging digital twins as strategic decision-making tools to enhance operational resilience, innovation, and competitiveness in rapidly evolving industrial landscapes.

Data Quality is Paramount: Digital twins heavily rely on data accuracy and quality. Inaccurate or incomplete data can lead to flawed simulations and predictions, undermining the effectiveness of the digital twin. Therefore, ensuring high-quality data collection, integration, and validation processes is crucial.

Interconnectivity and Integration: Successful implementation requires seamless integration between various systems and processes within an organization. This includes connecting digital twins with IoT devices, production machinery, supply chain management systems, and other relevant data sources to create a holistic digital representation of the physical system.

Real-Time Monitoring and Feedback Loops: Digital twins provide for real-time tracking and evaluation of resources, processes, and systems. Developing efficient cycles of feedback helps firms to rapidly discover and respond to variations, improve processes, and make data-driven choices in near real-time.

Predictive Maintenance and Optimization: By leveraging historical data and predictive analytics, digital twins can anticipate equipment failures and performance issues before they occur. This capability enables proactive maintenance strategies, minimizing downtime, reducing maintenance costs, and optimizing asset performance.

Simulation and Scenario Planning: Digital twins facilitate virtual simulations and scenario planning, allowing organizations to test different strategies, optimize processes, and evaluate the impact of potential changes or disruptions without risking physical assets or operations. This capability enhances decision-making and enables agile responses to evolving market conditions.

Cybersecurity and Data Privacy: As digital twins involve the collection, processing, and transmission of sensitive data, cybersecurity and data privacy are critical considerations. Adopting strong security mechanisms, encryption methods, access controls, and regulations is vital for securing digital twin environments from cyber-attacks and ensuring the safety of information and privacy.

Scalability and Flexibility: Organizations must design digital twin solutions that are scalable and adaptable to accommodate growth, changes in operations, and evolving technological landscapes. This requires adopting modular architectures, flexible data models, and interoperable standards to support seamless scalability and integration with existing and future systems and technologies.

Human–Machine Collaboration: Despite the advanced capabilities of digital twins, human expertise remains invaluable. Integrating human insights, domain knowledge, and decision-making capabilities with digital twin technologies enhances collaboration between humans and machines, fostering innovation, creativity, and continuous improvement across various industrial domains.

Overall, the integration of digital twins in Industry 4.0 and beyond has underscored the importance of data quality, interconnectivity, real-time monitoring, predictive analytics, cybersecurity, scalability, and human–machine collaboration in driving operational excellence, agility, and competitiveness in the digital age.

8.7 THE FUTURE RESEARCH DIRECTIONS FOR THE INTEGRATION OF DIGITAL TWINS IN INDUSTRIES 4.0 AND 5.0

Future research directions stemming from the integration of digital twins in Industry 4.0 and the evolving landscape of Industry 5.0 are multifaceted. One key area of focus involves advancing the sophistication and intelligence of digital twin models by integrating developing technologies like intelligent machines and machine learning, and edge computing. Research efforts will aim to enhance predictive capabilities, enabling digital twins to anticipate and mitigate complex operational challenges with greater accuracy and efficiency. Additionally, there will be a continued emphasis on addressing cybersecurity and privacy concerns to ensure the secure exchange and protection of sensitive data within digital twin ecosystems. Furthermore, research will explore novel applications of digital twins beyond traditional manufacturing domains, including healthcare, smart cities, and sustainable energy systems, driving innovation and addressing societal challenges through interconnected digital twin networks. Overall, future research endeavors will seek to deepen our understanding of digital twin technologies and their transformative potential, paving the way for more resilient, adaptive, and intelligent industrial ecosystems in the Fourth and Fifth Industrial Revolutions.

The integration of digital twins into Industries 4.0 and 5.0 opens up numerous avenues for future research and development. One crucial direction involves enhancing the interoperability and standardization of digital twin frameworks to facilitate seamless integration across diverse industrial sectors and technologies. This includes developing common data models, communication protocols, and interoperability standards to enable effective data exchange and collaboration between different digital twin instances and stakeholders. Additionally, there is a need to advance the capabilities of digital twins through the integration of emerging technologies such as artificial intelligence, machine learning, blockchain, and quantum computing.

Research efforts will focus on enhancing predictive analytics, autonomous decision-making, and self-optimization capabilities of digital twins to enable more proactive and adaptive control of complex industrial systems. Furthermore, there is a growing emphasis on addressing ethical, legal, and societal implications of digital twin technologies, including privacy concerns, data ownership, and algorithmic bias, to ensure responsible and ethical deployment in Industry 4.0 and beyond. Overall, future research directions will continue to explore innovative applications, technical advancements, and governance frameworks to unlock the full potential of digital twins in driving operational efficiency, resilience, and sustainability in the Fourth and Fifth Industrial Revolutions. Here are several potential future research directions for integrating digital twins in Industries 4.0 and 5.0:

Interoperability and Standardization: Research can focus on developing common frameworks, data models, and communication protocols to enhance interoperability and facilitate seamless integration of digital twins across different industrial domains and technologies.

Advanced Analytics and AI Integration: Future studies may explore the integration and use of modern analytics methods, such as machine learning, deep learning, and statistical analysis, to improve the skills of digital twins in data analysis, decision-making, and optimization.

Edge Computing and Real-Time Processing: Research could investigate the integration of edge computing technology that will enable actual time processing and assessment of data created by digital twins, resulting in quicker reaction times and more agile decision-making.

Cybersecurity and Data Privacy: There is a need for research focusing on enhancing the cybersecurity measures and data privacy protections of digital twin ecosystems to safeguard against cyber threats, data breaches, and privacy violations.

Ethical and Societal Implications: Future research may explore the ethical, legal, and societal implications of digital twin technologies, including issues related to data ownership, algorithmic bias, and the impact on employment and society.

Human–Machine Interaction: Studies can investigate methods for improving human–machine interactions within digital twin environments, including user interfaces, augmented reality (AR), virtual reality (VR), and natural language processing (NLP) interfaces.

Lifecycle Management and Sustainability: Research could focus on developing digital twin frameworks for the entire lifecycle of products and systems, including design, manufacturing, operation, and end-of-life management, with a focus on sustainability and environmental impact reduction.

Resilience and Risk Management: Future studies may explore the use of digital twins for enhancing resilience and risk management in industrial systems, including the ability to simulate and mitigate the impacts of disruptions, disasters, and unforeseen events.

Cross-Sectoral Applications: Research can explore the application of digital twins beyond traditional manufacturing sectors, including healthcare, smart cities, transportation, energy, and agriculture, to address broader societal challenges and promote interdisciplinary collaboration.

Business Models and Economic Implications: There is a need for research on new business models, economic implications, and value creation opportunities enabled by digital twin technologies, including cost savings, revenue generation, and competitive advantage.

These research directions could help advance the capabilities, applications, and adoption of digital twins in Industry 4.0 and beyond, driving innovation, efficiency, and sustainability in various industrial sectors.

8.8 CONCLUSION

The integration of digital twins is a game-changer for factories, from Industry 4.0 to Industry 5.0. These virtual twins unlock a new era of optimization, innovation, and sustainability. By mirroring real-world machines and processes, they enable real-time tracking, predict problems, and help companies make smarter choices. As factories get more digital, digital twins work even better with AI, the IoT, and blockchain. This technology combination rewrites the rules of manufacturing, making it faster, more adaptable, and more reliable. In Industry 4.0, digital twins are instrumental in optimizing operational efficiency by facilitating predictive maintenance, enhancing product development through simulation and prototyping, and enabling agile manufacturing practices. The synergy between digital twins and emerging technologies such as the IoT and AI amplifies their capabilities, leading to streamlined workflows and improved resource utilization. As Industry 5.0 emerges, the focus shifts toward human–machine collaboration and sustainable practices. Digital twins continue to play a pivotal role in this evolution, augmenting human capabilities, fostering creativity, and supporting sustainability initiatives by optimizing energy consumption and reducing waste. However, the widespread adoption of digital twins also brings forth cybersecurity challenges, necessitating robust measures to safeguard data integrity and operational continuity. In essence, the integration of digital twins in Industries 4.0 and 5.0 represents a transformative force, reshaping industrial operations, driving innovation, and laying the foundation for a more effective, flexible, and resilient future.

REFERENCES

[1] Lu, Y., Huang, X., Zhang, K., Maharjan, S., & Zhang, Y. (2020). Low-latency federated learning and blockchain for edge association in digital twin-empowered 6G networks. *IEEE Transactions on Industrial Informatics*, *17*(7), 5098–5107.

[2] Bellavista, P., Giannelli, C., Mamei, M., Mendula, M., & Picone, M. (2021). Application-driven network-aware digital twin management in industrial edge environments. *IEEE Transactions on Industrial Informatics*, *17*(11), 7791–7801.

[3] Qin, Y., Wu, X., & Luo, J. (2021). Data-model combined driven digital twin of life-cycle rolling bearing. *IEEE Transactions on Industrial Informatics*, *18*(3), 1530–1540.

[4] Dai, Y., Zhang, K., Maharjan, S., & Zhang, Y. (2020). Deep reinforcement learning for stochastic computation offloading in digital twin networks. *IEEE Transactions on Industrial Informatics*, *17*(7), 4968–4977.

[5] Awotunde, J. B., Ayo, E. F., Ajamu, G. J., Jimoh, T. B., & Ajagbe, S. A. (2023). The influence of industry 4.0 and 5.0 for distance learning education in times of pandemic for a modern society. In *Advances in Distance Learning in Times of Pandemic* (pp. 177–214). Chapman and Hall/CRC.

[6] Brunheroto, P. H., Tomanek, D. P., & Deschamps, F. (2021). Implications of Industry 4.0 to companies' performance: A comparison between Brazil and Germany. *Brazilian Journal of Operations & Production Management*, *18*(3), 1–10.

[7] Bonaccorsi, A., Chiarello, F., Fantoni, G., & Kammering, H. (2020). Emerging technologies and industrial leadership. A Wikipedia-based strategic analysis of Industry 4.0. *Expert Systems with Applications*, *160*, 113645.

[8] Beier, G., Matthess, M., Guan, T., Grudzien, D. I. D. O. P., Xue, B., de Lima, E. P., & Chen, L. (2022). Impact of Industry 4.0 on corporate environmental sustainability: Comparing practitioners' perceptions from China, Brazil and Germany. *Sustainable Production and Consumption*, *31*, 287–300.

[9] Shan, S., Wen, X., Wei, Y., Wang, Z., & Chen, Y. (2020). Intelligent manufacturing in industry 4.0: A case study of Sany heavy industry. *Systems Research and Behavioral Science*, *37*(4), 679–690.

[10] Barari, A., de Sales Guerra Tsuzuki, M., Cohen, Y., & Macchi, M. (2021). Intelligent manufacturing systems towards industry 4.0 era. *Journal of Intelligent Manufacturing*, *32*, 1793–1796.

[11] Xu, X., Lu, Y., Vogel-Heuser, B., & Wang, L. (2021). Industry 4.0 and Industry 5.0—Inception, conception and perception. *Journal of manufacturing systems*, *61*, 530–535.

[12] Mourtzis, D. (2021). Towards the 5th industrial revolution: A literature review and a framework for process optimization based on big data analytics and semantics. *Journal of Machine Engineering*, *21*(3), 5–39.

[13] Nain, G., Pattanaik, K. K., & Sharma, G. K. (2022). Towards edge computing in intelligent manufacturing: Past, present and future. *Journal of Manufacturing Systems*, *62*, 588–611.

[14] Mandolla, C., Petruzzelli, A. M., Percoco, G., & Urbinati, A. (2019). Building a digital twin for additive manufacturing through the exploitation of blockchain: A case analysis of the aircraft industry. *Computers in Industry*, *109*, 134–152.

[15] Židek, K., Piteľ, J., Adámek, M., Lazorík, P., & Hošovský, A. (2020). Digital twin of experimental smart manufacturing assembly system for industry 4.0 concept. *Sustainability*, *12*(9), 3658.

[16] Cheng, J., Zhang, H., Tao, F., & Juang, C. F. (2020). DT-II: Digital twin enhanced industrial internet reference framework towards smart manufacturing. *Robotics and Computer-Integrated Manufacturing*, *62*, 101881.

[17] Bao, J., Guo, D., Li, J., & Zhang, J. (2019). The modelling and operations for the digital twin in the context of manufacturing. *Enterprise Information Systems*, *13*(4), 534–556.

[18] Alexopoulos, K., Nikolakis, N., & Chryssolouris, G. (2020). Digital twin-driven supervised machine learning for the development of artificial intelligence applications in manufacturing. *International Journal of Computer Integrated Manufacturing*, *33*(5), 429–439.

[19] Redelinghuys, A. J. H., Basson, A. H., & Kruger, K. (2020). A six-layer architecture for the digital twin: a manufacturing case study implementation. *Journal of Intelligent Manufacturing*, *31*(6), 1383–1402.

[20] Kamble, S. S., Gunasekaran, A., Parekh, H., Mani, V., Belhadi, A., & Sharma, R. (2022). Digital twin for sustainable manufacturing supply chains: Current trends, future perspectives, and an implementation framework. *Technological Forecasting and Social Change*, *176*, 121448.

[21] Lee, J., Azamfar, M., Singh, J., & Siahpour, S. (2020). Integration of digital twin and deep learning in cyber-physical systems: Towards smart manufacturing. *IET Collaborative Intelligent Manufacturing*, *2*(1), 34–36.

[22] Lv, Z. (2023). Digital twins in industry 5.0. *Research*, *6*, 0071.

[23] Lu, D. (2024). Industrial structure and regional development. In *Regional Development and Its Spatial Structure* (pp. 71–105). Springer Nature Singapore.

[24] Yadav, R., Parwez, Z., Parimala, R. S., Priya, U., Rathore, S. K., & Deepak, S. S. K. (2023). Analysis and prediction of future research trends in the state of industry 5.0. *Res Militaris* , *13*(3), 2330–2339.

[25] Javaid, M., Haleem, A., Singh, R. P., & Sinha, A. K. (2024). Digital economy to improve the culture of industry 4.0: A study on features, implementation and challenges. *Green Technologies and Sustainability*, *2*(2), May 2024, 100083, 1–19.

[26] Sharma, M., Tomar, A., & Hazra, A. (2024). Edge computing for industry 5.0: Fundamental, applications and research challenges. *IEEE Internet of Things Journal, 11*(11), 19070–19093, 1 June, 2024, doi: 10.1109/JIOT.2024.3359297.

[27] Qi, Y., Sajadi, S. M., Baghaei, S., Rezaei, R., & Li, W. (2024). Digital technologies in sports: Opportunities, challenges, and strategies for safeguarding athlete wellbeing and competitive integrity in the digital era. *Technology in Society*, *77*, 2024, 102496, ISSN 0160-791X, https://doi.org/10.1016/j.techsoc.2024.102496

[28] Rath, K. C., Khang, A., & Roy, D. (2024). The role of internet of things (IoT) technology in industry 4.0 economy. In *Advanced IoT Technologies and Applications in the Industry 4.0 Digital Economy* (pp. 1–28). CRC Press.

[29] Ciliberto, C., Szopik-Depczyńska, K., Tarczyńska-Łuniewska, M., Ruggieri, A., & Ioppolo, G. (2021). Enabling the circular economy transition: A sustainable lean manufacturing recipe for Industry 4.0. *Business Strategy and the Environment*, *30*(7), 3255–3272.

[30] Sharma, R., & Villányi, B. (2022). Consistent round hash optimized SRP-6a-based end-to-end mutual authentication for secure data transfer in industry 4.0. *Internet of Things and Cyber-Physical Systems*, *2*, 170–179.

[31] Javaid, M., Haleem, A., Singh, R. P., & Suman, R. (2022). Enabling flexible manufacturing system (FMS) through the applications of industry 4.0 technologies. *Internet of Things and Cyber-Physical Systems*, *2*, 49–62.

[32] Javaid, M., & Haleem, A. (2020). Critical components of Industry 5.0 towards a successful adoption in the field of manufacturing. *Journal of Industrial Integration and Management*, *5*(03), 327–348.

[33] Mourtzis, D., & Doukas, M. (2014). The evolution of manufacturing systems: From craftsmanship to the era of customisation. In *Handbook of research on design and management of lean production systems* (pp. 1–29). IGI Global.

[34] Sengupta, J., Ruj, S., & Bit, S. D. (2020). A secure fog-based architecture for industrial internet of things and industry 4.0. *IEEE Transactions on Industrial Informatics*, *17*(4), 2316–2324.

[35] Awotunde, J. B., Oguns, Y. J., Amuda, K. A., Nigar, N., Adeleke, T. A., Olagunju, K. M., & Ajagbe, S. A. (2023). Cyber-physical systems security: analysis, opportunities, challenges, and future prospects. In: Maleh, Y., Alazab, M., Romdhani, I. (eds) *Blockchain for Cybersecurity in Cyber-Physical Systems*, (pp. 21–46). *102*. Springer, Cham. https://doi.org/10.1007/978-3-031-25506-9_2

[36] Abikoye, O. C., Bajeh, A. O., Awotunde, J. B., Ameen, A. O., Mojeed, H. A., Abdulraheem, M., ... & Salihu, S. A. (2021). Application of internet of thing and cyber physical system in Industry 4.0 smart manufacturing. In *Emergence of Cyber*

Physical System and IoT in Smart Automation and Robotics: Computer Engineering in Automation (pp. 203–217). Springer International Publishing.

[37] Krugh, M., & Mears, L. (2018). A complementary cyber-human systems framework for industry 4.0 cyber-physical systems. *Manufacturing letters*, *15*, 89–92.

[38] Bajeh, A. O., Mojeed, H. A., Ameen, A. O., Abikoye, O. C., Salihu, S. A., Abdulraheem, M., ... & Awotunde, J. B. (2021). Internet of robotic things: Its domain, methodologies, and applications. In *Emergence of Cyber Physical System and IoT in Smart Automation and Robotics: Computer Engineering in Automation* (pp. 135–146). Springer International Publishing.

[39] Ajagbe, S. A., Awotunde, J. B., Opadotun, A. T., & Adigun, M. O. (2023, March). Cybersecurity in the supply chain and logistics industry: A concept-centric review. In *International Conference on Advances in IoT and Security with AI* (pp. 39–50). Singapore: Springer Nature Singapore.

[40] Ślusarczyk, B., Tvaronavičienė, M., Haque, A. U., & Oláh, J. (2020). Predictors of Industry 4.0 technologies affecting logistic enterprises' performance: International perspective from economic lens. *Technological and Economic Development of Economy*, *26*(6), 1263–1283.

[41] Li, L. (2020). Education supply chain in the era of Industry 4.0. *Systems Research and Behavioral Science*, *37*(4), 579–592.

[42] Castelo-Branco, I., Cruz-Jesus, F., & Oliveira, T. (2019). Assessing Industry 4.0 readiness in manufacturing: Evidence for the European Union. *Computers in Industry*, *107*, 22–32.

[43] Sader, S., Husti, I., & Daróczi, M. (2019). Industry 4.0 as a key enabler toward successful implementation of total quality management practices. *Periodica Polytechnica Social and Management Sciences*, *27*(2), 131–140.

[44] Mourtzis, D., Angelopoulos, J., & Panopoulos, N. (2022). A Literature review of the challenges and opportunities of the transition from industry 4.0 to Society 5.0. *Energies*, *15*(17), 6276.

[45] Liao, H., Zhou, Z., Liu, N., Zhang, Y., Xu, G., Wang, Z., & Mumtaz, S. (2022). Cloud-edge-device collaborative reliable and communication-efficient digital twin for low-carbon electrical equipment management. *IEEE Transactions on Industrial Informatics*, *19*(2), 1715–1724.

[46] Zhou, Z., Jia, Z., Liao, H., Lu, W., Mumtaz, S., Guizani, M., & Tariq, M. (2021). Secure and latency-aware digital twin assisted resource scheduling for 5G edge computing-empowered distribution grids. *IEEE Transactions on Industrial Informatics*, *18*(7), 4933–4943.

[47] Zemtsov, S., Barinova, V., & Semenova, R. (2019). The risks of digitalization and the adaptation of regional labor markets in Russia. *Форсайт*, *13*(2 (eng)), 84–96.

[48] Leng, J., Sha, W., Wang, B., Zheng, P., Zhuang, C., Liu, Q., ... & Wang, L. (2022). Industry 5.0: Prospect and retrospect. *Journal of Manufacturing Systems*, *65*, 279–295.

[49] Kaasinen, E., Anttila, A. H., Heikkilä, P., Laarni, J., Koskinen, H., & Väätänen, A. (2022). Smooth and resilient human–machine teamwork as an Industry 5.0 design challenge. *Sustainability*, *14*(5), 2773.

[50] Asad, U., Khan, M., Khalid, A., & Lughmani, W. A. (2023). Human-centric digital twins in industry: A comprehensive review of enabling technologies and implementation strategies. *Sensors*, *23*(8), 3938.

[51] Ayo, F. E., Ogundele, L. A., Olakunle, S., Awotunde, J. B., & Kasali, F. A. (2024). A hybrid correlation-based deep learning model for email spam classification using fuzzy inference system. *Decision Analytics Journal*, *10*, 100390.

[52] Attaran, S., Attaran, M., & Celik, B. G. (2024). Digital twins and industrial internet of things: Uncovering operational intelligence in industry 4.0. *Decision Analytics Journal*, *10*, 100398.

[53] Piras, G., Agostinelli, S., & Muzi, F. (2024). Digital twin framework for built environment: A review of key enablers. *Energies*, *17*(2), 436.

[54] Ajagbe, S. A., Awotunde, J. B., & Florez, H. (2023). Ensuring Intrusion detection for IoT services through an improved CNN. *SN Computer Science*, *5*(1), 49.

[55] Gaber, T., Awotunde, J. B., Torky, M., Ajagbe, S. A., Hammoudeh, M., & Li, W. (2023). Metaverse-IDS: Deep learning-based intrusion detection system for Metaverse-IoT networks. *Internet of Things*, *24*, 100977.

[56] Javaid, M., & Haleem, A. (2023). Digital twin applications toward industry 4.0: A review. *Cognitive Robotics*, *3*, 71–92.

[57] Aheleroff, S., Xu, X., Zhong, R. Y., & Lu, Y. (2021). Digital twin as a service (DTaaS) in industry 4.0: An architecture reference model. *Advanced Engineering Informatics*, *47*, 101225.

[58] Nath, S. V., Van Schalkwyk, P., & Isaacs, D. (2021). *Building Industrial Digital Twins: Design, Develop, and Deploy Digital Twin Solutions for Real-World Industries Using Azure Digital Twins*. Packt Publishing Ltd.

[59] Awotunde, J. B., Bhoi, A. K., Jimoh, R. G., Ajagbe, S. A., Ayo, F. E., & Adebisi, O. A. (2023). Internet of things based enabled convolutional neural networks in healthcare. In *IoT-Enabled Convolutional Neural Networks: Techniques and Applications* (pp. 329–357). River Publishers.

[60] Alimam, H., Mazzuto, G., Tozzi, N., Ciarapica, F. E., & Bevilacqua, M. (2023). The resurrection of digital triplet: A cognitive pillar of human-machine integration at the dawn of industry 5.0. *Journal of King Saud University-Computer and Information Sciences*, *35*(10), 101846. ISSN 1319-1578, https://doi.org/10.1016/j.jksuci.2023.101846

[61] Awotunde, J. B., Ajagbe, S. A., & Florez, H. (2022, October). Internet of things with wearable devices and artificial intelligence for elderly uninterrupted healthcare monitoring systems. In *International Conference on Applied Informatics* (pp. 278–291). Cham: Springer International Publishing.

[62] Awouda, A., Traini, E., Bruno, G., & Chiabert, P. (2024). IoT-Based framework for digital twins in the industry 5.0 era. *Sensors*, *24*(2), 594.

[63] Abiodun, M. K., Imoize, A. L., Awotunde, J. B., Lee, C. C., Adeniyi, A. E., Chioma, U., & Li, C. T. (2023). Analysis of a double-stage encryption scheme using hybrid cryptography to enhance data security in cloud computing systems. *Journal of Library & Information Studies*, *21*(2), 1–26.

[64] Mihai, S., Yaqoob, M., Hung, D. V., Davis, W., Towakel, P., Raza, M., ... & Nguyen, H. X. (2022). Digital twins: A survey on enabling technologies, challenges, trends and future prospects. *IEEE Communications Surveys & Tutorials*, *24*(4), 2255–2291.

[65] Alcaraz, C., & Lopez, J. (2022). Digital twin: A comprehensive survey of security threats. *IEEE Communications Surveys & Tutorials*, *24*(3), 1475–1503.

[66] Teng, S. Y., Touš, M., Leong, W. D., How, B. S., Lam, H. L., & Máša, V. (2021). Recent advances on industrial data-driven energy savings: Digital twins and infrastructures. *Renewable and Sustainable Energy Reviews*, *135*, 110208.

[67] Awotunde, J. B., Jimoh, R. G., Ogundokun, R. O., Misra, S., & Abikoye, O. C. (2022). Big data analytics of iot-based cloud system framework: Smart healthcare monitoring systems. In *Artificial Intelligence for Cloud and Edge Computing* (pp. 181–208). Springer International Publishing.

[68] Awotunde, J. B., Ogundokun, R. O., & Misra, S. (2021). Cloud and IoMT-based big data analytics system during COVID-19 pandemic. In *Efficient Data Handling for Massive Internet of Medical Things: Healthcare Data Analytics* (pp. 181–201). Springer International Publishing.

[69] Reddy, C. K. K., Anisha, P. R., Khan, S., Hanafiah, M. M., Pamulaparty, L., & Mohana, R. M. (Eds.). (2024). *Sustainability in Industry 5.0: Theory and Applications*. CRC Press.

[70] Awotunde, J. B., Adeniyi, A. E., Ogundokun, R. O., Ajamu, G. J., & Adebayo, P. O. (2021). MIoT-based big data analytics architecture, opportunities and challenges for enhanced telemedicine systems. In: Marques, G., Kumar Bhoi, A., de la Torre Díez, I., Garcia-Zapirain, B. (eds) *Enhanced Telemedicine and e-Health: Advanced IoT Enabled Soft Computing Framework*, (pp. 199–220). *410*. Springer, Cham. https://doi.org/10.1007/978-3-030-70111-6_10

[71] Kaur, M. J., Mishra, V. P., & Maheshwari, P. (2020). The convergence of digital twin, IoT, and machine learning: Transforming data into action. In: Farsi, M., Daneshkhah, A., Hosseinian-Far, A., Jahankhani, H. (eds) *Digital Twin Technologies and Smart Cities*, 3–17. Springer, Cham. https://doi.org/10.1007/978-3-030-18732-3_1

[72] Dihan, M. S., Akash, A. I., Tasneem, Z., Das, P., Das, S. K., Islam, M. R., ... & Hasan, M. M. (2024). Digital twin: Data exploration, architecture, implementation and future. *Heliyon. 10*(5) March 15, 2024, e26503.

[73] AbdulRaheem, M., Oladipo, I. D., Imoize, A. L., Awotunde, J. B., Lee, C. C., Balogun, G. B., & Adeoti, J. O. (2024). Machine learning assisted snort and zeek in detecting DDoS attacks in software-defined networking. *International Journal of Information Technology, 16*(3), 1627–1643.

[74] Rathore, M. M., Shah, S. A., Shukla, D., Bentafat, E., & Bakiras, S. (2021). The role of ai, machine learning, and big data in digital twinning: A systematic literature review, challenges, and opportunities. *IEEE Access, 9*, 32030–32052.

[75] Huang, Z., Shen, Y., Li, J., Fey, M., & Brecher, C. (2021). A survey on AI-driven digital twins in industry 4.0: Smart manufacturing and advanced robotics. *Sensors, 21*(19), 6340.

[76] Adel, A. (2023). Unlocking the future: Fostering human–machine collaboration and driving intelligent automation through industry 5.0 in smart cities. *Smart Cities, 6*(5), 2742–2782.

[77] Ordieres-Meré, J., Gutierrez, M., & Villalba-Díez, J. (2023). Toward the industry 5.0 paradigm: Increasing value creation through the robust integration of humans and machines. *Computers in Industry, 150*, 103947.

[78] Awotunde, J. B., Arowolo, M. O., Imoize, A. L., Farhaoui, Y., & Adeniyi, A. E. (2022, November). A machine learning-based model for energy efficiency classification of an unmanned aerial vehicle. In *The International Conference on Artificial Intelligence and Smart Environment* (pp. 54–63). Cham: Springer International Publishing.

[79] Ehrhard, T. P. (2001). *Unmanned aerial vehicles in the United States armed services: A comparative study of weapon system innovation*. The Johns Hopkins University.

[80] Wang, B., Zhou, H., Li, X., Yang, G., Zheng, P., Song, C., ... & Wang, L. (2024). Human digital twin in the context of industry 5.0. *Robotics and Computer-Integrated Manufacturing, 85*, 102626.

[81] Verdugo-Cedeño, M., Jaiswal, S., Ojanen, V., Hannola, L., & Mikkola, A. (2023). Simulation-based digital twins enabling smart services for machine operations: An

industry 5.0 approach. *International Journal of Human–Computer Interaction*, 1–17. https://doi.org/10.1080/10447318.2023.2254607

[82] Skobelev, P. O., & Borovik, S. Y. (2017). On the way from Industry 4.0 to Industry 5.0: From digital manufacturing to digital society. *Industry 4.0*, *2*(6), 307–311.

[83] Liu, X. (2023). A new perspective on digital twin-based mechanical design in industrial engineering. *Innovations in Applied Engineering and Technology*. *2*(1). https://doi.org/10.58195/iaet.v2i1.134

[84] Anandaraj, A. P. S., Dhivya, R., Ateeq, K., & Subramaniam, S. (2024). A survey of AI integration in unmanned aerial vehicles (UAVs) using digital twin technology: Advancements and applications. In *Digital Twin Technology and AI Implementations in Future-Focused Businesses* (pp. 14–26). IGI Global.

[85] Geng, R., Li, M., Hu, Z., Han, Z., & Zheng, R. (2022). Digital twin in smart manufacturing: Remote control and virtual machining using VR and AR technologies. *Structural and Multidisciplinary Optimization*, *65*(11), 321.

[86] Künz, A., Rosmann, S., Loria, E., & Pirker, J. (2022, March). The potential of augmented reality for digital twins: A literature review. In *2022 IEEE Conference on Virtual Reality and 3D User Interfaces (VR)* (pp. 389–398). IEEE. Christchurch, New Zealand, doi: 10.1109/VR51125.2022.00058.

[87] Guo, Z., Zhou, D., Zhou, Q., Zhang, X., Geng, J., Zeng, S., ... & Hao, A. (2020). Applications of virtual reality in maintenance during the industrial product lifecycle: A systematic review. *Journal of Manufacturing Systems*, *56*, 525–538.

[88] Yin, Y., Zheng, P., Li, C., & Wang, L. (2023). A state-of-the-art survey on Augmented reality-assisted digital twin for futuristic human-centric industry transformation. *Robotics and Computer-Integrated Manufacturing*, *81*, 102515.

[89] Coronado, E., Ueshiba, T., & Ramirez-Alpizar, I. G. (2024). A path to industry 5.0 digital twins for human–robot collaboration by bridging NEP+ and ROS. *Robotics*, *13*(2), 28.

[90] Adeniyi, J. K., Adeniyi, T. T., Awotunde, J. B., Abiodun, M. K., & Atanda, O. G. (2023, April). Agrolend: A blockchain implementation approach of smart contract farming platform. In *2023 International Conference on Science, Engineering and Business for Sustainable Development Goals (SEB-SDG)* (Vol. 1, pp. 1–7). IEEE. Omu-Aran, Nigeria, doi: 10.1109/SEB-SDG57117.2023.10124467.

[91] Lee, D., Lee, S. H., Masoud, N., Krishnan, M. S., & Li, V. C. (2021). Integrated digital twin and blockchain framework to support accountable information sharing in construction projects. *Automation in Construction*, *127*, 103688.

[92] Putz, B., Dietz, M., Empl, P., & Pernul, G. (2021). Ethertwin: Blockchain-based secure digital twin information management. *Information Processing & Management*, *58*(1), 102425.

[93] Leng, J., Ruan, G., Jiang, P., Xu, K., Liu, Q., Zhou, X., & Liu, C. (2020). Blockchain-empowered sustainable manufacturing and product lifecycle management in industry 4.0: A survey. *Renewable and Sustainable Energy Reviews*, *132*, 110112.

[94] Teisserenc, B., & Sepasgozar, S. (2021). Project data categorization, adoption factors, and non-functional requirements for blockchain based digital twins in the construction industry 4.0. *Buildings*, *11*(12), 626.

[95] Leng, J., Zhu, X., Huang, Z., Xu, K., Liu, Z., Liu, Q., & Chen, X. (2023). ManuChain II: Blockchained smart contract system as the digital twin of decentralized autonomous manufacturing toward resilience in industry 5.0. *IEEE Transactions on Systems, Man, and Cybernetics: Systems*, *53*(8), 4715–4728.

[96] Leng, J., Chen, Z., Huang, Z., Zhu, X., Su, H., Lin, Z., & Zhang, D. (2022). Secure blockchain middleware for decentralized iiot towards industry 5.0: A review of architecture, enablers, challenges, and directions. *Machines*, *10*(10), 858.
[97] Sasikumar, A., Vairavasundaram, S., Kotecha, K., Indragandhi, V., Ravi, L., Selvachandran, G., & Abraham, A. (2023). Blockchain-based trust mechanism for digital twin empowered industrial internet of things. *Future Generation Computer Systems*, *141*, 16–27.
[98] Awotunde, J. B., Misra, S., & Pham, Q. T. (2022, November). A secure framework for internet of medical things security based system using lightweight cryptography enabled blockchain. In *International Conference on Future Data and Security Engineering* (pp. 258–272). Singapore: Springer Nature Singapore.
[99] Ogundokun, R. O., Awotunde, J. B., Imoize, A. L., Li, C. T., Abdulahi, A. T., Adelodun, A. B., ... & Lee, C. C. (2023). Non-orthogonal multiple access enabled mobile edge computing in 6G communications: A systematic literature review. *Sustainability*, *15*(9), 7315.
[100] Escamilla-Ambrosio, P. J., Rodríguez-Mota, A., Aguirre-Anaya, E., Acosta-Bermejo, R., & Salinas-Rosales, M. (2018). Distributing computing in the internet of things: cloud, fog and edge computing overview. In: Maldonado, Y., Trujillo, L., Schütze, O., Riccardi, A., Vasile, M. (eds) *NEO 2016: Results of the Numerical and Evolutionary Optimization Workshop NEO 2016 and the NEO Cities 2016 Workshop held on September 20-24, 2016 in Tlalnepantla, Mexico* (pp. 87–115). vol 731. Springer International Publishing, Cham. https://doi.org/10.1007/978-3-319-64063-1_4
[101] Hamdan, S., Ayyash, M., & Almajali, S. (2020). Edge-computing architectures for internet of things applications: A survey. *Sensors*, *20*(22), 6441.
[102] Ghosh, A. M., & Grolinger, K. (2020). Edge-cloud computing for Internet of Things data analytics: Embedding intelligence in the edge with deep learning. *IEEE Transactions on Industrial Informatics*, *17*(3), 2191–2200.
[103] Aheleroff, S., Huang, H., Xu, X., & Zhong, R. Y. (2022). Toward sustainability and resilience with Industry 4.0 and Industry 5.0. *Frontiers in Manufacturing Technology*, *2*, 951643.

9 Computational Intelligence in Big Data Analytics

Kingsley Theophilus Igulu,
Daniel Dauda Wisdom, Micheal Olaolu Arowolo,
and Thipendra P. Singh

9.1 INTRODUCTION

9.1.1 Definition of Big Data Analytics

Big data analytics involves examining extensive and intricate datasets to identify valuable patterns, correlations, and insights that can inform both strategic and tactical business decision-making. Data mining entails utilizing advanced analytic tools to sift through vast quantities of structured, unstructured, and semistructured data to extract valuable insights. Organizations can improve their growth and competitive advantage through data-driven decisions due to an enhanced comprehension of their customers, products, operations, and market trends thanks to this analysis [1].

Big data analytics is defined by its capacity to manage massive amounts of data. The magnitude and complexity of the data that can be analyzed with conventional tools and methods can be prohibitive [2]. However, the inception of big data analytics was geared toward timely processing and analyzing immense volumes of data, regardless of its original structure. Datasets that are too large, too varied, or too rapidly changing for conventional methods can now be managed by businesses [3,4].

Big data analytics also takes into account both structured and unstructured data. The phrase "structured data" is commonly used to refer to data that are stored in a database or spreadsheet in a manner that allows for easy retrieval of specific information. Unstructured data include text documents, social media posts, images, videos, and sensor data, and they can prove challenging to organize and search through. To derive valuable insights from unstructured data sources, big data analytics employs methods like natural language processing, machine learning, and computer vision [2,4]. These techniques enable the extraction of meaningful information from diverse data formats, contributing to a more comprehensive understanding of the underlying patterns and trends within the data. By analyzing both structured and unstructured

DOI: 10.1201/9781003581963-9

data, organizations can gain valuable insights that can inform strategic decision-making processes and drive innovation.

Many different types of business utilize the findings from big data analytics. To name just a few examples, businesses can use this information to better segment and target customers, optimize marketing campaigns, identify fraud and security threats, boost operational efficiency, and fuel innovation. In order to stay ahead of the competition, businesses are increasingly turning to big data analytics to help them gain a comprehensive view of their customers, markets, and internal operations [2].

Leveraging big data analytics is a powerful strategy for extracting insights from massive datasets. Data of any size or format can be processed, analyzed, and interpreted with the help of state-of-the-art analytic methods and tools. Businesses can boost growth, efficiencies, and customer satisfaction with the help of these insights. Big data analytics is becoming increasingly crucial in the business world as the volume and variety of data grow exponentially [1].

9.1.2 Overview of Computational Intelligence in Big Data Analytics

The field of big data analytics relies heavily on the application of computational intelligence. As the amount of data created increases at an exponential rate, businesses must figure out how to make sense of it all [5]. Computational intelligence comes into play here by providing the means for processing and analyzing large datasets. Organizations can gain insights into previously unseen patterns, trends, and correlations by utilizing computational intelligence methods like machine learning, data mining, and artificial intelligence. Insights like these help businesses make better decisions, boost efficiency, and gain a competitive edge [5].

Computational intelligence's capacity to deal with complex and unstructured data is a major plus in big data analytics [5]. Unstructured data, such as text, images, and videos, may pose challenges for analysis using traditional methods [6]. However, computational intelligence methods can efficiently analyze and glean useful insights from such data. Customer reviews and feedback, for instance, can be analyzed with natural language processing algorithms to learn more about customers' attitudes and preferences, improve product quality and advertising, and support with the data collected [7,8].

The speed and quantity of big data can be daunting, but computational intelligence methods can help. The rise of the Internet of Things (IoT) and the widespread use of connected devices has resulted in an explosion in data production [9]. This massive data influx in real time could overwhelm conventional analytical methods. Computational intelligence relies on advanced algorithms that have the capability to process and evaluate data streams in real time. This enables businesses to make timely decisions and take immediate action based on precise and reliable information [10]. This is especially important in sectors where real-time insights are crucial for risk management, fraud detection, and customer satisfaction, such as the financial, healthcare, and telecommunications sectors.

The capacity for uncertainty management and prediction is another key feature of CI in big data analytics. The quality and consistency of big data can vary significantly due to its diverse origins from various sources [11–13]. Fuzzy logic and neural networks are two examples of computational intelligence methods that work well with incomplete or unreliable data. These algorithms can model and analyze complex systems with impressive accuracy, drawing conclusions and offering suggestions based on the data at hand. Algorithms based on predictive analytics, for instance, can be utilized to do things like optimize resource allocation, predict future demand, and find hidden risks [14,15].

With the help of computational intelligence, large datasets can be processed, analyzed, and insights can be drawn. Organizations can gain an edge in the market and discover previously unseen patterns by implementing computational intelligence algorithms. Computational intelligence will become increasingly crucial as data volume and velocity continue to rise, allowing businesses to use big data for strategic decision-making and expansion growth [9,16–19].

9.1.3 Overview of Industry 4.0 and 5.0 Applications

Significant developments in the field of industrial automation and digitization include the concepts of "Industry 4.0" and "Industry 5.0" [20–22]. These ideas represent the development of manufacturing processes and technologies that help companies increase their efficiency, productivity, and competitiveness on the global market [20].

The goal of Industry 4.0, sometimes termed the "Fourth Industrial Revolution," is to more fully incorporate digital technologies into the production process. The term "smart factory" refers to an industrial setting that has been upgraded with state-of-the-art automation, AI/ML, and IoT technologies. In an Industry 4.0 setting, the interconnectivity of machines and systems enables the seamless exchange and examination of data. This facilitates immediate data transfer and analysis. Because of this, manufacturers can enhance product quality, streamline production, and reduce costs [22].

Predictive maintenance, in which machines are monitored continuously using sensors and data analytics to predict maintenance requirements and prevent breakdowns, is one of the key applications of Industry 4.0, as stated in Refs. [20,23–25]. As a result, less time is wasted, and more is accomplished. Smart logistics is another area where IoT-enabled devices and systems are put to use to better manage stock levels, streamline distribution, and speed up shipping. This ensures that goods arrive on time and reduces expenses.

Improvements in robotics and automation are yet another byproduct of Industry 4.0 [26–28]. In the manufacturing sector, collaborative robots, also referred to as cobots, are increasingly being used to supplement human labor. These robots can do the heavy lifting, so humans can focus on more strategic and imaginative work. This boosts efficiency and ensures the wellbeing of employees [27–29].

Industry 5.0, on the other hand, is where manufacturing is headed: it's the coming together of humans and machines to increase output [30,31]. The goal of Industry 5.0 is to enhance human productivity by combining cutting-edge technology with workers' natural cognitive abilities.

Human–robot cooperation is a central concept in the Fifth Industrial Revolution [32,33]. In this scenario, humans and robots collaborate to maximize productivity. Humans should focus on higher-order thinking and problem solving, while robots take care of the mundane, repetitive work. Working together, we've been able to boost output and enhance quality [34,35].

Industry 5.0 encompasses personalized manufacturing, which presents significant opportunities [36]. Recent technological advancements have made it possible to produce customized goods on a large scale. By utilizing data analytics and artificial intelligence, manufacturers can gain valuable insights into customer preferences and tailor their products accordingly. This capability to meet the distinct needs and desires of individual customers ultimately results in increased customer satisfaction and loyalty [32,33].

Upskilling and reskilling workers is a major theme in discussions of Industry 5.0. There will be a change in the kinds of workers needed as automation and digitization advance. In order to keep up with these shifts, workers will need to expand their skill sets. Maintaining a competitive and technologically adept workforce is a central focus of Industry 5.0's emphasis on lifelong learning and development [31].

Integrating cutting-edge technologies and giving factory workers more agency, Industries 4.0 and 5.0 are reshaping the manufacturing sector. Companies can use these ideas to enhance production efficiency, boost product quality, and adapt to changing consumer preferences. Companies can maintain their competitive edge in the global market and contribute to economic growth by adopting these innovations [31].

9.1.4 Similarities and Differences between Industries 4.0 and 5.0

The terms "Industry 4.0" and "Industry 5.0" are frequently used interchangeably when talking about the development of industrial technology. However, there are distinct differences between the two concepts, as well as similarities [20,22–24,33,36–39].

The term "Industry 4.0" describes the widespread adoption of digital technologies throughout the manufacturing sector. It involves the automation and enhancement of manufacturing processes, incorporating technologies such as artificial intelligence, big data analytics, and the Internet of Things (IoT). The goal of "Industry 4.0" is to modernize manufacturing by developing connected and intelligent "smart factories."

However, Industry 5.0 is the next step forward for manufacturing. "Industry 5.0" expands upon its predecessor by placing a greater emphasis on interactions between humans and automated systems. In contrast to the mechanization and machine-to-machine conversation emphasized in Industry 4.0, the priority of Industry 5.0 is to utilize the best powers of both humans and machines to develop a system that prioritizes the needs of workers.

The emphasis on automation as opposed to collaboration is a key distinction between "Industry 4.0" and "Industry 5.0." The idea of "Industry 4.0" centers on the replacement of human labor with automation and cutting-edge technologies. In contrast, the goal of "Industry 5.0" is to complement human abilities instead of replacing them with technology, acknowledging the value and relevance of human skills as well as creativity.

Data collection and analysis methods are another area where "Industry 4.0" and "Industry 5.0" diverge. The focus of "Industry 4.0" is to enhance operational efficiency and decision-making by collecting data from various sensors and machines within the manufacturing environment and analyzing them. This data-driven strategy enables preventative maintenance, continuous monitoring, and efficient production.

While data collection and analysis remain vitally important in Industry 5.0, the emphasis shifts to utilizing data to aid in human decision-making and teamwork. Workers can make better decisions and collaborate more efficiently with machines thanks to the real-time data and insights provided by Industry 5.0. By working together, businesses can better tailor their offerings to individual consumers and respond rapidly to market shifts.

In spite of these distinctions, the principles of "Industry 4.0" and "Industry 5.0" share many similarities. The improvements of industrial processes' productivity, efficiency, and competitiveness are common goals for both ideas. Communication and integration across the entire value chain are also enabled by digital technologies and connectivity.

In addition, both "Industry 4.0" and "Industry 5.0" can find application in a diverse range of contexts. The concepts presented possess the capability to completely transform the manner in which businesses operate across various industries and provide value to their customers, from manufacturing and logistics to energy and healthcare. Industry 4.0, for instance, can pave the way for the creation of smart factories that can manage production processes autonomously, while Industry 5.0 can equip workers with augmented reality tools that increase output and accuracy of judgment.

Finally, the goals of "Industry 4.0" and "Industry 5.0" are similar: to use digital technologies to radically alter traditional manufacturing processes. However, the two models differ in their relative weighting of automation and collaboration, as well as their methods for analyzing data. Business owners can better navigate the changing landscape of industrial technology and take advantage of its growth and innovation potential if they have a firm grasp on how these two ideas are similar and how they differ.

9.2 BIG DATA ANALYTICS: CHALLENGES AND OPPORTUNITIES

9.2.1 Volume, Velocity, Variety, and Veracity of Big Data

The term "big data" refers to the vast amount of data, both structured and unstructured, that is generated from a variety of sources including sensors, social media, mobile devices, and digital platforms. The distinguishing features of big data, known as the four V's (velocity, volume, variety, and veracity), set it apart from traditional data sets [4,40,41].

Firstly, volume denotes the sheer magnitude of data being produced and gathered. With technological advancements and widespread adoption of digital platforms, data volume is experiencing exponential growth. Organizations now have access to vast quantities of data, providing them with invaluable insights and analysis and decision-making opportunities. In order to effectively harness the strength of big data, organizations need to address the challenge of handling and processing these massive data volumes [6].

The second characteristic, velocity, emphasizes the rate of data generation and processing. At an unprecedented rate, data are generated in the current digital age. The need to process and analyze data in near real time arises from real-time data streams originating from social media platforms, transactional systems, and various other sources. This enables them to make rapid decisions and respond promptly to changing conditions [41].

Variety encompasses the diverse data types and formats available for analysis. Big data comprises unstructured data types like social media posts, emails, videos, images, and sensor data in addition to structured data such as spreadsheets and databases. Capturing and analyzing a variety of data types is essential for organizations seeking a comprehensive understanding of their customers, market trends, and operational performance [40].

Finally, veracity pertains to the quality and dependability of the data. Given the increasing velocity, volume, and variety of data, maintaining the data's accuracy and reliability becomes a formidable challenge. Data may be insufficient, inconsistent, erroneous, or contain biases. Organizations must implement robust data quality processes and employ data validation techniques to ensure that the analyzed data are trustworthy and can be used to make informed decisions [4].

The four V's of big data are essential attributes that define the nature and difficulties of dealing with large and complex datasets. In the contemporary business landscape driven by data, organizations proficient in managing and harnessing big data stand to acquire valuable insights, enhance decision-making processes, and attain a competitive edge [40,42].

9.2.2 Traditional Data Analytics vs. Big Data Analytics

As per Ref. [41], conventional data analytics refers to the examination of structured data using traditional tools and techniques. This approach involves gathering, arranging, and evaluating data from various sources to derive valuable insights and make informed choices. Traditional data analytics focuses primarily on small to medium-sized datasets that are easily manageable and analyzable using conventional database management systems and statistical instruments, utilizing statistical methods such as regression analysis, hypothesis testing, and data visualization to extract meaningful patterns and relationships from data [40–42].

Big data analytics, on the contrary, is a more advanced and intricate method that deals with extensive amounts of unstructured and semistructured data. Big data analytics entails processing, analyzing, and interpreting vast quantities of data to reveal hidden patterns, trends, and insights. Specialized tools and technologies are necessary for this type of analytics, as they need to be able to handle the vast amount, speed, diversity, and reliability of big data. Machine learning, natural language processing, and predictive analytics are commonly employed to interpret large quantities of data [4,43].

The amount of data being analyzed is a key difference between both analytics approaches. Typically, traditional data analytics focuses on relatively small datasets that are readily handled by conventional database management systems. Big data analytics, on the contrary, deals with massive amounts of data that are difficult for analysis using conventional or traditional analytics tools and methods [41,44].

There is also a distinction in the types of data being analyzed. Traditional data analytics is primarily concerned with structured, predefined data organization. This type of data is typically stored in relational databases or spreadsheets and can be processed using conventional methods with relative ease. Big data analytics, on the other hand, deals with unstructured and semistructured data that does not conform to a predefined schema. This includes social media posts, sensor data, log files, audio and video recordings, and other textual and multimedia information [6,19,45,46].

Traditional data analytics and big data analytics also differ in their respective analysis methods. Traditional data analytics employs statistical methods to extract insights from data. This includes regression analysis, hypothesis testing, and data visualization techniques. In contrast, big data analytics frequently entails more advanced techniques such as machine learning, natural language processing, and predictive analytics. These techniques enable the discovery of complex patterns and relationships in the data that are most often undiscernible utilizing conventional statistical methods [6].

9.2.3 Challenges in Big Data Analytics

In the contemporary era of technology, companies consider big data analytics an essential tool, crucial for their operations and decision-making processes. Insights can be mined, and decisions can be made based on the collected data. However, there are a few major obstacles that businesses must overcome in order to fully benefit from big data analytics [6,14,16,17,40,43,44,47,48].

Some challenges in big data analytics include:

i. Dealing with the immense amount of data produced by different sources poses a significant challenge. The storage, management, and processing of large-scale data necessitate scalable infrastructure and solutions.
ii. The swift and real-time generation of big data originates from diverse sources such as social media, sensors, and Internet of Things (IoT). Real-time analysis and insight extraction from streaming data can be difficult because it requires efficient data ingestion, processing, and analysis capabilities.
iii. Big data exists in diverse formats, encompassing structured, semistructured, and unstructured information. Text, images, and videos are typically difficult for conventional data analysis methods to process. Advanced analytic techniques and tools are required to derive valuable insights from a multitude of data sources and formats.
iv. The veracity or dependability of big data is an additional challenge. Data quality issues, such as inaccuracies, inconsistencies, and missing values, can have a substantial effect on the precision and dependability of analytics results. Ensuring data quality and resolving data integrity issues are indispensable for gaining insightful knowledge.

v. Sources of Data: Diverse sources of data, including internal systems, external databases, social media, and third-party sources, are common for big data. Complex and time-consuming, integrating and harmonizing data from disparate sources requires data integration and data management strategies.

vi. Privacy and Security: Big data analytics involves working with vast quantities of private and sensitive information. Significant challenges include ensuring data privacy, complying with regulations (e.g., GDPR), implementing strong security measures is crucial in order to protect data from unauthorized access and potential breaches. It is imperative to have robust safeguards in place to ensure the safety and integrity of sensitive information.

vii. Scalability: As data volumes continue to expand exponentially, scalability becomes a significant obstacle. It is essential to scale up analytics infrastructure, including storage, computing power, and network bandwidth, to accommodate increasing data loads and future growth.

viii. Skill Gap: Big data analytics requires data scientists, data engineers, and domain experts with specialized skills. There is frequently a dearth of skilled professionals who can effectively extract insights from large data sets and appropriately apply analytical techniques.

ix. Ethical Concerns: Big data analysis raises ethical concerns, specifically in data privacy, surveillance, and potential algorithmic bias. In big data analytics, ensuring ethical data practices and addressing potential biases are crucial considerations.

x. Cost Management: Implementing and maintaining an infrastructure for big data analytics can be costly. The costs associated with storage, computing resources, software licenses, and skilled personnel must be carefully managed by organizations.

xi. Complexity: Big data analytics frequently involves complex datasets and sophisticated analytic models. Developing and implementing machine learning models and complex algorithms can be difficult and requires proficiency in programming, statistics, and mathematics. It also can be difficult to interpret and communicate the results of complex analyses to non-technical stakeholders.

xii. Integrating data from numerous sources and systems can pose a challenging task. Data often reside in diverse formats, databases, or data warehouses, creating complexities in unifying and analyzing the information. Including data cleansing, transformation, and matching, data integration processes necessitate meticulous planning and execution.

xiii. Big data analytics requires the management of sensitive and valuable data assets. It is essential to establish robust data governance standards, for instance data access controls, data ownership, data quality standards, and data lifecycle management. Compliance with regulatory requirements and ethical considerations increases the difficulty of data governance.

xiv. Real-Time Analytics: Real-time analytics, in which insights are derived from streaming data as they are generated, presents unique difficulties. Data ingestion, processing, and analytics must be efficient for real-time processing of data and analysis. Providing real-time analytics with low latency and high throughput is a technical challenge that organizations must overcome.

xv. Cultural and Organizational Difficulties: Adopting a data-driven culture and transforming the organization's mentality in order to embrace data-driven decision-making can be difficult. Change resistance, a lack of data literacy among employees, and organizational silos can impede the successful adoption of big data analytics initiatives. It is essential to promote data literacy, foster a culture of experimentation and learning, and align analytics efforts with business objectives.

xvi. Data Storage and Retrieval: Storing and managing vast quantities of data can be a challenging task. Important considerations include selecting appropriate storage technologies, implementing efficient data retrieval mechanisms, and ensuring data accessibility and availability. Strategies for data archiving and data lifecycle management are essential for optimizing storage costs and preserving data integrity.

xvii. Data Privacy and Ethics: Big data analytics raises data privacy concerns, particularly when dealing with personally identifiable information (PII). To build customer and stakeholder trust in organizations it is imperative to ensure compliance with privacy regulations, employ data anonymization techniques when needed, and establish transparent practices for handling data.

xviii. Bias and Interpretability of Data: Inadvertently introducing biases into big data analytics processes can result in skewed or unfair outcomes. It is essential to comprehend and mitigate biases in data collection, feature selection, and algorithmic decision-making. Interpreting and explaining the results of complex analytical models to stakeholders can be difficult, particularly when AI and machine learning are employed.

xix. Scalability of Analytics Infrastructure: As data volumes and analytics demands increase, scalability of analytics infrastructure becomes crucial. Organizations must ensure that their analytics infrastructure, which includes storage, computing power, and network bandwidth, is scalable to accommodate growing workloads. Adopting cloud-based solutions and utilizing distributed computing frameworks can assist in addressing scalability issues.

xx. Costs of Data Storage: Storing large volumes of data can incur substantial storage expenses. Organizations must carefully manage their data storage needs, including implementing data compression techniques, tiered storage systems, and data archiving strategies, in order to optimize costs and maintain data accessibility.

xxi. Integration of Data Across Departments: In organizations with multiple departments or business units, it can be difficult to integrate data across silos. Each department may have its own data systems, formats, and processes, making a unified view of data difficult. Comprehensive analytics requires dismantling data silos and establishing cross-departmental data integration processes.

xxii. Data Visualization and Communication: It can be difficult to present complex analytical findings in a clear and understandable manner. To communicate insights to stakeholders and make them accessible to non-technical audiences, effective data visualization techniques and tools must be employed. Complex analyses must be condensed into meaningful and actionable visual representations.

xxiii. Data Ownership and Sharing: When multiple organizations or entities are involved in data sharing or collaboration, data ownership and sharing agreements can be problematic. Successful data collaborations require establishing data ownership rights, ensuring data security during sharing, and maintaining stakeholder trust.

xxiv. The landscape of big data technologies is constantly evolving, with new tools, frameworks, and platforms emerging on a regular basis. Staying abreast of the most recent innovations, evaluating and adopting new technologies, and managing technology transitions can be difficult for organizations.

xxv. Talent Retention and Recruitment: Big data analytics professionals are in high demand, but there is a talent shortage in the field. The recruitment and retention of skilled data scientists, data engineers, and analysts is difficult for organizations. This challenge can be mitigated by providing ongoing training and development opportunities, competitive compensation packages, and fostering a data-driven culture.

xxvi. Measuring Business Impact: It can be difficult to determine the actual business impact and return on investment of big data analytics initiatives. Measuring the success of big data analytics projects requires defining appropriate metrics, establishing a feedback loop to measure the impact of analytics-driven decisions, and aligning analytics efforts with business objectives.

9.2.4 Opportunities for Computational Intelligence in Big Data Analytics

The field of big data analytics has witnessed the emergence of computational intelligence as a potent tool. Large and complex datasets present a challenge for organizations as data generation and storage continue to rise at an exponential rate. This is where AI from computers can help. It encompasses a broad spectrum of methods for analyzing and comprehending large datasets, incorporating techniques like machine learning, artificial intelligence, and data mining. Insights, patterns, and trends can all be uncovered, and data-driven decisions can be made with the help of computational intelligence [5,9,10,30,40,41,43,44,49–52].

Predictive analytics is a promising area for computational intelligence in big data analysis. In predictive analytics, past or historic data are mined for clues on what will occur in the future. Using computational intelligence methods, businesses can create predictive models to sift through mountains of data in search of hidden trends and correlations that humans might miss. Organizations can attain a competitive advantage in the market and make more prudent choices when they have access to reliable forecasts of future trends and events [52].

The field of anomaly detection is another promising area for computational intelligence in big data analytics. Finding anomalies in data, such as those caused by fraud or a malfunctioning system, is the goal of anomaly detection. Anomaly detection in large and complex datasets may not respond well to conventional rule-based approaches. However, artificial intelligence tools like neural networks and genetic algorithms can automatically learn to recognize and report anomalous patterns and behaviors. Organizations can use this to proactively locate and eliminate threats [51].

In addition, the field of sentiment analysis is again another domain where computational intelligence can be put to use. Customer reviews, social media posts, and survey responses are all examples of text data that can be used in a sentiment analysis. Businesses can leverage computational intelligence methods such as NLP and machine learning to analyze vast amounts of text data. This facilitates the extraction of insights into customer preferences, satisfaction levels, and brand perception. Companies can use this information to improve their products and services by responding to customer feedback [10].

The field of recommendation systems can also benefit from the application of computational intelligence. E-commerce platforms, streaming services, and content websites all often employ recommendation systems to assist users in discovering the most relevant products and content based on their preferences and behavior. Organizations can analyze large amounts of user data and produce tailored suggestions by employing computational intelligence methods like collaborative filtering and content-based filtering. This can help businesses boost user engagement, sales, and satisfaction.

9.3 FUNDAMENTALS OF COMPUTATIONAL INTELLIGENCE

9.3.1 Overview of Computational Intelligence Techniques

Computational intelligence focuses on the developing intelligent systems capable of simulating human-like behavior and performing tasks requiring intelligence. It includes subfields like machine learning, evolutionary computation, neural networks, and fuzzy logic. Computational intelligence's primary focus is to create algorithms and methods that can solve complex problems by learning from data, adapting to changing environments, and making decisions based on uncertain or incomplete information [10,52,53]. The general composition of CI is given in Figure 9.1 [242,243].

One major aspect of computational intelligence is machine learning, which involves the creation of algorithms capable of acquiring knowledge from data and enhancing their performance progressively. Substantial volumes of data can be processed by machine learning algorithms to identify patterns, trends, and relationships that are not immediately obvious to humans. These algorithms can then utilize this information to make predictions, categorize new data, or make decisions. Supervised learning, reinforcement learning, and unsupervised learning are common machine learning techniques [54–62].

Neural networks, which take inspiration from the organization and operation of the human brain, play a significant role within the field of computational intelligence. Information is processed and transmitted by interconnected nodes or artificial

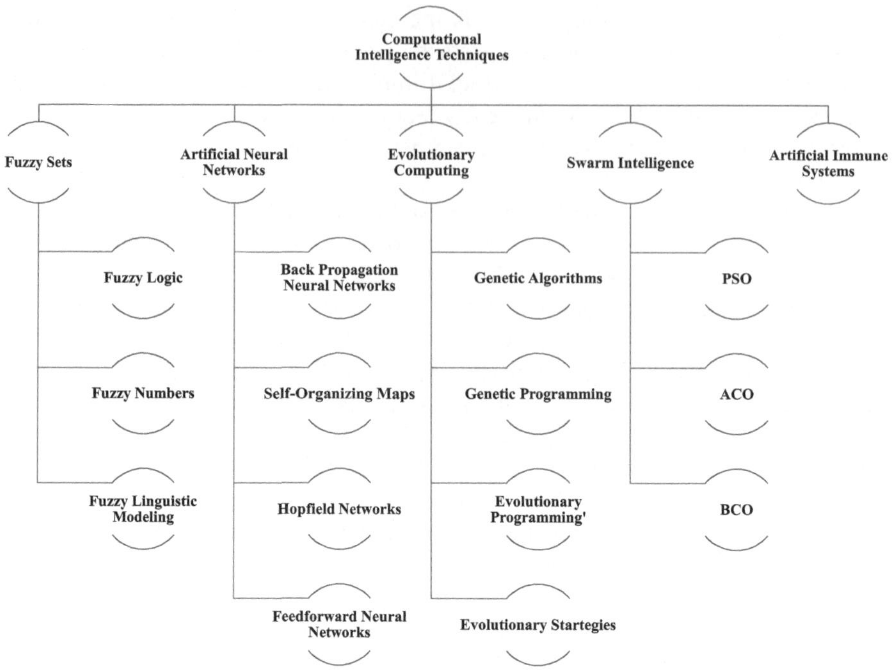

FIGURE 9.1 General compositions of computational intelligence [242].

neurons in neural networks. Neural networks can learn from examples and perform activities such as image recognition and natural language processing, and speech synthesis by adjusting the weights and connections between neurons. Deep learning, a subset of neural networks, has garnered tremendous interest in recent times as a result of its capacity to comprehend intricate data representations and attain cutting-edge performance across diverse [56–65].

Another area of computational intelligence that draws inspiration from natural selection is evolutionary computation. It employs evolutionary algorithms to address optimization challenges by simulating the evolutionary process. A population of candidate solutions undergoes genetic operations such as mutation and crossover to produce offspring in evolutionary computation. The best offspring are then chosen for reproduction in the next generation based on their adaptability to the problem at hand. This iterative process eventually converges on optimal or near-optimal solutions [66–68].

Fuzzy logic is a subfield of computational intelligence concerned with reasoning and decision-making in the presence of ambiguity or uncertainty. Unlike conventional binary logic, which only permits true or false values, fuzzy logic allows degrees of truth between 0 and 1. This allows fuzzy logic systems to process imprecise or ambiguous data and make decisions based on fuzzy rules. There are numerous applications for fuzzy logic, including control systems, expert systems, and pattern recognition [68].

9.3.2 Neural Networks and Deep Learning

Artificial neural networks (ANNs) are a type of machine learning model whose structure and functionality are inspired by the human brain [58,69]. ANNs consist of interconnected nodes, often called "neurons," that work together to process and analyze data. Each neuron receives input from several other neurons, performs calculations, and then transmits its output to additional neurons. Through this process, ANNs can acquire knowledge and generate predictions by recognizing patterns and associations within the data. The structure of an ANN as well as a biological NN are given in Figure 9.2.

Each layer of an artificial neural network structure contains a different number of neurons. The input layer receives the initial data, which then goes through the hidden layers before reaching the output layer. Each neuron in a hidden layer determines its output by performing a weighted calculation on its inputs and applying an activation function. In the process of training, the network's performance is enhanced by adjusting the weights and biases between neurons [60,61].

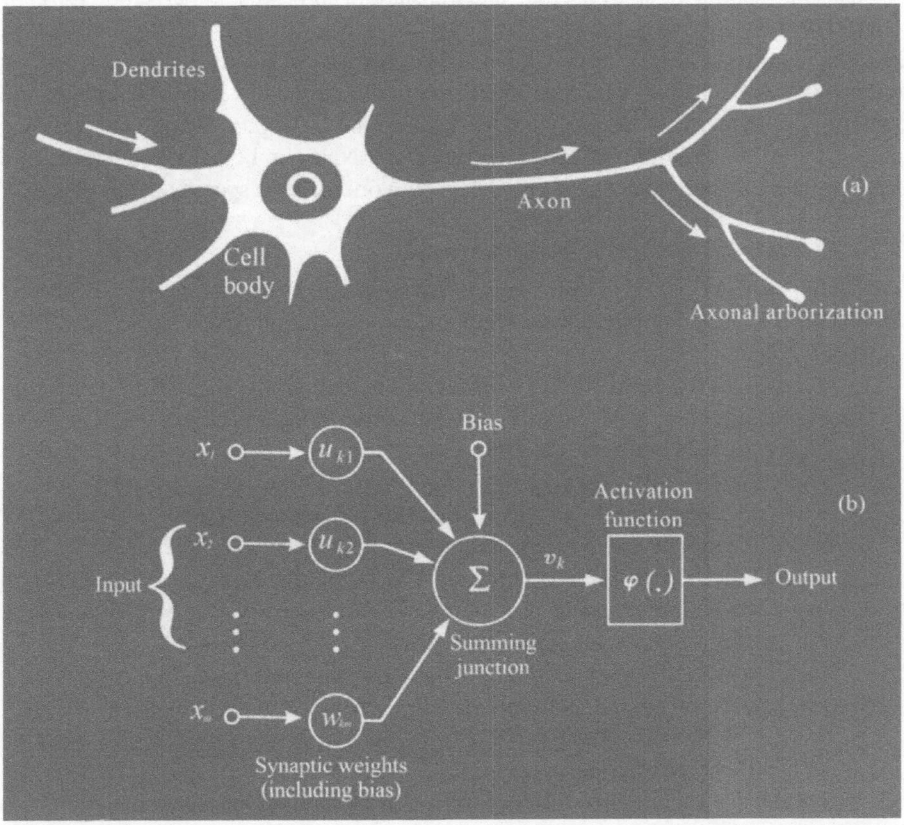

FIGURE 9.2 Structure of (a) biological neural networks and (b) artificial neural networks.

The capability of ANNs to learn from data is a defining characteristic. This is accomplished through a process known as "training," in which the network is exposed to a collection of labeled examples and its weights and biases are adjusted based on the errors it makes. The objective of training is to reduce the disparity between the forecasted network outputs and the actual labels of the examples. By iteratively adjusting the weights and biases, the network gradually increases its accuracy and is able to make more precise predictions on unseen data [61].

Speech recognition, image recognition, NLP, and financial forecasting are just some of the fields and tasks where artificial neural networks have been utilized. For instance, in image recognition, ANNs can be trained to classify images based on their content. By feeding the network with a huge amount of dataset of labeled images, the network learns to recognize characteristics and patterns that are characteristic of particular objects or categories. Once trained, the network is capable of accurately classifying images it has never seen [70].

ANNs can also be used to analyze and generate human language in the context of NLP. Through training on a tremendous amount of text, a network can learn to comprehend the meaning and context of words and sentences. This enables the network to carry out tasks like sentiment analysis, machine translation, and text summarization [70].

Despite their widespread success, artificial neural networks have certain limitations. Training requires large quantities of labeled data, and may be relatively time-consuming and costly to acquire. In addition, ANNs are computationally intensive and require powerful hardware, such as graphics processing units (GPUs), for efficient training and operation. In addition, the inner workings of ANNs can be hard to interpret, and thereby making it hard to comprehend why a network makes a specific prediction [70].

9.3.2.1 Types of Artificial Neural Networks

Various types of ANNs exist, each designed to solve specific problems and exhibiting distinct architectural configurations. Here are some common ANN types:

1. Feedforward Neural Networks (FNN): This represents the simplest and fundamental form of ANN. In FNNs, information is transmitted in a one-way direction, moving from the input layer, passing through one or more hidden layers, and finally reaching the output layer. These networks are devoid of loops or connections that provide feedback, which makes them well-suited for tasks like identifying patterns and performing classification [71,72].
2. Convolutional Neural Networks (CNN): CNNs find extensive application in image and visual data processing. They utilize shared weights and spatial hierarchies, often comprising convolutional layers, pooling layers, and fully connected layers. CNNs are highly proficient in tasks like categorizing images, identifying objects, and dividing images into segments [73,74].
3. Recurrent Neural Networks (RNNs): The RNNs were specifically invented to handle sequential data, where the output at each step is dependent on the previous computations. RNNs have recurrent connections that enable them to store and use information from previous inputs. RNNs are commonly used in various applications such as natural language processing, speech recognition, and time series analysis [69,75,76].

4. LSTMs, also known as Long Short-Term Memory Networks, are a specific type of RNN that were created to address the issue of vanishing gradients. These networks are equipped with memory cells, input gates, output gates, and forget gates, which allow them to effectively capture long-term relationships in sequential data. LSTMs have proven to be highly useful in tasks that require modeling of extended temporal dependencies.
5. Generative Adversarial Networks (GANs) are composed of two neural networks, namely a generator network and a discriminator network. The primary function of the generator network is to generate artificial data samples, while the discriminator network is designed to distinguish between real and generated samples. GANs find applications in various tasks such as image synthesis, data augmentation, and generative modeling.
6. Self-Organizing Maps (SOMs): SOMs are unsupervised learning models that map input data onto a lower-dimensional grid or lattice. They are commonly used for clustering, visualization, and exploratory data analysis tasks. SOMs enable the identification of underlying patterns and the discovery of relationships within the data [81–84].
7. Radial Basis Function Networks (RBFNs): RBFNs utilize radial basis functions as activation functions. They are frequently employed in tasks involving function approximation, pattern recognition, and time series prediction. RBFNs are adept at capturing non-linear relationships and prove suitable for problems characterized by non-linear decision boundaries [85–88].
8. Modular Neural Networks: Modular neural networks consist of several interlinked subnetworks or modules, with a dedicated module specializing in a specific task or subproblem. These modules work collaboratively to solve complex problems. Modular networks allow for modularization of the network architecture, making it easier to understand, train, and debug [89–91].
9. Spiking Neural Networks (SNNs): SNNs are inspired by the biological behavior of neurons, where information is encoded in the form of discrete spiking events. Instead of using continuous activation values like in traditional ANNs, SNNs simulate the firing of neurons in discrete time steps. SNNs are particularly useful in modeling biological neural systems, cognitive tasks, and brain-inspired computing [92,93].
10. Deep Belief Networks (DBNs): DBNs represent a form of generative deep neural network consisting of stacked layers of restricted Boltzmann machines (RBMs). They integrate both unsupervised and supervised learning approaches. DBNs are applied in tasks like dimensionality reduction, feature learning, and generative modeling [94–96].
11. Radial Basis Probabilistic Neural Networks (RBPNNs): RBPNNs merge components of radial basis function networks (RBFNs) and probabilistic neural networks (PNNs) to create a unified system. They leverage the advantages of both models by incorporating probabilistic information in the RBFN framework. RBPNNs are often used in classification and pattern recognition tasks [28].

12. Echo State Networks (ESNs) are a particular form of recurrent neural network. In ESNs, the recurrent connections are randomly created and remain unaltered during the training process. The only connections that are learned are those between the input layer and the reservoir (hidden layer). ESNs are known for their computational efficiency and are commonly used in time series prediction, signal processing, and reservoir computing [98–100].
13. Hopfield Networks: Hopfield networks are recurrent neural networks with symmetric connections between neurons. They are used for associative memory tasks and can recover stored patterns from partial or noisy inputs. Hopfield networks have applications in content-addressable memory, optimization problems, and patterns [101,102].

9.3.2.2 Deep Learning

Deep learning (DL) is a subset of machine learning focused on constructing and training artificial neural networks with multiple layers, known as deep neural networks, to comprehend and extract intricate patterns from data [63,88,103,104].

Due to its remarkable performance in a good number of domains, such as computer vision, speech recognition, NLP, and reinforcement learning, deep learning has gained considerable attention and popularity. Deep learning employs neural networks with numerous intermediate (hidden) layers positioned between the input and output layers. Each layer is composed of interconnected nodes (neurons) that transform and process the incoming data. The network's depth enables the acquisition of increasingly abstract and intricate representations of the input. Deep learning has accomplished remarkable advances and state-of-the-art performance in a variety of domains. Examples include image classification with CNNs, machine translation with RNNs, and speech recognition with CNNs and RNNs combined in hybrid architectures [104,105].

Deep learning models can automatically discover hierarchical data representations, beginning with low-level features and progressing to higher-level abstractions. This is accomplished by repeatedly applying non-linear transformations to the hidden layers, which capture increasingly complex characteristics and patterns. The backpropagation algorithm is commonly utilized to train deep neural networks. The network's weights and biases are adjusted iteratively by propagating error gradients backwards through the layers. This procedure enables the network to adjust its parameters on the basis of the difference between forecasted and real outputs, thereby gradually minimizing the total loss [104,105].

Tremendous volumes of labeled data are optimal for training deep learning algorithms. The availability of large datasets, in conjunction with advances in computing power and distributed computing, has been essential to the success of deep learning. It enables the models to capture a broad range of patterns and generalize effectively to new, unseen instances. Deep learning models are well suited when learning automatically meaningful and discriminative features or properties from raw data. Deep learning algorithms differ from conventional machine learning models by extracting relevant features directly from the data, eliminating the reliance on manual feature engineering. This approach reduces the requirement for human domain expertise [106–108].

Deep learning models exhibit exceptional adaptability and scalability, allowing them to tackle a wide variety of tasks and increasingly complex problems. They can manage a good number of data types, such as video audio, text, image, and can be scaled to accommodate huge chunks of data and intricate architectures [108].

However, deep learning is not without its drawbacks, including the requirement for a substantial volume of labeled data, resources, and the possibility of overfitting in complex models. Despite this, ongoing research and advances in deep learning continue to extend the boundaries of what can be achieved in AI and ML [88,104].

In big data analytics, the capability of ANNs and DL to handle large and complex datasets is one of their primary benefits. Traditional statistical methods frequently struggle with high-dimensional datasets or those that contain non-linear relationships. Neural networks, in contrast, are designed to work well with such data. Using a network of interconnected neurons, deep learning models have the ability to autonomously uncover patterns and information, and adapt to the data's underlying patterns. This makes them particularly useful for tasks requiring sophisticated pattern recognition capabilities, such as NLP, speech recognition, and image recognition [45].

In big data analytics, the ability of neural networks and DL to uncover hidden insights and make accurate predictions is an additional advantage. Traditional analytics methods frequently rely on predefined data models or assumptions, which may not fully capture the complexity of real-world phenomena. Neural networks, on the other hand, are capable of learning directly from the data, without any prior assumptions. This enables them to recognize new patterns and associations that may not be obvious to human analysts. By leveraging this capability, organizations can derive meaningful observations regarding customer behavior, market trends, and various factors influencing performance [18,109].

In addition, neural networks and deep learning can help businesses improve their decision-making by providing more precise and timely forecasts. Through the analysis of extensive historical data, these models can discern patterns and trends, enabling the prediction of future outcomes. For example, deep learning models find applications in predicting stock prices, detecting fraudulent transactions, and assessing credit risk within the financial services industry. In healthcare, they can aid in disease diagnosis, patient outcome prediction, and individualized treatment. By utilizing these forecasts, organizations can enhance decision-making and implement proactive measures to optimize their operations and enhance their business performance [110–114].

9.3.3 Evolutionary Algorithms

Evolutionary algorithms (EAs) represent a category of optimization algorithms inspired by natural evolution and genetics. They replicate the principles of natural selection to iteratively pursue optimal solutions for complex problems. EAs function with a population of candidate solutions, emulating selection, reproduction, and mutation mechanisms across successive generations to navigate the search for improved solutions. The following are essential characteristics of evolutionary algorithms [67,115–119]:

1. EAs manage a group of potential solutions, usually depicted as individuals or chromosomes, where each individual represents a possible solution to the given problem. The population undergoes evolution across multiple generations, and the algorithm employs variation operators to generate new individuals, guided by the idea of natural selection.
2. Fitness Evaluation: In order to assess the suitability or competence of every individual within the population, a fitness function is employed. The fitness function measures how well an individual solves the problem or achieves the desired objective. It serves as the guiding criterion for selection and drives the evolutionary process, as individuals with higher fitness are more inclined to contribute to the next generation.
3. Selection: The selection process in EAs mimics the survival-of-the-fittest idea.
4. Individuals with superior fitness scores are more inclined to be chosen for reproduction. Various selection mechanisms are used, such as tournament selection, roulette wheel selection, or rank-based selection, to choose individuals that will contribute to the next generation.
5. Reproduction and Variation: EAs employ reproduction operators, like crossover and mutation, to generate new individuals from the selected parents. Crossover entails exchanging genetic information between two or more parents to produce offspring, resembling genetic recombination. Mutation is responsible for introducing random alterations to the genetic material of the offspring, facilitating exploration of new regions within the search space.
6. Iterative Optimization: EAs operate iteratively over multiple generations, applying selection, reproduction, and variation operators to evolve the population. The process continues until a specific condition is fulfilled, such as reaching the maximum limit of iterations or achieving a desirable outcome.

Figure 9.3 depicts the sequence of a typical EA process.

EAs are able to effectively explore search space, particularly in complex and multimodal problem domains, which is one of their strengths. By maintaining a diverse population and incorporating stochastic variation operators, EAs are able to navigate through various regions of the search space, allowing for the discovery of globally optimal or near-optimal solutions.

EAs have found successful applications in a wide range of optimization problems across diverse domains. They are ideal for problems with a large and complex search space, non-linearity, multiple objectives, or noisy and uncertain environments. EAs

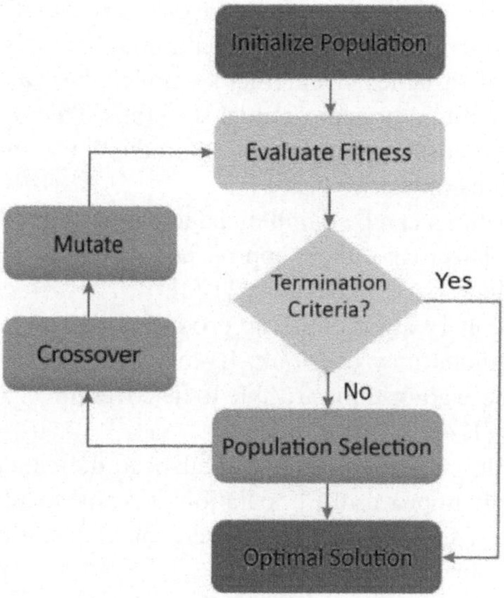

FIGURE 9.3 Evolutionary algorithms process flow.

have been utilized in numerous fields, including engineering design, scheduling, data mining, and finance.

Examples of popular evolutionary algorithms include genetic programming (GP), genetic algorithms (GAs), particle swarm optimization (PSO), and evolution strategies (ESs). These algorithms differ in their representation of solutions, variation operators, and specific implementation details [34–36].

9.3.3.1 Evolutionary Algorithms in Big Data Analytics

As organizations strive to make sense of the extensive quantities of data at their disposal, evolutionary algorithms offer a promising alternative to conventional data analysis techniques. By emulating the process of evolution, these algorithms are able to sift through large volumes of data, uncover concealed patterns, and generate valuable insights [115–117].

Using evolutionary algorithms in big data analytics provides a number of important benefits. First and foremost, these algorithms are exceptional at managing complex and high-dimensional datasets. Traditional data analysis methods may become inefficient or impractical as the volume and variety of data continue to expand. In contrast, evolutionary algorithms can effectively navigate vast amounts of data, revealing hidden patterns and relationships [122,123].

Secondly, evolutionary algorithms can account for data uncertainty and noise. Frequently, data from the real world contain inconsistencies or missing values, which can hinder conventional analysis methods. Nevertheless, evolutionary algorithms can adapt to noisy data and deal with uncertainty, making them robust and trustworthy tools for big data [123].

The ability of evolutionary algorithms to optimize solutions is an additional benefit. Whether it's optimizing resource allocation in a supply chain or finding the optimal combination of variables in a predictive model, these algorithms can search a vast search space for optimal or near-optimal solutions. This optimization capability can result in substantial cost savings, increased productivity, and improved decision-making across numerous industries [120].

Evolutionary algorithms can be parallelized and scaled in order to process extensive volumes of data. This makes them appropriate for big data analytics, where data volumes continue to increase exponentially [122].

In addition, evolutionary algorithms can produce novel and exploratory solutions that conventional methods may overlook. By exploring a variety of solutions and adapting over time, these algorithms are able to discover novel and efficient solutions to complex problems [124].

Additionally, evolutionary algorithms can adapt to the data and learn from it. As the algorithm iteratively improves the population, it is able to adapt its search strategy to concentrate on promising areas of the search space, resulting in quicker convergence and improved solutions [120].

9.3.3.2 Examples of Successful Applications of Evolutionary Algorithms in the Industry

The application of evolutionary algorithms in big data analytics has yielded impressive results across various industries. Let's explore some notable examples:

1. **Healthcare**: Evolutionary algorithms have been utilized in healthcare to enhance the treatment plans offered to individuals. These algorithms are able to generate personalized treatment plans for patients by taking into account multiple variables, such as patient demographics, medical history, and treatment options. These plans are designed to maximize therapeutic efficacy while minimizing adverse effects [123,125].
2. **Portfolio Optimization**: The financial industry has found uses for evolutionary algorithms in the process of portfolio optimization. This is a process in which the objective is to select a combination of assets that maximizes return while minimizing risk. These algorithms are able to identify optimal portfolios that strike a healthy balance between risk and return by taking into account historical market data, risk profiles, and investment objectives [126,127].
3. **Manufacturing**: The use of evolutionary algorithms in the manufacturing industry has enabled production processes and resource allocation to be optimized. These algorithms are able to generate production schedules that minimize downtime, reduce costs, and maximize throughput by taking into consideration a variety of factors, including machine availability, production capacity, and order [128–130].
4. **Transportation**: The optimization of routing and scheduling in transportation systems has been accomplished adopting evolutionary algorithms. These EA algorithms can generate efficient routes and schedules that minimize travel

time, fuel consumption, and transportation costs by taking into consideration factors like traffic conditions, delivery deadlines, and vehicle capacity [116,131–134].

These examples demonstrate the versatility and effectiveness of evolutionary algorithms in solving complex, real-world problems in a wide range of industries.

9.3.3.3 How Businesses Can Leverage Evolutionary Algorithms for Better Data Insights

To harness the power of evolutionary algorithms for improved data insights, businesses must adopt a systematic methodology [115,120,125,127,135]:

1. **Identify the problem:** Precisely articulate the problem you aim to address or the objective you want to achieve. This could be anything from predicting customer behavior to optimizing supply chain operations.
2. **Data collection and preprocessing:** Collect pertinent data and preprocess it to guarantee its quality and consistency. To achieve this, you must undertake various activities, including data cleansing, rectifying any missing values, and modifying variables if necessary.
3. **Algorithm selection:** Choose the appropriate evolutionary algorithm based on the problem at hand. There are various forms of EAs, such as, GP, GA, and PSO. Consider the specific requirements of your problem and select the algorithm that best suits your needs.
4. **Parameter tuning:** Fine-tune the parameters of the selected algorithm to optimize its performance. Parameters or features such as the size of the population, rate of mutation, and crossover probability can significantly impact the algorithm's convergence and solution quality.
5. **Model evaluation and validation:** Evaluate or assess the performance of the evolved models by adopting suitable metrics and validate their effectiveness using test data or cross-validation techniques. This step ensures that the models are robust and reliable.
6. **Deployment and monitoring:** Once the models are ready, deploy them into your production environment and monitor their performance over time. Continuously update and retrain the models as new data become available to ensure their effectiveness.

By following these steps, businesses can effectively leverage evolutionary algorithms to extract valuable insights from their big data and drive data-driven decision-making.

9.3.3.4 Case Studies of Companies Using Evolutionary Algorithms in Their Data Analytics Processes

Incorporating evolutionary algorithms into data analytics processes has improved efficiency and decision-making at a number of companies. Let's look at a few examples [128–130]:

1. Netflix: Netflix, the popular streaming platform, uses evolutionary algorithms to optimize its recommendation system. By considering user preferences, viewing history, and content metadata, these algorithms help personalize the recommendations and improve user satisfaction.
2. Google: Google leverages evolutionary algorithms in its advertising platform to optimize bidding strategies. These algorithms consider factors such as user behavior, ad relevance, and bidding constraints to determine the optimal bid for each ad placement, maximizing the return on investment for advertisers. Google has also employed evolutionary algorithms for optimizing their data center operations. They used a genetic algorithm to determine the most efficient configuration of data center components such as cooling systems, servers, and workload allocations. By evolving these configurations over time, Google successfully decreased energy consumption and enhanced the overall efficiency of their data centers.
3. Uber: Uber uses evolutionary algorithms to optimize its dynamic pricing system. By considering factors such as supply and demand, traffic conditions, and user behavior, these algorithms determine the optimal pricing strategy that balances profitability and user demand. They have also utilized evolutionary algorithms for route optimization. They employed a genetic algorithm to dynamically evolve and optimize routes based on the current state of traffic, the number of passengers requesting rides, and the availability of drivers. This approach helped Uber drivers save time and fuel by identifying the most efficient routes for pickups and drop-offs.
4. Siemens: Siemens, a multinational conglomerate, has implemented evolutionary algorithms in their data analytics processes for optimizing manufacturing operations. They used genetic algorithms to optimize production schedules, machine configurations, and supply chain logistics. By evolving these parameters, Siemens was able to improve production efficiency, minimize downtime, and reduce costs.
5. Santander Bank: Santander Bank, a global financial institution, utilized evolutionary algorithms for credit risk assessment. They employed a genetic programming approach to evolve mathematical models that could predict credit default probabilities relying on historical data and considering other pertinent factors. This allowed Santander Bank to improve the accuracy of their credit risk assessments and make more informed lending decisions.
6. Procter & Gamble (P&G): P&G, a consumer goods company, has applied evolutionary algorithms in their product design and optimization processes. They used genetic algorithms to evolve and optimize product formulations, packaging designs, and supply chain configurations. By employing these algorithms, P&G was able to create more cost-effective and sustainable products while meeting customer preferences and regulatory requirements.
7. Boeing: Boeing, the aerospace company, has employed evolutionary algorithms for aircraft design optimization. They used genetic algorithms to evolve and optimize wing shapes, material distributions, and structural configurations. By leveraging these algorithms, Boeing was able to improve

aerodynamic performance, reduce fuel consumption, and enhance overall aircraft efficiency.

8. Amazon: Amazon, the e-commerce giant, has utilized evolutionary algorithms for supply chain optimization. They employed genetic algorithms to optimize inventory management, warehouse layouts, and delivery routes. By evolving these parameters, Amazon was able to streamline their operations, reduce shipping costs, and improve order fulfillment efficiency.
9. General Electric (GE): GE, a multinational conglomerate, has applied evolutionary algorithms in their predictive maintenance processes. They used genetic programming to evolve predictive models that could detect equipment failures and recommend maintenance actions. By leveraging these algorithms, GE was able to reduce downtime, enhance equipment reliability, and optimize maintenance schedules.
10. Ford: Ford, the automotive company, has applied evolutionary algorithms in vehicle design optimization. They used genetic algorithms to evolve and optimize vehicle architectures, engine configurations, and component placements. By leveraging these algorithms, Ford was able to improve vehicle performance, fuel efficiency, and safety while reducing manufacturing costs.

These case studies highlight the real-world impact of evolutionary algorithms in improving business processes and delivering value to customers [127].

9.3.3.5 Challenges and Limitations of Using Evolutionary Algorithms in Big Data Analytics

While evolutionary algorithms offer numerous benefits for big data analytics, they also have limitations. Let's explore some of the common ones [129,130]:

1. Evolutionary algorithms can require a high amount of computational resources, especially when applied to large datasets. As the problem or population size grows, so can the time and space needed to process it. Effective implementation and parallelization strategies are required to overcome this difficulty.
2. The success of evolutionary algorithms is highly sensitive to the values chosen for their tuning parameters. Finding the best parameter values can be difficult and time consuming, necessitating a lot of trial and error and specific knowledge.
3. When an algorithm converges on a less-than-ideal solution before exhausting its search space, this phenomenon is known as premature convergence. This can be avoided, and the best solutions can be found by maintaining an equilibrium between exploration and exploitation within the algorithm.
4. Complex models or solutions are common outcomes of evolutionary algorithms, making them challenging to interpret. This can be a problem in fields like healthcare and finance where interpretability is essential. It may be necessary to use additional methods, like model simplification or post-processing, to improve interpretability.

5. Understanding the problem domain and how to properly frame it are prerequisites for successfully implementing evolutionary algorithms. The fitness function, problem representation, and domain knowledge all play crucial roles in the algorithm's effectiveness.
6. Scalability issues may arise when dealing with extremely high-dimensional or streaming data, despite the fact that evolutionary algorithms can manage massive datasets. These difficulties may necessitate the use of specialized methods, such as dimensionality reduction or online learning.

Nevertheless, evolutionary algorithms are constantly developing and improving to overcome these obstacles. The potential of these algorithms is constantly being expanded as a result of ongoing research and technological developments in the field.

9.3.4 Fuzzy Logic and Fuzzy Systems

In the ever-changing world of data analysis, fuzzy logic has emerged as a potent tool that challenges binary thinking. As the amount and intricacy of data continue to expand rapidly, cooperations are searching for novel approaches to extract insightful information. With its capacity to handle uncertainty and imprecision, fuzzy logic offers a novel approach to data interpretation. Fuzzy logic empowers decision-makers to confidently navigate the complexities of big data by incorporating degrees of truth and reasoning similar to that of humans. This chapter will explore the fascinating world of fuzzy logic and its applications in a variety of industries. From healthcare to finance, fuzzy logic has the potential to revolutionize how we analyze and interpret the vast quantities of data available to us [136–139].

9.3.4.1 What Are Fuzzy Logic and Fuzzy Systems?

Fuzzy logic and fuzzy systems are mathematical frameworks that deal with imprecision and uncertainty in data and reasoning processes. In the 1960s, Lotfi Zadeh created them as an extension of classical Boolean logic to deal with situations where precise values or boundaries are not applicable [136–139].

Fuzzy logic introduces fuzzy sets, which permit degrees of membership as opposed to strict membership in a set. Fuzzy sets assign membership values between 0 and 1 to indicate the degree of membership, as opposed to classical sets where an element either belongs or does not belong to a set. This enables a more adaptable representation of data that incorporates uncertainty, vagueness, and partial truths.

Fuzzy systems, in contrast, are computational systems that model and reason with imprecise or uncertain information using fuzzy logic. There are three primary components: fuzzification, fuzzy inference, and defuzzification, as depicted in Figure 9.4 [47,140–142].

1. Fuzzification: Fuzzification involves the mapping of crisp input values into fuzzy sets by assigning appropriate membership degrees. It involves

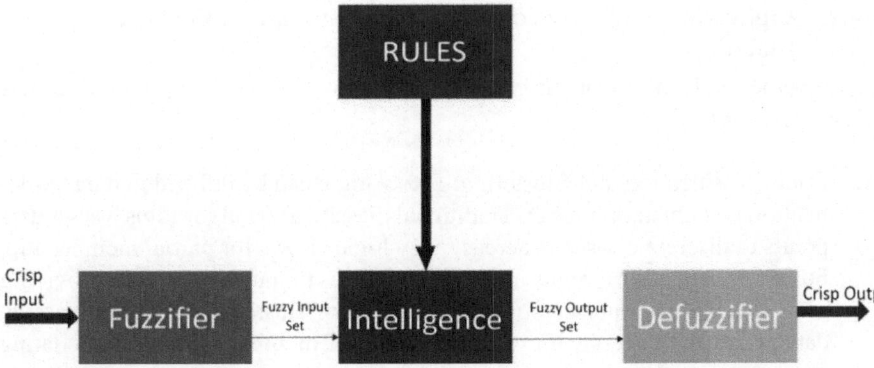

FIGURE 9.4 Components of a fuzzy system.

transforming numerical data into linguistic variables that capture the subjective or vague nature of the information.

2. Fuzzy Inference: Fuzzy inference is the core reasoning process of fuzzy systems. It applies fuzzy logic rules to fuzzy input variables to derive fuzzy output variables. Fuzzy rules play a crucial role in establishing connections between input and output variables by utilizing linguistic terms and fuzzy sets. Fuzzy inference combines these rules using fuzzy logic operators (such as AND, OR, and NOT) to make inferences and draw conclusions.
3. Defuzzification: Defuzzification transforms fuzzy output variables back into crisp values, making them suitable for decision-making or additional analysis. Several defuzzification methods, including centroid, weighted average, or maximum membership, can be employed to derive a single crisp value from the fuzzy output.

Fuzzy logic has numerous applications, including decision support systems, control systems, pattern recognition, data mining, artificial intelligence, and data analytics. In the context of big data analytics, fuzzy logic can be very helpful in the interpretation and extraction of insights from vast and complex datasets. It permits the consideration of multiple factors and their relative importance, allowing for a more comprehensive understanding of the data. Fuzzy logic provides a valuable tool for dealing with the inherent noise and variability in big data by incorporating uncertainty and imprecision [85].

When data are incomplete, inconsistent, or uncertain, fuzzy logic is particularly useful. In healthcare, for instance, patient symptoms and test results may not always provide definitive answers. Considering the uncertainty and imprecision of the data, fuzzy logic can be utilized to evaluate the likelihood of various diagnoses based on the available data. Similarly, fuzzy logic can be utilized in finance to evaluate investment risks, taking into account market volatility, economic indicators, and past performance. By incorporating fuzzy logic into big data analytics, businesses can gain a greater insight into complex phenomena and make more informed decisions [12,143].

9.3.4.2 Applications of Fuzzy Logic and Fuzzy Systems in Big Data Analytics

Here are some applications of fuzzy logic and fuzzy systems in big data analytics [12,128,144–149]:

1. Data Classification and Clustering: Fuzzy logic can be utilized in data classification and clustering tasks. Traditional classification algorithms assign data points to discrete classes, whereas fuzzy logic allows for partial membership. Fuzzy classification assigns membership values to multiple classes, providing a more nuanced representation of data. Fuzzy clustering algorithms assign data points to clusters with varying degrees of membership, accommodating overlapping and uncertain data patterns.
2. Uncertain Data Processing: In big data analytics, dealing with uncertain or incomplete information is common. Fuzzy logic provides a framework to handle such uncertainty. Fuzzy systems can model and process uncertain data, allowing for more robust analysis. Fuzzy sets and fuzzy rules enable the representation and reasoning of imprecise and incomplete information, enabling more flexible and accurate data analysis.
3. Decision Support Systems: Fuzzy logic plays a crucial role in decision support systems (DSSs) that deal with complex and uncertain data. Fuzzy DSSs employ fuzzy logic to represent decision criteria, preferences, and uncertainties. By incorporating fuzzy rules and fuzzy inference, these systems can assist in decision-making processes, particularly when faced with incomplete or ambiguous data.
4. Rule-Based Systems: Fuzzy logic is often used in rule-based systems for big data analytics. These systems use fuzzy rules to model complex relationships and decision-making processes. By combining fuzzy sets, fuzzy logic operators, and fuzzy inference, rule-based systems can handle data with uncertainty, vagueness, and imprecision, making them suitable for analyzing large and heterogeneous datasets.
5. Text Mining and Sentiment Analysis: Fuzzy logic has applications in text mining and sentiment analysis, where the interpretation of human language involves inherent vagueness and ambiguity. Fuzzy logic techniques can be employed to model linguistic variables, fuzzy sets, and fuzzy rules to capture the subjective and imprecise nature of textual data. This enables sentiment analysis algorithms to provide more nuanced and context-aware sentiment analysis results.

Fuzzy logic and fuzzy systems provide a useful framework for big data analytics, enabling the management of complex and uncertain data. Incorporating fuzzy logic techniques enables analysts to process, model, and reason with imprecise information, resulting in more accurate and trustworthy insights from large-scale datasets.

9.3.4.3 Advantages of Using Fuzzy Logic in Big Data Analytics

Using fuzzy logic in big data analytics has several advantages over binary approaches. Initially, fuzzy logic permits the representation of data uncertainty and imprecision.

Data are not always precise or easily quantifiable in many real-world situations. Fuzzy logic provides a method for capturing and modeling these uncertainties, allowing for a more precise data analysis. Fuzzy logic can handle incomplete or missing data by considering degrees of truth, providing a more robust framework for decision-making [144].

Secondly, fuzzy logic incorporates reasoning similar to that of humans into data analysis. Complex situations are frequently oversimplified by traditional binary approaches, resulting in limited insights and potentially flawed decisions. Fuzzy logic, on the other hand, imitates how humans think and reason, enabling a more nuanced and comprehensive analysis of data. By taking multiple factors and their interactions into account, fuzzy logic can capture the complexity of real-world phenomena and provide deeper insights [145].

In big data analytics, fuzzy logic's ability to handle non-linear relationships and complex data patterns is an additional benefit. Traditional linear models may not always be appropriate for capturing the complex dependencies and interactions present in large datasets. These non-linear relationships can be effectively captured by fuzzy logic algorithms, such as fuzzy clustering and fuzzy rule-based systems, allowing for a more precise analysis of the data [146].

In addition, fuzzy logic provides a framework that is adaptable to changing conditions and evolving data. In numerous instances of the real world, data is dynamic and subject to constant change. Fuzzy logic enables the updating and refining of models as new data becomes available, ensuring that the analysis remains relevant and accurate.

The benefits of using fuzzy logic in big data analytics are its ability to deal with uncertainty, incorporate human-like reasoning, capture non-linear relationships, and adapt to changing data. By leveraging these benefits, businesses can gain deeper insights, make more informed decisions, and ultimately achieve better outcomes [147].

9.3.4.4 Implementing Fuzzy Logic in Big Data Analytics

To effectively incorporate fuzzy logic into big data analytics, a range of tools, techniques, and specialized knowledge are needed. The process of implementing fuzzy logic within the realm of big data analytics involves several essential steps [144,146]:

1. **Data preprocessing**: Preprocessing the data is a critical step in any data analytics project. This involves activities like data cleansing, resolving missing values, and transforming the data into a suitable format for analysis. In fuzzy logic, preprocessing may also involve converting crisp data into fuzzy representations, allowing for the representation of uncertainty and imprecision.
2. **Fuzzy logic modeling**: Once the data are preprocessed, the subsequent phase involves developing a fuzzy logic model. This includes the definition of fuzzy sets, membership functions, and fuzzy rules to encapsulate the relationships and patterns within the data. The selection of a fuzzy logic model depends on the particular problem and domain at hand.

3. **Fuzzification**: Fuzzification involves the conversion of crisp data into fuzzy representations. This step is essential for incorporating uncertainty and imprecision into the analysis. Fuzzification involves assigning membership values to data points based on their degree of membership to various fuzzy sets.
4. **Inference and reasoning**: After fuzzification, a fuzzy logic model is utilized to perform inference and reasoning. This involves applying fuzzy rules to the fuzzified data to derive meaningful insights and conclusions. The output or result of the inference mechanism may be fuzzy sets or crisp values, depending on the specific problem.
5. **Defuzzification**: Defuzzification is the process of transforming fuzzy outputs into crisp values. This step is necessary to obtain actionable insights and make informed decisions.
6. **Evaluation and validation**: After the implementation of the fuzzy logic model, it is crucial to assess and validate its performance. This involves assessing the accuracy, precision, and reliability utilizing appropriate evaluation metrics. Validation may also involve comparing the results or outputs of the fuzzy logic model with established benchmarks or expert opinions.
7. **Deployment and integration:** After the fuzzy logic model is evaluated and validated, it can be deployed and integrated into the existing data analytics infrastructure. This may involve integrating the fuzzy logic model with other machine learning algorithms, visualization tools, or decision support systems.

Organizations can successfully implement fuzzy logic in big data analytics by adhering to these steps and making use of the appropriate tools and techniques. Success requires familiarity with the problem space, accurate data modeling, and on-going adjustment of the fuzzy logic model considering experience and new information.

9.3.4.5 Challenges and Limitations of Fuzzy Logic in Big Data Analytics

While there are many benefits to using fuzzy logic for big data analytics, there are also some drawbacks. Here are some of the drawbacks [147–149]:

1. **Computational complexity:** Fuzzy logic models can be computationally intensive, especially when dealing with large and complex datasets. The processing and analysis of fuzzy logic models may require significant computational resources and time. Organizations need to consider the scalability and efficiency of fuzzy logic algorithms when working with big data.
2. **Interpretability:** While fuzzy logic models offer transparency and interpretability, they can also be complex and challenging to interpret. The linguistic nature of fuzzy logic can make it difficult to explain the reasoning behind the model's decisions. Organizations need to develop techniques and tools for visualizing and explaining fuzzy logic models to enhance their interpretability.
3. **Data quality and preprocessing:** Fuzzy logic heavily relies on the quality and preprocessing of the data. Incomplete or inaccurate data can lead to unreliable and misleading results. Organizations need to invest in data quality

management and preprocessing techniques to ensure that the data used in fuzzy logic models are accurate and representative.

4. **Expert knowledge and domain expertise:** Fuzzy logic models often require expert knowledge and domain expertise to develop and interpret. The success of fuzzy logic in big data analytics depends on the availability of experts who can define appropriate fuzzy sets, membership functions, and fuzzy rules. Organizations need to invest in training and collaboration with domain experts to leverage the full potential of fuzzy logic.
5. **Scalability and real-time processing:** Fuzzy logic models may face challenges in scalability and real-time processing. As big data continues to grow, organizations need to ensure that fuzzy logic algorithms can handle large volumes of data efficiently. Real-time processing of data requires fast and responsive fuzzy logic models, which may require optimization and parallel processing techniques.

9.3.4.6 Future Trends and Advancements in Fuzzy Logic for Big Data Analytics

The field of fuzzy logic for big data analytics is continuously evolving, with several future trends and advancements on the horizon. Let's explore some of these trends [144,145]:

1. **Hybrid models**: An emerging trend in fuzzy logic involves the creation of hybrid models that integrate fuzzy logic with other machine learning techniques. Hybrid models leverage the strengths of different approaches, allowing for more accurate and robust analysis of big data. For example, fuzzy logic can be combined with deep learning algorithms to handle the complexity and scale of big data.
2. **Explainable AI:** As the demand for transparency and interpretability in AI systems grows, explainable AI becomes increasingly important. Fuzzy logic, with its transparent and interpretable nature, can play a crucial role in developing explainable AI systems. Future advancements in fuzzy logic may focus on improving the explainability and interpretability of fuzzy logic models, allowing stakeholders to comprehend and trust the decisions made by fuzzy models.
3. **Real-time analytics:** With the increasing speed and volume of data, real-time analytics becomes essential in big data analytics. Fuzzy logic models need to adapt to real-time data streams and provide timely insights and decisions. Future advancements may focus on developing fast and scalable fuzzy logic algorithms that can handle real-time data processing efficiently.
4. **Automated fuzzy logic modeling:** Developing fuzzy logic models often requires expert knowledge and domain expertise. Future advancements may focus on automating the process of fuzzy logic modeling, making it more accessible to non-experts. This can involve techniques such as automated rule generation, intelligent fuzzy set selection, and model optimization.
5. **Integration with the IoT and edge computing:** The proliferation of IoT devices and edge computing opens new opportunities for fuzzy logic in big

data analytics. Fuzzy logic can be applied at the edge to analyze data in real time, reducing the need for data transfer and enabling faster decision-making. Future advancements may focus on integrating fuzzy logic with IoT platforms and edge computing architectures, enabling distributed and intelligent analytics.

These future trends and advancements highlight the exciting possibilities for fuzzy logic in big data analytics. As the field persists to evolve, organizations can anticipate seeing more sophisticated and efficient fuzzy logic models, enabling deeper insights and more.

9.3.5 Hybrid Computational Intelligence Approaches

Multiple computational techniques, such as ANNs, EC techniques, and fuzzy logic, are combined by hybrid computational intelligence to produce a more robust and accurate analytical model. These techniques complement one another's strengths and overcome their respective weaknesses. For instance, artificial neural networks are effective at learning patterns from data, whereas genetic algorithms can optimize the model's parameters. By combining these methods, hybrid computational intelligence is able to process large datasets with high precision and efficiency [5,150,151].

Predictive modeling is one area where hybrid computational intelligence is used extensively in big data analytics. Building a model that can predict future outcomes based on historical data is predictive modeling. It is possible that traditional statistical models cannot handle the complexity and volume of big data. Predictive modeling is more adaptable and scalable when utilizing hybrid computational intelligence techniques. A hybrid model combining artificial neural networks and genetic algorithms, for instance, can learn complex patterns from large datasets and optimize the model parameters to increase accuracy [53].

Anomaly detection is another application of hybrid computational intelligence in big data analytics. Anomaly detection is the procedure of recognizing patterns or events that deviate substantially from the anticipated behavior. Identifying anomalies is essential in big data analytics for detecting fraud, network intrusions, and equipment failures. By combining multiple detection algorithms, hybrid techniques for computational intelligence can detect anomalies effectively. A hybrid model combining fuzzy logic and genetic algorithms, for instance, can identify outliers in large datasets by simultaneously considering multiple factors [10,152].

In addition, hybrid computational intelligence can be used for feature selection in large-scale data analytics. Feature selection is the identification of the most pertinent features or variables in a dataset that significantly contribute to the desired outcome. With the vast amount of data available in big data analytics, it is vital to choose the suitable features to improve the accuracy and efficiency of analytical models. Combining the strengths of different feature selection algorithms, hybrid techniques for artificial intelligence can automatically select the most informative features.

Lastly, hybrid computational intelligence offers a promising strategy for addressing the difficulties of big data analytics. Hybrid models can handle large and complex datasets with high precision and efficiency by combining multiple computational techniques. They are especially advantageous for predictive modeling, anomaly detection, and feature selection. As the volume of data continues to increase, hybrid computational intelligence will play an increasingly vital role in gleaning valuable insights from big data. To enhance the efficacy of big data analytics, researchers and practitioners in the field should continue to investigate and develop new hybrid models.

9.4 COMPUTATIONAL INTELLIGENCE TECHNIQUES IN BIG DATA PREPROCESSING

The initial step in analyzing and utilizing large amounts of data involves preprocessing. This crucial stage encompasses the cleansing, transformation, and integration of raw data to guarantee its quality and suitability for further analysis. However, as big data becomes more complex and voluminous, traditional preprocessing techniques often struggle to maintain efficiency and accuracy. Consequently, computational intelligence techniques have emerged as a promising solution to address these challenges.

9.4.1 Data Cleaning and Data Integration

Cleansing and integrating data are two essential steps in the preprocessing of big data. Before big data can be analyzed or modeled, it must undergo a series of preprocessing steps, including data cleansing and data integration [153–156].

Data cleansing is the process of detecting and rectifying mistakes and discrepancies within the data. This is crucial because big data frequently comes from multiple sources and may contain missing values, duplicate records, outliers, or errors. These errors can negatively impact the quality and dependability of any data analysis or modeling. Therefore, the aim of data cleansing is to ensure that the data are precise, comprehensive, consistent, and error-free [154,157].

In big data preprocessing, there are numerous techniques and tools available for data cleansing. Among these are outlier detection algorithms, missing value imputation techniques, deduplication algorithms, and error detection and correction methods. Outlier detection algorithms assist in identifying and removing outliers, which are data points that significantly deviate from the norm of the data. Using statistical techniques or machine learning algorithms, missing value imputation methods help fill in missing values. Deduplication algorithms assist in identifying and removing duplicate records that may result from combining data from multiple sources. Error detection and correction techniques enable the identification and correction of data errors such as misspellings and inconsistent formatting [10,153,154,157].

In contrast, data integration involves the merging of data from various sources into a single dataset. The sources of big data are frequently diverse, including databases, text files, social media feeds, sensor networks, and web scraping. Data integration aims to produce a single, exhaustive dataset used for modeling or analysis. This step is necessary because different sources may have varying formats, structures, or semantics, making it difficult to combine them seamlessly [5,53].

Techniques for data integration involve mapping and transforming data from diverse sources into a uniform format or schema. This may involve identifying and resolving schema conflicts, such as variations in attribute names, data types, or units of measurement. It may also involve resolving semantic conflicts, such as disagreements in the data's meaning or interpretation. Data integration methods include data fusion, schema matching, entity resolution, and ontology mapping.

The objective of data cleansing is to ensure the accuracy, completeness, and error-free nature of the data. Conversely, data integration focuses on combining data from different sources to create a cohesive dataset. These two steps are relevant for maintaining the quality, dependability, and usability of big data for purposes of analysis and modeling. For data cleaning and data integration in big data preprocessing, a variety of techniques and tools are available to address issues such as outliers, missing values, duplicates, schema conflicts, and semantic conflicts [53].

9.4.2 Feature Selection and Extraction

The selection and extraction of features are crucial steps in the preprocessing of large datasets. Recently, it has gained growing significance to efficiently process and analyze large datasets occasioned by the exponential expansion of data. Nonetheless, working with big data presents unique challenges, such as a great number of features or variables. These characteristics may be redundant, irrelevant, or noisy, resulting in an increase in computational complexity and a decrease in the precision of data analysis tasks. To decrease the dimensionality of the dataset and retain only the most relevant and informative features, feature selection and extraction techniques are employed [158,159].

Feature selection involves identifying and selecting a subset of the original dataset's features that significantly contribute to the predictive ability of a machine learning model. Statistical measures such as correlation coefficients, information gain, and chi-square tests are typically utilized in this procedure. Feature selection reduces computational complexity and improves the interpretability and generalizability of a model by eliminating irrelevant or redundant features. In addition, it mitigates the issue of overfitting, in which the model becomes overly specific to the training data and does not perform effectively on novel data [160,161].

Feature extraction seeks to convert the original set of features into a new set; a set of lower-dimensional features that covers the majority of relevant details. This is accomplished by projecting the data onto a new feature space using mathematical techniques such as linear discriminant analysis (LDA) or principal component analysis (PCA). The extracted features are linear transformations or combinations of the original features and are selected based on their ability to explain the maximum variance or discriminate between different data classes. When working with high-dimensional datasets where feature selection alone may not be sufficient, or when interpretability or visualization of the transformed data is required, feature extraction is particularly useful [158].

Both feature selection and extraction techniques play a crucial role in big data preprocessing because they help to reduce dimensionality, improve computational efficiency, and improve the precision and interpretability of machine learning models.

They are applicable to a variety of data types, including structured and unstructured data, and can be incorporated into various stages of the data analysis pipeline. In addition, these techniques are not limited to a particular domain or application and can be utilized in a variety of fields, including healthcare, finance, marketing, and social sciences [158,159].

Lastly, both feature selection and extraction contribute to the reduction of dimensionality, enhancement of computational efficiency, and improvement of the accuracy and interpretability of models. By selecting or transforming the most pertinent characteristics, these techniques enable more efficient and effective data analysis, resulting in improved insights and decisions. As big data continues to expand in both volume and intricacy, the importance of feature selection and extraction will only increase. These tools are becoming increasingly essential in the field of data science [160].

9.5 COMPUTATIONAL INTELLIGENCE TECHNIQUES FOR BIG DATA ANALYSIS

9.5.1 Clustering Algorithms for Pattern Recognition

Clustering algorithms facilitate the organization and categorization of data into groups or clusters based on their similarities, thereby easing the analysis process. These algorithms play a crucial role in uncovering hidden patterns and connections within the data, which can be applied for various reasons including market segmentation, anomaly detection, and recommendation systems [164,165].

The k-means algorithm stands out as one of the most popular clustering algorithms. The objective of the algorithm is to divide the dataset into k separate clusters. It achieves this by repeatedly assigning each data point to the centroid closest to it and then updating the centroids based on the newly formed clusters. This procedure is repeated until convergence is reached. The k-means algorithm is suitable for large datasets and is computationally efficient. However, it has a few drawbacks, including sensitivity to initial cluster centers and difficulty with non-convex clusters [158,166].

The hierarchical clustering algorithm is one of the most widely used clustering algorithms. Hierarchical clustering, unlike k-means, does not demand a predefined number of clusters. Instead, it builds a hierarchy of these clusters through iterative merging and splitting based on their similarities This produces a dendrogram that depicts the relationships between clusters at various granularity levels. When the number of clusters is unknown or the data have a hierarchical structure, hierarchical clustering is advantageous. However, it is computationally expensive and inappropriate for large datasets.

In big data analytics, density-based clustering algorithms are also frequently used for pattern recognition. These algorithms identify dense partitions within the data space and classify all points within these regions as belonging to the same cluster. Density-Based Spatial Clustering of Applications with Noise (DBSCAN) is one such algorithm that does the clustering of data points with a sufficient number of neighbors that are close to one another. DBSCAN is noise-resistant and capable of discovering clusters of any shape. However, it necessitates the correct parameter setting and may struggle with datasets of varying densities [167–169].

With the emergence of deep and neural networks recently, clustering algorithms have been combined with these methods to improve pattern recognition in big data analytics. Deep clustering algorithms utilize the power of deep neural networks to learn meaningful representations of the data and then cluster the data based on the learned representations. This strategy has demonstrated promising results in domains such as image segmentation and document clustering [170–172].

Lastly, clustering algorithms are vital in big data analytics pattern recognition. They facilitate the organization and categorization of data into clusters, thereby facilitating the identification of hidden patterns and relationships. Therefore, many clustering algorithms, such as k-means, density-based clustering, hierarchical clustering, and deep clustering, have distinct advantages and disadvantages. The selection of an algorithm is determined by the requirements and characteristics of the dataset. As big data continues to grow, it will be essential to develop more efficient and scalable clustering algorithms to extract valuable insights from enormous datasets [170,171].

9.5.2 Classification and Prediction Models

Classification is a core method in the field of big data analysis, which entails grouping data into distinct classes or categories according to specific attributes or features. Its purpose is to forecast or categorize new data by identifying patterns and connections within the already existing data. Classification in big data analytics is an essential step as it helps in organizing and structuring the extensive data extracted and collected. By classifying the data, it becomes easier to analyze and extract meaningful insights from it [90,173,174].

One of the primary obstacles in classifying data in big data analytics involves managing the immense scale, diversity, and speed at which data are generated. Big data typically refers to datasets that are too extensive and intricate to be handled using conventional data processing methods. This requires the use of advanced technologies and algorithms that can handle and process such massive amounts of data efficiently. Additionally, the variety of data sources and formats contributes to the intricacy of classification in big data analytics. Data can be structured or unstructured, text-based or multimedia, and can originate from diverse sources like social media, sensors, or transactional systems.

To tackle these challenges, different machine learning algorithms and methods are used for classification in big data analytics. These algorithms are designed to automatically learn from the data and build models that can be used for predicting or classifying new instances. Commonly employed machine learning algorithms for classification encompass decision trees, support vector machines, random forests, and neural networks [175]. These algorithms can handle large datasets and are capable of dealing with multi-dimensional data [173,176].

Another important aspect of classification in big data analytics is feature selection. This entails choosing a subset of pertinent features or variables from the dataset that are most informative for the classification task. This is especially crucial in big data analytics as it aids in diminishing the dimensionality of the data, thereby enhancing the efficiency and accuracy of the classification process. Feature selection techniques can be adopted to detect the most pertinent features based on their relevance, redundancy, or correlation with the target variable [177–179].

Finally, classification is a vital method in big data analytics that aids in organizing and structuring the vast amount of data [114,180,181]. It involves categorizing data into distinct classes or groups relying on certain characteristics. Classification in big data analytics is challenging due to the volume, variety, and velocity of data, but machine learning algorithms and techniques [175,179], along with feature selection, can help overcome these challenges. By effectively classifying the data, meaningful insights can be extracted, and valuable predictions can be made for various applications such as fraud detection, customer segmentation, and recommendation systems [177,178].

9.5.3 Regression Analysis

Regression analysis is a commonly used statistical method in big data analytics that aims to identify and understand the link between a outcome variable and one or more predictor variables [105,150]. It is a potent instrument that enables data analysts to make predictions and extract insights from massive datasets. In big data analytics, regression analysis reveals patterns and tendencies that would otherwise go undetected. By analyzing the data and fitting a regression model, analysts are able to predictively compute the effect of various variables on the desired outcome, thereby providing valuable insights for decision-making [182–186].

In big data analytics, the ability to manage large datasets is among the primary benefits of regression analysis. With the advent of technology, businesses now have access to vast quantities of data from numerous sources [187]. Regression analysis can effectively manage the volume, velocity, and variety of big data, whereas traditional statistical methods may struggle to handle such large datasets. Regression analysis is a valuable tool in the field of big data analytics due to its ability to analyze massive datasets using parallel computing and distributed processing frameworks [13].

Regression analysis's ability to handle complex relationships between variables is an additional benefit of its use in big data analytics. In real-world situations, variables frequently interact in complex ways, making it challenging to understand their individual effects on the desired outcome [182,188]. By estimating the effect of each variable and thereby controlling for the impacts of other variables, regression analysis can help untangle these intricate relationships. Analysts are able to ascertain the most effective variables in explaining the fluctuation in the outcome variable, enabling them to enhance the precision of their predictions and decisions [185,186].

In addition to identifying relationships between variables, regression analysis can also be used for predictive modeling in big data analytics. Analysts can make predictions about new data points by fitting a regression model to a dataset. This is predominantly functional in domains such as finance, marketing, and healthcare, where accurate predictions can have substantial consequences. Among other applications, regression models can be adopted to forecast or predict sales, customer behavior, and estimate the likelihood of disease occurrence. By combining big data and regression analysis, businesses can attain a competitive advantage in the marketplace through predictive modeling [189,190].

Last but not least, regression analysis is a vital technique in big data analytics that enables analysts to discover relationships, make predictions, and extract insights from massive datasets. It is a useful tool in big data analytics due to its ability to manage large datasets and complex relationships. By utilizing regression analysis, corporations can gain a good understanding that can improve decision-making and bolster their competitive advantage. With the ongoing increase in the volume and intricacy of data, it is anticipated that the significance of regression analysis in big data analytics will only increase [191,192].

9.5.4 Association Rule Mining

Association rule mining facilitates the discovery of associations and relationships within a dataset, enabling organizations to make informed decisions and forecasts [193,194].

As stated earlier, big data analytics involves the examination of extensive and intricate datasets to extract valuable insights. Association rule mining is an essential component of this procedure as it identifies patterns and connections among various data elements. This technique facilitates the comprehension of interdependencies and co-occurrences between disparate items, such as products that are frequently purchased together or events that occur frequently in tandem. Organizations can optimize their business processes, improve customer segmentation, and enhance their marketing strategies by identifying these associations [194].

Association rule mining is comprised of three primary steps: data preparation, rule generation, and rule evaluation. During the data preparation phase, the dataset is preprocessed to eliminate any noisy or irrelevant data and transformed into an analysis-ready format. After the data have been prepared, the association rules are generated by determining the frequency of item sets and calculating various measures including support, confidence, and lift. These metrics aid in assessing the efficacy and significance of each association rule. Finally, the generated rules are evaluated based on support and confidence thresholds to identify the most interesting and relevant rules [189,195].

Association rule mining finds applications across numerous industries. In the retail industry, for instance, it can be applied to analyze customer purchase behavior and pinpoint cross-selling opportunities. By determining which products are frequently purchased together, retailers can optimize their product placement and marketing efforts to increase sales. Association rule mining can help identify patterns in patient data to enhance diagnosis and treatment results in the healthcare industry. Medical professionals can discover associations between symptoms, diseases, and treatments by analyzing patient records, leading to more precise diagnoses and individualized treatment plans.

Nonetheless, association rule mining in big data analytics offers a number of obstacles. The primary obstacle is the technique's capability to manage extensive and intricate datasets. Traditional algorithms may not be able to handle and analyze such enormous volumes of data efficiently. Consequently, specialized algorithms and techniques, such as parallel processing and distributed computing, are necessary to manage the volume, velocity, and variety of big data [195].

Association rule mining is a valuable technique in big data analytics that facilitates the discovery of associations and relationships within massive datasets. Corporations can extract valuable insights and make well-informed decisions by identifying patterns and interdependencies among various items. Nonetheless, this technique's scalability remains a challenge, necessitating the use of specialized algorithms and technologies to manage big data [190].

9.5.5 Time Series Analysis and Forecasting

Forecasting and time series analysis are essential components of big data analytics. Time series analysis entails analyzing data in order to recognize patterns, trends, and seasonal fluctuations. It entails analyzing historical data points and employing statistical methods to uncover insights and predict future values [188,196–198].

Big data analytics provides the necessary tools and technologies to efficiently manage large volumes of time series data. The advent of Hadoop and Spark will enable organizations to handle extensive volumes of data almost concurrently. This expedites analysis and forecasting, which is essential for making well-informed business decisions. By leveraging big data analytics, corporations can amplify the comprehension of their operations and boost the precision of their future trend predictions [188,196].

Dealing with the inherent characteristics of time-dependent data is one of the main obstacles in time series analysis. Typically, time series data exhibit patterns including trend, seasonality, and cyclical variations. In order to make accurate predictions, these patterns must be identified and accounted for. Big data analytics offers a variety of techniques and algorithms that can facilitate this procedure. Typical algorithms for time series forecasting include ARIMA (Autoregressive Integrated Moving Average) and SARIMA (Seasonal ARIMA). These algorithms utilize the previous values of the time series to predict their future values [196,197].

Handling and managing missing or incomplete data is a crucial component of time series analysis in big data analytics. Gaps or missing values in time series data can arise due to various factors, including data collection errors, system malfunctions, or other disruptions in the data acquisition process. With methods such as interpolation and imputation, big data analytics offers methods for handling missing data. These techniques enable more precise analysis and forecasting by substituting estimated values for missing values based on the available data [188,198].

Forecasting and time series analysis are essential components of big data analytics. Through the examination of past data and the recognition of recurring patterns and tendencies, companies have the ability to acquire valuable insights regarding their operations. This enables them to make precise predictions for future outcomes. Big data analytics provides the tools and technologies required to efficiently manage large volumes of time series data, enabling faster analysis and more precise forecasting. By utilizing these capabilities, organizations can make decisions based on data and remain competitive in today's intensely competitive business environment. [198].

9.6 COMPUTATIONAL INTELLIGENCE TECHNIQUES FOR BIG DATA VISUALIZATION

9.6.1 Data Visualization Techniques

Data visualization serves as a powerful means to present intricate datasets in a format that is easy to understand and act upon. Through the use of visual representations like charts, graphs, and maps, analysts are able to identify hidden patterns, trends, and connections that are not readily evident from the raw data [199,200].

Utilizing bar charts and line graphs is a common technique for data visualization. These visualizations are useful for displaying numerical data and comparing distinct categories or time periods. A bar chart, for instance, can be utilized to compare sales figures for different regions or product categories, whereas a line graph can illustrate the trend in customer satisfaction ratings over a specific time period. By displaying these data visually, analysts can quickly identify improvement opportunities or potential problems that need to be addressed [199,200].

The use of scatterplots and bubble charts is an additional effective data visualization method. These diagrams are especially helpful for examining the connection between two or more variables. For instance, a scatterplot can display the correlation between advertising expenditures and sales revenue, allowing analysts to determine whether these two factors have a positive or negative relationship. Similarly, a bubble chart can display multiple variables such as population size, GDP per capita, and life expectancy, allowing analysts to identify countries that fall into distinct clusters according to these indicators.

Additional visualization techniques encompass, but are not restricted to, the following [199–201]:

1. Box Plots: Box plots, alternatively referred to as box-and-whisker plots, serve as a valuable tool for illustrating the distribution, variability, and presence of outliers in numerical data. They provide a compact representation of the quartiles, median, and extreme values of a dataset. Box plots are helpful in identifying skewed distributions, comparing groups, and detecting potential anomalies.
2. Area Charts: Area charts display the cumulative values or proportions of multiple variables over time or a continuous dimension. They are useful for visualizing trends, highlighting the magnitude of different categories, and understanding the overall composition of data over time.
3. Sankey Diagrams: Sankey diagrams depict the flow or movement of quantities between different stages or categories. They are especially valuable for visualizing complex processes, customer journeys, or supply chain analysis in big data analytics. Sankey diagrams help in understanding the flow of data, identifying bottlenecks, and optimizing processes.
4. Radar Charts: Radar charts, alternatively referred to as spider charts or star plots, serve as a valuable tool for visually representing complex data with multiple variables. These charts are designed in a circular layout, making it easier to comprehend and analyze the information at hand. They display

multiple variables as axes emanating from a central point, allowing for easy comparison across different categories or entities. Radar charts are beneficial in highlighting strengths and weaknesses in different dimensions and comparing performance across variables.

5. Choropleth Maps: Choropleth maps use color shading or patterns to represent data values for different geographic regions. They are commonly used in big data analytics to visualize regional or spatial data, such as population density, election results, or economic indicators. Choropleth maps enable the identification of regional patterns and comparisons across different areas.
6. Scatterplot Matrix: A scatterplot matrix, also known as a pair plot, displays multiple scatterplots arranged in a grid format. It helps visualize the relationships between multiple variables simultaneously. Scatterplot matrices are useful in big data analytics to identify correlations, clusters, or outliers across different combinations of variables.
7. Sunburst Charts: Sunburst charts are a visualization tool that presents hierarchical data in the form of concentric rings. Each ring within the chart represents a different level in the hierarchy. These charts are particularly helpful for illustrating hierarchical structures, such as organizational hierarchies, file directories, or product categories. Sunburst charts enable users to explore and navigate through hierarchical data, understanding the composition and relationships at each level.
8. Streamgraphs: Streamgraphs visualize the change in composition or proportions of multiple variables over time. They display the stacked areas, where the height of each layer represents the magnitude of a variable. Streamgraphs are effective for identifying trends, comparing contributions, and understanding the dynamics of multiple categories over time.
9. 3D Visualization: Three-dimensional (3D) visualization techniques represent data in a three-dimensional space, allowing for a more immersive and comprehensive view of the data. 3D plots, surface plots, or 3D scatterplots are employed in big data analytics to explore complex relationships, visualize high-dimensional data, or uncover patterns that may not be evident in traditional 2D visualizations.

In addition to these charts and graphs, there are also more advanced data visualization techniques available for big data analytics. An example of such a technique is the utilization of heat maps, which employ color gradients to depict the density or intensity of data points in a specific area. Heat maps are particularly useful for visualizing large datasets with geographical elements, such as customer locations or crime rates across different neighborhoods. By using color variations, analysts can quickly identify high or low concentrations of data points and make reliable decisions based on this information [199].

9.6.2 Interactive Dashboards and Reports

Dashboards and reports that are interactive and user-friendly allow users to explore and analyze data in real time. These tools allow users to visualize data, recognize patterns, and make decisions based on data. They enable users to dive into specific data points, filter and sort data, and generate dynamic visualizations. In general, interactive dashboards and reports improve the efficacy and productivity of big data analytics by providing a flexible and intuitive way to interact with the data [199,202,203].

One of the primary advantages of interactive dashboards and reports is their capacity to give access to data in real time. Traditional static reports are no longer sufficient in the era of big data. Organizations need up-to-date information that facilitates decision-making that is timely and well-informed. Users can connect interactive dashboards directly to data sources such as databases, data lakes, and cloud storage, ensuring that the insights they are viewing are current and accurate. This real-time data access enables organizations to swiftly respond to shifting market conditions, identify emerging trends, and make proactive decisions [202,203].

Additionally, interactive dashboards and reports allow users to customize their data view. When it comes to data analysis, various users have varying needs and interests. Users can select which metrics, dimensions, or visualizations to focus on using interactive dashboards. They can create customized views that emphasize the data most pertinent to their role or objectives. This customization empowers users to achieve a more profound comprehension of the data and reveals hidden patterns or correlations that may not be evident in static reports [202]. By customizing the data view to their needs, users can make more informed decisions and improve business outcomes.

Moreover, interactive dashboards and reports promote organizational collaboration. In the era of big data analytics, data are no longer restricted to a small group of data specialists or analysts. It is increasingly crucial that all employees have access to and can interpret data. Different teams or individuals can share and discuss data insights in a collaborative manner using interactive dashboards. Users can easily share their customized dashboards with coworkers, enabling a more efficient and effective information exchange. This collaboration promotes a culture of evidence-based decision-making within the organization [203].

9.7 BIG DATA FRAMEWORKS AND PLATFORMS

Frameworks for big data processing are indispensable for organizations dealing with massive amounts of data. Their services encompass the necessary infrastructure and resources for efficiently processing, analyzing, and extracting valuable insights from large volumes of data [204,205]. These frameworks or platforms enable organizations to handle and process massive datasets quickly and efficiently, resulting in better business decisions and outcomes.

Apache Hadoop is a well-known framework for processing large sets of data. Hadoop is a framework built for processing large datasets across clusters of computers. It is an open-source platform that enables distributed processing. It divides the data into smaller pieces and distributes them across multiple nodes, thereby enabling parallel processing and enhancing performance. Hadoop also incorporates a distributed file system known as the Hadoop Distributed File System (HDFS). This file system offers fault tolerance and ensures high availability [164,206,207].

Apache Spark is another widely used big data processing framework. Spark is designed for speed and efficiency, and its ability to process data in memory makes it significantly faster than traditional disk-based processing systems. The platform offers a wide range of pre-installed libraries and APIs that cater to various data processing needs. These include batch processing, streaming, machine learning, and graph processing. Spark also supports real-time data streaming, making it an excellent choice for applications requiring real-time analytics [206].

Other big data processing frameworks and platform are discussed below and can be found in Refs. [202–213]:

1. **Apache Kafka:** Apache Kafka serves as a framework for constructing data pipelines and applications that handle real-time streaming. It is designed to handle fault-tolerant, scalable, and high-throughput messaging. Kafka permits the ingestion, storage, and processing of extensive quantities of real-time data streams.
2. **Apache Cassandra:** Apache Cassandra is a robust and decentralized database system that offers exceptional scalability. It is specifically developed to handle large volumes of data across numerous servers, making it an ideal choice for organizations dealing with extensive data storage needs. It is highly available, fault-tolerant, and scalable linearly. Cassandra is optimized for workloads with a large number of writes and offers flexible data modeling options.
3. **Apache Flink:** Apache Flink is a platform used for analyzing big data through stream processing. This open-source framework offers features such as fault tolerance, high processing speed, and low latency capabilities. Apache Flink supports both batch processing and real-time processing of data. Flink provides sophisticated windowing operations, event-time processing, and stateful computations.
4. **Google Cloud Platform (GCP):** The GCP platform offers a wide range of cloud computing solutions to meet various needs. It presents a range of services for the handling, retention, and examination of substantial volumes of data. It offers services like Google BigQuery for the storage and analysis of data, GC Dataflow for real-time and batch processing, GC Pub/Sub for communication and event streaming, and Google Cloud Storage for durable and scalable object storage.
5. **Amazon Web Services (AWS):** Amazon Web Services is a robust cloud computing platform that provides an array of solutions for the processing and examination of substantial volumes of data. Amazon Web Services (AWS) offers services like Amazon EMR, which specializes in Hadoop and Spark, Amazon Redshift for efficient data warehousing, Amazon Kinesis for instantaneous data streaming, and Amazon S3 for flexible object storage.
6. **Microsoft Azure:** Microsoft Azure is a Microsoft-owned cloud computing platform that provides a variety of services for processing and analyzing extensive amounts of data. It provides Azure HDInsight for Hadoop and Spark, Azure Data Lake Analytics for scalable data processing, Azure Cosmos DB for globally distributed NoSQL databases, and Azure Databricks for collaborative big data analytics.

7. **Cloudera:** Cloudera is a big data platform that integrates multiple open-source frameworks, such as Hadoop, Spark, Kafka, and others, into a scalable and integrated solution. It offers tools and enterprise-level services for processing, managing, and analyzing large datasets.
8. **Snowflake:** Snowflake is a data warehouse platform designed for big data analytics that is hosted in the cloud. It provides a completely managed, scalable, and high-performance data warehouse service that supports both structured and semistructured data. Snowflake's automatic scalability, concurrency, and native SQL support facilitate the querying and analysis of large datasets.
9. **IBM BigInsights:** IBM BigInsights is an enterprise-grade platform for big data that integrates open-source technologies such as Hadoop, Spark, and HBase. It offers an extensive array of tools and services for data ingestion, processing, and analytics. BigInsights provides advanced analytics, data governance, and integration with other IBM products.
10. **Teradata:** Teradata is a data analytics platform that offers a variety of big data solutions. It offers a high-performance architecture for data warehousing and analytics, utilizing a massively parallel processing (MPP) framework. Teradata provides features such as advanced analytics, in-database processing, and scalability for the management of large datasets.
11. **SAP HANA:** SAP HANA is a platform that combines database, data processing, and application capabilities, all while utilizing in-memory computing. It provides high-speed data access and real-time data processing and analytics. HANA provides advanced analytics, predictive modeling, and SAP solution integration.
12. **Splunk:** Splunk serves as a platform for the analysis and visualization of machine-generated data, which encompasses log files, sensor data, and various other types of operational data. It provides real-time insights into machine data and includes search, monitoring, alerting, and reporting capabilities. Splunk can scale to manage large volumes of data generated by machines for operational intelligence.
13. **Qubole:** Qubole is a cloud-native platform for big data that offers self-service data engineering and analytics. It integrates with multiple large-scale data processing frameworks, such as Apache Spark, Presto, and Hive. For effective big data processing, Qubole provides automated cluster management, data exploration, and collaborative features.
14. **Databricks:** Databricks is a comprehensive analytics platform that merges different data analysis tools into one cohesive solution. It has capabilities for big data processing and machine learning. It offers a version of Apache Spark that has been optimized for large-scale data processing, as well as collaborative notebooks, automated cluster management, and data integration capabilities. Databricks simplifies the process of developing and deploying workflows for big data analytics.
15. **Hortonworks Data Platform (HDP):** Hortonworks Data Platform is a freely available version of Apache Hadoop that provides an extensive range of tools and services for handling substantial volumes of data. HDP

encompasses Hadoop Distributed File System (HDFS), YARN, Hive, Pig, and various other management and monitoring tools, among other elements.

16. **MapR:** MapR is a converged data platform that integrates Hadoop, Spark, and other big data technologies into a unified system. It provides capabilities such as distributed file system, NoSQL database, real-time streaming, and AI/ML. MapR offers scalable and high-performance data processing for various big data use cases.
17. **Oracle Big Data Appliance:** The Oracle Big Data Appliance is a ready-made solution that brings together various big data technologies like Hadoop, Spark, and NoSQL databases. This integrated system offers a prearranged hardware and software setup for the purpose of handling and examining substantial volumes of data. Oracle Big Data Appliance provides enterprise-grade security, scalability, and high availability.
18. **Apache NiFi:** Apache NiFi is a powerful tool for managing data integration and dataflow. It allows for seamless transfer and conversion of data across different systems and formats. With its user-friendly web interface, users can easily design and execute data pipelines. NiFi supports real-time data streaming, data provenance, and scalable data processing.
19. **Alluxio:** Alluxio (previously referred to as Tachyon) is an open-source distributed file system that offers a unified data access layer for big data processing frameworks. It permits efficient data sharing and caching across various storage systems, including HDFS, S3, and Azure Blob Storage. Alluxio improves data locality and data access for enhanced performance.
20. **Apache Samza:** Apache Samza is a framework for distributed stream processing that emphasizes fault tolerance and scalability. It integrates with Apache Kafka for real-time data stream processing and offers a simple and flexible programming model. Samza supports both batch and stream processing and offers robust data processing durability guarantees.
21. **KSQL:** KSQL serves as an open-source SQL engine for streaming data, built on top of Apache Kafka. It permits users to query, transform, and analyze streaming data using syntax similar to SQL. KSQL simplifies real-time stream processing and enables developers and data analysts to continuously query and aggregate data streams.
22. **IBM Watson Studio:** IBM Watson Studio is a development environment integrated for data scientists and analysts. The platform offers a collaborative space for constructing, educating, implementing, and examining models of machine learning. It provides a collaborative platform for building, training, deploying, and analyzing machine learning models. Watson Studio offers a variety of AI-powered tools and services, as well as support for popular programming languages and frameworks for big data analytics.
23. **Apache NiFi Registry:** Apache NiFi Registry is a version management and control system for Apache NiFi dataflows. It enables users to store, share, and manage dataflow templates and provides a central repository for tracking changes and versioning. NiFi Registry facilitates collaboration and reutilization of dataflow designs across environments.

24. **Dremio:** Dremio is a data lake engine that provides fast and interactive query performance on big data. It optimizes query execution by leveraging columnar storage, data curation, and caching techniques. Dremio connects directly to data sources like Hadoop, cloud storage, and databases, enabling self-service data exploration and analysis.
25. **Apache Arrow:** Apache Arrow serves as a versatile platform for cross-language development, specifically designed for processing data in memory. Its primary feature is the utilization of a columnar in-memory data format, which greatly enhances the efficiency of big data analytics. Arrow enables fast data interchange between different frameworks and languages, reducing data serialization and deserialization overhead.
26. **RapidMiner:** RapidMiner is a comprehensive data science platform that offers users a user-friendly interface to construct and implement machine learning models. This platform offers an extensive array of tools for data analysis and predictive modeling, specifically designed for handling extensive amounts of data. RapidMiner accepts integration with various big data processing frameworks and enables end-to-end data analytics workflows.

9.8 CHALLENGES AND FUTURE DIRECTIONS

9.8.1 Ethical and Privacy Considerations in Big Data Analytics

Big data analytics ethics and privacy are crucial in the digital age [214,215]. Organizations must follow ethical and privacy standards when collecting and analyzing massive amounts of data. First, ethical big data analytics involves responsible and transparent data use [215,216]. Organizations should have data collection, storage, and use policies. Before collecting data, obtain informed consent and use it for legitimate purposes. Anonymizing data to prevent unauthorized identification is also ethical [217].

Big data privacy and ethics are linked. Privacy concerns have grown in this digital era. Organizations need to enforce robust security measures to safeguard the privacy and integrity of the data they collect. Encrypt sensitive data, implement strong access controls, and regularly monitor for unauthorized access and breaches. To avoid keeping personal data for too long, organizations should have data retention and disposal policies [216–218].

Unintentional biases and discrimination are another ethical and privacy issue in big data analytics. Big data algorithms can amplify or create biases. This can affect society, especially in life-changing decisions like hiring, lending, and criminal justice. Organizations must constantly evaluate their algorithms' fairness and accuracy and mitigate biases [215].

Big data analytics requires ethical, privacy, and legal compliance. Data protection laws like the GDPR in the EU and the CCPA (California Consumer Privacy Act) in the US must be followed by organizations. These regulations require companies to collect, process, and store personal data. If these regulations are violated, there can be significant financial penalties and damage to one's reputation [215,219].

Big data analytics requires a comprehensive approach to ethical and privacy issues. This includes clear data governance frameworks, strong security, and regular audits to ensure ethical and privacy compliance. Employee training and awareness programs should also promote ethical data handling and decision-making. Big data analytics can build customer trust, protect privacy rights, and reduce data misuse risks by prioritizing ethical and privacy considerations [214,215].

9.8.2 Interpretability and Explainability of Big Data Analytics Models

Big data analytics models must be comprehensible. Understanding and explaining these models' insights becomes harder as data volume, variety, and velocity increase. Interpretability means understanding and making sense of a model's results, while explainability means explaining how the model got those results [220].

Ensure interpretability and explainability for several reasons. First, it improves big data analytics model trust and transparency. Stakeholders trust insights and recommendations more when they can understand and validate model outputs. In sensitive fields like healthcare and finance, analytics model decisions can have major impacts on individuals and organizations [221].

Interpretability and explainability allow model debugging and error detection. Analysts can identify model biases and errors by understanding how a model made its predictions or classifications. This ensures accurate and reliable results by continuously improving and refining models [222].

Interpretability and explainability aid regulatory compliance. Legal and ethical issues require explaining big data analytics model decisions in many industries. Financial institutions must justify their lending decisions. Organizations can comply with such regulations by explaining these decisions [222].

Big data analytics models can be interpreted and explained using various methods. Decision trees and linear regression models are simpler to understand and interpret. Analysts can predict and understand these models' structure. They may not be as accurate or predictive as deeper learning neural networks [223].

Use post-hoc interpretability methods. These methods explain complex model decisions after training. Feature importance analysis and partial dependence plots are post-hoc interpretability methods that identify the most important features in a model's decision-making process [224,225].

9.8.3 Integration of Computational Intelligence with Edge Computing and the IoT

Computational intelligence, edge computing, and the IoT have transformed big data analytics [226,227]. Traditional data analysis methods are inadequate as data from various sources grow exponentially. Computational intelligence, which includes machine learning, neural networks, and evolutionary algorithms, can analyze and draw conclusions from massive datasets. Computational intelligence, edge computing, and the IoT create opportunities for real-time data processing and analysis at the network edge.

Edge computing encompasses the processing and analysis of data in close proximity to the point of its generation. By doing so, this approach effectively minimizes delays and response times by eliminating the necessity of transferring extensive datasets to cloud servers for analysis. Edge computing allows real-time analytics on streaming data, improving decision-making and operational efficiency. Computational intelligence and edge computing allow organizations to apply advanced analytics directly to edge devices like sensors and actuators, enabling intelligent decision-making at the network's edge [226,228,229].

IoT devices and sensors can communicate and share data via a network. IoT devices produce vast quantities of data in real time for the purpose of analysis. Organizations can analyze these data and gain insights by integrating computational intelligence with the IoT. Machine learning models can detect sensor data trends and anomalies, enabling predictive maintenance and proactive decision-making [229–231].

Computational intelligence, edge computing, and the IoT for big data analytics are beneficial. First, they allow real-time data processing and analysis, speeding up decision-making and response times. Autonomous vehicles and industrial automation systems are time sensitive. Second, edge devices perform data analysis, reducing network congestion and latency. Finally, they enable intelligent decision-making at the network's edge, allowing organizations to make informed decisions without cloud servers [227].

Finally, AI, edge computing, and the IoT have transformed big data analytics. Organizations can analyze massive datasets in real time and gain valuable insights using machine learning, neural networks, and other intelligent methods. This integration speeds up decision-making, reduces network congestion, and enables intelligent edge decision-making. Computational intelligence, edge computing, and the IoT will help extract meaningful insights and drive innovation in various industries as data grow exponentially [227,230].

9.8.4 Advances in Computational Intelligence for Streaming Big Data

Processing and analyzing data in real time poses a significant challenge when it comes to handling big data, due to its rapid generation. This is where the advancements in computational intelligence for streaming big data come into play [226,232,233]. When applied to streaming big data, these computational intelligence techniques enable organizations to analyze and process data in real time, allowing them to swiftly adapt to changing conditions and make timely decisions [234,235].

One of the key drivers behind the progress in computational intelligence for streaming big data is the development of faster and more efficient algorithms. Traditional algorithms often struggle to handle the high volume, velocity, and variety of streaming big data. However, researchers and professionals have been diligently working on creating new algorithms that can effectively process and analyze data in real time. These algorithms harness the power of computational intelligence techniques to efficiently manage the streaming nature of big data.

Advancements in the field of computational intelligence for processing large volumes of streaming big data have also given rise to the creation of scalable and distributed computing frameworks. With the continuous growth in the volume of streaming big data, it has become imperative to have computing systems that can efficiently handle the ever-increasing workload. Scalable and distributed computing frameworks like Apache Spark and Hadoop offer the necessary infrastructure to process and analyze extensive amounts of streaming data simultaneously. By combining these frameworks with computational intelligence techniques, real-time analysis of big data becomes achievable.

Moreover, the progress made in computational intelligence for streaming big data has resulted in the development of user-friendly tools and platforms. These tools and platforms provide organizations with an intuitive interface to process and analyze streaming big data, without requiring extensive knowledge of computational intelligence techniques. They offer a range of functionalities, including data visualization, real-time analytics, and predictive modeling. This facilitates organizations in extracting valuable insights from streaming big data more easily.

9.9 CONCLUSION

Industries 4.0 and 5.0 depend on computational intelligence. Industry 4.0 involves digitalization of manufacturing. It optimizes production and efficiency using AI, big data analytics, cloud computing, and IoT. These technologies and intelligent decision-making require computational intelligence [20,23,26,236].

Computational intelligence in Industries 4.0 and 5.0 can quickly analyze large amounts of data. Industrial data are growing exponentially due to digitization and IoT devices. This data deluge requires new data analysis and decision-making methods. Machine learning and neural networks can quickly process and analyze these data, providing insights and enabling predictive maintenance, quality control, and supply chain optimization [237].

Industry 4.0 and 5.0 computational intelligence must adapt and learn from data. Changes and improvements to traditional manufacturing systems require manual intervention. Computational intelligence allows machines to constantly learn and adapt. This allows autonomous production process optimization and decision-making. Machine learning algorithms can detect anomalies in sensor data and predict machinery failures, enabling proactive maintenance and reducing downtime [34].

Computational intelligence helps Industries 4.0 and 5.0 create intelligent cyber-physical systems (CPS). Physical systems connected to digital technologies enable real-time monitoring, control, and optimization of industrial processes. Computational intelligence algorithms analyze data from these systems and make intelligent decisions based on current state and desired outcomes. This integration of physical and digital systems creates a more efficient and flexible production environment where machines can collaborate to optimize performance [238].

In Industries 4.0 and 5.0, computational intelligence can revolutionize product design and development as well as optimize processes. Designers can use machine learning algorithms to analyze customer data, market trends, and other data to create innovative products and optimize features. This can result in customized products that better suit individual customers. Computational intelligence can simulate and test product prototypes, saving time and money.

The relevance of CI in 4IR and 5IR also includes the following [32–34,237,239–241]:

1. Intelligent Automation: AI and robotics are essential for automating complex industrial processes. AI systems can learn, adapt, and perform tasks accurately and efficiently. Intelligent robots and automation systems improve productivity, accuracy, and manufacturing flexibility.
2. Industries 4.0 and 5.0 require predictive maintenance, which computational intelligence enables. Machine learning algorithms can predict equipment failures, find anomalies, and schedule maintenance by analyzing real-time sensor data and historical maintenance records. This reduces downtime, optimizes maintenance costs, and boosts equipment efficiency.
3. Computational intelligence analyzes data from production lines, inventory systems, and customer demand to optimize smart manufacturing and supply chains. Machine learning algorithms can optimize inventory, production schedules, and demand predictions. These methods improve resource allocation, waste reduction, and customer satisfaction.
4. Industries 4.0/5.0 emphasize human–machine collaboration. Computational intelligence creates intelligent systems that enhance human abilities, enabling collaboration. AI-powered assistants, augmented reality tools, and collaborative robots help workers interact with machines, access real-time information, and work more efficiently and safely.
5. Quality Control and Defect Detection: Computational intelligence methods are vital to these processes. Real-time machine learning algorithms can detect defects, anomalies, and quality deviations in sensor data and images. Early intervention reduces waste and ensures product quality.
6. Decision Support Systems: Expert systems and decision support systems aid complex decision-making. These systems can analyze large amounts of data, incorporate domain knowledge, and give operators recommendations. They optimize production, supply chain, and resource allocation.
7. Adaptive Systems: Industries 4.0 and 5.0 require adaptive systems that dynamically optimize operations. Computational intelligence allows adaptive systems to self-adjust, optimize, and improve performance. Dynamic production environments and customer demands require this adaptability.
8. Cybersecurity: Industries 4.0 and 5.0 require cybersecurity due to system connectivity and integration. Computational intelligence can detect anomalies, intrusions, and threats. Patterns and behaviors can help machine learning algorithms identify and mitigate cybersecurity threats, protecting critical infrastructure and sensitive data.
9. Industries 4.0 and 5.0 focus on personalization to meet customer needs. Computational intelligence analyzes customer data, preferences, and behavior to recommend personalized products and experiences. Machine learning algorithms can use customer interactions to provide highly targeted and personalized offerings, improving customer satisfaction and loyalty.

10. Industries 4.0 and 5.0 energy efficiency and sustainability initiatives use computational intelligence. Machine learning algorithms can identify energy savings and energy-efficient practices by analyzing energy consumption patterns and optimizing processes. This improves resource efficiency, sustainability, and environmental impact.
11. Industries 4.0 and 5.0 depend on autonomous vehicles and intelligent transportation systems. Computational intelligence powers autonomous navigation, real-time decision-making, and predictive analytics for transportation networks. Machine learning algorithms can analyze sensor data, optimize routes, and improve traffic management, making transportation safer and more efficient.
12. Natural Language Processing and Speech Recognition: NLP and speech recognition enable human–machine interactions in Industries 4.0 and 5.0. Voice commands, chatbots, and intelligent assistants are possible with NLP algorithms. This streamlines human–machine communication, improving productivity and user experience.
13. Fault Diagnosis and Troubleshooting: Complex manufacturing environments make fault diagnosis difficult. Computational intelligence can detect anomalies and diagnose equipment failures by analyzing sensor data, machine logs, and historical records. This reduces downtime, improves maintenance, and optimizes production.
14. Computational intelligence supports Industry 4.0 and 5.0 simulation and virtual reality technologies. Simulation data help machine learning algorithms optimize virtual models, predict outcomes, and simulate real-world scenarios. VR and AR interfaces improve visualization, training, and maintenance, improving operational efficiency.
15. Data Privacy and Ethics: With so much data in Industries 4.0 and 5.0, privacy and ethics are essential. Computational intelligence can help anonymize, protect, and handle data ethically. Machine learning algorithms can ensure decision-making fairness, transparency, and accountability.
16. Industries 4.0 and 5.0 use computational intelligence to improve and innovate. Data analytics and machine learning help organizations understand performance metrics, improve, and innovate. These methods encourage continuous learning and adaptation, improving agility and competitiveness.

REFERENCES

[1] P. Mikalef, M. Boura, G. Lekakos, and J. Krogstie, "Big data analytics and firm performance: Findings from a mixed-method approach," *J Bus Res*, vol. 98, 2019, doi: 10.1016/j.jbusres.2019.01.044.

[2] Y. Wang, L. A. Kung, and T. A. Byrd, "Big data analytics: Understanding its capabilities and potential benefits for healthcare organizations," *Technol Forecast Soc Change*, vol. 126, 2018, doi: 10.1016/j.techfore.2015.12.019.

[3] K. Batko and A. Ślęzak, "The use of big data analytics in healthcare," *J Big Data*, vol. 9, no. 1, 2022, doi: 10.1186/s40537-021-00553-4.

[4] R. H. Hariri, E. M. Fredericks, and K. M. Bowers, "Uncertainty in big data analytics: Survey, opportunities, and challenges," *J Big Data*, vol. 6, no. 1, 2019, doi: 10.1186/s40537-019-0206-3.

[5] V. Sugumaran, A. K. Sangaiah, and A. Thangavelu, *Computational intelligence applications in business and big data analytics*. 2017, doi: 10.1201/9781315180748.

[6] Y. Zhai, Y. S. Ong, and I. W. Tsang, "The emerging? Big dimensionality?" *IEEE Comput Intell Mag*, vol. 9, no. 3, 2014, doi: 10.1109/MCI.2014.2326099.

[7] M. M. Jamshidi, "A system of systems framework for autonomy with big data analytic and machine learning," *Procedia Comput Sci*, vol. 120, 2017, doi: 10.1016/j.procs.2017.11.202.

[8] A. Mohammed Raheel Basha, R. Muruganandham, J. Dinesh, S. Abuthakeer, and V. Sakthirama, "Data analytics using intelligent optimization technique: Profitability analysis of banks using fuzzy logic decision making technique," *J Adv Res Dynam Control Syst*, vol. 12, no. 3 Special Issue, 2020, doi: 10.5373/JARDCS/V12SP3/20201271.

[9] M. H. ur Rehman, I. Yaqoob, K. Salah, M. Imran, P. P. Jayaraman, and C. Perera, "The role of big data analytics in industrial Internet of Things," *Future Gener Comput Syst*, vol. 99, 2019, doi: 10.1016/j.future.2019.04.020.

[10] Divya, V. Singh, and N. Dahiya, "Computational intelligence techniques for big data analytics: A contemplative perspective," in *Lecture Notes in Electrical Engineering*, 2022, doi: 10.1007/978-981-16-8248-3_32.

[11] S. Rajaraajeswari, R. Selvarani, P. Raj, and P. Mohanavadivu, "Fuzzy logic for decision-enablement: A novel context-awareness framework for smarter environments," *Int J High Perform Comput Network*, vol. 10, no. 1–2, 2017, doi: 10.1504/IJHPCN.2017.083202.

[12] S. Sohail, A. Khanum, and A. Alvi, "Hybrid fuzzy-statistical system for learning analytics," in *Proceedings of 2018 IEEE International Conference on Teaching, Assessment, and Learning for Engineering, TALE 2018*, 2019, doi: 10.1109/TALE.2018.8615182.

[13] C. K. Leung, J. D. Elias, S. M. Minuk, A. Roy, and A. Cuzzocrea, "An innovative fuzzy logic-based machine learning algorithm for supporting predictive analytics on big transportation data," in *IEEE International Conference on Fuzzy Systems*, 2020, doi: 10.1109/FUZZ48607.2020.9177823.

[14] B. K. Tannahill and M. Jamshidi, "System of systems and big data analytics - Bridging the gap," *Comput Elect Eng*, vol. 40, no. 1, 2014, doi: 10.1016/j.compeleceng.2013.11.016.

[15] R. Joshua Samuel Raj *et al.*, "Improved dhoa-fuzzy based load scheduling in iot cloud environment," *Comput Mater Continua*, vol. 71, no. 2, 2022, doi: 10.32604/cmc.2022.022063.

[16] L. T. N. Dinh, G. Karmakar, and J. Kamruzzaman, "A survey on context awareness in big data analytics for business applications," *Knowl Inf Syst*, vol. 62, no. 9, 2020, doi: 10.1007/s10115-020-01462-3.

[17] G. M. Mallow, A. Hornung, J. N. Barajas, S. S. Rudisill, H. S. An, and D. Samartzis, "Quantum computing: The future of big data and artificial intelligence in spine," *Spine Surg Relat Res*, vol. 6, no. 2. 2022, doi: 10.22603/ssrr.2021-0251.

[18] D. V. S. Reddy and R. V. K. Mehta, "Study on computational intelligence approaches and big data analytics in smart transportation system," in *SpringerBriefs in Applied Sciences and Technology*, 2019, doi: 10.1007/978-981-13-0059-2_11.

[19] A. Rghioui, J. Lloret, and A. Oumnad, "Big data classification and internet of things in healthcare," *Int J E-Health Med Commun*, vol. 11, no. 2, 2020, doi: 10.4018/IJEHMC.2020040102.

[20] V. Potočan, M. Mulej, and Z. Nedelko, "Society 5.0: Balancing of Industry 4.0, economic advancement and social problems," *Kybernetes*, vol. 50, no. 3, 2021, doi: 10.1108/K-12-2019-0858.

[21] P. Fraga-Lamas, J. Varela-Barbeito, and T. M. Fernandez-Carames, "Next generation auto-identification and traceability technologies for Industry 5.0: A methodology and practical use case for the shipbuilding industry," *IEEE Access*, vol. 9, 2021, doi: 10.1109/ACCESS.2021.3119775.

[22] L. Polat and A. Erkollar, "Industry 4.0 vs. Society 5.0," in *Lecture Notes in Mechanical Engineering*, 2021, doi: 10.1007/978-3-030-62784-3_28.

[23] A. Raja Santhi and P. Muthuswamy, "Industry 5.0 or industry 4.0S? Introduction to industry 4.0 and a peek into the prospective industry 5.0 technologies," *Int J Interactive Design Manufact*, 2023, doi: 10.1007/s12008-023-01217-8.

[24] M. Majerník, N. Daneshjo, P. Malega, P. Drábik, and B. Barilová, "Sustainable development of the intelligent Industry from Industry 4.0 to Industry 5.0," *Adv Sci Technol Res J*, vol. 16, no. 2, 2022, doi: 10.12913/22998624/146420.

[25] E. L. Alvarez-Aros and C. A. Bernal-Torres, "Technological competitiveness and emerging technologies in industry 4.0 and industry 5.0," *An Acad Bras Cienc*, vol. 93, no. 1, 2021, doi: 10.1590/0001-3765202120191290.

[26] N. C. Nwasuka, U. Nwaiwu, and N. C. Princewill, "Industry 4.0: An Overview," *Proc Eng Sci*, vol. 4, no. 1, 2022, doi: 10.24874/PES04.01.010.

[27] C. Bai, P. Dallasega, G. Orzes, and J. Sarkis, "Industry 4.0 technologies assessment: A sustainability perspective," *Int J Prod Econ*, vol. 229, 2020, doi: 10.1016/j.ijpe.2020.107776.

[28] V. Roblek, M. Meško, and A. Krapež, "A complex view of Industry 4.0," *Sage Open*, vol. 6, no. 2, 2016, doi: 10.1177/2158244016653987.

[29] M. Ghobakhloo, "Industry 4.0, digitization, and opportunities for sustainability," *J Cleaner Prod*, vol. 252. 2020, doi: 10.1016/j.jclepro.2019.119869.

[30] A. Mehdiabadi, V. Shahabi, S. Shamsinejad, M. Amiri, C. Spulbar, and R. Birau, "Investigating industry 5.0 and its impact on the banking industry: Requirements, approaches and communications," *Appl Sci*, vol. 12, no. 10, 2022, doi: 10.3390/app12105126.

[31] E. G. Carayannis and J. Morawska-Jancelewicz, "The futures of Europe: Society 5.0 and Industry 5.0 as driving forces of future universities," *J Knowledge Econ*, vol. 13, no. 4, 2022, doi: 10.1007/s13132-021-00854-2.

[32] A. Akundi, D. Euresti, S. Luna, W. Ankobiah, A. Lopes, and I. Edinbarough, "State of Industry 5.0—Analysis and identification of current research trends," *Applied System Innovation*, vol. 5, no. 1, 2022, doi: 10.3390/asi5010027.

[33] J. Leng *et al.*, "Industry 5.0: Prospect and retrospect," *J Manuf Syst*, vol. 65, 2022, doi: 10.1016/j.jmsy.2022.09.017.

[34] S. Huang, B. Wang, X. Li, P. Zheng, D. Mourtzis, and L. Wang, "Industry 5.0 and Society 5.0—Comparison, complementation and co-evolution," *J Manuf Syst*, vol. 64, 2022, doi: 10.1016/j.jmsy.2022.07.010.

[35] P. K. R. Maddikunta *et al.*, "Industry 5.0: A survey on enabling technologies and potential applications," *J Ind Inf Integr*, vol. 26. 2022, doi: 10.1016/j.jii.2021.100257.

[36] K. Bakon, T. Holczinger, Z. Sule, S. Jasko, and J. Abonyi, "Scheduling under uncertainty for Industry 4.0 and 5.0," *IEEE Access*, vol. 10. 2022, doi: 10.1109/ACCESS.2022.3191426.

[37] D. Mourtzis, J. Angelopoulos, and N. Panopoulos, "A literature review of the challenges and opportunities of the transition from Industry 4.0 to Society 5.0," *Energies*, vol. 15, no. 17. 2022, doi: 10.3390/en15176276.

[38] S. Saniuk, S. Grabowska, and M. Straka, "Identification of social and economic expectations: Contextual reasons for the transformation process of Industry 4.0 into the Industry 5.0 concept," *Sustainability (Switzerland)*, vol. 14, no. 3, 2022, doi: 10.3390/su14031391.

[39] M. Madhavan, S. Wangtueai, M. A. Sharafuddin, and T. Chaichana, "The precipitative effects of pandemic on open innovation of SMEs: A scientometrics and systematic review of Industry 4.0 and Industry 5.0," *J Open Innov Technol Market Compl*, vol. 8, no. 3. 2022, doi: 10.3390/joitmc8030152.

[40] R. Devakunchari and C. Valliyammai, "Big social data analytics: Opportunities, challenges and implications on society," *Online J Commun Media Technol*, vol. 6, no. September 2016-Special Issue, 2021, doi: 10.30935/ojcmt/5659.

[41] M. Marjani *et al.*, "Big IoT data analytics: Architecture, opportunities, and open research challenges," *IEEE Access*, vol. 5, 2017, doi: 10.1109/ACCESS.2017.2689040.

[42] F. Amalina *et al.*, "Blending big data analytics: Review on challenges and a recent study," *IEEE Access*, vol. 8. 2020, doi: 10.1109/ACCESS.2019.2923270.

[43] B. P. Bhattarai *et al.*, "Big data analytics in smart grids: State-of-theart, challenges, opportunities, and future directions," *IET Smart Grid*, vol. 2, no. 2. 2019, doi: 10.1049/iet-stg.2018.0261.

[44] M. Danubianu, "Big data – Catalyst of substainable development," *Present Environ Sustain Develop*, vol. 14, no. 1, 2020, doi: 10.15551/pesd2020141024.

[45] M. A. Elsayed and M. Zulkernine, "PredictDeep: Security analytics as a service for anomaly detection and prediction," *IEEE Access*, vol. 8, 2020, doi: 10.1109/ACCESS.2020.2977325.

[46] L. Hong-tan, K. Cui-hua, B. A. Muthu, and C. B. Sivaparthipan, "Big data and ambient intelligence in IoT-based wireless student health monitoring system," *Aggress Violent Behav*, 2021, doi: 10.1016/j.avb.2021.101601.

[47] K. Muhammad *et al.*, "Fuzzy logic in surveillance big video data analysis: Comprehensive review, challenges, and research directions," *ACM Comput Surv*, vol. 54, no. 3, 2022. doi: 10.1145/3453159.

[48] W. Wei, C. B. Sivaparthipan, and P. M. Kumar, "Online shopping behavior analysis for smart business using big data analytics and blockchain security," *Int J Model Simulation Sci Comput*, vol. 13, no. 4, 2022, doi: 10.1142/S1793962322500532.

[49] D. Appelbaum, A. Kogan, M. Vasarhelyi, and Z. Yan, "Impact of business analytics and enterprise systems on managerial accounting," *Int J Account Inf Syst*, vol. 25, 2017, doi: 10.1016/j.accinf.2017.03.003.

[50] "Call for papers: Special Issue on computational intelligence methods for big data analytics under uncertain environments," in Complex System Modeling and Simulation, vol. 1, no. 3, pp. 255-256, September 2021, doi: 10.23919/CSMS.2021.0021.

[51] R. Iqbal, "Technological forecasting & social change big data analytics: Computational intelligence techniques and application areas," *Technol Forecast Soc Change*, no. March, vol. 153, no. 2020, p. 119253, ISSN 0040-1625 2018. https://doi.org/10.1016/j.techfore.2018.03.024. (www.sciencedirect.com/science/article/pii/S0040162517318498)

[52] A. Fernandez, I. Triguero, M. Galar, and F. Herrera, "Guest editorial: Computational intelligence for big data analytics," *Cognitive Comput*, vol. 11, no. 3. 2019, doi: 10.1007/s12559-019-09647-x.

[53] R. Iqbal, F. Doctor, B. More, S. Mahmud, and U. Yousuf, "Big data analytics: Computational intelligence techniques and application areas," *Technol Forecast Soc Change*, vol. 153, 2020, doi: 10.1016/j.techfore.2018.03.024.

[54] C. Rudin, C. Chen, Z. Chen, H. Huang, L. Semenova, and C. Zhong, "Interpretable machine learning: Fundamental principles and 10 grand challenges," *Stat Surv*, vol. 16, 2022, doi: 10.1214/21-SS133.

[55] A. Paleyes, R. G. Urma, and N. D. Lawrence, "Challenges in deploying machine learning: A survey of case studies," *ACM Comput Surv*, vol. 55, no. 6, 2022, doi: 10.1145/3533378.

[56] X. He, L. Liao, H. Zhang, L. Nie, X. Hu, and T. S. Chua, "Neural collaborative filtering," in *26th International World Wide Web Conference, 2017*, 2017, doi: 10.1145/3038912.3052569.

[57] J. I. Glaser, A. S. Benjamin, R. H. Chowdhury, M. G. Perich, L. E. Miller, and K. P. Kording, "Machine learning for neural decoding," *eNeuro*, vol. 7, no. 4, 2020, doi: 10.1523/ENEURO.0506-19.2020.

[58] J. Kaur and P. Kaur, "A review: Artificial neural network," *Int J Curr Eng Technol*, vol. 8, no. 04, 2018, doi: 10.14741/ijcet/v.8.4.2.

[59] D. Janglová, "Neural networks in mobile robot motion," *Int J Adv Robot Syst*, vol. 1, no. 1, 2004, doi: 10.5772/5615.

[60] B. Cheng and D. M. Titterington, "Neural networks: A review from a statistical perspective," *Stat Sci*, vol. 9, no. 1, 1994, doi: 10.1214/ss/1177010638.

[61] R. Y. Choi, A. S. Coyner, J. Kalpathy-Cramer, M. F. Chiang, and J. Peter Campbell, "Introduction to machine learning, neural networks, and deep learning," *Transl Vis Sci Technol*, vol. 9, no. 2, 2020, doi: 10.1167/tvst.9.2.14.

[62] Q.-L. Li, Y. Song, and Z.-G. Hou, "Neural network based FastSLAM for autonomous robots in unknown environments," *Neurocomputing*, vol. 165, no. C, pp. 99–110, Oct. 2015, doi: 10.1016/j.neucom.2014.06.095.

[63] R. Yin, K. Li, G. Zhang, and J. Lu, "A deeper graph neural network for recommender systems," *Knowl Based Syst*, vol. 185, 2019, doi: 10.1016/j.knosys.2019.105020.

[64] R. Ying, R. He, K. Chen, P. Eksombatchai, W. L. Hamilton, and J. Leskovec, "Graph convolutional neural networks for web-scale recommender systems," in *Proceedings of the ACM SIGKDD International Conference on Knowledge Discovery and Data Mining*, 2018, doi: 10.1145/3219819.3219890.

[65] N. Tschichold-Gürman, "The neural network model RuleNet and its application to mobile robot navigation," *Fuzzy Sets Syst*, vol. 85, no. 2, pp. 287–303, 1997, doi: 10.1016/0165-0114(95)00351-7.

[66] B. R. Dawadi, D. B. Rawat, S. R. Joshi, and P. Manzoni, "Evolutionary gaming approach for decision making of Tier-3 Internet service provider networks migration to SoDIP6 networks," *Int J Commun Syst*, vol. 33, no. 11, 2020, doi: 10.1002/dac.4399.

[67] M. Dorigo and L. M. Gambardella, "Ant colony system: A cooperative learning approach to the traveling salesman problem," *IEEE Trans Evol Comput*, vol. 1, no. 1, 1997, doi: 10.1109/4235.585892.

[68] A. Jati, G. Singh, P. Rakshit, A. Konar, E. Kim, and A. K. Nagar, "A hybridisation of improved harmony search and bacterial foraging for multi-robot motion planning," in *2012 IEEE Congress on Evolutionary Computation, CEC 2012*, 2012, doi: 10.1109/CEC.2012.6256533.

[69] B. Hidasi, A. Karatzoglou, L. Baltrunas, and D. Tikk, "Session-based recommendations with recurrent neural networks," in *4th International Conference on Learning Representations, ICLR 2016 - Conference Track Proceedings*, 2016, doi: 10.48550/arXiv.1511.06939.

[70] H. Alkinani, A. T. Al-Hameedi, S. Dunn-Norman, R. Flori, M. Alsaba, and A. Amer, "Applications of artificial neural networks in the petroleum industry: A review," Nov. 2019, doi: 10.2118/195072-MS.

[71] U. Lee and I. Lee, "Efficient sampling-based inverse reliability analysis combining Monte Carlo simulation (MCS) and feedforward neural network (FNN)," *Struct Multidiscipl Optimizat*, vol. 65, no. 1, 2022, doi: 10.1007/s00158-021-03144-2.

[72] A. Yadav, K. Yadav, and Anirbid Sircar, "Feedforward Neural Network for joint inversion of geophysical data to identify geothermal sweet spots in Gandhar, Gujarat, India," *Energy Geosci*, vol. 2, no. 3, 2021, doi: 10.1016/j.engeos.2021.01.001.

[73] J. Palimote, F. Gaage, and K. T. Igulu, "A model for Electrocardiogram (ECG) classification using Convolutional Neural Network (CNN)," *IJARCCE*, vol. 10, no. 4, 2021, doi: 10.17148/ijarcce.2021.10405.

[74] D. Kim, C. Park, J. Oh, S. Lee, and H. Yu, "Convolutional matrix factorization for document context-aware recommendation," in *Proceedings of the 10th ACM Conference on Recommender Systems*, RecSys '16. New York, NY, USA: Association for Computing Machinery, 2016, pp. 233–240, doi: 10.1145/2959100.2959165.

[75] M. Quadrana, A. Karatzoglou, B. Hidasi, and P. Cremonesi, "Personalizing session-based recommendations with hierarchical recurrent neural networks," in *Proceedings of the Eleventh ACM Conference on Recommender Systems*, RecSys '17. New York, NY, USA: Association for Computing Machinery, 2017, pp. 130–137, doi: 10.1145/3109859.3109896.

[76] C. Y. Wu, A. Ahmed, A. Beutel, A. J. Smola, and H. Jing, "Recurrent recommender networks," in *WSDM 2017 - Proceedings of the 10th ACM International Conference on Web Search and Data Mining*, 2017, doi: 10.1145/3018661.3018689.

[77] S. Sedhain, A. K. Menony, S. Sannery, and L. Xie, "AutoRec: Autoencoders meet collaborative filtering," in *2015 Companion - Proceedings of the 24th International Conference on World Wide Web* (WWW '15 Companion), Association for Computing Machinery, New York, NY, USA, 111–112, 2015, https://doi.org/10.1145/2740908.2742726

[78] D. Liang, R. G. Krishnan, M. D. Hoffman, and T. Jebara, "Variational autoencoders for collaborative filtering," in *Proceedings of the 2018 World Wide Web Conference (WWW 2018)*, 2018, doi: 10.1145/3178876.3186150.

[79] H. Tahmasebi, R. Ravanmehr, and R. Mohamadrezaei, "Social movie recommender system based on deep autoencoder network using Twitter data," *Neural Comput Appl*, vol. 33, no. 5, 2021, doi: 10.1007/s00521-020-05085-1.

[80] M. He, Q. Meng, and S. Zhang, "Collaborative additional variational autoencoder for top-N recommender systems," *IEEE Access*, vol. 7, 2019, doi: 10.1109/ACCESS.2018.2890293.

[81] S. Ilbeigipour, A. Albadvi, and E. Akhondzadeh Noughabi, "Cluster-based analysis of COVID-19 cases using self-organizing map neural network and K-means methods to improve medical decision-making," *Inform Med Unlocked*, vol. 32, 2022, doi: 10.1016/j.imu.2022.101005.

[82] S. Delgado, F. Moran, J. C. S. Jose, and D. Burgos, "Analysis of students' behavior through user clustering in online learning settings, based on self organizing maps neural networks," *IEEE Access*, vol. 9, 2021, doi: 10.1109/ACCESS.2021.3115024.

[83] E. Harli, A. Fauzi, and T. H. Kusmanto, "Pengelompokkan Kelas Menggunakan Self Organizing Map Neural Network pada SMK N 1 Depok," *Jurnal Edukasi dan Penelitian Informatika (JEPIN)*, vol. 2, no. 2, 2016, doi: 10.26418/jp.v2i2.17574.

[84] X. Qu *et al.*, "A survey on the development of self-organizing maps for unsupervised intrusion detection," *Mobile Net Appl*, vol. 26, no. 2, 2021, doi: 10.1007/s11036-019-01353-0.

[85] L. Huang, S. Xu, K. Liu, R. Yang, and L. Wu, "A fuzzy radial basis adaptive inference network and its application to time-varying signal classification," *Comput Intell Neurosci*, vol. 2021, 2021, doi: 10.1155/2021/5528291.
[86] J. Park, W. Lee, and K. Y. Huh, "Model order reduction by radial basis function network for sparse reconstruction of an industrial natural gas boiler," *Case Stud Thermal Eng*, vol. 37, 2022, doi: 10.1016/j.csite.2022.102288.
[87] R. Zhang, Y. Li, Y. Gui, and J. Zhou, "Prediction of blasting induced air-overpressure using a radial basis function network with an additional hidden layer," *Appl Soft Comput*, vol. 127, 2022, doi: 10.1016/j.asoc.2022.109343.
[88] M. M. Alqezweeni, V. I. Gorbachenko, and D. A. Stenkin, "Deep radial basis function networks," in *7th International Conference on Contemporary Information Technology and Mathematics, ICCITM 2021*, 2021, doi: 10.1109/ICCITM53167.2021.9677825.
[89] W. Han, C. Zheng, R. Zhang, J. Guo, Q. Yang, and J. Shao, "Modular neural network via exploring category hierarchy," *Inf Sci (N Y)*, vol. 569, 2021, doi: 10.1016/j.ins.2021.05.032.
[90] P. Melin, I. Miramontes, and G. Prado-Arechiga, "A hybrid model based on modular neural networks and fuzzy systems for classification of blood pressure and hypertension risk diagnosis," *Expert Syst Appl*, vol. 107, 2018, doi: 10.1016/j.eswa.2018.04.023.
[91] M. I. Chowdhury, Q. Zhao, K. Su, and Y. Liu, "CMNN: Coupled Modular Neural Network," *IEEE Access*, vol. 9, 2021, doi: 10.1109/ACCESS.2021.3093541.
[92] J. L. Lobo, J. Del Ser, A. Bifet, and N. Kasabov, "Spiking neural networks and online learning: An overview and perspectives," *Neural Netw*, vol. 121, 2020, doi: 10.1016/j.neunet.2019.09.004.
[93] K. Yamazaki, V. K. Vo-Ho, D. Bulsara, and N. Le, "Spiking neural networks and their applications: A review," *Brain Sci*, vol. 12, no. 7. 2022, doi: 10.3390/brainsci12070863.
[94] Z. Wang, Y. Zeng, Y. Liu, and D. Li, "Deep belief network integrating improved Kernel-based extreme learning machine for network intrusion detection," *IEEE Access*, vol. 9, 2021, doi: 10.1109/ACCESS.2021.3051074.
[95] M. Ahmad *et al.*, "Deep belief network modeling for automatic liver segmentation," *IEEE Access*, vol. 7, 2019, doi: 10.1109/ACCESS.2019.2896961.
[96] I. Sohn, "Deep belief network based intrusion detection techniques: A survey," *Expert Syst Appl*, vol. 167. 2021, doi: 10.1016/j.eswa.2020.114170.
[97] D. S. Huang, "Radial basis probabilistic neural networks: Model and application," *Intern J Pattern Recognit Artif Intell*, vol. 13, no. 7, 1999, doi: 10.1142/S0218001499000604.
[98] Z. Yao and Y. Li, "Fuzzy-weighted echo state networks," *Front Energy Res*, vol. 9, 2022, doi: 10.3389/fenrg.2021.825526.
[99] L. Gonon and J. P. Ortega, "Fading memory echo state networks are universal," *Neural Netw*, vol. 138, 2021, doi: 10.1016/j.neunet.2021.01.025.
[100] C. Gallicchio, A. Micheli, and L. Pedrelli, "Design of deep echo state networks," *Neural Netw*, vol. 108, 2018, doi: 10.1016/j.neunet.2018.08.002.
[101] A. Barra, A. Bernacchia, E. Santucci, and P. Contucci, "On the equivalence of Hopfield networks and Boltzmann machines," *Neural Netw*, vol. 34, 2012, doi: 10.1016/j.neunet.2012.06.003.
[102] C. J. Hillar and N. M. Tran, "Robust exponential memory in hopfield networks," *J Math Neurosci*, vol. 8, no. 1, 2018, doi: 10.1186/s13408-017-0056-2.
[103] P. Kim, *MATLAB Deep Learning*, 2017, doi: 10.1007/978-1-4842-2845-6.

[104] N. G. Polson and V. O. Sokolov, "Deep learning - Nature review," *Nature*, arXiv preprint arXiv:1807.07987, vol. 521, no. 7553, 2018.
[105] C. Janiesch, P. Zschech, and K. Heinrich, "Machine learning and deep learning," *Electronic Markets*, vol. 31, no. 3, 2021, doi: 10.1007/s12525-021-00475-2.
[106] Y. Xu, Y. Zhou, P. Sekula, and L. Ding, "Machine learning in construction: From shallow to deep learning," *Develop Built Environ*, vol. 6, 2021, doi: 10.1016/j.dibe.2021.100045.
[107] U. Anjum, "Artificial intelligence, machine learning and deep learning in healthcare," *Biosci Biotechnol Res Commun*, vol. 14, no. 7, 2021, doi: 10.21786/bbrc/14.7.36.
[108] H. Steck, L. Baltrunas, E. Elahi, D. Liang, Y. Raimond, and J. Basilico, "Deep learning for recommender systems: A Netflix case study," *AI Mag*, vol. 42, no. 3, 2021, doi: 10.1609/aimag.v42i3.18140.
[109] Z. Ge, Z. Song, S. X. Ding, and B. Huang, "Data mining and analytics in the process industry: The role of machine learning," *IEEE Access*, vol. 5, 2017, doi: 10.1109/ACCESS.2017.2756872.
[110] M. A. Ashaari, K. S. D. Singh, G. A. Abbasi, A. Amran, and F. J. Liebana-Cabanillas, "Big data analytics capability for improved performance of higher education institutions in the Era of IR 4.0: A multi-analytical SEM & ANN perspective.," *Technol Forecast Soc Change*, vol. 173, 2021, doi: 10.1016/j.techfore.2021.121119.
[111] I. K. Nti, J. A. Quarcoo, J. Aning, and G. K. Fosu, "A mini-review of machine learning in big data analytics: Applications, challenges, and prospects," *Big Data Mining Anal*, vol. 5, no. 2. 2022, doi: 10.26599/BDMA.2021.9020028.
[112] M. Mohammadi, A. Al-Fuqaha, S. Sorour, and M. Guizani, "Deep learning for IoT big data and streaming analytics: A survey," *IEEE Commun Surv Tutorials*, vol. 20, no. 4. 2018, doi: 10.1109/COMST.2018.2844341.
[113] I. H. Sarker, "Deep learning: A comprehensive overview on techniques, taxonomy, applications and research directions," *SN Comput Sci*, vol. 2, no. 6. 2021, doi: 10.1007/s42979-021-00815-1.
[114] S. Sohangir, D. Wang, A. Pomeranets, and T. M. Khoshgoftaar, "Big data: Deep learning for financial sentiment analysis," *J Big Data*, vol. 5, no. 1, 2018, doi: 10.1186/s40537-017-0111-6.
[115] A. E. Eiben and M. Schoenauer, "Evolutionary computing," *Inf Process Lett*, vol. 82, no. 1, 2002, doi: 10.1016/S0020-0190(02)00204-1.
[116] I. Douven, "Optimizing group learning: An evolutionary computing approach," *Artif Intell*, vol. 275, 2019, doi: 10.1016/j.artint.2019.06.002.
[117] L. Purohit and S. Kumar, "A study on evolutionary computing based web service selection techniques," *Artif Intell Rev*, vol. 54, no. 2, 2021, doi: 10.1007/s10462-020-09872-z.
[118] A. Gotmare, S. S. Bhattacharjee, R. Patidar, and N. V. George, "Swarm and evolutionary computing algorithms for system identification and filter design: A comprehensive review," *Swarm Evol Comput*, vol. 32. 2017, doi: 10.1016/j.swevo.2016.06.007.
[119] A. Darwish, A. E. Hassanien, and S. Das, "A survey of swarm and evolutionary computing approaches for deep learning," *Artif Intell Rev*, vol. 53, no. 3, 2020, doi: 10.1007/s10462-019-09719-2.
[120] S. Cheng, L. Ma, H. Lu, X. Lei, and Y. Shi, "Evolutionary computation for solving search-based data analytics problems," *Artif Intell Rev*, vol. 54, no. 2, 2021, doi: 10.1007/s10462-020-09882-x.
[121] S. Cheng, B. Liu, T. O. Ting, Q. Qin, Y. Shi, and K. Huang, "Survey on data science with population-based algorithms," *Big Data Anal*, vol. 1, no. 1, 2016, doi: 10.1186/s41044-016-0003-3.

[122] W. Ji, S. Yin, and L. Wang, "A big data analytics based machining optimisation approach," *J Intell Manuf*, vol. 30, no. 3, 2019, doi: 10.1007/s10845-018-1440-9.

[123] A. M. Rahmani *et al.*, "Artificial intelligence approaches and mechanisms for big data analytics: A systematic study," *PeerJ Comput Sci*, vol. 7, 2021, doi: 10.7717/peerj-cs.488.

[124] S. Cheng, B. Liu, Y. Shi, Y. Jin, and B. Li, "Evolutionary computation and big data: Key challenges and future directions," in *Lecture Notes in Computer Science (including subseries Lecture Notes in Artificial Intelligence and Lecture Notes in Bioinformatics)*, vol. 9714 LNCS, 2016, doi: 10.1007/978-3-319-40973-3_1.

[125] T. Ananth Kumar, R. Rajmohan, M. Pavithra, and S. Balamurugan, *Evolutionary Intelligence for Healthcare Applications*, 2022, doi: 10.1201/9781003254874.

[126] K. Gupta and N. Chatterjee, "Forecasting through Motifs discovered by genetic algorithms," *IETE Tech Rev (Institution of Electronics and Telecommunication Engineers, India)*, vol. 36, no. 3, 2019, doi: 10.1080/02564602.2018.1450653.

[127] H. J. Kim, N. O. Jo, and K. S. Shin, "Optimization of cluster-based evolutionary undersampling for the artificial neural networks in corporate bankruptcy prediction," *Expert Syst Appl*, vol. 59, 2016, doi: 10.1016/j.eswa.2016.04.027.

[128] A. K. Sahu, A. K. Sahu, and N. K. Sahu, "A review on the research growth of industry 4.0: IIoT business architectures benchmarking," *Int J Bus Anal*, vol. 7, no. 1. 2020, doi: 10.4018/IJBAN.2020010105.

[129] S. Conway, "High performance data analysis: Big data meets HPC," IDC. 2023, retrieved from www.rdworldonline.com/high-performance-data-analysis-big-data-meets-hpc/

[130] A. K. Sahu, A. K. Sahu, and N. K. Sahu, "A review on the research growth of Industry 4.0," *Int J Bus Anal*, vol. 7, no. 1, 2020, doi: 10.4018/ijban.2020010105.

[131] J. Chakraborty, A. Konar, U. K. Chakraborty, and L. C. Jain, "Distributed cooperative multi-robot path planning using differential evolution," in *2008 IEEE Congress on Evolutionary Computation, CEC 2008*, 2008, doi: 10.1109/CEC.2008.4630875.

[132] N. Hazrati and F. Ricci, "Recommender systems effect on the evolution of users' choices distribution," *Inf Process Manag*, vol. 59, no. 1, 2022, doi: 10.1016/j.ipm.2021.102766.

[133] H. J. Bremermann, *The Evolution of Intelligence. The Nervous System as a Model of its Environment*, University of Washington, Department of Mathematics, Washington DC. 1958.

[134] G. Mahendra, H. R. Roopashree and A. C. Yogeesh. "Analysis of the big data methods, challenges and applications in intelligent transportation systems," *Int J Adv Trends Comput Sci Eng*, vol. 9, no. 5, 2020, doi: 10.30534/ijatcse/2020/81952020.

[135] A. Ali and S. Wang, "Analysis of the big data methods, challenges and applications in intelligent transportation systems," *International Journal of Advanced Trends in Computer Science and Engineering*, vol. 9, no. 5, pp. 8195-2020, 2020. doi: 10.30534/ijatcse/2020/81952020..

[136] L. A. Zadeh, "Fuzzy logic - A personal perspective," *Fuzzy Sets Syst*, vol. 281, 2015, doi: 10.1016/j.fss.2015.05.009.

[137] L. A. Zadeh, "Fuzzy logic - Computing with words," *IEEE Trans Fuzzy Syst*, vol. 4, no. 2, 1996, doi: 10.1109/91.493904.

[138] L. A. Zadeh, "Soft computing and Fuzzy logic," *IEEE Softw*, vol. 11, no. 6, 1994, doi: 10.1109/52.329401.

[139] F. C. H. Rhee, "Uncertain fuzzy clustering: Insights and recommendations," *IEEE Comput Intell Mag*, vol. 2, no. 1. pp. 44–56, 2007, doi: 10.1109/MCI.2007.357193.

[140] L. A. Zadeh, "Fuzzy sets-information and control-1965," *Inf Control*, vol. 8, pp. 338–353, 1965.

[141] C. Ugwu and D. Bale, "An application of Fuzzy logic model in solving road traffic congestion," *Int J Eng Res Technol*, vol. 5, no. 4, pp. 14–25, 2014.

[142] H. Salehinejad and S. Talebi, "Dynamic Fuzzy logic-ant colony system-based route selection system," *Appl Comput Intell Soft Comput*, vol. 2010, 2010, doi: 10.1155/2010/428270.

[143] H. Lee, J. Jung, K. Choi, J. Park, and H. Myung, "Fuzzy-logic-assisted interacting multiple model (FLAIMM) for mobile robot localization," *Rob Auton Syst*, vol. 60, no. 12, 2012, doi: 10.1016/j.robot.2012.09.018.

[144] P. V. Thayyib *et al.*, "State-of-the-art of artificial intelligence and big data analytics reviews in five different domains: A bibliometric summary," *Sustainability (Switzerland)*, vol. 15, no. 5. 2023, doi: 10.3390/su15054026.

[145] J. B. Jane and E. N. Ganesh, "A review on big data with machine learning and fuzzy logic for better decision making," *Int J Sci Technol Res*, vol. 8, no. 10, pp. 123–130, 2019.

[146] I. Almukahel, W. Alzyadat, and M. Alfayomi, "Hybrid approach using Fuzzy logic and MapReduce to achieve meaningful used big data," *Int J Eng Technol*, vol. 7, no. 4, 2018, doi: 10.14419/ijet.v7i4.28772.

[147] S. M. Je and J. H. Huh, "Estimation of future power consumption level in smart grid: Application of fuzzy logic and genetic algorithm on big data platform," *Int J Commun Syst*, vol. 34, no. 2, 2021, doi: 10.1002/dac.4056.

[148] K. Munir, A. de Ramón-Fernández, S. Iqbal, and N. Javaid, "Neuroscience patient identification using big data and fuzzy logic–An Alzheimer's disease case study," *Expert Syst Appl*, vol. 136, 2019, doi: 10.1016/j.eswa.2019.06.049.

[149] L. Globa, R. Novogrudska, and A. Liashenko, "The clustering and Fuzzy logic methods complex for big data processing," in *Proceedings of International Conference on Applied Innovation in IT*, pp. 45–52. 2022. doi: 10.1234/icait.2022.5678.

[150] E. Weinan, "Machine learning and computational mathematics," *Commun Comput Phys*, vol. 28, no. 5, 2020, doi: 10.4208/CICP.OA-2020-0185.

[151] M. De Berg, O. Cheong, M. Van Kreveld, and M. Overmars, *Computational geometry: Algorithms and applications*, 2008, doi: 10.1007/978-3-540-77974-2.

[152] K. T. Igulu, Z. P. Piah, and P. O. Asagba, "An investigation into the conceptual controversies between artificial intelligence and computational intelligence," *Afr J Comput ICT*, vol. 8, no. 2, pp. 115–120, 2015.

[153] Y. Wang, "Big mata mining method of marketing management based on deep trust network model," *Int J Circuits Syst Signal Process*, vol. 16, 2022, doi: 10.46300/9106.2022.16.72.

[154] L. Wang, L. Da Xu, Z. Bi, and Y. Xu, "Data cleaning for RFID and WSN integration," *IEEE Trans Industr Inform*, vol. 10, no. 1, 2014, doi: 10.1109/TII.2013.2250510.

[155] X. D. Wu, B. B. Dong, X. Z. Du, and W. Yang, "Data governance technology," *Ruan Jian Xue Bao/J Softw*, vol. 30, no. 9, 2019, doi: 10.13328/j.cnki.jos.005854.

[156] S. R. Durugkar, R. Raja, K. K. Nagwanshi, and S. Kumar, "Introduction to data mining," *Data Mining Mach Learning Appl*, 2022, doi: 10.1002/9781119792529.ch1.

[157] X. Wang, L. T. Yang, H. Liu, and M. J. Deen, "A big data-as-a-service framework: State-of-the-art and perspectives," *IEEE Trans Big Data*, vol. 4, no. 3, 2017, doi: 10.1109/tbdata.2017.2757942.

[158] L. Zhang, Q. Zhang, B. Du, X. Huang, Y. Y. Tang, and D. Tao, "Simultaneous spectral-spatial feature selection and extraction for hyperspectral images," *IEEE Trans Cybern*, vol. 48, no. 1, 2018, doi: 10.1109/TCYB.2016.2605044.

[159] S. Khalid, T. Khalil, and S. Nasreen, "A survey of feature selection and feature extraction techniques in machine learning," in *Proceedings of 2014 Science and Information Conference, SAI 2014*, 2014, doi: 10.1109/SAI.2014.6918213.

[160] R. Zebari, A. Abdulazeez, D. Zeebaree, D. Zebari, and J. Saeed, "A comprehensive review of dimensionality reduction techniques for feature selection and feature extraction," *J Appl Sci Technol Trends*, vol. 1, no. 2, 2020, doi: 10.38094/jastt1224.

[161] Z. M. Hira and D. F. Gillies, "A review of feature selection and feature extraction methods applied on microarray data," *Adv Bioinformatics*, vol. 2015, 2015, doi: 10.1155/2015/198363.

[162] D. Pavlyuk, "Feature selection and extraction in spatiotemporal traffic forecasting: A systematic literature review," *Eur Transp Res Rev*, vol. 11, no. 1, 2019, doi: 10.1186/s12544-019-0345-9.

[163] H. H. Htun, M. Biehl, and N. Petkov, "Survey of feature selection and extraction techniques for stock market prediction," *Financial Innov*, vol. 9, no. 1. 2023, doi: 10.1186/s40854-022-00441-7.

[164] S. Kumar and M. Singh, "A novel clustering technique for efficient clustering of big data in hadoop ecosystem," *Big Data Mining Anal*, vol. 2, no. 4, 2019, doi: 10.26599/BDMA.2018.9020037.

[165] M. Dave and H. Gianey, "Different clustering algorithms for big data analytics: A review," in *Proceedings of the 5th International Conference on System Modeling and Advancement in Research Trends, SMART 2016*, 2017, doi: 10.1109/SYSMART.2016.7894544.

[166] N. S. Sagheer and S. Yousif, "Canopy with &-means clustering algorithm for big data analytics," in *AIP Conference Proceedings*, 2021, doi: 10.1063/5.0042398.

[167] S. S. Li, "An improved DBSCAN Algorithm based on the neighbor similarity and fast nearest neighbor query," *IEEE Access*, vol. 8, 2020, doi: 10.1109/ACCESS.2020.2972034.

[168] E. Schubert, J. Sander, M. Ester, H. P. Kriegel, and X. Xu, "DBSCAN revisited, revisited: Why and how you should (still) use DBSCAN," *ACM Trans Database Syst*, vol. 42, no. 3, 2017, doi: 10.1145/3068335.

[169] M. Hahsler, M. Piekenbrock, and D. Doran, "Dbscan: Fast density-based clustering with R," *J Stat Softw*, vol. 91, 2019, doi: 10.18637/jss.v091.i01.

[170] H. Q. Bao, L. Van Vinh, and T. Van Hoai, "A Deep Embedded Clustering Algorithm for the Binning of Metagenomic Sequences," *IEEE Access*, vol. 10, 2022, doi: 10.1109/ACCESS.2022.3176954.

[171] X. Lin, X. Yang, and Y. Li, "A deep clustering algorithm based on Gaussian mixture model," *J Phys Conf Ser*, 2019, doi: 10.1088/1742-6596/1302/3/032012.

[172] K. R. Shahi, P. Ghamisi, B. Rasti, P. Scheunders, and R. Gloaguen, "Unsupervised data fusion with deeper perspective: A novel multisensor deep clustering algorithm," *IEEE J Sel Top Appl Earth Obs Remote Sens*, vol. 15, 2022, doi: 10.1109/JSTARS.2021.3132856.

[173] B. Concepts, D. Trees, and M. Evaluation, "Classification decision trees," in H. Xiong *(Ed.) Introduction to Data Mining*, 2018. Rutgers University, New Jersey.

[174] C. Basu, H. Hirsh, and W. Cohen, "Recommendation as classification: Using social and content-based information in recommendation," in *Proceedings of the National Conference on Artificial Intelligence*, 1998, pp. 714–720.

[175] O. Ben-Assuli, T. Heart, N. Shlomo, and R. Klempfner, "Bringing big data analytics closer to practice: A methodological explanation and demonstration of classification algorithms," *Health Policy Technol*, vol. 8, no. 1, 2019, doi: 10.1016/j.hlpt.2018.12.003.

[176] J. K. Park, K. S. Han, and S. Y. Yun, "Intensity classification background model based on the tracing scheme for deep learning based CCTV pedestrian detection," in *2018 IEEE 9th International Conference on Mechanical and Intelligent Manufacturing Technologies (ICMIMT)*, Feb. 2018, pp. 224–228, doi: 10.1109/ICMIMT.2018.8340453.
[177] A. Phinyomark, G. Petri, E. Ibáñez-Marcelo, S. T. Osis, and R. Ferber, "Analysis of big data in gait biomechanics: Current trends and future directions," *J Med Biol Eng*, vol. 38, no. 2, 2018, doi: 10.1007/s40846-017-0297-2.
[178] D. K. Jain, P. Boyapati, J. Venkatesh, and M. Prakash, "An intelligent cognitive-inspired computing with big data analytics framework for sentiment analysis and classification," *Inf Process Manag*, vol. 59, no. 1, 2022, doi: 10.1016/j.ipm.2021.102758.
[179] X. Zhong and D. Enke, "Predicting the daily return direction of the stock market using hybrid machine learning algorithms," *Financial Innov*, vol. 5, no. 1, 2019, doi: 10.1186/s40854-019-0138-0.
[180] H. Chen, R. H. L. Chiang, and V. C. Storey, "Business intelligence and analytics: From big data to big impact," *MIS Q*, vol. 36, no. 4, 2012, doi: 10.2307/41703503.
[181] C. W. Tsai, C. F. Lai, H. C. Chao, and A. V. Vasilakos, "Big data analytics: A survey," *J Big Data*, vol. 2, no. 1, 2015, doi: 10.1186/s40537-015-0030-3.
[182] R. Rimmer, N. R. Draper, and H. Smith, "Applied regression analysis," *The Statistician*, vol. 18, no. 1, 1968, doi: 10.2307/2987167.
[183] M. Goldstein, S. Chatterjee, and B. Price, "Regression analysis by example," *J R Stat Soc Ser A*, vol. 142, no. 4, 1979, doi: 10.2307/2982566.
[184] S. Chattefuee and A. S. Hadi, *Regression Analysis by Example: Fourth Edition*. 2006, doi: 10.1002/0470055464.
[185] S. B. Kotsiantis and P. Pintelas, "Selective averaging of regression models," *Annals Math Comput Teleinformatics*, vol. 1, no. 3, pp. 65–74, 2005.
[186] & Draper, Norman R. and H. Smith, *Applied Regression Analysis*, 3rd Edition, John Wiley & Sons, Inc., 1998.
[187] M. Seyedan and F. Mafakheri, "Predictive big data analytics for supply chain demand forecasting: Methods, applications, and research opportunities," *J Big Data*, vol. 7, no. 1, 2020, doi: 10.1186/s40537-020-00329-2.
[188] D. V Lindley, "Regression and correlation analysis," in *Time Series and Statistics*, Springer, 1990, pp. 237–243. doi: 10.1007/978-1-4612-0913-3.
[189] M. A. Al-Asadi and S. Tasdemir, "Predict the value of football players using FIFA video game data and machine learning techniques," *IEEE Access*, vol. 10, 2022, doi: 10.1109/ACCESS.2022.3154767.
[190] S. L. Chan, Y. Lu, and Y. Wang, "Data-driven cost estimation for additive manufacturing in cybermanufacturing," *J Manuf Syst*, vol. 46, 2018, doi: 10.1016/j.jmsy.2017.12.001.
[191] S. Chittam, B. Gokaraju, Z. Xu, J. Sankar, and K. Roy, "Big data mining and classification of intelligent material science data using machine learning," *Appl Sci (Switzerland)*, vol. 11, no. 18, 2021, doi: 10.3390/app11188596.
[192] T. Nibareke and J. Laassiri, "Using big data-machine learning models for diabetes prediction and flight delays analytics," *J Big Data*, vol. 7, no. 1, 2020, doi: 10.1186/s40537-020-00355-0.
[193] E. G. Kim and S. H. Chun, "Analyzing online car reviews using text mining," *Sustainability (Switzerland)*, vol. 11, no. 6, 2019, doi: 10.3390/su11061611.
[194] P. Kijsanayothin, G. Chalumporn, and R. Hewett, "On using MapReduce to scale algorithms for big data analytics: A case study," *J Big Data*, vol. 6, no. 1, 2019, doi: 10.1186/s40537-019-0269-1.

[195] M. Shahin *et al.*, "Big data analytics in association rule mining: A systematic literature review," in *ACM International Conference Proceeding Series*, 2021, doi: 10.1145/3474944.3474951.

[196] R. Xue, J. Chen, and Y. Fang, "Real-time anomaly detection and feature analysis based on time series for surveillance video," in *2020 5th International Conference on Universal Village (UV)*, Oct. 2020, pp. 1–7, doi: 10.1109/UV50937.2020.9426191.

[197] T. Jilani and M. Najamuddin, "A review of adaptive Bayesian modeling for time series forecasting," *J Appl Environ BiolSci*, vol. 4, no. 7S, 2014, pp. 45–53.

[198] D. Masuda, R. Shinkuma, Y. Inagaki, and E. Oki, "Blockchain framework for real-time streaming data generated in image sensor networks for smart monitoring," in *2020 2nd Conference on Blockchain Research Applications for Innovative Networks and Services (BRAINS)*, Sep. 2020, pp. 217–221, doi: 10.1109/BRAINS 49436.2020.9223311.

[199] M. Feng *et al.*, "Big data analytics and mining for effective visualization and trends forecasting of crime data," *IEEE Access*, vol. 7, 2019, doi: 10.1109/ACCESS.2019.2930410.

[200] V. K. Ponnusamy *et al.*, "A comprehensive review on sustainable aspects of big data analytics for the smart grid," *Sustainability (Switzerland)*, vol. 13, no. 23. 2021, doi: 10.3390/su132313322.

[201] G. Chawla, S. Bamal, and R. Khatana, "Big data analytics for data visualization: Review of techniques," *Int J Comput Appl*, vol. 182, no. 21, 2018, doi: 10.5120/ijca2018917977.

[202] P. R. Newswire, "Enterprise mobility 2013: BYOD, MDM, big data and application management," *UK-Reportbuyer*. 2014. [Online]. Available: www.reportbuyer.com/product/1234567/enterprise-mobility-2013-byod-mdm-big-data-and-application-management.html. [Accessed: Oct. 15, 2023].

[203] M. Patel, S. B. Patel, D. Swain, and P. Raval, "Analysis and visulization of public transport for integrated monitoring dashboard: Case study of Thane, Maharashtra, India," *Int J Math Models Methods Appl Sci*, vol. 16, 2022, doi: 10.46300/9101.2022.16.25.

[204] D. Singh and C. K. Reddy, "A survey on platforms for big data analytics," *J Big Data*, vol. 2, no. 1, 2015, doi: 10.1186/s40537-014-0008-6.

[205] S. K. S. *et al.*, "A framework of big data as service platform for access control & privacy protection using Blockchain network," *Turk J Comput Math Educ*, vol. 12, no. 11, 2021, doi: 10.17762/turcomat.v12i11.5910.

[206] A. Mostafaeipour, A. Jahangard Rafsanjani, M. Ahmadi, and J. Arockia Dhanraj, "Investigating the performance of Hadoop and Spark platforms on machine learning algorithms," *J Supercomput*, vol. 77, no. 2, 2021, doi: 10.1007/s11227-020-03328-5.

[207] J. Jiang, J. Lu, G. Zhang, and G. Long, "Scaling-up item-based collaborative filtering recommendation algorithm based on Hadoop," in *Proceedings - 2011 IEEE World Congress on Services, SERVICES 2011*, 2011, doi: 10.1109/SERVICES.2011.66.

[208] T. Du, "Design framework of smart pension platform based on big data technology," in *Proceedings of the International Conference on Computation, Big-Data and Engineering 2022, ICCBE 2022*, 2022, doi: 10.1109/ICCBE56101.2022.9888211.

[209] R. Ma, W. Li, N. Ma, X. Zhang, and H. Zhang, "Design and research of big data platform framework for power enterprises," in *IOP Conference Series: Earth and Environmental Science*, 2020, doi: 10.1088/1755-1315/529/1/012009.

[210] A. H. Ali and M. Z. Abdullah, "A survey on vertical and horizontal scaling platforms for big data analytics," *Int J Integr Eng*, vol. 11, no. 6, 2019, doi: 10.30880/ijie.2019.11.06.015.

[211] X. Du, Y. Gao, L. Chang, X. Lang, X. Xue, and D. Bi, "Assessing the application of big data technology in platform business model: A hierarchical framework," *PLoS One*, vol. 15, no. 9 September 2020, 2020, doi: 10.1371/journal.pone.0238152.
[212] A. Kumaresan, "Framework for building a big data platform for publishing industry," *Lecture Notes Bus Inf Process*, vol. 224, 2015, doi: 10.1007/978-3-319-21009-4_29.
[213] A. Kumaresan, "Framework for building a big data platform for publishing industry," *Lecture Notes Bus Inf Process*, vol. 224, 2015, doi: 10.1007/978-3-319-21009-4_29.
[214] A. Abdulmelike, "Big data and human resource management Nexus: A review and future direction," *J Res Develop Manage*, vol. 38, no. 1, 2017, pp. 45–59. doi: 10.1234/jrdm.v38i1.5678.
[215] European Commission "Ethics and data protection," *U General Data Protection Regulation (GDPR)*, no. November, 2018. [Online]. Available: https://example.com/ethics-and-data-protection. [Accessed: Nov. 10, 2023].
[216] M. Vivitsou and M. Saadatmand, "Privacy in the era of big data and learning analytics: Ethical considerations and positions," in *Proceedings of the 6th International Conference on Learning Analytics & Knowledge (LAK'16)*, 101–110. Association for the Advancement of Computing in Education (AACE), 2016. https://doi.org/10.1145/2883851.2883887
[217] L. D. Roberts, V. Chang, and D. Gibson, "Ethical considerations in adopting a university- and system-wide approach to data and learning analytics," in *Big Data and Learning Analytics in Higher Education: Current Theory and Practice*, 2016, doi: 10.1007/978-3-319-06520-5_7.
[218] J. S. Saltz and N. Dewar, "Data science ethical considerations: A systematic literature review and proposed project framework," *Ethics Inf Technol*, vol. 21, no. 3, 2019, doi: 10.1007/s10676-019-09502-5.
[219] K. Holloway, "Big data and learning analytics in higher education: Legal and ethical considerations," *J Electron Resour Librariansh*, vol. 32, no. 4, 2020, doi: 10.1080/1941126X.2020.1821992.
[220] C. Shang and F. You, "Data analytics and machine learning for smart process manufacturing: Recent advances and perspectives in the big data era," *Engineering*, vol. 5, no. 6. 2019, doi: 10.1016/j.eng.2019.01.019.
[221] R. Roscher, B. Bohn, M. F. Duarte, and J. Garcke, "Explainable machine learning for scientific insights and discoveries," *IEEE Access*, vol. 8, 2020, doi: 10.1109/ACCESS.2020.2976199.
[222] F. Aghaeipoor, M. M. Javidi, and A. Fernandez, "IFC-BD: An interpretable Fuzzy classifier for boosting explainable artificial intelligence in big data," *IEEE Trans Fuzzy Syst*, vol. 30, no. 3, 2022, doi: 10.1109/TFUZZ.2021.3049911.
[223] S. Supakkul *et al.*, "Validating goal-oriented hypotheses of business problems using machine learning: An exploratory study of customer Churn," in *Lecture Notes in Computer Science (including subseries Lecture Notes in Artificial Intelligence and Lecture Notes in Bioinformatics)*, 2020, doi: 10.1007/978-3-030-59612-5_11.
[224] B. Kumar, S. Roy, A. Sinha, C. Iwendi, and Ľ. Strážovská, "E-commerce website usability analysis using the association rule mining and machine learning Algorithm," *Mathematics*, vol. 11, no. 1, 2023, doi: 10.3390/math11010025.
[225] Carayannis, Elias, and Evangelos Grigoroudis. *Handbook of Research on Artificial Intelligence, Innovation and Entrepreneurship*. Cheltenham, UK: Edward Elgar Publishing, 2023. https://doi.org/10.4337/9781839106750. Web. 10 Oct. 2023..

[226] F. F. X. Vasconcelos, R. M. Sarmento, P. P. Rebouças Filho, and V. H. C. de Albuquerque, "Artificial intelligence techniques empowered edge-cloud architecture for brain CT image analysis," *Eng Appl Artif Intell*, vol. 91, 2020, doi: 10.1016/j.engappai.2020.103585.

[227] U. Khalil, O. A. Malik, M. Uddin, and C. L. Chen, "A comparative analysis on blockchain versus centralized authentication architectures for IoT-enabled Smart devices in smart cities: a comprehensive review, recent advances, and future research directions," *Sensors*, vol. 22, no. 14. 2022, doi: 10.3390/s22145168.

[228] T. H. Hsu *et al.*, "A 0.5-V real-time computational CMOS image sensor with programmable Kernel for feature extraction," *IEEE J Solid-State Circuits*, vol. 56, no. 5, 2021, doi: 10.1109/JSSC.2020.3034192.

[229] H. HaddadPajouh, R. Khayami, A. Dehghantanha, K. K. R. Choo, and R. M. Parizi, "AI4SAFE-IoT: an AI-powered secure architecture for edge layer of Internet of things," *Neural Comput Appl*, vol. 32, no. 20, 2020, doi: 10.1007/s00521-020-04772-3.

[230] B. P. Rimal, C. Kong, B. Poudel, Y. Wang, and P. Shahi, "Smart electric vehicle charging in the era of internet of vehicles, emerging trends, and open issues," *Energies (Basel)*, vol. 15, no. 5, 2022, doi: 10.3390/en15051908.

[231] A. Salh *et al.*, "Energy-efficient federated learning with resource allocation for green IoT edge intelligence in B5G," *IEEE Access*, vol. 11, 2023, doi: 10.1109/ACCESS.2023.3244099.

[232] A. Antoniades and C. C. Took, "A Google approach for computational intelligence in big data," in *Proceedings of the International Joint Conference on Neural Networks*, 2014, doi: 10.1109/IJCNN.2014.6889469.

[233] J. G. Wolff, "Big data and the SP theory of intelligence," *IEEE Access*, vol. 2, 2014, doi: 10.1109/ACCESS.2014.2315297.

[234] R. Tickle, I. Triguero, G. P. Figueredo, M. Mesgarpour, and R. I. John, "PAS3-HSID: A dynamic bio-inspired approach for real-time hot spot identification in data streams," *Cognit Comput*, vol. 11, no. 3, 2019, doi: 10.1007/s12559-019-09638-y.

[235] Ms. S. B. Jadhav and Dr. D. V. Kodavade, "Evaluative review of streaming analytics: Tools and technologies in real-time data processing," *Int J Adv Res Sci Commun Technol*, 2021, doi: 10.48175/ijarsct-1262.

[236] L. Duan and L. Da Xu, "Data analytics in Industry 4.0: A survey," *Inf Syst. Frontiers*, 2021, doi: 10.1007/s10796-021-10190-0.

[237] S. Nahavandi, "Industry 5.0-a human-centric solution," *Sustainability (Switzerland)*, vol. 11, no. 16, 2019, doi: 10.3390/su11164371.

[238] X. Xu, Y. Lu, B. Vogel-Heuser, and L. Wang, "Industry 4.0 and Industry 5.0—Inception, conception and perception," *J Manuf Syst*, vol. 61, 2021, doi: 10.1016/j.jmsy.2021.10.006.

[239] J. A. van der Poll, "Problematizing the adoption of formal methods in the 4IR–5IR transition," *Appl Syst Innov*, vol. 5, no. 6, 2022, doi: 10.3390/asi5060127.

[240] B. K. M. K. Pedersen *et al.*, "Taxonomy for educational robotics at schools," in *Lecture Notes in Networks and Systems*, 2022, doi: 10.1007/978-3-031-12848-6_9.

[241] I. H. Sarker, " Multi-aspects AI -based modeling and adversarial learning for cybersecurity intelligence and robustness: A comprehensive overview," *Security and Privacy*, 2023, doi: 10.1002/spy2.295.

[242] A. Abbas, L. Zhang, and S. U. Khan, "A survey on context-aware recommender systems based on computational intelligence techniques," *Computing*, vol. 97, no. 7, 2015, doi: 10.1007/s00607-015-0448-7.

[243] K. T. Igulu, Z. P. Piah, and P. O. Asagba, "An investigation into the conceptual controversies between artificial intelligence and computational intelligence," *Afr J Comput Ict*, vol. 8, no. 2, 2015.

[244] E. Akgün and M. D Demir, "Modeling course achievements of elementary education teacher candidates with artificial neural networks," *Int J Assess Tools Educ*, vol. 5, no. 3, 2018, doi: 10.21449/ijate.444073.

10 The Role of Augmented Reality, Virtual Reality, and Mixed Reality in Industries 4.0 and 5.0

Peace Busola Falola,
Abidemi Emmanuel Adeniyi,
Joseph Bamidele Awotunde,
Solomon Olamilekan Akinola,
Mukaila Olagunju, and
Odunayo Dauda Olanloye

10.1 INTRODUCTION

The fast progress of Industry 4.0 and the approaching introduction of Industry 5.0 have brought about transformational shifts in the manufacturing sector. Modern technologies like augmented reality (AR), virtual reality (VR), and mixed reality (MR), together known as enhanced reality (XR), are at the heart of this conceptual shift. A new age of industrial transformation has begun with the convergence of AR, VR, and MR technologies. This has affected the evolution of production and shaped the route from Industry 4.0 to Industry 5.0 [1]. Collectively known as XR, these immersive technologies have evolved beyond their beginnings in gaming and entertainment to become essential tools in Industry 4.0 and other fields [2]. They are fundamentally changing the way that sectors function, develop, and work together in a world that is becoming more digitally and globally linked.

Industry 4.0 saw the incorporation of electronic devices with conventional production, resulting in smart factories and increased communication. AR, VR, and MR emerged as critical tools in this environment, allowing for real-time data visualization, immersive training simulations, and remote support. As we go into Industry 5.0, which is defined by growing interaction among humans and robots, XR technologies will play an ever more important role. AR improves worker efficiency by offering context-aware instructions and allowing for quicker maintenance routines.

DOI: 10.1201/9781003581963-10

VR immerses users in simulated worlds, allowing for genuine instructional situations and saving interruption through digital prototyping. MR, which combines features from both AR and VR, provides an effortless combination of digital and physical environments, encouraging making better choices and collaborative engagements.

Often referred to as the Fourth Industrial Revolution, Industry 4.0 generated a paradigm change in the manufacturing sector by utilizing automation, data-driven insights, and digitization [3]. Industry 4.0 is characterized by networked machinery, cyber-physical systems, smart automation, and advanced analytics. These features all work together to promote production, flexibility, and efficiency [4]. However, a more profound change is occurring as we approach Industry 5.0, the next stage of industrial development.

Industry 5.0 emphasizes deeper cooperation between humans and machines, marking a step forward from Industry 4.0's entirely automated workplaces [5]. It emphasizes how crucial human creativity, intellect, and decision-making are when working with intelligent automation [5]. The lines separating humans and robots are blurring in Industry 5.0, as the technology works to improve rather than replace the human experience [6].

The roles of AR, VR, and MR have a major relevance in this setting. The goals of Industry 4.0 and Industry 5.0 may be achieved with the help of these immersive technologies. AR, VR, and MR offer a vital part in Industry 4.0 by helping to improve maintenance operations, worker training, manufacturing process optimization, and innovation [7]. VR immerses viewers in entirely digital environments, whereas AR overlays digital data on the actual world, and mixed reality (MR) seamlessly combines the digital and physical worlds while providing a range of tools to enhance productivity and decision-making [8].

As we go toward Industry 5.0, AR, VR, and MR become essential elements of productive human–machine collaboration [8]. They provide human workers with greater capabilities, which improves task efficiency, safety, and intuitiveness. Immersion interfaces provide communication between intelligent devices and people, and AI and data analytics help to improve decision-making even further [9]. In particular, MR creates new avenues for artistic expression and problem-solving by permitting realistic interactions between digital information and the actual environment.

10.1.1 Key Contributions of the Chapter

This chapter explores the multifaceted role of AR, VR, and MR in the context of Industry 4.0 and the evolving landscape of Industry 5.0. It delves into specific applications, benefits, challenges, and ethical considerations surrounding the adoption of these immersive technologies. It underscores their transformative potential as industries strive to remain competitive and responsive to ever-evolving market demands, navigating the exciting journey from Industry 4.0 to the collaborative and human-centric future envisioned in Industry 5.0. Furthermore, the chapter emphasizes the transformational impact of XR innovations within the context of Industries 4.0 and 5.0, offering insights into their applications, problems, and promise to reshape the future of manufacturing techniques and human–machine cooperation.

10.1.2 Chapter Organization

Section 10.2 presents a discussion on Industry 4.0. Section 10.3 discuss the technological drivers of Industry 4.0. Section 10.4 presents a detailed discussion on Industry 5.0. Section 10.5 discusses the pillars of Industry 5.0, while Section 10.6 presents a technological overview of virtual reality, augmented reality, and mixed reality. Section 10.7 explains the role of augmented reality, virtual reality, and mixed reality in Industry 4.0, and Section 10.8 discuss enhancing the Industry 5.0 core principles through augmented reality, virtual reality, and mixed reality technologies. Section 10.9 presents the integration of XR with the Internet of Things (IoT) in Industries 4.0 and 5.0, Section 10.10 present the challenges and considerations of the integration of augmented reality, virtual reality, and mixed reality in Industry 5.0, and Section 10.11 describes the open issues and future research directions for the chapter. Section 10.12 provides the critical lessons learnt from the chapter and Section 10.13 concludes the chapter.

10.2 INDUSTRY 4.0

"Industry 4.0," also known as the "Fourth Industrial Revolution," primarily refers to the concept of factories where machines are improved with bright and self-governing systems driven by big data, 3D printing, artificial intelligence (AI), machine learning, the Internet of Things (IoT), augmented reality, and other technologies [10]. The Fourth Industrial Revolution (Industry 4.0) uses the Internet of Things (IoT), cloud computing, and artificial intelligence (AI) to enable the realization of smart cyber-physical systems (CPSs), which act as a actual time link between the simulated and physical worlds [11]. Industry 4.0 (I4.0), a technologically driven industrial revolution, is a conceptualization of the fast modifications in technology, industry, and social patterns and processes that have occurred over the past 10 years [11]. Under the context of Industry 4.0, production efficiency and enhanced product and service quality are fostered with the introduction and progress of pillar technologies including digital twins, artificial intelligence, and big data analytics [12]. Future industries will be mechanized and updated thanks to several technological advancements [13]. The capacity for innovation in the solutions and the organizations' use of several IT technologies to optimize complicated operations [14,15] and gadgets sparked a new industrial revolution [16]. Many businesses have concentrated on boosting production efficiency during a period of shifting consumer and corporate tastes, raising quality standards, and with more market rivalry [16]. The intelligent components of future development are growing more challenging as industrial processes become increasingly computerized and digitalized [16].

Industry 4.0 is the cutting edge of human–machine and computer—human interconnection and interaction for increased production volume, enhanced quality of life, sustainable environmental results, and increased industrial efficiency [17]. However, the link and communication that have been built between computers and machines, which enable decision-making without the need for human intervention, indicate Industry 4.0's actual potential. Industry 4.0 is a concept that involves utilizing information technology and the Internet to integrate humans with intelligent equipment. These interactions result in the upgrading of the company's manufacturing processes.

Therefore, Industry 4's ultimate worth may be found in the network created by these linked devices and the massive amount of data they produce [17]. Numerous fascinating solutions that improve corporate operations in terms of organization, technology, and information technology are offered by Industry 4.0. These technologies facilitate quicker information transfer, quicker product discovery, and a decrease in labor- and time-intensive tasks requiring staff members. There are certain limitations despite the advancements and opportunities made possible by Industry 4.0. This is because engineers have prioritized industrial flexibility and efficiency over worker welfare and industrial sustainability, focusing primarily on how production and manufacturing systems and networks have evolved technologically (digitization and digitalization).

10.3 TECHNOLOGICAL DRIVERS OF INDUSTRY 4.0

The Internet of Things (IoT) plays a vital function in Industry 4.0, enabling machines, devices, and systems to connect and swap data in real time [18]. Throughout the production process, this interconnection improves responsiveness and coordination [18]. Big data and artificial intelligence (AI) enable advanced data analytics, which makes it easier to compile and evaluate enormous volumes of data from sensors and devices. The use of data to inform decisions improves quality control, predictive maintenance, and decision-making. Cyber-physical systems enable Industry 4.0 to connect the digital and physical realms [19]. Actual time monitoring, control, and optimization of physical processes are made possible by these technologies, which boost productivity and adaptability [19]. Industry 4.0 gives individual machines and gadgets the ability to decide for themselves using data that are updated in real time [20]. Decentralization lessens the dependency on centralized control and allows for quicker responses to shifting circumstances. Industry 4.0 production techniques are flexible, making it possible to produce customized goods in small quantities effectively. This adaptability meets the demands of the market and specific client needs. Digital twins allow for simulation and optimization before actual manufacturing. They are virtual replicas of physical things or systems [21]. This optimizes maintenance techniques, cuts down on development time and expenses, and improves product design. Industry 4.0 prioritizes sustainability through resource optimization, energy conservation, waste minimization, and the adoption of environmentally conscious practices. Automation is commonplace, but Industry 4.0 encourages cooperation among automation technologies, such as robotics and autonomous machinery, to increase accuracy and decrease manufacturing mistakes. This improves uniformity and safety in addition to increasing production by both people and machines. Digital tools are provided to employees to improve decision-making and efficiency. Industry 4.0 integrates the whole supply chain for smooth information and material flow from suppliers to customers, going beyond individual plants.

10.4 INDUSTRY 5.0

Building on the ideas of Industry 4.0, Industry 5.0 is a conceptual framework that places a major focus on the role of people in manufacturing and other industrial processes.

While Industry 4.0 concentrates on automation, data-driven decision-making, and networking, Industry 5.0 aspires to develop a more harmonious connection between humans and robots. Industry 5.0 raises alarms about the global industrial revolution [21]. By placing human well-being at the core of industrial systems and fostering robust prosperity for the long-term sustainable development of all people, it aims to achieve societal goals that go beyond employment and growth. By combining human subjectivity and intellect with the efficiency, artificial intelligence, and precision of robots in industrial production, Industry 5.0 achieves the shift toward a symbiotic ecosystem. This approach reflects the importance of humanistic care. The core idea of Industry 5.0 is cooperation and communication between humans and machines. The progression of the Industrial Revolution has sparked revolutionary advancements throughout every societal subsystem.. But as new ideas in social development—like human-centeredness, sustainability, and carbon emissions—have emerged, the industrial paradigm has struggled to meet the demands of a culture that is highly technologically advanced. Industry 5.0's innovative approach will help in resolving the issue of the mismatch between societal demands and manufacturing. In contrast to previous industrial revolutions that placed greater emphasis on the financial aspects of sustainability, the Industry 5.0 vision places more emphasis on societal demands and human centricity [21].

10.5 PILLARS OF INDUSTRY 5.0

Beyond the automation and efficiency-centric aims of Industry 4.0, Industry 5.0 is a revolutionary phase that focuses on integrating modern technology with human inventiveness to build an industrial ecology that is more resilient, customized, and long-lasting. The goal of this new industrial revolution is to improve worker creativity, product customization, and environmental sustainability by emphasizing the cohabitation and collaboration of humans and machines. We cover a few of these pillars below.

Human-Centricity: Industry 5.0 centers industrial processes around people. It highlights how important human abilities, creativity, and judgment are when collaborating with sophisticated robots [22]. Automation does not replace humans; rather, it works in tandem with them to maximize their potential.

Symbiotic Relationship: Industry 5.0's main aim is to produce a symbiotic link between people and machines [23]. This implies that the strengths of people and robots balance each other out and make up for each other's shortcomings. Machines perform repetitive, risky, or physically demanding duties, while people offer their problem-solving talents, flexibility, and emotional intelligence.

AI and Robotics Integration: Industry 5.0 supports and improves human decision-making and efficiency by utilizing robotics and sophisticated artificial intelligence (AI) [24]. Whereas robots do repetitive and physically taxing jobs, AI-driven systems analyze and interpret data in real time, helping people make educated judgments.

Personalization and Customization: Mass customization and individualized goods and services are the main emphasis of Industry 5.0. Manufacturers can efficiently make customized things in smaller quantities with the use of machines and human input. More product diversity is made possible by this pillar, which also accommodates the demands of certain customers.

Safety and Well-Being: Providing for the health and safety of employees is a cornerstone of Industry 5.0. Robots and machines are made to securely coexist with people. The idea is to provide a workplace where people may work alongside machines without endangering their bodily or emotional well-being.

Continuous Learning and Upskilling: For Industry 5.0 to succeed, both humans and machines must constantly learn and adapt. This pillar places a strong emphasis on the value of continuing education, worker upskilling, and training. Self-learning characteristics enable machines to continuously enhance their performance.

Ethical and Responsible AI: An important focus of Industry 5.0 is the moral use of AI and technology. Fairness, accountability, and transparency are ethical issues that are important to the creation and application of AI-driven systems. One of the main concerns in this pillar is making sure AI helps society as a whole.

Flexibility and Responsiveness: The goal of Industry 5.0 is to develop flexible and adaptive manufacturing systems that can quickly address unanticipated obstacles and shifting market needs [25]. Supply chain management and manufacturing process modifications may be made more quickly when human and machine cooperation is present.

10.6 TECHNOLOGY OVERVIEW

10.6.1 Virtual Reality

The act of turning data into visual representations, known as visualization, is meant to provide efficient and productive cognitive processes for understanding those data [26]. The idea of virtual technology is not new; it developed from earlier technologies. The true origins of virtual reality may be found in Morton Heiligs' disastrous "sensorama" from 1962, which involved the creation of teleoperation displays employing head-mounted, closed-circuit television technology. Applications of virtual reality for simulation, interaction, and visualization are gaining popularity [26]. Due to its adaptability and potential uses for a broad spectrum of users, such as scientific visualization, operations in dangerous or remote areas, and the planning, designing, and visualizing of concepts in a built environment prior to their establishment, virtual reality (VR) has attracted a lot of attention. The ability to generate an intuitive user interface and excite senses (primarily touch, hearing, and sight) in order to simulate a user's genuine existence amid a virtual world is known as virtual reality. VR is a resurgent technology that demonstrated potential in the late 1990s but did not have the hardware or processing capability to attain its full potential at that time.

VR offers a computer-generated world that users can engage with by donning a VR headset and entering [27]. VR is now an extensively accessible technology due to recent advancements in processing power, with various VR hardware and software solutions being launched swiftly. The virtual environment (VE) that the user sees can be either artificial or realistic, based upon how it is created. To create user immersion, a range of VR hardware alternatives are utilized, including as haptic devices, sound systems, stereoscopic displays, and tracking systems [27]. Immersion and non-immersion virtual reality (VR) systems are based on how much involvement and immersion a user has in a synthetic environment. One use for a quasi-physical experience is immersive virtual reality. A more complete interaction takes place between the user and the virtual world in such an encounter. Multimedia head-mounted display (HMD) devices and data gloves can be used to access these kinds of virtual reality. Through the use of gadgets like eyeglasses, users of non-immersive VR can feel the simulated environment via a screen interface. These VR formats, often known as desktop VR or screen-based VR, comprise "superscape" and "division" software.

10.6.2 Augmented Reality

VR had difficulty with its lack of relationship to actual space, but AR technology addressed this issue and offered a new visualization technique that allowed computer-generated material to be added to the real environment. With the use of this technology, the user can interact with an enhanced reality [27]. To improve engagement, people must get nonvisible information about an item they are interacting with as soon as feasible and in an intelligible way. For this reason, augmented reality (AR) technology has been regarded as a cutting-edge method of engagement. Humans may now explore beyond what their five senses can detect, thanks to augmented reality. AR's primary goal is to improve how humans perceive their surroundings by superimposing extra computer-generated visual data over the user's field of view using specialized devices like smartphone cameras, head-mounted displays (HMDs), projection systems, etc. Texts, sounds, spoken commands, movies, photos, and 3D models are examples of computer-generated visual information. By superimposing this type of augmentation onto their actual vision, the user may access hidden information about things that interact with one another or the surrounding area. This makes AR a practical technology for a range of uses, such as in sports, gaming, advertising, education, the military, medical treatments, and the industrial sector.

Combining real and virtual things in a real setting, allowing users to interact with them in real time, and identifying (coordinating) real and virtual objects are the three main characteristics of augmented reality. The augmentation's added information could be useful to a user when carrying out duties in the actual world. AR has the potential to significantly meet industrial expectations with these qualities. Moreover, industry interest in AR has increased due to advancements in hardware and software systems.

10.6.3 Mixed Reality

Even while augmented reality is important, it can be difficult to distinguish between the actual and virtual worlds. This issue lowers the degree of user immersion in augmented reality settings. Mixed reality (MR) arose to address this issue by developing the MR environment. This configuration blends the virtual and physical worlds together to

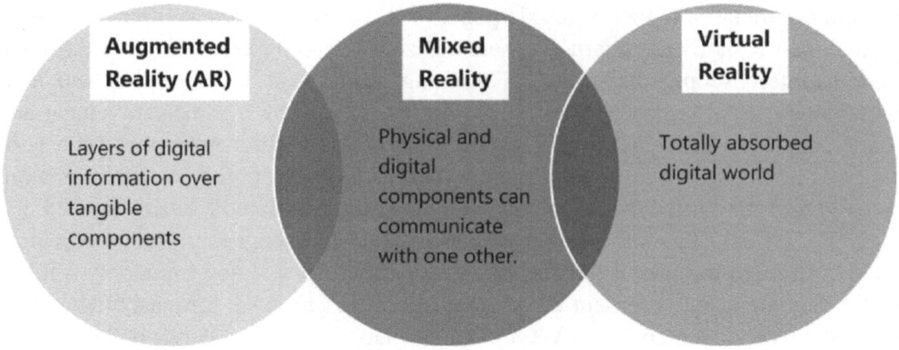

FIGURE 10.1 Intersection of AR, MR, and VR technologies.

create an opening between them. Consequently, a virtual object and a real-world item communicate to carry out useful scenarios for the user. Mixed reality is the blending of actual and digital reality to provide new environments and representations where real-time communication and the coexistence of digital and physical items occur [28]. Following the emergence of VR and AR technologies in the graphics industry, MR technology is a new multidisciplinary frontier. It combines VR and AR in 3D applications with the use of state-of-the-art control devices. Figure 10.1 shows the interception of VR, AR, and MR. Every MR system should include these three crucial components: (1) merging the digital and actual world objects; (2) engaging in actual time interaction; and (3) creating a connection to enable communication between the digital and real items.

Mixed reality is accessed using head-mounted see-through glasses, whereas augmented reality is presented through a portable mobile device like a tablet or smartphone. When Microsoft debuted the Microsoft HoloLens in 2016, it coined the phrase "mixed reality." Mixed reality is different from augmented reality in addition to being head-elevated. It can place holographic pictures in the actual space and has a more advanced understanding of it.

Extended reality (XR) and hybrid reality are other names for mixed reality. A headset form factor tracks the user's gaze to map out their real surroundings and apps. It then uses deep learning algorithms to link digital data to particular locations inside the story. Digital things may interact with actual objects through MR software development, and individuals can interact with digital materials as though they were tangible. This implies that a regular desktop computer may be transformed into a responsive internet touchscreen, or an MR-generated movie character could perch on the homeowner's living room sofa.

With MR, you may superimpose text, photos, videos, and music on top of preexisting images or spaces [29]. The mix of actual and virtual items, actual time interaction, and three-dimensional registration make the MR environment special. It can facilitate the smooth transition between the digital and actual worlds. MR gives people the ability to see what's around them in the actual world as well as the digital elements (digital objects) that are displayed on the screens [30]. The lines separating the actual world from the digital are blurring, suggesting limitless potential for innovation in medical applications. To increase the sensation of reality in the user experience, MR technology presents and incorporates computer virtual models into the actual world as seen by users. It also creates an interactive feedback loop between the digital and actual worlds [30]. MR technology has garnered a lot of interest because of its potential for use in several novel fields [31].

Even though MR proponents list several benefits, research on consumers' adoption of the technology is still lacking. The ability to comprehend the elements impacting users' adoption of MR technology, particularly in the educational setting, aids developers in creating practical MR applications.

10.7 INTEGRATION INTO INDUSTRY 4.0

The integration of AR, VR, and MR into Industry 4.0 processes is ushering in a new era of smart manufacturing and industrial operations. These immersive technologies are revolutionizing the way businesses operate, innovate, and interact with the digital and physical worlds.

10.7.1 Role of Augmented Reality, Virtual Reality, and Mixed Reality in Industry 4.0

The Industry 4.0 strategy makes use of AR. AR is one way to enhance the labor experience in an industrial setting that is focused on people [32]. Through an additional layer of data placed on top of the real environment, this technology allows humans to access the digital world. The MR framework places AR between VR and the actual world. AR enhances, but does not replace, the actual world [32]. In contrast, with VR, all information is shown virtually. There is a wide range of uses throughout several sectors. AR has applications in design, production, and assembly processes, as well as instructional and as a digital operator assistance system [33]. "Pick-by-vision" is a well-known logistics idea that uses augmented reality to show selecting locations and amounts [34]. AR is frequently utilized for upkeep and repairs. To increase productivity and accuracy, technicians may access digital manuals, schematic overlays, and step-by-step repair instructions via mobile devices or AR glasses. Workers may engage in immersive, practical learning experiences through AR-based training programs. To prepare for real-world scenarios, they may hone their assembly, maintenance, and troubleshooting abilities in a virtual setting. Warehouse operations are among the other domains in which AR can find use. Other well-known application domains include through-life engineering services, supervisory control and data acquisition (SCADA) jobs, quality assurance, and instruction visualization. In the last several years, there has also been a noticeable trend toward the application of AR technology in human–robot cooperation, such as safety enhancement and automobile case studies. As a result, operators may be fully immersed in the digital world of Industry 4.0 technologies by using AR to naturally display information on-site as soon as they start to depend on it (in actual time).

Among the technologies connected to Industry 4.0 is VR, which helps the product development process without requiring a physical setting by simulating the real world on a computer [35]. The virtual environment, interactive elements, sensory input, and immersion—the fundamental components of virtual reality—can be utilized to help the digital factory accomplish its objectives [36]. VR offers a multitude of visual, aural, and even tactile inputs, which can enhance the efficacy and appeal of cognitive processes [37]. These procedures can be categorized either broadly or narrowly. In the first instance, they are speaking of higher-order brain processes that enable the nervous system to process information. These functions include gathering, storing, converting, and introducing information into the surrounding environment [37]. In the second instance, they discuss characteristics of post-cognitive mechanisms for generating, building, and altering environmental information. In light of VR systems' high degree of immersion, it can be said that this technology generally supports cognitive processes in both. With virtual reality technology, people may experience situations that are similar to or even the same as the actual world, while simultaneously being in a completely fictional place. Many approaches are now being researched that can "transfer" and "immerse" the user in the virtual reality environment to differing degrees. Owing to its characteristics, VR is becoming increasingly popular each year across a range of industries, including entertainment, business, education, science, and research. One of the most important of these areas is Industry 4.0. In this instance, virtual reality technology may be specifically used to conduct training procedures as well as test and validate individual devices, whole processes, and industrial technologies. VR cuts down on development time and costs by allowing engineers and designers to build and test prototypes in a virtual setting. It provides a realistic representation of goods and procedures, facilitating incremental advancements. Virtual reality enables teams who are geographically separated to collaborate remotely. In a virtual environment, engineers and specialists from different places may collaborate to plan projects, debate designs, and solve problems. The utilization of VR as a sophisticated and interactive visualization tool can expedite and lower the cost of layout, verification, and administration improvement. Additionally, complicated and dynamic trends may be effectively replicated because of VR's adaptability and scalability. When combined with an intuitive interface, virtual reality's capacity to depict models with the highest level of realism helps streamline and expedite tasks. VR has the ability to improve a number of industrial tasks, such as planning factory layouts, designing products, maintaining equipment, using CNC machining, designing assembly lines, and more. Owing to the vast potential advantages that the industry can reap from the widespread adoption of VR, numerous businesses, academic institutions, and scientific organizations are working on research and development projects to create entirely new solutions and acquire new functionalities in the VR technology space.

The industrial landscape is undergoing a change. Industry 4.0, which is propelled by the amalgamation of intelligent technologies, networked systems, and data-derived understanding, prioritizes automation, effectiveness, and instantaneous optimization [38]. However, in the middle of this technological upsurge, a new mixed reality (MR) player appears. Combining the real and virtual worlds, MR has enormous potential to advance and change Industry 4.0 in several ways. In Industry 4.0, MR, which combines digital and physical surroundings, is revolutionizing the industry. It offers a dynamic and immersive connection between the real and virtual worlds, marking a significant turning point in the growth of manufacturing and industrial processes [39,40]. MR technology is becoming increasingly popular across a range of industries because it may deliver a superior information presentation by fusing digital and real-world data. By superimposing digital instructions and visual assistance on actual workplaces, MR improves assembly operations. Errors can be decreased by workers following instructions more precisely and quickly. Engineers and customers may see items in actual settings thanks to MR.

For example, architects can evaluate the viability of a design by placing virtual building models on construction sites. MR creates a hybrid environment by superimposing digital information over the physical world, in contrast to its virtual reality cousin. Its smooth mixing makes training and visualization possible. With AR glasses, engineers can alter 3D models of items in real time, and technicians may receive step-by-step instructions overlaid on actual apparatus. This allows for intuitive cooperation and rapid learning. By visualizing internal components, providing real-time access to manuals and diagnostics, and even providing remote expert help through shared MR settings, MR enables personnel to diagnose and fix complicated equipment [39]. AR overlays provide workers with dynamic instructions and real-time quality feedback, which optimize processes and minimize mistakes in assembly lines. MR speeds up design iterations and lowers the cost of physical production by enabling product development and testing in virtual settings [39]. By visualizing goods in actual environments, designers may improve market fit and consumer understanding. Not only may MR be integrated into Industry 4.0 to increase efficiency, but it also causes a paradigm change. By putting resources and knowledge at their fingertips, MR helps employees make better decisions by lowering mental fatigue and increasing their independence in making decisions [40]. Teams who are geographically separated may collaborate easily thanks to shared machine learning environments, which promote ideation, problem-solving, and cooperative design work [41]. MR serves as a link between the digital and physical realms, enabling real-time data gathering and processing, enabling predictive maintenance and continuous process improvement

10.7.2 Challenges and Applications of Augmented Reality, Virtual Reality, and Mixed Reality in Industry 4.0

It can be costly to integrate AR, VR, and MR technologies due to the price of the necessary gear, software, and training. Secure data management is required while using immersive technology to safeguard private data and intellectual property [42]. To utilize AR, VR, and MR products efficiently, employees must get training, which can be challenging. High-quality content creation for AR, VR, and MR applications necessitates proficiency in 3D modeling, design, and programming [43].

Porsche uses augmented reality glasses in its service facilities so that technicians may view technical data and maintenance instructions without using their hands [44]. Errors and repair times have significantly decreased as a result. Siemens uses VR to model and simulate production processes [45]. This aids in streamlining manufacturing processes, cutting down on lead times, and raising productivity. When assembling airplanes, Airbus employs MR. Microsoft HoloLens is a mixed-reality gadget that can display data and even create a virtual environment in real time on a three-dimensional platform through the use of several sensors and holographic processing [46]. With technology developing quickly and virtual learning becoming more popular,

HoloLens technology can be an essential tool for surgical planning and dentistry education [46]. Workers wear HoloLens headsets, which provide digital overlays of instructions and part placements. This has led to a 25% reduction in assembly time [47]. Ford employs VR for vehicle design and prototyping [48]. Designers may see and work with automobile models in a virtual setting, which expedites the creation process and enhances the caliber of the final result [48]. Successful implementations in companies like Porsche, Siemens, Airbus, and Ford demonstrate the tangible benefits and potential of these technologies in reshaping the future of manufacturing and industry.

10.7.3 Anticipated Role of Augmented Reality, Virtual Reality, and Mixed Reality in Industry 5.0

AR, VR, and MR technologies possess the capacity to greatly improve various aspects of Industry 5.0, including human–machine collaboration, customization, sustainability, flexibility, and remote collaboration.

Human-Machine Collaboration: It is anticipated that AR, VR, and MR will improve human–machine cooperation by establishing engaging and dynamic work environments [49]. Employees can engage with digital interfaces, robotics, and machinery more naturally. By offering real-time data, instructions, and visual assistance, augmented reality glasses and headsets can simplify difficult jobs [49]. This can reduce mistakes and increase overall productivity.

Customization and Personalization: Real-time product customization can be made possible by AR by superimposing virtual design options on tangible goods. The ability for customers to see and customize items fits with Industry 5.0's mass customization trend. VR may be used to provide more engaging and personalized shopping experiences by enabling customers to explore and modify items in a virtual environment.

Sustainability and Green Manufacturing: By saving waste in industrial processes and maximizing resource use, AR, VR, and MR may support sustainability initiatives. VR simulation and modeling may aid in the design of environmentally friendly manufacturing processes, while AR can help with real-time energy usage monitoring and optimization.

Flexible and Agile Manufacturing: Robot programming and quick production line reconfiguration are made possible by these technologies [50]. By guiding workers through setup and process modifications, downtime may be minimized [51]. A dynamic and responsive manufacturing environment, where machinery and procedures adjust instantly to changing production requirements, can be made possible by MR.

Remote Collaboration and Expert Assistance: By establishing virtual meeting rooms where professionals and employees from various locations may engage as if they were in the same physical environment, VR and MR can facilitate distant cooperation. Using AR gear, professionals may view what workers are seeing on-site and give real-time instruction and help. This is known as remote assistance.

While mixed reality is currently forming in its early phases, a variety of businesses are already using it for instructional materials. For example, airline businesses are utilizing MR to inexpensively prepare repair staff [52]. Rather than eliminating a combustion chamber from an aircraft for training, experts can view a holographic projection of an engine through specialized headphones and communicate with it using motion, direct vision, voice user interface (VUI) directions, altering viewpoints, and layer-by-layer extraction of critical information. With the expectation that online digital displays and three-dimensional projections would be important components of MR, headsets are typically used to deliver the most recent mixed reality information. Due to the high processing needs and strong computer vision and image recognition capabilities of the technology, creating consumer goods that benefit from the MR spectrum was previously unaffordable. Big data, cloud computing, and significant advances in artificial intelligence (AI) are working to lower the cost of MR features; as a result, it is anticipated that MR will significantly change the human–computer interface (HCI).

10.8 ENHANCING INDUSTRY 5.0 CORE PRINCIPLES THROUGH AUGMENTED REALITY, VIRTUAL REALITY, AND MIXED REALITY TECHNOLOGIES

Big data, cloud computing, and noteworthy advances in artificial intelligence (AI) are working to lower the cost of MR features; as a result, it is anticipated that MR will significantly change the human–computer interface (HCI). AR, VR, and MR technologies are critical to accomplishing Industry 5.0's goals because they promote innovation, enhance sustainability, ease customization, and enhance human–machine connection. To foster a more customized, effective, and sustainable industrial future, these technologies provide immersive, interactive experiences that close the divide between the actual and online worlds. The following section discusses a few of the concepts that AR, VR, and MR support.

Human–Machine Collaboration: By allowing employees to see digital overlays of actual things, AR can improve productivity and safety by guiding workers through difficult tasks, maintenance, or training [53]. For instance, a technician may display predicted maintenance instructions for machinery right on the apparatus. VR provides immersive training settings where workers may practice using machines or carrying out activities in a secure, virtual environment [54]. This lowers the risk of damage while also enabling the investigation of intricate situations that would be rigid or unfeasible to replicate in real life. By combining elements of both AR and VR, MR builds environments where real-world objects and digital ones coexist and interact. This permits more natural interactions between intelligent machines and people, facilitating inventive and cooperative problem-solving.

Customization: With the use of AR, designers and consumers may preview real-time adjustments and how a product will seem and work before it is produced [55]. This may be especially helpful in fields where customization is important, such as interior design, furniture, and the automobile industry. VR enables the rapid iteration of precise virtual prototypes, which minimizes the time and expense associated with physical prototyping. This allows manufacturers to provide a greater level of flexibility by enabling them to respond to specific consumer requirements more quickly. Through the use of MR, designers, engineers, and clients may collaborate in real time, facilitating a participatory design process. Because stakeholders may engage with virtual prototypes in a shared mixed reality arena, making adjustments and viewing outcomes instantly, this could result in more customized goods and services.

Sustainability and Efficiency: By giving employees real-time information and directions, AR can maximize operational efficiency by lowering mistakes and material waste [55]. It may also be utilized to provide remote help, which eliminates the need to go on-site, reducing travel time and costs. VR simulations may be used to reduce the environmental effect of production by optimizing layouts and processes for energy efficiency [56]. Without the requirement for tangible resources, it may also be used to instruct staff members on sustainable practices. Through the use of MR, more participatory and iterative approaches to product design and production processes may be optimized [57]. This may spark inventions that boost product sustainability and cut waste.

Enhancing Creativity and Problem-Solving: AR, VR, and MR all provide distinctive means of seeing issues and potential solutions, encouraging original thought and invention. They promote an innovative culture by enabling designers, engineers, and laborers to test concepts in a low-risk setting.

10.9 THE INTEGRATION OF XR WITH THE INTERNET OF THINGS (IOT) IN INDUSTRIES 4.0 AND 5.0

Within the Industrial Internet of Things (IIoT), XR is developing as a potential emerging technology. Its numerous applications have the potential to alter many elements of Industry 4.0 and set the basis for Industry 5.0 [57]. However, a number of challenges, notably the finite resources accessible to processing and distributing huge and intricate data, preclude current systems from providing consumers with an excellent experience.

The combination of extended reality (XR) and the Internet of Things (IoT) is a key component in the progress of Industry 4.0 and the next Industry 5.0. In Industry 4.0, the confluence of XR and IoT technologies has ushered in a new age of intelligent production [58]. XR improves the display of data provided by IoT devices, delivering real-time information on the state of equipment, manufacturing processes, and general factory activities. AR displays important details onto the real world, allowing workers to engage seamlessly with IoT-generated data, improving decision-making, and aiding maintenance forecasting [59].

As the industrial environment transitions to Industry 5.0, the synergy between XR and the IoT becomes ever more apparent. The integration creates a full and integrated environment in which both digital and physical components interact together. VR simulations may use data from IoT devices to generate realistic training situations, hence improving worker skills and productivity. Mixed reality enhances this integration by providing a dynamic and responsive environment in which real-world data from IoT devices may be smoothly merged with virtual features, resulting in a more natural and collaborative human–machine interaction.

Nevertheless, this integration presents a number of obstacles, including guaranteeing privacy of information, standardized protocols for communication, and addressing compatibility concerns. The study examines these issues and presents solutions for realizing the full potential of XR and IoT in Industries 4.0 and 5.0. By integrating XR's immersive characteristics with the huge data created by the IoT, companies may not only optimize their operations, but also advance toward a future where intelligent choices and adaptable production are the norm.

As Industry 4.0 advances into Industry 5.0, the revolutionary potential of AR, VR, and MR becomes more apparent in transforming the landscape of manufacturing procedures and human–machine cooperation [60]. The varied influence of XR innovations on the prospects of production, with a focus on improving effectiveness, cooperation, and overall operating paradigms, is transformative. In the framework of Industry 4.0, AR, VR, and MR have been shown to be useful in constructing intelligent factories based on data. AR's capacity to overlay multimedia content onto an actual setting enables real-time data visualization and context-aware support, leading to a more agile and responsive workforce. VR involves people in virtual settings and provides genuine experiments for instruction, prototyping, and architecture, lowering time-to-market and operational expenses. MR, as a convergence of AR and VR, delivers a seamless integration of digital and physical aspects, ushering in new opportunities for collaborative solving issues and making choices.

As companies move into the collaboration phase of Industry 5.0, XR equipment will become ever more important. AR, VR, and MR have helped to improve human–machine cooperation by building interactive interactions, allowing remote support, and encouraging a symbiotic interaction between individuals and intelligent machines. The combination of XR with the IoT, AI, and sophisticated robots increases the possibility for real-time data interchange, proactive upkeep, and adaptable manufacturing operations [61]. Case investigations and practical implementations of XR in industrial settings have shown that it improves worker safety while also increasing development.

10.10 CHALLENGES AND CONSIDERATIONS OF INTEGRATION OF AUGMENTED REALITY, VIRTUAL REALITY, AND MIXED REALITY IN INDUSTRY 5.0

Technologies like AR, VR, and MR have the possibility to greatly improve several Industry 5.0 features. However, issues like cost, infrastructure, security, labor preparedness, and health and safety must be resolved if they are to be successfully integrated and deployed. These technologies are anticipated to be crucial facilitators of Industry 5.0's key tenets and goals as it develops.

Cost and Infrastructure: Some firms may find it difficult to invest in the hardware, software, and network infrastructure needed to implement AR, VR, and MR systems.

Integration Complexity: It can be difficult to integrate new technologies with current systems and procedures, which could result in incompatibilities and the hiring of qualified IT staff [62,63].

Data Security and Privacy: Ensuring data security and managing confidentiality issues are crucial when it comes to the collection and transfer of data. Accessing confidential data without authorization might pose a danger.

Workforce Training and Acceptance: The workforce may need to undergo training and upskilling to be prepared to use AR, VR, and MR efficiently. Upskilling and reskilling the workforce is necessary for integrating new technology, yet it can be costly and time-consuming. To fully profit from new technologies, workers must feel at ease using them. Considerable challenges might also be brought about by resistance to change and worries about job displacement.

Health and Safety: VR headset use for extended periods might cause pain or health problems, which need to be addressed. It is important to develop safety procedures for the application of MR and AR in industrial environments.

Accessibility and Affordability: The cost of current AR, VR, and MR gear prevents their widespread adoption, particularly in smaller businesses and underdeveloped nations. Furthermore, it might be expensive to maintain dependable network access and infrastructure for easy remote communication.

Technical Immaturity: Even though they are developing quickly, many immersive technologies may not have the haptic feedback or accuracy required for specific Industry 5.0 applications, such as simulations of dangerous environments or intricate assembly jobs.

Battery Life and Latency: Workflows and user experience might be negatively impacted by headsets' short battery life and possible latency problems, particularly for important jobs.

Specific Challenges for each Technology are highlighted below:

AR: Accurately recording digital information in complicated real-world environments—especially while outdoors—can be challenging. Concerns concerning user attention and safety when wearing AR glasses while completing jobs [64].

VR: Prolonged usage may cause motion sickness and discomfort, making it unsuitable for several worker jobs and activities [65]. High development costs for creating realistic and immersive VR experiences.

MR: The intricacy involved in effectively integrating the digital and physical realms, especially when it comes to haptic feedback integration. Limited availability of customized MR tools and platforms for specific industry applications.

Although there are obstacles along the way, realizing them and actively working toward solutions is essential to maximizing the potential of AR, VR, and MR in Industry 5.0. By addressing these challenges, we may use these immersive technologies to build an industry that is more collaborative, human-centered, and sustainable—a future in which people and machines coexist together. Some of the mitigation strategies to combat the challenges are discussed below.

Government and industry collaboration: Governments and business partners must work together to invest in infrastructure, R&D, and other areas to lower costs and speed up development.

Focus on user experience and training: Prioritizing user comfort, user-friendly interfaces, and thorough training programs can help reduce adoption barriers and address security issues.

Ethical governance and standards: For responsible development and use, it is imperative to establish explicit ethical guidelines and regulations regarding data privacy, user safety, and algorithm bias.

Open-source software and standardization: Encouraging cooperation and the creation of interoperable systems across various businesses and technologies may be achieved by supporting open-source development platforms and data formats.

10.11 OPEN ISSUES AND FUTURE RESEARCH DIRECTIONS

Investigate how AR, VR, and MR may effortlessly interact with other Industry 4.0 innovations such as the IoT, cyber-physical structures, and big data analytics to improve general productivity and effectiveness [66]. Connectivity with Industry 4.0 innovations such as AR, VR, and MR within the framework of Industry 4.0 and 5.0 entails a combination of interactive technologies with the larger ecosystem of intelligent production [67,68]. As Industry 4.0 replaces conventional industrial processes with networked systems, cyber-physical structures, and the IoT, AR, VR, and MR play critical roles in accelerating this digital transformation. These interactive solutions may seamlessly integrate with streams of information from IoT devices, sensors, and associated machines. This connection provides users with realistic representations of real-time data, simplifies hands-on training, and allows for collaborative cooperation in virtual settings. As Industry 4.0 develops into Industry 5.0, the combination of AR, VR, and MR is projected to be beneficial to increasingly more advanced and linked industrial ecosystems, supporting creativity, effectiveness, and intelligent choices in the manufacturing environment [69].

1. **Human–Machine Interaction and Collaboration:** Discover new techniques of communicating with machines in AR, VR, and MR settings. This incorporates gesture detection, voice commands, and other intuitive interfaces to improve the user experience. Investigate collaborative ecosystems in which both real and virtual entities may interact, resulting in improved communication and collaboration in Industry 4.0 situations. Develop more advanced human–machine interfaces for AR, VR, and MR in Industries 4.0 and 5.0. This comprises natural language processing, recognition of gestures, brain–computer interactions, and other intuitive connection approaches to improve the user satisfaction and effectiveness.
2. **Real-Time Data Visualization and Analysis:** Create innovative visualization approaches for real-time data processing in AR, VR, and MR systems. This can improve decision-making on the work floor and in other industrial

contexts. Real-time data visualization and analysis in AR, VR, and MR as part of Industry 4.0 entail using immersive methods to give live and engaging visualizations of complicated industrial data. Real-time sensor data, production metrics, and other pertinent information may be integrated into AR, VR, or MR experiences to provide users with quick insights and make educated decisions. These innovations provide a transformational approach to analyzing information by allowing users to view sophisticated processes physically and chronologically, promoting faster resolving issues and enhancing operational effectiveness. In Industry 4.0 contexts, the effortless incorporation of current information visualization into fully immersive settings improves awareness of circumstances, enabling proactively tracking, proactive upkeep, and production procedure improvement.

3. **Security and Privacy Concerns:** Analyze the safety and privacy concerns of incorporating AR, VR, and MR into Industry 4.0. Investigate methods for securing communication and preservation, as well as protecting sensitive knowledge in online environments [70]. Security and privacy issues in AR, VR, and MR in the setting of Industry 4.0 center on potential weaknesses caused by the combination of immersive technologies with significant manufacturing procedures and data. As these technologies become more integrated into production and smart business environments, there is a greater need to manage concerns like illegal access to vital systems, security breaches, and the possible exposure of confidential data [71]. Furthermore, the immersive characteristics of AR, VR, and MR improve privacy issues concerning the gathering, preservation, and dissemination of private and operational information, requiring the creation of strong security procedures, encoding processes, and moral standards that guarantee the safeguarding of both information assets and user confidentiality in the Industry 4.0 landscape [72].
4. **Skill Training and Knowledge Transfer:** Investigate the application of interactive technologies for skill development as well as skill transmission in Industry 4.0 scenarios. Develop successful training programs integrating AR, VR, and MR to increase worker abilities.
5. **Cost-effective Hardware Solutions:** Explore and build more affordable and user-friendly AR, VR, and MR equipment for industrial use. Cost-effective hardware options in AR, VR, and MR for Industries 4.0 and 5.0 are critical for broad acceptance and adaptability. As these technological innovations grow more common in factories, addressing hardware prices and availability is critical for promoting widespread industry use. The creation of more inexpensive and efficient AR, VR, and MR systems requires breakthroughs in technological elements such as sensors, screens, and computing units. The objective is to create a balance between performance and affordability, making these technologies available to a larger variety of businesses. In the constantly changing environment of Industry 5.0, the focus on affordability in hardware alternatives is likely to remain, encouraging the incorporation of interactive technologies into a wide range of business environments, from big factories to smaller businesses looking for efficient and affordable ways to improve their operations.

6. **Standardization and Interoperability:** Work on standardizing and interoperability of AR, VR, and MR technologies to enable compatibility and easy integration across multiple Industry 4.0 ecosystems. Industries 4.0 and 5.0 require standardization and compatibility in AR, VR, and MR to provide effortless integration as well as cooperation across varied applications and platforms. Developing universal norms for equipment interactions, file formats, and protocol connections is critical for enabling AR, VR, and MR devices to interact with other elements of the Industry 4.0 and upcoming Industry 5.0 environments. Interoperability allows diverse gadgets and platforms to operate together seamlessly, resulting in a more integrated industrial landscape in which information can be transmitted easily. As these fully immersive technologies develop, an integrated structure for compatibility not only streamlines execution but also encourages creativity by allowing different groups to develop and combine appropriate approaches, eventually speeding up the wider acceptance of AR, VR, and MR in manufacturing environments.
7. **Ethical and Social Implications:** Investigate the ethical and social consequences of the broad use of immersive technologies in business, such as employment relocation, concerns regarding privacy, and the influence on work–life balance. Examine the ethical and societal consequences of broad AR, VR, and MR use in Industries 4.0 and 5.0. This involves investigating the implications for employment positions, labor dynamics, and society attitudes toward immersive technology.
8. **Scalability and Deployment Challenges:** Address the scalability and deployment problems that come with adopting AR, VR, and MR solutions across various industrial sizes and industries. Sustainability and implementation problems in AR, VR, and MR within the domains of Industries 4.0 and 5.0 include the complications associated with growing the usage of these technological innovations across varied industrial contexts. Scalability entails resolving challenges such as hardware reliability, network connectivity, and computing power to maintain comparable efficiency across different scales of installation, from small businesses to big industrial plants. Furthermore, the deployment issues include developing adaptive platforms that can meet the particular demands and processes of various sectors. User training, maintenance, and the integration of AR, VR, and MR technologies with current equipment are critical factors in meeting these problems. In the shift from Industry 4.0 to Industry 5.0, boosting scalability and overcoming deployment problems will be critical for the widespread use of immersive technologies, stimulating creativity and efficiency across a spectrum of industrial applications.
9. **Context-Aware and Adaptive Environments:** Investigate the creation of context-aware AR, VR, and MR systems that can respond to changing industrial contexts. This comprises systems that may dynamically change information, interfaces, and interactions in response to real-time data and user context.
10. **Cognitive Load Management:** Look into ways for controlling cognitive load in immersive situations. This involves refining information display, removing

extraneous distractions, and using adaptive strategies to fit users' cognitive capacities.

11. **Digital Twins and Simulation:** Investigate the use of AR, VR, and MR with digital twin technologies to create more realistic simulations and virtual representations of physical systems. This can improve the ability to test, monitor, and optimize industrial processes.
12. **Blockchain Integration for Security:** Investigate the use of blockchain-based technologies to improve security and trust in AR, VR, and MR technologies for Industries 4.0 and 5.0. This can assist in protecting data transfers, operations, and user identities in immersive settings. Blockchain integration for protection in AR, VR, and MR, as part of Industries 4.0 and 5.0, entails exploiting blockchain technology's decentralized and impermeable nature to improve the security of information exchanges and interactions in fully immersive settings. By integrating blockchain procedures, these advancements can protect the integrity and anonymity of crucial information shared throughout industrial networks. In Industry 4.0, this connection can strengthen the reliability of data connected to augmented and virtual experiences, limiting unwanted access and alteration. As industries transition to the era of Industry 5.0, blockchain's role in securing the absorbed computing surroundings is expected to evolve, providing secure alternatives for safeguarding private information, checking opinions, and laying the groundwork for the widespread use of AR, VR, and MR in a variety of industrial applications.
13. **Edge Computing for Low Latency:** Look at the usage of edge computing to minimize latency in AR, VR, and MR uses, providing real-time performance in changing industrial contexts. Edge computing for low latency in AR, VR, and MR within the structures of Industries 4.0 and 5.0 implies the decentralization of data closer to the source, lowering latency in enabling real-time applications. Edge computing reduces information processing and transmission latency by bringing computational chores closer to AR, VR, and MR devices. This strategy is critical in Industry 4.0 applications to ensure responsive and immersive experiences, especially for time-sensitive industrial operations. As businesses transition into the era of Industry 5.0, the integration of edge computing is expected to play a critical role in further reducing latency and allowing enhanced interaction and dynamic applications spanning a wide range of industrial contexts, from production floors to collaborating virtual workspaces.
14. **Intelligent Data Analysis:** Create advanced analytics and machine learning algorithms to extract useful insights from the massive volumes of data produced by AR, VR, and MR devices in industrial environments. This incorporates analytics that are predictive for maintenance and quality control. Smart data analysis in AR, VR, and MR within the framework of Industries 4.0 and 5.0 entails using sophisticated analytics as well as machine learning approaches to extract useful insights from the massive amounts of data created by these technological innovations. By incorporating real-time data analytics into AR, VR, and MR surroundings, companies may get vital insights for better decision-making, maintenance planning, and process efficiency. As Industry

4.0 grows into Industry 5.0, the emphasis on cognitive data analytics broadens to include increasingly complex models capable of reacting to changing industrial circumstances. These innovations not only provide for a greater knowledge of operational processes but also assist businesses to extract significant patterns, trends, and forecasts, supporting a data-driven strategy geared to productivity and creativity in industrial applications.

15. **Wearable and Mobile AR/VR Devices:** Investigate the creation of more lightweight, portable, and user-friendly AR/VR systems appropriate for industrial application. This includes improvements in optics, longevity of batteries, and form factors that increase user versatility and mobility. Wearable and handheld AR/VR devices in AR, VR, and MR as part of Industries 4.0 and 5.0 signify a trend toward a more lightweight and user-friendly immersive technology. In Industry 4.0, the invention of compact and adaptable AR/VR devices is intended to improve user accessibility and adaptability in business environments by facilitating operations such as repair, instruction, and collaborating. As companies migrate to Industry 5.0, the focus on wearable and mobile solutions is projected to continue, enabling increasing accessibility and acceptance across a variety of applications in industry. These gadgets do not only deliver full immersion, but also help to evolve more dynamic and adaptable processes, giving workers on-the-go access to essential knowledge and enhanced capabilities in innovative production settings.
16. **Robust Multi-User Collaborative Environments:** Investigate and create strong multi-user working environments in AR, VR, and MR for industrial use. This includes handling issues such as synchronization, interaction, and collaboration in shared virtual environments. Robust multi-user cooperative environments in AR, VR, and MR within the framework of Industries 4.0 and 5.0 need the development of intelligent technologies that permit smooth interaction as well as collaboration among users in shared virtual worlds. In Industry 4.0, collaborative AR/VR environments offer real-time interaction and information sharing, improving team cooperation for activities like design reviews, training modeling, and remote help. As companies develop toward Industry 5.0, the emphasis on multi-user collaboration expands to include increasingly sophisticated capabilities such as improved perception of space, constantly changing information sharing, and real-time collaborating on multimedia assets. These settings are critical for breaking down barriers of distance, enabling cross-disciplinary cooperation, and exploiting team experience, contributing to the evolution of industrial processes and exchange of information frameworks.
17. **Human Factors and Ergonomics:** Conduct studies on the human aspects and ergonomics of prolonged use of AR, VR, and MR in industrial contexts, with an emphasis on user comfort, tiredness, and potentially long-term impacts. Address challenges of user safety and ergonomics in complete immersion. Investigate solutions to alleviate pain, weariness, and other health hazards associated with the extended use of AR, VR, and MR equipment in work environments.

10.12 CRITICAL LESSONS LEARNED

Numerous essential lessons have been learnt about the roles of augmented reality (AR), virtual reality (VR), and mixed reality (MR) in Industry 4.0 and the emerging environment of Industry 5.0. To begin, the most successful incorporation of these immersive innovations occurs when they are linked to particular industrial scenarios and procedures, highlighting the necessity of tailored applications for optimum impact. Second, user training and acceptability are critical, and effective deployment necessitates prioritizing user experience, comfort, and offering suitable training programs. Third, compatibility and standardization are important; providing smooth connection with current systems and devices is necessary for the broad acceptance of AR, VR, and MR in Industry 4.0 and beyond. Furthermore, the security and privacy concerns of immersive technology must be carefully considered in order to safeguard sensitive data. Finally, the ongoing expansion of hardware, software, and analytics capabilities emphasizes the importance of flexibility and scalability in AR, VR, and MR systems for meeting the changing needs of Industries 4.0 and 5.0. The following are the lessons learnt in this chapter:

1. **Targeted Applications for Maximum Impact:** AR, VR, and MR deployments in Industries 4.0 and 5.0 are most effective when they are strategically applied to particular commercial use cases and processes. A tailored strategy ensures that innovative technologies directly solve operational difficulties, resulting in increased efficiency and meaningful benefits.
   Instructions for users and acceptability are crucial. User experience, comfort, and instructional initiatives are all important aspects in the success of AR, VR, and MR acceptance in industrial settings. Businesses have realized that offering extensive training for users and dealing with issues about comfort and usability are vital for ensuring smooth integration and adoption of new technologies across the workforce.
2. **Interoperability and Standardization Are Vital:** The seamless integration of AR, VR, and MR with current systems and devices is critical. Lessons learnt emphasize the necessity of compatibility and uniformity in allowing for seamless communication across diverse technologies, resulting in a more unified and productive Industry 4.0 and 5.0 environment.
   Safety and confidentiality concerns are essential. The immersive nature of AR, VR, and MR creates major confidentiality and safety problems. Organizations have realized that protecting critical data and maintaining safe communications in these immersive settings is critical. Addressing security and privacy concerns is critical for garnering confidence and mainstream adoption.
3. **Adaptability and Scalability Are Key:** The fast expansion of hardware, software, and analytics capabilities highlights the importance of flexibility and scalability in AR, VR, and MR applications. Lessons learnt highlight the necessity of adaptable frameworks that can accept technological improvements and changes, enabling firms to remain nimble in the dynamic world of Industries 4.0 and 5.0.

These key lessons emphasize the practical insights acquired from experiences in deploying AR, VR, and MR in the context of Industry 4.0 and the coming Industry 5.0 paradigm.

10.13 CONCLUSION

This chapter explores the critical role of augmented reality (AR), virtual reality (VR), and mixed reality (MR) technologies in the progression from Industry 4.0 to Industry 5.0. It explores how these immersive technologies develop smart manufacturing paradigms, improve human–machine interactions, and transform industrial processes. With an emphasis on streamlining processes, cutting downtime, and supporting employee development, these technologies play a critical role in enabling remote maintenance and cooperation, which boosts productivity and resilience in Industry 4.0. The combination of AR, VR, and MR promises to further human-centricity as we move toward Industry 5.0 by linking the digital and physical domains and highlighting symbiotic human–machine connections. The advancement of Industry 4.0 and Industry 5.0's fundamental ideas is greatly aided by the integration of AR, VR, and MR technologies. These technologies presents a new degree of human-centricity and machine–human collaboration in Industry 5.0, in addition to improving operational efficiency and workforce training in Industry 4.0.

REFERENCES

[1] H. M. Kamdjou, D. Baudry, V. Havard & S. Ouchani. "Resource-Constrained Extended Reality Operated with Digital Twin in Industrial Internet of Things," *IEEE Open Journal of the Communications Society*. 2024. https://doi.org/10.1109/OJCOMS.2024.3356508.

[2] N. Partarakis & X. Zabulis. "A Review of Immersive Technologies, Knowledge Representation, and AI for Human-Centered Digital Experiences". *Electronics*. 2024. vol 13, issue 2. https://doi.org/10.3390/electronics13020269

[3] M. Andronie, G. Lăzăroiu, R. Ştefănescu C. Uţă & I. Dijmărescu. "Sustainable, Smart, and Sensing Technologies for Cyber-Physical Manufacturing Systems: A Systematic Literature Review". *Sustainability*. 2021. vol 3, issue 10. https://doi.org/10.3390/su13105495

[4] M. Andronie, G. Lăzăroiu, M. Iatagan, C. Uţă, R. Ştefănescu & M. Cocoşatu. "Artificial Intelligence-Based Decision-Making Algorithms, Internet of Things Sensing Networks, and Deep Learning-Assisted Smart Process Management in Cyber-Physical Production Systems". *Electronics*. 2021. vol 10, issue 20. https://doi.org/10.3390/electronics10202497

[5] M. Yaqot, B. Menezes, & A. Mohamed, M. Kimberly & L. Cochrane. "Navigating the Nexus of Intelligent Manufacturing and Service Systems: Conflict between Technology and Humanity". *SSRN*. 2021. http://dx.doi.org/10.2139/ssrn.4669779

[6] A. E. Adeniyi, M. Olagunju, J. B. Awotunde, M. K Abiodun, J. Awokola, & M. O. Lawrence. "Augmented Intelligence Multilingual Conversational Service for Smart Enterprise Management Software". In *International Conference on Computational Science and Its Applications* (pp 476–488), 2022. Cham: Springer International Publishing.

[7] H. Alimam, G. Mazzuto, N. Tozzi, F. E. Ciarapica, & M. Bevilacqua. "The Resurrection of Digital Triplet: A Cognitive Pillar of Human-Machine Integration at the Dawn of Industry 5.0". *Journal of King Saud University - Computer and Information Sciences*. 2023. vol 35, issue 10. https://doi.org/10.1016/j.jksuci.2023.101846

[8] Y. P. Su, X.Q. Chen, C. Zhou, L. H. Pearson C. G. Pretty & J. G. Chase. "Integrating Virtual, Mixed, and Augmented Reality into Remote Robotic Applications: A Brief Review of Extended Reality-Enhanced Robotic Systems for Intuitive Telemanipulation and Telemanufacturing Tasks in Hazardous Conditions". *Applied Sciences*. 2023. vol 13, issue 22. https://doi.org/10.3390/app132212129

[9] R. Nitin, C. Saurabh & R. Jayesh. "Enhanced Product Design and Development Using Artificial Intelligence (AI), Virtual Reality (VR), Augmented Reality (AR), 4D/5D/6D Printing, Internet of Things (IoT), and Blockchain: A Review". *SSRN*. 2023. http://dx.doi.org/10.2139/ssrn.4644059

[10] A. Aoun, A. Ilinca, M. Ghandour, & H. Ibrahim. "A Review of Industry 4.0 Characteristics and Challenges, with Potential Improvements using Blockchain Technology". *Computers & Industrial Engineering*. 2021. vol 162, pp 107746, https://doi.org/10.1016/j.cie.2021.107746.

[11] D. Mourtzis, J. Angelopoulos & N. Panopoulos. "A Literature Review of the Challenges and Opportunities of the Transition from Industry 4.0 to Society 5.0." *Energies*. 2023. vol 15, issue 6276, pp 1–29. https://doi.org/10.3390/en15176276

[12] J. Angelopoulos & D. Mourtzis. "An Intelligent Product Service System for Adaptive Maintenance of Engineered-to-Order Manufacturing Equipment Assisted by Augmented Reality". *Applied Sciences*. 2021. vol 12, issue 11, https://doi.org/10.3390/app12115349

[13] J. B. Awotunde, A. L. Imoize, A. E. Adeniyi, K. M. Abiodun, E. F. Ayo, K. V. Kavitha, K. ... & R. O. Ogundokun. "Explainable Machine Learning (XML) for Multimedia-Based Healthcare Systems: Opportunities, Challenges, Ethical and Future Prospects". *Explainable Machine Learning for Multimedia Based Healthcare Applications*, 2023, pp 21–46. https://doi.org/10.1007/978-3-031-38036-5_2

[14] C. Laiton-Bonadiez, J.W. Branch-Bedoya, J. Zapata-Cortes, E. Paipa-Sanabria & M. Arango-Serna. "Industry 4.0 Technologies Applied to the Rail Transportation Industry: A Systematic Review". *Sensors*. 2022. vol 22, issue 7, p 2491. https://doi.org/10.3390/s22072491

[15] B. Jeong, & J. Yoon. Competitive Intelligence Analysis of Augmented Reality Technology Using Patent Information. *Sustainability*. 2017. vol 9, issue 4, p 497. https://doi.org/10.3390/su9040497

[16] E. A. Adeniyi, S. A. Ajagbe, O. A. Oki, A. O. Adebayo, & O. Olasupo. "Application of Machine Learning Algorithm in Cloud-to-edge Computing: Analysis and Limitations". *2023 IEEE AFRICON*, Nairobi, Kenya, 2023, pp. 1–6, doi: 10.1109/AFRICON55910.2023.10293346.

[17] N. H. Nguyen, G. Lasa, & I. Iriarte. "Human-Centred Design in Industry 4.0: Case Study Review and Opportunities for Future Research". *Journal of Intelligent Manufacturing*. 2022. vol 33, issue 1, pp 35–76.

[18] K. C. Rath, A. Khang, D. Roy. *The Role of Internet of Things (IoT) Technology in Industry 4.0 Economy In Advanced IoT Technologies and Applications in the Industry 4.0 Digital Economy*. Taylor & Francis Group. 2024. https://doi.org/10.1201/9781003434269-1

[19] A. Nounou, H. Jaber & R. Aydin. "A cyber-physical system architecture based on lean principles for managing industry 4.0 setups". *International Journal of*

Computer Integrated Manufacturing. 2022. vol 35, issue 8, pp 890–908. https://doi.org/10.1080/0951192X.2022.2027016

[20] M. Javaid, A. Haleem, R. P. Singh & R. Rajiv Suman. "Enabling flexible manufacturing system (FMS) through the applications of industry 4.0 technologies". *Internet of Things and Cyber-Physical Systems*. 2022. vol 2, pp 49–62. https://doi.org/10.1016/j.iotcps.2022.05.005

[21] J. Leng, W. Sha, B. Wang, P. Zheng, C. Zhuang, Q. Liu, T. Wuest, D. Mourtzis & L. Wang. "Industry 5.0: Prospect and Retrospect". *Journal of Manufacturing Systems*. vol 65, pp 279–295. https://doi.org/10.1016/j.jmsy.2022.09.017.

[22] M. Polakova, J. H. Suleimanova, P. Madzík. L. Copus, I. Molnarovab, & J. Polednovab. "Soft Skills and Their Importance in the Labour Market Under the Conditions of Industry 5.0." *Heliyon*. 2023. vol 9, issue 8. https://doi.org/10.1016/j.heliyon.2023.e18670

[23] F. Longo, A. Padovano & S. Umbrello. "Value-Oriented and Ethical Technology Engineering in Industry 5.0: A Human-Centric Perspective for the Design of the Factory of the Future". *Applied Sciences*. 2022. vol 10, issue 12. https://doi.org/10.3390/app10124182

[24] A. Chandel & B. Sharma. "Technology Aspects of Artificial Intelligence: Industry 5.0 for Organization Decision Making". In: Garg, L., et al. *Information Systems and Management Science* (vol 521, pp 79–90), 2023. Cham: Springer. https://doi.org/10.1007/978-3-031-13150-9_7

[25] P. K. Maddikunta, Q. Pham, B. Prabadevi, N. Deepa, K. Dev, T. R. Gadekallu. R. Rukhsana & M. Liyanage. "Industry 5.0: A Survey on Enabling Technologies and Potential Applications". *Journal of Industrial Information Integration*. 2022. vol 26. https://doi.org/10.1016/j.jii.2021.100257.

[26] E. Jamei, M. Mortimer, M. Seyedmahmoudian, B. Horan & A.Stojcevski. "Investigating the Role of Virtual Reality in Planning for Sustainable Smart Cities". *Sustainability*. 2017. vol 9, p 2006. https://doi.org/10.3390/su9112006

[27] S. Rokhsaritalemi, A. Sadeghi-Niaraki & M. Choi. "A Review on Mixed Reality: Current Trends, Challenges and Prospects". *Applied Sciences*. 2020. vol 10, issue 2, p. 636. https://doi.org/10.3390/app10020636

[28] B. Alojaiman. "Technological Modernizations in the Industry 5.0 Era: A Descriptive Analysis and Future Research Directions". *Processes*. 2023. vol 11. https://doi.org/10.3390/pr11051318

[29] C.M. Y. Rasimah, M. Nurazean, M.D. Salwani, M. Z. Norziha, & I. Roslina. "A Systematic Literature Review of Factors Influencing Acceptance on Mixed Reality Technology". *ARPN Journal of Engineering and Applied Sciences*. 2015. vol 10, pp 18239–18246.

[30] H. Hu X. Feng Z. Shao, M. Xie, S. Xu, X. Wu, Z. Zhe-wei. "Application and Prospect of Mixed Reality Technology in Medical Field". *Current Medical Science*. 2019. vol 39, pp 1–6. https://doi.org/10.1007/s11596-019-1992-8

[31] X. Hu, V. Nanjappan & G. V. Georgiev. "Bursting Through the Blocks in the Human Mind: Enhancing Creativity with Extended Reality Technologies". *The Digital Library is published by the Association for Computing Machinery*. 2021. vol 28, issue 3, pp 57–61. https://doi.org/10.1145/3460114

[32] T. Masooda & J. Eggera. "Augmented Reality in Support of Industry 4.0—Implementation Challenges and Success Factors". *Robotics and Computer Integrated Manufacturing*. 2019. vol 58, pp 181–195. https://doi.org/10.1016/j.rcim.2019.02.003

[33] M. Eswaran, A. K. Gulivindala, A. K. Inkulu, & M. V. A. Raju Bahubalendruni. "Augmented Reality-Based Guidance in Product Assembly and Maintenance/ Repair Perspective: A State of the Art Review on Challenges and Opportunities". *Expert Systems with Applications*. 2023. vol 213, https://doi.org/10.1016/ j.eswa.2022.118983

[34] M. Eswaran & R. Bahubalendruni. "Challenges and Opportunities on AR/VR Technologies for Manufacturing Systems in the Context of Industry 4.0: A State of the Art Review". *Journal of Manufacturing Systems*. 2022. vol 65, pp 260–278, https://doi.org/10.1016/j.jmsy.2022.09.016

[35] A. C. Firu, A.I. Tapîrdea, A. I. Feier, G. Drăghici. "Virtual Reality in the Automotive Field in Industry 4.0." *Materials Today: Proceedings*. vol 45, pp 4177–4182. https:// doi.org/10.1016/j.matpr.2020.12.037

[36] S. C. Sekaran, H. J. Yap, S. N. Musa, K. E. Liew, C. H. Tan & A. Aman. "The Implementation of Virtual Reality in Digital Factory—A Comprehensive Review". *The International Journal of Advanced Manufacturing Technology*. 2021. vol 115, pp 1349–1366. https://doi.org/10.1007/s00170-021-07240-x

[37] A. Paszkiewicz, M. Salach, P. Dymora, M. Bolanowski, G. Budzik & P. Kubiak. "Methodology of Implementing Virtual Reality in Education for Industry 4.0". *Sustainability*. 2021. vol 13, issue 9, p 5049. https://doi.org/10.3390/su1 3095049

[38] M. Tseng, T. P. T. Tran, H. Hien Minh, T. Bui, & M. K. Lim. "Sustainable industrial and operation engineering trends and challenges Toward Industry 4.0: A data driven analysis". *Journal of Industrial and Production Engineering*. 2021. vol 38, issue 8, pp 581–598. https://doi.org/10.1080/21681015.2021.1950227

[39] Y. Yin, P. Zheng, C. Li & L. Wang. "A State-of-the-Art Survey on Augmented Reality-Assisted Digital Twin for Futuristic Human-Centric Industry Transformation". *Robotics and Computer-Integrated Manufacturing*. 2023. vol 81, p 102515. https:// doi.org/10.1016/j.rcim.2022.102515

[40] Y. Yin, P. Zheng, C. Li, J. Cong & L. Wang. "An Empirical Study of An MR-Enhanced Kinematic Prototyping Approach for Articulated Products". *Advanced Engineering Informatics*. 2023. vol 58. https://doi.org/10.1016/j.aei.2023.102203

[41] C. K. Nuraini, C. K. Mohd, F. Shahbodin, M. M. Sedek, T. N. T. Zakaria, A. Anggrawan & H. M. Kasim. "Unveiling the Potential of Mixed Reality: Opportunities, Challenges, And Future Prospects". *Journal of Theoretical and Applied Information Technology*. 2023. vol 101 , issue 20, pp 6650–6662.

[42] O. A. Ruzakova & E. S. Grin. "Intellectual Property Protection in The Field of Virtual and Augmented Reality Technologies". *Perm University of Herald Juridicial Sciences*. 2020. vol 49. https://doi.org/10.17072/1995-4190-2020-49-502-523

[43] M. Venkatesan, H. Mohan, J. R. Ryan, C. M. Schurch, G.P. Nolan, D. H. Frakes, & F. Ahmet, A.F. Coskun. "Virtual and Augmented Reality for Biomedical Applications". *Cell Reports Medicine*. 2021. https://doi.org/10.1016/j.xcrm.2021.100348

[44] C. E. Mendoza-Ramírez, J. C. Tudon-Martinez, L. C. Félix-Herrán, J. D. Lozoya-Santos, & A. Vargas-Martínez. "Augmented Reality: Survey". *Applied Sciences*. 2023. vol 13, issue 18, p 10491.

[45] V. K. Annanth, M. Abinash, L. B. Rao. "Intelligent Manufacturing in the Context of Industry 4.0: A Case Study of Siemens Industry". *Journal of Physics: Conference Series*. 2021. https://doi.org/10.1088/1742-6596/1969/1/012019

[46] J. Blanchard, S. Koshal, S. Morley, & M. McGurk. "The Use of Mixed Reality in Dentistry". *British Dental Journal*. 2022. vol 233, pp 261–265. https://doi.org/ 10.1038/s41415-022-4451-z

[47] Y. Qin, E. Bloomquist, T. Bulbul, J. Gabbard & K. Tanous. "Impact of Information Display on Worker Performance for Wood Frame Wall Assembly Using AR HMD Under Different Task Conditions". *Advanced Engineering Informatics*. 2021. vol 50. https://doi.org/10.1016/j.aei.2021.101423.

[48] R. E. Petruse, G. Meixner & S. Ćuković. *Revolutionizing Computer-Aided Design with Virtual Reality in Smart VR/AR/MR Systems for Professionals*. CRC Press. 2024. pp 24–33. https://doi.org/10.1201/9781003306078

[49] G. Costa, M. R. Petry, & A.P. Moreira. "Augmented Reality for Human–Robot Collaboration and Cooperation in Industrial Applications: A Systematic Literature Review". *Sensors*. 2022. vol 22. https://doi.org/10.3390/s22072725

[50] M. Javaid, A. Haleem, R. P. Singh, R. Suman & E. S. Gonzalez. Understanding the Adoption of Industry 4.0 Technologies in Improving Environmental Sustainability. *Sustainable Operations and Computers*. 2023. vol 3, pp 203–217. https://doi.org/10.1016/j.susoc.2022.01.008.

[51] M. Javaid, A. Haleem, R. P. Singh & R. Rajiv Suman. Substantial Capabilities of Robotics in Enhancing Industry 4.0 Implementation. *Cognitive Robotics*. vol 1, pp 58–75. https://doi.org/10.1016/j.cogr.2021.06.001.

[52] B. Alojaiman. "Technological Modernizations in the Industry 5.0 Era: A Descriptive Analysis and Future Research Directions". *Processes*. 2023. vol 11. https://doi.org/10.3390/pr11051318

[53] E. Marino, L. Barbieri, B. Colacino, A. K. Fleri, & F. Fa Bruno. "An Augmented Reality Inspection Tool to Support Workers in Industry 4.0 Environments". *Computers in Industry*. 2021. vol 127. https://doi.org/10.1016/j.compind.2021.103412

[54] U. Radhakrishnan, K. Koumaditis & F. Chinello. "A Systematic Review of Immersive Virtual Reality for Industrial Skills Training". *Behaviour & Information Technology*. 2021. vol 40, issue 12, pp 1310–1339. https://doi.org/10.1080/0144929X.2021.1954693

[55] A. Sharma, R. Mehtab, S. Mohan, and M. K. Mohd Shah. "Augmented Reality – An Important Aspect of Industry 4.0, Industrial Robot". 2021. vol 49 issue 3, pp 428–441. https://doi.org/10.1108/IR-09-2021-0204

[56] Z. W. Lie, Q. L. Zheng, S. Zhou & H. L. Rauf. "Virtual Energy-Saving Environmental Protection Building Design and Implementation". *International Journal of System Assurance Engineering and Management*. 2022. vol 13, pp 263–272. https://doi.org/10.1007/s13198-021-01387-2

[57] P. Wang, S. Zhang, M. Billinghurst, X. Bai, W. He, S. Wang, M. Sun & X. Zhang. "A Comprehensive Survey of AR/MR-Based Co-Design in Manufacturing". *Engineering with Computers*. 2021. vol 36, pp 1715–1738. https://doi.org/10.1007/s00366-019-00792-3

[58] O. C. Abikoye, A. O. Bajeh, J. B. Awotunde, A. O. Ameen, H. A. Mojeed, M. Abdulraheem, ... & S. A. Salihu. "Application of Internet of Thing and Cyber Physical System in Industry 4.0 Smart Manufacturing". In *Emergence of Cyber Physical System and IoT in Smart Automation and Robotics: Computer Engineering in Automation* (pp 203–217), 2021. Cham: Springer International Publishing.

[59] C. E. Mendoza-Ramírez, J. C. Tudon-Martinez, L. C. Félix-Herrán, J. Lozoya-Santos, A. Vargas-Martínez. "Augmented Reality: Survey". *Applied Science*. 2023. vol 13. https://doi.org/10.3390/app131810491

[60] J. B. Awotunde, F. E. Ayo, R. Panigrahi, A. Garg, A. K. Bhoi, & P. Barsocchi. "A Multi-level Random Forest Model-Based Intrusion Detection Using Fuzzy Inference System for Internet of Things Networks". *International Journal of Computational Intelligence Systems*. 2023. vol 16, issue 1, p 31.

[61] A. O. Bajeh, H. A. Mojeed, H. A., Ameen, A. O., Abikoye, O. C., Salihu, S. A., Abdulraheem, M., ... & Awotunde, J. B. "Internet of Robotic Things: Its Domain, Methodologies, and Applications". In *Emergence of Cyber Physical System and IoT in Smart Automation and Robotics: Computer Engineering in Automation* (pp 135–146), 2021. Cham: Springer International Publishing.

[62] M. Eswaran, A. K. Gulivindala, A. K. Inkulu, & M. V. A. Raju Bahubalendruni. "Augmented Reality-Based Guidance in Product Assembly and Maintenance/ Repair Perspective: A State of the Art Review on Challenges and Opportunities". *Expert Systems with Applications*. 2023. vol 213. https://doi.org/10.1016/j.eswa.2022.118983

[63] M. Eswaran & R. Bahubalendruni. "Challenges and Opportunities on AR/VR Technologies for Manufacturing Systems in the Context of Industry 4.0: A State of the Art Review". *Journal of Manufacturing Systems*. 2022. vol 65, pp 260–278. https://doi.org/10.1016/j.jmsy.2022.09.016

[64] S. Aromaa, A. Väätänen, I. Aaltonen, V. Goriachev, K. Helin & J. Karjalainen. "Awareness of the Real-World Environment When Using Augmented Reality Head-Mounted Display". *Applied Ergonomics*. 2020. vol 88. https://doi.org/10.1016/j.apergo.2020.103145

[65] T. Porcino, D. Trevisan & E. Clua. "Minimizing Cybersickness in Head-Mounted Display Systems: Causes and Strategies Review". *22nd Symposium on Virtual and Augmented Reality (SVR)* (pp 154–163), 2020. Brazil: Porto de Galinhas. https://doi.org/10.1109/SVR51698.2020.00035

[66] Z. You, & L. Feng. "Integration of Industry 4.0 Related Technologies in Construction Industry: A Framework of Cyber-Physical System". *IEEE Access*. 2020. vol 8, pp 122908–122922.

[67] H. Alimam, G. Mazzuto, N. Tozzi, F. E. Ciarapica, & M. Bevilacqua. "The resurrection of digital triplet: A cognitive pillar of human-machine integration at the dawn of industry 5.0." *Journal of King Saud University-Computer and Information Sciences*. 2023. vol 35, issue 10, p 101846.

[68] O. C. Abikoye, E. T. Oladipupo, A. L. Imoize, J. B. Awotunde, C. C. Lee, & C. T. Li. "Securing Critical User Information Over the Internet of Medical Things Platforms Using a Hybrid Cryptography Scheme". *Future Internet*. 2023. vol 15, issue 3, p 99.

[69] A. Adel, "Unlocking the Future: Fostering Human–Machine Collaboration and Driving Intelligent Automation through Industry 5.0 in Smart Cities". *Smart Cities*. 2023. vol 6, issue 5, pp 2742–2782.

[70] J. B. Awotunde, A. L. Imoize, R. G. Jimoh, E. A. Adeniyi, M. Abdulraheem, I. D. Oladipo, & P. B. Falola. "AIoMT Enabling Real-Time Monitoring of Healthcare Systems: Security and Privacy Considerations". In *Handbook of Security and Privacy of AI-Enabled Healthcare Systems and Internet of Medical Things* (pp 97–133), 2024. IET Publisher, United Kingdom.

[71] A. E. Adeniyi, R. G. Jimoh, R. G., & Awotunde, J. A Review on Elliptic Curve Cryptography Algorithm for Internet of Things: Categorization, Application Areas, and Security. Application Areas, and Security. http://dx.doi.org/10.2139/ssrn.4683742

[72] M. Abdulraheem, E. A. Adeniyi, J. B. Awotunde, A. L. Imoize, R. G. Jimoh, I. D. Oladipo, & P. B. Falola. "Artificial Intelligence of Medical Things for Medical Information Systems Privacy and Security". In *Handbook of Security and Privacy of AI-Enabled Healthcare Systems and Internet of Medical Things* (pp 63–96), 2024. CRC Press.

11 Industry 4.0 Design Principles, Technologies, and Applications

Lokaiah Pullagura, Biswajit Brahma, N. Vinaya Kumari, L. Ravikumar, Siva Kumar Gowda Katta, and Ronald Chiwariro

11.1 INTRODUCTION

Industry 4.0, often referred to as the Fourth Industrial Revolution, marks a paradigm shift in the manufacturing landscape. This transformative concept envisions the integration of cutting-edge technologies to create intelligent, interconnected, and highly efficient production systems. Unlike its predecessors, Industry 4.0 is characterized by the convergence of digital, physical, and biological domains, reshaping the way products are designed, produced, and delivered. At its core, Industry 4.0 embraces a set of design principles aimed at enhancing the agility, adaptability, and responsiveness of manufacturing processes. Interoperability, one of these principles, ensures seamless communication among devices and systems, fostering a cohesive and integrated environment. Information transparency guarantees the accessibility and reliability of real-time data throughout the supply chain, while decentralized decision-making empowers machines to make autonomous choices, optimizing operations with unprecedented speed. Key enabling technologies, such as the Internet of Things (IoT), artificial intelligence (AI), and big data analytics, play pivotal roles in realizing the Industry 4.0 vision [1–5].

IoT devices embedded in machinery and products collect vast amounts of data, which, when analyzed through sophisticated algorithms, yield actionable insights. AI and machine learning algorithms drive predictive analytics, allowing manufacturers to anticipate maintenance needs, optimize production schedules, and enhance overall decision-making. Cloud computing provides the scalable infrastructure necessary for processing and storing the immense volumes of data generated in Industry 4.0 environments [6–8]. Cyber-physical systems (CPSs) integrate physical processes with computational elements, creating intelligent systems capable of real-time adaptation. Additive manufacturing, commonly known as 3D printing, enables not only rapid prototyping but also on-demand production and customization, revolutionizing traditional manufacturing methods.

DOI: 10.1201/9781003581963-11

Applications of Industry 4.0 are diverse and impactful. From predictive maintenance and digital twins to smart supply chains and autonomous robots, these applications redefine efficiency and productivity. Human–machine collaboration, facilitated by collaborative robots and augmented reality, enhances the capabilities of the workforce in this new era of smart manufacturing. As Industry 4.0 continues to evolve, its influence extends across industries, promising a future where innovation, connectivity, and intelligence converge to shape the way we conceive and execute industrial processes. The journey into Industry 4.0 is an exploration of technological frontiers that promise not just increased efficiency but a fundamental transformation of the manufacturing landscape [9–12].

In the tapestry of industrial evolution, Industry 4.0 stands as a transformative force, weaving together digital technologies and smart systems to redefine the very fabric of manufacturing. This Fourth Industrial Revolution is not merely a progression but a revolution marked by the fusion of cyber-physical systems, data analytics, and automation, unleashing a new era of efficiency, customization, and interconnectedness. At the heart of Industry 4.0 lies a commitment to interoperability, transcending the limitations of disparate systems by establishing a universal language for seamless communication. This interconnectedness paves the way for an ecosystem where machines, devices, and humans collaborate harmoniously, each contributing to a symphony of synchronized operations. Information transparency, another cornerstone of Industry 4.0, goes beyond data availability. It involves the creation of a transparent digital thread weaving through the entire value chain, providing stakeholders with real-time insights into production processes, supply chain dynamics, and product lifecycles. Blockchain technology emerges as a robust solution, ensuring data integrity and security in this era of heightened connectivity. Decentralized decision-making, empowered by edge computing, signifies a departure from centralized control. Machines at the edge of the network process data autonomously, enabling quicker responses and reducing dependence on a central decision-making hub. This shift toward decentralized intelligence amplifies the agility of manufacturing processes, allowing real-time adjustments to changing conditions [13–16].

The technical assistance rendered by augmented reality and virtual reality technologies opens new dimensions in human–machine interaction. Workers equipped with AR devices receive contextual information, aiding them in complex tasks, training, and maintenance. This augmentation of human capabilities amplifies efficiency and precision in the manufacturing environment. Smart objects, embedded with sensors and identification technologies, usher in a new era of traceability and connectivity. From raw materials to finished products, these smart objects provide a granular view of the entire production chain, enabling real-time monitoring, quality control, and a heightened level of responsiveness to market demands [17,18].

The technological backbone of Industry 4.0 is fortified by the IoT, where a myriad of devices and sensors forms a network, generating a continuous stream of data [19,20]. Big data analytics, propelled by artificial intelligence and machine learning, transforms this data deluge into actionable insights, fostering predictive maintenance, optimized resource allocation, and data-driven decision-making [21]. Cloud computing, as the cornerstone of Industry 4.0 infrastructure, serves as the backbone for scalable and flexible data storage and processing. This allows for the seamless deployment of applications, facilitates collaboration, and ensures accessibility to critical information across the manufacturing ecosystem. As the manufacturing landscape evolves, Industry 4.0 applications become increasingly diverse. Predictive maintenance algorithms anticipate equipment failures, minimizing downtime and extending machinery lifespan. Digital twins provide a virtual mirror of physical assets, enabling real-time analysis and optimization. Smart supply chains leverage interconnected systems to enhance transparency, reduce inefficiencies, and respond swiftly to market fluctuations.

Autonomous robots, guided by artificial intelligence, redefine the factory floor. These machines perform tasks with precision, consistency, and adaptability, working alongside human counterparts to create a harmonious blend of human ingenuity and machine efficiency [22,23]. Collaborative robots, or cobots, exemplify the synergy between human and machine, sharing the workspace and responsibilities seamlessly. Blockchain technology, beyond ensuring transparency in the supply chain, introduces trust and security [24]. Through a decentralized and tamper-proof ledger, blockchain establishes a verifiable record of transactions, assuring the authenticity of products and transactions in an interconnected manufacturing landscape [25]. As Industry 4.0 advances, it resonates not only with technological prowess but with a promise of a future where innovation, efficiency, and sustainability converge. The journey into Industry 4.0 is an exploration of uncharted territories, where the fusion of digital and physical realms heralds a new industrial epoch. The impact of Industry 4.0 extends far beyond the factory floor, influencing how we conceptualize and actualize production, ultimately shaping the way we live and work.

In the annals of industrial evolution, the advent of Industry 4.0 represents a watershed moment, ushering in a new era of intelligent manufacturing. This chapter delves into the transformative landscape of Industry 4.0, exploring its foundational principles, the technological tapestry that underpins it, diverse applications across industries, and the profound impact it wields on the future of production.

11.2 FOUNDATIONS OF INDUSTRY 4.0

11.2.1 Interoperability: The Language of Connectivity

At the core of Industry 4.0 lies the principle of interoperability, transcending traditional barriers by establishing a universal language for seamless communication. This section explores the significance of interoperability in creating an integrated manufacturing ecosystem. In the landscape of Industry 4.0, interoperability emerges as a critical enabler, providing the necessary framework for seamless integration and communication across diverse systems, devices, and stakeholders [26,27]. At its core, interoperability breaks down operational silos, fostering a unified environment where data can flow effortlessly, facilitating collaboration and driving efficiency. In essence, it serves as the backbone of modern manufacturing, laying the foundation for intelligent and interconnected production ecosystems. The significance of interoperability within Industry 4.0 cannot be overstated. It is the key to unlocking the full potential of emerging technologies such as artificial intelligence, the IoT, and big data analytics [28,29]. By establishing common standards and protocols for communication, interoperability enables disparate components to work together harmoniously, driving innovation and agility in manufacturing processes. Without interoperability, the promises of increased automation, predictive maintenance, and personalized manufacturing experiences remain unattainable.

Central to the concept of interoperability are standardized communication protocols and data formats. Protocols like OPC UA and MQTT provide a common language for devices and systems to exchange information, ensuring compatibility regardless of manufacturer or origin [30,31]. Similarly, standardized data formats and models define common structures and semantics, allowing for consistent interpretation of information across platforms. This semantic interoperability goes beyond mere syntactic compatibility, focusing on the meaningful interpretation of data to ensure a shared understanding among different systems. Furthermore, interoperability extends to the realm of application programming interfaces (APIs), which facilitate interaction between software applications. Well-defined APIs enable seamless integration between various components, from the shop floor to enterprise-level systems, allowing for efficient data exchange and process orchestration. Additionally, reference architectures such as RAMI 4.0 provide a structured approach to designing interoperable systems, defining standardized layers and interfaces to guide implementation efforts.

Practically, interoperability finds application across a spectrum of use cases within Industry 4.0. In supply chain integration, interoperability enables real-time collaboration between suppliers, manufacturers, and distributors, optimizing inventory management and reducing lead times. Smart manufacturing systems leverage interoperability to ensure seamless communication between diverse production systems, enhancing efficiency and flexibility. Collaborative robotics (cobots) exemplify the importance of interoperability, as these robots need to communicate with human operators and other machines to perform tasks collaboratively and safely.

Moreover, interoperability facilitates cross-platform data exchange, allowing for seamless transfer of information between different software tools and systems. For instance, product design data created in one software tool can be effortlessly transferred to another tool for simulation or prototyping purposes. Additionally, interoperability plays a crucial role in integrating cloud and edge computing resources, ensuring that data collected at the edge are seamlessly transferred to the cloud for analysis, and insights derived from the cloud are effectively utilized at the edge for real-time decision-making.

Despite its transformative potential, interoperability also presents challenges and considerations that need to be addressed. Security and privacy concerns loom large, as interoperability increases the surface area for potential cyber threats. Ensuring secure and encrypted communication channels and implementing robust access control mechanisms are paramount in mitigating these risks. Furthermore, integrating legacy systems with modern Industry 4.0 technologies poses a significant challenge, often requiring the development of middleware solutions to bridge the gap between old and new systems.

Standardization efforts play a crucial role in addressing interoperability challenges, with industry consortia and standard-setting organizations driving the development and adoption of common standards and protocols. These efforts aim to ensure interoperability across disparate systems and technologies, fostering a more cohesive and interconnected manufacturing ecosystem [32,33]. Moreover, interoperability must be considered throughout the entire lifecycle of systems and devices, from design and implementation to operation and maintenance. This lifecycle approach ensures continued compatibility and adaptability as technologies evolve and requirements change over time.

In conclusion, interoperability serves as the linchpin of Industry 4.0, enabling seamless communication and collaboration among diverse systems, devices, and stakeholders. Its importance cannot be overstated, as it lays the foundation for the intelligent and interconnected manufacturing ecosystems of the future. By addressing challenges, leveraging standardized protocols, and adopting a lifecycle approach, manufacturers can unlock the full potential of interoperability and realize the transformative benefits of Industry 4.0.

11.2.2 Information Transparency: Beyond Data Availability

Information transparency within Industry 4.0 transcends the mere availability of data; it encompasses the integrity, security, and accessibility of information across the entire value chain. At the forefront of ensuring this transparency is blockchain technology, which revolutionizes data management by providing a decentralized, immutable ledger system. Unlike traditional centralized databases, blockchain operates on a distributed network of nodes, where each transaction is verified and recorded in a transparent and tamper-resistant manner. This inherent transparency fosters trust among stakeholders, as it allows for real-time visibility into the origin, ownership, and history of data.

One of the primary benefits of blockchain in ensuring information transparency is its ability to establish a single source of truth. By decentralizing data storage and employing consensus mechanisms, blockchain eliminates the need for intermediaries and central authorities, thereby reducing the risk of data manipulation or fraud. This transparency engenders confidence in the accuracy and reliability of information, enabling stakeholders to make informed decisions based on verified data. Moreover, blockchain's cryptographic principles ensure data security, as each transaction is cryptographically linked to the previous one, making it virtually impossible to alter historical records without consensus from the network participants. Furthermore, blockchain enhances transparency by enabling seamless data sharing and collaboration among disparate entities. Through smart contracts, self-executing agreements coded on the blockchain, stakeholders can automate processes and enforce predefined rules without the need for intermediaries. This automation streamlines workflows, reduces administrative overhead, and ensures compliance with regulations, thereby enhancing transparency and efficiency across the value chain. Additionally, blockchain's transparent nature promotes accountability and traceability, as every transaction is timestamped and traceable to its point of origin. This traceability is particularly crucial in industries such as supply chain management, where stakeholders need to track the movement of goods and verify their authenticity.

11.2.3 Decentralized Decision-Making: Empowering Machines

Decentralized decision-making, propelled by the advent of edge computing, represents a fundamental departure from traditional centralized control paradigms. In the context of Industry 4.0, this shift toward decentralized intelligence is reshaping the landscape of manufacturing, enabling autonomous decision-making at the edge of the network. At its core, decentralized decision-making distributes computational power and decision authority closer to where data are generated, fostering agility, responsiveness, and efficiency in industrial processes.

Edge computing serves as the cornerstone of decentralized decision-making, empowering devices and machines with the computational capabilities to process data locally, without relying solely on centralized data centers or cloud infrastructure [34]. By bringing computing resources closer to the point of data generation, edge computing minimizes latency and bandwidth constraints, enabling real-time analysis and decision-making at the network edge. This paradigm shift is particularly transformative in manufacturing environments, where split-second decisions can significantly impact operational performance and productivity [35].

One of the key advantages of decentralized decision-making is its ability to enhance agility and responsiveness in manufacturing operations [36]. By decentralizing decision-making authority to individual machines or devices, manufacturers can enable autonomous adaptation to dynamic production conditions and unforeseen disruptions. For example, in a smart factory equipped with edge-enabled sensors and actuators, machines can autonomously adjust production parameters in response to fluctuations in demand, material availability, or machine health, without requiring explicit human intervention. This agility enables manufacturers to optimize production efficiency, minimize downtime, and respond swiftly to changing market demands.

Moreover, decentralized decision-making fosters resilience and robustness in manufacturing systems by reducing reliance on centralized points of failure. Traditional centralized control architectures are vulnerable to disruptions such as network outages or data center failures, which can have cascading effects on production operations. In contrast, decentralized decision-making distributes decision authority across a distributed network of edge devices, mitigating the risk of single points of failure and enhancing system resilience. This decentralized approach ensures that manufacturing processes can continue seamlessly even in the event of localized failures or network interruptions, thereby improving overall system reliability and uptime.

11.2.4 Technical Assistance: Augmenting Human Capabilities

The integration of augmented reality (AR) and virtual reality (VR) technologies represents a transformative advancement in human–machine interaction, offering a new dimension of technical assistance in manufacturing environments [37]. Augmented reality overlays digital information onto the physical world, while virtual reality creates immersive simulated environments, both enhancing worker capabilities in various facets of complex tasks, training, and maintenance within Industry 4.0 [38].

In complex manufacturing tasks, AR and VR technologies serve as invaluable tools for providing real-time guidance and contextual information to workers. AR-enabled smart glasses or headsets can overlay digital instructions, schematics, or real-time data onto the physical workspace, aiding workers in performing intricate assembly tasks or troubleshooting machinery [37,38]. This hands-free access to information enhances productivity and accuracy while reducing the need for paper-based instructions or manual data lookup. Similarly, VR simulations offer immersive training environments where workers can practice operating complex machinery, performing maintenance procedures, or simulating hazardous scenarios in a safe and controlled manner. These virtual training environments provide realistic hands-on experience, accelerating the learning curve and ensuring that workers are well-prepared to handle diverse operational challenges [39].

Furthermore, AR and VR technologies facilitate remote technical assistance and collaboration, enabling experts to provide guidance and support to on-site personnel regardless of geographical location [38]. Through AR-enabled video calls or remote assistance applications, off-site experts can visualize the field of view of on-site technicians, annotate real-world objects, and provide step-by-step instructions in real time. This remote assistance capability reduces downtime, minimizes travel costs, and enhances the efficiency of troubleshooting and maintenance activities [37]. Additionally, AR and VR technologies support predictive maintenance initiatives by enabling workers to visualize equipment performance data, identify potential issues proactively, and schedule maintenance tasks preemptively, thereby optimizing asset uptime and reliability [37–39].

Beyond task execution and maintenance, AR and VR technologies also foster continuous learning and skill development among workers. VR-based training modules offer immersive simulations of complex scenarios or hazardous environments, allowing workers to develop critical skills and procedural knowledge in a safe and controlled setting. AR-enabled performance support tools provide contextual information and guidance directly within the workflow, empowering workers to access relevant information on-demand and troubleshoot issues effectively in real time. This integration of AR and VR technologies into the fabric of everyday work enhances worker capabilities, fosters a culture of innovation and continuous improvement, and ultimately drives operational excellence in the digital age.

11.2.5 Smart Objects: Tracing the Connected Supply Chain

Smart objects, equipped with sensors and identification technologies, are revolutionizing traceability and connectivity in the supply chain, ushering in a new era of real-time monitoring, quality control, and responsiveness [40]. These intelligent devices, ranging from RFID tags to IoT-enabled sensors, imbue physical assets with digital capabilities, enabling unprecedented visibility and transparency throughout the supply chain.

At the heart of smart objects is the ability to capture and transmit data in real time, providing stakeholders with instantaneous insights into the status and whereabouts of goods as they move through the supply chain. RFID tags, for instance, allow for automated tracking and identification of items at various stages of production and distribution, from manufacturing facilities to warehouse shelves. This real-time visibility enables manufacturers and logistics providers to optimize inventory management, minimize stockouts, and streamline order fulfillment processes, thereby enhancing overall supply chain efficiency.

Furthermore, smart objects facilitate proactive quality control measures by continuously monitoring environmental conditions, such as temperature, humidity, and vibration, to ensure product integrity throughout transit. IoT-enabled sensors embedded in packaging or shipping containers can detect deviations from predefined thresholds and trigger alerts in case of potential quality issues. By proactively identifying and addressing quality concerns in real time, manufacturers can mitigate the risk of product spoilage, reduce waste, and uphold brand reputation.

Additionally, smart objects enhance supply chain responsiveness by enabling dynamic rerouting and real-time decision-making in response to unforeseen disruptions or changing market conditions. For example, GPS-enabled tracking devices provide real-time location data, allowing logistics managers to monitor shipment progress and adjust routes to avoid delays or congestion. Similarly, sensors embedded in perishable goods can detect transit delays and automatically alert stakeholders, enabling swift corrective actions to minimize the impact on product freshness and shelf-life (Figure 11.1).

11.3 TECHNOLOGIES DRIVING INDUSTRY 4.0

11.3.1 Internet of Things (IoT): The Network of Connectivity

A comprehensive exploration of how IoT devices and networks form the backbone of Industry 4.0, generating a continuous stream of data that fuels real-time decision-making, is provided next. The principles of the IoT form the foundation for the widespread adoption and integration of connected devices across various domains. At its core, the IoT is driven by the overarching goal of enabling connectivity everywhere, transforming ordinary objects into intelligent entities capable of collecting, processing, and exchanging data in real time. This principle underscores the pivotal role of embedding sensors and communication devices into physical objects, thereby facilitating the seamless flow of information and unlocking new opportunities for innovation and efficiency (Figure 11.2).

Sensor integration lies at the heart of the IoT, empowering devices with the ability to perceive and interact with the physical world [41]. IoT devices are equipped with a diverse array of sensors, including temperature sensors, accelerometers, gyroscopes, and more. These sensors gather a wealth of real-time data, providing a granular understanding of the surrounding environment and enabling informed decision-making [42]. Whether monitoring environmental conditions in smart homes, tracking inventory levels in warehouses, or optimizing energy consumption in industrial

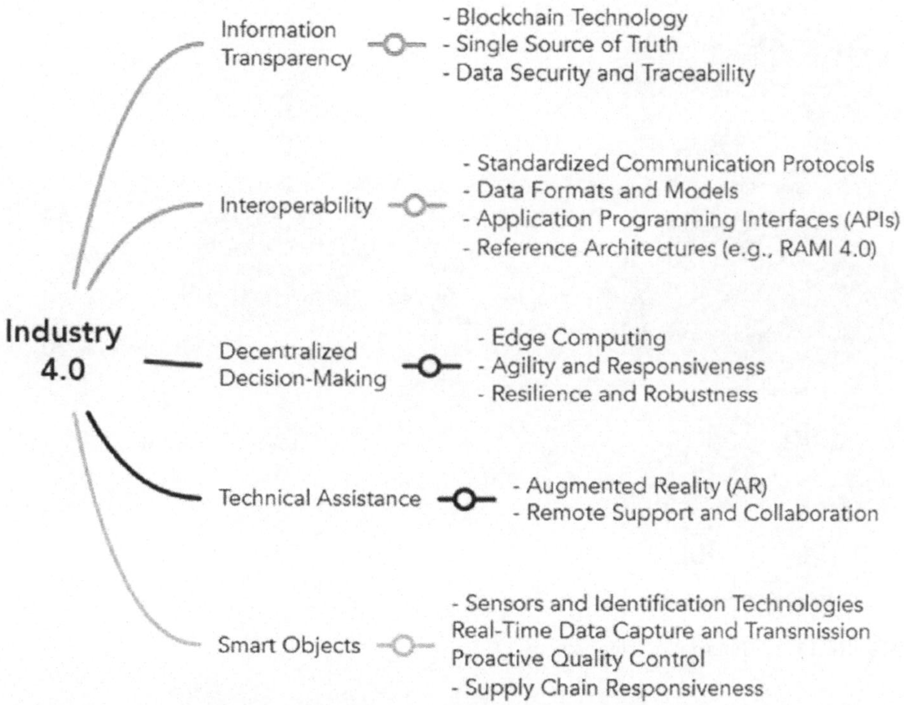

FIGURE 11.1 Conceptual framework.

settings, sensor integration enables IoT devices to capture valuable insights and drive actionable outcomes.

Central to the principles of the IoT is the reliance on wireless communication technologies to facilitate seamless connectivity between devices. Wi-Fi, Bluetooth, Zigbee, and cellular networks are among the most commonly used wireless communication protocols in IoT ecosystems [43]. These protocols enable devices to communicate autonomously without the constraints of physical connections, allowing for greater flexibility, scalability, and interoperability. Whether transmitting sensor data, receiving commands from centralized control systems, or coordinating with other IoT devices in a network, wireless communication forms the backbone of IoT connectivity, enabling devices to stay interconnected in diverse environments and scenarios [44].

Furthermore, the principles of the IoT emphasize the importance of interoperability and standardization to ensure the seamless integration of heterogeneous devices and systems. By adhering to common communication protocols and data formats, IoT devices can exchange information effortlessly, regardless of their manufacturer or origin [41]. This interoperability fosters collaboration, innovation, and the development of robust ecosystems where diverse IoT devices can work together to achieve common objectives [43].

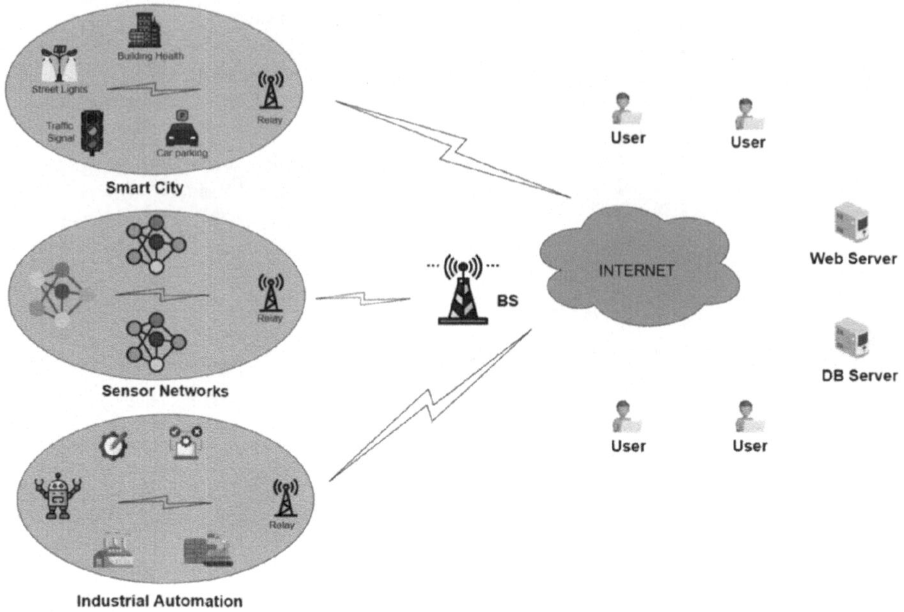

FIGURE 11.2 Internet of Things network.

11.3.2 Components of the Internet of Things

IoT devices represent a pivotal component of the interconnected infrastructure driving Industry 4.0, equipped with sensors, actuators, and communication modules to enable seamless data exchange and automation across diverse applications (Figure 11.3) [5,45]. These devices span a wide spectrum, ranging from smart sensors embedded in everyday objects to wearables and sophisticated industrial IoT devices powering smart factories [46]. IoT devices use connectivity protocols like MQTT, CoAP, and HTTP/HTTPS to facilitate efficient data transmission across distributed environments, meeting specific requirements and constraints [47]. A key paradigm shift in the IoT is the adoption of edge computing, which involves processing data closer to the source rather than relying solely on centralized cloud servers. This approach reduces latency, enabling faster real-time decision-making and alleviating bandwidth constraints associated with transmitting large volumes of data to the cloud [48]. While edge computing handles immediate data processing needs, cloud platforms serve as repositories for storing, analyzing, and further processing IoT data. These platforms offer scalable infrastructure and advanced analytics tools to derive actionable insights from the substantial volumes of data generated by IoT devices.

Advanced analytics and machine learning algorithms are instrumental in extracting valuable insights, identifying patterns, and making predictions from IoT data. Predictive maintenance, for instance, utilizes IoT sensors to gather data on machinery performance, enabling algorithms to forecast potential failures and trigger proactive

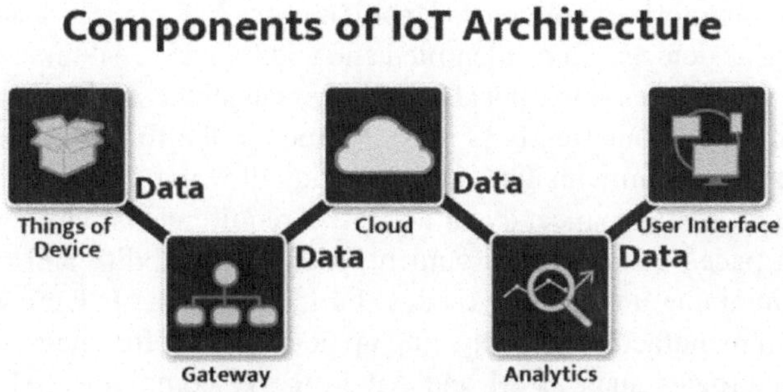

FIGURE 11.3 Components of the Internet of Things.

maintenance measures, thus minimizing downtime and optimizing asset utilization. In smart manufacturing environments, the IoT facilitates real-time communication and collaboration among machines, devices, and systems, leading to enhanced efficiency, adaptive manufacturing processes, and improved resource allocation. Similarly, in supply chain management, the IoT enables end-to-end visibility by leveraging RFID tags and sensors for real-time tracking, optimizing logistics, and enhancing overall efficiency.

Quality control in manufacturing is bolstered by IoT devices monitoring and collecting data during the production process. Any deviations from standard parameters trigger alerts, enabling immediate corrective actions and ensuring adherence to quality standards. Furthermore, the IoT contributes to energy management efforts by monitoring energy usage in manufacturing facilities and adjusting operations based on real-time demand and availability. Moreover, the IoT enables precise asset tracking within manufacturing facilities, facilitating the monitoring of asset location, condition, and usage [46]. This includes tracking tools, equipment, and inventory, thereby enhancing operational efficiency and resource optimization. In essence, IoT devices, coupled with advanced connectivity protocols, edge computing capabilities, and analytics tools, are driving transformative changes across industries, revolutionizing processes, optimizing resource utilization, and enabling the realization of Industry 4.0's vision of intelligent, interconnected ecosystems [42].

11.3.3 The Internet of Things' Impact on Manufacturing

The integration of the IoT into manufacturing processes has ushered in a new era of enhanced efficiency, cost savings, improved quality, and innovation opportunities, driving the evolution of Industry 4.0. By leveraging IoT-driven data analytics and real-time monitoring, operational efficiency is significantly enhanced, enabling production processes to become more agile and responsive to changing demands. With IoT-enabled predictive maintenance and efficient resource utilization, cost savings are realized as unplanned downtime is minimized, and energy consumption is optimized, thereby contributing to overall financial efficiency.

Continuous monitoring and control facilitated by IoT devices lead to improved product quality, as defects can be identified and addressed in real time. This proactive approach not only reduces waste but also enhances customer satisfaction by delivering high-quality products consistently [47,48]. Moreover, the IoT enables agile production by providing real-time insights into demand, allowing for rapid adjustments in manufacturing processes to meet dynamic market requirements. This agility is crucial in today's fast-paced business environment, where adaptability and responsiveness are key to maintaining a competitive edge. Furthermore, the IoT creates innovation opportunities in manufacturing by opening up new avenues for integrating with other emerging technologies such as AI and AR [49]. By combining IoT data with AI algorithms, manufacturers can gain deeper insights into production processes, optimize resource allocation, and automate decision-making, leading to unprecedented levels of efficiency and productivity. Similarly, integrating the IoT with AR technologies enables workers to access real-time information, instructions, and visualizations, enhancing productivity and reducing errors in tasks such as assembly and maintenance [50].

11.3.4 Big Data and Analytics: Transforming Data into Insights

Big data analytics, augmented by AI and ML, represents a transformative force in modern industries, converting vast volumes of raw data into actionable insights [51]. This convergence of technologies unlocks a plethora of opportunities for organizations to enhance operational efficiency, drive innovation, and gain a competitive edge in today's data-driven world [52]. By harnessing the power of big data analytics, companies can unlock valuable insights that enable predictive maintenance, optimize resource allocation, and facilitate data-driven decision-making across various domains (Figure 11.4) [53].

Predictive maintenance, a key application of big data analytics, leverages AI and ML algorithms to forecast equipment failures before they occur, thereby minimizing

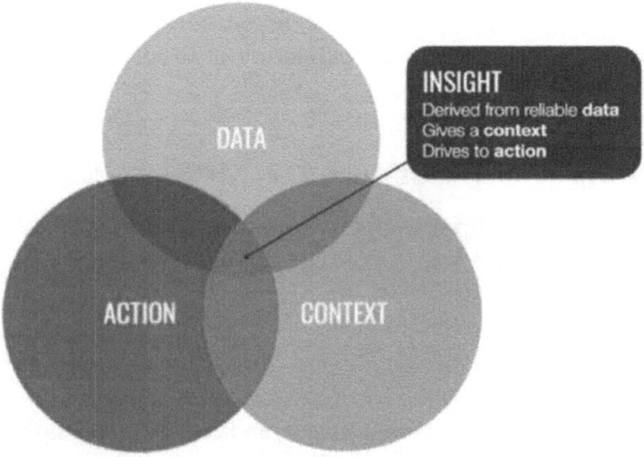

FIGURE 11.4 Transforming data into actionable insights.

downtime and maximizing asset uptime. By analyzing historical performance data, sensor readings, and other relevant factors, predictive maintenance models can identify patterns indicative of impending failures and trigger proactive maintenance actions. This proactive approach not only reduces maintenance costs but also enhances operational reliability and extends the lifespan of critical assets, resulting in significant cost savings and improved productivity.

Furthermore, big data analytics enables optimized resource allocation by providing organizations with real-time insights into resource utilization, demand patterns, and operational inefficiencies. By analyzing large datasets encompassing various aspects of business operations, including production, inventory management, and supply chain logistics, organizations can identify optimization opportunities and allocate resources more effectively. For instance, AI-driven demand forecasting models can predict future demand trends with high accuracy, enabling organizations to adjust production schedules, inventory levels, and procurement strategies accordingly. This optimization leads to reduced inventory holding costs, minimized stockouts, and improved customer satisfaction through timely order fulfillment.

Moreover, big data analytics facilitates data-driven decision-making by empowering organizations with actionable insights derived from diverse sources of data [52]. By integrating data from internal systems, IoT devices, external sources, and social media platforms, organizations can gain a comprehensive understanding of market trends, customer preferences, and competitive dynamics [53]. AI and ML algorithms analyze these data to uncover hidden patterns, correlations, and trends, enabling stakeholders to make informed decisions with confidence. Whether optimizing marketing campaigns, identifying new revenue opportunities, or mitigating operational risks, data-driven decision-making driven by big data analytics enables organizations to stay agile, responsive, and competitive in today's fast-paced business environment.

11.3.5 Big Data and Analytics in Industry 4.0

Big data and analytics are foundational pillars of Industry 4.0, transforming the manufacturing landscape by converting vast amounts of data into actionable insights that drive innovation, efficiency, and competitiveness. At the core of this transformation lie the foundational principles of big data, encompassing the three Vs: volume, velocity, and variety [54]. In Industry 4.0, these principles are harnessed to manage the substantial flow of data originating from a multitude of sensors and devices embedded within manufacturing processes. These sensors generate a massive volume of data at high velocity, originating from diverse sources and in various formats, highlighting the importance of embracing the diversity of data in driving informed decision-making [50].

To effectively harness the power of big data, Industry 4.0 relies on robust storage and management solutions, such as data lakes and warehouses. These repositories serve as central hubs for storing extensive volumes of structured and unstructured data, facilitating analytics and enabling informed decision-making processes [53]. Real-time data processing is paramount in Industry 4.0, enabling timely insights and rapid responses to changing conditions on the factory floor. Advanced analytics

FIGURE 11.5 Big data and analytics in Industry 4.0.

solutions operate on streaming data, allowing manufacturers to extract valuable insights in real time, thereby enhancing agility and responsiveness in production environments (Figure 11.5) [54].

Key components of big data and analytics in Industry 4.0 encompass data acquisition, storage, and management, along with sophisticated analytics tools and algorithms [55]. Data acquisition involves the continuous collection of data from diverse origins, including IoT sensors, production equipment, and enterprise systems. Once collected, data are stored in robust storage solutions, organized, cleaned, and prepared for analysis [56]. Analytics tools and algorithms, such as machine learning models and statistical techniques, are then employed to derive significant insights from the vast datasets, uncovering patterns, correlations, and trends that inform decision-making processes. Data visualization tools play a crucial role in transforming complex data into visually intuitive representations, facilitating better decision-making across different levels of the organization [57].

In the context of Industry 4.0, big data and analytics find application across various domains, including predictive maintenance, quality control, supply chain optimization, energy management, demand forecasting, and process optimization [49]. Predictive maintenance leverages big data analytics to examine historical and real-time data from machinery, enabling proactive maintenance strategies and minimizing downtime. Quality control involves analyzing data from sensors and production processes to identify patterns associated with quality issues, ensuring that only high-quality products reach the market. Supply chain optimization leverages big data analytics to streamline logistics, shorten lead times, and enhance resilience across the entire supply chain, while energy management optimizes energy usage through continuous monitoring and analysis of energy consumption patterns [55–57].

The transformative impact of big data and analytics on manufacturing is profound, enabling agile decision-making, cost reduction, efficiency, innovation, quality improvement, and competitive advantage. Real-time data analytics empowers manufacturers to respond promptly to changing conditions, fostering adaptability and resilience. By identifying inefficiencies, reducing downtime, and optimizing resource allocation, big data analytics contributes to significant cost reductions and improved operational efficiency. Moreover, the analysis of customer feedback, market trends, and competitor activities provides valuable insights for innovation and product development, positioning manufacturers as industry leaders in the era of Industry 4.0.

11.3.6 Cloud Computing: The Scalable Infrastructure

Cloud computing stands as the cornerstone of Industry 4.0, providing the scalable infrastructure essential for processing and storing the immense volumes of data generated by interconnected devices and systems. In this era of digital transformation, where data have become the lifeblood of modern manufacturing, cloud computing offers unparalleled agility, scalability, and accessibility, enabling organizations to harness the power of big data analytics and drive innovation at unprecedented speeds. At its core, cloud computing entails the delivery of computing resources such as servers, storage, databases, networking, software, and analytics over the internet on a pay-as-you-go basis. This on-demand model eliminates the need for organizations to invest in and maintain costly on-premises infrastructure, allowing them to scale their computing resources up or down dynamically to meet fluctuating demand.

One of the primary benefits of cloud computing in the context of Industry 4.0 is its ability to handle the massive scale of data generated by IoT devices, sensors, and production systems. Cloud providers offer robust storage solutions capable of housing petabytes of data, along with high-performance computing resources for processing and analyzing these data in real time. This scalability ensures that organizations can effectively manage and derive insights from their ever-expanding datasets without worrying about infrastructure limitations. Furthermore, cloud computing enables seamless integration and interoperability across disparate systems and devices within Industry 4.0 environments. By providing standardized APIs and data formats, cloud platforms facilitate the exchange of information between different components of the manufacturing ecosystem, including IoT devices, enterprise systems, and third-party applications. This interoperability fosters collaboration, innovation, and agility, driving the evolution of connected and intelligent manufacturing processes.

Moreover, cloud computing offers unmatched flexibility and agility, empowering organizations to innovate rapidly and experiment with new technologies and business models. With access to a vast ecosystem of cloud services, including AI and machine learning tools, data analytics platforms, and IoT development kits, manufacturers can leverage cutting-edge technologies to optimize production processes, enhance product quality, and deliver personalized customer experiences. In addition to scalability and flexibility, cloud computing enhances security and resilience in Industry

4.0 environments. Cloud providers invest heavily in state-of-the-art security measures, including encryption, authentication, and access control, to safeguard sensitive data and protect against cyber threats. Furthermore, cloud platforms offer built-in redundancy and disaster recovery capabilities, ensuring business continuity even in the face of unexpected disruptions or outages.

11.3.7 Cyber-Physical Systems: Bridging the Digital and Physical

Cyber-physical systems (CPSs) represent a pivotal component of Industry 4.0, seamlessly integrating physical processes with computational control to create intelligent and adaptive manufacturing systems [57]. At their core, CPSs blur the boundaries between the digital and physical worlds, harnessing advanced technologies such as sensors, actuators, embedded systems, and connectivity to orchestrate complex interactions between machinery, equipment, and human operators. One of the key features of cyber-physical systems is their ability to monitor, analyze, and respond to real-time data from physical processes [58]. By deploying an array of sensors throughout manufacturing facilities, CPSs capture vital information about machine performance, environmental conditions, and product quality. These data are then processed and analyzed in real time, enabling CPSs to adapt manufacturing operations dynamically based on changing conditions and requirements. Moreover, CPSs leverage computational control to optimize manufacturing processes and enhance overall system performance [59]. Advanced algorithms and decision-making logic embedded within CPSs enable predictive maintenance, proactive fault detection, and autonomous decision-making, thereby minimizing downtime, reducing waste, and improving operational efficiency. For example, in a smart factory environment, CPSs can adjust production schedules, reconfigure production lines, and allocate resources in response to fluctuating demand or unexpected disruptions, ensuring continuous operation and maximizing productivity [60].

Furthermore, CPSs facilitate human–machine collaboration by providing interfaces and interaction mechanisms that enable seamless communication and cooperation between humans and machines. Through intuitive user interfaces, augmented reality displays, and collaborative robotics, CPSs empower operators to monitor, control, and interact with manufacturing processes in real time, enhancing productivity, safety, and flexibility on the factory floor [59,60]. In essence, cyber-physical systems represent a paradigm shift in manufacturing, bridging the gap between the digital and physical realms to create intelligent, adaptive, and interconnected manufacturing ecosystems. By integrating physical processes with computational control, CPSs enable manufacturers to achieve unprecedented levels of efficiency, agility, and responsiveness, driving the evolution of Industry 4.0 and shaping the future of modern manufacturing [57].

11.3.8 Additive Manufacturing (3D Printing): Revolutionizing Production

Additive manufacturing, commonly known as 3D printing, stands at the forefront of technological innovation, revolutionizing traditional production methods and unlocking new possibilities across various industries. Unlike conventional subtractive manufacturing processes that involve cutting, drilling, or molding raw materials to create a final product, additive manufacturing builds objects layer by layer from digital designs, offering unparalleled flexibility, speed, and customization. One of the most significant advantages of additive manufacturing is its ability to facilitate rapid prototyping. By translating digital designs into physical prototypes with remarkable speed and precision, 3D printing enables designers and engineers to iterate on concepts rapidly, test functionality, and validate designs before committing to full-scale production. This accelerated prototyping process not only reduces time-to-market but also lowers development costs, fostering innovation and driving product evolution in dynamic market environments.

Moreover, additive manufacturing enables on-demand production, eliminating the need for large-scale inventory storage and minimizing waste associated with traditional manufacturing methods. With 3D printing, manufacturers can produce parts and components as needed, in response to specific customer orders or changing market demands, thereby optimizing inventory management and reducing excess inventory costs. This on-demand production model also facilitates just-in-time manufacturing, enabling companies to respond quickly to fluctuations in demand and customize products to meet individual customer preferences. Furthermore, additive manufacturing empowers customization and personalization, allowing manufacturers to create unique, tailor-made products to suit individual needs and preferences. By leveraging digital design capabilities and advanced materials, 3D printing enables the production of highly complex geometries, intricate patterns, and customized features that would be impractical or impossible to achieve using traditional manufacturing methods. This customization capability opens up new opportunities for product differentiation, brand loyalty, and enhanced customer satisfaction in diverse industries, from aerospace and automotive to healthcare and consumer goods.

11.4 APPLICATIONS OF INDUSTRY 4.0

11.4.1 Predictive Maintenance: Anticipating Equipment Needs

Predictive maintenance stands as a foundational element in Industry 4.0, providing a proactive and data-driven method for equipment maintenance. By leveraging advanced technologies like machine learning and IoT sensors, predictive maintenance algorithms anticipate equipment failures, minimize downtime, and extend machinery lifespan. At the core of predictive maintenance lie several foundational principles, key components, applications, and considerations essential for its effective implementation and utilization.

Foundational Principles: Predictive maintenance relies on continuous condition monitoring of equipment, facilitated by sensors and IoT devices. These sensors gather real-time data on various parameters such as temperature, vibration, and wear, allowing predictive maintenance systems to analyze equipment health and performance trends. Advanced data analytics, particularly machine learning algorithms, play a crucial role in predictive maintenance by analyzing collected data to identify patterns and predict potential failures. Historical data analysis further enhances the accuracy of predictions by providing context and insights into equipment behavior over time.

Key Components: The deployment of sensors is essential for effective condition monitoring in predictive maintenance systems. Various types of sensors, including accelerometers and pressure sensors, capture data on different aspects of equipment performance. IoT connectivity enables seamless data transmission from sensors to centralized systems for analysis, facilitating real-time monitoring and decision-making. Machine learning algorithms form the backbone of predictive maintenance systems, analyzing complex datasets to predict equipment failures accurately. Cloud computing provides the scalable infrastructure needed for processing and storing large volumes of data generated by predictive maintenance systems, allowing organizations to access advanced analytics capabilities and scale resources as needed.

Challenges and Considerations: The success of predictive maintenance hinges on the quality and integrity of the collected data. Poor-quality or incomplete data can lead to faulty predictions, jeopardizing the efficacy of the maintenance strategy. Integrating predictive maintenance systems with existing enterprise systems can be challenging, requiring seamless integration to ensure a holistic view of maintenance needs. Change management strategies are essential to ensure that maintenance teams embrace data-driven approaches and adapt to new workflows. Cybersecurity is a critical consideration, as predictive maintenance systems involve the transmission and analysis of sensitive equipment data. Ensuring the security of data during transmission and storage is paramount. Lastly, the scalability of predictive maintenance solutions is vital for organizations with diverse and expanding equipment portfolios, allowing them to effectively manage growing volumes of data and adjust to changing requirements.

Predictive maintenance stands as a transformative approach to equipment maintenance in Industry 4.0, leveraging advanced technologies and data-driven insights to optimize maintenance practices, minimize downtime, and enhance equipment reliability. As organizations continue to adopt predictive maintenance strategies, addressing challenges and leveraging opportunities will be crucial to maximizing its benefits and ensuring long-term success in the era of Industry 4.0.

11.4.2 Digital Twin: Real-Time Simulation for Optimization

Digital twin technology revolutionizes manufacturing by creating virtual replicas of physical assets, enabling real-time analysis and optimization of processes [61]. At its core, a digital twin is a digital representation of a physical object, system, or process. It captures the behavior, performance, and characteristics of its physical counterpart through data collection, sensors, and modeling techniques. In the context of Industry 4.0, digital twins serve as powerful tools for monitoring, analyzing, and simulating manufacturing operations, leading to enhanced efficiency, productivity, and innovation (Figure 11.6) [60].

The creation of a digital twin begins with the collection of data from sensors embedded in physical assets. These sensors gather real-time information on various

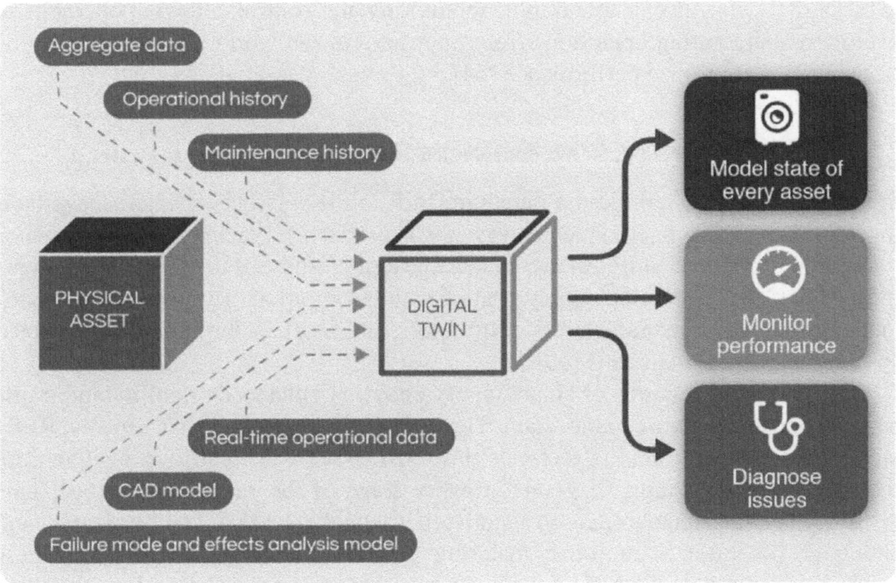

FIGURE 11.6 Digital twin working process.

parameters such as temperature, pressure, vibration, and energy consumption [61]. The data collected are then transmitted to a digital platform where they are processed, analyzed, and used to create a virtual representation of the physical asset. This virtual replica incorporates detailed information about the asset's geometry, material properties, and operational characteristics, providing a comprehensive view of its behavior and performance [62]. Once the digital twin is created, it serves as a dynamic simulation environment where different scenarios can be tested, analyzed, and optimized in real time. By simulating various operating conditions, process parameters, and maintenance strategies, manufacturers can identify opportunities for improvement, optimize resource allocation, and mitigate risks before implementing changes in the physical environment [63]. For example, in a manufacturing plant, a digital twin of a production line can be used to simulate different production schedules, identify bottlenecks, and optimize workflow to maximize throughput and minimize downtime [61,63].

One of the key benefits of digital twins is their ability to enable predictive maintenance strategies. By continuously monitoring the performance of physical assets through their digital counterparts, manufacturers can detect early signs of equipment degradation or failure and take proactive measures to address issues before they impact production. Predictive maintenance algorithms analyze data from the digital twin to predict potential failures, optimize maintenance schedules, and ensure that equipment operates at peak performance. Moreover, digital twins facilitate continuous improvement and innovation by providing insights into the behavior and performance of manufacturing processes. By analyzing data collected from digital twins, manufacturers can identify inefficiencies, optimize workflows, and develop innovative solutions to enhance product quality, reduce costs, and meet customer demands

[61]. Digital twins also enable remote monitoring and control, allowing operators to oversee manufacturing operations from anywhere in the world and make real-time adjustments to optimize performance [64].

11.4.3 Smart Supply Chain: Enhancing Transparency and Efficiency

Smart supply chains represent a paradigm shift in the way businesses manage their logistics, leveraging interconnected systems and advanced technologies to enhance transparency, reduce inefficiencies, and enable agile responses to market fluctuations [65]. At the heart of a smart supply chain lies the integration of various components, including suppliers, manufacturers, distributors, and retailers, through interconnected systems and digital platforms [65].

One of the key features of smart supply chains is enhanced visibility and transparency across the entire value chain. Through the integration of IoT sensors, RFID tags, and advanced tracking technologies, businesses gain real-time insights into the movement and status of goods at every stage of the supply chain [66]. This visibility enables stakeholders to identify bottlenecks, track inventory levels, and anticipate potential disruptions, fostering greater efficiency and responsiveness to changing market conditions. Furthermore, smart supply chains leverage data analytics and predictive algorithms to optimize inventory management, demand forecasting, and resource allocation [65,66]. By analyzing historical data, market trends, and customer behavior, businesses can anticipate demand fluctuations, optimize production schedules, and ensure the right products are available at the right time and place. This proactive approach not only reduces inventory carrying costs but also minimizes stockouts and overstock situations, improving overall supply chain efficiency [65].

In addition to enhancing operational efficiency, smart supply chains enable swift responses to market fluctuations and unexpected events. Through real-time data analytics and collaboration platforms, businesses can quickly adapt to changes in demand, supply disruptions, or regulatory requirements [67]. For example, in response to sudden shifts in consumer preferences or disruptions in the transportation network, smart supply chains allow businesses to reroute shipments, adjust production schedules, or source alternative suppliers in a timely manner, minimizing the impact on customer satisfaction and business continuity [68]. Moreover, smart supply chains promote collaboration and visibility among supply chain partners, fostering trust and accountability across the ecosystem. By sharing relevant data and insights in a secure and transparent manner, stakeholders can collaborate more effectively, streamline processes, and drive continuous improvement initiatives [65]. This collaborative approach not only strengthens relationships between suppliers and customers but also enables the co-creation of value-added services and innovative solutions to address evolving market demands [68].

11.4.4 Autonomous Robots: Redefining the Factory Floor

Autonomous robots, empowered by AI and advanced robotics technology, are revolutionizing the factory floor by redefining traditional manufacturing processes

FIGURE 11.7 Autonomous robots.

(Figure 11.7) [69]. These robots operate independently, without direct human intervention, and are capable of performing a wide range of tasks with precision, consistency, and adaptability. One of the key benefits of autonomous robots is their ability to improve operational efficiency and productivity. Unlike traditional manufacturing methods that rely heavily on manual labor, autonomous robots can execute tasks more quickly and accurately, leading to faster production cycles and reduced lead times. Whether it's assembly, packaging, material handling, or quality inspection, autonomous robots excel in repetitive tasks, ensuring consistency and reliability in manufacturing operations [70].

Moreover, autonomous robots offer greater flexibility and adaptability in response to changing production requirements. Unlike fixed automation systems, which are designed for specific tasks or processes, autonomous robots can be easily reprogrammed or reconfigured to handle different products, production volumes, or configurations [69,70]. This versatility allows manufacturers to quickly adapt to market demands, introduce new products, or scale production up or down as needed, without the need for costly retooling or reprogramming. Additionally, autonomous robots contribute to improved workplace safety by performing hazardous or strenuous tasks in place of human workers. By automating tasks that pose risks to worker health and safety, such as heavy lifting, repetitive motions, or exposure to hazardous materials, autonomous robots help reduce the incidence of workplace injuries and create a safer working environment for employees [71].

Furthermore, autonomous robots enable data-driven decision-making and predictive maintenance through the integration of sensors and AI algorithms. By collecting real-time data on equipment performance, environmental conditions, and production metrics, autonomous robots can identify anomalies, predict potential failures, and proactively address maintenance issues before they lead to costly downtime. This predictive capability helps manufacturers optimize equipment uptime, extend asset lifespan, and minimize unplanned disruptions in production [66,71].

11.4.5 Human–Machine Collaboration: Synergy in Manufacturing

Autonomous robots, empowered by AI and advanced robotics technology, are revolutionizing the factory floor by redefining traditional manufacturing processes [70]. These robots operate independently, without direct human intervention, and are capable of performing a wide range of tasks with precision, consistency, and adaptability. One of the key benefits of autonomous robots is their ability to improve operational efficiency and productivity [52]. Unlike traditional manufacturing methods that rely heavily on manual labor, autonomous robots can execute tasks more quickly and accurately, leading to faster production cycles and reduced lead times [59]. Whether it's assembly, packaging, material handling, or quality inspection, autonomous robots excel in repetitive tasks, ensuring consistency and reliability in manufacturing operations. Moreover, autonomous robots offer greater flexibility and adaptability in response to changing production requirements. Unlike fixed automation systems, which are designed for specific tasks or processes, autonomous robots can be easily reprogrammed or reconfigured to handle different products, production volumes, or configurations [36]. This versatility allows manufacturers to quickly adapt to market demands, introduce new products, or scale production up or down as needed, without the need for costly retooling or reprogramming [45].

Additionally, autonomous robots contribute to improved workplace safety by performing hazardous or strenuous tasks in place of human workers. By automating tasks that pose risks to worker health and safety, such as heavy lifting, repetitive motions, or exposure to hazardous materials, autonomous robots help reduce the incidence of workplace injuries and create a safer working environment for employees. Furthermore, autonomous robots enable data-driven decision-making and predictive maintenance through the integration of sensors and AI algorithms [68]. By collecting real-time data on equipment performance, environmental conditions, and production metrics, autonomous robots can identify anomalies, predict potential failures, and proactively address maintenance issues before they lead to costly downtime. This predictive capability helps manufacturers optimize equipment uptime, extend asset lifespan, and minimize unplanned disruptions in production [71].

In conclusion, autonomous robots are reshaping the factory floor by revolutionizing manufacturing processes with their precision, consistency, and adaptability. As AI and robotics technologies continue to advance, autonomous robots will play an increasingly pivotal role in driving efficiency, productivity, and innovation in modern manufacturing environments. By embracing autonomous robots, manufacturers can unlock new opportunities for growth, competitiveness, and sustainability in the era of Industry 4.0 (Figure 11.8) [69–71].

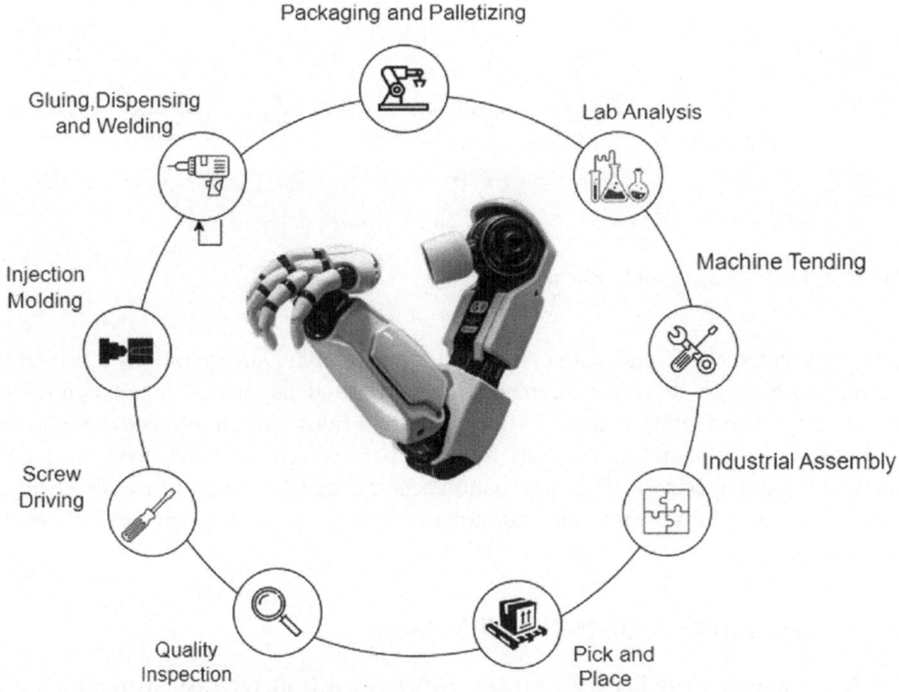

FIGURE 11.8 Collaborative robots.

11.4.6 Blockchain for Supply Chain: Ensuring Trust and Transparency

Blockchain technology is revolutionizing supply chain management by providing a secure, transparent, and immutable ledger for recording and tracking transactions across the entire supply chain [25]. At its core, blockchain is a distributed ledger that stores transactional data in a decentralized network of computers, ensuring that all participants have access to the same information in real time. One of the key features of blockchain technology is its ability to guarantee trust and transparency in transactions [72]. By using cryptographic techniques and consensus mechanisms, blockchain ensures that transactions recorded on the ledger are tamper-proof and verifiable, eliminating the risk of fraud, manipulation, or unauthorized alterations. This transparency instills confidence among supply chain stakeholders, as they can trace the origin, journey, and ownership of products from the point of origin to the final destination (Figure 11.9) [73].

Moreover, blockchain enables greater traceability and visibility within the supply chain, allowing companies to track the movement and status of goods at every stage of the production and distribution process. By recording key information such as product provenance, batch numbers, and temperature controls on the blockchain, companies can verify the authenticity, quality, and compliance of products, ensuring that they meet regulatory requirements and consumer expectations. Blockchain also

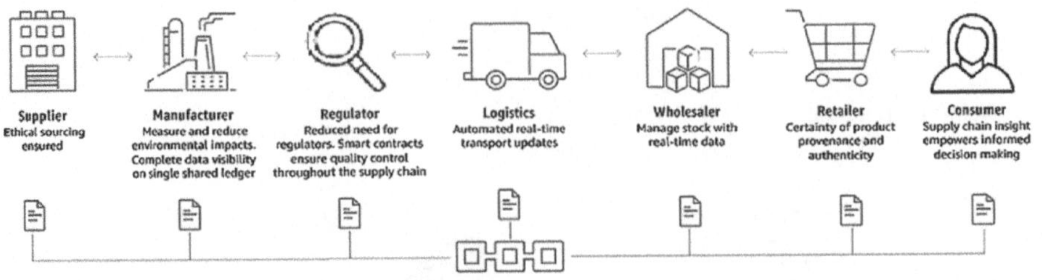

FIGURE 11.9 Benefits of blockchain.

facilitates greater efficiency and collaboration in supply chain operations by streamlining processes such as procurement, invoicing, and payments. Smart contracts, which are self-executing contracts with predefined rules written into code, automate and enforce contractual agreements between parties, reducing the need for intermediaries and paperwork. This automation accelerates transaction processing times, reduces administrative costs, and minimizes disputes, leading to greater efficiency and cost savings across the supply chain.

11.5 THE IMPACT OF INDUSTRY 4.0

11.5.1 Beyond the Factory Floor: Industry 4.0 in Diverse Sectors

Industry 4.0, characterized by the integration of advanced technologies and data-driven processes, extends its influence far beyond manufacturing, permeating various sectors including healthcare, logistics, energy, agriculture, finance, retail, education, and urban development. In healthcare, Industry 4.0 ushers in a new era of connected healthcare devices, telemedicine platforms, and predictive analytics for disease management. Connected medical devices enable remote patient monitoring, personalized treatment plans, and early detection of health issues. Telemedicine platforms leverage Industry 4.0 technologies to enable virtual consultations and remote diagnostics, enhancing healthcare accessibility. Predictive analytics and machine learning contribute to early disease detection, personalized treatment recommendations, and effective population health management.

In logistics and supply chain management, Industry 4.0 brings about smart logistics solutions, blockchain-enabled transparent supply chains, and automated warehousing systems. Real-time tracking, predictive maintenance, and data-driven route optimization optimize logistics operations, leading to improved efficiency and reduced costs. Blockchain technology ensures transparency and traceability in the supply chain, reducing fraud and providing a tamper-proof record of transactions. Automated warehouse systems, guided by the IoT and AI, streamline order fulfillment processes, minimizing errors and reducing human intervention. In the energy sector, Industry 4.0 transforms traditional energy grids into smart grids, enabling optimized energy distribution and the integration of renewable energy sources. Predictive maintenance techniques ensure the reliability of energy infrastructure, minimizing downtime and extending asset lifespan. Precise monitoring and control of energy consumption lead to optimized energy usage and reduced environmental impact. In agriculture, Industry 4.0 facilitates precision agriculture practices, autonomous farming equipment, and supply chain traceability solutions. IoT sensors and data analytics optimize planting, irrigation, and harvesting processes, enhancing crop yield and resource efficiency. Autonomous farming equipment, guided by AI and GPS technologies, performs tasks with precision, reducing labor demands and improving efficiency. Blockchain ensures traceability in the agricultural supply chain, addressing concerns related to food safety and authenticity. Across various sectors such as finance, retail, education, and urban development, Industry 4.0 drives digital transformation, personalized experiences, and data-driven insights. From blockchain-enabled secure transactions in finance to personalized shopping experiences in retail, from digital learning platforms in education to intelligent transportation systems in smart cities, Industry 4.0 technologies revolutionize processes, enhance efficiency, and improve quality of life across diverse sectors. As these technologies continue to evolve, their impact on industries and society at large is poised to grow, shaping the future of work, commerce, and urban living.

11.5.2 Shaping the Future: Industry 4.0 as a Catalyst for Innovation

Industry 4.0 stands as a transformative force, serving as a catalyst for innovation across various sectors and reshaping our perspectives and implementation approaches. At its core, Industry 4.0 drives digital transformation by enabling comprehensive connectivity, integrating cyber-physical systems, and promoting data-driven decision-making. This digital revolution extends beyond manufacturing processes, influencing areas such as supply chain management, workforce collaboration, sustainability, and business models.

Innovations in manufacturing processes under Industry 4.0 include additive manufacturing (3D printing), collaborative robotics (cobots), and the emergence of smart factories. Additive manufacturing revolutionizes traditional production methods by enabling rapid prototyping, on-demand production, and intricate design possibilities. Collaborative robots work alongside human operators, enhancing flexibility, efficiency, and safety in manufacturing environments. Smart factories leverage advanced technologies like the IoT, AI, and automation to create agile, responsive, and intelligent production environments.

Human–machine collaboration is redefined through technologies such as augmented reality (AR), virtual reality (VR), and digital twins. AR enhances real-world experiences with additional digital information, while VR creates immersive environments for training, maintenance, and design purposes. Digital twins facilitate simulation, analysis, and optimization by providing virtual replicas of physical objects or systems, enhancing understanding and decision-making processes.

Supply chain innovation is propelled by Industry 4.0, with advancements in areas like blockchain for transparency, predictive analytics for demand forecasting, and the development of dynamic and responsive supply chains. Blockchain technology ensures transparency, traceability, and security in supply chains, reducing fraud and building trust among stakeholders. Predictive analytics leverages data to forecast demand accurately, optimizing inventory and reducing lead times. Dynamic supply chains adapt quickly to changes in demand, disruptions, and market trends, enhancing resilience and efficiency.

Sustainability and energy efficiency are paramount considerations in Industry 4.0, with initiatives focusing on smart energy management, green manufacturing practices, and circular economy initiatives. Smart energy management optimizes energy consumption through real-time monitoring and analysis, contributing to sustainability goals by minimizing waste and environmental impact. Green manufacturing practices leverage technologies like the IoT and data analytics to optimize processes and resource usage, while circular economy initiatives promote resource efficiency, recycling, and the reuse of materials.

$$\textbf{Energy efficiency} = \textbf{Output/Input}$$

Description: This equation calculates energy efficiency, where the output represents the desired outcome (e.g., production output) and the input represents the energy consumed. Higher energy efficiency values indicate better optimization and resource utilization.

Economic and business model innovation is driven by Industry 4.0, enabling mass customization, servitization, and collaborative ecosystems. Mass customization is achieved through flexible manufacturing processes, allowing organizations to tailor products to individual customer needs without sacrificing efficiency. Servitization involves offering services alongside products, with outcome-based models emerging where customers pay for the value or results delivered. Collaborative ecosystems foster shared innovation among diverse stakeholders, leading to the creation of new value propositions and business opportunities.

Despite the promises of Industry 4.0, challenges and considerations persist, including data security and privacy concerns, workforce transformation needs, and the imperative for interoperability and standardization. Addressing these challenges is crucial to realizing the full potential of Industry 4.0 and ensuring its continued evolution as a driver of innovation in the global economy. Through strategic initiatives and collaborative efforts, industries can overcome these obstacles and harness the transformative power of Industry 4.0 to create a more connected, efficient, and sustainable future.

11.6 CONCLUSION

In conclusion, this chapter has provided an in-depth exploration of Industry 4.0, unraveling its principles, technologies, applications, and the transformative impact it holds for the future. As we navigate this industrial revolution, the convergence of digital and physical realms continues to redefine the boundaries of what is possible in the world of manufacturing. In conclusion, Industry 4.0 stands at the forefront of a revolutionary era, fundamentally transforming the landscape of diverse industries. The seamless integration of cutting-edge technologies, including the IoT, AI, and data analytics, has given rise to interconnected systems that redefine how we conceptualize and approach manufacturing. This paradigm shift extends beyond the factory floor, permeating healthcare, logistics, energy, agriculture, finance, retail, education, and smart cities, showcasing its universal impact. The digital thread woven by Industry 4.0 fosters unprecedented levels of connectivity, ushering in an era of real-time data exchange and informed decision-making. The marriage of human ingenuity with intelligent machines, exemplified by augmented reality and digital twins, heralds a new age of innovation and productivity. Supply chains are reimagined, economic models evolve, and sustainability becomes a cornerstone, emphasizing the holistic transformation Industry 4.0 instigates. As this transformative journey unfolds, challenges emerge, from data security to workforce adaptation. Navigating these challenges demands a strategic and collaborative approach, ensuring that the benefits of Industry 4.0 are maximized while mitigating potential risks. Ultimately, Industry 4.0 shapes a future where technology not only augments our capabilities but becomes an integral force propelling us toward greater efficiency, sustainability, and economic prosperity. The legacy of Industry 4.0 is one of innovation, collaboration, and a dynamic redefinition of what is possible in the ever-evolving landscape of modern industries.

REFERENCES

[1] Bermúdez, G. M., Sánchez-Castañeda, A., & Villalobos, P. K. (2021). *Industry 4.0: Labor and Social Security*. Universidad Nacional AutÓnoma de Mexico. ISBN 978-607-30-4439-4.

[2] Awotunde, J. B., Ayo, E. F., Ajamu, G. J., Jimoh, T. B., & Ajagbe, S. A. (2023). The influence of industry 4.0 and 5.0 for distance learning education in times of pandemic for a modern society. In: Joanna Rosak Szyrocka, Justyna Żywiołek, Anand Nayyar, Mohd Naved (eds). *Advances in Distance Learning in Times of Pandemic* (pp. 177–214). Chapman and Hall/CRC.

[3] Brahma, B., Kamila, N. K., Dhal, S. K., Pani, S. K., Mahesh, N., & Majhi, S. K. (2021, May 12). An extensive evolutional survey of medical domain data analytics & decision improvisation systems. SSRN. www.papers.ssrn.com/sol3/ papers.cfm?abstract_id=3842573

[4] Brahma, B., & Bhuyan, H. K. (2022). Soft computing and machine learning techniques for e-health data analytics. In: Mishra, S., González-Briones, A., Bhoi, A. K., Mallick, P. K., & Corchado, J. M. (eds). *Connected e-Health. Studies in Computational Intelligence*, vol 1021. Cham: Springer. https://doi.org/10.1007/978-3-030-97929-4_4

[5] Abikoye, O. C., Bajeh, A. O., Awotunde, J. B., Ameen, A. O., Mojeed, H. A., Abdulraheem, M., ... & Salihu, S. A. (2021). Application of internet of thing and cyber physical system in Industry 4.0 smart manufacturing. In: *Emergence of Cyber Physical System and IoT in Smart Automation and Robotics: Computer Engineering in Automation* (pp. 203–217). Cham: Springer International Publishing.

[6] Epicor. What is Industry 4.0—The Industrial Internet of Things (IIoT)?. www.epicor.com/en-us/blog/what-is-industry-4-0/

[7] Gartner. Definition of Digitalization. www.gartner.com/en/information-technology/glossary/digitalization

[8] Hermann, M., Pentek, T., & Otto, B. (2015). *Design Principles for Industrie 4.0 Scenarios: A Literature Review*. Technische Universität Dortmund. https://doi.org/10.13140/RG.2.2.29269.22248

[9] Awotunde, J. B., Folorunso, S. O., Imoize, A. L., Odunuga, J. O., Lee, C. C., Li, C. T., & Do, D. T. (2023). An ensemble tree-based model for intrusion detection in industrial internet of things networks. *Applied Sciences*, *13*(4), 2479.

[10] Kagermann, H., Wahlster. W. & Johannes, H. (2013). *Recommendations for Implementing the Strategic Initiative INDUSTRIE 4.0*. Forschungsunion.

[11] Bhuyan, H.K., Pullagura, L., Brahma, B., Reddy, C.S. (2023). Impact of node radiation on human health using IoMT. In: Jain, S., Marriwala, N., Tripathi, C.C., & Kumar, D. (eds). *Emergent Converging Technologies and Biomedical Systems. ETBS 2022. Lecture Notes in Electrical Engineering*, vol 1040. Singapore: Springer. https://doi.org/10.1007/978-981-99-2271-0_42

[12] Brahma, B. (2021). Mathematical model for analysis of COVID-19 outbreak using VON Bertalanffy Growth Function (VBGF). *Turkish Journal of Computer and Mathematics Education (TURCOMAT)*, *12*(11), 6063–6075. www.turcomat.org/index.php/turkbilmat/article/view/6925

[13] Neugebauer, R., Hippmann, S., Leis, M., & Landherr, M. (2016). Industrie 4.0—From the perspective of applied research. *Procedia CIRP,* 57, pp 2–7.

[14] Nexus Integra. Why is big data the core of the 4.0 industry? www.nexusintegra.io/big-data-industry-4-0/

[15] Pereira, A. C. & Romero, F. (2017). A review of the meaning and the implications of the Industry 4.0 concept. *Procedia Manufacturing,* 13. https://doi.org/10.1016/j.promfg.2017.09.032

[16] Salkin, C., Oner, M., Ustundag, A., & Cevikcan, E. (2018). *A Conceptual Framework for Industry 4.0. Industry 4.0: Managing The Digital Transformation*. Springer Series in Advanced Manufacturing.

[17] Schwab, K. (2016). *The Fourth Industrial Revolution*. World Economic Forum.

[18] Soldatos, J. (2019). *Introduction to Industry 4.0 and the Digital Shopfloor Vision. The Digital Shopfloor: Industrial Automation in the Industry 4.0 Era*. https://doi.org/10.13052/rp-978877022040

[19] Yang, K. (2024). *Quality in the Era of Industry 4.0: Integrating Tradition and Innovation in the Age of Data and AI*. John Wiley & Sons.

[20] Alabadi, M., Habbal, A., & Guizani, M. (2024). An innovative decentralized and distributed deep learning framework for predictive maintenance in the industrial Internet of Things. *IEEE Internet of Things Journal, 11*(11), 20271–20286.

[21] Awotunde, J. B., Jimoh, R. G., Ogundokun, R. O., Misra, S., & Abikoye, O. C. (2022). Big data analytics of IoT-based cloud system framework: Smart healthcare monitoring systems. In: Misra, S., Kumar Tyagi, A., Piuri, V., Garg, L. (Eds.) *Artificial Intelligence for Cloud and Edge Computing* (pp. 181–208). Cham: Springer International Publishing.

[22] Mathew, D., Brintha, N. C., & Jappes, J. W. (2023). Artificial intelligence powered automation for industry 4.0. In: *New Horizons for Industry 4.0 in Modern Business* (pp. 1–28). Cham: Springer International Publishing.

[23] Awotunde, J. B., Sur, S. N., Jimoh, R. G., Aremu, D. R., Do, D. T., & Lee, B. M. (2023). FL_GIoT: Federated learning enabled edge-based green Internet of Things system: A comprehensive survey. *IEEE Access*, *11*, 136150–136165.

[24] Vazquez Melendez, E. I., Bergey, P., & Smith, B. (2024). Blockchain technology for supply chain provenance: Increasing supply chain efficiency and consumer trust. *Supply Chain Management: An International Journal, 29*(4), 706–730.

[25] Awotunde, J. B., Gaber, T., Prasad, L. N., Folorunso, S. O., & Lalitha, V. L. (2023). Privacy and security enhancement of smart cities using hybrid deep learning-enabled blockchain. *Scalable Computing: Practice and Experience*, *24*(3), 561–584.

[26] Onu, P., Mbohwa, C., & Pradhan, A. (2024). Internet of production: Unleashing the full potential of Industry 4.0–A comprehensive review of trends, drivers, and challenges. *Procedia Computer Science*, *232*, 2049–2056.

[27] Attaran, S., Attaran, M., & Celik, B. G. (2024). Digital twins and industrial Internet of Things: Uncovering operational intelligence in industry 4.0. *Decision Analytics Journal*, *10*, 100398.

[28] Gaber, T., Awotunde, J. B., Folorunso, S. O., Ajagbe, S. A., & Eldesouky, E. (2023). Industrial internet of things intrusion detection method using machine learning and optimization techniques. *Wireless Communications and Mobile Computing*, *2023*, 1–15.

[29] Wanyama, J., Bwambale, E., Kiraga, S., Katimbo, A., Nakawuka, P., Kabenge, I., & Oluk, I. (2024). A systematic review of fourth industrial revolution technologies in smart irrigation: Constraints, opportunities, and future prospects for Sub-Saharan Africa. *Smart Agricultural Technology*, 100412, 1–14.

[30] Lakshminarayana, S., Praseed, A., & Thilagam, P. S. (2024). Securing the IoT application layer from an MQTT protocol perspective: Challenges and research prospects. *IEEE Communications Surveys & Tutorials*, 1–1.

[31] Folgado, F. J., Calderón, D., González, I., & Calderón, A. J. (2024). Review of Industry 4.0 from the perspective of automation and supervision systems: Definitions, architectures and recent trends. *Electronics*, *13*(4), 782.

[32] Awotunde, J. B., Misra, S., & Pham, Q. T. (2022, November). A secure framework for Internet of medical things security based system using lightweight cryptography enabled blockchain. In: Dang, T. K., Küng, J., Chung, T. M. (Eds.) *International Conference on Future Data and Security Engineering* (pp. 258–272). Singapore: Springer Nature Singapore.

[33] Awotunde, J. B., Misra, S., Ayoade, O. B., Ogundokun, R. O., & Abiodun, M. K. (2022). Blockchain-based framework for secure medical information in internet of things system. In: Misra, S., Kumar Tyagi, A. (Eds.) *Blockchain Applications in the Smart Era* (pp. 147–169). Cham: Springer International Publishing.

[34] Sharma, M., Tomar, A., & Hazra, A. (2024). Edge computing for Industry 5.0: Fundamental, applications and research challenges. *IEEE Internet of Things Journal*, *11*(11), 19070–19093.

[35] Ajani, S. N., Khobragade, P., Dhone, M., Ganguly, B., Shelke, N., & Parati, N. (2024). Advancements in computing: Emerging trends in computational science with next-generation computing. *International Journal of Intelligent Systems and Applications in Engineering*, *12*(7s), 546–559.

[36] Ogundokun, R. O., Arowolo, M. O., Misra, S., & Awotunde, J. B. (2022). Machine learning, IoT, and blockchain integration for improving process management application security. In: *Blockchain Applications in the Smart Era* (pp. 237–252). Cham: Springer International Publishing.

[37] Hassan, A., Dutta, P. K., Gupta, S., Mattar, E., & Singh, S. (Eds.). (2024). *Human-Centered Approaches in Industry 5.0: Human-Machine Interaction, Virtual Reality Training, and Customer Sentiment Analysis: Human-Machine Interaction, Virtual Reality Training, and Customer Sentiment Analysis*. IGI Global.

[38] Prathibha, S., Palanikumar, K., Ponshanmugakumar, A., & Kumar, M. R. (2024). Application of augmented reality and virtual reality technologies for maintenance and repair of automobile and mechanical equipment. In *Machine Intelligence in Mechanical Engineering* (pp. 63–89). Academic Press.

[39] Morales Méndez, G., & del Cerro Velázquez, F. (2024). Augmented reality in Industry 4.0 assistance and training areas: A systematic literature review and bibliometric analysis. *Electronics*, *13*(6), 1147.

[40] Ajagbe, S. A., Awotunde, J. B., Opadotun, A. T., & Adigun, M. O. (2023, March). Cybersecurity in the supply chain and logistics industry: A concept-centric review. In: *International Conference on Advances in IoT and Security with AI* (pp. 39–50). Singapore: Springer Nature Singapore.

[41] Pramanik, P. K. D., Upadhyaya, B. K., Pal, S., & Pal, T. (2019). Internet of things, smart sensors, and pervasive systems: Enabling connected and pervasive healthcare. In: Nilanjan Dey, Amira S. Ashour, Chintan Bhatt, Simon James Fong (Eds.) *Advances in ubiquitous sensing applications for healthcare, Healthcare, Data Analytics and Management, Academic Press,* (pp. 1–58). Academic Press. ISBN 9780128153680, https://doi.org/10.1016/B978-0-12-815368-0.00001-4.

[42] Oladipupo, E. T., Abikoye, O. C., Imoize, A. L., Awotunde, J. B., Chang, T. Y., Lee, C. C., & Do, D. T. (2023). An efficient authenticated elliptic curve cryptography scheme for multicore wireless sensor networks. *IEEE Access*, *11*, 1306–1323.

[43] Sofi, M. A. (2016). Bluetooth protocol in Internet of Things (IoT), security challenges and a comparison with Wi-Fi protocol: A review. *International Journal of Engineering and Technical Research*, *5*, 461–467.

[44] Awotunde, J. B., Ogundokun, R. O., Adeniyi, A. E., Ayo, F. E., Ajamu, G. J., Abiodun, M. K., & Ogundokun, O. E. (2022). Cloud-IoMT-based wearable body sensors network for monitoring elderly patients during the COVID-19 pandemic. In: Valentina Emilia Balas, Oana Geman (Eds.) *Biomedical Engineering Applications for People with Disabilities and the Elderly in the COVID-19 Pandemic and Beyond* (pp. 33–48). Academic Press. ISBN 9780323851749, https://doi.org/10.1016/B978-0-323-85174-9.00028-5

[45] Munirathinam, S. (2020). Industry 4.0: Industrial internet of things (IIOT). In: Pethuru Raj and Preetha Evangeline (Eds) *Advances in Computers* (Vol. 117, No. 1, pp. 129–164). Elsevier.

[46] Aheleroff, S., Xu, X., Lu, Y., Aristizabal, M., Velásquez, J. P., Joa, B., & Valencia, Y. (2020). IoT-enabled smart appliances under industry 4.0: A case study. *Advanced Engineering Informatics*, *43*, 101043.

[47] Al-Masri, E., Kalyanam, K. R., Batts, J., Kim, J., Singh, S., Vo, T., & Yan, C. (2020). Investigating messaging protocols for the Internet of Things (IoT). *IEEE Access*, *8*, 94880–94911.

[48] Wu, H., Sun, Y., & Wolter, K. (2018). Energy-efficient decision making for mobile cloud offloading. *IEEE Transactions on Cloud Computing*, *8*(2), 570–584.

[49] Alcácer, V., & Cruz-Machado, V. (2019). Scanning the industry 4.0: A literature review on technologies for manufacturing systems. *Engineering Science and Technology, An International Journal*, *22*(3), 899–919.

[50] Sahu, C. K., Young, C., & Rai, R. (2021). Artificial intelligence (AI) in augmented reality (AR)-assisted manufacturing applications: A review. *International Journal of Production Research*, *59*(16), 4903–4959.

[51] Majdzadeh, R. (2024). Big data revolution: Transforming business landscapes through data-driven decision making. *Social Sciences Spectrum*, *3*(1), 115–125.

[52] Awotunde, J. B., Adeniyi, A. E., Ogundokun, R. O., Ajamu, G. J., & Adebayo, P. O. (2021). MIoT-based big data analytics architecture, opportunities and challenges for enhanced telemedicine systems. *Enhanced Telemedicine and e-Health: Advanced IoT Enabled Soft Computing Framework*, *410*, 199–220.

[53] Stephenson, D. (2018). *Big Data Demystified: How to Use Big Data, Data Science and AI to Make Better Business Decisions and Gain Competitive Advantage.* Pearson UK.

[54] Aceto, G., Persico, V., & Pescapé, A. (2020). Industry 4.0 and health: Internet of things, big data, and cloud computing for healthcare 4.0. *Journal of Industrial Information Integration*, *18*, 100129.

[55] Tseng, M. L., Tran, T. P. T., Ha, H. M., Bui, T. D., & Lim, M. K. (2021). Sustainable industrial and operation engineering trends and challenges Toward Industry 4.0: A data driven analysis. *Journal of Industrial and Production Engineering*, *38*(8), 581–598.

[56] Awotunde, J. B., Jimoh, R. G., Oladipo, I. D., Abdulraheem, M., Jimoh, T. B., & Ajamu, G. J. (2021). Big data and data analytics for an enhanced COVID-19 epidemic management. In *Artificial Intelligence for COVID-19* (pp. 11–29). Cham: Springer International Publishing.

[57] Javaid, M., Haleem, A., Singh, R. P., & Suman, R. (2023). An integrated outlook of cyber–physical systems for Industry 4.0: Topical practices, architecture, and applications. *Green Technologies and Sustainability*, *1*(1), 100001.

[58] Monostori, L., Kádár, B., Bauernhansl, T., Kondoh, S., Kumara, S., Reinhart, G., ... & Ueda, K. (2016). Cyber-physical systems in manufacturing. *Cirp Annals*, *65*(2), 621–641.

[59] Dafflon, B., Moalla, N., & Ouzrout, Y. (2021). The challenges, approaches, and used techniques of CPS for manufacturing in Industry 4.0: A literature review. *The International Journal of Advanced Manufacturing Technology*, *113*, 2395–2412.

[60] Dafflon, B., Moalla, N., & Ouzrout, Y. (2021). The challenges, approaches, and used techniques of CPS for manufacturing in Industry 4.0: A literature review. *The International Journal of Advanced Manufacturing Technology*, *113*, 2395–2412.

[61] Mihai, S., Yaqoob, M., Hung, D. V., Davis, W., Towakel, P., Raza, M., ... & Nguyen, H. X. (2022). Digital twins: A survey on enabling technologies, challenges, trends and future prospects. *IEEE Communications Surveys & Tutorials*, *24*(4), 2255–2291.

[62] Stojanovic, N., & Milenovic, D. (2018, December). Data-driven digital twin approach for process optimization: An industry use case. In: *2018 IEEE International Conference on Big Data (Big Data)*, Seattle, WA, USA, 2018, (pp. 4202–4211). IEEE. doi: 10.1109/BigData.2018.8622412.

[63] Lampropoulos, G., & Siakas, K. (2023). Enhancing and securing cyber-physical systems and Industry 4.0 through digital twins: A critical review. *Journal of Software: Evolution and Process*, *35*(7), e2494.

[64] Aheleroff, S., Xu, X., Zhong, R. Y., & Lu, Y. (2021). Digital twin as a service (DTaaS) in industry 4.0: An architecture reference model. *Advanced Engineering Informatics*, *47*, 101225.

[65] Tripathi, S., & Gupta, M. (2020). Transforming towards a smarter supply chain. *International Journal of Logistics Systems and Management*, *36*(3), 319–342.

[66] Hofmann, E., Sternberg, H., Chen, H., Pflaum, A., & Prockl, G. (2019). Supply chain management and Industry 4.0: Conducting research in the digital age. *International Journal of Physical Distribution & Logistics Management*, *49*(10), 945–955.

[67] Pan, S., Trentesaux, D., McFarlane, D., Montreuil, B., Ballot, E., & Huang, G. Q. (2021). Digital interoperability in logistics and supply chain management: State-of-the-art and research avenues towards Physical Internet. *Computers in Industry*, *128*, 103435.

[68] Accorsi, R., Bortolini, M., Baruffaldi, G., Pilati, F., & Ferrari, E. (2017). Internet-of-things paradigm in food supply chains control and management. *Procedia Manufacturing*, *11*, 889–895.

[69] Ravi, P. R., Sarumathi, S., & Ramaswamy, R. (2022). Design principles, modernization and techniques in artificial intelligence for IoT: Advanced technologies, development and challenges. In: *Artificial Intelligence for Internet of Things* (pp. 315–333). CRC Press.

[70] Soori, M., Dastres, R., Arezoo, B., & Jough, F. K. G. (2024). Intelligent robotic systems in Industry 4.0: A review. *Journal of Advanced Manufacturing Science and Technology*, *4*, 2024007.

[71] Leng, J., Zhong, Y., Lin, Z., Xu, K., Mourtzis, D., Zhou, X., ... & Shen, W. (2023). Towards resilience in Industry 5.0: A decentralized autonomous manufacturing paradigm. *Journal of Manufacturing Systems*, *71*, 95–114.

[72] Centobelli, P., Cerchione, R., Del Vecchio, P., Oropallo, E., & Secundo, G. (2022). Blockchain technology for bridging trust, traceability and transparency in circular supply chain. *Information & Management*, *59*(7), 103508.

[73] Loebbecke, C., Lueneborg, L., & Niederle, D. (2018). Blockchain technology impacting the role of trust in transactions: Reflections in the case of trading diamonds. European Conference on Information Systems.

12 Industry 4.0 and Computational Intelligence for Fighting COVID-19

A Case Study

Lokaiah Pullagura, Biswajit Brahma, R. S. M. Lakshmi Patibandla, Dontha Madhusudhana Rao, Siva Kumar Gowda Katta, and Ronald Chiwariro

12.1 INTRODUCTION

The convergence of Industry 4.0, deep learning, and computational intelligence has ushered in a new era of transformative possibilities, especially in the context of addressing global challenges such as the COVID-19 pandemic. Industry 4.0 represents the Fourth Industrial Revolution, characterized by the integration of digital technologies, the Internet of Things (IoT), and smart manufacturing. This paradigm shift enables the creation of intelligent, interconnected systems that can adapt and optimize processes in real time. Machine learning techniques, such as deep learning (DL), are inspired by the architecture and operations of the human brain, and have emerged as a powerful tool within the Industry 4.0 framework. Its ability to automatically learn and represent intricate patterns in data makes it particularly well-suited for complex tasks, ranging from predictive maintenance to quality control. This work explores the intersection of Industry 4.0, DL, and computational intelligence in the context of combating the COVID-19 pandemic.

The integration of these technologies is not only pivotal for optimizing industrial processes but also proves instrumental in creating innovative solutions for public health challenges [1,2]. In the study, it is observed that the risk of diabetes and retinopathy can be reduced by changing diet, and adding physical activities reduces the risk of cardiovascular disorders [3]. Techniques proposed suggest that different features of data can be used for effectively decreasing irrelevant features [4]. The utilization of DL in Industry 4.0 is a cornerstone in enhancing automation, efficiency,

DOI: 10.1201/9781003581963-12

and decision-making processes. From intelligent robotics to predictive analytics, DL algorithms leverage massive datasets to uncover hidden patterns and provide insights that were previously unattainable. In the context of Industry 4.0, deep learning empowers systems to adapt to changing conditions, optimize production workflows, and facilitate data-driven decision-making. The COVID-19 pandemic necessitates novel and agile responses [5–9]. Computational intelligence, which encompasses a range of intelligent algorithms, is employed to analyze epidemiological data, model virus spread, and optimize resource allocation.

This adaptive approach is crucial in the face of a dynamically evolving public health crisis. The case study presented in this chapter investigates the practical application of Industry 4.0 principles and computational intelligence techniques in a comprehensive strategy to combat COVID-19. It delves into the integration of smart manufacturing, data analytics, and DL for real-time monitoring and decision support. The case study illustrates the effectiveness of this combined approach in enhancing situational awareness, optimizing healthcare resource allocation, and facilitating proactive interventions during a global health crisis [10–12]. The study describes retinopathy grading and manual annotation, as possible solutions are standardized direct retinal findings [13]. Techniques such as deep CNN are used to identify the infected area and classified into either COVID-19 or non-COVID-19. Smartphones are increasingly used in diabetic retinopathy screening and testing, and images captured through these devices can be accessed remotely [14].

12.1.1 Key Contributions of the Chapter

This chapter explores the synergies between Industry 4.0, DL, and computational intelligence in the fight against COVID-19. The case study provides practical insights into the application of these technologies, not only in industrial contexts but also in addressing pressing global challenges, highlighting the potential for a smarter, more adaptive future.

12.1.2 Chapter Organization

Section 12.2 presents the related works on the applicability of explainable artificial intelligence in medical decision support systems, while Section 12.3 describes the technologies in action. Section 12.4 describes the challenges and ethical considerations, while Section 12.5 presents the proposed framework. Section 12.6 discusses the application of Industry 4.0 and deep learning models for fighting COVID-19, and Section 12.7 presents the performance evaluation of the models. Section 12.8 presents he results and discussion, and finally, section 12.9 concludes the chapter with future scope described.

12.2 RELATED WORK

Artificial intelligence and image processing are crucial to the advancement of humanity. Precision health makes heavy use of various image processing and artificial intelligence approaches. The COVID-19 pandemic has been the subject of numerous investigations recently. This section describes a few image identification and decision-making strategies linked to the COVID-19 radiography examination. Improved digital solutions to combat COVID-19 issues could be made possible by Industry 4.0 technology [25]. Telemedicine and remote health monitoring are made possible by these digital technologies [26,55]. Artificial intelligence (AI) is a rapidly developing health technology from Industry 4.0 that has proven useful in forecasting the likelihood of illness and the likelihood of recovery during pandemics [27,57].

The COVIDX-NET model was proposed in the work by Hamdanet et al. [28]. In order to discover COVID-19, the authors conducted a comparative analysis of six DL classifiers: MobileNet V2, ResNet V2, DenseNet 201, Inception-V3, Xception, and Inception ResNet-V2. They employed a binary dataset for their investigation. Twenty-five of the 50 X-ray images show healthy individuals, whereas the other 25 show COVID-19 sufferers. Tests conducted on X-ray pictures revealed that DenseNet 201 and VGG19 produced the best accuracy (90%) of any method. However, because of the small dataset, their analysis has several drawbacks.

Additionally, Apostolopoulos et al. [29] worked with X-ray imaging to identify COVID-19. VGG19 has been utilized. Open-source repositories are the source of this dataset. There have been four datasets utilized, each from a separate data repository. In all, 1427 X-ray scans were employed in their investigation. A total of 504 of these images were considered "baseline" images, meaning they were unrelated to any specific ailment; 700 patients had pneumonia; and 224 patients had COVID-19. Research was conducted on both binary and multiclass categories. For the binary class, they were able to attain a maximum accuracy of 98.75%, and for the multiclass, 93.48%. VGG19 performed more accurately than the other models.

DarkNet, a deep neural network, was proposed by Ozturk et al. [30] to diagnose COVID-19 from X-ray images. In their study, binary and multiclass classifications were carried out using two datasets. For object detection, they suggested the "YOLO" model, a leaky ReLu activation function, and a 17-layer convolutional network model. For the binary class, they obtained an accuracy of 98.08%, and for the multiclass, 82.02%. When it came to classification performance, DarkNet outperformed other models. With the limited dataset, they were able to obtain a respectable level of accuracy.

X-ray image-based COVID-19 diagnosis using ResNet and DenseNet models has shown impressive results. Minaee et al. [31] used the Deep-Covid model with DenseNet121, squeeze Net, ResNet50, and ResNet18. Five thousand chest X-rays made up the dataset that was used in the research. For the binary classification, they obtained 97.5% specificity and 90% sensitivity. They used 5000 photos from the non-COVID category and 100 from the COVID-19 category. The dataset was severely unbalanced as a result. A model, Covid-CAPS, was proposed by Afsher et al. [32]. This is a capsule network with three capsule layers and four CNNs. In their research, they have employed two datasets. Their research was greatly skewed by the datasets they used. At 95.7%, they had the highest accuracy. An autonomous DL-based model was created by Narin et al. [33] to identify COVID-19 from X-ray pictures. Three distinct DL architectures were employed. They made use of 50 X-ray images of patients with COVID-19 and 50 X-ray images of patients without COVID-19. They did not enlarge the images beyond 224 × 224 pixels. Their solution to the dataset's limited size was the application of DL techniques. Of the total data, 80% was used for training, and 20% was used for testing. The three CNN models they employed to identify COVID-19 from the X-ray images were ResNet50, Inception V3, and ResNet V2. The cross-validation approach also employed the k-fold method with k = 5. In their work, they also applied DL. ResNet50 was able to attain a maximum accuracy of 98%.

COVID-19 patients were identified from the other pneumonia (viral and bacterial) patients by Farooq et al. [34]. They made use of a dataset that included 2839 patients' 5941 chest X-rays. Their dataset has been split up into four subgroups: normal (1203 images), bacterial (660 images), viral (931 images), and COVID-19 (48 images). With a classification accuracy of 96.23%, ResNet had the best results. Using chest X-ray images, Zhang et al. [35] suggested a DL algorithm to identify COVID-19 in healthy individuals. There are three parts to their suggested system: (1) Backbone network: High-level characteristics were extracted from the chest X-ray images using an 18-layer residue CNN. The classification score p_{cls} is produced by the classification head. (2) It uses the backbone network's extracted features as input. (3) Anomaly detection: a scalar anomaly score P is produced. The threshold T was used to determine the ultimate judgment after the anomaly score and categorization score were computed. According to their findings, the sensitivity dropped as long as the threshold T's value dropped. For the 0.5 value of T, they attained a sensitivity value of 96%.

A comparative analysis of the most recent DL models for COVID-19 identification from chest X-rays was done by Khalid el Asnaoui et al. [36]. They looked at DenseNet 201, ResNet 50, Inception-ResNet V2, MobileNet V2, VGG16, and VGG19, which have all been employed in their research. They made use of a CT dataset in addition to a collection of 6087 chest X-ray images. According to their findings, Inception-ResNet-V2 identified COVID-19 from X-ray images with an accuracy of 88.09%, whereas DenseNet201 attained an accuracy of 92.18%. For the same objective, Irfan Ullah Khan et al. [37] used four DL models: VGG16, VGG19, DenseNet121, and ResNet 50. In their investigation, they employed three distinct types of datasets and discovered that the VGG16 and VGG19 outperformed the other DL models in terms of performance. They attained a 99% accuracy rate.

A small collection of X-ray images was used by Shi et al. [38] to categorize COVID-19 patients. The model can only be trained with a certain quantity of images. Since results from smaller datasets are difficult to generalize, it is challenging to assess the robustness and accuracy of their research due to the tiny number of images used. They had an 83.50% accuracy rate. A system named COVINet was proposed by Umer et al. [39]. In order to extract the features from the chest X-ray images, they used CNN architecture. Three distinct scenarios, each with a different number of classes, were used for the studies. For two, three, and four classes, they attained accuracy rates of 97%, 90%, and 85%, respectively.

12.3 INDUSTRY 4.0 TECHNOLOGIES IN ACTION

12.3.1 Innovative Technologies in Industry 4.0 to Combat the COVID-19 Pandemic

The COVID-19 pandemic presented unprecedented challenges, placing a burden on society and healthcare institutions. However, Industry 4.0 technologies emerged as useful tools throughout the crisis, offering innovative solutions to a variety of issues. Some key Industry 4.0 innovations helped address some of the most important problems during the pandemic [15]. To provide ideal testing circumstances, diagnostics and testing on the Internet of Things (IoT) rely on linked sensors in testing booths that communicate real-time data on temperature, humidity, and air quality.

Wearable technology allowed for remote patient monitoring, which reduced needless hospital stays. By examining sizable patient datasets and virus features, big data analytics can detect high-risk populations [16–20], forecast future outbreaks, and improve testing protocols. Automation of robots to conduct repetitive tasks, such as collecting swabs, lowers worker exposure for healthcare providers, and increases testing capacity. Virtual models of PPE designs known as "digital twins" enable quicker iteration and optimization while enhancing functionality and safety through the use of real-world data. With the use of blockchain technology in supply chain management, PPE production and distribution became more transparent and traceable, guaranteeing effective resource allocation and lowering the risk of counterfeit goods [21].

The production and development of vaccines have been expedited by artificial intelligence (AI), which uses algorithms to analyze large molecular databases and forecast possible candidates for vaccines. Scientists around the world can communicate and share knowledge more quickly because of augmented reality (AR), which is used to support remote cooperation in laboratories [22]. Cyber-physical systems (CPSs), and smart factories with automated and optimized vaccine production facilitated by CPS, guarantee quality and optimize output. Patient monitoring as well as care are all part of telemedicine, and doctors could virtually consult with patients through video conferencing platforms, reducing the amount of time that patients and healthcare professionals are exposed to each other. Wearable technology and sensors are used in remote patient monitoring (RPM) to continually collect patient data (such as oxygen levels and vital signs), allowing for rapid treatments and remote monitoring. AI-powered chatbots help patients by offering information and support around the clock, relieving pressure on healthcare systems, and calming patients' fears. Contact tracking and containment are provided by location-based services (LBS), which are smartphone apps that use anonymized location data to help trace contacts and isolate infected people. Through the use of big data analytics, tailored interventions were made possible by the analysis of GPS data mobility patterns, which revealed information about potential hotspots for infections and population movement. Drones fitted with thermal cameras allowed for early detection and separation of those suspected of having fevers in large crowds using drone-based surveillance [23].

These are just a few examples of how combating COVID-19 has been transformed by Industry 4.0 technologies. Integrating the rapid adoption of these innovative tools demonstrates Industry 4.0's immense potential to enhance healthcare systems and prepare for future global health crises. However, issues such as data protection and ethical considerations require careful attention. By continuing to innovate and integrate new technology responsibly, we can, to everyone's benefit, build a more responsive and resilient healthcare environment.

12.3.2 Computational Intelligence for Data-Driven Insights

Massive volumes of data were generated by the COVID-19 pandemic, ranging from patient demographics to viral mutations. Despite the enormous potential of the data, extracting meaningful information to influence critical decisions proved to be very challenging. Thankfully, computational intelligence (CI), which uses data to inform the infection approach, proved to be a game-changer.

12.3.2.1 Unlocking Machine Learning's Capabilities for Forecasting Case Increases

Machine learning algorithms examined both historical data and current patterns to make more accurate predictions about upcoming epidemics. Proactive resource allocation made possible by this foresight allowed healthcare institutions to get ready for spikes in demand. Using social contact, age, and pre-existing disease data, CI models identified those who were more likely to suffer a serious illness. By identifying high-risk groups, this targeted strategy helped to optimize resource allocation and guide personalized interventions [23]. Through the optimization of treatment strategies and the analysis of large patient outcome databases, CI has been able to predict possible adverse responses, identify effective therapy combinations, and provide more individualized and superior patient care.

12.3.2.2 Artificial Intelligence Shows Hidden Patterns

AI systems scoured through enormous molecular databases to identify possible vaccine candidates, which accelerated the search for new medications. As a result, it took much less time to create and implement essential interventions in the fields of drug discovery and vaccine development. Through contact tracing on a broader scale, using social media interactions and anonymized movement data, AI-powered systems find possible contacts outside of the reach of conventional tracing techniques. This increased reach made it easier to contain outbreaks. Attitude analysis for public health insights that are AI-processed social media chatter, evaluate public attitudes toward health standards and discover misinformation hotspots. This addressed vaccination skepticism and made targeted communication efforts possible.

12.3.2.3 Overcoming Algorithms: Human–Machine Collaboration

Although AI models produced insightful results, developing trust and guaranteeing ethical use required knowledge of their logic. Explainable AI approaches promote accountability and transparency by providing insight into the inner workings of these models. AI recommendations for human-in-the-loop decision-making were never intended to replace human expertise. Rather, CI was a potent instrument that enhanced and enriched human decision-making, resulting in more sophisticated and knowledgeable actions. Ensuring data privacy and security became crucial as data started to serve as the engine for CI applications [24]. In data privacy and security, ethical concerns and strong data governance frameworks were essential for safeguarding personal information and fostering public confidence in these technologies.

CI's effects went well beyond these examples. Its applications were numerous and varied, ranging from supply chain and logistics optimization to hospital operations efficiency. However, difficulties remain. To fully utilize CI for upcoming public health problems, it will be imperative to address data quality, algorithmic biases, and ethical issues.

Researchers can uncover data's latent potential and use it as a potent weapon in the fight against pandemics, paving the path for a healthier, more resilient future.

12.4 CHALLENGES AND ETHICAL CONSIDERATIONS

Industry 4.0 technologies were very helpful in the fight against COVID-19, but putting them into practice came with some difficult decisions and moral dilemmas. To ensure the responsible and sustainable use of these potent instruments in upcoming healthcare endeavors, these concerns must be addressed.

12.4.1 The Data Dilemma

Privacy concerns regarding potential abuse and individual privacy were raised by the vast amount of data collected for the study. Effective data governance frameworks and effective user permission methods are necessary to strike a balance between individual privacy and data-driven insights. Data bias, with algorithms trained on biased data, have the potential to sustain discriminating results. To reduce unjust results, addressing data bias requires transparent algorithms, diversified datasets, and human oversight. Data networks and linked devices pose a security risk since they are more susceptible to hackers. To protect sensitive patient data, strong cybersecurity measures, data encryption, and routine audits are necessary.

12.4.2 Ethical Implementation

Algorithmic details and "black box" transparency of certain AI models have sparked questions around explainability and responsibility. Encouraging human decision-making in the loop and putting explainable AI into practice are essential for ethical and transparent use. Equity and access: During the pandemic, not everyone had equal access to resources and technology. In order to ensure fair access to healthcare and reduce the digital divide, focused interventions and inclusive technology development are needed. Automation brought about by Industry 4.0 technology has sparked worries about job displacement in the healthcare industry. Initiatives to reskill the workforce, social safety nets, and ethical technology deployment are necessary to address this.

12.4.3 Regulatory Frameworks

The advent of new data-driven technologies calls for flexible regulatory frameworks that strike a balance between innovation and data security, a concept known as data governance. Harmonizing data governance policies and collaborating internationally is essential. To direct research and implementation, it is essential to define explicit ethical norms that cover justice, accountability, and transparency for the development and application of AI. To address concerns about new technologies and foster trust, public involvement is crucial. Public engagement is open discourse. Encouraging public acceptance and collaboration requires openness and the accessibility of information.

12.4.4 Navigating the Path Forward

Even though there are many obstacles to overcome, doing so is essential to guaranteeing the ethical and responsible application of Industry 4.0 technology in the healthcare sector. Researchers can use these tools to our advantage if we adopt transparent algorithms, thorough data governance, and ethical guidelines. Researchers can create a future where technology benefits mankind fairly and responsibly by encouraging broad access, reducing job displacement, and putting strong regulatory frameworks in place.

12.5 PROPOSED FRAMEWORK

Compared to conventional machine learning models, DL-based models are starting to take the lead. Deep neural networks are functioning well with picture data and displaying higher accuracy values. These characteristics have drawn a lot of attention recently and make DL-based models the top choice for researchers. Nonetheless, a framework is necessary for the effective integration of DL with a human–machine system [40–42].

The most effective tool for computer vision tasks is CNN. Convolutional, pooling, and fully linked layers make up CNN models. In the CNN paradigm, every layer has a distinct purpose. Convolutional layers, for instance, extract local features from the input image using a fixed-size filter or kernel. Convolution is applied to the resultant image each time a fresh input image is obtained. The features in this convolutional image were taken from the final layer's output. Assuming $f(x, y)$ is the 2D kernel utilized for the convolution and $I(x, y)$ is the two-dimensional input picture, the conversion may be written as [43]:

$$y(i,j) = (I,f)(x,y) = \sum_{-\infty}^{\infty}\sum_{-\infty}^{\infty} I(x-u, y-v)f(u,v) \qquad (12.1)$$

The pixel values at the edges are either ignored when applied as a convolution or some padding is applied. A non-linear activation function [44] can be used to convert the convolution process's output.

$$sigmoid(x) = \frac{1}{1+e^{-x}} \tag{12.2}$$

CNN also includes fully linked and pooling layers in addition to convolutional layers. The convolutional layer is summarized by a pooling layer. By breaking up convolutional layers into smaller subsamples, it reduces the feature map's overall size. The CNN model's pooling layer determines the convolutional layer's average or maximum function. Either max pooling or average pooling can be used with this layer.

Image pixels are spaced by pooling. Rectified linear units (ReLUs) are frequently used in pooling layers in place of a specific activation function. The way to figure out the average in a pooling convolutional layer is [45]:

$$X_{ij}^{l} = \frac{1}{MN}\sum_{m}^{M}\sum_{n}^{N} X_{iM+m,jN+n}^{l-1} \tag{12.3}$$

where positions on the output map are denoted by i and j, while M and N stand for the pooling sample's dimensions. A fully connected layer is superior to the pooling and convolutional layers in terms of classification. Because this layer is interrelated, it incorporates different weights and demands a lot of processing resources. The suggested CNN model's structure is shown in Figure 12.1.

12.6 APPLICATION OF INDUSTRY 4.0 AND DEEP LEARNING MODELS FOR FIGHTING COVID-19

The COVID-19 pandemic has catalyzed the integration of cutting-edge technologies, notably Industry 4.0 and DL, to develop innovative solutions for combating the spread of the virus and managing its impact on society. This case study explores the application of Industry 4.0 principles and DL models in a comprehensive strategy to fight COVID-19, emphasizing their collective role in optimizing industrial processes and providing intelligent solutions for public health challenges.

12.6.1 Industry 4.0 in Pandemic Response

Industry 4.0, characterized by the fusion of digital technologies and smart manufacturing, serves as the foundation for a responsive and adaptive pandemic management system. Smart sensors, IoT devices, and real-time data analytics enable the monitoring and optimization of manufacturing processes. This infrastructure is repurposed to support public health initiatives, providing a dynamic platform for data-driven decision-making and resource allocation.

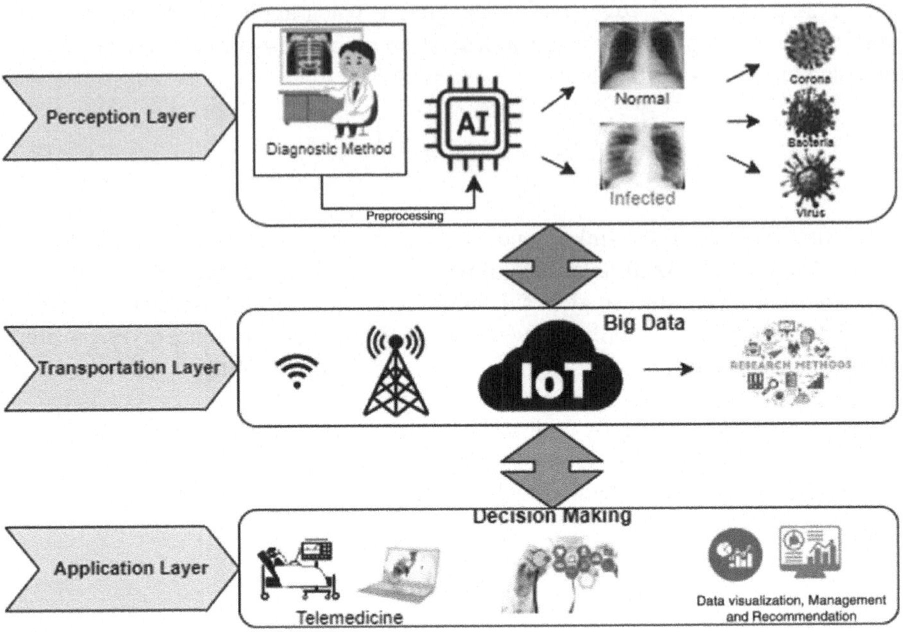

FIGURE 12.1 COVID-19 pandemic and Industry 4.0.

12.6.2 Deep Learning for Intelligent Insights

Deep learning models, a subset of machine learning, prove invaluable in extracting meaningful insights from vast and complex datasets. In the context of COVID-19, these models analyze epidemiological data, medical records, and social dynamics to enhance predictive capabilities and decision support systems. DL applications include predicting infection trends, identifying potential outbreak hotspots, and optimizing healthcare resource distribution [46].

12.6.3 The Integrative Approach

This case study demonstrates the synergies between Industry 4.0 and deep learning in a unified strategy to combat COVID-19. The manufacturing infrastructure of Industry 4.0 is utilized to collect and process real-time data from various sources, including healthcare systems, social media, and community sensors. DL models then leverage these data to predict the spread of the virus, optimize testing and treatment strategies, and provide actionable insights for public health interventions [47].

12.6.4 Key Findings and Outcomes

The findings of the case study reveal the efficacy of the integrated Industry 4.0 and DL approach in responding to the dynamic challenges posed by the pandemic. The system's adaptability, real-time monitoring, and intelligent decision-making contribute to enhanced situational awareness and resource optimization. The case study highlights successful applications in supply chain management, vaccine distribution, and public health communication [48].

As industries embrace the transformative potential of Industry 4.0 and DL, their collaborative application emerges as a robust solution for fighting the complexities of a global pandemic. This case study illustrates the adaptability and responsiveness of an integrated system, setting a precedent for future crises where the synergy of advanced technologies can play a pivotal role in safeguarding public health and societal well-being [49,56].

12.7 PERFORMANCE EVALUATION OF THE MODELS

Area under the curve (AUC), recall, accuracy, precision, sensitivity, specificity, and F score were the performance evaluation metrics employed in this study. These measures are based on four terms: false negative (FN), false positive (FP), true positive (TP), and true negative (TN).

A patient who tests positive and has the condition is considered a true positive (TP). A patient who tests negative and does not have COVID-19 is said to have true negativity (TN). False positive (FP): a patient who tests positive but does not have COVID-19. False negative (FN): A patient who tests negative yet has COVID-19 (Figure 12.2) [50].

The researchers may assess accuracy, precision, recall, sensitivity, specificity, and F-score based on these terms.

$$Sensitivity = \frac{TP}{TP + FN} \tag{12.4}$$

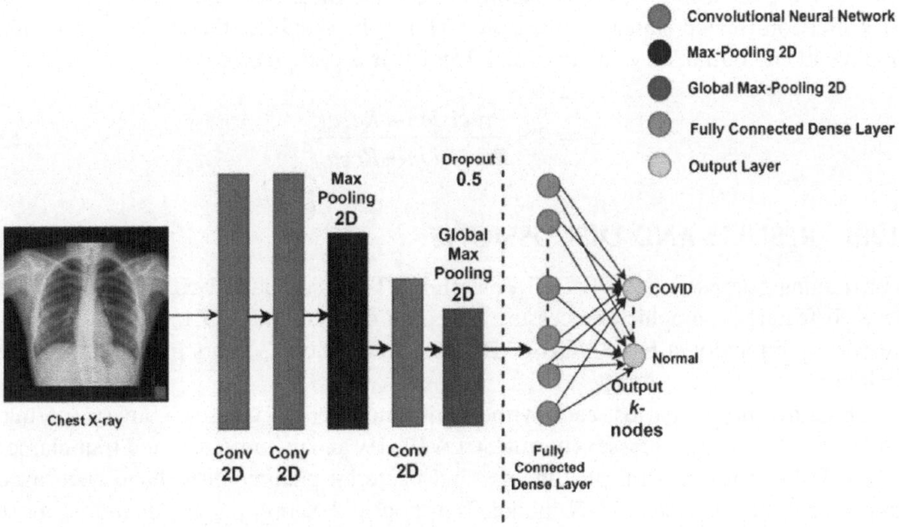

FIGURE 12.2 A framework for detection of COVID-19.

A 100% sensitivity indicates that all positive cases of the disease have been correctly diagnosed by the classifier [52]. When identifying a serious illness, a high sensitivity value is crucial.

Evaluating accuracy, precision, recall, sensitivity, specificity, and F-score is the definition of specificity.

$$Specificity = \frac{TN}{TN + FP} \tag{12.5}$$

AUC has also been utilized in our model evaluation process. The area under the ROC curve, or AUC, ranges from 0 to 1. According to the ROC curve hypothesis, a binary classification model with a high AUC value performs well. The model prefers to equivocate the class when the AUC is less than 0.5. The AUC and ROC schemes are displayed graphically [51].

One often-used metric for assessing classifier performance is accuracy. It is computed using

$$Accuracy = \frac{TP + TN}{TP + TN + FP + FN} \tag{12.6}$$

Recall and precision are often used as metrics to assess classifier performance. The projected positive situations that are actually positive are expressed with precision [52]. It is computed as

$$Precision = \frac{TP}{TP + FP} \tag{12.7}$$

The F-score is also computed using all of the measures listed above. It is a classification-related statistical measure [53,54]. It calculates the model's precision and recall and outputs a value between 0 and 1. It is computed as

$$F = 2 \times \frac{Precision \times Recall}{Precision + Recall} \tag{12.8}$$

12.8 RESULTS AND DISCUSSIONS

For training purposes, a 2 GB Dell PowerEdge T430 computer was utilized in these tests. It features a graphics processing unit on a dual-core, 2.4 GHz Intel Xeon processor. Additionally, it has 32 GB of DDR4 RAM. About 7 hours passed during the training.

Three distinct scenarios, each with varying numbers of classes—binary (normal and COVID-19), three classes (normal, COVID-19, and pneumonia), and four classes (COVID-19, normal, viral pneumonia, and bacterial pneumonia)—have been used to evaluate the suggested CNN model. Ten thousand X-ray images, including those of 79 patients with bacterial and viral pneumonia, were used to train and test the

TABLE 12.1
Result Comparison of Proposed CNN with DL Models with Two Classes

Model	Accuracy	Precision	Sensitivity	F-Score	Specificity	AUC
VGG16	96.31%	97.73%	97.47%	96.13%	95.93%	97.88%
AlexNet	68.56%	68.85%	91.43%	80.83%	55.80%	67.47%
InceptionV3	95.42%	96.88%	96.14%	96.33%	95.19%	95.83%
Proposed CNN	96.68%	98.21%	97.74%	99.08%	97.32%	98.97%

TABLE 12.2
Result Comparison of Proposed CNN with DL Models with Three Classes

Model	Accuracy	Precision	Sensitivity	F-Score	Specificity	AUC
VGG16	88.95%	90.51%	96.97%	94.98%	91.62%	56.71%
AlexNet	88.78%	92.01%	93.83%	94.91%	91.46%	58.37%
InceptionV3	87.20%	91.12%	95.84%	93.98%	91.19%	58.96%
Proposed CNN	89.25%	92.61%	97.72%	96.21%	96.40%	55.41%

suggested model. For training and testing, the data splitting ratios are 80% and 20%, respectively. This experiment makes use of 12 epochs. Evaluation criteria that have been employed include accuracy, precision, recall/sensitivity, F-score, specificity, and AUC.

The researchers employed two binary classes in the first experiment: normal and COVID-19. Table 12.1 displays the outcomes of the suggested CNN model with two classes. In this research, three DL-based classification models were employed: InceptionV3, VGG16, and AlexNet.

The suggested CNN model performs best for binary classification, achieving 96.68% accuracy, 98.21% precision, 97.74% sensitivity, 99.08% F-score, and 97.32% specificity, AUC with a 98.97% score, VGG16 has the highest specificity. With a 95.22% score, the suggested model comes in second.

In the second experiment, the model is trained and tested on three classes. Pneumonia and COVID-19 are typical classes.

Table 12.2 shows the outcomes of the suggested model along with three alternative deep learning models: Inception-V3, VGG16, and AlexNet.

Observations show that when it came to classifying X-ray images into three classes, the proposed CNN model and the VGG16 model performed quite similarly, achieving 88.95% accuracy, 90.51% precision, 94.98% F-score, and 56.71% AUC. The suggested CNN model achieves the maximum sensitivity and specificity at 97.72% and 98.40%, respectively. With 58.96%, Inception v3 achieves the highest AUC value. Comparable findings have been shown by AlexNet with 88.78%, 92.61%, 96.21%, and 96.40% in terms of accuracy, precision, F-score, and specificity, respectively.

TABLE 12.3
Result Comparison of Proposed CNN with DL Models with Four Classes

Model	Accuracy	Precision	Sensitivity	F-Score	Specificity	AUC
VGG16	83.58%	88.92%	96.32%	91.90%	91.21%	58.28%
AlexNet	82.94%	88.92%	96.95%	93.60%	92.87%	57.98%
InceptionV3	85.64%	89.32%	97.99%	94.50%	93.49%	57.28%
Proposed CNN	85.76%	89.19%	98.79%	94.69%	92.49%	58.68%

Four classes were employed for testing and training in the third trial. These categories include viral pneumonia, bacterial pneumonia, COVID-19, and normal. Table 12.3 displays the outcomes of the suggested model as well as three deep learning models: Inception-V3, VGG16, and AlexNet.

The suggested CNN model performs better than the other models and has the greatest results, scoring 94.69% F-score, 58.68% AUC, 98.79% sensitivity, 89.19% precision, and 85.76% accuracy. With 85.76% accuracy, 89.19% precision, 98.79% sensitivity, 94.69% F-score, 92.49% specificity, and 58.68% AUC, Inception v3 also produced impressive results.

As illustrated in Figure 12.3, a comparative study of the experimental outcomes demonstrates that the suggested CNN model effectively diagnoses COVID-19 illness from chest X-ray images when used in conjunction with a human–machine system. The effectiveness of the model is measured by a variety of evaluation metrics, including F-score, AUC, sensitivity, specificity, recall, accuracy, and precision.

12.9 CONCLUSIONS AND FUTURE SCOPE

The global COVID-19 pandemic has underscored the imperative for innovative approaches, and this case study illuminates the symbiotic relationship between Industry 4.0 principles and computational intelligence in combating the virus's spread and mitigating its societal impact. Industry 4.0's integration of cyber-physical systems, the IoT, and data-driven decision-making presents a transformative framework, while computational intelligence, encompassing machine learning and artificial intelligence, provides intelligent solutions for data analysis and decision support. Through the application of Industry 4.0 technologies like smart sensors and data analytics, coupled with computational intelligence methods for large-scale data analysis and dynamic resource optimization, the case study illustrates a comprehensive COVID-19 response strategy. This integrated framework not only enhances situational awareness and resource utilization but also facilitates proactive, adaptive measures in healthcare, supply chain management, and public health interventions.

The key findings underscore the efficacy of Industry 4.0 and computational intelligence in bolstering the agility and resilience of systems during public health crises. The proposed framework not only addresses immediate health concerns through data-driven decision-making but also contributes to the establishment of more robust, adaptive systems for future challenges. This research augments the existing body

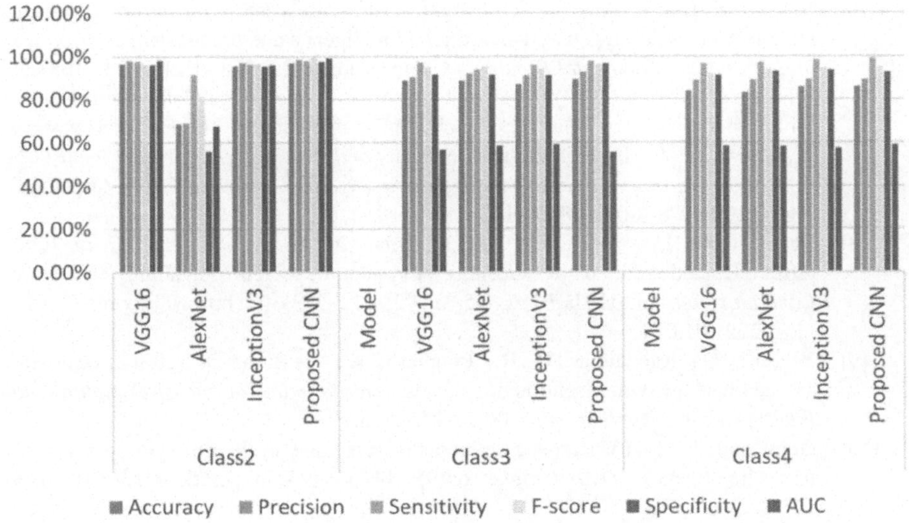

FIGURE 12.3 Comparison of proposed CNN with different classes.

of literature, offering practical insights into the implementation of Industry 4.0 and computational intelligence in pandemic response strategies. As the world continues to grapple with the long-term impacts of the pandemic, these technologies stand poised not only to mitigate immediate crises but also to lay the foundation for a more resilient and responsive global health infrastructure.

REFERENCES

[1] Yenduri, G., Kaluri, R., Rajput, D. S., Lakshmanna, K., Gadekallu, T. R., Mahmud, M., & Brown, D. J. (2023). From assistive technologies to metaverse–technologies in inclusive higher education for students with specific learning difficulties: A review. *IEEE* Access, 11, 64907–64927.

[2] Bryl, A., Mrugacz, M., Falkowski, M., & Zorena, K. (2022). The effect of diet and lifestyle on the course of diabetic retinopathy—A review of the literature. *Nutrients,* 14(6). https://doi.org/10.3390/nu14061252.

[3] Bhuyan, H. K., Saikiran, M., Tripathy, M., & Ravi, V. (2023). Wide-ranging approach-based feature selection for classification. *Multimedia Tools and Applications*, 82(15), 23277–23304.

[4] Jones, A., Vijayan, T. B., Subbarayan, S., & John, S. (2022). A systematic review on screening of diabetic retinopathy and maculopathy using artificial intelligence. *Lecture Notes in Electrical Engineering*, 929, 249–257. https://doi.org/10.1007/978-981-19-5550-1_24.

[5] Yenduri, G., Ramalingam, M., Selvi, G. C., Supriya, Y., Srivastava, G., Maddikunta, P. K., Raj, G. D., Jhaveri, R. H., Prabadevi, B., Wang, W., Vasilakos, A. V., & Gadekallu, T. R. (2023). GPT (Generative Pre-Trained Transformer)— A Comprehensive Review on Enabling Technologies, Potential Applications, Emerging Challenges, and Future Directions. *IEEE Access, 12*, 54608–54649.

[6] Ji, Y., Ji, Y., Liu, Y., Zhao, Y., & Zhang, L. (2023). Research progress on diagnosing retinal vascular diseases based on artificial intelligence and fundus images. *Frontiers in Cell and Developmental Biology,* 11. https://doi.org/10.3389/fcell.2023.1168327.

[7] Srivastava, G. et al. (2023). Federated Learning Enabled Edge Computing Security for Internet of Medical Things: Concepts, Challenges and Open Issues. In: Srivastava, G., Ghosh, U., & Lin, J. C. W. (eds). *Security and Risk Analysis for Intelligent Edge Computing. Advances in Information Security*, vol 103. Springer, Cham. https://doi.org/10.1007/978-3-031-28150-1_3.

[8] Egunsola, O., Dowsett, L. E., Diaz, R., Brent, M. H., Rac, V., & Clement, F. M. (2021). Diabetic retinopathy screening: A systematic review of qualitative literature. *Canadian Journal of Diabetes*, 45(8), 725.e12–733.e12. https://doi.org/10.1016/j.jcjd.2021.01.014.

[9] Yenduri, G., Rajakumar, B. R., Praghash, K., & Binu, D. (2021). Heuristic-assisted bert for twitter sentiment analysis. *International Journal of Computational Intelligence and Applications*, 20(03), 2150015.

[10] Grauslund, J. (2022). Diabetic retinopathy screening in the emerging era of artificial intelligence. *Diabetologia,* 65(9), 1415–1423. https://doi.org/10.1007/s00125-022-05727-0.

[11] Supriya, Y., Yenduri, G., Srivastava, G., & Gadekallu, T. R. (2023). Firefly Optimized Federated SVM Model for Breast Cancer Prediction. *2023 IEEE Canadian Conference on Electrical and Computer Engineering (CCECE)* (pp. 130–135), Regina, SK, Canada. https://doi.org/10.1109/CCECE58730.2023.10288828.

[12] Nakayama, L. F., Ribeiro, L. Z., Gonçalves, M. B., Ferraz, D. A., dos Santos, H. N. V., Malerbi, F. K., Morales, P. H., Maia, M., Regatieri, C. V. S., & Mattos, R. B. (2022). Diabetic retinopathy classification for supervised machine learning algorithms. *International Journal of Retina and Vitreous*, 8(1). https://doi.org/10.1186/s40942-021-00352-2.

[13] Bhuyan, H. K., Chakraborty, C., Shelke, Y., & Pani, S. K. (2022). COVID-19 diagnosis system by deep learning approaches. *Expert Systems*, 39(3), e12776.

[14] Pieczynski, J., Kuklo, P., & Grzybowski, A. (2021). The role of telemedicine, in-home testing and artificial intelligence to alleviate an increasingly burdened healthcare system: Diabetic retinopathy. *Ophthalmology and Therapy,* 10(3), 445–464. https://doi.org/10.1007/s40123-021-00353-2.

[15] Chengoden, R., et al. (2023). Metaverse for healthcare: A survey on potential applications, challenges and future directions. *IEEE Access*, 11, 12765–12795, https://doi.org/10.1109/ACCESS.2023.3241628.

[16] Ajamu, G. J., et al. (2024). Online Teaching Sustainability and Strategies during the COVID-19 Epidemic. In *The Role of Sustainability and Artificial Intelligence in Education Improvement* (pp. 106–132). Chapman and Hall/CRC.

[17] Olatinwo, S. O., & Joubert, T. -H. (2022). Deep learning for resource management in Internet of Things networks: A bibliometric analysis and comprehensive review. *IEEE Access*, 10, 94691–94717. https://doi.org/10.1109/ACCESS.2022.3195898.

[18] Awotunde, J. B., Adeniyi, A. E., Abiodun, K. M., Ajamu, G. J., & Matiluko, O. E. (2022). Application of cloud and IoT technologies in battling the COVID-19 pandemic. In: *Machine Learning for Critical Internet of Medical Things: Applications and Use Cases* (pp. 1–29). Springer International Publishing, Cham.

[19] Agrawal, S., et al. (2022). Federated Learning for intrusion detection system: Concepts, challenges and future directions. *Comput Commun*, 195, 346–361, ISSN 0140-3664. https://doi.org/10.1016/j.comcom.2022.09.012.

[20] Joseph Bamidele Awotunde, Roseline Oluwaseun Ogundokun, Abidemi Emmanuel Adeniyi, Femi Emmanuel Ayo, Gbemisola Janet Ajamu, Moses Kareem Abiodun, Opeyemi Eyitayo Ogundokun (2022). Cloud-IoMT-Based Wearable Body Sensors Network for Monitoring Elderly Patients During the COVID-19 Pandemic. In: *Biomedical Engineering Applications for People with Disabilities and the Elderly in the COVID-19 Pandemic and Beyond* (pp. 33–48). Academic Press. ISBN 9780323851749, https://doi.org/10.1016/B978-0-323-85174-9.00028-5

[21] Bashir, K., et al. Federated learning for the healthcare metaverse: Concepts, applications, challenges, and future directions. *IEEE Internet of Things Journal*. https://doi.org/10.1109/JIOT.2023.3304790.

[22] Pranata, R., Vania, R., & Victor, A. A. (2021). Statin reduces the incidence of diabetic retinopathy and its need for intervention: A systematic review and meta-analysis. *European Journal of Ophthalmology*, 31(3), 1216–1224. https://doi.org/10.1177/1120672120922444.

[23] Folorunso, S. O., Ogundepo, E. A., Awotunde, J. B., Ayo, F. E., Banjo, O. O., & Taiwo, A. I. (2022). A Multi-Step Predictive Model for COVID-19 Cases in Nigeria Using Machine Learning. In: *Decision Sciences for COVID-19: Learning Through Case Studies* (pp. 107–136). Springer International Publishing, Cham.

[24] Han, J., Lando, L., Skowronska-Krawczyk, D., & Chao, D. L. (2019). Genetics of diabetic retinopathy. *Current Diabetes Reports*, 19(9). https://doi.org/10.1007/s11892-019-1186-6.

[25] Grasselli, G., Pesenti, A., & Cecconi, M. (2020). Critical care utilization for the COVID-19 outbreak in lombardy, Italy: early experience and forecast during an emergency response. *JAMA*, 323(16), 1545–1546.

[26] Haleem, A., Javaid, M., & Vaishya, R. (2020). Effects of Covid 19 pandemic in daily life. Current Medicine Research and Practice, *10*(2), 78–79, ISSN 2352-0817, https://doi.org/10.1016/j.cmrp.2020.03.011.

[27] Naudé, Wim (2020). Artificial Intelligence Against Covid-19: An Early Review. IZA Discussion Paper No. 13110, http://dx.doi.org/10.2139/ssrn.3568314.

[28] Hemdan, E. E.-D., Shouman, M. A., & Karar, M. E. (2020). Covidx-net: A framework of deep learning classifiers to diagnose Covid-19 in X-ray images. *ArXiv, abs/2003.11055.*

[29] Apostolopoulos, I. D., & Mpesiana, T. A. (2020). Covid-19: Automatic detection from x-ray images utilizing transfer learning with convolutional neural networks. *Physical and Engineering Sciences in Medicine*, 43(2), 635–640.

[30] Ogundokun, R. O., Awotunde, J. B., Adeniyi, E. A., & Misra, S. (2022). Application of the Internet of Things (IoT) to fight the COVID-19 Pandemic. In: *Intelligent Internet of Things for Healthcare and Industry* (pp. 83–103). Springer International Publishing, Cham.

[31] Minaee, S., Kafieh, R., Sonka, M., Yazdani, S., & Soufi, G. J. (2020). Deep-covid: Predicting COVID-19 from chest x-ray images using deep transfer learning. *Medical Image Analysis*, 65, Article 101794.

[32] Awotunde, J. B., Jimoh, R. G., AbdulRaheem, M., Oladipo, I. D., Folorunso, S. O., & Ajamu, G. J. (2021). IoT-based wearable body sensor network for COVID-19 pandemic. *Advances in Data Science and Intelligent Data Communication Technologies for COVID-19: Innovative Solutions against COVID-19, Studies in Systems, Decision and Control*. 253–275.

[33] Narin, A., Kaya, C., & Pamuk, Z. (2021). Automatic detection of Coronavirus disease (Covid-19) using X-rRay images and deep convolutional neural networks, *Pattern Anal Appli, 24*, 1207–1220. https://doi.org/10.1007/s10044-021-00984-y.

[34] Farooq, M. S., & Hafeez, A. (2020). Covid-resnet: A deep learning framework for screening of COVID-19 from radiographs, *ArXiv, abs/2003.14395*.
[35] Zhang, J., Xie, Y., Li, Y., Shen, C., & Xia, Y. (2020). Covid-19 screening on chest X-Ray images using deep learning based anomaly detection, *arXiv preprint arXiv:2003.12338*, *27*(10.48550)..
[36] Awotunde, J. B., Ajagbe, S. A., Idowu, I. R., & Ndunagu, J. N. (2021). An enhanced cloud-IoMT-based and machine learning for effective COVID-19 diagnosis system. *Intelligence of Things: AI-IoT Based Critical-Applications and Innovations*, 55–76.
[37] Khan, I. U., & Aslam, N. (2020). A deep-learning-based framework for automated diagnosis of COVID-19 using x-ray images. *Information*, 11(9), 419.
[38] Shi, F., Wang, J., Shi, J., Wu, Z., Wang, Q., Tang, Z., He, K., Shi, Y., & Shen, D. (2021). Review of artificial intelligence techniques in imaging data acquisition, segmentation and diagnosis for COVID-19. IEEE Reviews in Biomedical Engineering, *14*, 4–15, doi: 10.1109/RBME.2020.2987975.
[39] Umer, M., Ashraf, I., Ullah, S., Mehmood, A., & Choi, G. S. (2021). Choi COVINet: A convolutional neural network approach for predicting COVID-19 from chest X-ray image. *Journal of Ambient Intelligence and Humanized Computing*, *13*(1), 535–547. https://doi.org/10.1007/s12652-021-02917-3
[40] Yenduri, G., et al. (2023). From assistive technologies to metaverse—Technologies in inclusive higher education for students with specific learning difficulties: A review. *IEEE Access*, 11, 64907–64927. https://doi.org/10.1109/ ACCESS.2023.3289496.
[41] Bu, Y., Shih, K. C., & Tong, L. (2022). The ocular surface and diabetes, the other 21st Century epidemic. *Experimental Eye Research*, 220. https://doi.org/10.1016/j.exer.2022.109099.
[42] Yenduri, G., Kaluri, R., Gadekallu, T. R., Mahmud, M., & J. Brown, D. (2023, January). Blockchain for Software Maintainability in Healthcare. In *Proceedings of the 24th International Conference on Distributed Computing and Networking* (pp. 420–424).
[43] Wang, Y., Wang, L., Zhou, H., Liao, Y., & Yi, Q. (2022). Application research of artificial intelligence screening system for diabetic retinopathy. *Journal of Healthcare Engineering*, 2022. https://doi.org/10.1155/2022/2185547.
[44] Yenduri, G., & Gadekallu, T. R. (2023, January). XAI for Maintainability Prediction of Software-Defined Networks. In *Proceedings of the 24th International Conference on Distributed Computing and Networking* (pp. 402–406).
[45] Yan, L., Vaghari-Tabari, M., Malakoti, F., Moein, S., Qujeq, D., Yousefi, B., & Asemi, Z. (2022). Quercetin: An effective polyphenol in alleviating diabetes and diabetic complications. *Critical Reviews in Food Science and Nutrition*. https://doi.org/10.1080/10408398.2022.2067825.
[46] Yenduri, G., & Gadekallu, T. R. (2022). *Recent Advancements in Network and Cyber Security Using RNN. Trust, Security and Privacy for Big Data*. CRC Press, Boca Raton, FL, USA, 129–143.
[47] Ramos, H., Hernández, C., Simó, R., & Simó-Servat, O. (2023). Inflammation: the link between neural and vascular impairment in the diabetic retina and therapeutic implications. *International Journal of Molecular Sciences,* 24(10). https://doi.org/10.3390/ijms24108796.
[48] Maddikunta, P. K. R., et al. (2022). Incentive techniques for the internet of things: A survey. *Journal of Network and Computer Applications*, 206, 103464.
[49] Kumar, P., Bhargava, S., Agarwal, P., Garg, A., & Khosla, A. (2019). Association of serum magnesium with type 2 diabetes mellitus and diabetic retinopathy. *Journal of*

Family Medicine and Primary Care, 8(5), 1671. https://doi.org/10.4103/jfmpc.jfmpc_83_19.

[50] Bhuyan, H. K., Ravi, V., Brahma, B., & Kamila, N. K. (2022). Disease analysis using machine learning approaches in healthcare system. *Health and Technology*, 12(5), 987–1005.

[51] Selvachandran, G., Quek, S. G., Paramesran, R., Ding, W., & Son, L. H. (2023). Developments in the detection of diabetic retinopathy: A state-of-the-art review of computer-aided diagnosis and machine learning methods. *Artificial Intelligence Review*, 56(2), 915–964. https://doi.org/10.1007/s10462-022-10185-6.

[52] Bhuyan, H. K., et al. (2023). Wide-ranging approach-based feature selection for classification. *Multimedia Tools Applications*, 82, 23277–23304. https://doi.org/10.1007/s11042-022-14132-z.

[53] Sanie-Jahromi, F., Zia, Z., & Afarid, M. (2023). A review on the effect of garlic on diabetes, BDNF, and VEGF as a potential treatment for diabetic retinopathy. Chinese Medicine, 18(1). https://doi.org/10.1186/s13020-023-00725-9.

[54] Bhuyan, H. K., & Ravi, V. (2023). An integrated framework with deep learning for segmentation and classification of cancer disease. *International Journal on Artificial Intelligence Tools*, 32(02), 2340002.

[55] Brahma, B., Kamila, N. K., Dhal, S. K., Pani, S. K., Mahesh, N., & Majhi, S. K. (2021, May 12). An extensive evolutional survey of medical domain data analytics & decision improvisation systems. SSRN. www.papers.ssrn.com/sol3/ papers.cfm?abstract_id=3842573

[56] Brahma, B., Bhuyan, H.K. (2022). Soft Computing and Machine Learning Techniques for e-Health Data Analytics. In: Mishra, S., González-Briones, A., Bhoi, A.K., Mallick, P.K., Corchado, J.M. (eds). *Connected e-Health. Studies in Computational Intelligence*, vol 1021. Springer, Cham. https://doi.org/10.1007/978-3-030-97929-4_4.

[57] Bhuyan, H.K., Pullagura, L., Brahma, B., Reddy, C.S. (2023). Impact of Node Radiation on Human Health Using IoMT. In: Jain, S., Marriwala, N., Tripathi, C.C., Kumar, D. (eds). *Emergent Converging Technologies and Biomedical Systems*. ETBS 2022. Lecture Notes in Electrical Engineering, vol 1040. Springer, Singapore. https://doi.org/10.1007/978-981-99-2271-0.

Index

D

E

F

G

H

I

L

M